MICROECONOMICS

ECONOMICS
Principles and Policy

THE DRYDEN SERIES IN ECONOMICS

Anderson	*Regional Economic Analysis: A Canadian Perspective*
Baker	*An Introduction to International Economics*
Boreham and Bodkin	*Money, Banking and Finance: The Canadian Context*
Brodie	*The Political Economy of Canadian Regionalism*
Brue	*Economic History*
Clower, Graves, and Sexton	*Intermediate Microeconomics*
Eastman	*Labour Market Theory and the Canadian Experience*
Eckert and Leftwich	*The Price System and Resource Allocation*
Gardner	*Comparative Economic Systems*
Glahe and Lee	*Microeconomics: Theory and Applications*
Griffin and Steele	*Energy Economics and Policy*
Hirsch and Rufolo	*Public Finance and Expenditure in a Federal System*
Hirschey and Pappas	*Fundamentals of Managerial Economics*
Hyman	*Public Finance: A Contemporary Application of Theory to Policy*
Keating and Wilson	*Managerial Economics*
Kennett and Lieberman	*Comparative Systems*
Kreinin	*International Economics: A Policy Approach*
Landsburg	*Price Theory and Applications*
Nicholson	*Intermediate Microeconomics and Its Application*
Nicholson	*Microeconomic Theory: Basic Principles and Extensions*
Norrie and Owram	*A History of the Canadian Economy*
Ormiston	*Intermediate Microeconomics*
Oser and Brue	*The Evolution of Economic Thought*
Pappas and Hirschey	*Managerial Economics*
Ramanathan	*Introductory Econometrics with Applications*
Rukstad	*Corporate Decision Making in the World Economy: Company Case Studies*
Rukstad	*Macroeconomic Decision Making in the World Economy: Text and Cases*
Samuelson and Marks	*Managerial Economics*
Scarth	*Macroeconomics: An Introduction to Advanced Methods*
Smith and Spudeck	*Interest Rates: Principles and Applications*
Strick	*Canadian Public Finance*
Vogt, Cameron, and Dolan	*Economics: Understanding the Canadian Economy*
Yarbrough and Yarbrough	*The World Economy: Trade and Finance*
Zimbalist, Sherman, and Brown	*Comparing Economic Systems: A Political Economic Approach*

MICROECONOMICS

ECONOMICS
Principles and Policy
FOURTH CANADIAN EDITION

WILLIAM J. BAUMOL
C.V. Starr Center for Applied Economics,
New York University

ALAN S. BLINDER
Princeton University

WILLIAM M. SCARTH
McMaster University

DRYDEN

Harcourt Brace & Company, Canada

Toronto Montreal Orlando Fort Worth San Diego
Philadelphia London Sydney Tokyo

Canadian Cataloguing in Publication Data

Baumol, William J.
    Economics: principles and policy, fourth
Canadian edition : microeconomics

Includes index.
ISBN 0-03-922974-2

1. Microeconomics. I. Blinder, Alan S. II. Scarth, William M., 1946–   . III. Title.

HB172.B3 1994   338.5   C93-094554-9

Publisher: Scott Duncan
Senior Editor and Marketing Manager: Ron Fitzgerald
Developmental Editor: Sarah J. Duncan
Director of Publishing Services: Jean Davies
Editorial Manager: Marcel Chiera
Supervising Editor: Semareh Al-Hillal
Production Manager: Sue-Ann Becker
Manufacturing Co-ordinator: Denise Wake
Copy Editor: Glenn Martin
Cover and Interior Design: Dave Peters
Cover Photograph: Susan Dobson
Typesetting and Assembly: Compeer Typographic Services Limited
Printing and Binding: Metropole Litho Inc.

♾ This book was printed in Canada on acid-free paper.

1 2 3 4 5 98 97 96 95 94

To my four children,
Ellen, Daniel,
and now Sabrina and Jim
W.J.B.

For Scott, who is now Beyond the Final Exam,
and William, who is on his way
A.S.B.

To Brian, David,
and the memory of Michael
W.M.S.

PREFACE

For decades, the "principles of economics" book has been expected to codify the entire discipline of economics. In recent years, this has become increasingly difficult, but also more imperative. The explosion of economic knowledge has made it impossible to put all of economics between two covers. But at the same time, more and more public policy issues either are basically economic in nature or involve important economic considerations. Intelligent citizens can no longer afford to be unaware of economics.

This dilemma has guided the preparation of this book in two ways. First, we have studiously avoided the encyclopedic approach and abandoned the fiction, so popular among textbook writers, that literally everything is of the utmost importance. Second, we have tried to highlight those important ideas that are likely to be of lasting significance—principles that you will want to remember long after the course is over because they offer insights that are far from obvious, because they are of practical importance, and because they are widely misunderstood by intelligent laypeople. Twelve of the most important of these ideas have been selected as **Ideas for Beyond the Final Exam** and are called to the reader's attention whenever they occur through the use of this icon: ▦ .

This method of highlighting key ideas has proved very popular with users of the previous editions of our book, many of whom have suggested that we go even further in this direction. In this edition and the previous edition, we decided to follow these suggestions. There seems to be an unwritten law that, with every new edition, a principles textbook will drift farther away from the focus that was its original raison d'être: New material is added, but old material has a habit of remaining in place, with the result that both readability and focus deteriorate. Because both students and instructors have told us that the comparative advantage of our textbook is precisely in its consistent focus and readability, we have increased our resolve to avoid this common pitfall.

This fourth edition builds on the extensive shortening that was achieved in the last edition by concentrating on presentation issues. We have improved the usability of the book in three ways: by extending the "12 Ideas" concept, by adding new material that interprets the analysis in terms of policy issues and episodes, and by moving to a four-colour format so that the diagrams are easier to understand.

An economics text must provide the reader with a basic level of economic literacy. To avoid losing sight of this objective, we now provide one-page introductions to start each of the seven parts of the book. The core of each introduction is the highlighting of four "election issues" that will be covered in that part. Of course, these are not the only applied topics addressed in each section of the book, but the whole point is to be selective. Besides whetting the reader's appetite in a focussed way, the election issues provide a convenient checklist that will be useful both at exam time and after the course is over. Now readers can conveniently review the "12 Ideas" (which are important general principles such as comparative advantage and marginal analysis) and the 28 "election issues" (which are much more specific topics, but ones which seem to be always in the news). Some of the 28 election issues concern: minimum wages, speculators, user charges, farm subsidies, marketing boards, emission taxes, free trade, welfare reform, tax shifting (for example, does labour really pay the taxes levied on capital?), unemployment insurance reform, sales taxes versus income taxes, interest rates and exchange rates, the crowding-out effect, twin deficits, the national debt, competitiveness, and deindustrialization.

The book contains many boxed inserts—an average of just over two per chapter. Forty percent of these inserts are either new to this edition or have been fundamentally revised. A consistent set of titles and background colours are used so that readers can clearly identify the category to which each box belongs (and therefore quickly decide when they want to read it). The categories are: Application, Further Detail, At the Frontier, Public Controversy, and Biographical Note. In this fourth edition, we have included discussion of broader issues in some of the Public Controversy boxes. Examples include Canadian sovereignty, the general dissatisfaction with governments, starvation in Africa, international competitiveness, and the challenges facing Eastern-bloc countries.

We remain committed to directly linking the material of mainstream economics to the more popular commentary that is stressed in the media. For example, we end the microeconomics half of the book with an economist's response to the criticisms (such as those often published by David Suzuki) of our discipline's approach to the issue of environmental protection. Also, in the macroeconomics section, we directly address the critique of mainstream economics that has been offered by the Canadian Council of Catholic Bishops. Further, we end the macro half of the book by discussing the popular writings of Michael Porter, Robert Reich, and Lester Thurow on the challenge of international competitiveness.

A large effort has gone into reorganizing the book's layout to make it more user friendly. We resisted the temptation to adopt a two-column design to make the book *appear* shorter, since we wanted to keep space available for the margin definitions and the reader's own annotations, and to avoid an intimidating format. For the first time in this edition, we have the option of more than one colour in the diagrams. Careful thought has gone into using this increased degree of freedom in a pedagogically helpful way. Broadly speaking, our strategy has been to use red as the basic colour to show the initial outcome in any market. Then, we consistently use blue to indicate the "new" position for any demand or supply curve after whatever event that is being examined has occurred. Finally, we use gold as "commentary" or highlighting, for example, to draw attention to various outcomes, such as the net efficiency gains that follow the removal of a tariff. By using colour in this consistent fashion, we hope that readers will move much more quickly to a state of comfort with our subject's comparative static methodology (that is, comparing the "before" and "after" graphic snapshots as a means of evaluating policy options).

READABILITY WITHOUT SACRIFICING RIGOUR

All modern economics textbooks abound with "real-world" examples, but we have tried to go beyond this, to elevate the examples to pre-eminence. For in our view, the policy issue or everyday economic problem ought to lead the student naturally to the economic principle, not the other way around. For this reason, many chapters (not just each broad section of the book) *start* with a real policy issue or a practical problem that may seem puzzling or paradoxical to non-economists. Each chapter then proceeds to describe the economic analysis required to remove the mystery. In doing this, we have tried to utilize technical jargon and diagrams only where there is a clear need for them, never for their own sake.

Still, economics is a somewhat technical subject and, except for a few rather light chapters, this is a book for the desk, not for the bed. We have, however, made strenuous efforts to simplify the technical level of the discussion as much as we could without sacrificing content. Fortunately, almost every important idea in economics can be explained in plain English, and this is what we have tried to do. Yet, even while reducing the technical difficulty of the book, we have incorporated some elements of economic analysis that have traditionally been left out of introductory books but that are really too important to omit.

Foremost among these is our extensive treatment of prices and inflation in Parts 5 through 7. For years, textbooks devoted many chapters to unrealistic, but presumably simpler, economic models, in which prices never rose. The original American edition of this book was the first introductory textbook to put inflation into the story from the very beginning, rather than as an afterthought—a practice we maintain and expand in this fourth Canadian edition.

Another example is our treatment of monetary and fiscal policy options for a small open economy such as Canada's. Unlike other textbooks, ours does not shy away from a full application of aggregate supply and demand analysis in this area. And instead of separating our explanation of theory from our discussion of historical policy episodes, we thoroughly integrate the two by making full and rigorous use of the analytical tools to explain the policy experiences.

A third example of our commitment to a rigorous study of central analytical issues is our treatment of the market mechanism's ability, under ideal circumstances, to allocate society's resources in the most efficient manner possible. Many introductory-textbook authors, thinking the topic too difficult for beginning students, give little more than some general hints about this important result. We offer a genuine proof and an extensive discussion of precisely what the result does—and does not—imply about the efficiency of real-world market economies.

To summarize, then, our revision has been guided by two objectives —readability and rigour. The majority of students taking a principles course in economics do not plan to specialize in the field. What they want and need is to obtain a basic level of literacy in economic affairs, so that they can think independently when evaluating public issues. A book cannot meet this need if it is too technical, and addresses itself only to those going on to advanced studies in economics. In a word, the book will fail if it is not readable. But an introductory economics textbook will also fail if it tries so hard to be accessible that it glosses over fundamental points. (After all, in economics, a little learning can be a particularly dangerous thing!) Hence, a book that purports to explain economic reasoning cannot sacrifice rigour any more than it can succeed without being readable. By combining an untiring effort to maintain the literary style that readers have appreciated in our earlier editions with a "hard line" on topic selection, we have tried to meet both objectives, and to achieve a consistent focus on central themes and rigorous analysis in the process.

MICROECONOMICS

The discussion of microeconomics is organized around the central theme that we believe deals with the most significant lessons to be learned in an introductory economics course: what a market system does well, and what it does poorly.

Part 1 introduces this central theme and some of the fundamental ideas of economics (such as scarcity, opportunity cost, markets, and prices). A host of topical examples are used to illustrate these concepts and to convey the power of supply and demand analysis. They include "green" products at grocery stores, the proliferation of materials for recycling, species extinction, minimum-wage laws, rent controls, interest rate ceilings, and the drug problem. Both the beginning (Chapters 2 and 3) and the end (Chapter 17) of the microeconomics portion of the book emphasize the fundamentally important issue of the environment. By starting with, and then returning to, this issue, we are able to maintain our focus on the theme of what the market does well and what it does poorly.

Our deeper excursion into microeconomic reasoning begins with Part 2. The chapters in this part of the book acquaint students with the central analytical tools of microeconomics and use those tools to explain how both consumers (Chapters 4 and 5) and producers (Chapters 6 and 7) make decisions that best serve their own interests. Great emphasis is placed on the trade-off between equity and efficiency throughout these chapters, and the issue is explained with the aid of graphs depicting consumer and producer surplus.

Part 3 examines how the decisions of consumers and firms interact in the marketplace, and provides an extensive examination of the virtues and vices of free markets. The early chapters (8 and 9) extol the remarkable accomplishments of an idealized system of markets, while the later chapters (10, 11, and 12) discuss some of the market system's principal failings, particularly in the areas of monopoly power and externality effects. Chapter 13 discusses the free trade debate. New to this edition is an explicit cost–benefit analysis of free trade, including consideration of adjustment costs. Chapter 13 ends with a clear, schematic explanation of how the government's main instruments of economic policy can best be assigned to our major economic goals. This important summary is presented in chart form on the inside back cover. We emphasize this chart for two reasons. First, we believe that no opportunity for helping the reader see the forest, and not just the trees, should be lost. Second, it is fundamentally important that we note how policy trade-offs can be minimized. The two broad strategies involved are: have as many policy instruments as goals, and assign the instruments to goals so that the power of self-interest becomes something that is harnessed by policy, rather than something that frustrates the success of the policy.

Part 3 sets the stage for Part 4, in which we address several important microeconomic policy issues. The four chapters in Part 4 are devoted to answering the following four questions of current concern:

- Chapter 14: What determines the distribution of income?

- Chapter 15: What sorts of reforms in the tax and welfare systems represent the most efficient ways of reducing the problems of poverty and discrimination?

- Chapter 16: How have our competition laws and our experience with government regulation of industry contributed to promoting competitive behaviour?

- Chapter 17: What guidance does economic analysis offer for solving the problems of pollution and resource depletion?

All four of these chapters maintain our fundamental emphasis on identifying the equity and the efficiency aspects of microeconomic policy issues. Only by exploring the implications of policy on these two fronts can we fully appreciate the differences in the views that are held on these issues. And only by stressing this distinction can we defend our preference for certain policies—that is, for the policies that promote our objectives of equity and equality with the least sacrifice of economic efficiency.

The microeconomics portion of the book is replete with topical discussions. For example, in the text there are discussions of tax reform (Chapter 15), the Free Trade Agreement (Chapter 13), and privatization in eastern-bloc countries (Chapter 9). Furthermore, there are new or revised boxed inserts on the following subjects:

- Opportunity cost and divorce settlements (page 39)

- Student attitudes on using the price system (page 83)

- Youth unemployment and the baby boom (page 91)

- User fees (page 110 and page 979)
- Just-in-time inventories (page 67)
- The minimum-differentiation principle (page 328)
- Public infrastructure (page 352)
- Trade creation versus trade diversion (page 391)
- GATT versus environmentalists (page 389)
- The definition of poverty (page 498)
- Sexual discrimination (page 514)
- Tradeable emissions permits (page 585)

We have also updated our "At the Frontier" series of boxed inserts in the microeconomics section of the book, which treat subjects such as the following:

- Experimental economics (page 77)
- Game theory (page 325)
- The theory of contestable markets (page 330)
- Asymmetric information and principal agents (page 350)
- Rent-seeking (page 429)

The issue of moral hazard is stressed in the discussion of reforming unemployment insurance and federal deposit insurance, and the asymmetric information material is expanded to include coverage of efficiency wages.

MACROECONOMICS

Students are invariably interested in learning enough macroeconomics within an introductory course to enable them to make sense of (or at least evaluate) such things as major statements by the Governor of the Bank of Canada. This is simply not possible without an analysis that stresses the cost-increasing effects of a lower Canadian dollar, which requires an integrated analysis of aggregate demand *and* supply. We use this integrated analysis directly in our discussion of policy episodes.

The macroeconomic section of the book starts with a brief history of macroeconomic events in Canada and an initial use of the aggregate demand and supply curves (Chapter 18). In the same chapter, there is a full discussion of the costs associated with unemployment and inflation, and an explanation of how national product (gross domestic product) is measured. In other words, measurement issues relating to all the major macroeconomic variables are contained within one chapter. The different parts of the chapter are self-contained, so that they can be read at any time during the term of study, at the instructor's discretion. In Chapters 19 through 23, we move on to multiplier theory, fiscal policy, and the supply-side effects of tax changes. The effects of personal income-tax changes, sales tax policy, and corporate tax concessions are thoroughly examined. This edition includes a specific numerical example that shows readers how the job-creating potential of a typical budget can be calculated.

Chapter 24 introduces financial considerations. Firms finance their investment expenditures in two ways: They sell stocks and bonds (this is the set of options discussed in Chapter 24), and they borrow from the banks. Chapter 25 introduces the student to the operations of the latter by explaining the money supply and the chartered banking system. The study of central banking that follows (Chapter 26) stresses that pegging the exchange rate forces the Bank of Canada to conduct "open-market operations" in the foreign-exchange market, in just the same way that it does in domestic bond markets when initiating monetary policy. The nature of the foreign-exchange market is explained at this stage, and monetary policy and exchange-rate policy are discussed simultaneously. The chapter ends with a full discussion of several public statements issued by the Governor of the Bank of Canada concerning the viability of an independent interest-rate policy for Canada and other aspects of monetary policy.

The next two chapters integrate the analyses of fiscal and monetary/exchange-rate policy. Chapter 27 provides an updated discussion of the monetarist–Keynesian debate from the perspective of a closed economy. This approach allows us to outline the policy options available to the United States, whose economy has such a direct impact on our own. Chapter 28 analyzes the relative effectiveness of monetary and fiscal policies under alternative exchange-rate regimes for a small open economy such as Canada's. Several policy episodes are used to illustrate the direct importance of the economic analysis. The potential use of exchange-rate policy to limit the damage caused by foreign trade restrictions is fully discussed in Chapter 28. Also, in this edition, we emphasize the implications of the small open economy framework for the co-ordination problems that face provincial governments.

The macroeconomics half of the book ends with four "issues" chapters, which can be read in any order. Each of these remaining four chapters deals with a central issue that is both highly topical and of enduring importance. The questions raised are as follows:

- Chapter 29: How was our international monetary system developed and why do we observe such vast swings in currency values?

- Chapter 30: Are large government budget deficits bad?

- Chapter 31: What is the nature of the trade-off between inflation and unemployment?

- Chapter 32: How can productivity growth and international competitiveness be increased in both the developed and the less developed economies?

This final chapter of the book focusses on the rise of the service sector in Western economies, the consequent concern about the phenomenon often referred to as "deindustrialization," and the challenge of reforming our method of providing public services (such as education and health) so that competitiveness can be increased without sacrificing compassion.

There are new or revised boxed inserts on many topical issues in macroeconomics, such as the following:

- Hidden unemployment (page 631)
- Reforming unemployment insurance (page 636)
- Corporate tax concessions (page 788)
- Reforming deposit-insurance and reserve-requirement regulations (page 842)
- Bank of Canada policy statements (page 869)
- Economic aspects of the Constitutional debate (page 924)
- Why the national debt is a burden (page 977 and page 979)
- Economists versus religious leaders on macroeconomic policy (page 1016)
- Labour's reaction to changes in the workplace (page 1032)
- The drive for competitiveness (page 1056)

All of our boxed inserts (both those on policy controversies and those on advanced topics such as co-ordination failures and the Lucas critique on estimated models) are intended to stimulate the student's interest and to demonstrate that investing a serious effort in understanding economic reasoning is a worthwhile and relevant endeavour.

CANADA AND THE REST OF THE WORLD

In both the micro and macro sections of the book, the material on the openness of the Canadian economy is given centre stage. In the microeconomics sections, the material on comparative advantage and tariff policy is not tucked away, but appears in the core set of chapters on the pros and cons of free markets. Also, since the legal approaches to limiting market power (that is, regulation and competition laws) have met with rather limited success in the past, it is frequently stressed that tariff cuts can be used to make Canadian markets contestable. Thus, tariff policy is discussed as one among several instruments for stimulating competition. Of course, the gains from international trade do not depend solely on Canada's small domestic markets and incomplete exploitation of the economies of large-scale production. The principle of comparative advantage in the standard situation of constant costs is fully explained in Chapter 13, which also contains two important sections: One discusses the advantages and disadvantages of the Free Trade Agreement with the United States and the other explains the proper assignment of policy instruments to goals, as noted earlier.

Perhaps the most popular feature of the previous editions of this book is the full integration of macroeconomic theory with the discussions of policy episodes in a way that properly emphasizes the fact that monetary policy and exchange-rate policy are one and the same thing.

NOTE TO THE STUDENT

Most courses will begin with Part 1, where we have touched most of the traditional bases while keeping the introductory materials briefer than they are in most other texts. Courses dealing with microeconomic theory and policy in the first term will proceed next to Parts 2 through 4, while courses commencing with macroeconomics will skip to Parts 5 through 7.

Whatever the nature of your course, we would like to offer one suggestion. Unlike some of the other courses you may be taking, principles of economics is cumulative — each week's lesson builds on what you have learned before. You will save yourself a lot of frustration (and also a lot of work) if you keep up on a week-to-week basis. To help you do this, there is a chapter summary, a list of important terms and concepts, and a selection of discussion questions at the end of each chapter. In addition to these aids, many students will find the *Study Guide*, designed specifically to accompany this text, helpful as a self-testing and diagnostic device. When you encounter difficulties in the *Study Guide*, you will know which sections of the text you need to review.

NOTE TO THE INSTRUCTOR

The ordering of chapters in the book is based on courses that treat microeconomics before macroeconomics (the opposite order from that in previous editions). But the book can be used equally well in courses that reverse the sequence. The following chart summarizes the book's basic structure:

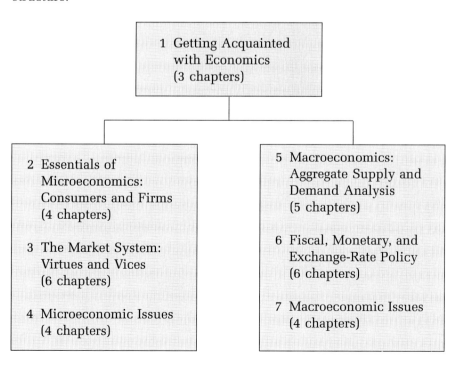

OUTLINE FOR A ONE-TERM COURSE IN MICROECONOMICS

Chapter Number	Material Covered
1	Methodology
2	Scarcity and choice
3 } 4	Basic supply and demand
5 } 6	Consumer theory
7	Theory of the firm
8	Perfect competition
9	Laissez faire versus planning
10	Monopoly
12	Other sources of market failure
13	Comparative advantage and free trade

Plus any *two* of the following:

14	Income distribution
15	Tax reform
16	Competition policy
17	Environmental issues

OUTLINE FOR A ONE-TERM COURSE IN MACROECONOMICS

Chapter Number	Material Covered
1	Methodology
3	Basic supply and demand
18	Measuring macroeconomic performance
19 20 21 22 23	Multiplier analysis, fiscal policy, aggregate demand and supply, the self-correcting mechanism
25 26	Money and banking
27 28	Integration of fiscal, monetary, and exchange-rate policy

Plus any *two* of the following:

29	International policy co-ordination
30	The deficit
31	Phillips curves
32	Productivity and growth

Given that a reasonable pace for covering material is roughly one chapter per week on average, the suggested course outlines presented on the opposite page should be suitable for many teaching situations.

Chapters 11 and 24 have been omitted from these course outlines. Chapter 11, on monopolistic competition and oligopoly, can be included by instructors who wish to place extra emphasis on theory, but its inclusion would necessitate the exclusion of one of the microeconomic "issues" chapters. However, it should be noted that the latter four microeconomic chapters are divided into self-contained sections to allow instructors to focus on particular issues without having to cover the complete chapter. For example, the topic of regulation occupies half of Chapter 16, and that of pollution occupies half of Chapter 17; this material can be combined to create the equivalent of one chapter, to the exclusion of the other sections in Chapters 16 and 17.

Chapter 24, on firms and the stock market, can (and most probably will) be read by students on their own. It is not demanding analytically, and most students are very interested in the subject.

Two things should be clear from our sample course outlines: (1) the book works very well for instructors who prefer to start their courses with macroeconomics; (2) it is structured to accommodate the time constraints that confront most instructors.

Concerning the *Study Guide*, and whether you should recommend it for your students, we offer the following advice. Since such a guide should be especially useful for the student who is having difficulty, the core material in our *Study Guide* is pitched at a fairly basic level. However, it does include a number of much more challenging questions, so that the *Study Guide* is of significant value to the more advanced students as well. Every chapter has two practice tests, each of which contains both true/false and multiple-choice questions. The first test is more basic, while the second is more challenging. More advanced students who are fairly confident that they understand the material may want to skim the Chapter Review, the Basic Exercises, the Definition Quiz, and the first practice test, and concentrate their attention on the more difficult practice test and the Supplementary Exercises. By structuring the *Study Guide* in this way, we have tried to ensure that students of varying levels of ability will be able to benefit from this learning aid. As instructors, we know that even the best students can benefit from extra practice.

One convenience that has been added to the *Study Guide* with this edition is that the "answers to questions" section now lists the page numbers in the text where each question's topic is covered, thus students who make mistakes can easily find the appropriate material to review.

As with previous editions, a computerized *Test Bank* is available for the use of instructors. The fourth edition of this teaching aid has been extensively revised. Previous users will see that this ancillary has been significantly improved, and this reflects our appreciation of the fact that instructors are being forced to place increased emphasis on prepared test banks. Also available is a fully revised *Instructor's Manual* and a set of *Transparency Masters*.

Once again, our textbook is available in separate, paperback *Micro-economics* and *Macroeconomics* editions. The introductory chapters (Part 1) and the chapter on free trade are included in both volumes. Users of these split editions will have no difficulty locating material in the textbook's ancillaries, as the chapter and page numbers in the paperback volumes conform exactly to those used in the combined text.

In trying to improve the book from one edition to the next, we rely heavily on our own experiences as teachers. But our experience using the book is small compared with that of the community of instructors who have been and who will be using it. If you encounter problems, or have suggestions for improving the book, we urge you to let us know by writing to Bill Scarth in care of the publisher. Such letters are invaluable, and we are glad to receive them, even if they are critical.

ACKNOWLEDGEMENTS

Finally, and with great pleasure, we turn to the customary acknowledgements of indebtedness. Some of these have been accumulating now through six American editions of the book. The many American instructors whose comments were invaluable in planning this edition have been individually listed in the sixth American edition. Friends and colleagues who have made helpful suggestions directly for the Canadian editions include: John Burbidge, Don Dawson, Martin Dooley, Paul Grootendorst, Carlos Leite, Wayne Lewchuk, Andy Muller, Arthur Sweetman, and Mike Veall of McMaster University; Doug Burgess of Burgess–Graham Securities; Michael Hare, Michael Krashinsky, and Knut Larsen of the University of Toronto; Tom Powrie, Brian Scarfe, and Sten Drugge of the University of Alberta; Hugh Young, Don Drummond, Peter Liebel, and Mario Albert of the Department of Finance in Ottawa; Tony Myatt and Charles Waddell of the University of New Brunswick; Peter Kennedy of Simon Fraser University; Waclaw Dajnowiec of Ryerson Polytechnic University; Irwin Gillespie of Carleton University; Jack Guthrie of Camosun College; Robert Allan of the University of British Columbia; Lionel Ifill of Algonquin College; Ted Horbulyck of the University of Calgary; Chris Debresson of Concordia University; John Sayre of Capilano College; Mary-Ann Dimond and Robert Dimond of Brock University; Maurice Boote of Trent University; John Farrugia of Mohawk College; Arnold Frenzel and Peter Sinclair of Wilfrid Laurier University; Robert Kerton of the University of Waterloo; Rob Jeacock and Raimo Marttala of Malaspina College; Thierry Neubert of John Abbott College; David Gray of the University of Ottawa; and Bram Cadsby of the University of Guelph. We wish to thank all of these individuals, as well as the many students who took the time to send their comments and suggestions to the publisher. Many of the suggestions made by instructors and students alike have been incorporated into this fourth edition. We are particularly indebted to Don

Dawson of McMaster University, who provided thorough and invaluable input for the chapter on industrial organization.

The book you hold in your hand was not done by us alone. Sarah Duncan, Alex Gault, and the other fine people in the college division at Harcourt Brace & Company, Canada, worked tirelessly and effectively to turn our manuscript into the book you see. In particular, valuable help (delivered with a tremendous amount of patience, support, and good humour) was contributed by Semareh Al-Hillal. Thanks also to the many others who worked behind the scenes to help produce this book.

And finally, there are our wives, Hilda Baumol, Madeline Blinder, and Kathy Scarth. They have helped us in so many ways. Their patience, good judgement, and love have made everything go more smoothly than we had any right to expect. We deeply appreciate their invaluable support.

William J. Baumol   Alan S. Blinder   William M. Scarth

A NOTE FROM THE PUBLISHER

Thank you for selecting *Economics: Principles and Policy*, Fourth Edition, by William J. Baumol, Alan S. Blinder, and William M. Scarth. The authors and publisher have devoted considerable time to the careful development of this book. We appreciate your recognition of this effort and accomplishment.

We want to hear what you think about *Economics: Principles and Policy*. Please take a few minutes to fill in the stamped reader reply card at the back of the book. Your comments and suggestions will be valuable to us as we prepare new editions and other books.

BRIEF CONTENTS

PART 1 **GETTING ACQUAINTED WITH ECONOMICS   1**

CHAPTER   1   THE PROBLEMS AND TOOLS OF THE ECONOMIST   3
CHAPTER   2   SCARCITY AND CHOICE   35
CHAPTER   3   SUPPLY AND DEMAND: AN INITIAL LOOK   57

PART 2 **ESSENTIALS OF MICROECONOMICS: CONSUMERS AND FIRMS   97**

CHAPTER   4   CONSUMER CHOICE AND THE INDIVIDUAL'S
              DEMAND CURVE   99
CHAPTER   5   MARKET DEMAND AND ELASTICITY   131
CHAPTER   6   INPUT DECISIONS AND PRODUCTION COSTS   159
CHAPTER   7   OUTPUT–PRICE DECISIONS AND MARGINAL ANALYSIS   199

PART 3 **THE MARKET SYSTEM: VIRTUES AND VICES   225**

CHAPTER   8   THE FIRM AND THE INDUSTRY UNDER
              PERFECT COMPETITION   227
CHAPTER   9   THE PRICE SYSTEM: LAISSEZ FAIRE VERSUS
              ECONOMIC PLANNING   253
CHAPTER 10   MONOPOLY   289
CHAPTER 11   BETWEEN COMPETITION AND MONOPOLY   311
CHAPTER 12   THE MARKET MECHANISM: SHORTCOMINGS AND
              REMEDIES   333
CHAPTER 13   COMPARATIVE ADVANTAGE: THE QUESTION OF
              FREE TRADE   361

PART 4 **MICROECONOMIC ISSUES   409**

CHAPTER 14   PRICING THE FACTORS OF PRODUCTION:
              INCOME DISTRIBUTION   411
CHAPTER 15   THE TAX SYSTEM AND INCOME INEQUALITY   471
CHAPTER 16   REGULATION OF INDUSTRY AND
              COMPETITION POLICY   525
CHAPTER 17   ENVIRONMENTAL PROTECTION AND
              RESOURCE CONSERVATION   567

PART 5   MACROECONOMICS: AGGREGATE SUPPLY AND DEMAND ANALYSIS   609

CHAPTER   18   NATIONAL PRODUCT, UNEMPLOYMENT, AND INFLATION   611

CHAPTER   19   INCOME AND SPENDING: THE POWERFUL CONSUMER   669

CHAPTER   20   DEMAND-SIDE CONSIDERATIONS: UNEMPLOYMENT OR INFLATION?   693

CHAPTER   21   CHANGES ON THE DEMAND SIDE: MULTIPLIER ANALYSIS   717

CHAPTER   22   SUPPLY-SIDE CONSIDERATIONS: UNEMPLOYMENT *AND* INFLATION?   733

PART 6   FISCAL, MONETARY, AND EXCHANGE-RATE POLICY   761

CHAPTER   23   FISCAL POLICY   763

CHAPTER   24   FIRMS AND THEIR FINANCING: STOCKS AND BONDS   795

CHAPTER   25   MONEY AND THE BANKING SYSTEM   819

CHAPTER   26   CENTRAL BANKING AND MONETARY POLICY   847

CHAPTER   27   STABILIZATION POLICY FOR A CLOSED ECONOMY   875

CHAPTER   28   STABILIZATION POLICY FOR A SMALL OPEN ECONOMY   911

PART 7   MACROECONOMIC ISSUES   931

CHAPTER   29   POLICY CO-ORDINATION IN THE WORLD ECONOMY   933

CHAPTER   30   BUDGET DEFICITS AND THE NATIONAL DEBT   957

CHAPTER   31   THE TRADE-OFF BETWEEN INFLATION AND UNEMPLOYMENT   983

CHAPTER   32   PRODUCTIVITY, GROWTH, AND DEVELOPMENT   1021

CONTENTS

This textbook appears in three versions. The full text, *Economics: Principles and Policy*, contains all 32 chapters, as listed below. The *Microeconomics* split edition contains Chapters 1–17. The *Macro-economics* split edition contains Chapters 1–3, 13, and 18–32.

PART 1   GETTING ACQUAINTED WITH ECONOMICS 1

CHAPTER 1   THE PROBLEMS AND TOOLS OF THE ECONOMIST 3

IDEAS FOR BEYOND THE FINAL EXAM   **3**

Idea 1: Rational Choice and True Economic Costs   4
Idea 2: Mutual Gains from Voluntary Exchange   5
Idea 3: Attempts to Repeal the Laws of Supply and Demand:
    The Market Strikes Back   5
Idea 4: The Importance of Marginal Analysis   6
Idea 5: Increasing Output May Require Sacrificing Equality   7
Idea 6: Externalities: A Shortcoming of the Market Cured by
    Market Methods   7
Idea 7: The Surprising Principle of Comparative Advantage   8
Idea 8: The Trade-Off between Inflation and Unemployment   9
Idea 9: The Illusion of High Interest Rates   9
Idea 10: The Consequences of Budget Deficits   10
Idea 11: The Overwhelming Importance of Productivity   10
Idea 12: The Cost Disease of the Service Sector   11
Epilogue   11

INSIDE THE ECONOMIST'S TOOL KIT   **12**

Economics as a Discipline   12
The Need for Abstraction   12
The Role of Economic Theory   16
What Is an Economic "Model"?   17
Reasons for Disagreements: Imperfect Information and
    Value Judgements   19

SUMMARY   20
CONCEPTS FOR REVIEW   21
QUESTIONS FOR DISCUSSION   21

APPENDIX TO CHAPTER 1: THE USE AND
  MISUSE OF GRAPHS — 22

CONSTRUCTING GRAPHS — **22**

Two-Variable Diagrams — 22
The Definition and Measurement of Slope — 23
Rays through the Origin and 45° Lines — 26
Squeezing Three Dimensions into Two: Contour Maps — 27

PERILS IN THE INTERPRETATION OF GRAPHS — **28**

The Interpretation of Growth Trends — 28
Distorting Trends by Choice of the Time Period — 29
Dangers of Omitting the Origin — 29
Unreliability of Steepness and Choice of Units — 30

SUMMARY — 32
CONCEPTS FOR REVIEW — 33
QUESTIONS FOR DISCUSSION — 33

CHAPTER 2   SCARCITY AND CHOICE — 35

The "Indispensable Necessity" Syndrome — 35
Scarcity, Choice, and Opportunity Cost — 36
Opportunity Cost and Money Cost — 37
Production, Scarcity, and Resource Allocation — 38
Scarcity and Choice for a Single Firm — 39
Scarcity and Choice for the Entire Society — 42
The Concept of Efficiency — 46
The Three Co-ordination Tasks of Any Economy — 48
Specialization, Division of Labour, and Exchange — 48
Markets, Prices, and the Three Co-ordination Tasks — 51
Radicalism, Conservatism, and the Market Mechanism — 53

SUMMARY — 54
CONCEPTS FOR REVIEW — 55
QUESTIONS FOR DISCUSSION — 55

CHAPTER 3   SUPPLY AND DEMAND: AN INITIAL LOOK — 57

Fighting the Invisible Hand — 57
Demand and Quantity Demanded — 60
Supply and Quantity Supplied — 62
Equilibrium of Supply and Demand — 63
Shifts of the Demand Curve — 67
Shifts of the Supply Curve — 72
Restraining the Market Mechanism: Price Ceilings — 78
Restraining the Market Mechanism: Price Floors — 84
Fixed Exchange Rates — 86
A Can of Worms — 87
A Simple but Powerful Lesson — 89

SUMMARY 92
CONCEPTS FOR REVIEW 93
QUESTIONS FOR DISCUSSION 93

PART 2 ESSENTIALS OF MICROECONOMICS: CONSUMERS AND FIRMS 97

CHAPTER 4 CONSUMER CHOICE AND THE INDIVIDUAL'S DEMAND CURVE 99

Marginal Analysis 99
Total and Marginal Utility 101
From Marginal Utility to the Demand Curve 105
The Diamond–Water Paradox: The Puzzle Resolved 106
Consumer Surplus 107

MORE ADVANCED TOPICS IN THE THEORY OF CONSUMER DEMAND 111

Prices, Income, and Quantity Demanded 111
Indifference Curve Analysis 115
The Consumer's Choice 122
Consequences of Income Changes: Inferior Goods 124
Consequences of Price Changes: Deriving the Demand Curve 124
Conclusion 125

SUMMARY 127
CONCEPTS FOR REVIEW 128
QUESTIONS FOR DISCUSSION 129

CHAPTER 5 MARKET DEMAND AND ELASTICITY 131

From Individual-Demand Curves to Market-Demand Curves 132
The "Law" of Demand 133
Application: Who Pays an Excise Tax? 134
Elasticity: The Measure of Responsiveness 138
Elasticity and the Shape of Demand Curves 141
Elasticity and Total Expenditure 143
What Determines Elasticity of Demand? 145
Elasticity Is a General Concept 146
Shifts in Demand Curves 151
The Time Dimension of the Demand Curve and
    Decision Making 152

SUMMARY 153
CONCEPTS FOR REVIEW 154
QUESTIONS FOR DISCUSSION 154

APPENDIX TO CHAPTER 5: STATISTICAL ANALYSIS OF
 DEMAND RELATIONSHIPS 156

 An Illustration: Did the Advertising Program Work? 157

CHAPTER 6 INPUT DECISIONS AND PRODUCTION COSTS 159

PRODUCTION, INPUT CHOICE, AND COST WITH ONE VARIABLE INPUT **161**

 Production: An Input's Total, Average, and Marginal
  Physical Products 161
 The "Law" of Diminishing Marginal Returns 164
 The Optimal Quantity of an Input 165
 The Firm's Three Cost Curves 167
 Fixed Costs and Variable Costs 169
 Shapes of the Average-Cost and Total-Cost Curves 172
 Long-Run versus Short-Run Costs 174

MULTIPLE INPUT DECISIONS: THE CHOICE OF INPUT COMBINATIONS **176**

 The Marginal Rule for Optimal Input Proportions:
  An Introduction 177
 Changes in Input Prices and Optimal Input Proportions 179
 The Production Function 179
 The Firm's Cost Curves 182
 Economies of Scale 183
 Diminishing Returns and Returns to Scale 186
 Historical Costs versus Analytical Cost Curves 187
 Cost Minimization in Theory and Practice 189

 SUMMARY 190
 CONCEPTS FOR REVIEW 191
 QUESTIONS FOR DISCUSSION 191

APPENDIX TO CHAPTER 6: A GRAPHIC ANALYSIS OF
 INPUT DECISIONS 193

 Characteristics of Isoquants 194
 The Choice of Input Combinations 194
 Cost Minimization, Expansion Path, and Cost Curves 195
 Effects of Changes in Input Prices 196

 SUMMARY 197
 CONCEPTS FOR REVIEW 198
 QUESTIONS FOR DISCUSSION 198

CHAPTER 7   OUTPUT–PRICE DECISIONS AND
             MARGINAL ANALYSIS   199

Price and Quantity: One Decision, Not Two   200
Do Firms Really Maximize Profits?   202
Total Profit: Keep Your Eye on the Goal   203
Profit Maximization: A Graphical Interpretation   206
Marginal Analysis and Maximization of *Total* Profit   208
Marginal Revenue and Marginal Cost: Guides to an Optimum   210
Marginal Analysis in Real Decision Problems   215
Conclusion: The Fundamental Role of Marginal Analysis   217
A Look Back and a Look Forward   218

SUMMARY   218
CONCEPTS FOR REVIEW   219
QUESTIONS FOR DISCUSSION   219

APPENDIX TO CHAPTER 7: THE RELATIONSHIPS AMONG
TOTAL, AVERAGE, AND MARGINAL DATA   221

Graphic Representation of Marginal and Average Curves   223
Questions for Discussion   224

PART 3   THE MARKET SYSTEM:
             VIRTUES AND VICES   225

CHAPTER 8   THE FIRM AND THE INDUSTRY UNDER
             PERFECT COMPETITION   227

Varieties of Market Structure: A Sneak Preview   228
Perfect Competition Defined   229
The Competitive Firm and Its Demand Curve   230
Short-Run Equilibrium of the Perfectly Competitive Firm   232
Short-Run Profit: Graphic Representation   234
The Case of Short-Term Losses   234
Shut-Down and Break-Even Analysis   235
The Short-Run Supply Curve of the Competitive Firm   238
The Short-Run Supply Curve of the Competitive Industry   238
Industry Equilibrium in the Short Run   239
Industry and Firm Equilibrium in the Long Run   241
The Long-Run Industry Supply Curve   245
Zero Economic Profit: The Opportunity Cost of Capital   245
Perfect Competition and Economic Efficiency   246
Cutting Pollution: The Carrot or the Stick?   248

SUMMARY   249
CONCEPTS FOR REVIEW   250
QUESTIONS FOR DISCUSSION   250

CHAPTER 9   THE PRICE SYSTEM: LAISSEZ FAIRE VERSUS
                   ECONOMIC PLANNING   253

EFFICIENCY AND FREE MARKETS   **254**

Efficient Resource Allocation: The Concept   254
Efficiency and the Public Interest   256
Scarcity and the Need to Co-ordinate Economic Decisions   258
Three Co-ordination Tasks in the Economy   260
Input–Output Analysis: The Virtual Impossibility of Perfect
    Central Planning   263
How Perfect Competition Achieves Efficiency: What to Produce   266
A Graphic Exposition of Efficiency   269
Other Roles of Prices: Income Distribution and Fairness   271
Toward Assessment of the Price Mechanism   272

ECONOMIC PLANNING   **273**

Alternative Economic Systems: What Are the Choices?   273
The Russian Economy   273
The Chinese Economy   277
The Amazing Japanese Economy   278
Is Japan a Planned Economy?   280
Postscript   281

SUMMARY   282
CONCEPTS FOR REVIEW   283
QUESTIONS FOR DISCUSSION   283

APPENDIX TO CHAPTER 9: THE INVISIBLE HAND IN THE
DISTRIBUTION OF GOODS AND IN
PRODUCTION PLANNING   285

Efficient Distribution of Commodities: Who Gets What?   285
Efficient Production Planning: Allocation of Inputs   287

SUMMARY   288
QUESTIONS FOR DISCUSSION   288

CHAPTER 10   MONOPOLY   289

Monopoly Defined   290
Causes of Monopoly: Barriers to Entry and Cost Advantages   291
Natural Monopoly   292
The Monopolist's Supply Decision   293
The Monopolist's Price and Marginal Revenue   294
Determining the Profit-Maximizing Output   296
Comparison of Monopoly and Perfect Competition   298
Can Anything Good Be Said about Monopoly?   301
Monopoly Policy   303
Monopoly and the Shifting of Pollution Charges   305

SUMMARY   307
CONCEPTS FOR REVIEW   308
QUESTIONS FOR DISCUSSION   308

CHAPTER 11 BETWEEN COMPETITION AND MONOPOLY   311

Monopolistic Competition   312
Price and Output Determination under Monopolistic
    Competition   314
The Excess-Capacity Theorem and Resource Allocation   316
Oligopoly   318
A Shopping List   319
Sales Maximization   322
Game Theory   324
Monopolistic Competition, Oligopoly, and Public Welfare   330

SUMMARY   331
CONCEPTS FOR REVIEW   332
QUESTIONS FOR DISCUSSION   332

CHAPTER 12 THE MARKET MECHANISM:
                SHORTCOMINGS AND REMEDIES   333

What Does the Market Do Poorly?   334
Efficient Resource Allocation: A Review   334
Externalities   337
Public Goods   343
Allocation of Resources between Present and Future   344
Some Other Sources of Market Failure   347
Market Failure and Government Failure   349
The Cost Disease of the Service Sector   354
Evaluative Comments   357

SUMMARY   358
CONCEPTS FOR REVIEW   359
QUESTIONS FOR DISCUSSION   359

CHAPTER 13 COMPARATIVE ADVANTAGE: THE QUESTION
                OF FREE TRADE   361

Issue: The Competition of "Cheap Foreign Labour"   362
Why Trade?   363
Mutual Gains from Trade   364
Comparative Advantage: The Fundamental Principle of
    Specialization   365
The Arithmetic of Comparative Advantage   366
The Graphics of Comparative Advantage   369
Supply–Demand Equilibrium and Pricing in Foreign Trade   372
Comparative Advantage and Competition of "Cheap
    Foreign Labour"   374

Tariffs, Quotas, and Other Interferences with Trade   374
How Tariffs and Quotas Work   377
Tariffs versus Quotas   379
Why Inhibit Trade?   381
Other Arguments for Protection   386
The Development of Trade Policy   388
The Canada–U.S. Free Trade Agreement   390
What Import Prices Benefit a Country?   395

MICROECONOMIC POLICY: A REVIEW AND A PREVIEW   399

The Proper Assignment of Policies to Goals   399

SUMMARY   401
CONCEPTS FOR REVIEW   402
QUESTIONS FOR DISCUSSION   402

APPENDIX TO CHAPTER 13: DISCOUNTING AND
PRESENT VALUE   405

SUMMARY   406
CONCEPTS FOR REVIEW   407
QUESTIONS FOR DISCUSSION   407

PART 4   MICROECONOMIC ISSUES   409

CHAPTER 14 PRICING THE FACTORS OF PRODUCTION:
            INCOME DISTRIBUTION   411

MARGINAL PRODUCTIVITY THEORY   412

The Principle of Marginal Productivity   412
The Derived Demand Curve for an Input   414
The Basic Determinants of Income Distribution   416
Issue: The Minimum Wage and Unemployment   417
The Determination of Rent   421
Generalization: What Determines Mario Lemieux's Salary?   425
Rent Controls: The Misplaced Analogy   428
Criticisms of Marginal Productivity Theory and
    Mainstream Economics   429

INTEREST AND PROFIT   435

The Issue of Usury Laws: Are Interest Rates Too High?   435
The Market Determination of Interest Rates   437
Issue: Are Profits Too High or Too Low?   441
What Accounts for Profits?   442

The Labour Market 445

The Supply of Labour 445
The Demand for Labour and the Determination of Wages 447
Why Wages Differ 447
Investment in Human Capital 449
Unions and Collective Bargaining 452
Unions as a Labour Monopoly 457
Monopsony and Bilateral Monopoly 460
Collective Bargaining and Strikes 462
Collective Bargaining in the Public Sector 464
Corporatism and Industrial Democracy 465

Summary 466
Concepts for Review 467
Questions for Discussion 468

Chapter 15 The Tax System and Income Inequality 471

Taxes in Canada 472

Some Facts and Definitions 472
The Personal Income Tax 473
Sales and Excise Taxes 476
Other Taxes 480
Fiscal Federalism 481
The Concept of Equity in Taxation 482
The Concept of Efficiency in Taxation 485
Shifting the Burden of Taxation: Tax Incidence 487
When Taxation Can Improve Efficiency 493
Equity, Efficiency, and the Optimal Tax 494

Poverty and the Welfare System 496

Poverty: The Facts 496
Inequality: The Facts 499
Depicting Income Distributions: The Lorenz Curve 500
Policies to Combat Poverty 503
The Negative Income Tax 504
Other Tax and Expenditure Programs 506

Discrimination 508

Discrimination: The Facts 508
Discrimination: The Theory 509
Policies to Combat Discrimination 512

Equality versus Efficiency 515

The Politics and Economics of Inequality 515
The Optimal Amount of Inequality 515
The Trade-Off between Equality and Efficiency 517
Postscript on the Distribution of Income 520

SUMMARY 520
CONCEPTS FOR REVIEW 522
QUESTIONS FOR DISCUSSION 523

CHAPTER 16 REGULATION OF INDUSTRY AND COMPETITION POLICY 525

MONOPOLY, REGULATION, AND NATIONALIZATION 526

The Degree of Regulation in Canada 526
Why Regulation? 527
Why Regulators Sometimes Raise Prices 533
Some Pricing Issues 535
Reactions to the Problems of Regulation 539
Some Effects of Deregulation 542
A Word on Nationalization 544
The Movement toward Privatization 546

THE COMPETITION ACT 548

The Origin and Development of Competition Policy 548
Current Legislation 550
Issues in Concentration of Industry 559
Evidence on Concentration in Industry 561

SUMMARY 564
CONCEPTS FOR REVIEW 565
QUESTIONS FOR DISCUSSION 566

CHAPTER 17 ENVIRONMENTAL PROTECTION AND RESOURCE CONSERVATION 567

THE ECONOMICS OF ENVIRONMENTAL PROTECTION 567

The Environment in Perspective: Is Everything Getting Steadily Worse? 568
The Law of Conservation of Matter and Energy 570
Environmental Damage as an Externality 571
Supply–Demand Analysis of Environmental Problems 573
Basic Approaches to Environmental Policy 577
Emissions Taxes versus Direct Controls 580
Other Financial Devices to Protect the Environment 583
Two Cheers for the Market 587

THE ECONOMICS OF ENERGY AND NATURAL RESOURCES 587

The Free Market and Pricing of Depletable Resources 589
The Free Market and Resource Depletion 593
On the Virtues of Rising Prices 595
Controversies over Canadian Resource Policy 597
Serious Problems Remain 601
Alternatives for the Future 602

SUMMARY	606
CONCEPTS FOR REVIEW	607
QUESTIONS FOR DISCUSSION	607

PART 5 MACROECONOMICS: AGGREGATE SUPPLY AND DEMAND ANALYSIS 609

CHAPTER 18 NATIONAL PRODUCT, UNEMPLOYMENT, AND INFLATION 611

GROSS DOMESTIC PRODUCT AND STABILIZATION POLICY **612**

Aggregation and Macroeconomics	612
Supply and Demand in Macroeconomics	614
Gross Domestic Product	616
Limitations of the GDP: What GDP Is Not	618
The Economy on a Roller Coaster	621
The Great Depression of the 1930s	623
From World War II to the Present	626
The Problem of Macroeconomic Stabilization	627

UNEMPLOYMENT **629**

Counting the Unemployed: The Official Statistics	630
Types of Unemployment	632
What Is "Full Employment"?	633
Unemployment Insurance: The Invaluable Cushion	634
The Economic Costs of High Unemployment	637

INFLATION **640**

Inflation as a Redistributor of Income and Wealth	644
Real versus Nominal Interest Rates	645
Inflation and the Tax System	646
Other Costs of Inflation	649
The Costs of Creeping versus Galloping Inflation	650
SUMMARY	651
CONCEPTS FOR REVIEW	652
QUESTIONS FOR DISCUSSION	652

APPENDIX A TO CHAPTER 18: NATIONAL INCOME ACCOUNTING 654

Defining GDP: Exceptions to the Rules	654
GDP as the Sum of Final Goods and Services	654
GDP as the Sum of All Factor Payments	656
GDP as the Sum of Values Added	657
Alternative Measures of the Income of the Nation	659

SUMMARY   660
CONCEPTS FOR REVIEW   661
QUESTIONS FOR DISCUSSION   661

APPENDIX B TO CHAPTER 18: HOW STATISTICIANS
    MEASURE INFLATION   663

Index Numbers for Inflation   663
The Consumer Price Index   664
How to Use a Price Index to "Deflate" Monetary Figures   665
The GDP Deflator   665

SUMMARY   666
CONCEPTS FOR REVIEW   666
QUESTIONS FOR DISCUSSION   666

CHAPTER 19 INCOME AND SPENDING:
                THE POWERFUL CONSUMER   669

Aggregate Demand, National Product, and National Income   670
The Circular Flow of Spending, Production, and Income   671
Demand Management and the Powerful Consumer   674
Consumer Spending and Income: The Important Relationship   676
The Consumption Function and the Marginal Propensity
    to Consume   680
Movements along versus Shifts of the Consumption Function   683
Other Determinants of Consumer Spending   683
Sales Tax Changes   687
The Predictability of Consumer Behaviour   688

SUMMARY   689
CONCEPTS FOR REVIEW   690
QUESTIONS FOR DISCUSSION   690

CHAPTER 20 DEMAND-SIDE CONSIDERATIONS:
                UNEMPLOYMENT OR INFLATION?   693

The Extreme Variability of Investment   694
A Simplified Circular Flow   695
The Meaning of Equilibrium GDP   697
Equilibrium on the Demand Side of the Economy   699
Constructing the Total Expenditure Schedule   700
The Mechanics of Income Determination   702
The Simple Algebra of Income Determination   704
The Aggregate Demand Curve   706
Demand-Side Equilibrium and Full Employment   708
The Co-ordination of Saving and Investment   710

SUMMARY   713
CONCEPTS FOR REVIEW   714
QUESTIONS FOR DISCUSSION   715

CHAPTER 21   CHANGES ON THE DEMAND SIDE:
             MULTIPLIER ANALYSIS   717

The Magic of the Multiplier   717
Demystifying the Multiplier: How It Works   720
Algebraic Statement of the Multiplier   721
The Multiplier Effect of Consumer Spending   724
The Multiplier in Reverse   725
The Paradox of Thrift   726
The Simple Algebra of the Multiplier   727
The Multiplier and the Aggregate Demand Curve   728

SUMMARY   730
CONCEPTS FOR REVIEW   731
QUESTIONS FOR DISCUSSION   731

CHAPTER 22   SUPPLY-SIDE CONSIDERATIONS:
             UNEMPLOYMENT *AND* INFLATION?   733

The Mystery of Stagflation   734
The Aggregate Supply Curve   734
Shifts of the Aggregate Supply Curve   736
The Shape of the Aggregate Supply Curve   739
Equilibrium of Aggregate Demand and Supply   739
Recessionary and Inflationary Gaps Revisited   741
Adjusting to an Inflationary Gap: Inflation   742
Demand Inflation and Stagflation   745
Adjusting to a Recessionary Gap: Deflation or Unemployment?   747
Does the Economy Have a Self-Correcting Mechanism?   750
Stagflation from Supply Shifts   752
Inflation and the Multiplier   754
A Role for Stabilization Policy   757

SUMMARY   757
CONCEPTS FOR REVIEW   758
QUESTIONS FOR DISCUSSION   758

PART 6   FISCAL, MONETARY, AND
             EXCHANGE-RATE POLICY   761

CHAPTER 23   FISCAL POLICY   763

Government Purchases and Equilibrium Income   763
Income Taxes and the Consumption Schedule   766
Tax Policy and Equilibrium Income   768

Multipliers for Tax Policy   770
Government Transfer Payments   771
The Multiplier Revisited   772
Equilibrium Income with Exports and Imports   776
The Canadian and World Economies   778
Planning Expansive Fiscal Policy   779
Planning Restrictive Fiscal Policy   780
The Choice between Spending Policy and Tax Policy   781
Some Harsh Realities   783
The Scope for Government Policy in Quantitative Terms   783
Taxes and the Aggregate Supply Schedule   784

SUMMARY   791
CONCEPTS FOR REVIEW   791
QUESTIONS FOR DISCUSSION   792

CHAPTER 24 FIRMS AND THEIR FINANCING:
            STOCKS AND BONDS   795

Firms in Canada   796
Financing Corporate Activity   800
Stocks and Bonds   801
Bond Prices and Interest Rates   803
Corporate Choice between Stocks and Bonds   803
Buying Stocks and Bonds   804
Following a Portfolio's Performance   805
Stock Exchanges and Their Functions   808
Stock Exchanges and Corporate Capital Needs   809
The Issue of Speculation   810
Stock Prices as Random Walks   814

SUMMARY   817
CONCEPTS FOR REVIEW   817
QUESTIONS FOR DISCUSSION   818

CHAPTER 25 MONEY AND THE BANKING SYSTEM   819

Policy Issue: Competition among Banks   819
Barter versus Monetary Exchange   821
The Conceptual Definition of Money   822
What Serves as Money?   822
How the Quantity of Money Is Measured   825
How Banking Began   828
Principles of Bank Management: Profits versus Safety   830
Bank Regulation   830
How Bankers Keep Books   831
The Limits to Money Creation by a Single Bank   832
Multiple Money Creation by a Series of Banks   835

The Process in Reverse: Multiple Contractions of the
    Money Supply 838
Why the Money-Creation Formula Is Oversimplified 840
The Need for Monetary Control 841

Summary 843
Concepts for Review 844
Questions for Discussion 844

Chapter 26 Central Banking and Monetary Policy 847

The Bank of Canada 847
The Independence of the Bank of Canada 848
Controlling the Money Supply 850
Flexible Exchange Rates: A Prerequisite for Independent
    Control of the Money Supply 854
Exchange-Rate Determination in a Free Market 855
Fixed Exchange Rates 857
The Money-Supply Mechanism: A Summary 860
The Demand for Money 862
Equilibrium in the Money Market When Foreign and Domestic
    Financial Markets Are Independent 864
Equilibrium in the Money Market When Foreign and Domestic
    Financial Markets Are Integrated 866
Conclusion and Preview 871

Summary 872
Concepts for Review 873
Questions for Discussion 873

Chapter 27 Stabilization Policy for a
                Closed Economy 875

Interest Rates and Total Expenditure 877
Monetary Policy in the Keynesian Model 877
Money and the Price Level in the Keynesian Model 881
Velocity and the Quantity Theory of Money 883
The Determinants of Velocity 885
Monetarism: The Quantity Theory Modernized 888
Reconciling the Keynesian and Monetarist Views 890
Should Stabilization Policy Rely on Fiscal or Monetary Policy? 892
Controversy Surrounding the Aggregate Supply Curve 895
Should We Have a Stabilization Policy at All? 898
Other Dimensions of the Rules-versus-Discretion Debate 902
Conclusion: What Should Be Done? 905

Summary 906
Concepts for Review 908
Questions for Discussion 908

CHAPTER 28 STABILIZATION POLICY FOR A SMALL
                OPEN ECONOMY   911

Fiscal Policy under a Fixed Exchange-Rate Regime   912
Fiscal Policy under a Flexible Exchange-Rate Regime   913
Monetary Policy under a Fixed Exchange-Rate Regime   914
Monetary Policy under a Flexible Exchange-Rate Regime   917
Review of Aggregate Demand Policy Options   919
Exchange Rates and Aggregate Supply   920
Review   922
Foreign Interest Rate Increases and Aggregate Supply   923
Foreign Trade Restrictions   926
A Concluding Comment   927

SUMMARY   927
CONCEPTS FOR REVIEW   928
QUESTIONS FOR DISCUSSION   929

PART 7   MACROECONOMIC ISSUES   931

CHAPTER 29 POLICY CO-ORDINATION
                IN THE WORLD ECONOMY   933

What Determines Exchange Rates?   933
Fixed Exchange Rates and the Definition of the Balance of
    Payments   939
The Canadian Balance-of-Payments Accounts   939
A Bit of History: The Gold Standard   940
The Bretton Woods System and the International
    Monetary Fund   941
Adjustment Mechanisms under the Bretton Woods System   943
Why Try to Fix Exchange Rates?   945
The Current Mixed System   946
Recent Developments in International Financial Markets   948
The Link between the Budget Deficit and the Trade Deficit   950
Concluding Comment   953

SUMMARY   953
CONCEPTS FOR REVIEW   955
QUESTIONS FOR DISCUSSION   955

CHAPTER 30 BUDGET DEFICITS AND THE NATIONAL DEBT   957

Should the Budget Be Balanced?   957
Deficits and Debt: Some Terminology   958
Some Facts about the National Debt   959
Interpreting the Budget Deficit   962

Bogus Arguments about the Burden of the Debt 968
Budget Deficits and Inflation 970
Deficits, Interest Rates, and Crowding Out 973
The True Burden of the National Debt 975
Conclusion: What Should Be Done about the Deficit? 976

SUMMARY 981
CONCEPTS FOR REVIEW 982
QUESTIONS FOR DISCUSSION 982

CHAPTER 31 THE TRADE-OFF BETWEEN INFLATION
AND UNEMPLOYMENT 983

Demand-Side Inflation versus Supply-Side Inflation: A Review 984
Applying the Model to a Growing Economy 986
Demand-Side Inflation and the Phillips Curve 987
Supply-Side Inflation and the Collapse of the Phillips Curve 992
What the Phillips Curve Is Not 994
Fighting Inflation with Fiscal and Monetary Policy 997
What Should Be Done? 999
Inflationary Expectations and the Phillips Curve 1002
The Theory of Rational Expectations 1005
Why Economists (and Politicians) Disagree 1008
The Dilemma of Demand Management 1008
Attempts to Reduce the Trade-Off Directly 1009
Incomes Policy 1010
Profit-Sharing 1013
Indexing 1014
Controversies over Stabilization Policy 1017

SUMMARY 1018
CONCEPTS FOR REVIEW 1019
QUESTIONS FOR DISCUSSION 1019

CHAPTER 32 PRODUCTIVITY, GROWTH,
AND DEVELOPMENT 1021

PRODUCTIVITY 1021

Vast Changes in Living Standards 1022
Significance of the Growth of Productivity 1024
Convergence in Productivity Performance 1025
Determinants of Productivity Growth 1026
Productivity and the Deindustrialization Thesis 1028
Unemployment and Productivity Growth 1029
The Real Cost of Lagging Productivity: Lagging Wages and
Living Standards 1030

GROWTH AND ITS COSTS AND BENEFITS   1033

Population Growth: Is Less Really More?   1033
The Crowded Planet: Exponential Population Growth   1035
Requirements for Increased Growth   1037
Sacrificing Current Consumption for Higher
    Future Consumption   1039
Growth without Sacrificing Consumption: Something
    for Nothing?   1040
Is More Growth Really Better?   1041

PROBLEMS OF THE LESS DEVELOPED COUNTRIES   1044

Living in the LDCs   1044
Recent Trends   1045
Impediments to Development in the LDCs   1048
Help from Industrialized Economies   1053
The "North–South" Controversy and Commodity
    Price Stabilization   1055

SUMMARY   1057
CONCEPTS FOR REVIEW   1058
QUESTIONS FOR DISCUSSION   1059

GLOSSARY   G-1

INDEX   I-1

CREDITS   C-1

1

GETTING
ACQUAINTED WITH
ECONOMICS

One of the fundamental purposes of an introductory text in economics is to provide the reader with a basic level of economic literacy. After all, without such knowledge, how can one have confidence that he or she is voting in an intelligent manner, when so many of the issues that we are asked to consider at election time are economic in nature? Of course, no text should pretend to instruct readers on how to vote. A good text should, however, explain clearly the key economic issues so that each individual can come to an informed opinion. A textbook will fail if the insights it provides on such topical issues are lost amid a mass of technical material and jargon. To avoid this problem, we start each of the seven major parts of this book by highlighting four key election issues that will be covered in that part. While these topics are not the only ones addressed in the text, they do constitute a list of 28 of the most important economic issues that political parties debate in almost every election.

The four topics for Part 1 are listed in the margin at right. They will be among the propositions you will understand after reading the book's first three chapters.

The profit motive can be harnessed to help clean up the environment. (pages 51, 76–78)

Rent controls worsen the housing shortage. (pages 79–81)

Minimum-wage laws cause unemployment. (page 86)

Speculators often serve the public interest. (page 88)

THE PROBLEMS AND TOOLS OF THE ECONOMIST

Economics is a broad-ranging discipline, both in the questions it asks and in the methods it uses to seek answers. Many definitions of economics have been proposed, but we prefer to avoid any attempt to define the discipline in a single sentence or paragraph. Instead, this chapter will introduce you to economics by letting the subject matter speak for itself.

The first part of this chapter is intended to give you some idea of the types of problems that can be approached through economic analysis and the kinds of solutions that economic principles suggest. Many of the world's most pressing problems are economic in nature. So a little knowledge of basic economics is essential to anyone who wants to understand the world in which he or she lives.

The second part briefly introduces the methods of economic inquiry and the tools that economists use, while the appendix zeroes in specifically on the use and misuse of graphs. These are tools you may find useful in your life as a citizen, consumer, and worker long after the course is over.

Why does public discussion of economic policy so often show the abysmal ignorance of the participants? Why do I so often want to cry at what public figures, the press, and television commentators say about economic affairs?

ROBERT M. SOLOW

IDEAS FOR BEYOND THE FINAL EXAM

As university professors, we realize it is inevitable that you will forget much of what you learn in this course—perhaps with a sense of relief—soon after the final exam. There is not much point in bemoaning this fact; elephants may never forget, but people do. Nevertheless, some economic ideas are so important that you will want to remember them well beyond the final exam. If you do not, you will have short-changed your own education. To help you pick out a few of the most crucial concepts, we have selected twelve ideas from among the many contained in this book. Some offer critical and enduring insights into the workings of the economy. Others bear on important policy issues that often appear in the newspapers. Still others point out common misunderstandings that occur among even the most thoughtful lay observers. As the quotation that opens this chapter suggests, many learned judges, politicians, business leaders, and university administrators who misused or failed to understand these economic principles could have made far wiser decisions than they did.

These twelve important ideas involve general issues, such as how two countries both gain from trading with each other, even when one of them is more efficient at producing everything! You will find often that one of these general insights forms the underlying rationale for the "election issues" that are highlighted in the introductions to each of the text's seven parts.

Each of the twelve "Ideas for Beyond the Final Exam" will be discussed in depth as it occurs in the course of the book; you should not expect to understand these ideas fully after reading this first chapter. Nonetheless, we think it useful to sketch them briefly here both to introduce you to economics and to provide a selective preview of what is to come.

▦ IDEA 1:
RATIONAL CHOICE AND TRUE ECONOMIC COSTS

Despite dramatic improvements in our standard of living since the Industrial Revolution, we have not come anywhere near a state of unlimited abundance, and so we must constantly make choices. If you purchase a house, you may not be able to afford to eat at expensive restaurants as often as in the past. If a firm decides to retool its factories, it may have to postpone plans for new executive offices. If a government expands its road networks, it may be forced to reduce its outlays on school buildings.

Economists say that the true costs of such decisions are not the number of dollars spent on the house, the new equipment, or the roads, but rather the value of what must be given up in order to acquire the item — the restaurant meals, the new executive offices, or the new schools. These are called *opportunity costs* because they represent the opportunities the individual, firm, or government must forego to make the desired expenditure. Economists maintain that opportunity costs must be considered in the decision-making process if rational choices are to be made (see Chapter 2).

The cost of a university or college education provides a vivid example that is probably close to your heart. How much do you think it costs to go to university? Most likely you would answer this question by totalling your expenditures on tuition, room and board, books, and the like and then deducting any scholarship funds or government grants you may receive. Economists would not. They would first want to know how much you could be earning if you were not attending university. This may sound like an irrelevant question, but because you give up these earnings by attending university, they must be added to your tuition bill as a cost of your education. Nor would economists accept the dormitory expense for room and board as a measure of your living costs. They would want to know by how much this exceeds what it would have cost you to live at home, and only this extra cost would be counted as an expense. On balance, a university or college education probably costs more than you think.

⌖ IDEA 2:

MUTUAL GAINS FROM VOLUNTARY EXCHANGE

One of the most fundamental ideas of economics is that, in a **voluntary exchange**, both parties must gain something, or at least expect to gain something. Otherwise, why would they both agree to the exchange? This principle may seem self-evident, but it is often ignored in practice.

For example, it was widely believed for centuries that governments should interfere with international trade because one country's gain from a swap must be the other country's loss (see Chapter 13). Analogously, some people feel instinctively that if Mr. A profits handsomely from a deal with Mr. B, then Mr. B must have been exploited. Laws sometimes prohibit mutually beneficial exchanges between buyers and sellers—for example, when rental housing units are eliminated because the rent is "too high" (Chapter 3), or when a willing worker cannot be hired because the wage rate is "too low" (Chapters 3 and 14).

In each of these cases and in many more, well-intentioned but misguided reasoning blocks the mutual gains that arise from voluntary exchange—and thereby interferes with one of the most basic functions of an economic system (see Chapter 2).

⌖ IDEA 3:

ATTEMPTS TO REPEAL THE LAWS OF SUPPLY AND DEMAND: THE MARKET STRIKES BACK

When a commodity is in short supply, its price naturally tends to rise. Sometimes disgruntled consumers badger politicians into "solving" the problem by imposing a legal ceiling on the price. Similarly, when supplies are abundant — say, when fine weather produces extraordinarily abundant crops — prices tend to fall. Naturally, this makes suppliers unhappy, and they often succeed in getting legislation enacted that prohibits low prices by imposing price floors. But such attempts to repeal the laws of supply and demand usually backfire and sometimes produce results virtually the opposite of those intended.

Where rent controls are adopted to protect tenants, housing grows scarce because the law makes it unprofitable to build and maintain apartments. When minimum-wage legislation is enacted to protect low-wage workers, low-wage jobs disappear. Price floors are placed under agricultural products, and surpluses pile up. History provides spectacular examples of the way in which free markets strike back at attempts to interfere with the way they would otherwise work. For example, when the Spanish army surrounded Antwerp in 1584, hoping to starve the city into submission, profiteers kept Antwerp going by smuggling food and supplies through enemy lines. However, when the city fathers adopted price controls to end their "unconscionable" prices, smuggling was no longer worthwhile, so supplies suddenly dried up and the city soon surrendered.

As we will see in Chapter 3 and elsewhere in this book, such consequences of interference with the price mechanism are no accident. They follow inevitably from the way free markets work. Despite the many examples from history, many policy-makers still call for interference with the price mechanism.

⌂ IDEA 4:
THE IMPORTANCE OF MARGINAL ANALYSIS

Many pages in this book will be spent explaining and extolling the virtues of a type of decision-making process called **marginal analysis** (see especially Chapters 4 and 7), which can best be illustrated by an example.

Suppose that an airline is told by its accountants that the full cost of transporting one passenger from Montreal to Edmonton is $350. Can the airline profit by offering a reduced rate of $250 to students who fly on a standby basis? The surprising answer is probably yes. The reason is that the airline is committed to pay most of the $350 cost per passenger whether the plane carries 20 passengers or 120 passengers. Marginal analysis says that full costs—which include costs of maintenance, landing rights, ground crews, and so on—are irrelevant to an airline interested in making as much profit as possible. The only costs that are relevant in deciding whether to carry standby passengers for reduced rates are the extra costs of writing and processing additional tickets, the food and beverages these passengers consume, the additional fuel required, and so on. These costs are called **marginal costs**, and they are probably quite small in this instance. Any passenger who pays the airline more than its marginal cost will add something to the company's profit, so it probably is more profitable to let the students ride for the reduced fare than to fly the plane with some empty seats.

In many real cases, decision-makers who failed to understand marginal analysis have rejected advantageous possibilities like the reduced fare in our hypothetical example. These people were misled by calculating in terms of average- rather than marginal-cost figures—an error that can be quite costly.

⌂ IDEA 5:

INCREASING OUTPUT MAY REQUIRE SACRIFICING EQUALITY

Many people support tax cuts on the grounds that they spur productivity and efficiency by providing greater incentives for working, saving, and investing. The provision of such incentives was one of the primary reasons the federal government has made the limits for contributions to registered retirement savings plans (RRSPs) much more generous.

But there is at least one problem with this approach: To provide stronger incentives for success in the economic game, the gaps between the "winners" and the "losers" must necessarily be widened. It is these gaps, after all, that provide the incentives to work harder, to save more, and to invest productively.

However, some observers feel that the unequal distribution of income in our society is unjust, that it is inequitable for the wealthy to sail yachts and give expensive parties while poor people live in slums and eat inadequate diets. People who hold this view are disturbed by the fact that tax cuts (like those involved in the RRSP provisions) are quite likely to make the distribution of income even more unequal.

This example illustrates a genuine and pervasive dilemma. A trade-off often exists between the *size* of a nation's output and the degree of *equality* with which that output is distributed. As illustrated by the example of tax cuts, programs that increase production often breed inequality. Further, as we shall see in Chapter 15, many policies designed to divide the proverbial economic pie more equally inadvertently cause the pie to shrink. But, as we shall also see, economists make many useful suggestions about how this trade-off can be minimized.

⌂ IDEA 6:

EXTERNALITIES: A SHORTCOMING OF THE MARKET CURED BY MARKET METHODS

Markets are very efficient in producing the goods that consumers want in the quantities in which they are desired. Markets do so by offering large financial rewards to those who respond to what consumers want to buy and who make these products available economically. Similarly, the market mechanism minimizes waste and inefficiency by causing inefficient producers to lose money.

This system works well as long as an exchange between a seller and a buyer affects only those two parties. But often an economic transaction affects third parties that were not consulted. Examples abound: The utility that supplies electricity to your home also produces soot and pollutants that despoil the air and affect the health of others; after a farmer sprays crops with toxic pesticides, the poison may seep into the ground water and affect the health of neighbouring communities.

Such social costs — called **externalities** because they affect parties external to the economic transaction that causes them—escape the control of the market mechanism, since there is normally no financial incentive motivating polluters to minimize the damage they do. The electric company and the farmer do not include environmental damage in their cost calculations. As a consequence, it pays firms to make their products as cheaply as possible, disregarding externalities that may damage the quality of life.

Yet, as we will learn in Chapters 12 and 17, there is a way for the government to use the market mechanism to control undesirable externalities. If the public utility and the farmer are charged for the harm they cause to the public, just as they are charged when they use tangible resources such as coal and fertilizer, they will have an incentive to reduce the amount of pollution they generate. Thus, in such cases, economists believe that market methods are often the best way to cure one of the market's most important shortcomings.

🏛 IDEA 7:
THE SURPRISING PRINCIPLE OF COMPARATIVE ADVANTAGE

The Japanese economy produces many products that Canadians buy in huge quantities, including cars, TV sets, cameras, and electronic equipment. Canadian manufacturers have complained about the competition and demanded protection against the flood of imports that, in their view, threatens the Canadian standard of living. Is this view justified?

Economists think not. But what if a combination of higher productivity and lower wages were to permit Japan to produce *everything* more cheaply than we could? Wouldn't most Canadians be out of work? Wouldn't our nation be impoverished?

A remarkable result, called the **law of comparative advantage**, shows that even in this extreme case the two nations should still trade and that each can gain as a result! We will explain this principle fully in Chapter 13 (where we will also note some potentially valid arguments in favour of protecting domestic industry). But, for now, a simple parable will make the reason clear.

Suppose Sam grows up on a farm and excels at ploughing, but is also a successful country singer who earns $2000 a performance at hotels and nightclubs. Should Sam refuse some singing engagements to leave time for ploughing? Of course not. Instead, he should hire Alfie, a much less efficient farmer, to plough for him. Sam is the better farmer, but he earns so much more by specializing in singing that it pays him to leave the farming to Alfie. Alfie, though a poorer farmer than Sam, is an even worse singer. Thus, Alfie earns a living by specializing in the job at which he at least has a *comparative* advantage (his farming is not quite as bad as his singing), and both Alfie and Sam gain. The same is true of two countries. Even if one of them is more efficient at everything, both countries can gain by producing the things they do best comparatively.

IDEA 8:
THE TRADE-OFF BETWEEN INFLATION AND UNEMPLOYMENT

At the start of the 1980s, Canadian policy-makers waged all-out war on inflation. The war was won: Inflation was reduced dramatically. But casualties were heavy: The national unemployment rate, which had averaged 6.8 percent during the 1970s, ran at a stunning 11.5 percent in 1982 and 1983, and remained above 9 percent until 1987.

Economists maintain that this conjunction of events was no coincidence. Owing to features of our economy that we will study in Parts 5, 6, and 7, there is an agonizing *trade-off* between inflation and unemployment in the short run, meaning that most policies that reduce inflation also cause unemployment to rise. Since this trade-off poses a fundamental dilemma of national economic policy, we will devote all of Chapter 31 to examining it in detail.

IDEA 9:
THE ILLUSION OF HIGH INTEREST RATES

Is it more costly to borrow money at 5 percent interest or at 13 percent interest? That would appear to be an easy question to answer, even without any knowledge of economics. But, in fact, it is not. An example will show why.

Around 1960, banks were lending money to home buyers at annual interest rates of about 5 percent. Twenty years later, those rates had risen to 13 percent. Yet economists maintain that it was actually cheaper to borrow in 1980 than in 1960. Why? Because inflation in 1980 was running at about 10 percent per year, while in 1960 it stood at only about 1 percent.

Why is information on inflation relevant to deciding how costly it is to borrow? Consider the position of a person who lends $100 for one year at a rate of 13 percent interest when the inflation rate is at 10 percent. At the end of the year, the lender gets back his $100 plus $13 interest. But over that same year, because of inflation, he loses $10 in terms of what his money can buy. That is, in terms of *purchasing power*, the lender gains only $3 on his $100 loan, or 3 percent.

Now consider someone who lends $100 at 5 percent interest when prices are rising only 1 percent a year. This lender gets back the original

$100 plus $5 in interest and loses only $1 in purchasing power from inflation—for a net gain of $4, or a 4 percent return on her loan.

As we will learn in Chapter 18, the failure by legislators to understand this principle has caused troubles for our tax laws, and in Chapter 30 we will see that it has even led to misunderstanding of the size and nature of the government budget deficit.

⛬ IDEA 10:
THE CONSEQUENCES OF BUDGET DEFICITS

Large federal budget deficits have been the focus of all of the Canadian government's budgets in recent years. The conflicting claims and counterclaims that have marked the debate over budget deficits are bound to confuse laypeople. Some critics claim that deficits hold dire consequences—including higher interest rates, more inflation, a stagnant economy, and a heavy burden on future generations of Canadians. Others deny these charges.

Who is right? In Chapter 30, we will learn that there is no easy answer —a budget deficit may be sound or unsound policy, depending on its size and on the reasons for its existence. However, whether or not the deficit represents sound policy, if it is generally believed to be unsound, its existence limits the government's ability to undertake new policies.

⛬ IDEA 11:
THE OVERWHELMING IMPORTANCE OF PRODUCTIVITY

In Geneva, a worker in a watch factory now turns out roughly one hundred times as many mechanical watches per year as his ancestor did three centuries ago. The **productivity** of labour (output per worker hour) in cotton production has probably increased by more than a thousandfold in the past two hundred years. It is estimated that production per hour of labour in North American manufacturing has gone up about seven times in the past century. This means that we can enjoy about seven times as much clothing, housewares, and luxury goods as were available to a typical citizen one hundred years ago.

Economic issues such as inflation, unemployment, and monopoly are important to us all and will receive great attention in this book. But in the long run, nothing has as great an effect on our material well-being and the amounts society can afford to spend on hospitals, schools, and social amenities as the rate of growth of productivity. Chapter 32 points out that, because productivity compounds like the interest on savings in a bank, what appears to be a small increase in productivity growth can have a huge effect on a country's standard of living over a long period of time. Since 1800, for example, productivity growth in North America is estimated to have averaged only slightly more than 1.5 percent a year. But that was enough to increase the output of manufactured goods per person about twenty times—a truly staggering amount.

﬙ IDEA 12:
THE COST DISEASE OF THE SERVICE SECTOR

There is a distressing phenomenon occurring throughout the industrialized world. Many community services have apparently been growing poorer — less-frequent postal deliveries, larger university classes, less-reliable garbage pickups—while the public is paying more and more for them. Indeed, the cost of providing public services has risen consistently faster than the rate of inflation. A natural response is to attribute the problem to government inefficiency. But this is certainly not the whole story, because private services have also grown more costly.

As we shall see in Chapter 12, one of the major causes of the problem is economic. It has nothing to do with the inefficiency (or corruption) of public employees; rather, it relates to the dazzling growth in efficiency of private manufacturing industries! Because technological improvements make workers more productive in manufacturing, wages rise. Further, they rise not only for the manufacturing workers, but also for postal workers, teachers, and other public employees because workers can leave industries with low-paying jobs and compete for jobs in high-paying industries. But for personal services, technology is not easily changed. Since it still takes one person to drive a postal truck and one teacher to teach a class, the cost of these services is forced to rise. The same sort of cost disease affects other services, such as medical care, restaurants, retailing, and automobile repair.

This is important to understand not because it excuses the financial record of our governments, but because an understanding of the problem suggests what we should expect the future to bring and, perhaps, indicates what policies should be advocated to correct the problem.

EPILOGUE

These, then, are a dozen of the more fundamental concepts to be found in this book — ideas that we hope you will retain "Beyond the Final Exam." Do not try to learn them perfectly right now, for you will hear much more about each of them as the book progresses. Instead, keep them in mind as you read—we will point them out to you as they occur by the use of this icon: ﬙ —and look back over this list at the end of the course. You may be amazed to see how natural, or even obvious, they will seem then.

INSIDE THE ECONOMIST'S TOOL KIT

Now that you have some idea of the kinds of issues economists deal with, you should know something about how they grapple with these problems.

ECONOMICS AS A DISCIPLINE

Economics has something of a split personality. Clearly the most rigorous of the social sciences, it nevertheless looks decidedly more "social" than "scientific" when compared with physics.

Economists are jacks of several trades, borrowing modes of investigation from numerous fields. They make extensive use of mathematical reasoning and historical study, but use neither in quite the same way as do mathematicians or historians. Statistical inference also plays an important role in economic inquiry, but economists have had to modify standard statistical procedures to fit the kinds of data they deal with—data that are not generated under the controlled conditions of the laboratory.

An introductory course in economics cannot make you an economist, but it should help you approach social problems from a pragmatic and dispassionate point of view. Answers to all of society's problems will not be found in this book. But you should learn how to pose questions in ways that will help produce answers that are both useful and illuminating.

THE NEED FOR ABSTRACTION

Some students find economics unduly abstract and unrealistic. The stylized world depicted by economic theory seems only a distant cousin to the world students see around them. There is an old joke about three people—a chemist, a physicist, and an economist—stranded on an isolated island with an ample supply of canned food but no implements with which to open the cans. In debating what to do, the chemist suggests lighting a fire under the cans, thus expanding their contents and causing the cans to burst. The physicist doubts that this will work and advocates building a catapult with which they can smash the cans against some nearby boulders. Then, they turn to the economist for his suggestion. He thinks for a moment and announces, "Let's assume we have a can opener."

Economists do make unrealistic assumptions, and you will encounter many of them in the pages that follow. But this propensity to abstract from reality results from the complexity of the real world, not from any fondness economists have for sounding absurd.

Compare the chemist's task of explaining the interactions of compounds in a chemical reaction with the economist's task of explaining the interactions of people in an economy. Are molecules ever motivated by greed or altruism, by envy or ambition? Do they ever emulate other molecules? Do forecasts about them influence their behaviour? People, of course, do all these things, and many, many more. It is therefore immeasurably more difficult to predict human behaviour than it is to predict chemical reactions. If economists tried to keep track of every aspect of human behaviour, they could surely never hope to understand the nature of the economy. This leads to the following principle:

Abstraction from details is necessary to understand the functioning of anything as complex as the economy.

To appreciate why the economist **abstracts** from details, put yourself in the following hypothetical situation. You have just arrived, for the first time in your life, in Montreal. You are now at Hôpital Jean-Talon. This is the point marked *A* in Figures 1-1 and 1-2, which are alternative maps of part of Montreal. You want to drive to the Hôpital St. Mary, marked *B* on each map. Which map would you find more useful? You will notice that Map 1 (Figure 1-1) has the full details of the Montreal road system. Consequently, reading it requires a major effort. In contrast, Map 2 (Figure 1-2) omits many minor roads so that the major arteries stand out more clearly.

ABSTRACTION means ignoring many details in order to focus on the most important factors in a problem.

FIGURE 1-1

MAP 1

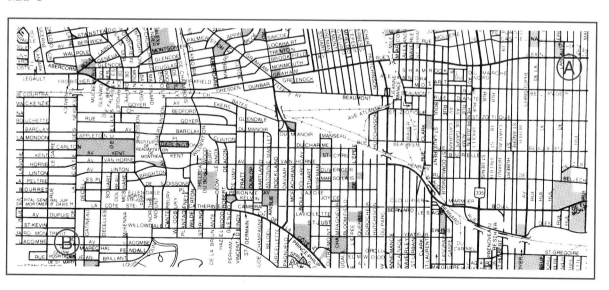

Map 1 gives complete details of the road system of Montreal. If you are like most people, you will find it hard to read and not very useful for figuring out how to get from Hôpital Jean-Talon (point *A*) to Hôpital St. Mary (point *B*). For this purpose, the map contains far too much detail, but for some other purposes (for example, locating some small street), it may be the best map available.

SOURCE: © 1990 Perly's Maps Ltd.

FIGURE 1-2

MAP 2

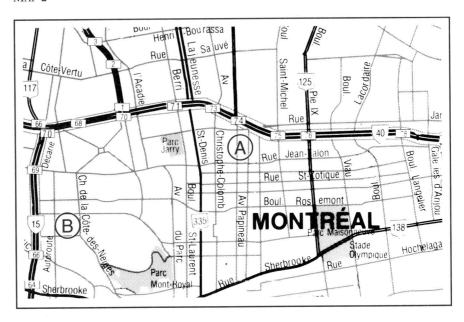

Map 2 shows a very different perspective of Montreal. Minor roads are eliminated—we might say, *assumed away*—in order to present a clearer picture of where the major arteries go. As a result of this simplification, several ways of getting from Hôpital Jean-Talon (point *A*) to Hôpital St. Mary (point *B*) stand out clearly. For example, we can drive west on Hwy. 40 to Hwy. 15 or take Rue Jean-Talon over to Chemin de la Côte-des-Neiges. While we might find a shorter route by poring over the details of Map 1, most of us will feel more comfortable with Map 2.

SOURCE: ©1990 Perly's Maps Ltd.

Most strangers to the city would prefer Map 2. With its guidance, they would be likely to find Hôpital St. Mary in a reasonable amount of time, even though a slightly shorter route might have been found by careful calculation and planning using Map 1. Map 2 seems to abstract successfully from a lot of confusing details while retaining the essential aspects of the city's geography. Economic theories strive to do the same.

Map 3 (Figure 1-3), which shows little more than the major routes that pass through the greater Montreal area, illustrates a danger of which all theorists must beware. Armed only with the information provided on this map, you might never find Hôpital St. Mary. Instead of a useful idealization of the Montreal road network, the map-makers have produced a map that is oversimplified for our purpose. Too much has been assumed away. Of course, this map was never intended to be used as a guide to Hôpital St. Mary, which brings us to a very important point:

There is no such thing as one "right" degree of abstraction for all analytic purposes. The optimal degree of abstraction depends on the objective of the analysis. A model that is a gross oversimplification for one purpose may be needlessly complicated for another.

FIGURE 1-3

MAP 3

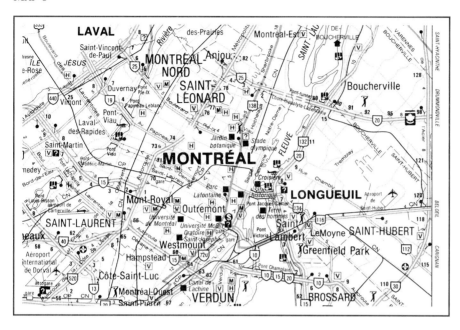

Map 3 strips away still more details of the Montreal road system. In fact, only major roads remain. This map may be useful for passing through the city or getting around it, but it will not help the tourist who wants to see the sights of Montreal. For this purpose, too many details are missing.

SOURCE: Ministère des Transports du Québec, *Carte routière du Québec*, version 1992–93, reproduction autorisée par Les Publications du Québec.

Economists are constantly treading the thin line between Map 2 and Map 3, between useful generalization about complex issues and gross distortions of the pertinent facts. How can they tell when they have abstracted from reality just enough? There is no objective answer to this question, which is why applied economics is as much art as science. One of the factors distinguishing good economics from bad economics is the degree to which analysts are able to find the factors that constitute the equivalent of Map 2 (rather than Map 1 or 3) for the problem at hand. It is not always easy to do.

For example, suppose you are interested in learning why different people have different incomes, why some are fabulously rich while others are pathetically poor. People differ in many ways—too many to enumerate, much less to study. The economist must ignore most of these details in order to focus on the important ones. The colour of a person's hair or eyes probably is not important to the problem at hand, but the colour of his or her skin might be (for example, blacks in the United States have less access to education, and so, on average, they earn lower incomes). Height and weight may not matter, but education probably does. Proceeding in this way, we can pare Map 1 down to the manageable simplicity of Map 2. But there is a danger of going too far. To make it easy to analyze a problem, we can end up stripping away some of the crucial features and be left with Map 3.

THE ROLE OF ECONOMIC THEORY

A person "can stare stupidly at phenomena; but in the absence of imagination they will not connect themselves together in any rational way." These words of renowned American philosopher–scientist C.S. Peirce succinctly express the crucial role of theory in scientific inquiry. What precisely do we mean by theory? To the economist or the natural scientist, the word *theory* does not mean what it does in common parlance. In scientific usage, a theory is not an untested assertion of alleged fact. The statement that saccharin causes cancer is not a theory; it is a *hypothesis* that will prove to be either true or false after the right experiments have been completed.

A **THEORY** is a deliberate simplification of factual relationships; its purpose is to explain how those relationships work.

Instead, a **theory** is a deliberate simplification (abstraction) of factual relationships that attempts to explain how those relationships work. It is an explanation of the mechanism behind observed phenomena. For example, astronomers' data describe the paths of the planets, and gravity forms the basis of theories that are intended to explain these data. Similarly, economists have data suggesting that government policies can affect the degree of a country's prosperity. Economic theory seeks to describe and explain how government policies affect the path of the national economy.

Economic theory has acquired an unsavoury public image in recent years — partly because of inaccurate predictions by some economists, partly because doctrinal disputes have spilled over into the news media, and partly because some politicians have found it expedient to scoff at economists. This bad image is unfortunate because theorizing is not a luxury but a necessity. Economic theory provides a logical structure for organizing and analyzing economic data. Without theory, economists would be able only to observe the world; with theory, they can attempt to understand it.

People who have never studied economics often draw a false distinction between theory and *practical policy*. Politicians and business people, in particular, often reject abstract economic theory as something that is best ignored by practical policy-makers. The irony of this statement can be expressed as follows:

It is precisely the concern for policy that makes economic theory so necessary and important.

If there were no possibility of changing the economy through public policy, economics might be a historical and descriptive discipline, asking, for example, What happened in Canada during the Great Depression of the 1930s? or, How is it that industrial pollution got to be so serious in the twentieth century?

But deep concern about public policy forces economists to go beyond such historical and descriptive questions. To analyze policy options, they are forced to deal with possibilities that have not actually occurred. For example, to learn how to prevent depressions, they must investigate whether the Great Depression could have been avoided by more astute government policies. Or, to determine what environmental programs will be most effective, they must understand how and why a market economy produces pollution and what might happen if government placed taxes on industrial waste discharges and automobile emissions. As Peirce pointed out, not even a lifetime of poring over real-world data will answer such questions.

Indeed, the facts can sometimes be highly misleading. Statistics often indicate that two variables behave very similarly, moving up and down together. But this correlation does not prove that either of these varia- bles *causes* the other. For example, in rainy weather, people tend to drive their cars more slowly, and there are also more traffic accidents. But this **correlation** does not mean that slow driving causes accidents. Rather, both phenomena can be attributed to a common underlying fac- tor (more rain) that leads both to more accidents and to slower driving. Thus, just looking at the degree of correlation (the degree of similarity) of two sets of statistics (like accidents and driving speeds) may not tell us much about cause and effect. We need to use theory as part of the analysis.

Two variables are said to be CORRELATED if they tend to go up or down together. But correlation need not imply causation.

Because most economic issues hinge on some question of cause and effect, only by using a combination of theoretical reasoning and data anal- ysis can economists hope to provide solutions. Simply observing corre- lations in data is not enough. We must understand how, if at all, different government policies will lead to a lower unemployment rate or how a tax on emissions will reduce pollution.

WHAT IS AN ECONOMIC "MODEL"?

An **economic model** is a representation of a theory or a part of a theory, often for the purpose of illuminating cause-and-effect relationships. The notion of a model is familiar enough to children, and economists (and other scientists) use the term in much the same way that children do.

An ECONOMIC MODEL is a simplified, small-scale version of some aspect of the econ- omy. Economic models are often expressed in equations, by graphs, or in words.

A child's model automobile or airplane looks and operates much like the real thing, but it is much smaller and much simpler, and so it is much easier to manipulate and understand. Engineers for General Motors and Boeing also build models of cars and planes. While their models are far bigger and much more elaborate than a child's toys, they use them for much the same purposes: to observe the workings of these vehicles up close and to experiment with them in order to see how they might behave under different circumstances ("What happens if I do this?"). From these experiments, they make educated guesses about how the real-life version will perform.

Economists use models for similar purposes. A.W. Phillips, the famous engineer-turned-economist who discovered the "Phillips curve" (discussed in Chapter 31), was talented enough to construct a working model of the determination of national income in a simple economy using coloured water flowing through pipes. For years this contraption, depicted in Figure 1-4, graced the basement of the London School of Economics. However, most economists lack Phillips's manual dexterity, so economic models are generally built with paper and pencil rather than with hammer and nails.

Because many of the models used in this book are depicted in diagrams, we explain the construction and use of various types of graphs in the appendix to this chapter. But sometimes economic models are expressed only in words. The statement "Business people produce the level of output that maximizes their profits" is the basis for a behavioural model whose consequences are explored in some detail in Parts 2 through 4. Don't be put off by seemingly abstract models. Think of them as useful road maps, and remember how hard it would be to find your way around Montreal without one.

FIGURE 1-4
THE PHILLIPS MACHINE

The late Professor A.W. Phillips, while teaching at the London School of Economics in the early 1950s, built this machine to illustrate Keynesian theory. This is the same theory that we will explain later in this book, using words and diagrams, but Phillips's background as an engineer enabled him to depict the theory with the help of tubes, valves, and pumps. Economists, on the whole, tend not to be very good plumbers; only Phillips and Irving Fisher before him used water and pipes to build models of this sort. Most economists rely on paper and pencil instead. But the two sorts of models perform the same function: They simplify reality in order to make it understandable.

REASONS FOR DISAGREEMENTS: IMPERFECT INFORMATION AND VALUE JUDGEMENTS

"If all the earth's economists were laid end to end, they could not reach an agreement," or so the saying goes. If economics is a scientific discipline, why do economists seem to quarrel so much? Politicians and reporters are fond of pointing out that economists can generally be found on both sides of every issue of public policy. Physicists, on the other hand, do not debate whether the earth revolves around the sun or vice versa.

The question reflects a misunderstanding of the nature of science. Disputes are normal at the frontier of any science. In fact, physicists once did argue over whether the earth revolves around the sun. Today, they argue about antimatter, the "big bang," and other esoteric phenomena. These arguments often go unnoticed by the public, because most of us do not understand what modern physicists are talking about. But because economics is a *social* science, its disputes are aired in public, and almost everyone is personally concerned with the subject matter. Sometimes it seems like anyone who has ever bought or sold anything fancies himself or herself an amateur economist.

Furthermore, there is much more agreement among economists than is commonly supposed. For example, virtually all economists, regardless of their politics, agree that taxing polluters is one of the best ways to protect the environment, and that free trade among nations is preferable to the erection of barriers through tariffs and quotas. The list could go on and on. It is probably true that the issues about which economists agree far exceed those about which they disagree.

Finally, many of the disputes among economists are not disputes at all. Economists, like everyone else, come in all political persuasions: conservative, middle-of-the-road, and radical. Each may have different values and hold a different view of what is best for society, so each may have a different opinion on the best solution to any problem of public policy. In addition, not all of the pertinent facts about the issue in question may be known.

While economists can contribute the best theoretical and factual knowledge there is on a particular issue, the final decision on policy questions often rests either on information that is not currently available or on tastes and ethical opinions (the things we call **value judgements**), or on both.

The following example concerning unemployment and inflation might help to illustrate why pure scientific analysis often fails to lead to a specific policy conclusion.

Government policies that succeed in shortening a recession are virtually guaranteed to cause higher inflation for a while. Using tools that we will describe in Parts 5 through 7, many economists believe they can even measure how much more inflation the economy will suffer as the price of fighting a recession. Is it worth it? An economist cannot answer this

VALUE JUDGEMENTS are propositions that cannot be proven true or false; they simply are or are not consistent with a particular moral code.

question: The decision rests on value judgements about the trade-off between inflation and unemployment (about who is made better and worse off in each case)—judgements that can be made only by the citizenry through its elected officials.

A **POSITIVE QUESTION** is one that can be assessed by evaluating its consistency with logic and factual evidence. A **NORMATIVE QUESTION** is one that involves a value judgement.

Many people use the distinction between **positive questions** and **normative questions** to explain the role of economists in public policy debates. How much inflation a job-creation policy will cause is a factual matter, a positive question; therefore, economists can attempt to use their expertise to answer it. But once the factual issue has been addressed, a normative question remains: Should society incur the cost of that much inflation to create the additional jobs? No scientist can answer this kind of question. All that can be said about a normative question is whether the proposition is or is not consistent with a particular set of value judgements. Scientists are individuals and therefore have personal values. Nevertheless, when they speak out in their role as economists, they should attempt to answer only positive questions.

Earlier in this chapter, we said that economics cannot provide all the answers, but it can teach you how to ask the right questions. Now you know some of the reasons why. By the time you finish studying this book, you should have a good understanding of when the right course of action turns on disputed facts, on value judgements, and on some combination of the two.

SUMMARY

1. To help you get the most out of your first course in economics, we have devised a list of twelve important ideas that you will want to remember "Beyond the Final Exam." Here we list them, very briefly, indicating where each idea occurs in the book.

   1) To make a rational decision, the opportunity cost of an action must be measured, because only this calculation will tell the decision-maker what he or she has given up. (Chapter 2)

   2) In a voluntary exchange, both parties must expect to benefit. (Chapters 3 and 14)

   3) Lawmakers who try to repeal the "law" of supply and demand are liable to open a Pandora's box of troubles they never expected. (Chapter 3)

   4) Decision making often requires the use of marginal analysis to isolate the costs and benefits of a particular decision. (Chapters 4 and 7)

   5) Most policies that equalize income will exact a cost by reducing the nation's output. (Chapter 15)

   6) Externalities cause the market mechanism to misfire, but this defect of the market can be remedied by market-oriented policies. (Chapters 12 and 17)

   7) Two nations can gain from international trade even if one is more efficient at making everything. (Chapter 13)

   8) Most government policies that reduce inflation are likely to intensify the unemployment problem, and vice versa. (Chapter 31)

9) Interest rates that appear very high may actually be very low if they are accompanied by rapid inflation. (Chapter 18)

10) Budget deficits may or may not be advisable, depending on circumstances. (Chapter 30)

11) In the long run, productivity is almost the only thing that matters for a nation's material well-being. (Chapter 32)

12) The operation of free markets is likely to lead to rising prices for public and private services. (Chapter 12)

2. Because of the great complexity of human behaviour, economists are forced to abstract from many details, make generalizations that they know are not quite true, and organize what knowledge they have according to some theoretical structure.

3. Economists use simplified models to understand the real world and predict its behaviour, much as a child uses a model railway to learn how trains work.

4. While these models, if skilfully constructed, can illuminate important economic problems, they can rarely answer the questions that confront policy-makers. This purpose requires value judgements, which the economist is no better equipped than anyone else to make.

5. A course in economics seeks to teach the student how to formulate the right questions, questions that point to the value judgements or unknown pieces of data that must be obtained in order to make an intelligent decision. It does not try to provide all the answers.

CONCEPTS FOR REVIEW

Voluntary exchange
Marginal analysis
Marginal costs
Externalities
Comparative advantage

Productivity
Abstraction and generalization
Theory
Correlation versus causation

Economic model
Value judgements
Positive versus normative
    questions

QUESTIONS FOR DISCUSSION

1. Think about how you would construct a model of how your university is governed. Which officers and administrators would you include and exclude from your model if the objective were
   a. to explain how decisions on tuition payments are made?
   b. to explain the quality of the football team?
   Relate this to the map example in the chapter.

2. Relate the process of abstraction to the way you take notes in a lecture. Why do you not try to transcribe every word the lecturer utters? Why do you not just write down the title of the lecture and stop there? How do you decide, roughly speaking, on the correct amount of detail?

3. Explain why a government policy-maker cannot afford to ignore economic theory.

APPENDIX TO CHAPTER 1

THE USE AND MISUSE OF GRAPHS

CONSTRUCTING GRAPHS

We have noted that economic models are often analyzed and explained with the help of graphs, but that is not the only reason for you to study how they work. You are likely to encounter them often, and in various areas of your life — from reading the daily newspaper to discussing your health with your physician.

In this appendix, first we show how to read a graph that depicts a relationship between two variables. Second, we define the term *slope* and describe how it is measured and interpreted. Third, we explain how the behaviour of three variables can be shown on a two-dimensional graph. Fourth, we discuss how misinterpretation is avoided by adjusting many economic graphs to accommodate changes in the purchasing power of the dollar, in the population of the nation, and in other pertinent developments. Finally, we examine several other common ways in which graphs can be misleading if not drawn and interpreted with care.

TWO-VARIABLE DIAGRAMS

Much of the economic analysis to be found in this and other books requires that we keep track of two **variables** simultaneously. For example, in studying the operation of markets, we will want to keep one eye on the price of a commodity and the other on the quantity that is bought and sold.

For this reason, economists frequently find it useful to display actual or hypothetical figures in a *two-dimensional graph*, which simultane-ously represents the behaviour of two economic variables. The numerical value of one variable is measured along the bottom of the graph (called the **horizontal axis**), starting from the **origin** (the point labelled "0"), and the numerical value of the other is measured along the side of the graph (called the **vertical axis**), also starting from the origin. Both variables are equal to zero at the origin.

Let us now develop such a graph. Consider the data in Table 1-1, which indicates the quan-tity of natural gas that customers want at various possible prices. The table shows that the higher the price, the less people consume this particu-lar fuel. A graphic summary of the same infor-mation can make this point more dramatically. In Figure 1-5, we measure the quantity of natural gas along the horizontal axis and the price for each unit of natural gas along the vertical axis. Each pair of observations in the table can then be recorded as a dot in the graph. Once all the dots are plotted in the graph, it becomes imme-diately apparent that there is an inverse rela-tionship between the two variables: the quantity of natural gas that people demand rises when the price they have to pay falls. This negative association is even more apparent when the dots are connected, as in Figure 1-5(b). Economists call this relationship the *demand curve* for natural gas.

Economic diagrams are generally read as one reads latitudes and longitudes on a map. On the demand curve in Figure 1-5, the point marked *a* represents a hypothetical combination of price and quantity demanded in Halifax. By drawing a horizontal line leftward from that point to the vertical axis, we learn that the average price for

TABLE 1-1

QUANTITIES OF NATURAL GAS DEMANDED AT
VARIOUS PRICES

Price ($ per thousand cubic metres)	20	30	40	50	60
Quantity demanded (millions of cubic metres)	120	80	60	40	22

gas in Halifax is $30 per thousand cubic metres.
By dropping a line straight down to the horizontal axis, we find that 80 million cubic metres are wanted by consumers at this price, just as the statistics in Table 1-1 show. The other points on the graph give similar information. For example, point *b* indicates that if natural gas in Halifax cost only $20 per thousand cubic metres, the quantity demanded would be higher—it would reach 120 million cubic metres.

Notice that information about price and quantity is all we can learn from the diagram. The demand curve will not tell us about the kinds of people who live in Halifax, the size of their homes, or the condition of their furnaces. It tells us the price and the quantity demanded at that price—no more, no less. But on that subject, it does tell us that when price declines, there is an increase in the amount of gas that consumers are willing and able to buy.

A diagram abstracts from many details, some of which may be quite interesting, in order to focus on the two variables of primary interest—in this case, the price of natural gas and the amount of gas that is demanded at each price. All the diagrams used in this book share this basic feature. They cannot tell the reader the "whole story," just as a map's latitude and longitude figures for a particular city cannot make someone an authority on that city.

THE DEFINITION AND MEASUREMENT OF SLOPE

One of the most important features of the diagrams used by economists is the rapidity with

FIGURE 1-5

A DEMAND CURVE FOR NATURAL GAS IN HALIFAX

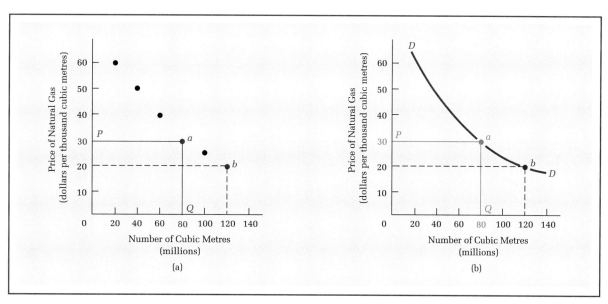

These figures show the relationship between the price of natural gas and the quantity of it that will be demanded. In Figure 1-5(a), each point represents one of the pairs of data given in Table 1-1. For example, the point labelled *a* indicates that at a price of $30 per thousand cubic metres (point *P*), the quantity demanded will be 80 million cubic metres (point *Q*). In Figure 1-5(b), the points have been connected by the coloured line. This curve gives us an easy-to-read image of the relationship between price and quantity demanded.

which the line, or curve, being sketched runs uphill or downhill as we move to the right. The demand curve in Figure 1-5 clearly slopes downhill (the price falls) as we follow it to the right (that is, as more gas is demanded because of the lower price). In such instances, we say that the curve has a **negative slope**, or is negatively sloped, because one variable falls as the other one rises.

The **slope of a straight line** is the ratio of the vertical change to the corresponding horizontal change as we move to the right along the line, or as is often said, the ratio of the "rise" over the "run."

The four panels of Figure 1-6 show all the possible slopes for a straight-line relationship between two unnamed variables called Y (measured along the vertical axis) and X (measured along the horizontal axis). Figure 1-6(a) shows a negative slope, much like our demand curve. Figure 1-6(b) shows a **positive slope**, because variable Y rises (we go uphill) as variable X rises (we move to the right). Figure 1-6(c) shows a **zero slope**, where the value of Y is the same, irrespective of the value of X. Figure 1-6(d) shows an **infinite slope**, meaning that the value of X is the same, irrespective of the value of Y.

Slope is a numerical concept, not just a qualitative one. The two panels of Figure 1-7 show two positively sloped straight lines with different slopes. The line in Figure 1-7(b) is clearly steeper. But by how much? The labels should help you compute the answer. In Figure 1-7(a), a horizontal movement, AB, of 10 units ($13 - 3$) corresponds to a vertical movement, BC, of 1 unit ($9 - 8$). So the slope is $BC/AB = \frac{1}{10}$. In Figure 1-7(b), the same horizontal movement of 10 units corresponds to a vertical movement of 3 units ($11 - 8$). So the slope is $\frac{3}{10}$, which is larger.

By definition, the slope of any particular straight line is the same no matter where on that line we choose to measure it. That is why we can pick any horizontal distance, AB, and the corresponding slope triangle, ABC, to measure slope. But this is not true of lines that are curved.

A curved line also has slope, but the numerical value of the slope is different at every point.

The four panels of Figure 1-8 provide some examples of **slopes of curved lines**. The curve in Figure 1-8(a) has a negative slope everywhere, while the curve in Figure 1-8(b) has a positive slope everywhere. But these are not the only possibilities. In Figure 1-8(c), we encounter a curve that has a positive slope at first but a negative slope later on. Figure 1-8(d) shows the opposite case: a negative slope followed by a positive slope.

FIGURE 1-6

DIFFERENT TYPES OF SLOPE OF A STRAIGHT-LINE GRAPH

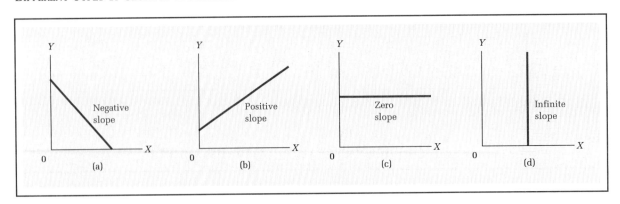

In Figure 1-6(a), the curve goes downward as we read from left to right, so we say it has a negative slope. The slopes in the other figures can be interpreted similarly.

FIGURE 1-7

HOW TO MEASURE SLOPE

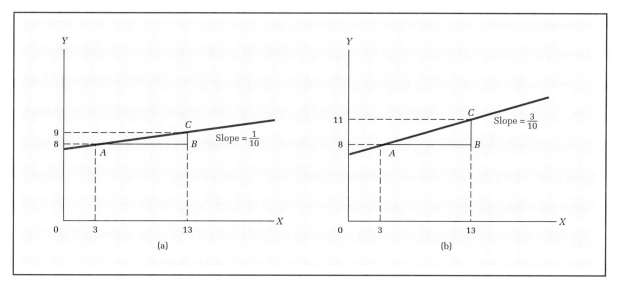

Slope indicates how much the graph rises per unit move from left to right. Thus, in Figure 1-7(b), as we go from point A to point B, we go $13 - 3 = 10$ units to the right. But in that interval, the graph rises from the height of point B to the height of point C; that is, it rises 3 units. Consequently, the slope of the line is $BC/AB = 3/10$.

It is possible to measure the slope of a smooth curved line numerically at any particular point. This is done by drawing a straight line that touches, but does not cut, the curve at the point in question. Such a line is called a **tangent to the curve**.

The slope of a curved line at a particular point is the slope of the straight line that is tangent to the curve at that point.

In Figure 1-9, we have constructed tangents to a curve at two points. Line tt is tangent at

FIGURE 1-8

BEHAVIOUR OF SLOPES IN CURVED GRAPHS

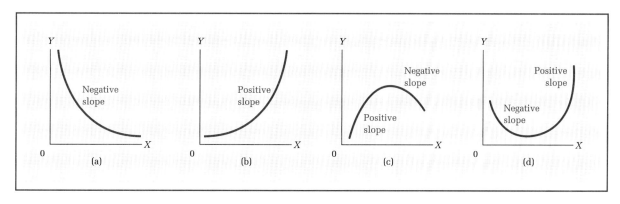

As Figures 1-8(c) and 1-8(d) indicate, where a graph is not a straight line it may have a slope that starts off as positive but becomes negative farther to the right, or vice versa.

point C, and line TT is tangent at point F. We can measure the slope of the curve at these two points by applying the definition. The calculation for point C, then, is as follows:

$$\text{Slope at point } C = \text{Slope of line } tt$$
$$= \frac{\text{Distance } BC}{\text{Distance } AB} = \frac{6-2}{10-0} = \frac{4}{10} = +0.4$$

A similar calculation yields the slope of the curve at point F, which, as we can see from Figure 1-9, must be smaller:

$$\text{Slope at point } F = \text{Slope of line } TT$$
$$= \frac{14-9}{50-0} = \frac{5}{50} = +0.1$$

EXERCISE

Show that the slope of the curve at point D is between $+0.1$ and $+0.4$.

What would happen if we tried to apply this graphical technique to the high point in Figure 1-8(c) or to the low point in Figure 1-8(d)? Take a ruler and try it. The tangents that you construct should be horizontal, meaning that they should have a slope of exactly zero. It is always true that where the slope of a smooth curve changes from positive to negative, or vice versa, there will be at least a single point with a zero slope.

Curves that have the shape of a hill, such as Figure 1-8(c), have a zero slope at their *highest* point. Curves that have the shape of a valley, such as Figure 1-8(d), have a zero slope at their *lowest* point.

RAYS THROUGH THE ORIGIN AND 45° LINES

The point at which a straight line cuts the vertical (Y) axis is called the **Y-intercept**. For example, the Y-intercept of line tt in Figure 1-9 is 2, while the Y-intercept of line TT is 9. Lines whose Y-intercept is zero have so many special

FIGURE 1-9

HOW TO MEASURE SLOPE AT A POINT ON A CURVED GRAPH

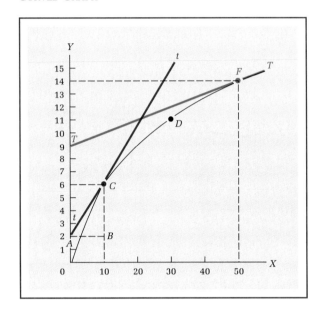

To find the slope at point F, draw the line TT, which is tangent to the curve at point F; then measure the slope of the straight-line tangent TT as in Figure 1-7. The slope of the tangent is the same as the slope of the curve at point F.

uses that they have been given a special name: a **ray through the origin**, or a **ray**.

Figure 1-10 contains three rays through the origin, and the slope of each is indicated in the diagram. The ray in the centre—whose slope is 1—is particularly useful in many economic applications because it marks off points where X and Y are equal (as long as X and Y are measured in the same units). For example, at point A, we have $X = 3$ and $Y = 3$; at point B, $X = 4$ and $Y = 4$; a similar relation holds at any other point on that ray.

How do we know that this is always true for a ray whose slope is 1? If we start from the origin (where both X and Y are zero) and the slope of the ray is 1, we know from the definition of slope that

$$\text{Slope} = \frac{\text{Vertical change}}{\text{Horizontal change}} = 1$$

FIGURE 1-10

RAYS THROUGH THE ORIGIN

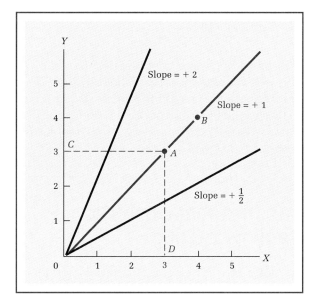

Rays are straight lines drawn through the zero point on the graph (the *origin*). Three rays with different slopes are shown. The middle ray, the one with slope = +1, has two properties that make it particularly useful in economics: (1) it makes a 45° angle with either axis, and (2) any point on that ray (for example, point *A*) is exactly equal in distance from the horizontal and vertical axes (length *DA* = length *CA*). So if the items measured on the two axes are in equal units, then at any point on that ray, such as *A*, the number on the *X*-axis (the abscissa) will be the same as the number on the *Y*-axis (the ordinate).

This implies that the vertical change and the horizontal change are always equal, so the two variables must always remain equal.

Rays through the origin with a slope of 1 are called **45° lines** because they form an angle of 45° with the horizontal axis. If a point representing some data is above the 45° line, we know that the value of *Y* exceeds the value of *X*. Conversely, whenever we find a point below the 45° line, we know that *X* is larger than *Y*.

SQUEEZING THREE DIMENSIONS INTO TWO: CONTOUR MAPS

Sometimes, because a problem involves more than two variables, two dimensions are not enough, which is unfortunate since paper is only two-dimensional. When we study the deci-

sion-making process of a business firm, for example, we may want to keep track simultaneously of three variables: how much labour it employs, how much machinery it uses, and how much output it creates.

Luckily, there is a well-known device for collapsing three dimensions into two, namely a **contour map**. Figure 1-11 is a contour map of Grotto Mountain, near Canmore, Alberta, on the eastern rim of Banff National Park. On several of the irregularly shaped "rings," we find a number indicating the height above sea level at that particular spot on the mountain. Thus, unlike the more usual sort of map, which gives only latitudes and longitudes, this contour map exhibits three pieces of information about each point: latitude, longitude, and altitude.

Figure 1-12 looks more like the contour maps encountered in economics. It shows how some

FIGURE 1-11

A GEOGRAPHIC CONTOUR MAP

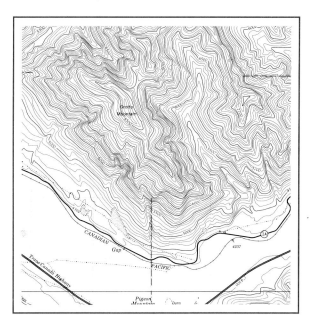

All points on any particular contour line represent geographic locations that are at the same height above sea level.

SOURCE: Based on information taken from the National Topographic System map sheet number NTS 82-0-3, Canmore, Edition 3, © 1980. Her Majesty The Queen in Right of Canada with permission of Energy, Mines and Resources Canada.

FIGURE 1-12

AN ECONOMIC CONTOUR MAP

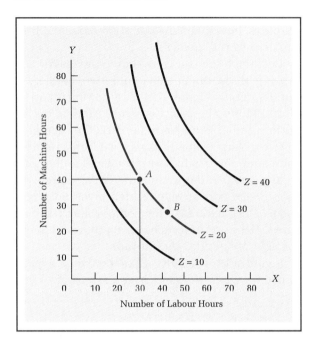

In this contour map, all points on a given contour line represent different combinations of labour and capital capable of producing a given output. For example, all points on the curve $Z = 20$ represent input combinations that can produce 20 units of output. Point A on that line means that the 20 units of output can be produced using 30 labour hours and 40 machine hours. Economists call such maps *isoquant maps* or *production indifference maps*.

third variable, called Z (think of it as a firm's output, for example), varies as we change either variable X (think of it as a firm's employment) or variable Y (think of it as the use of a firm's machines). Just as with the map of Grotto Mountain, any point on the diagram conveys three pieces of data. At point A, we can read off the values of X and Y in the conventional way (X is 30 and Y is 40), and we can also note the value of Z by checking to see on which contour line point A falls. (It is on the $Z = 20$ contour.) So point A is able to tell us that 30 hours of labour and 40 hours of machine time produce 20 units of output.

While most of the analyses presented in this book are based on the simpler two-variable diagrams, contour maps find applications as well, especially in Chapter 4 and the appendix to Chapter 6.

PERILS IN THE INTERPRETATION OF GRAPHS

The preceding materials contain just about all you will need in order to understand the simple graphics used in economic models. We turn now to the second objective of this appendix: to show how statistical data are portrayed on graphs and some of the pitfalls to avoid.

THE INTERPRETATION OF GROWTH TRENDS

Probably the most common form of graph in empirical economics is a year-by-year (or perhaps a month-by-month) depiction of the behaviour of some economic variable — such as the percentage of the labour force that has been unemployed. **Time-series graphs** are a type of two-variable diagram in which time is always the variable measured along the horizontal axis. Such graphs can be quite illuminating, offering an instant visual grasp of the course of the relevant events. However, if misused, they can easily mislead those who are not experienced in dealing with them, and misinterpretations can easily, if unintentionally, be caused by people who draw graphs without sufficient care.

A fine example of such problems can be seen by referring ahead to Figures 30-1 and 30-2 on pages 960 and 961. The first of these figures shows a time-series chart of Canada's national debt that illustrates the possibility of misinterpretation. Consider the increase in the national debt from the mid-1950s to the mid-1970s — it appears to be substantial. But this oversimplified chart fails to alert the reader to two relevant facts: (1) there was substantial population growth in Canada during that decade, and (2) Canadians' incomes were rising rapidly at the time, with a consequent increase in the quantity of all sorts of debts, such as home mortgages. The real issue involved in the question of the national debt is whether it rises *more rapidly* than do the population and the average income per person, and Figure 30-1 essentially ignores that central issue. The relevant factors can, however, be accounted for if the national debt is expressed as a *fraction* of national income (that is, national product), and the results of this correction are shown in Figure 30-2. There, we see that the national debt, when measured as a fraction of the income Canadians had available to service that debt, actually declined over the two decades in question. There is a general lesson to be learned from this example:

The facts, as portrayed in a time-series graph, most assuredly do not "speak for themselves." Because almost everything grows in a growing economy, one must use judgement in interpreting growth trends. Depending on what kind of data are being analyzed, it may be essential to correct for population growth, for rising prices, for rising incomes, or for all three.

DISTORTING TRENDS BY CHOICE OF THE TIME PERIOD

In addition to watching for possible misinterpretations of growth trends, users of statistical data must be on guard for distortions of trends caused by unskilfully chosen first and last periods for the graph. A brief reference to the stock market price indexes that we hear discussed on the nightly news should be sufficient to make this point. Suppose you were presented with a time-series graph of the Toronto Stock Exchange (TSE) price index from 1929 to 1932 or from August to December 1987. Most people know that there were major stock market crashes during these periods. But suppose you didn't know this. If all the information you had was the dramatic downhill pictures for these years, you would conclude that stocks are a terrible investment. On the other hand, if you saw a time-series graph covering the entire period from the 1920s to the 1990s, you would see the true picture: investment in stocks is profitable at some times and unprofitable at others, but over the long term, the general increase in stock prices has been dramatic.

Users of graphs must constantly watch for the deliberate or inadvertent distortion resulting from an unfortunate or unscrupulous choice of time period.

There are no rules that can give absolute protection from this difficulty, but several precautions can be helpful:

1. Make sure that the first date shown on the graph is not an exceptionally high or low point. In comparison with 1929—a year of unusually high stock market prices — the years immediately following are bound to give the impression of a downward trend.

2. For the same reason, make sure that the graph does not end in a year that is extraordinarily high or low (although this may be unavoidable if the graph simply ends with figures that are as up-to-date as possible).

3. In the absence of some special justification, make sure that the graph does not depict only a very brief period, which can easily be atypical.

DANGERS OF OMITTING THE ORIGIN

Frequently, the value of an economic variable described on a graph does not fall anywhere near zero during the period under consideration. For example, Canada's bank rate (the interest rate that the chartered banks must pay to the Bank of Canada when borrowing reserves) rose during early 1990 from 12.15 percent to 12.8 percent. This means that a graph representing the behaviour of the bank rate in early 1990 would have a good deal of wasted space between the horizontal axis of the graph, where the interest rate would be zero, and the level of the graph that would represent a 12 percent interest rate. In that area, there would simply be no data to plot. It is therefore tempting simply to eliminate this wasted space by beginning the graph just below the 12 percent interest rate level. This was done at the time by *Maclean's*, as reproduced in our Figure 1-13.

What is wrong with the drawing? The answer is that it vastly exaggerates the size of the increase in the interest rate that is depicted. The graph makes the interest rate appear to have quadrupled. In fact, however, the bank rate increased by only about one-twentieth of its initial value during this period.

Omitting the origin in a graph is dangerous because it always exaggerates the magnitude of the changes that have taken place.

Sometimes, however, the inclusion of the full graph would waste so much space that it is undesirable to include it. In that case, a good practice is to put a very clear warning on the graph to remind the reader that some space has been omitted. Figure 1-14 shows one way of doing so.

EXERCISE

Using the data shown in Figure 1-13, draw the *full* graph, from the point of zero interest rate, on a sheet of graph paper. Notice the difference in its effect from that of Figure 1-13. Notice also the amount of wasted space.

UNRELIABILITY OF STEEPNESS AND CHOICE OF UNITS

The last problem we will consider has consequences very similar to the one we have just discussed. The problem is that we can never trust the impression we get from the steepness of an economic graph. A graph of stock market prices

FIGURE 1-13

A GRAPH SHOWING OMISSION OF THE ORIGIN

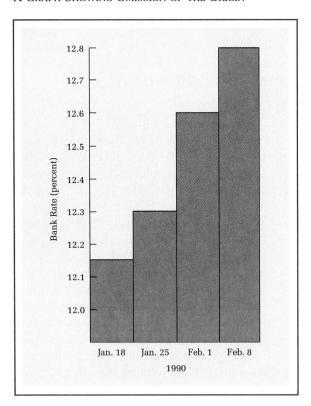

A hasty glance at this figure seems to show that the bank rate quadrupled during the first few weeks of 1990.

SOURCE: Adapted from *Maclean's*, February 19, 1990, page 35.

FIGURE 1-14

A BREAK IN A GRAPH

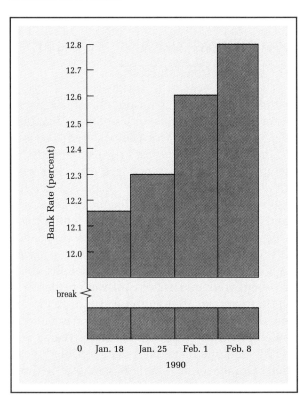

A good way of warning the reader that the full graph has not been included is to put a break in the graph, as illustrated here.

that moves uphill sharply (has a large positive slope) appears to suggest that prices are rising rapidly, while another graph in which the rate of climb is much slower seems to imply that prices are going up sluggishly. Yet, depending on how one draws the graph, exactly the same statistics can produce a graph that rises very quickly or one that climbs very slowly.

One reason for this is that 100 points on the stock market index, for example, can be represented in a graph by a height of either, say, one centimetre or three centimetres. Clearly, if the larger size is chosen to represent a one-unit change in the variable, the movement of that variable up or down will appear much more dramatic than it would if the smaller size were used. Another reason graphs are rather arbitrary is that, in economics, there are no fixed units of measurement. Coal production can be measured in kilograms, hundredweight (hundreds of pounds), or tons. Prices can be measured in cents, dollars, or millions of dollars. Time can be measured in days, months, or years. Any of these choices is perfectly legitimate, but the unit chosen makes all the difference to the rapidity with which a graph using the resulting figures rises or falls.

An example will illustrate the point. Suppose we have the following (imaginary) figures on daily coal production from a mine, which we measure both in hundredweight and in tons (remembering that 1 ton = 20 hundredweight):

FIGURE 1-15

SLOPE DEPENDS ON UNITS OF MEASUREMENT

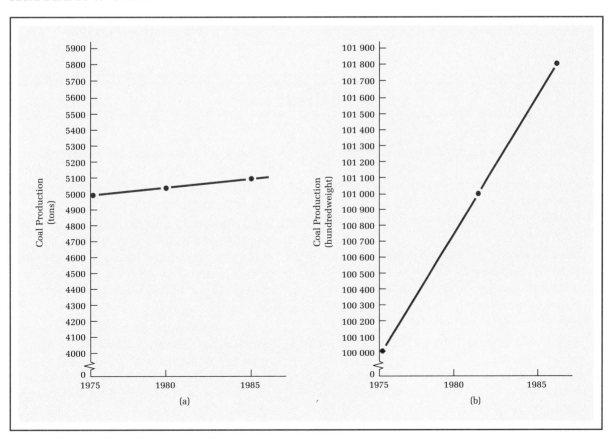

(a) Coal production is measured in tons, and production seems to be rising very slowly. (b) Production is measured in hundredweight (hundred-pound units), so the same facts now seem to say that production is rising spectacularly.

Year	Production in Tons	Production in Hundredweight
1975	5000	100 000
1980	5050	101 000
1985	5090	101 800

Look at Figures 1-15(a) and 1-15(b) on the previous page, one graph showing the figures in tons and the other showing them in hundredweight. The line looks quite flat in Figure 1-15(a) but quite steep in Figure 1-15(b).

Unfortunately, we cannot solve the problem by agreeing always to stick to the same measurement units. Litres may be the right unit for measuring demand for milk, but they will not do for measuring demand for cloth or coal. A penny may be the right monetary unit for jelly beans, but it is not a very convenient unit for the cost of airplanes or cars.

A change in units of measurement stretches or compresses the axis on which the information is represented, which automatically changes the slope of a graph. Therefore, we must never place much faith in the apparent implications of the slope of an ordinary graph in economics.

In Chapter 5, on demand analysis, we present an approach that economists have adopted to deal with this problem. Instead of calculating changes in "absolute" terms — such as tons of coal — they use as their common unit the *percentage* increase. By using percentages rather than absolute figures, we can avoid the problem. The reason is simple. If we look at our hypothetical figures on coal production again, we see that whether we measure the increase in output from 1975 to 1980 in tons (from 5000 to 5050) or in hundredweight (from 100 000 to 101 000), the percentage increase is the same. Fifty is 1 percent of 5000, and 1000 is 1 percent of 100 000. Since a change in units affects both numbers proportionately, the result is a washout—it does nothing to the percentage calculation.

SUMMARY

1. Because graphs are used so often to portray economic models, it is important for students to acquire some understanding of their construction and use. Fortunately, the graphics used in economics are usually not very complex.

2. Most economic models are depicted in two-variable diagrams. We read data from these diagrams just as we read the latitude and longitude on a map: each point represents the values of two variables at the same time.

3. In a few instances, three variables must be shown at once. In these cases, economists use contour maps, which, as the name suggests, show "latitude," "longitude," and "altitude" at the same time.

4. Often the most important property of a line or curve drawn on a diagram will be its slope, which is defined as the ratio of the "rise" over the "run," or the vertical change

divided by the horizontal change. Curves that go uphill as we move to the right have positive slopes, while curves that go downhill have negative slopes.

5. By definition, a straight line has the same slope wherever we choose to measure it. The slope of a curved line changes, but the slope at any point on the curve can be calculated by measuring the slope of a straight line tangent to the curve at that point.

6. A time-series graph is a particular type of two-variable diagram that is useful in depicting statistical data. Time is measured along the horizontal axis, and some variable of interest is measured along the vertical axis.

7. While time-series graphs are invaluable in helping us condense a great deal of information in a single picture, they can be quite misleading if they are not drawn and inter-

preted with care. For example, growth trends can be exaggerated by inappropriate choice of units of measurement or by failure to correct for some obvious source of growth (such as rising population). Omitting the origin can make the ups and downs in a time series appear much more extreme than they actually are. Or, by a clever choice of the starting and ending points for the graphs, the same data can be made to tell very different stories. Readers of such graphs — and they include anyone who ever reads a newspaper — must be on guard for problems like these or they may find themselves misled by "the facts."

CONCEPTS FOR REVIEW

Variable
Two-variable diagram
Horizontal and vertical axes
Origin (of a graph)
Slope of a straight (or curved)
    line

Negative, positive, zero, and
    infinite slope
Tangent to a curve
Y-intercept
Ray through the origin, or
    ray

45° line
Contour map
Time-series graph

QUESTIONS FOR DISCUSSION

1. Look for a graph in your local newspaper, on the financial page or elsewhere. What does the graph try to show? Is someone trying to convince you of something with this graph? Check to see if the graph is distorted in any of the ways mentioned in this appendix.

2. Portray the following hypothetical data on a two-variable diagram:

ENROLLMENT DATA: UNIVERSITY OF NOWHERE

Academic Year	Total Enrollment	Enrollment in Economics Courses
1990–1991	3000	300
1991–1992	3100	325
1992–1993	3200	350
1993–1994	3300	375
1994–1995	3400	400

Using a ruler, draw in a straight line to summarize the trend in the data in your graph. Measure the slope of this line, and explain what this number means.

3. Sam believes the number of dates he gets per week depends on the number of dabs of aftershave lotion he uses. He concludes from experience that the following figures are typical:

Number of dabs 0 1 2 3 4
Number of dates 1 3 4 5 6

Put these numbers into a graph like Figure 1-5(a). Measure and interpret the slopes between adjacent dots.

4. Suppose that, between 1991 and 1992, expenditures on dog food rose from $35 million to $70 million and the price of dog food doubled. What do these facts imply about the popularity of dog food?

5. Suppose that, between 1980 and 1990, the population of North America went up 10 percent and the number of people attending professional wrestling matches rose from 3 000 000 to 3 100 000. What do these facts imply about the growth in popularity of professional wrestling?

SCARCITY AND CHOICE

This chapter examines a subject that many economists consider to be the fundamental issue of economics: the fact that since virtually no resource is available in unlimited supply, people must consequently make decisions consistent with their limited means. A wild-eyed materialist may dream of a world in which everyone owns a yacht and five automobiles, but the earth almost certainly lacks the resources needed to make that dream come true. The scarcity of resources, both natural and synthetic, makes it vital that we stretch our limited resources as far as possible.

This chapter introduces a method of analyzing the choices available to decision-makers, given the resources at their command. The same sort of analysis, based on the concept of opportunity cost, will be shown to apply to the decisions of business firms, of governments, and of society as a whole. Many of the most basic ideas of economics—such as efficiency, division of labour, exchange, and the role of markets—are introduced here for the first time and are shown to be means for making the unpleasant choices forced upon us by the scarcity of resources constraining all economic decisions. This chapter also introduces a broad question that constitutes the central theme of this text:

What does the market do well and what does it do poorly?

THE "INDISPENSABLE NECESSITY" SYNDROME

It is natural but not rational for people to try to avoid facing up to the hard choices that scarcity makes necessary. This has happened, for example, as countries such as Russia and Poland have been forced by extreme scarcity of foreign currency to tighten their belts sharply during the 1990s. Shortages of foreign currency meant that these governments and their people had to cut down severely the quantities of consumer goods and productive inputs they bought from abroad.

Budget cuts force politicians and administrators to make some hard decisions about which services to cut. As they struggle with these decisions, they learn to their dismay that their constituents are often unwilling to accept *any* reductions. It seems that any proposal for cuts that would bring us closer to living within our means is met with the cry that each of the items slated for reduction is absolutely essential.

Yet, regrettable as it is to have to give up anything, reduced budgets mean that something must go. If everyone reacts by declaring everything to be indispensable, the decision-maker is in the dark and will likely end up making cuts that are bad for everyone. When the budget must be reduced, it is critical to determine which cuts are likely to prove least damaging to the people affected.

It is nonsense to assign top priority to everything. No one can afford everything. An optimal decision is one that chooses the most desirable alternative among the possibilities permitted by the quantities of scarce resources available.

SCARCITY, CHOICE, AND OPPORTUNITY COST

RESOURCES are the instruments, provided by nature or by people, that are used to obtain the goods and services humans want. Natural resources include minerals, the soil (usable for agriculture, building land, and so on), water, and air. Labour is another resource that is scarce, partly because of time limitations (the day having only 24 hours). Factories and machines are resources made by men and women. These three types of resources are often referred to as "land, labour, and capital."

One of the basic themes of economics is that the **resources** of decision-makers, no matter how large they may be, are always limited, and that as a result everyone has some hard decisions to make. The federal government agonizes over difficult budget decisions every year, even though it spends billions of dollars annually. Even Philip II, of Spanish Armada fame and ruler of one of the greatest empires of history, had to cope with rebellions by his troops, whom he was often unable to pay or to supply with even the most basic provisions. His government actually went bankrupt about half a dozen times.

But far more fundamental than the scarcity of funds is the scarcity of physical resources. The supply of fuel, for example, has never been limitless, and an increased scarcity of fuel would force us to make some hard choices. We might have to keep our homes cooler in winter and warmer in summer, live closer to our jobs, or give up such fuel-using conveniences as dishwashers. While energy is the most widely discussed scarcity these days, the general principle of scarcity applies to all the earth's resources—iron, copper, uranium, and so on.

Even goods that can be produced are in limited supply because their production requires fuel, labour, and other scarce resources. Wheat and rice can be grown, but nations have nonetheless suffered famines because the land, labour, fertilizer, and water needed to grow these crops were unavailable. We can increase our output of cars, but the increased use of labour, steel, and fuel in auto production will mean that something else, perhaps the production of refrigerators, will have to be cut back. This all adds up to the following fundamental principle of economics, one we will encounter again and again in this text:

Virtually all resources are scarce, meaning that humanity has less of them than we would like. So choices must be made among a limited set of possibilities, in full recognition of the inescapable fact that a decision to have more of one thing means we must give up some of another thing.

In fact, one popular definition of economics is "the study of how best to use limited means in the pursuit of unlimited ends." While this definition, like any short statement, cannot possibly cover the scope of the entire discipline, it does convey the flavour of the type of problem that is the economist's stock in trade.

The Principle of Opportunity Cost

Economics examines the options left open to households, business firms, governments, and entire societies by the limited resources at their command, and it studies the logic of how **rational decisions** can be made from among the competing alternatives. One overriding principle governs this logic—a principle we have already introduced in Chapter 1 as one of the twelve Ideas for Beyond the Final Exam. With limited resources, a decision to have more of something is simultaneously a decision to have less of something else. Hence, the relevant cost of any decision is its *opportunity cost*—the value of the next best alternative that is given up. Rational decision making, be it in industry, government, or households, must be based on opportunity-cost calculations.

To illustrate opportunity cost, we can continue the example in which production of additional cars requires the production of fewer refrigerators. While the production of a car may cost $15 000 per vehicle, or some other money amount, its real cost to society is the refrigerators that must be foregone to get an additional car. If the labour, steel, and fuel needed to make a car are sufficient to make eight refrigerators, we say that the opportunity cost of a car is eight refrigerators. The principle of opportunity cost is of such general applicability that we devote most of this chapter to elaborating it.

A **RATIONAL DECISION** is one that best serves the objective of the decision-maker, whatever that objective may be. The term *rational* connotes neither approval nor disapproval of the objective itself.

OPPORTUNITY COST AND MONEY COST

Since we live in a market economy where (almost) everything "has its price," students often wonder about the connection between the opportunity cost of an item and its market price. What we just said seems to divorce the two concepts. We stressed that the true cost of a car is not its market price but the value of the other things (like refrigerators) that could have been made instead. This **opportunity cost** is the true sacrifice that society makes to get a car.

But isn't the opportunity cost of a car related to its money cost? The answer is that the two are often very closely tied because of the way a market economy sets the prices of the steel and electricity that go into the production of cars. Steel is valuable because it can be used to make other goods. If the items that can be made from steel are themselves

The **OPPORTUNITY COST** of any decision is the foregone value of the next best alternative that is not chosen.

valuable (that is, if those items are valued highly by consumers), the price of steel will be high. But if the goods that can be made from steel have very little value, the price of steel will be low. Thus, if a car has a high opportunity cost, a well-functioning price system will assign high prices to the resources that are needed to produce cars, and therefore a car will also command a high price. This concept can be summarized as follows:

If the market is functioning well, goods that have high opportunity costs will tend to have high money costs, and goods that have low opportunity costs will tend to have low money costs.

Yet it would be a mistake to treat opportunity costs and explicit money costs as identical. For one thing, there are times when the market does *not* function well and hence does not assign prices that accurately reflect opportunity costs. Many such examples will be encountered in this book, especially in Chapters 12 and 17.

Moreover, some valuable items may not bear explicit price tags at all. We have already encountered one example of this in Chapter 1, where we contrasted the opportunity cost of going to college or university with the explicit money cost. We learned that one important item typically omitted from the money-cost calculation is the value of the student's time —that is, the wages he or she could have earned by working instead of attending university. These foregone wages, which are given up by students in order to acquire an education, are part of the opportunity cost of a postsecondary education just as surely as are tuition payments.

Other common examples are goods and services that are given away "free," such as certain medical services. You incur no explicit money cost to acquire such a service, but society still has to give up something else by providing the medical care. Yet another example of the applicability of opportunity cost is the use of this concept in court cases (see the boxed insert on the next page).

PRODUCTION, SCARCITY, AND RESOURCE ALLOCATION

Consumers do not obtain all the goods and services they would want to acquire if those goods and services were provided free (at a zero price); that is what we mean when we say that outputs are scarce. Scarcity forces consumers to make choices. The scarcity of goods and services is, in turn, attributable to the scarcity of the land, labour, and capital used to produce **outputs**.

OUTPUTS are the goods and services that consumers want to acquire. **INPUTS** or **MEANS OF PRODUCTION** are the natural resources, labour, and produced plant and equipment used to make the outputs.

These resources are, after all, the means (instruments) of production —the **inputs** whose services co-operate in the production process, on the farm and in the factory, to yield the commodities that people consume as well as the produced means of production (machines, locomotives, and so on).

Scarcity of such input resources, then, means that the economy cannot produce all the bread, hats, cars, and computers that consumers would want if they could be made available in limitless amounts at a zero price.

A P P L I C A T I O N

OPPORTUNITY COST IN DIVORCE COURT

It is customary in divorce settlements for the husband to make child support payments after the breakup of the marriage, if the child remains primarily with the wife and if the wife did not have a job outside the home during the marriage. But a 1992 settlement in the Hamilton-Wentworth courts involved an additional payment to the wife—compensation for "lost economic opportunities" resulting from the marriage.

The wife's claim ran as follows. She lost wages for the years that they were married, and when she eventually returned to her former job, she was earning less than she would have received if her career had not been interrupted. This lower income that she received upon return to work meant that her entire stream of earnings until retirement would be lower. The settlement involved calculating the present value of this entire stream of foregone earnings and having the husband compensate the wife with a payment of one-half of that amount (on the grounds that income loss due to a marriage breakdown is a risk that should be shared equally by the two parties).

No doubt the husband in this case was unimpressed with the fact that an economist testified during the proceedings. With the concept of opportunity cost brought to the court's attention, the husband's settlement was much higher. His lump-sum compensation payment to his wife for this consideration alone was greater than his annual (pre-tax) income!

Somehow it must be decided whether or not to assign more fuel to the production of refrigerators, which will mean having less fuel to use in the production of airplanes, washing machines, or toys.

The decision regarding how to **allocate resources** among the production of commodities and among the organizations that produce them is made in different ways in different types of economies. In a centrally planned economy, such as that of the former Soviet Union, many such decisions were made by government bureaus. In a market economy, such as that of Canada, the United States, or Great Britain, no one group or individual makes such resource-allocation decisions explicitly. Rather, they are made automatically, often unobserved, by what are called "the forces of supply and demand." For example, if consumers want more beef than farmers now supply, scarcity will make it profitable for ranchers to hire more labour to increase their herds, thus reallocating labour and other inputs away from other production activities and into increased production of beef.

The **ALLOCATION OF RESOURCES** refers to the decision regarding how to divide the economy's scarce input resources among the different outputs produced in the economy and among the different firms or other organizations that produce those outputs.

SCARCITY AND CHOICE FOR A SINGLE FIRM

The nature of opportunity cost is perhaps clearest in the case of a single business firm that produces two outputs from a fixed supply of inputs.

Given the existing technology and the limited resources at the firm's disposal, the more of one good it produces, the less of the other it will be able to produce. Further, unless management carries out an explicit comparison of the available choices, weighing the desirability of each against the others, it is unlikely to make rational production decisions.

Consider the example of a farmer whose available supplies of land, machinery, labour, and fertilizer are capable of producing the various combinations of soybeans and wheat listed in Table 2-1. Obviously, the more land and other resources he devotes to production of soybeans, the less wheat he will be able to produce. Table 2-1 indicates, for example, that if he produces only soybeans, he can harvest 40 000 bushels. But, when soybean production is reduced to only 30 000 bushels, the farmer can also grow 38 000 bushels of wheat. Thus, the opportunity cost of obtaining 38 000 bushels of wheat is 10 000 fewer bushels of soybeans. Or, alternatively, the opportunity cost of 10 000 bushels of soybeans is 38 000 bushels of wheat. The other numbers in Table 2-1 have similar interpretations.

Figure 2-1 is a graphical representation of the same information. Point A corresponds to the first line of Table 2-1, point B to the second, and so on. Curves like AE appear at several points in this book; they are called **production possibilities frontiers**. Any point *on or below* the production possibilities frontier is attainable. Points above the frontier cannot be achieved with the available resources and technology.

The production possibilities frontier always slopes downward to the right. Why? Because resources are limited. The farmer can increase his wheat production (move to the right in Figure 2-1) only by devoting more of his land and labour to growing wheat, meaning that he must simultaneously reduce his soybean production (move downward), since less of his land and labour is available for growing soybeans.

Notice that in addition to having a negative slope, our production possibilities frontier, curve AE, has another characteristic—it is "bowed outward." Let us consider a little more carefully what this curvature means.

Suppose our farmer is initially producing only soybeans, so that he uses for this purpose even land that is much more suitable for wheat cultivation (point A). Now suppose he decides to switch some of his land from soybean production to wheat production. Which part of his land will he switch? Obviously, if he is sensible, he will use the part best

A **PRODUCTION POSSIBILITIES FRONTIER** shows the different combinations of various goods that a producer can turn out, given the available resources and existing technology.

TABLE 2-1
PRODUCTION POSSIBILITIES OPEN TO A FARMER

Bushels of Soybeans	Bushels of Wheat	Label in Figure 2-1
40 000	0	A
30 000	38 000	B
20 000	52 000	C
10 000	60 000	D
0	65 000	E

FIGURE 2-1

PRODUCTION POSSIBILITIES FRONTIER FOR PRODUCTION BY A SINGLE FIRM

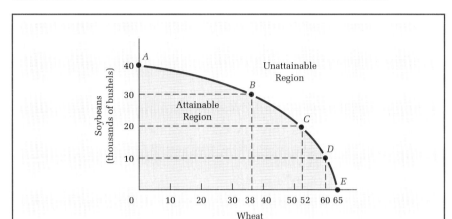

With a given set of inputs, the firm can produce only those output combinations given by points in the shaded area. The production possibilities frontier, *AE*, is not a straight line but one that curves more and more as it nears the axes. That is, when the firm specializes in only one product, those inputs that are especially adapted to the production of the other good lose at least part of their productivity.

suited to wheat growing. If he shifts to point *B*, soybean production falls from 40 000 bushels to 30 000 bushels as wheat production rises from zero to 38 000. A sacrifice of only 10 000 bushels of soybeans "buys" 38 000 bushels of wheat.

Imagine now that the farmer wants to produce still more wheat. Figure 2-1 tells us that the sacrifice of an additional 10 000 bushels of soybeans (from 30 000 to 20 000) will yield only 14 000 more bushels of wheat (see point *C*). Why? The main reason is that inputs tend to be specialized. As we noted, at point *A*, the farmer was using resources for soybean production that were much more suitable for growing wheat. Consequently, the productivity of those resources in soybeans was relatively low, and when they were switched into wheat production, the yield was very high. But this cannot continue forever. As more wheat is produced, the farmer must use land and machinery that are better suited to producing soybeans and less well suited to producing wheat. This is why the first 10 000 bushels of foregone soybeans buys the farmer 38 000 bushels of wheat while the second 10 000 bushels of soybeans buys him only 14 000 bushels of wheat. Figure 2-1 and Table 2-1 show that these returns continue to decline as wheat production expands: the next 10 000-bushel reduction in soybean production yields only 8000 bushels of additional wheat, and so on.

We can now see that the *slope* of the production possibilities frontier represents graphically the concept of opportunity cost. Between points *C* and *B*, for example, the opportunity cost of acquiring 10 000 additional bushels of soybeans is 14 000 bushels of foregone wheat, and between points *B* and *A*, the opportunity cost of 10 000 bushels of soybeans is 38 000 bushels of foregone wheat. In general, as we move upward to the left along the production possibilities frontier (toward more soybeans and less wheat), the opportunity cost of soybeans in terms of wheat increases. In other words, as we move downward to the right, the opportunity cost of acquiring wheat by giving up soybeans increases.

THE PRINCIPLE OF INCREASING COSTS

The **PRINCIPLE OF INCREASING COSTS** states that as the production of a good expands, the opportunity cost of producing another unit of this good generally increases.

We have just described a very general phenomenon that is applicable well beyond farming. The **principle of increasing costs** states that as the production of a good expands, the opportunity cost of producing another unit of this good generally increases.

This principle does not apply universally; there can be exceptions to it. But it does seem to apply regularly to a wide range of economic activities. As our example of the farmer suggests, the principle of increasing costs is based on the fact that resources tend to be specialized, at least in part, so that some of their productivity is lost when they are transferred from doing what they are relatively good at doing to what they are relatively bad at doing. In terms of diagrams like Figure 2-1, the principle simply asserts that the production possibilities frontier is bowed outward.

Perhaps the best way to understand this idea is to contrast it with a case in which there are no specialized resources. Figure 2-2 depicts a production possibilities frontier for producing black shoes and brown shoes. Because the labour and capital used to produce black shoes are just as good at producing brown shoes, the frontier is a straight line. If the firm cuts back its production of black shoes by 10 000 pairs, it always gets 10 000 additional pairs of brown shoes. No productivity is lost in the switch because resources are not specialized.

The production possibilities frontier is the first of many graphs you will encounter in this book. Most, like the production possibilities frontier, are used to summarize ideas, not the actual data involved in a specific application. Graphs of ideas are simply helpful summaries. For example, the image of a negatively sloped, bowed-out production possibilities frontier reminds us at a glance of two important concepts: opportunity cost (that is, more of one thing involves less of another) and the principle of increasing costs (that is, selecting more of a thing makes its opportunity cost higher). So, while this picture may not be worth a thousand words, it certainly saves quite a few. We encourage you to become familiar with using graphs to summarize ideas. If you have been uncomfortable trying to understand these last few pages, review the appendix to Chapter 1.

SCARCITY AND CHOICE FOR THE ENTIRE SOCIETY

Like an individual firm, the entire economy is also constrained by its limited resources and technology. If society wants more aircraft and

FIGURE 2-2

A PRODUCTION POSSIBILITIES FRONTIER WITH NO SPECIALIZED RESOURCES

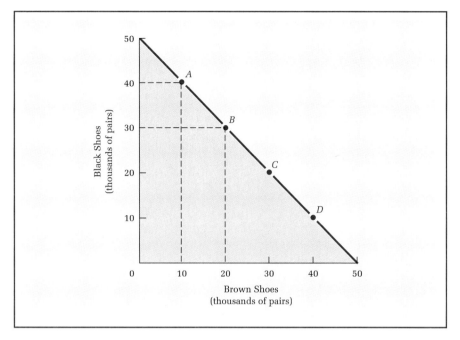

Resources that produce black shoes are just as good at producing brown shoes. So there is no loss of productivity when black-shoe production is decreased in order to increase brown-shoe production. For example, if the firm moves from point *A* to point *B*, black-shoe output falls by 10 000 pairs and brown-shoe output rises by 10 000 pairs. The same would be true if it moved from point *B* to point *C* or from point *C* to point *D*. The production possibilities frontier is therefore a straight line.

tanks, it will have to give up some boats and automobiles. If it wants to build more factories and stores, it will have to build fewer homes and sports arenas.

The position and shape of the production possibilities frontier that constrains the choices of the economy are determined by the economy's physical resources, its skills and technology, its willingness to work, and its investments in factories, research, and innovation.

Since the debate over environmental issues has been so active in recent years, let us illustrate the nature of society's choices using the example of the choice between clean air and manufactured goods. Just like a single firm, the economy as a whole has a production possibilities frontier for these items, determined by its technology and the available resources of land, labour, capital, and raw materials. This production possibilities frontier may look like curve *BC* in Figure 2-3.

If most workers are employed at factories, coal mines, and refineries, the production of manufactured goods will be large but the availability of clean air will be small. If resources are transferred from the mines and factories to emission treatment operations, the mix of output can be shifted toward cleaner air at some sacrifice of manufactured goods (the

FIGURE 2-3

THE PRODUCTION POSSIBILITIES FRONTIER FOR THE ENTIRE ECONOMY

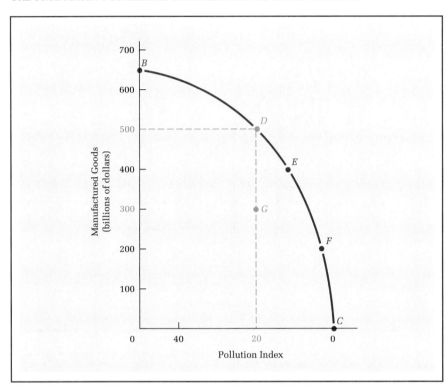

This production possibilities frontier is curved because resources are not perfectly transferable from goods production to emission treatment operations. The limits on available resources place a ceiling, *C*, on the availability of clean air (a reading of zero on the pollution index), and a ceiling, *B*, on the output of manufactured goods.

move from *D* to *E*). However, something is likely to be lost in the transfer process—some of the machines and chemicals that helped produce the manufactured goods will not help in the emission treatment operations. As summarized in the description of the principle of increasing costs, physical resources tend to be specialized, so the production possibilities frontier will probably curve downward and toward the axes.

We may even reach a point where the only resources left are items that are not very useful outside factories. In that case, even a very large additional sacrifice of goods would yield very little cleaner air. That is the meaning of the steep segment, *FC*, on the frontier. At point *C*, the air is only slightly cleaner than at *F*, even though at *C* goods production has been foregone entirely.

The downward slope of society's production possibilities frontier implies that hard choices must be made. Our nation's pollution problems can be solved only by decreasing material consumption, not by rhetoric nor wishful thinking. The curvature of the production possibilities frontier implies that, as emission treatment increases, it becomes progressively more expensive to "buy" cleaner air by sacrificing manufactured goods.

APPLICATION: ECONOMIC GROWTH IN CANADA AND JAPAN

Among the economic choices that any society must make, one very important choice illustrates well the concept of opportunity cost. This choice is embodied in the question, "How fast should the economy grow?" At first, the question may seem ridiculous. Since **economic growth** means, roughly, that the average citizen has more and more goods and services, is it not self-evident that faster growth is always better? (Economic growth will be studied in detail in Chapter 32.)

ECONOMIC GROWTH occurs when an economy is able to produce more goods and services for each consumer.

Again, the fundamental problem of scarcity intervenes. Economies do not grow by magic. Scarce resources must be devoted to the process of growth. Cement and steel that could be used to make swimming pools and stadiums must be diverted to build more machinery and factories. Wood that could be made into furniture and toys must be used for hammers and ladders instead. Grain that could be eaten must be used as seed to plant additional acres. By deciding how large a quantity of resources to devote to future needs rather than to current consumption, society in effect *chooses* (within limits) how fast it will grow.

In diagrammatic terms, economic growth means that the economy's production possibilities frontier shifts outward—that is, it moves further away from the origin in the graph, as in the move from *FF* to *GG* in Figure 2-4(a). Why? Because such a shift means that the economy can produce more of both outputs shown in the graph. Thus, in the figure, after growth has occurred, it is possible to produce the combination of products represented by point *N* (or any other point between the old frontier, *FF*, and the new frontier, *GG*). Before growth occurred, point *N* was beyond the economy's means because it was outside the production possibilities frontier.

How does growth occur? That is, what shifts an economy's production frontier outward? There are many ways in which this can occur. For example, workers may acquire greater skill and learn to produce more output in an hour. Perhaps even more important, the economy may construct more capital goods, temporarily giving up some consumption goods to provide the resources to build factories and machines. Finally, inventions like the steam engine, AC electricity, and industrial robots can and do increase the economy's productive capacity, thereby shifting the production frontier outward.

Figure 2-4 illustrates the nature of the choice by depicting production possibilities frontiers of two different societies for **consumption goods** (like food and electricity), which are consumed immediately, versus **capital goods** (like farm equipment and electricity generating plants), which provide for future consumption.

A CONSUMPTION GOOD is an item that is available for immediate use by households and that satisfies wants of members of households without contributing directly to future production by the economy.

Figure 2-4(a) depicts a society like Canada's, which devotes a relatively small quantity of resources to growth, preferring current consumption instead. This society chooses a point like *A* on this year's production possibilities frontier, *FF*. At *A*, consumption is relatively high and production of capital goods is relatively low, so the production possibilities frontier shifts only to *GG* next year. Figure 2-4(b) depicts a society much more enamoured of growth, like Japan's. This society selects a point like

A CAPITAL GOOD is an item that is used to produce other goods and services in the future, rather than being consumed today. Factories and machines are examples.

FIGURE 2-4

GROWTH IN TWO ECONOMIES

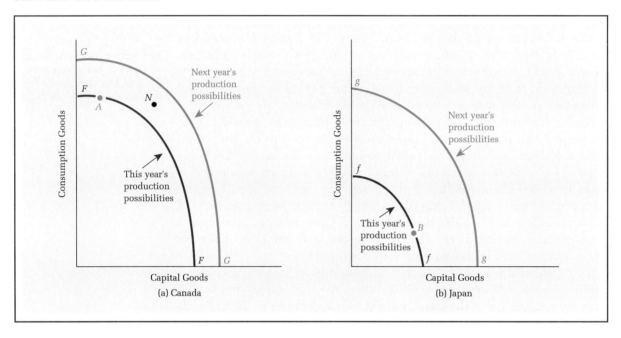

Growth shifts the production possibilities frontiers *FF* and *ff* (red) outward to the frontiers *GG* and *gg* (blue), meaning that each economy can produce more of both goods than it could before. If the shift in both economies occurs in the same period of time, then the Japanese economy (b) is growing faster than the Canadian economy (a) because the outward shift in (b) is much greater than the one in (a).

B on its production possibilities frontier, *ff*. At *B*, consumption is lower and investment is higher, so the production possibilities frontier moves all the way to *gg* by next year. Over the years, Japan has grown faster than Canada, but this faster growth has had a price—an opportunity cost. The Japanese must forego some of the current consumption that Canadians enjoy.

An economy grows by foregoing some current consumption and producing capital goods instead for the future. The more capital it produces, the faster will its production possibilities frontier shift outward over time.

It should be noted, however, that the production of capital goods is not the only way to shift the economy's production possibilities frontier outward. New technology—the process of invention and innovation—is probably the primary means by which economies have increased the output they can produce with a given quantity of resources. Increased education and training of the labour force is generally believed to yield a similar result.

THE CONCEPT OF EFFICIENCY

So far in our discussion of scarcity and choice, we have assumed that either the single firm or the whole economy always operates *on* its production possibilities frontier rather than below it. In other words, we have tacitly assumed that, whatever the firm or economy decides to do, it does so efficiently. Economists define **efficiency** as the absence of waste. An efficient economy uses all of its available resources and produces the maximum amount of output that its technology permits.

To see why any point on the economy's production possibilities frontier in Figure 2-3 represents an efficient decision, suppose for a moment that society has decided to settle for air with a purity level of 20. According to the production possibilities frontier, if this level of clean air is to be attained, the maximum amount of manufactured goods that can be made is $500 billion (point D in Figure 2-3). The economy is therefore operating efficiently if it actually produces $500 billion worth of goods rather than some smaller amount, such as $300 billion (as at point G). Point D is efficient while point G is not.

Note that the concept of efficiency does not tell us which point on the production possibilities frontier is best; it only tells us that no point that is *not* on the frontier can be best, because any such point represents wasted resources. For example, should society ever find itself at point G, the necessity of making hard choices would (temporarily) disappear. It would be possible to increase both the production of goods and air purity by moving to a point such as E.

Why, then, would an economy ever find itself at a point below its production possibilities frontier? There are a number of ways in which resources are wasted in real life. One of the most important, unemployment, is an issue that will take up a substantial part of this book (much of Parts 5 through 7). When many workers are unemployed, the economy finds itself at a point like G, below the frontier, because by putting the unemployed to work in both manufacturing and emission treatment jobs, the economy could produce more goods and have cleaner air. The economy would then move from point G to the right (cleaner air) and upward (more goods) toward a point like E on the production possibilities frontier. Only when no resources are wasted by unemployment or misuse is the economy *on* the frontier.

Inefficiency can also occur in other ways (even with full employment). A prime example is failure to assign inputs to the right task—as when wheat is grown on land best adapted to soybean growing while soybeans are grown on land best suited to wheat production. Another important type of inefficiency occurs when large firms produce goods or services that are best turned out by small enterprises able to pay closer attention to detail, or when small firms produce outputs best suited to large-scale production. A final example is the outright waste that occurs as a result of favouritism (for example, the promotion of an incompetent brother-in-law), discrimination (for example, the promotion of a man when a more-competent woman is available for the job), or wasteful job creation (for example, when union rules require a railway to continue to employ a firefighter on a diesel locomotive even though there is no longer a need for one). Each of these inefficiencies results in the community's obtaining less output than it could, given the amounts of input used in the production process.

THE THREE CO-ORDINATION TASKS OF ANY ECONOMY

In deciding how to use its scarce resources, society must somehow make three sorts of decisions. First, as we have just emphasized, it must figure out how to use its resources efficiently; that is, it must find a way to get on its production possibilities frontier. Second, it must decide what combination of goods to produce—what quantity of manufactured goods versus cleaner air, and so on; that is, it must select one specific point on the production possibilities frontier. Third, it must decide how much of each good to distribute to each person, and do so in a sensible way so that meat does not go to vegetarians and wine to teetotallers.

Certainly, each of these decisions could be made by a central planner who would tell people how to produce, what to produce, and what to consume. But many of the decisions can also be made without central direction, through a system of prices and markets whose directions are dictated by the demands of consumers and the costs of producers. Let us consider each task in turn.

SPECIALIZATION, DIVISION OF LABOUR, AND EXCHANGE

Efficiency in production is one of the economy's three basic tasks. Many features of society contribute to efficiency; others interfere with it. While different societies pursue the goal of economic efficiency in different ways, one source of efficiency is so fundamental that we must single it out for special attention: the tremendous gains in productivity that stem from **specialization**, and the consequent **division of labour**.

DIVISION OF LABOUR means breaking up a task into a number of smaller, more **SPECIALIZED** tasks so that each worker can become more adept at his or her particular job.

Adam Smith, the founder of modern economics, first marvelled at this mainspring of efficiency and productivity on a visit to a pin factory. In a famous passage near the beginning of his monumental book *The Wealth of Nations* (1776), he described what he saw:

> One man draws out the wire, another straightens it, a third cuts it, a fourth points it, a fifth grinds it at the top for receiving the head; to make the head requires two or three distinct operations; to put it on is a peculiar business, to whiten the pins is another; it is even a trade by itself to put them into the paper.[1]

Smith observed that when the work to be done was divided in this way, each worker became quite skilled in a particular specialty, and the productivity of the group of workers as a whole was enhanced enormously. Smith related it as follows:

---

1. Adam Smith, *The Wealth of Nations* (New York: Random House, Modern Library Edition, 1937), page 4.

> I have seen a small manufactory of this kind where ten men only were
> employed. . . . Those ten persons . . . could make among them upwards of
> forty-eight thousand pins in a day. . . . But if they had all wrought separately
> and independently, . . . they certainly could not each of them have made
> twenty, perhaps not one pin in a day.[2]

In other words, through the miracle of division of labour and specialization, ten workers accomplished what would otherwise have required
thousands. An enormous increase in specialization was the secret of the
Industrial Revolution, which helped lift humanity out of the abject poverty that had for so long been its lot.

But specialization created a problem. With division of labour, people
no longer produced only what they wanted to consume themselves. The
workers in the pin factory had no use for the thousands of pins they
produced each day; they wanted to trade them for things like food, clothing, and shelter. Specialization thus made it necessary to have some
mechanism by which workers producing pins could **exchange** their wares
with workers producing such things as cloth and potatoes.

Without a system of exchange, the productivity miracle achieved by
the division of labour would have done society little good. With it, standards of living rose enormously. Recall what we observed in Chapter 1:

Mutual Gains from Voluntary Exchange

Unless there is deception or misunderstanding of the facts, a voluntary
exchange between two parties must benefit both parties. Even though
no additional goods are produced by the act of trading, the welfare of
society is increased because each individual acquires goods that are
more suited to his or her needs and tastes. This simple but fundamental precept of economics is one of our twelve Ideas for Beyond the
Final Exam.

While goods can be traded for other goods, a system of exchange works
better when everyone agrees to use some common item (such as pieces
of paper) for buying and selling goods and services. Enter *money*. Then
workers in pin factories, for example, can be paid in money rather than
in pins, and they can use this money to purchase cloth and potatoes.
Textile workers and farmers can do the same.

These two principles — specialization and exchange (assisted by
money)—working in tandem led to a vast improvement in the well-being
of humanity. This process of specialization and exchange is extended
when one country's citizens trade with those of other countries. Indeed,
it can be shown that even if the citizens of one country are more efficient
at producing *everything* than are the citizens of the other country, both

---

2. Smith, *The Wealth of Nations*, page 5.

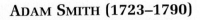

BIOGRAPHICAL NOTE

ADAM SMITH (1723–1790)

Adam Smith, who was to become the leading advocate of freedom of international trade, was born the son of a customs official in 1723 and ended his career in the well-paid post of collector of customs for Scotland. He received an excellent education at Glasgow College, where, for the first time, some lectures were being given in English rather than Latin. A fellowship to Oxford University followed, and for six years he studied there mostly by himself; at that time, teaching at Oxford was virtually nonexistent.

After completing his studies, Smith was appointed professor of logic at Glasgow College and, later, professor of moral philosophy, a field which then included economics as one of its branches. Fortunately, he was a popular lecturer, because in those days a Glasgow professor's pay depended on the number of students who chose to attend his lectures. At Glasgow, Smith was responsible for helping young James Watt find a job as an instrument maker. Watt later invented a key improvement in the steam engine, which made its use possible in factories, trains, and ships. In this and many other respects, Smith was present virtually at the birth of the Industrial Revolution; he was destined to become its prophet.

After thirteen years at Glasgow, Smith accepted a highly paid post as a tutor to a young Scottish nobleman with whom he spent several years in France, a customary way of educating nobles in the eighteenth century. Primarily because he was bored during these years in France, Smith began working on *The Wealth of Nations*. In 1776, several years after his return to England, the book was published and rapidly achieved popularity.

The Wealth of Nations contains many brilliantly written passages. It was one of the first systematic treatises in economics, contributing to both theoretical and factual knowledge about the subject. Among the main points made in the book are the importance for a nation's prosperity of freedom of trade and the division of labour permitted by more widespread markets; the dangers of governmental protection of monopolies and imposition of tariffs; and the superiority of self-interest—the instrument of the "invisible hand"—over altruism as a means of improving the economy's service to the general public.

The British government was grateful for the ideas for new tax legislation that Smith proposed, and to show its appreciation, appointed him to the lucrative sinecure of collector of customs. This position, together with the lifetime pension awarded him by his former pupil, left him very well off financially, although he eventually gave away most of his money to charitable causes.

In the eighteenth century, the intellectual world was small, and among Smith's acquaintances were David Hume, Samuel Johnson, James Boswell, Benjamin Franklin, and Jean-Jacques

(continued)

(continued)
Rousseau. Smith got along well with everyone except Johnson, who was noted for his dislike of Scots. Smith was absent-minded and apparently timid with women, being visibly embarrassed by the public attention of the eminent ladies of Paris during his visits there. He never married and lived with his mother most of his life. When he died, the Edinburgh newspapers recalled only that when Smith was four years old, he was kidnapped by gypsies. But thanks to his writings, he is remembered for a good deal more than that.

countries benefit from specializing and trading. We explain this *principle of comparative advantage* fully in Chapter 13. We show there that a country can obtain points beyond its own production possibilities frontier by engaging in foreign trade.

MARKETS, PRICES, AND THE THREE CO-ORDINATION TASKS

We have emphasized that two important principles—specialization and exchange—have led to a vast improvement in material welfare. But what forces induce workers to join together so that the fruits of the division of labour can be enjoyed? Further, what forces establish a smoothly functioning system of exchange so that each person can acquire what he or she wants to consume? One alternative is to have a central authority telling people what to do. But Adam Smith explained and extolled another way of organizing and co-ordinating economic activity—the use of markets and prices.

Smith noted that people were very good at pursuing their own self-interest, and that a **market system** was a very good way to harness this self-interest. As he put it, with clear religious overtones, in doing what is best for themselves, people are "led by an invisible hand" to promote the economic well-being of society.

Since we live in a market economy, the outlines of the process by which the invisible hand works are familiar to all of us. Firms are encouraged by the profit motive to use inputs efficiently. Valuable resources (such as energy) command high prices, so producers do not use them wastefully. The market system also guides firms' output decisions and, hence, those of society. A rise in the price of wheat, for example, will persuade farmers to produce more wheat and fewer soybeans. A rise in the price of environmentally friendly products will persuade firms to produce more of these items as well, as the boxed insert on page 52 illustrates. Indeed, this profit incentive seems to be more effective than public exhortations that call for some change in human nature. It was surely the lure of profits that motivated McDonald's to discontinue using the styrofoam clamshell as a packaging material.

A **MARKET SYSTEM** is a form of organization of the economy in which decisions on resource allocation are made independently by individual producers and consumers acting in their own best interest without central direction.

FIRMS CASH IN ON CONSUMERS' GREEN AWARENESS

"Green is such a selling point that it is in businesses' own interest to appear environmentally friendly," said a spokesman for Friends of the Earth, a British environmental group. The organization said it gets 30 to 40 calls a day from companies asking "How can I go green?"

The supermarket is the most visible representative of green awareness.

This summer, the Canadian grocery chain Loblaws introduced a line of environmentally friendly products under the brand name Green that includes re-refined motor oil, toilet paper made from recycled fibre, biodegradable soaps and cleansers, and phosphate-free detergents—all packaged in recycled paper.

In four weeks Loblaws sold $5 million worth of these products, double the company's forecast.

Britain's Body Shop chain promotes natural cosmetic products that are not tested on animals and are packaged in refillable containers.

From an initial investment of $12 500 in 1976, Body Shop has grown to a network of 400 stores in 34 countries that grossed $125 million last year.

In Sweden concern about chlorine emissions has caused shops to run out of supplies of unbleached paper, and the country's huge forestry export industry has revamped its pulp and paper production technology in line with environmental demands.

SOURCE: Catherine Arnst, *The Mail-Star*, Halifax, December 2, 1989, page C2. Reprinted with the permission of Reuters.

Finally, a price system determines who gets what goods through a series of voluntary exchanges. All consumers use their own income to buy the things they like best among those they can afford. But the ability to buy goods is not divided equally. Workers with valuable skills and owners of scarce resources are able to sell what they have at attractive prices. With the incomes they earn, they can then purchase the goods and services they want most, within the limits of their budgets. Those with less to sell must live more frugally.

This, in broad terms, is how a market economy solves the three basic problems facing any society: how to produce any given combination of goods efficiently, how to select an appropriate combination of goods, and how to distribute these goods sensibly among the people. As we proceed through the following chapters, you will learn much more about these issues. You will see that they constitute the central theme that permeates not only this text but the work of economists in general. As you progress through the book, keep in mind the following two questions: What does the market do well? What does it do poorly? There are plenty of answers to both questions. You will learn the following in coming chapters:

1. Society has many important goals. Some of them, such as producing goods and services with maximum efficiency (minimum waste), can in certain circumstances be achieved extraordinarily well by letting markets operate more or less freely.

2. Free markets will not, however, achieve all of society's goals. For example, as we will see in Part 5, they often have trouble keeping unemployment and inflation low. There are even some goals—such as protection of the environment—for which the unfettered operation of markets may be positively harmful.

3. But even in cases where the market does not perform at all well, there may be ways of harnessing the power of the market mechanism to remedy its own deficiencies, as you will learn in Part 4 of this book.

RADICALISM, CONSERVATISM, AND THE MARKET MECHANISM

Since economic debates often have political and ideological overtones, we think it important to close this chapter by stressing that the central theme that we have just outlined is neither a defence of nor an attack upon the capitalist system. Nor is it a "right-wing" position. One does not have to be a conservative to recognize that the market mechanism can be a helpful instrument for the pursuit of economic goals. Most of the formerly staunch socialist countries of Europe are now working hard to "marketize" their economies, and even the People's Republic of China now seems to be moving in that direction.

The point is not to confuse means and ends in deciding on how much to rely on market forces. Radicals and conservatives surely have different goals, and they may also differ in the means they advocate to pursue these goals. But means should be chosen on the basis of how effective they are in achieving the adopted goals, not on some ideological prejudgement.

For example, many people assign a higher priority to pollution control than some conservatives do. Consequently, these individuals may support very strict controls even if such controls cut into business profits; conservatives may prefer things the other way around. Nevertheless, for reasons explained in Chapter 17, each side may want to use the market mechanism to achieve its goals. Indeed, each side may conclude that, if it loses the political struggle and the other side's position is adopted, less damage will be done to its own goals if market methods are used.

Certainly, the market cannot deal with all economic problems. Indeed, we have just noted that the market is the *source* of a number of significant problems. But the evidence leads economists to believe that many economic problems are best handled by market techniques. The analysis in this book is intended to help you identify the strengths and weaknesses of the market mechanism. We urge you to forget the slogans you have heard—whether from the left or from the right—and make up your own mind after you have learned the material covered in this book.

SUMMARY

1. Supplies of all resources are limited. Because resources are scarce, a rational decision is one that chooses the best alternative among the options that are possible with the available resources.

2. It is irrational to assign highest priority to everything. No one can afford everything, and so hard choices must be made.

3. With limited resources, if we decide to obtain more of one item, we must give up some of another item. What we give up is called the opportunity cost of what we get; this is the true cost of any decision. The concept of opportunity cost is one of the twelve Ideas for Beyond the Final Exam.

4. The allocation of resources refers to the division of the economy's scarce inputs (fuel, minerals, machines, labour, and so on) among the economy's different outputs and the enterprises that produce them.

5. When the market is functioning effectively, firms are led to use resources efficiently and to produce the things that consumers want most. In such cases, opportunity costs and money costs (prices) correspond closely. When the market performs poorly or when important items of cost do not get price tags, opportunity costs and money costs can be quite different.

6. A firm's production possibilities frontier shows the combinations of goods that the firm can produce with a given quantity of resources, given the state of technology. The frontier usually is not a straight line but is bowed outward because resources tend to be specialized.

7. The principle of increasing costs states that as the production of a good expands, the opportunity cost of producing another unit of this good generally increases.

8. The economy as a whole has a production possibilities frontier whose position is determined by the economy's technology and by the available resources of land, labour, capital, and raw materials.

9. If a firm or an economy ends up at a point below its production possibilities frontier, it is using its resources inefficiently or wastefully. This is what happens, for example, when there is unemployment.

10. Economic growth means there is an outward shift in the economy's production possibilities frontier. The faster the growth, the faster this shift will occur. But growth requires a sacrifice of current consumption, and this is its opportunity cost.

11. Efficiency is defined by economists as the absence of waste. It is achieved primarily by gains in productivity brought about through specialization, division of labour, and a system of exchange.

12. If an exchange is voluntary, both parties must benefit even though no new goods are produced. This is another of the twelve Ideas for Beyond the Final Exam.

13. Every economic system must find a way to answer three basic questions: How can goods be produced most efficiently? How much of each good should be produced? How should goods be distributed?

14. The market system works very well in solving some of society's basic problems, but it fails to remedy others and may even create some of its own. The questions of where and how it succeeds and fails constitute the theme of this book and characterize the work of economists in general.

CONCEPTS FOR REVIEW

Scarcity
Choice
Opportunity cost
Outputs
Inputs (means of production)
Allocation of resources

Production possibilities frontier
Principle of increasing costs
Economic growth
Consumption goods
Capital goods

Efficiency
Specialization
Division of labour
Exchange
Market system
Three co-ordination tasks

QUESTIONS FOR DISCUSSION

1. Discuss the resource limitations that affect
   a. The poorest person on earth.
   b. The richest person on earth.
   c. A firm in Switzerland.
   d. A government agency in China.
   e. The population of the world.

2. If you were president of your university, what would you change if your budget were cut by 5 percent? By 20 percent? By 50 percent?

3. If you were to drop out of university, what things would change in your life? What, then, is the opportunity cost of your education?

4. A person rents a house for which she pays the landlord $10 000 a year. Money invested in a savings certificate earns 6 percent interest a year. The house is offered for sale at $75 000. Is this a good deal for the potential buyer? Where does opportunity cost enter the picture?

5. Construct graphically the production possibilities frontier for the Grand Republic of Glubstania given in the table below. Does the principle of increasing cost hold in the Glubstanian economy?

GLUBSTANIA'S 1995 PRODUCTION POSSIBILITIES

Pork Muffins (millions per year)	Noodle Machines (thousands per year)
75	0
60	12
45	22
30	30
15	36
0	40

6. Consider two alternatives for Glubstania in the year 1995. In case (a), its inhabitants eat 60 million pork muffins and build only 12 000 noodle-making machines. In case (b), the population eats only 15 million pork muffins but builds 36 000 noodle machines. Which case will lead to a more favourable production possibilities frontier for Glubstania in 1995? (*Note*: In Glubstania, noodle machines are used to produce pork muffins.)

7. Sam's Snack Shop sells two brands of potato chips. Brand X costs Sam 75 cents per bag, and Brand Y costs him $1. Draw Sam's production possibilities frontier if he has $60 budgeted to spend on potato chips. Why is it not bowed out?

CHAPTER 3

SUPPLY AND DEMAND: AN INITIAL LOOK

Reformers have the idea that change can be achieved by brute sanity.

GEORGE BERNARD SHAW

If the issues of scarcity, choice, and co-ordination constitute the basic problem of economics, then the mechanism of supply and demand is its basic investigative tool. Supply and demand analysis is used in this book to study issues as seemingly diverse as inflation and unemployment, the international value of the dollar, government regulation of business, and protection of the environment. Therefore, careful study of this chapter will pay rich dividends.

The chapter describes the rudiments of supply and demand analysis in steps. We begin with demand, then add supply, and finally put the two sides together. Supply and demand curves—graphs that relate price to quantity supplied and quantity demanded, respectively — are explained and used to show how prices and quantities are determined in a free market. Influences that shift either the demand curve or the supply curve are catalogued briefly. The analysis is used to explain such things as why airlines often run "sales" and why the prices of personal computers and recycled items have recently fallen so dramatically. Our discussion also involves several examples of government involvement in markets, such as rent controls, minimum-wage laws, subsidization of our court system, and certain aspects of our drug laws.

Indeed, one major theme of this chapter is that governments around the globe and throughout recorded history have attempted to tamper with the price mechanism. We will see that these bouts with Adam Smith's "invisible hand" have often produced undesired side effects that surprised and dismayed the authorities. Further, we will show that many of these unfortunate effects were not accidents but inherent consequences of interfering with the operation of free markets. The invisible hand fights back!

FIGHTING THE INVISIBLE HAND

Adam Smith was a great admirer of the price system. He extolled its accomplishments—both as a producer of goods and as a guarantor of individual freedoms. Many people since Smith's time have shared his enthusiasm, but many others have not, and they have tried to do better by legislative decree. There have been countless instances in which the public's sense of justice was outraged by the prices charged on the open market, particularly when the sellers of the expensive items did not enjoy great popularity—landlords, moneylenders, and oil companies are good examples.

Attempts to control interest rates (which may be thought of as the price of borrowing money) go back hundreds of years before the birth of Christ, at least to the code of laws compiled under Hammurabi in Babylonia about 1800 B.C. Our historical legacy also includes a rather long list of price ceilings on foods and other products imposed in the reign of Diocletian, emperor of the declining Roman Empire. More recently, Canadians have been offered the "protection" of a variety of price controls. Ceilings have been placed on prices of some items (such as energy, apartment rents, and insurance premiums) to protect buyers, while floors have been placed under prices of other items (such as farm products) to protect sellers. Many if not most of these measures were adopted in response to popular opinion, and there is a great outcry whenever it is proposed that any one of them be weakened or eliminated.

Yet, somehow, everything such regulation touches seems to end up in even greater disarray than it was before. For example, rent controls lead to a decreased supply of rental accommodation, and surplus agricultural products have had to be destroyed or stored indefinitely. The list could go on. Still, legislators continue to turn to controls whenever the economy does not work to their satisfaction. We still have rent controls in four Canadian provinces, and agricultural price-support schemes abound. A web of controls over energy prices was dismantled only in the 1980s.

Interferences with the "Law" of Supply and Demand

Public opinion frequently encourages legislative attempts to "repeal" the law of supply and demand by controlling prices. The consequences are usually quite unfortunate, exacting heavy costs from the general public and often aggravating the problem that the legislation was intended to cure. This is another of the twelve Ideas for Beyond the Final Exam, and it will occupy our attention throughout this chapter.

To understand what goes wrong when markets are tampered with, we must first learn how they operate when they are unfettered. This chapter takes a first step in that direction by studying the machinery of supply and demand. Then, at the end of the chapter, we return to the issue of price controls, presenting case studies of rent controls and the minimum wage to illustrate the problems that can arise.

Every market has both buyers and sellers. We begin our analysis on the consumers' side of the market.

APPLICATION

PRICE CONTROLS IN THE EIGHTEENTH CENTURY

The following excerpts illustrate the unfortunate results that have followed from two of the many attempts to override market forces with legislation that have occurred over the years. In these examples, price ceilings made it unprofitable for suppliers to operate, so that scarcities and lost jobs were the unintended by-products.

The French Revolution

During the twenty months between May 1793 and December 1794, the Revolutionary Government of the new French Republic tried almost every experiment in wage and price controls which has been attempted before or since. . . .

[The] first Law of the Maximum, as it was called, provided that the price of grain and flour in each district of France should be the average of local market prices which were in effect from January to May 1793. . . .

By the summer of 1794, demands were coming from all over the country for the immediate repeal of the Law. In some towns in the South the people were so badly fed that they were collapsing in the streets from lack of nourishment. The department of the Nord complained bitterly that their shortages all began just after the passage of the by now hated Law of the Maximum. "Before that time," they wrote to the Convention in Paris, "our markets were supplied, but as soon as we fixed the price of wheat and rye we saw no more of those grains. The other kinds not subject to the maximum were the only ones brought in. The deputies of the Convention ordered us to fix a maximum for all grains. We obeyed and henceforth grain of every sort disappeared from the markets. What is the inference? This, that the establishment of a maximum brings famine in the midst of abundance. What is the remedy? Abolish the maximum.". . .

When Robespierre and his colleagues were being carried through the streets of Paris on their way to their executions, the mob jeered their last insult: "There goes the dirty Maximum."

Early Canada—Louisbourg

During 1750 rules were made as to the price that must be charged for fresh cod fish. It was, by this order, explicitly forbidden for fishermen to refuse to sell their fish at the posted price provided only that the buyer was solvent. To appreciate the serious nature of this law, it is necessary to remember that the bulk of New France's wealth was derived from the cod fishery. Of course, from time to time this regulation led to desperate circumstances for the fishermen and there is some reason to believe that it was responsible for the decline in the fishery in that area of New France.

SOURCE: Robert L. Schuettinger, "The Historical Record: A Survey of Wage and Price Controls over Fifty Centuries," in *Tax-Based Incomes Policies — A Cure for Inflation?* edited by M. Walker (Vancouver: The Fraser Institute, 1982), pages 67, 73–76. Reprinted with permission.

DEMAND AND QUANTITY DEMANDED

People who are not economists are apt to think of consumer demands as fixed amounts. For example, when the production of a new type of machine tool is proposed, management asks, "What is its market potential? How many will we be able to sell?" Similarly, government bureaus conduct studies to determine how many engineers will be required in succeeding years.

Economists respond that such questions are not well posed—that there is no single answer to such a question. Rather, they say, the "market potential" for machine tools or the number of engineers that will be required depends on a great number of things, including the price that will be charged for each.

The **quantity demanded** of any product normally depends on its price. Quantity demanded also has a number of other determinants, including population size, consumer incomes, tastes, and the prices of other products.

Because of the central role of prices in a market economy, we begin our study of demand by focussing on the relationship between quantity demanded and price. Shortly, we will bring the other determinants of quantity demanded back into the picture.

Consider, as an example, the quantity of milk demanded. Almost everyone purchases at least some milk. However, if the price of milk is very high, its market potential may be very small. People will find ways to get along with less milk, perhaps by switching to tea or coffee. If the price declines, people will be encouraged to drink more milk. They may give more milk to their children or switch away from juices and sodas.

There is no one demand figure for milk, for machine tools, or for engineers. Rather, there is a different quantity demanded for each possible price.

THE DEMAND SCHEDULE

A **DEMAND SCHEDULE** is a table showing how the quantity demanded of some product during a specified period of time changes as the price of that product changes, holding all other determinants of quantity demanded constant.

Table 3-1 displays this information for milk in what we call a **demand schedule**, which shows how much consumers are able and willing to buy (during a specified time period) at different possible prices. The table indicates the quantity of milk that will be demanded in a year at prices ranging from $1 to 40¢ per litre. We see, for example, that at a relatively low price, like 50¢ per litre, customers wish to purchase 70 million litres per year. But if the price rises to, say, 90¢ per litre, quantity demanded falls to 50 million litres.

Common sense tells us why this should be so. First, as prices rise, some customers will reduce their consumption of milk. Second, higher prices will induce some customers to drop out of the market entirely—for example, by switching to soda or juice. On both counts, quantity demanded will decline as the price rises.

TABLE 3-1

DEMAND SCHEDULE FOR MILK

Price (dollars per litre)	Quantity Demanded (millions of litres per year)	Label in Figure 3-1
1.00	45	A
0.90	50	B
0.80	55	C
0.70	60	E
0.60	65	F
0.50	70	G
0.40	75	H

FIGURE 3-1

DEMAND CURVE FOR MILK

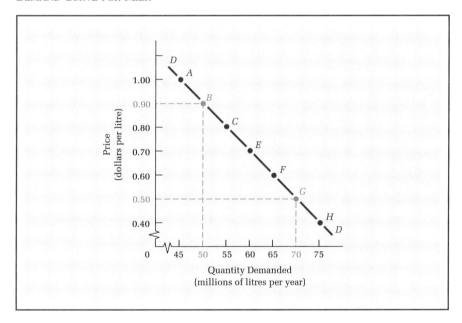

This curve shows the relationship between price and quantity demanded. To sell 70 million litres per year, the price must be only 50¢ (point *G*). If, instead, the price is 90¢, only 50 million litres will be demanded (point *B*). To sell more milk, the price must be reduced. That is what the negative slope of the demand curve means.

As the price of an item rises, the quantity demanded normally falls. As the price falls, the quantity demanded normally rises.

THE DEMAND CURVE

The information contained in Table 3-1 can be summarized in a graph, which we call a **demand curve**, displayed in Figure 3-1. Each point in the graph corresponds to a line in the table. For example, point *B* cor-

A **DEMAND CURVE** is a graphical depiction of a demand schedule. It shows how the quantity demanded of some product during a specified period of time will change as the price of that product changes, holding all other determinants of quantity demanded constant.

responds to the second line in the table, indicating that at a price of 90¢ per litre, 50 million litres per year will be demanded. Since the quantity demanded declines as the price increases, the demand curve has a negative slope.

Notice the last phrase in the definitions of demand schedule and demand curve: "holding all other determinants of quantity demanded constant." These other determinants include consumer incomes and preferences, the prices of soda and juice, and perhaps even advertising by the dairy association. We will examine the influences of these factors later in the chapter. First, however, let's look at the sellers' side of the market.

SUPPLY AND QUANTITY SUPPLIED

Like quantity demanded, the quantity of milk supplied by dairy farmers is not a fixed number; it also depends on many things. Obviously, if there are more dairy farms, or larger ones, we expect more milk to be supplied. Or, if bad weather deprives the cows of their feed, they may give less milk. As before, however, let's turn our attention first to the relationship between **quantity supplied** and one of its major determinants—price.

Economists generally suppose that a higher price calls forth a greater quantity supplied. Why? Remember our analysis of the principle of increasing costs in Chapter 2 (page 42). According to that principle, as more of any farmer's (or the nation's) resources are devoted to milk production, the opportunity cost of obtaining another litre of milk increases. Farmers will therefore find it profitable to raise milk production only if they can sell the milk at a higher price—high enough to cover the higher costs incurred when milk production expands.

Alternatively, we have just concluded that higher prices normally will be required to persuade farmers to raise milk production. This idea is quite general and applies to the supply of most goods and services. As long as suppliers want to make profits and the principle of increasing costs holds, the following will be true:

As the price of an item rises, the quantity supplied normally rises. As the price falls, the quantity supplied normally falls.

THE SUPPLY SCHEDULE AND THE SUPPLY CURVE

The relationship between the price of milk and its quantity supplied is recorded in Table 3-2, which we call a **supply schedule**. The table shows that a low price like 50¢ per litre will induce suppliers to provide only 40 million litres, while a higher price like 80¢ will induce them to provide much more: 70 million litres.

As you might have guessed, when information like this is plotted on a graph, it is called a **supply curve**. Figure 3-2 is the supply curve corresponding to the supply schedule in Table 3-2. It slopes upward because quantity supplied is higher when price is higher.

A **SUPPLY SCHEDULE** is a table showing how the quantity supplied of some product during a specified period of time changes as the price of that product changes, holding all other determinants of quantity supplied constant.

A **SUPPLY CURVE** is a graphical depiction of a supply schedule. It shows how the quantity supplied of some product during a specified period of time will change as the price of that product changes, holding all other determinants of quantity supplied constant.

TABLE 3-2

SUPPLY SCHEDULE FOR MILK

Price (dollars per litre)	Quantity Supplied (millions of litres per year)	Label in Figure 3-2
1.00	90	a
0.90	80	b
0.80	70	c
0.70	60	e
0.60	50	f
0.50	40	g
0.40	30	h

FIGURE 3-2

SUPPLY CURVE FOR MILK

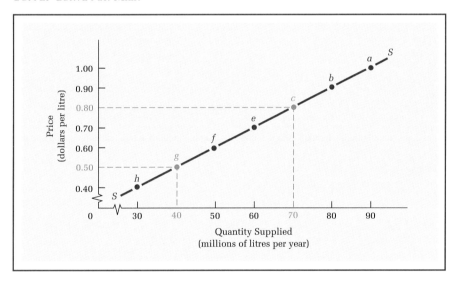

This curve shows the relationship between the price of milk and the quantity supplied. To stimulate a greater quantity supplied, price must be increased. That is the meaning of the positive slope of the supply curve.

Notice again the same phrase in the definition: "holding all other determinants of quantity supplied constant." We will return to these other determinants a bit later. But first we are ready to put demand and supply together.

EQUILIBRIUM OF SUPPLY AND DEMAND

To analyze how price is determined in a free market, we must compare the desires of consumers (demand) with the desires of producers (supply) and see whether the two sets of plans are consistent. Table 3-3 and Figure 3-3 are designed to help us do this.

Table 3-3 brings together the demand schedule from Table 3-1 and the supply schedule from Table 3-2. Similarly, Figure 3-3 puts together the demand curve from Figure 3-1 and the supply curve from Figure 3-2 on a single graph. Such a graphic device is called a **supply–demand diagram**, and we will encounter many of them in this book. Notice that, for reasons already discussed, the demand curve has a negative slope and the supply curve has a positive slope. Most supply–demand diagrams are drawn with slopes like these.

There is only one point in Figure 3-3, point *E*, at which the supply curve and the demand curve intersect. At the price corresponding to

TABLE 3-3

DETERMINATION OF THE EQUILIBRIUM PRICE AND QUANTITY OF MILK

Price (dollars per litre)	Quantity Demanded (millions of litres per year)	Quantity Supplied (millions of litres per year)	Surplus or Shortage?	Price Will:
1.00	45	90	Surplus	Fall
0.90	50	80	Surplus	Fall
0.80	55	70	Surplus	Fall
0.70	60	60	Neither	Remains the same
0.60	65	50	Shortage	Rise
0.50	70	40	Shortage	Rise
0.40	75	30	Shortage	Rise

FIGURE 3-3

SUPPLY–DEMAND EQUILIBRIUM

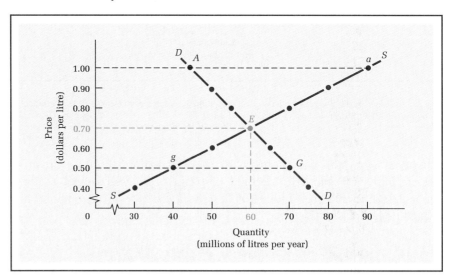

In a free market, price and quantity are determined by the intersection of the supply curve and the demand curve. In this example, the equilibrium price is 70¢ and the equilibrium quantity is 60 million litres of milk per year. Any other price is inconsistent with equilibrium. For example, at a price of 50¢, quantity demanded is 70 million litres (point *G*), while quantity supplied is only 40 million litres (point *g*), so that price will be driven up by the unsatisfied demand.

point *E*, which is 70¢ per litre, the quantity supplied is equal to the quantity demanded. This means that, at a price of 70¢ per litre, consumers are willing to buy just what producers are willing to sell.

At a lower price, such as 50¢, only 40 million litres of milk will be supplied (point *g*), whereas 70 million litres will be demanded (point *G*). Thus, quantity demanded will exceed quantity supplied. There will be a **shortage** equal to 70 − 40 = 30 million litres. Alternatively, at a higher price, such as $1, quantity supplied will be 90 million litres (point *a*) while quantity demanded will be only 45 million (point *A*). Quantity supplied will exceed quantity demanded, so there will be a **surplus** equal to 90 − 45 = 45 million litres.

Since 70¢ is the price at which quantity supplied and quantity demanded are equal, we say that 70¢ per litre is the equilibrium price in this market. Similarly, 60 million litres per year is the equilibrium quantity of milk.

The term **equilibrium** merits a little explanation, since it arises so frequently in economic analysis. An equilibrium is a situation in which there are no inherent forces that produce change—that is, a situation that does not contain the seeds of its own destruction. Think, for example, of a pendulum at rest at its centre point. If no outside force (such as a person's hand) comes to push it, the pendulum will remain where it is; it is in equilibrium.

But if someone gives the pendulum a shove, its equilibrium will be disturbed and it will start to move upward. When it reaches the top of its arc, the pendulum will, for an instant, be at rest again. But this is not an equilibrium position. A force known as gravity will pull the pendulum downward, and thereafter its motion from side to side will be governed by gravity and friction. Eventually, we know, the pendulum must return to the point at which it started, which is its only equilibrium position. At any other point, inherent forces will cause the pendulum to move.

The concept of equilibrium in economics is similar and can be illustrated by our supply and demand example. Why is no price other than 70¢ an equilibrium price in Table 3-3 or Figure 3-3? What forces will change any other price?

Consider first a low price like 50¢, at which quantity demanded (70 million) exceeds quantity supplied (40 million). If the price were this low, there would be many frustrated customers unable to purchase the quantities they desire. They would compete with one another for the available milk. Some would offer more than the prevailing price and, as customers tried to outbid one another, the market price would be forced up. In other words, a price below the equilibrium price cannot persist in a free market because a shortage sets in motion powerful economic forces that push price upward.

Similar forces operate if the market price is *above* the equilibrium price. If, for example, the price should somehow become $1, Table 3-3 tells us that quantity supplied (90 million) would far exceed quantity demanded (45 million). Producers would be unable to sell their desired quantities of milk at the prevailing price, and some would find it in their

A SHORTAGE is an excess of quantity demanded over quantity supplied. When there is a shortage, buyers cannot purchase the quantities they desire.

A SURPLUS is an excess of quantity supplied over quantity demanded. When there is a surplus, sellers cannot sell the quantities they desire to supply.

An EQUILIBRIUM is a situation in which there are no inherent forces that produce change. Changes away from an equilibrium position will occur only as a result of outside events that disturb the status quo.

interest to undercut their competitors by reducing price. This process of competitive price-cutting would continue as long as the surplus persisted — that is, as long as quantity supplied exceeded quantity demanded. Thus, a price above the equilibrium price cannot persist indefinitely.

We are left with only one conclusion. The price 70¢ per litre and the quantity 60 million litres is the only price–quantity combination that does not sow the seeds of its own destruction. It is the only equilibrium. Any lower price must rise, and any higher price must fall. It is as if natural economic forces place a magnet at point E that attracts the market, just as gravity attracts the pendulum.

The analogy to a pendulum is worth pursuing further. Most pendulums are more frequently in motion than at rest. However, unless pendulums are repeatedly buffeted by outside forces (which, of course, is exactly what happens to pendulums used in clocks), they gradually return to their resting points. The same is true of price and quantity in a free market. Markets are not always in equilibrium, but, if they are not interfered with, we have good reason to believe that they normally are moving *toward* equilibrium.

There is also good reason to believe that as computers are used more extensively by firms to adjust the supplies they have available at the retail level, markets will move more quickly toward equilibrium. Developments in this area are summarized in the boxed insert opposite.

The Law of Supply and Demand

In a free market, the forces of supply and demand generally push price toward its equilibrium level — the price at which quantity supplied and quantity demanded are equal.

Like most economic "laws," the law of supply and demand is occasionally disobeyed. Markets sometimes display shortages or surpluses for long periods of time. Prices sometimes fail to move toward equilibrium. But, by and large, the law seems a fair generalization. It is right far more often than it is wrong.

The last interesting aspect of the analogy concerns the outside forces of which we have spoken. A pendulum that is being blown by the wind or pushed by a hand does not remain in equilibrium. Similarly, many outside forces can disturb a market equilibrium. A frost in Florida will disturb equilibrium in the market for oranges. A strike by miners will disturb equilibrium in the market for coal.

Many of these outside influences actually change the equilibrium price and quantity by shifting either the supply curve or the demand curve. If you look again at Figure 3-3, you can see clearly that any event that causes either the demand curve or the supply curve to shift will also cause the equilibrium price and quantity to change. Such events constitute the "other determinants" that we held constant in our definitions of

FURTHER DETAIL

SUPPLY AND COMMAND

The following excerpt from The Globe and Mail *illustrates how modern technology, when operating in tandem with the price system, can go a long way toward eliminating shortages almost before they appear.*

The giant Price Club warehouse in Mississauga is jammed with bargain-hungry shoppers on a pre-Christmas afternoon. They're carting away everything from portable stereos to pet food.

At the cash register, the product codes whiz by at a dizzying pace. . . .

A four-slice Black & Decker toaster slides across the counter. Lucy taps out the code and the toaster is automatically deducted from the store's inventory.

That sets off an electronic chain reaction that reverberates from Montreal to Baltimore, Md. — and sends the toaster's replacement hurtling down the supply chain. Within days, a truck rolls out of Black & Decker Canada Inc.'s manufacturing and distribution centre in Brockville, Ont., carrying 30 four-slice toasters bound for the Mississauga Price Club.

No paper is ever exchanged. After Lucy's code-punching, the toaster order is untouched by human hands. For this is the revolutionary world of electronic data interchange, a lightning-fast, computer-based communications system that is rapidly transforming the way companies and governments do business.

EDI, as it's popularly known, eliminates the flow of documents between suppliers and their customers. The results: faster delivery, reduced inventories, fewer human errors and lower costs. It's the grease that makes just-in-time manufacturing and delivery run smoothly.

It also alters the nature of business relationships, as suppliers and customers lock together with unusual intimacy. Price Club and Black & Decker are separate companies, but in the realm of product orders and delivery, they act as one big enterprise. . . .

SOURCE: John Heinzl, "Supply and Command," *The Globe and Mail*, December 1992, page B2. Reprinted with the permission of *The Globe and Mail*.

supply and demand curves. We are now ready to analyze how these outside forces affect the equilibrium of supply and demand, beginning on the demand side.

SHIFTS OF THE DEMAND CURVE

Returning to our example of milk, we noted earlier that the quantity of milk demanded is probably influenced by a variety of things other than the price of milk. Changes in population, consumer income, and the prices of alternative beverages, such as soda and juice, presumably cause changes in the quantity of milk demanded, even if the price of milk is unchanged.

Since the demand curve for milk depicts only the relationship between the quantity of milk demanded and the price of milk, holding all other factors constant, a change in any of these other factors produces a shift of the entire demand curve.

A change in the price of a good produces a **movement along a fixed demand curve**. By contrast, a change in any other variable that influences quantity demanded produces a **shift of the demand curve**. If consumers want to buy more at any given price than they wanted previously, the demand curve shifts to the right (or outward). If they desire less at any given price, the demand curve shifts to the left (or inward).

Figure 3-4 shows this distinction graphically. If the price of a litre of milk falls from 80¢ to 60¢ and quantity demanded rises accordingly, we move along demand curve D_0D_0 from point C to point F, as shown by the black arrow. If, on the other hand, consumers suddenly decide that they like milk better than they did formerly, the entire demand curve shifts outward from D_0D_0 to D_1D_1, as indicated by the gold arrows. To make this general principle more concrete and to show some of its many applications, let us consider some specific examples.

FIGURE 3-4

MOVEMENT ALONG VERSUS SHIFT OF A DEMAND CURVE

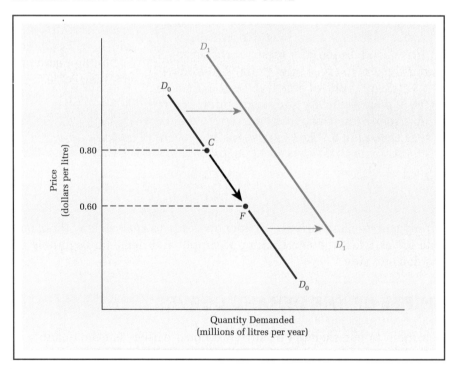

If quantity demanded increases because the price of a commodity falls, the market moves along a fixed demand curve such as D_0D_0 (see the movement from C to F). If, on the other hand, quantity demanded increases due to a change in one of its other determinants (such as consumer tastes or incomes), the entire demand curve shifts outward, as shown here by the shift from D_0D_0 to D_1D_1.

1. **Consumer incomes.**   If average incomes increase, consumers may purchase more of many foods, including milk, even if the price of milk remains the same. That is, increases in income normally shift demand curves outward to the right, as depicted in Figure 3-5(a). In this example, the quantity demanded at the old equilibrium price of 70¢ increases from 60 million litres per year (point E on demand curve $D_0 D_0$) to 75 million (point R on demand curve $D_1 D_1$). We know that 70¢ is no longer the equilibrium price, since at this price quantity demanded (75 million) exceeds quantity supplied (60 million). To restore equilibrium, price will have to rise. The diagram shows the new equilibrium at point T, where the price is 80¢ per litre and the quantity (demanded and supplied) is 70 million litres per year. This illustrates a general result.

Any factor that causes the demand curve to shift outward to the right and does not affect the supply curve will raise both the equilibrium price and the equilibrium quantity.

Everything works in reverse if consumer incomes fall. Figure 3-5(b) depicts a leftward (inward) shift of the demand curve that results from a decline in consumer incomes. For example, the quantity demanded at the previous equilibrium price (70¢) falls from 60 million litres (point E) to 45 million (point L on demand curve $D_2 D_2$). At the initial price, quantity supplied must begin to fall. The new

FIGURE 3-5

THE EFFECTS OF SHIFTS OF THE DEMAND CURVE

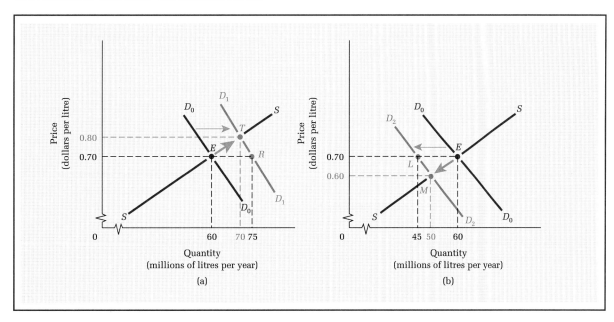

A shift of the demand curve will change the equilibrium price and quantity in a free market. In part (a), the demand curve shifts outward from $D_0 D_0$ to $D_1 D_1$. As a result, equilibrium moves from point E to point T; both price and quantity rise. In part (b), the demand curve shifts inward from $D_0 D_0$ to $D_2 D_2$, and equilibrium moves from point E to point M; both price and quantity fall.

equilibrium will eventually be established at point *M*, where the price is 60¢ and both quantity demanded and quantity supplied are 50 million.

In general, any factor that shifts the demand curve inward to the left and does not affect the supply curve will lower both the equilibrium price and the equilibrium quantity.

2. ***Population.*** Population growth should affect quantity demanded in more or less the same way as do increases in average incomes. A larger population will presumably wish to consume more milk, even if the price of milk and average incomes are unchanged, thus shifting the entire demand curve to the right, as in Figure 3-5(a). The equilibrium price and quantity both rise. Similarly, a decrease in population should shift the demand curve for milk to the left, as in Figure 3-5(b), causing equilibrium price and quantity to fall.

3. ***Consumer preferences.*** If the dairy industry mounts a successful advertising campaign extolling the benefits of drinking milk, families may decide to raise their quantities demanded. This would shift the entire demand curve for milk to the right, as in Figure 3-5(a). Alternatively, a medical report on the dangers of high cholesterol may persuade consumers to drink less milk, thereby shifting the demand curve inward, as in Figure 3-5(b).

   Again, these are quite general phenomena. If consumer preferences shift in favour of a particular item, that item's demand curve will shift outward to the right, causing both equilibrium price and quantity to rise. Conversely, if consumer preferences shift away from an item, that item's demand curve will shift inward to the left, causing equilibrium price and quantity to fall.

4. ***Prices and availability of related goods.*** Because soda, juice, and coffee are popular drinks that compete with milk, a change in the price of any of these beverages can be expected to shift the demand curve for milk. If any of these alternative drinks become cheaper, some consumers will switch away from milk. Thus, the demand curve for milk will shift to the left, as in Figure 3-5(b). The introduction of an entirely new beverage — say, coconut milk — can be expected to have a similar effect.

   But other price changes shift the demand curve for milk in the opposite direction. For example, suppose that cookies, a commodity that goes well with milk, become less expensive. This may induce some consumers to drink more milk and thus shift the demand curve for milk to the right, as in Figure 3-5(a).

   Common sense normally will tell us in which direction a price change for a related good will shift the demand curve for the good in question. Increases in the prices of goods that are substitutes for the good in question (as soda is for milk) move the demand curve to the right, thus raising both the equilibrium price and quantity. Increases in the prices of goods that are normally used together with the good in question (such as cookies and milk) shift the demand curve to the left, thus lowering both the equilibrium price and quantity.

APPLICATIONS

(1) WHY AIRLINES RUN SALES

Anyone who travels knows that airline companies reduce fares sharply to attract more customers at certain times of the year when air traffic is light. Yet there is no reason to think that air transportation gets any cheaper at these times. Our supply and demand diagram makes it easy to understand why airlines run such sales.

Given the number of planes in the airlines' fleets, the supply of seats is relatively fixed, as indicated by the steep supply curve SS in Figure 3-6, and it is more or less the same in all seasons. During times when people want to travel less, the demand curve for seats shifts leftward from its normal position, D_0D_0, to a position such as D_1D_1. Hence, equilibrium in the air traffic market shifts from point E to point A. Thus, both price and quantity decline at certain times of the year, not because of the generosity of the airlines but because of the discipline of the market.

FIGURE 3-6

SEASONAL CHANGES IN AIRLINE FARES

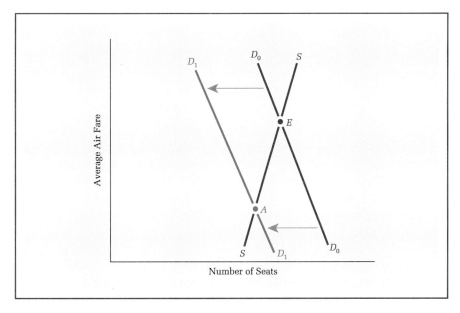

During seasons of slack demand for air travel, the demand curve shifts leftward from D_0D_0 to D_1D_1. In consequence, the market equilibrium point shifts from E to A, causing both price and quantity to decline.

(2) WHY HOUSING PRICES VARY

The same analysis can be used to explain variations in housing prices. During the period of high oil prices in the 1970s, average incomes rose in Alberta and so did the size of the province's population. The demand curve for homes, especially in Calgary and Edmonton, shifted to the right, and there was much building and big increases in housing prices. Then, a period of low oil prices followed in the 1980s; average incomes and the size of the population fell in Alberta. The demand curve for houses shifted back to the left, so housing prices fell.

(3) WHY THE WEATHER AFFECTS PRICES

December 1989 saw record cold temperatures in southern Ontario, and the price for heating fuels jumped by 20 percent in January 1990. It is easy to understand why: just think of Figure 3-6, applying it to the example of heating fuel and envisioning it in reverse. The cold weather caused a large rightward shift in the demand curve for heating fuels, and since the supply curve is relatively fixed in the short run, the price rose significantly.

SHIFTS OF THE SUPPLY CURVE

Like quantity demanded, the quantity supplied on a market typically responds to a great number of influences other than price. The weather, the cost of feed, the number and size of dairy farms, and a variety of other factors all influence how much milk will be brought to market. Since the supply curve depicts only the relationship between the price of milk and the quantity of milk demanded, holding all other factors constant, a change in any of these other factors will cause the entire supply curve to shift.

A change in the price of the good causes a **movement along a fixed supply curve**. But price is not the only influence on quantity supplied. If any of these other influences changes, **the entire supply curve shifts**.

Figure 3-7 once again depicts the distinction graphically. A rise in price from 60¢ to 80¢ will raise quantity supplied by moving along supply curve S_0S_0 from point f to point c. But any rise in quantity demanded attributable to a factor other than price will shift the entire supply curve outward to the right from S_0S_0 to S_1S_1, as shown by the gold arrows. Let us consider what some of these other factors are, and how they shift the supply curve.

1. *Size of the industry.* We begin with the most obvious factor. If more farmers enter the milk industry, the quantity supplied at any given price probably will increase. For example, if each farm provides 60 000 litres of milk per year when the price is 70¢ per litre, then 1000 farmers will provide 60 million litres and 1300 farmers will

FIGURE 3-7

MOVEMENT ALONG VERSUS SHIFT OF A SUPPLY CURVE

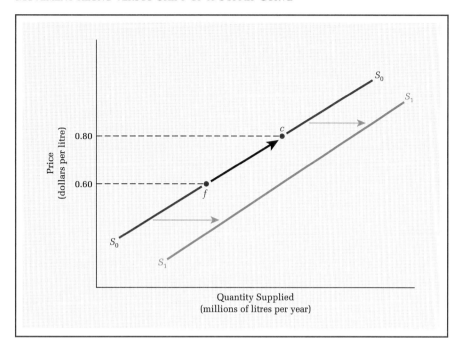

If quantity supplied rises because the price increases, we move along a fixed supply curve such as S_0S_0 (see the black arrow from point f to point c). If, on the other hand, quantity supplied rises because some other factor influencing supply improves, the entire supply curve shifts outward to the right from S_0S_0 to S_1S_1 (see the gold arrows).

provide 78 million. Thus, the more farms that are attracted to the industry, the greater will be the quantity of milk supplied at any given price and, hence, the farther to the right will be the supply curve.

Figure 3-8(a) illustrates the effect of an expansion of the industry from 1000 farms to 1300 farms—a rightward shift of the supply curve from S_0S_0 to S_1S_1. Notice that at the initial price of 70¢, the quantity supplied after the shift is 78 million litres (point I on supply curve S_1S_1), which exceeds the quantity demanded of 60 million (point E on supply curve S_0S_0). We can see in the graph that the price of 70¢ is too high to be the equilibrium price, so price must fall. The diagram shows the new equilibrium at point J, where the price is 60¢ per litre and the quantity is 65 million litres.

Generally, any factor that shifts the supply curve outward to the right and does not affect the demand curve will lower the equilibrium price and raise the equilibrium quantity.

This must *always* be true if the industry's demand curve has a negative slope, because the greater quantity supplied can be sold only if price is decreased to induce customers to buy more.

Figure 3-8(b) illustrates the opposite case: a contraction of the industry from 1000 farms to 625 farms. The supply curve shifts inward to the left and equilibrium moves from point E to point V, where price is 90¢ and quantity is 50 million litres.

Generally, any factor that shifts the supply curve inward to the left and does not affect the demand curve will raise the equilibrium price and will reduce the equilibrium quantity.

Even if no farmers enter or leave the industry, results like those depicted in Figure 3-8 can be produced by expansion or contraction of the existing farms. If farms get larger by adding more land, expanding the herds, and so on, the supply curve shifts to the right, as in Figure 3-8(a). If farms get smaller, the supply curve shifts to the left, as in Figure 3-8(b).

2. **Technological progress.** Another influence that shifts supply curves is technological change. Suppose someone discovers that cows give more milk if Mozart is played during milking. Then, at any given price of milk, farmers will be able to provide a larger quantity of output; that is, the supply curve will shift outward to the right, as in Figure 3-8(a). Again, this illustrates a quite general influence that applies to most industries: cost-reducing technological progress shifts the supply curve outward to the right. Thus, as Figure 3-8(a)

FIGURE 3-8
EFFECTS OF SHIFTS OF THE SUPPLY CURVE

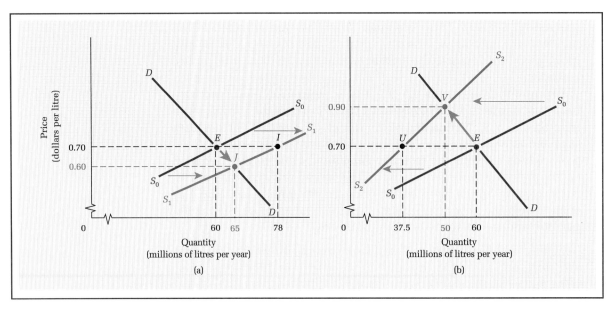

A shift of the supply curve will change the equilibrium price and quantity in a market. In part (a), the supply curve shifts outward to the right, from S_0S_0 to S_1S_1. As a result, equilibrium moves from point E to point J; price falls as quantity increases. Part (b) illustrates the opposite case—an inward shift of the supply curve from S_0S_0 to S_2S_2. Equilibrium moves from point E to point V, which means that price rises as quantity falls.

shows, the usual consequences of technological progress are lower prices and greater output.

3. ***Prices of inputs.***   Changes in input prices also shift supply curves. Suppose that farm workers become unionized and win a raise. Farmers will have to pay higher wages and consequently will no longer be able to provide 60 million litres of milk profitably at a price of 70¢ per litre (point E in Figure 3-8(b)). Perhaps they will provide only 37.5 million (point U on supply curve S_2S_2). This example illustrates that increases in the prices of inputs suppliers must buy will shift the supply curve inward to the left.

4. ***Prices of related outputs.***   Dairy farms produce more than milk. If cheese prices rise sharply, farmers may decide to use some raw milk to make cheese, thereby reducing the quantity of milk supplied. On a supply–demand diagram, the supply curve would shift inward, as in Figure 3-8(b).

Similar phenomena occur in other industries, and sometimes with the opposite effect. For example, suppose the price of beef goes up, which increases the quantity of meat supplied. That, in turn, will cause a rise in the number of cowhides supplied at any given price of leather. Thus, a rise in the price of beef will lead to a rightward shift in the supply curve of leather. In general, a change in the price of one good produced by a multiproduct industry may be expected to shift the supply curves of all the other goods produced by that industry.

APPLICATIONS

(1) A COMPUTER IN EVERY HOME?

A few decades ago, no one owned a home computer. Now there are millions in North America, and enthusiasts look toward the day when computers will be as commonplace as television sets. What happened to bring the computer from the laboratory into the home? Did people suddenly develop a craving for computers?

Hardly. What actually happened is that scientists in the early 1970s invented the microchip—a major breakthrough that drastically reduced both the size of computers and, more important, the cost of manufacturing them. Within a few years, microcomputers were in commercial production. Microchip technology continued to improve throughout the 1970s and 1980s, leading to ever smaller, better, and cheaper computers. Today, for less than a thousand dollars, you can buy a desktop machine with computing powers rivalling those of the giant computers of the early 1960s.

In terms of our supply and demand diagrams, the rapid technological progress in computer manufacturing shifted the supply curve dramatically to the right. As Figure 3-9 shows, a large outward shift of the supply

FIGURE 3-9

TECHNOLOGICAL CHANGE AND THE COMPUTER MARKET

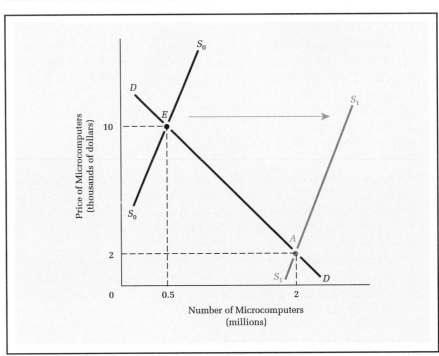

The invention of the microchip and subsequent improvements in microchip technology caused the supply curve of microcomputers to shift outward to the right—moving from S_0S_0 to S_1S_1. Consequently, equilibrium shifted from point E to point A. The price of microcomputers fell from $10 000 to $2000, and the quantity increased from 0.5 million to 2 million per year.

curve should bring down the equilibrium price and increase the equilibrium quantity—which is just what happened in the computer industry. The figure calls attention to the fact that consumers naturally buy more computers as the price of computers falls (a movement along demand curve *DD* from *E* to *A*), even if the demand curve does not shift.

(2) A GLUT OF RECYCLED ITEMS

Concern for the environment has led to the organization of recycling programs for numerous items such as newsprint and glass bottles. Initially these schemes made money, but with the dramatic increase in people's willingness to participate by separating their garbage, the market for such goods became flooded. With the supply curve shifting dramatically to the right (as more "suppliers" entered the market), the price for recycled items has fallen to very low levels, and some municipalities are simply storing them until the price rises again, or dumping them as before.

The price can be expected to rise when more factories become equipped to process the used products. For example, the machines that paper mills need to produce newsprint from used paper are different from

EXPERIMENTAL ECONOMICS

In theory, supply and demand curves determine price. But does reality work the way theory claims? One way of answering this question is to consider some actual historical events. This is what we have been doing in this chapter, and we have seen that supply and demand analysis explains observed variations in the price of a range of items, from houses to recycled goods, very well. But another way of answering the question is to run controlled experiments the way physicists do.

For a long time, it was believed that the option of laboratory experimentation was not available to economists. How can an economist re-create an entire economy, or even a single market, in a laboratory? How can one supply realistic motivation for the people who participate in such an experiment, so that they will act as they would in making an actual decision, with real money at stake?

Because economists have long felt that experimental methods were beyond their grasp, they have relied mostly on statistical inference to test their theories. But the statistical approach is an imperfect solution because it does not allow us to isolate perfectly just one influence at a time, as in a scientifically controlled experiment.

This view of experimentation in economics has recently begun to change. Economists still rely mainly on statistical analysis, but they have also begun to experiment. Market ex-

periments are now conducted to test theories about the behaviour of large firms, about economic incentives to help protect the environment, about the responses of consumers to changing tax rules, about government programs that provide financial assistance to poor people, and about a wide variety of other subjects. Dozens of experiments are now under way.

Who are the subjects of these experiments? You guessed it. They are often university students who volunteer to participate. What leads them to volunteer? One reason may be that the experiments are interesting; but there is also money to be earned. In fact, that is what provides the motivation for the participants to act as they would in a real market. Let's look at one such experiment, conducted at two schools in the United States.* The objective was to see whether demand and supply curves do in fact determine price in the way the theory claims.

Students were divided into two groups, sellers and buyers. Each was given some money to start, and the amount of money remaining at the end depended on the purchases and sales he or she made. Sellers acquired "goods" from the experimenter (who acted like a wholesaler) at a price, and then

(continued)

*See C.R. Plott, "Externalities and Corrective Policies in Experimental Markets," *The Economic Journal*, vol. 93, March 1983, pages 106–27.

(continued)

tried to sell them to one of the buyers. Sellers could pocket any difference between the price they paid to the experimenter and the price they received for selling the good. Similarly, buying students could maximize the amount of money they took away from the game by paying the lowest price possible for the goods they purchased. Since the experimenter specified how these gains to the buying students depended on the prices they paid, he was able to derive, at the theoretical level, what the market-clearing price would be.

How did the actual prices turn out in the experiment? Each time a sale was completed by voluntary interaction of buyers and sellers, the agreed-upon price was recorded. The experiment was repeated five times, with each repetition involving about 15 to 25 transactions. The actual prices were generally lower than the theoretical equilibrium value, but they were almost always very close. In each of the five experiments, the price came closer and closer to the theoretical figure as more transactions were completed and students acquired more experience. In the last two experiments, the average prices were within 2.2 percent of the predicted equilibrium. Apparently, the experiments do work, and so does the theory — as a reasonable approximation of reality.

the ones they currently own, which produce newsprint from pulp. Until more of the new machines are built, the recycled paper cannot be used in large quantities. Although this temporary outcome is discouraging for environmentalists, the current low prices for recycled items are indeed inducing firms to build the new equipment that will enable them to take advantage of these low prices. In the long run, this is exactly what environmentalists want. Another reason that the price for recycled items will not remain depressed for too long is that laws are being passed that effectively push the demand curve to the right. Thirty states south of the border now have some form of compulsory recycling laws. In Canada, a similar trend is evident; for example, the city of Toronto passed a law, effective January 1991, requiring 50 percent recycled content in the newsprint used by its newspapers.

RESTRAINING THE MARKET MECHANISM: PRICE CEILINGS

As we have noted already, lawmakers and rulers have often been dissatisfied with the outcomes of the operation of the market system. Through the ages, legislators have done battle with the invisible hand. Sometimes, rather than trying to make adjustments in the workings of the market, governments have sought to raise or lower the prices of specific commodities by decree. In many of these cases, those in authority felt that the prices set by the market mechanism were, in some sense, immorally low or immorally high. Penalties were therefore imposed on anyone offering the commodities in question at prices lower or higher than those determined by the authorities.

But the market has proven itself a formidable foe that strongly resists attempts to circumvent its workings. In case after case where **price ceilings** are imposed, virtually the same set of consequences ensues:

A **PRICE CEILING** is a legal maximum on the price that may be charged for a commodity.

1. The economy develops a persistent shortage of the items that have controlled prices. Queuing, direct rationing, or any of a variety of other devices, usually inefficient and unpleasant, have to be substituted for the distribution process provided by the price mechanism. *Example:* In 1990, consumers in the former Soviet Union were placing orders for sitting-room furniture that were scheduled for delivery in 2011.

2. An illegal or "black" market often arises to supply the commodity. There are usually some individuals who are willing to take the risks involved in meeting unsatisfied demands illegally, if legal means will not do the job. *Example:* Although ticket scalping is illegal in most places, it occurs at most popular sporting events.

3. The prices charged on the black market are almost certainly higher than those that would prevail in a free market. After all, black marketeers expect compensation for the risk of being caught and punished. *Example:* Goods that are illegally smuggled into a country, such as drugs, are normally quite expensive.

4. In each case, a substantial portion of the price falls into the hands of the black-market supplier instead of going to those who produce the good or perform the service. *Example:* A constant complaint in the series of hearings that have marked the history of theatre ticket price controls in New York City has been that the "ice" (the illegal excess charge) falls into the hands of ticket scalpers rather than going to those who invested in, produced, or acted in the play.

These points and others are best illustrated by considering some concrete examples of price ceilings.

CASE STUDIES

(1) RENT CONTROLS

New York is the only major city in North America that has had rent controls continuously since World War II. The objective of rent control is, of course, to protect the consumer from high rents. But more than 95 percent of Canadian economists believe that rent control does not help cities or their inhabitants and that, in the long run, it costs almost everyone. Let's use supply–demand analysis to see what actually happens.

Figure 3-10 is a supply–demand diagram for rental units in New York. Curve *DD* is the demand curve and curve *SS* is the supply curve. Without controls, equilibrium would be at point *E*, where rents average $1000 per month and 3 million units are occupied. Effective rent controls must set

FIGURE 3-10

SUPPLY–DEMAND DIAGRAM FOR HOUSING

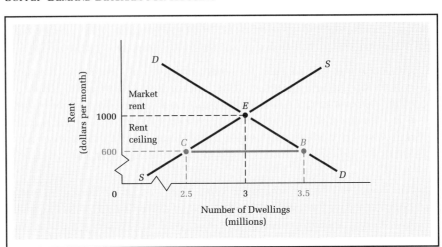

When market forces are permitted to set rents, the quantity of dwellings supplied will equal the quantity demanded. But when a rent ceiling forces rent below the market level, the number of dwellings supplied (point *C*) will be less than the number demanded (point *B*). Thus, rent ceilings induce housing shortages.

a ceiling price below the equilibrium price of $1000, because otherwise the rent level would simply settle at the point determined by market forces. But with a low ceiling such as, say, $600, the quantity of housing demanded will be 3.5 million (point *B*) while the quantity supplied will be only 2.5 million (point *C*).

The diagram shows a shortage of 1 million apartments. This theoretical concept of a "shortage" shows up in New York City as an abnormally low vacancy rate—typically about half the U.S. national urban average.

As we expect, rent controls have spawned a lively black market in New York. The black market works to raise the effective price of rent-controlled apartments in many ways, including bribes, "key money" paid to move up on waiting lists, and requirements that prospective tenants purchase worthless furniture at inflated prices.

According to the diagram, rent controls reduce the quantity supplied from 3 million to 2.5 million apartments. What do we see in New York? First, some property owners, discouraged by the low rents, have converted apartment buildings into office space or other uses. Second, some apartments have not been maintained adequately. After all, rent controls create a shortage that makes even dilapidated apartments easy to rent. Third, some landlords have actually abandoned their buildings rather than pay rising tax and fuel bills. These abandoned buildings rapidly become eyesores and eventually pose threats to public health and safety.

With all these problems, why do rent controls persist in New York City? Why did Canada have rent controls in all ten provinces in 1975, and why do we still have controls in four provinces today? Part of the explanation is that many people simply do not understand the problems that rent controls cause. Also, landlords are unpopular politically. But another, and important, part of the explanation is that not everyone is hurt by rent controls, and those who benefit from controls fight hard to preserve them. In New York, for example, many tenants pay rents that are only a fraction of what their apartments would fetch on the open market. This last point illustrates another very general phenomenon:

Virtually every price ceiling or floor creates a class of people with a vested interest in preserving the regulations because they benefit from them. These people naturally use their political influence to protect their gains, which is one reason why it is so hard to eliminate price ceilings or floors.

The effects of rent control in New York and in several European cities have prompted Swedish economist Assar Lindbeck to quip, "Next to bombing, rent control seems in many cases to be the most efficient technique so far known for destroying cities. . . ."[1]

Canadian cities have not, however, been "destroyed" by rent controls. One reason is that provincial government subsidies for apartment construction were increased at the same time. A study of rent controls in Toronto reported that the proportion of apartment starts that depended on government support increased from 13 percent in 1974 to 91 percent in 1977, after rent control was introduced.[2]

(2) SERVICES PROVIDED OUTSIDE THE MARKET

There are numerous other examples of price ceilings throughout the economy. Just think of where there are long waiting periods—in the judicial system, at airports, and even in the area of human organ transplants. In each of these cases, which we elaborate below, shortages have emerged because the institutional arrangements have not permitted market forces to determine an appropriate price—or, in the economist's jargon, a "market-clearing price." In a number of these cases, the most extreme form of price ceiling prevails—the rule that no price is permitted at all. (In a supply and demand diagram, the effect of this is to push the maximum price line down to the level of the quantity axis.)

Waits of several years for a trial date are not uncommon in our judicial system. Individuals cannot pay a fee to move their case forward in the queue; that is, the maximum allowed price for acquiring an earlier time in the schedule is zero. Despite this maximum price within the government-run court system, individuals do have a private-sector alternative that allows them to pay a higher price for a speedy settlement. This option is possible because much of the backlog in our court system is caused by the numerous civil suits that must be heard. These cases do not involve any alleged violation of law; rather, one private citizen brings suit against another over some disagreement. Many of these cases are

---

1. Assar Lindbeck, *The Political Economy of the New Left: An Outsider's View*, 2nd ed. (New York: Harper & Row, 1977), page 39.
2. Basil A. Kalymon, "Apartment Shortages and Rent Control," in *Rent Control: Myths and Realities*, ed. W. Block and E. Olsen (Vancouver: The Fraser Institute, 1981), page 241.

already being settled out of court (that is, without the involvement of a judge), but the demand on judges' time could be further reduced if private arbitrators were more commonly used. Some arbitration mechanisms are now in operation in Canada, and more than twenty U.S. states have successfully opted for a court-annexed arbitration system to relieve pressure on the judicial system. But it is difficult for private arbitration options to develop more fully when their overhead costs are not subsidized, as they are within the publicly funded judicial system. In any event, the growing popularity of the private alternative *despite* this cost disadvantage proves that the price ceiling of zero that prevails in the public system causes the perpetual "shortage" of judicial services.

Airport congestion is an example of what is known as a peak-load problem. Airlines and individual airplane owners must pay fees established by the government for using the various services offered by airport terminals—use of runways, ground services, and so on—and these fees are set at a level that allows the market for the services to clear at most times during the week. But because the government does not allow the charges to be increased temporarily at peak-demand times during the week, there is no incentive for smaller airlines and individual airplane owners to schedule their flights during less busy times. Consequently, severe congestion occurs at most major airports during rush hours.

Our final example is perhaps the most controversial. Present law prohibits the sale of human organs for transplant, and thereby sets a maximum price of zero for such transactions. It is hard to think of an arrangement that could maximize excess demand (that is, create a shortage) more effectively. With the added incentive of financial reward, more people would be likely to become donors; under the current system, far too many would-be recipients must wait for their transplants for long periods of time, or do without. Admittedly, this issue is sensitive and subject to persuasive ethical arguments against changing the present law. Nonetheless, the existing shortages can certainly be attributed to the zero price ceiling.

It is important to note here that economic analysis can be brought to bear only on positive questions (propositions that can be proved or disproved), not on normative issues (propositions that involve value judgements). We are not arguing that human organs *should* be sold at a market-determined price; we are simply noting that a number of the problems in this area follow inexorably from our ethical preference to disallow this practice. It *is* the economist's job to inform people of the trade-offs involved—but the economist cannot make the choices.

For twenty years, one economics instructor has been surveying his students' attitudes toward allowing a market price to be used to eliminate shortages. He described the results in an article in *The Globe and Mail* (see the boxed insert on the next page).

All of these examples of shortage show that numerous inefficiencies and inequities could be lessened if prices were allowed to be more flexible. Some of the outcomes are not regarded as fair, but we must remember that income can also be redistributed in ways that do *not* override market forces (as we will see in Chapter 15).

STUDENT ATTITUDES TOWARD THE PRICE SYSTEM

I teach economics at an Ontario community college and my students like the idea that resources should be allocated by all-wise, all-powerful civil servants who know what's best and do what's fair. And that's not because of what I teach them. They come to me this way.

Early in every course, I start a class with "a shortage problem." Students are asked to read the problem, to spend a few minutes thinking about it and to write down two or three possible solutions on separate cards. I suggest no solutions beforehand.

A shortage problem. A medical school has received 300 applications from students who want to enrol. The school has the capacity to accept only 120 new students. All the 300 applicants have at least the minimum academic requirements. All have sent cheques for the $6,000 tuition fee. How is the decision made to determine who gets in? . . .

Here are typical solutions ranked roughly from most popular to least popular. The titles and words are mine but the ideas are from the students.

The subsidy solution. A government grants or loans the medical school enough funds to permit extra classes to be held.

The subsidy solution is a crowd-pleaser that causes many young heads to nod wisely, and some not so young. On one occasion a mature student blurted out the need for subsidies before the cards were distributed. She was genuinely angry that government tolerates unfair shortages and she demanded that government intervene. The rest of the class was convinced; very few other solutions were offered that time around.

The queue solution. The applications with the earliest postmarks are accepted first. In other words, first come, first served.

The queue solution is the rival for most popular. Many students who have spent time lining up for movie or rock-concert tickets somehow look upon this as being fair.

The lottery solution. All 300 names are put in a hat and fairly shuffled. A blindfolded official randomly pulls out 120.

The lottery solution is somehow considered less fair because being early doesn't count. Students see some merit in making the effort to be first in line.

The merit solution. The applicants with the best academic backgrounds and highest marks are chosen first.

The merit of being first in line nearly always wins out over the merit of studying hard and earning good grades. . . .

The quota solution. The decision is made to fill quotas, such as 50 per cent women, 30 per cent non-white, 20 per cent native, 20 per cent challenged and 10 per cent left-handed.

The quota solution was never mentioned years ago but is coming on strong. It always encourages heated debate, with more angry words about the categories and percentages than about its overall fairness.

The following solutions tend to come from the more cynical and worldly-wise students.

The graft solution. The key admissions officer accepts bribes of $1,000 each to process some applicants first.

Interestingly enough, most students tend to think the graft solution is a market solution. They know from my introduction to the course that we will be spending a lot of time on markets and prices. And at this early stage in the course, the students often confuse the free-market system with the world of black markets, economic crimes and corruptible civil servants. It goes without saying that students who believe in the fairness of queues tend to look upon scalpers as criminals.

(continued)

(continued)

The nepotism solution. The medical school personnel allow their own family members and the sons and daughters of their friends and relatives in first.

The nepotism solution makes sense in a world of Senate appointees and too many other examples of taking care of your own. At this point in the class, some student will usually pipe up about how his friend got the high-wage summer job at Hydro or The Beer Store.

The lazy solution. The admissions officer simply reaches for the first 120 applications closest at hand and ignores the rest.

The lazy solution is hardly ever mentioned, but when it is, I always make a point of finding out who made this contribution. In any subsequent classroom debates, that student is nearly always worth drawing out.

There are many variations on the above themes, and there have been a few bizarre solutions through the years, such as shutting down the medical schools to make more room for chiropractors and midwives. Twice, students have earnestly explained astrological solutions.

But the solution I want to hear, if only because it leads into the next part of the course, is sometimes missing.

The price solution. Announce a sudden increase in tuition fee of, say, another $4,000 to a new total of $10,000.

Last semester, the entire second-year advertising class of about 55 students missed the price solution. When I flashed the foregoing words on the overhead, some students reacted with hostility. This solution was dismissed as unfair. "Only the children of the rich could become doctors," is a typical comment.

When I asked the class to identify the benefits of this solution, there was silence. I was the one to point out that the school could use the extra money to lay on extra classes and to build larger facilities. But my voice sounded lame. And as for the extra fee being an incentive to work hard to earn it, and a way to separate out the students who were not as keen on becoming doctors, forget it. My students' eyes glassed over. . . .

SOURCE: James L. Whyte, "Free-Market Mandarins in the Making," *The Globe and Mail*, January 6, 1993, page A16. Reprinted with the permission of *The Globe and Mail*.

RESTRAINING THE MARKET MECHANISM: PRICE FLOORS

A **PRICE FLOOR** is a legal minimum on the price that may be charged for a commodity.

Interferences with the market mechanism are not always designed to keep prices low. Agricultural price supports and minimum wages are two notable examples of how the law keeps prices above free-market levels. **Price floors** are typically accompanied by a standard set of symptoms:

1. A surplus develops as some sellers cannot find buyers. *Example:* Empty seats on airlines were the norm, not the exception, before the airline industry was deregulated in the 1970s and 1980s.

2. Where goods, rather than services, are involved, the surplus creates a problem of disposal. Something must be done about the excess of quantity supplied over quantity demanded. *Example:* The government has often been forced to purchase, and then store, large amounts of surplus agricultural commodities.

3. To get around the regulations, sellers may offer discounts in disguised—and often unwanted—forms. *Example:* With transatlantic air fares heavily regulated, airlines offer bargains on the land portions of package holidays to the United Kingdom that are often not fully used.

4. Regulations that keep prices artificially high encourage overinvestment in the industry. Even inefficient businesses whose high operating costs would doom them in an unrestricted market can survive beneath the shelter of a generous price floor. *Example:* This is why the airline and trucking industries both underwent painful "shakeouts" of the weaker companies in the 1980s, following deregulation.

Once again, some specific examples might be useful.

CASE STUDIES

(1) FARM PRICE SUPPORTS

Perhaps you have seen news items about farmers having to throw away surplus eggs, milk, or other agricultural products. The surpluses are by-products of various government programs designed to raise the incomes of farmers. For many products, a price higher than the equilibrium price is maintained through the provincial marketing boards, which stipulate production limits for each farmer. For other products, a high price is maintained because the government buys up any output that the market does not absorb at the higher price.

One example is the Canadian Dairy Commission, under Agriculture Canada. One of its purposes is to stabilize the price of dairy products at a level high enough to permit reasonable incomes to be earned by all existing dairy farmers. Generally, this involves a support price well above the free-market level, which causes a surplus to develop, as indicated in Figure 3-11. To maintain the price above the free-market level, the government must buy the surplus milk and other dairy products. But this creates a problem. Milk is so highly perishable that it must be turned into cheese or butter or dried milk before it can be stored. Buying and storing these products is costly, so the products are often simply disposed of. Even given this practice, the Organization for Economic Co-operation and Development (OECD) has estimated that Canadian taxpayers spend $100 000 per worker in the farm industries in Canada that are supported by policies of this sort. Similar problems have developed in the United States and Europe. One solution to the surplus wine that has resulted from price-support programs in Europe has been to convert it to automobile fuel (gasohol), at much expense to the taxpayer (a situation that wine-lovers find discouraging).

This analysis does not imply that individual farm incomes should be lower than they are. It simply shows how the basic forces of supply and demand lead to inefficiencies under the current methods for maintaining farm incomes.

FIGURE 3-11

PRICE SUPPORTS FOR MILK

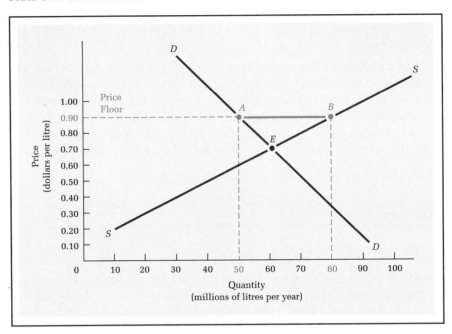

In this diagram, which repeats the supply and demand curves from Figure 3-3, the support price for milk (90¢ per litre) is above the equilibrium price (70¢). Quantity supplied is 80 million litres per year (point *B*), while quantity demanded is only 50 million (point *A*). To keep the price at 90¢, the government must buy 30 million litres of milk per year and store it as cheese or milk powder, or dispose of it.

(2) THE MINIMUM WAGE

We can use Figure 3-11 once again, to discuss the effects of minimum-wage legislation. Imagine that units of unskilled labour are measured along the quantity axis, and the wage paid to unskilled labour along the price axis. If the market-clearing wage (given by point *E*) is deemed "unacceptably low" by legislators, a minimum wage (at the height on the price axis of line *AB*) can be imposed. Employment (the quantity of labour demanded) falls to the quantity represented by point *A*, while the supply of labour increases to the quantity represented by point *B*. Unemployment (that is, excess supply of labour) therefore rises from zero to the amount represented by distance *AB*. We will analyze minimum-wage laws more thoroughly in Chapter 14; for now, just read the boxed insert in that chapter entitled "Minimum-Wage Law No Help to Unskilled" (page 420). It shows that youth unemployment in Canada is highest in the provinces that have the highest minimum wages, just as our supply and demand analysis predicts.

FIXED EXCHANGE RATES

The **EXCHANGE RATE** states the price at which one currency can be bought in terms of another currency.

One price that is often set by government policy is the international value of the Canadian dollar, known as the **exchange rate**. Through its agent, the Bank of Canada, the federal government often stands ready to buy or sell quantities of foreign currencies in whatever amounts are required to stabilize the price of the Canadian dollar. For example, in September 1992, during the Constitutional debate preceding the referendum on the Charlottetown agreement, many foreign lenders feared political uncertainty in Canada, and they withdrew their funds. Our government tried to keep the value of the Canadian dollar from falling much below a price of 80 cents (U.S.). It tried to maintain this price floor by trading currencies in the foreign-exchange market. Whenever private traders who desired U.S. dollars or other foreign currencies could not find a trader who would buy Canadian dollars at this price (exchange rate), the Canadian authorities would buy up the otherwise unwanted Canadian currency. The authorities did this by selling off one-quarter of their entire foreign-currency reserves in that month. Thus, the foreign-exchange rate can be fixed in precisely the same manner as in the milk-price supports discussed above. The only difference is that there are no direct storage costs for holding inventories of foreign currencies. Because of this, and because a fluctuating value of the Canadian dollar is often thought to deter foreign trade, this price is heavily managed and sometimes absolutely fixed.

Unfortunately, we must wait until Chapters 28 and 29 to assess the costs and benefits of this form of market intervention. We will learn that it greatly determines which government policies the minister of finance can or cannot use to fight unemployment and inflation.

A CAN OF WORMS

Our case studies illustrate some of the major side effects of price floors and ceilings but barely hint at others. There are yet more difficulties that we have not even mentioned. The market mechanism is a tough bird that imposes suitable retribution on those who seek to circumvent it by legislative decree. Here is a partial list of other problems that may arise when prices are controlled.

FAVOURITISM AND CORRUPTION

When price ceilings create a shortage, someone must decide who gets the limited quantity that is available. This can lead to political favouritism, to corruption in government, or even to discrimination along racial or religious lines.

UNENFORCEABILITY

Attempts to control prices are almost certain to fail in industries with numerous suppliers, simply because the regulating agency must monitor the behaviour of so many sellers. Ways will be found to evade or to violate the law, and something akin to the free-market price will generally re-emerge. But there is a difference: because the evasion mechanism, whatever its form, will have some operating costs, those costs must be borne by someone. That someone is normally the consumer.

AUXILIARY RESTRICTIONS

Fears that a system of price controls will break down invariably lead to regulations designed to shore up the shaky structure. Consumers may be told when and from whom they are permitted to buy. The powers of the police and the courts may be used to prevent the entry of new suppliers. Occasionally, an intricate system of market subdivision is imposed, giving each class of firms its protected category of operations in which others are not permitted to compete. Laws banning conversion of rent-controlled apartments to condominiums are one example.

LIMITATION OF VOLUME OF TRANSACTIONS

To the extent that controls succeed in affecting prices, they can be expected to reduce the volume of transactions that occur. Curiously, this is true whether the regulated price is above or below the free market's equilibrium price. If the regulated price is set above the equilibrium price, quantity demanded will be below the equilibrium quantity. On the other hand, if the imposed price is set below the free-market level, quantity supplied will be cut down. Since sales volume cannot exceed either the quantity supplied or the quantity demanded, a reduction in the volume of transactions (and, hence, in employment) is likely to result.

In some markets, price naturally fluctuates significantly because of such things as variations in the weather. For example, in a bad season when crops grow poorly, the supply curve for agricultural products shifts to the left and prices are high. Similarly, when harvests are good, the supply curve is far over to the right and prices are low. Speculators try to make a profit by keeping an inventory of these products. They sell off some of their inventory when prices are high, and they replenish their inventory when prices are low. This is a socially helpful thing to do. When speculators buy during the low-price period, they cause the demand curve to shift to the right, so that prices are not so low after all. Similarly, when speculators sell during the high-price periods, they shift the supply curve to the right, so prices are not so high after all. In other words, speculators decrease the amount of price volatility that would otherwise occur, and they make commodities more available in the scarce periods. Simply allowing speculators to perform this service can often "control" prices more effectively than a deliberate price-regulation policy. Also, this "natural" solution does not lower the average level of transactions.

MISALLOCATION OF RESOURCES

Departures from free-market prices are likely to produce misuse of the economy's resources because the connection between production costs and prices is broken. Also, just as more complex locks lead to more sophisticated burglary tools, more complex regulations lead to the use of even more resources for their avoidance. New jobs are created for executives, lawyers, and economists. One may well argue that at least some of the expensive services of these professionals could be used more productively elsewhere.

Economists put it this way. Free markets are capable of dealing with the three basic co-ordination tasks outlined in Chapter 2: deciding *what* to produce, *how* to produce it, and *to whom* it should be distributed. Price controls throw a monkey wrench into the market mechanism. Though the market is surely not flawless and government intervention often has praiseworthy goals, good intentions are not enough. Any government that sets out to repair what it sees as a defect in the market mechanism must take care lest it cause serious damage elsewhere. As a prominent economist once quipped, societies that are too willing to interfere with the operation of free markets soon find that the invisible hand is nowhere to be seen.

A SIMPLE BUT POWERFUL LESSON

The lessons you have learned in this chapter may seem elementary, even obvious. In many respects, they are. But they are also very important and indispensable. Although the law of supply and demand is one of the simplest principles in economics, it is also one of the most powerful. Yet, astonishing as it may seem, many people in authority, even highly intelligent people, fail to understand it or apply it accurately to concrete situations.

For example, not long ago, *The New York Times* carried a dramatic front-page picture of the president of Kenya setting fire to a large pile of elephant tusks that had been confiscated from poachers. The accompanying story explained that the burning was intended as a symbolic act to persuade the world to halt the ivory trade.[3] As economists, we are in no position to comment on the likely psychological impact of burning elephant tusks, although we doubt that it touched the consciences of poachers. The economic effect, however, was clear. By reducing the supply of ivory on the world market, the burning of tusks will force up the price of ivory, which will raise the illicit rewards reaped by those who slaughter elephants. That can only encourage more poaching — precisely the opposite of what the Kenyan government sought to accomplish.

Similar reasoning has been applied to cast doubt on the efficacy of the ongoing war on drugs. To the extent that drug-interdiction programs succeed in stopping illegal drugs at the border, they reduce the supply and drive up street prices. But that, in turn, raises the rewards for potential smugglers and attracts more criminals to the "industry." Many economists believe that any successful antidrug program must concentrate on

---

3. *The New York Times*, July 19, 1989, page A-1.

PUBLIC CONTROVERSY

ECONOMICS AND DRUGS

Current events in the drug trade are reminiscent of the alcohol business in the United States back in the 1920s under Prohibition. The Colombian drug lords compare with Al Capone and the other underworld figures, who were the object of intense police crackdowns. But the liquor continued to flow. . . .

In the end, we all know, Al Capone and the criminals were driven out of the liquor trade. But it is only through legend and television that we came to believe that flying squads of gun-wielding law enforcement agents shut down the underworld business. . . .

The historical reality, of course, is that Al Capone and his associates were driven out of the business by an economic development: deregulation. With the legalization of alcohol, the criminals were quickly replaced by legitimate corporations.

Imagine what would happen if cocaine were deregulated and legalized. The first result would be an end to the violence, both in the producing countries such as Colombia and on the streets of our cities. The guns and the killing are not the consequence of drugs, they are the result of governments trying to use force to stop the production and sale of a product for which there is a demand.

Another effect would be the saving of billions of dollars — the money now spent by law enforcement agencies and police departments across North America to stop the import, distribution, and sale of drugs. Economically, legalization would also remove the vast black-market profits that are the major attraction to those who get into the business.

The social consequences of drug deregulation were suggested recently by Kildare Clarke, associate medical director of the emergency department at Kings County Hospital in New York. In an article in *The New York Times* favouring legalization, Dr. Clarke wrote: "By removing black-market profits, it would substantially reduce the violence that goes with the illegal trade and the street crime that supports drug habits. It would stop the killing of police officers and innocent bystanders caught in the crossfire. It would allow better controls, reducing the chance of death by overdose or transmission of AIDS by dirty needles."

Dr. Clarke says legalization would probably lead to an initial increase in drug use, but education and training would be part of the deregulation process. He cites alcohol as an example. "Today, we are educating the public about the long-term effects of alcohol, providing treatment for those in need and, over all, dealing with alcohol in a far more rational fashion than we are coping with drugs."

SOURCE: Adapted from Terence Corcoran, "Economic Thinking on Drug Trade Leads to Deregulation Conclusion," *The Globe and Mail*, September 2, 1989, page B2. Used with the permission of *The Globe and Mail*.

THE BABY BOOM

Many changing events during this century can be explained by the supply and demand framework, once the changing age distribution of the population each decade is taken into consideration. The baby boom generation is that cohort of 9 million Canadians that were born between 1947 and 1966. This cohort is dramatically larger than any other age group, so it is no wonder that Canada witnessed crowded classrooms and school expansion in the 1960s, apartment shortages in the 1970s, and overheated housing markets in the 1980s. The demand curve for each of these items shifted to the right by a dramatic amount as the baby boom generation got older. (Incidently, this analysis means that in general, there will not be the same capital gains in residential housing in the years to come. Nevertheless, since many baby boomers have yet to buy a recreational property such as a cottage, we can expect this demand curve to shift to the right as the bulk of the baby boomers reach this age and affluence.)

In terms of supply and demand, people born in the peak of the baby boom (between 1957 and 1963) picked the worst possible time to be born this century. They have been labelled the "Me Generation", but it is not surprising that they have had to be more worried about their own prospects. There are simply so many of them competing for jobs, and the early baby boomers had already moved into many of the good careers and the affordable housing. The parents of these late baby boomers sometimes wonder why their sons and daughters do not "make a success of things" as they did. But these parents are members of a very small population cohort. Not so many people were born during the depression of the 1930s and the early war years, so these individuals faced much less competition. No wonder so many were a success in their careers.

Demographers now discuss the "baby boom echo"—which stems from the fact that so many baby boomers have produced children born after 1976. Elementary schools are already more crowded than they were 10 years ago. The greater numbers involved in this cohort means that these individuals will face stiffer competition after college and university than do those graduating today. While milder in effect, this is just what the parents of these individuals faced, and it is just what basic supply and demand analysis predicts.

reducing *demand*, which would lower the street price of drugs, not on reducing supply, which can only raise it. The newspaper excerpt from *The Globe and Mail* in the boxed insert opposite shows an appreciation of this reasoning. We included it to help you see the broad applicability of supply and demand analysis. We do not mean to suggest that legalization of drugs is a better way to lower prices than a program of education. Indeed, the vastly lower street prices of drugs that would surely follow legalization would increase drug use. Thus, while legalization would almost certainly reduce crime, it would also produce more addicts. The key question here

—to which no one has a good answer—is, How many more addicts? If you think the increase in quantity demanded would be large, and if you think the demand curve for drugs would not shift much to the left with an education program that made people more aware of the harmful effects, you are unlikely to find legalization an attractive option.

Many students are worried about their job prospects; they sense that their chances of a satisfying career are lower than what was available to their parents. The boxed insert on page 91 explains how the basic analysis of supply and demand can shed light on these concerns.

SUMMARY

1. The quantity of a product that is demanded is not a fixed number. Rather, quantity demanded depends on such factors as the price of the product, consumer incomes, and the prices of other products.

2. The relationship between quantity demanded and price, holding all other things constant, can be displayed graphically on a demand curve.

3. For most products, the higher the price, the lower the quantity demanded. Thus, the demand curve usually has a negative slope.

4. The quantity of a product that is supplied also depends on its price and many other influences. A supply curve is a graphical representation of the relationship between quantity supplied and price, holding all other influences constant.

5. For most products, the supply curve has a positive slope, meaning that higher prices call forth greater quantities supplied.

6. A market is said to be in equilibrium when quantity supplied is equal to quantity demanded. The equilibrium price and quantity are shown by the point on a graph where the supply and demand curves intersect. In a free market, price and quantity will tend to gravitate to this point.

7. A change in quantity demanded that is caused by a change in the price of the good is represented by a movement along a fixed demand curve. A change in quantity demanded that is caused by a change in any other determinant of quantity demanded is represented by a shift of the demand curve.

8. The same distinction applies to the supply curve: Changes in price lead to movements along a fixed supply curve; changes in other determinants of quantity supplied lead to shifts of the whole supply curve.

9. Changes in consumer incomes, tastes, technology, prices of competing products, and many other influences cause shifts in either the demand curve or the supply curve and produce changes in price and quantity that can be determined from supply–demand diagrams.

10. An attempt by government to force prices below or above their equilibrium levels is likely to lead to shortages or surpluses, black markets in which goods are sold at illegal prices, and a variety of other problems. This is one of the twelve Ideas for Beyond the Final Exam.

CONCEPTS FOR REVIEW

Quantity demanded	Supply curve	Shifts in versus movements
Demand schedule	Supply–demand diagram	along supply and demand
Demand curve	Shortage	curves
Quantity supplied	Surplus	Price ceiling
Supply schedule	Equilibrium	Price floor
		Exchange rate

QUESTIONS FOR DISCUSSION

1. How often do you go to the movies? Would you go less often if a ticket cost twice as much? Distinguish between your demand curve for movie tickets and your "quantity demanded" at the current price.

2. What would you expect to be the shape of a demand curve
   a. For a medicine that means life or death for a patient?
   b. For the gasoline sold by Sam's gas station, which is surrounded by many other gas stations?

3. The following are the assumed supply and demand schedules for T-shirts in British Columbia:

Demand Schedule		Supply Schedule	
Price (dollars)	Quantity Demanded (per month)	Price (dollars)	Quantity Supplied (per month)
16	60 000	16	180 000
14	80 000	14	140 000
12	100 000	12	100 000
10	120 000	10	60 000
8	140 000	8	20 000

   a. Plot the supply and demand curves and indicate the equilibrium price and quantity.
   b. What effect will a decrease in the price of cotton (a production input) have on the equilibrium price and quantity of T-shirts, assuming all other determinants remain constant? Explain your answer with the help of a diagram.
   c. What effect will a decrease in the price of sweatshirts (a substitute commodity) have on the equilibrium price and quantity of T-shirts, assuming again that all other determinants are held constant? Use a diagram in your answer.

4. Assume that the supply and demand schedules for soybeans in Glubstania are the following:

Price (dollars)	Quantity Demanded	Quantity Supplied
	(millions of bushels per year)	
3.50	10	75
3.00	25	55
2.50	40	40
2.00	55	20
1.50	70	15

   a. What is the equilibrium price and quantity of soybeans?
   b. In order to protect the incomes of farmers, the government sets a minimum price of $3 per bushel. How many bushels will be sold now?
   c. Consumers protest and, as a result, the government abolishes the $3 per bushel

price floor and imposes instead a $2 maximum price per bushel. How many bushels of soybeans will be sold now?

d. While this price ceiling is in effect, a drought reduces the soybean crop. What effects will this have on the soybean market?

5. Show how the following demand curves are likely to shift in response to the indicated changes:

a. The effect on the demand curve for umbrellas when rainfall decreases.

b. The effect on the demand curve for apple juice when the price of orange juice declines.

c. The effect on the demand curve for coffee when sugar prices fall.

6. Drinking water is costly to supply. Draw a supply–demand diagram showing how much water would be bought if water were supplied by a private industry controlled by supply and demand. In the same diagram, show how much would be consumed if water were supplied by a city government at zero charge. What do you conclude from these results about areas of the country in which water is in short supply?

7. On page 88, it is claimed that either price floors or price ceilings reduce the actual quantity exchanged in a market. Use a diagram, or diagrams, to support this conclusion. Explain the common sense behind it.

8. The same rightward shift of the demand curve may produce a very small or very large increase in quantity, depending on the slope of the supply curve. Explain with diagrams.

9. The two diagrams to the right show supply and demand curves for two substitute commodities: compact discs (CDs) and tapes.

a. On diagram (a), show what happens when technological progress makes it cheaper to produce CDs.

b. On diagram (b), show what happens to the market for tapes.

10. (More difficult.) Consider the market for milk discussed in this chapter (Tables 3-1

through 3-3 and Figures 3-1 through 3-3). Suppose the government decides to fight kidney stones by levying a tax of 30¢ per litre on sales of milk. Follow these steps to analyze the effects of the tax:

a. Construct the new supply curve (to replace Table 3-2) that relates quantity supplied to the price consumers pay. (*Hint:* Before the tax, when consumers paid 70¢, farmers supplied 60 million litres. With a 30¢ tax, when consumers pay 70¢, farmers will receive only 40¢. Table 3-2 tells us they will provide only 30 million litres at this price. This is one point on the new supply curve. The rest of the curve can be constructed in the same way.)

b. Graph the new supply curve constructed in part (a) on the supply–demand diagram depicted in Figure 3-3. What are the new equilibrium price and quantity?

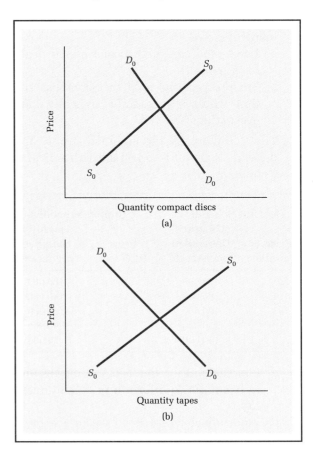
(a)

(b)

   c. Does the tax achieve its goal of reducing the consumption of milk?

   d. How much does the equilibrium price increase? Is the price rise greater than, equal to, or less than the 30¢ tax?

   e. Who actually pays the tax, consumers or producers? (This may be a good question to discuss in class.)

11. Use a supply–demand diagram to examine the legalization of marijuana. Explain how each curve would shift. On the basis of your analysis, what would you predict concerning the price of marijuana and the quantity of it that is used?

12. Often, when the price of a product rises significantly, some consumers suggest boycotting the product. The idea is to reduce producer profits by forcing the price lower through reduced demand.

   a. Who gains from such a boycott?

   b. Would you join such a boycott?

   c. How would your analysis be different if the commodity were fresh fish as opposed to wine?

2

ESSENTIALS OF MICROECONOMICS: CONSUMERS AND FIRMS

It is clear from our initial look at supply and demand in Chapter 3 that if we are to understand how markets function and how they react to changes in the economic environment, we will have to delve more deeply into the nature of both demand and supply. What influences determine the shapes and positions of the demand and supply curves? How do the curves shift in response to various events? The purpose of Part 2 is to answer questions like these and thereby provide the analytical tools we will need to pursue the central theme of this book: the virtues and shortcomings of the market mechanism.

We begin on the demand side of the market and explore the logic underlying the choices made by households. We develop an important analytical approach called marginal analysis. Then we turn our attention to supply, and embark on a detailed examination of profit-maximizing firms.

The four chapters in this part represent an important excursion behind demand and supply curves, an excursion that will allow you to appreciate better the logical underpinnings of these tools. But this material is not just background; it will yield many insights that are directly relevant to everyday issues that must be considered in the political arena. We have selected the four issues outlined in the margin at right to whet your appetite for Part 2.

Many people, misunderstanding the effects of user charges, reject them prematurely as a means of controlling the cost of providing government services. (pages 109–10)

Governments impose the highest tax rates on alcohol and tobacco probably because taxes on these commodities, more than on others, are "passed on" from sellers to buyers. (pages 137–38)

Governments often aid farmers in a way that may seem cheaper than the alternatives, but is really more expensive. (pages 150–51)

Some taxes levied on a firm will not be passed on to consumers, even if the firm has no competitors. (pages 211–15)

CHAPTER 4

CONSUMER CHOICE AND THE INDIVIDUAL'S DEMAND CURVE

Everything is worth what its purchaser will pay for it.

PUBLILIUS SYRUS
(first century B.C.)

This chapter explores the logic behind the individual's demand curve. It is a lengthy chapter, but only the material preceding "More Advanced Topics in the Theory of Consumer Demand" on page 111 is necessary for understanding the material in the remainder of the text. Thus, unless you wish to delve into the logic of what economists call "the theory of consumer behaviour" in more detail, you can move on to Chapter 5 after reaching page 111.

A PUZZLE: SHOULD WATER BE WORTH MORE THAN DIAMONDS?

When Adam Smith was lecturing at Glasgow College in the 1760s, he introduced the study of demand by posing a puzzle. Common sense, he said, suggests that the price of a commodity must somehow depend on what that good is worth to consumers—that is, on the amount of *utility* that commodity offers. Yet, Smith pointed out, there are cases in which a good's utility apparently has little influence on its price.

Two examples he gave were diamonds and water. He noted that water, which is essential to life and therefore undoubtedly of enormous value to most consumers, generally sells at a very low price; diamonds, on the other hand, cost thousands of dollars even though they are by no means a necessity. A century later, this puzzle, called the **diamond–water paradox**, helped stimulate the invention of what is perhaps the most powerful set of tools in the economist's tool kit — *marginal analysis*. Fortunately, we need wait only a few pages, not a century, to learn how marginal analysis — a general method for making optimal decisions — helps to resolve the paradox.

MARGINAL ANALYSIS

The intuition behind **marginal analysis** is very straightforward. Suppose you have $100 of spending money available for the coming month and you are trying to decide how to divide this entire budget between two items: beer and pizza. (We are not suggesting that you *should* limit your purchases to these two items! We have just chosen two commonly consumed items to provide a simple exposition of the basic idea behind marginal analysis.) Both beer and pizza yield satisfaction (or utility) but is seems that for virtually everyone, the additional satisfaction obtained from the tenth piece of pizza is less than that obtained from the first piece. Assuming, then, that the addition to satisfaction falls as you consume either more pizza or more beer, it is not likely to be rational for you to exhaust your budget on just one item or the other.

But how do you decide the optimal combination of beer and pizza? You will maximize the total satisfaction that can be obtained from your $100 if you arrange your purchases so that the additional satisfaction you get from spending the very last dollar is the same whether you spend it on beer or pizza. If this is not the case, you will have made a mistake. For example, if you are getting, say, 10 units of satisfaction per dollar spent on pizza and only 5 units of satisfaction per dollar spent on beer, it means two things. First, you should spend your next dollar on pizza; second, you could have had more satisfaction if you had spent your last dollar on pizza instead of beer. But as you transfer more of your expenditure over to pizza, you will move closer to satiation, and the amount of satisfaction you derive per unit of pizza will begin to fall. Your transfer of funds toward pizza should therefore stop when the additional amount of satisfaction per dollar spent on pizza falls to the point where it is no longer greater than that for beer. Thus, if you made no mistakes (that is, if your judgement was not clouded by the consumption of the beer itself), you could have maximized satisfaction only by arranging your purchases so that, in the end, the additional satisfaction per dollar spent on both (or all) commodities was the same. In the economist's language, this means that sensible buyers will equalize the "marginal utility per dollar spent" on all commodities, in accordance with the *optimal purchase rule.*

There are two ways we can make this discussion of a household's optimal purchase rule more concrete, and each method has advantages and disadvantages. The advantages of the first formal analysis, which assumes that any one good is a very small part of an individual's whole budget (income), are that it affords a simple derivation of the optimal purchase rule and that it can be used to explain *consumer surplus.* This concept will arise frequently in later chapters to explain why various distortions such as monopoly, tariffs, price regulations, and various taxes are "bad" on efficiency grounds. The disadvantages of this "one-good-at-a-time" analysis are that it gives insufficient emphasis to the fact that a consumer's budget is limited, and it may give the mistaken impression that economists have to treat utility as a cardinal concept (and that consumers need to be able to measure units of satisfaction). The second formalization of the optimal purchase rule, which we refer to as *indifference curve analysis* (discussed in the final sections of this chapter), avoids these problems. The disadvantage of this second approach is that it is more advanced. However, this book is written in such a way that these sections can be omitted without threatening your understanding of later chapters.

TOTAL AND MARGINAL UTILITY

As noted above, economists have constructed a simple theory of consumer choice based on the hypothesis that each consumer spends his or her income in the way that yields the greatest amount of satisfaction, or *utility*. This seems to be a reasonable starting point, since it says little more than that people do what they prefer. To describe the theory precisely, we need a way to measure utility.

A century ago, economists thought that utility could be measured directly in some kind of psychological units (sometimes called "utils"), after somehow reading the consumer's mind. But gradually economists realized that this task was unnecessary and perhaps impossible. How many utils did you get from the last movie you saw? You probably cannot answer that question because you have no idea what a util is.

But you may be able to answer a different question, such as, How many hamburgers would you give up to get that movie ticket? If your answer is three, we still do not know how many utils you get from a movie. But we do know that you get more than you get from a hamburger. Hamburgers, rather than utils, become the unit of measurement, and we can say that the utility of a movie (to you) is three hamburgers.

Early in the twentieth century, economists concluded that this more indirect way of measuring utility was all they needed to build a theory of consumer choice. We can measure the utility of a movie ticket by asking how much of some other commodity (like hamburgers) you are willing to give up for it. Any commodity will do for this purpose. But the simplest choice, and the one we will use in this book, is money income.[1]

Thus, we are led to define the **total utility** of some bundle of goods to a consumer as the largest sum of money income he or she will voluntarily give up in exchange for it. For example, suppose Jennifer is considering purchasing six kilograms of bananas. She has determined that she will not buy them if they cost more than $4.44, but she will buy them if they cost $4.44 or less. Thus, the total utility of six kilograms of bananas to her is $4.44—the maximum amount she is willing to spend to have them.

Total utility measures the benefit Jennifer derives from her purchases. It is total utility that really matters. But to understand which decisions most effectively promote total utility, we must consider the related concept of **marginal utility**. This term refers to the additional utility that an individual derives by consuming one more unit of any good.

The **TOTAL UTILITY** of a quantity of goods to a consumer (measured in money terms) is the maximum amount of money income that he or she is willing to give in exchange for it.

The **MARGINAL UTILITY** of a commodity to a consumer (measured in money terms) is the maximum amount of money that he or she is willing to pay for one more unit of it.

---

1. *NOTE TO INSTRUCTORS:* You will recognize that, although we are not using the terms, we are distinguishing between neoclassical *cardinal utility* and *ordinal utility*. Moreover, throughout the book, "marginal utility in money terms" and "money marginal utility" simply mean the marginal rate of substitution between money and the commodity in question.

Table 4-1 helps clarify the distinction between marginal utility and total utility and shows how the two are related. The first two columns show how much *total* utility (measured in money terms) Jennifer derives from various quantities of bananas ranging from zero to eight kilograms. For example, a single kilogram is worth (no more than) $1.20 to her, two kilograms are worth $2.32, and so on. The *marginal* utility is the difference between any two successive total-utility figures. For example, if the consumer already has three kilograms (worth $3.20 to her), an additional kilogram brings her total utility up to $3.92. Her marginal utility is therefore the difference between the two, or 72¢.

Remember, whenever we use the expressions *total utility* and *marginal utility*, we are defining them in terms of the consumer's willingness to part with money for the commodity — not in some unobservable (and imaginary) psychological units.

The "Law" of Diminishing Marginal Utility

With these definitions, we can now state in precise terms the simple hypothesis about consumer tastes that we mentioned above: The more of a good a consumer has, the less will be the marginal utility of an additional unit.

In general, this is a plausible proposition. The idea is based on the assertion that every person has a hierarchy of uses to which he or she will put a particular commodity. All of these uses are valuable, but some are more valuable than others. Let's consider bananas again. Jennifer may use them to give to her family to eat, to feed a pet monkey, to make banana cream pie (which is a bit rich for her tastes), or to give to a brother-in-law for whom she has no deep affection. If she has only one kilogram, the bananas will be used solely for the family to eat. If she has more, the second, third, and fourth kilograms may be used to feed the monkey; and the fifth may go into the banana cream pie. But the only use she has for the sixth kilogram, alas, is to give it to her brother-in-law.

Table 4-1

Total and Marginal Utility of Bananas (Measured in Money Terms)

Number of Kilograms	Total Utility (in dollars)	Marginal Utility (in dollars)	Point in Figure 4-1
0	0		
1	1.20	1.20	A
2	2.32	1.12	B
3	3.20	0.88	C
4	3.92	0.72	D
5	4.28	0.36	E
6	4.44	0.16	F
7	4.52	0.08	G
8	4.52	0	H

The point is obvious: Each kilogram of bananas contributes something to the satisfaction of Jennifer's needs for the product. But each additional kilogram contributes less (relative to money) than did its predecessor because the use to which it can be put has a lower priority. This, in essence, is the logic behind the **"law" of diminishing marginal utility**.

The third column of Table 4-1 illustrates this concept. The marginal utility (MU) of the first kilogram of bananas is $1.20; that is, Jennifer is willing to pay up to $1.20 for the first kilogram. The second kilogram is worth no more than $1.12, the third kilogram only 88¢, and so on until, after the fifth kilogram, the consumer is willing to pay only 16¢ for an additional kilogram (the MU of the sixth kilogram is 16¢).

The numbers in the first and third columns in the table are shown in Figure 4-1 by points A, B, C, and so on. Note that as we move to the right in the graph, the height of the points falls (for example, point B is lower than point A). This again illustrates the law: marginal utility diminishes as the quality of product obtained by the consumer rises.

The assumption upon which this law is based is plausible for most consumers and for most commodities. But, like most laws, there are exceptions. For some people, the more they have of some good that is particularly significant to them, the more they want. Consider the needs of collectors and addicts, for example. The stamp collector who has a few stamps may consider the acquisition of one more to be mildly amusing. The person who has a large and valuable collection may be prepared to go to the ends of the earth for another stamp. Similarly, the alcoholic who finds a dry martini quite pleasant when he first starts drinking may find one more to be absolutely irresistible once he has already consumed

The **"LAW" OF DIMINISH-ING MARGINAL UTILITY** asserts that additional units of a commodity are worth less and less to a consumer in money terms. As the individual's consumption increases, the marginal utility of each additional unit declines.

FIGURE 4-1

A TYPICAL MARGINAL UTILITY OR DEMAND CURVE

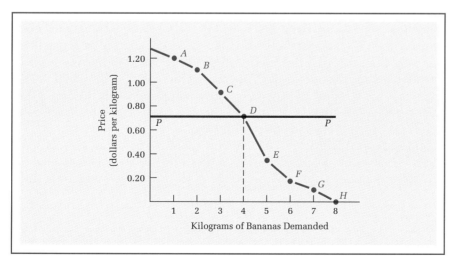

This demand curve is derived from the consumers' table of marginal utilities by following the optimal purchase rule. The points in the graph correspond to the numbers in Table 4-1.

four or five. Economists, however, generally treat such cases of increasing marginal utility as anomalies. For most goods and most people, marginal utility declines as consumption increases.

THE OPTIMAL PURCHASE RULE

Now let us put the concept of marginal utility to work in analyzing consumer choice. Every consumer has a limited amount of money to spend. Which items will he or she buy, and in what quantities? The theory of consumer choice is based on the hypothesis that consumers will spend their money in the way that maximizes their total utility. This hypothesis leads to the following **optimal purchase rule**:

It always pays the consumer to buy more of any commodity whose marginal utility (measured in money) exceeds its price, and less of any commodity whose marginal utility is less than its price. When possible, the consumer should buy the quantity of each good at which price (P) and marginal utility (MU) are exactly equal; that is, at which

$$P = \text{MU}$$

The reason is that only these quantities will maximize the total utility he or she gains from the purchases, given the fact that the money available must be divided up among all the goods bought.[2]

Notice that while our concern is with *total* utility, the rule is framed in terms of *marginal* utility. Marginal utility is not important for its own sake, but rather as an instrument for calculating the level of purchases that maximizes total utility.

To see why this rule works, refer to the table and graph of marginal utilities of bananas (Table 4-1 and Figure 4-1). Suppose the supermarket is selling bananas for 72¢ a kilogram (line *PP* in the graph) and Jennifer considers buying only two kilograms. We see that this is not a wise decision, because the marginal utility of the third kilogram of bananas (88¢) is greater than its 72¢ price. If Jennifer were to increase her purchase to three kilograms, the additional kilogram would cost 72¢ but yield 88¢ in marginal utility (point *C*); thus, the additional purchase would bring her a clear net gain of 16¢. Obviously, at the 72¢ price, she is better off with three kilograms of bananas than with two.

Similarly, at this price, five kilograms (point *E*) is *not* an optimal purchase because the marginal utility of the fifth kilogram is less than its 72¢ price. Jennifer would be better off with only four kilograms, since

---

2. We can equate a dollar price with marginal utility only because we measure marginal utility in money terms (or, as the matter is usually put by economists, because we deal with the marginal rate of substitution of money for the commodity in question). If marginal utility were measured in some psychological units not directly translatable into money terms, a comparison of *P* and MU would have no meaning. However, MU could also be measured in terms of any commodity other than money. (*Example:* How much root beer is Jennifer willing to trade for an additional banana?)

that would save her 72¢ with only a 36¢ loss in utility—a net gain of 36¢ from the decision to buy one kilogram less. In sum, our rule for optimal purchases tells us that Jennifer should not end up buying a quantity at which MU is far higher than price (points *A*, *B*, and *C*) because from any such point, she is better off buying more. Similarly, she should not end up at point *E*, *F*, *G*, or *H*, where MU is below price, because from any such point, she is better off buying less. Rather, Jennifer should buy four kilograms (point *D*), where *P* = MU, since any purchase above this amount yields a marginal utility that is less than price, and any purchase below this amount leaves MU greater than *P*.

It should be noted that price is an objective, observable figure determined by the market, while marginal utility is subjective and reflects the tastes of the consumer. Since consumers lack the power to influence the price, they must adjust their purchases to make the marginal utility of each good equal to the price determined by the market.

FROM MARGINAL UTILITY TO THE DEMAND CURVE

We can use the optimal purchase rule to show that the law of diminishing marginal utility implies that demand curves typically slope downward to the right; that is, they have negative slopes. For example, it is possible to use the list of marginal utilities in Table 4-1 to determine precisely how many bananas Jennifer would buy at any particular price. Table 4-2 gives several alternative prices and the optimal purchase quantity corresponding to each. (To make sure you understand the logic behind the optimal purchase rule, verify that the entries in the right-hand column of Table 4-2 are in fact correct. Note that for simplicity of explanation, the illustrative prices have been chosen to equal the marginal utilities in Table 4-1. In-between prices would make the optimal choices involve fractions of a kilogram.) This demand schedule, which relates quantity demanded to price, may be translated into Jennifer's demand curve shown in Figure 4-1. This demand curve is simply the line connecting

TABLE 4-2
LIST OF OPTIMAL QUANTITY TO PURCHASE AT ALTERNATIVE PRICES

Price (in dollars)	Quantity to Purchase
0.08	7
0.16	6
0.36	5
0.72	4
0.88	3
1.12	2
1.20	1

the marginal utility points, *A*, *B*, *C*, and so on. You can see that it has the characteristic negative slope commonly associated with demand curves.

Let us examine the logic underlying the negatively sloped demand curve a bit more carefully. If Jennifer is purchasing the optimal number of bananas and then the price falls, she will find that her marginal utility of bananas is now above the suddenly reduced price. For example, Table 4-1 tells us that at a price of 88¢ per kilogram, it is optimal to buy three kilograms, because the MU of the fourth kilogram is 72¢. But if price is reduced to anything less than 72¢, it then pays to purchase the fourth kilogram because its MU exceeds its price. This additional kilogram of bananas will lower the marginal utility of the next (fifth) kilogram of bananas to 36¢ in the example, so if the price exceeds 36¢, it will not pay the consumer to buy the fifth kilogram, just as is prescribed in the optimal purchase rule.

Note the critical role of the law of diminishing marginal utility. If *P* falls, a consumer who wishes to maximize total utility will see to it that MU falls. According to the law of diminishing marginal utility, the only way to do this is to increase the quantity purchased.

While this explanation is a bit abstract and mechanical, it can easily be rephrased in practical terms. We have seen that the various uses to which an individual puts a commodity have different priorities. For Jennifer, giving bananas to her family has a higher priority than using them to make pie, which in turn is of higher priority than giving them to her brother-in-law. If the price of bananas is high, Jennifer will buy only enough for the high-priority uses—those that offer a high marginal utility. When price declines, however, it pays to purchase more of the good—enough for some lower-priority uses. This is the essence of the analysis. It tells us that the same assumption about consumer psychology underlies both the law of diminishing marginal utility and the negative slope of the demand curve. They are really two different ways of describing the same response of consumers.

THE DIAMOND–WATER PARADOX: THE PUZZLE RESOLVED

We can use marginal utility analysis to solve Adam Smith's diamond–water paradox — his observation that the price of diamonds is much higher than the price of water even though water seems to offer far more utility. The resolution of the diamond–water paradox is based on the distinction between marginal and total utility.

The *total* utility of water — its life-giving benefit — is indeed much higher than that of diamonds, just as Smith observed. But price, as we have seen, is not related directly to total utility. Rather, the optimal purchase rule tells us that price will tend to be equal to *marginal* utility. Further, there is every reason to expect the marginal utility of water to be very low while the marginal utility of diamonds is very high. Water is extremely plentiful in many parts of the world, so its price is generally quite low. Consumers use correspondingly large quantities of water. By the principle of diminishing marginal utility, therefore, the marginal utility of water to a typical household will be pushed down to a very low level.

On the other hand, diamonds are very scarce. As a result, the quantity of diamonds consumed is not large enough to drive the MU of diamonds down very far, so buyers are willing to pay high prices for them. The scarcer the commodity, the higher its marginal utility and its market price, regardless of the size of its total utility.

Thus, like many paradoxes, the diamond–water puzzle has a straightforward explanation. In this case, all one has to remember is the following:

Scarcity raises price and marginal utility but not necessarily total utility.

CONSUMER SURPLUS

Economists often want to calculate how much consumers are hurt by having to pay high prices for the commodities that they purchase. For example, because we sometimes levy taxes on imported goods and because these tariff costs are included in the price that individuals pay for the goods, consumers are not receiving the benefits of the lower prices that would exist without trade restrictions. How can we estimate the magnitude of these consumer losses?

We can use marginal utility analysis to explain how economists answer this question. Let's return briefly to the numerical example given in Table 4-1. At the price of 72¢ per kilogram, Jennifer decides to buy four kilograms of bananas for a total payment of 4 × 72¢ = $2.88. But how much is Jennifer actually willing to pay for these four kilograms? The answer is equal to the total utility she derives from the four kilograms of bananas, which is $3.92. Her total willingness to pay exceeds what she has to pay since the value to her of the first few kilograms exceeds the addition to her utility provided by that last (or marginal) unit she purchases. This surplus exists because of the law of diminishing marginal utility. Economists note that all consumers receive a surplus of utility when the market allows them to buy more than one unit of any commodity at a constant price that equals their marginal utility. Economists call this **consumer surplus**. In our example, Jennifer's consumer surplus is the difference between the total utility she receives from the four kilograms of bananas ($3.92) and the total amount she must pay for the four kilograms ($2.88), or $1.04. These amounts are readily recognizable in Figure 4-2. The total utility received from consuming four kilograms of bananas is approximated by the area under the marginal utility curve up to quantity level 4. This is because the sum of the marginal utilities for all four kilograms gives the total utility received. This area is shaded in Figure 4-2, partly gold and partly blue. But Jennifer has to pay only four times the going market price (4 × 72¢ = $2.88). This total expenditure is equal to

CONSUMER SURPLUS is the amount by which an individual's total willingness to pay for an item exceeds what he or she has to pay to buy it.

FIGURE 4-2

CONSUMER SURPLUS

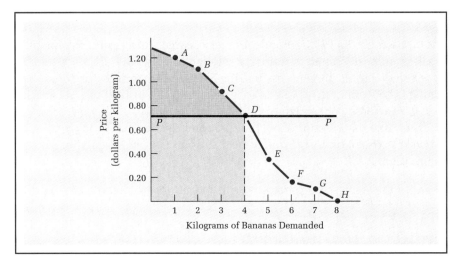

Given this demand curve, which is the same as that shown in Figure 4-1, the total utility from buying four kilograms of bananas is equivalent to the whole shaded area. But the total expenditure is only the portion of the shaded area below the price line, *PP*. The upper, triangular portion is the surplus utility gained by the consumer.

the gold part of the shaded region in Figure 4-2—that is, the part below line *PP*, the line that defines the going market price. Consumer surplus is the leftover (blue) part of the shaded region—that is, the triangle below the marginal utility curve but above the market price line, *PP*.

We can now see how economists use the concept of consumer surplus. Suppose new trade restrictions raise the price of bananas from 72¢ per kilogram to $1.50 per kilogram. How much is Jennifer, our representative consumer, hurt by this development? The price has risen so much that Jennifer decides not to purchase any bananas. The total utility she could have derived from banana consumption falls by $3.92. But that amount overstates her loss, because she now has the $2.88 (which she previously spent on bananas) available to spend on other commodities. Thus, her net losses are equal to the consumer surplus that she previously enjoyed ($1.04). In later chapters, we will use this insight to discuss the burden imposed by several specific taxes and tariffs, as well as by monopoly. As long as economists can obtain a statistical estimate of the demand curve for any commodity, the consumer surplus can be measured easily.

Economists are not the only ones who recognize and use the concept of consumer surplus. Many firms use pricing policies that offer lower prices only to customers who buy relatively large quantities in each market period. (One method is to sell large and small boxes of an item, with the per-kilogram price lower for the large boxes than for the small boxes. Another method is the quantity discount: one pair of socks for $6, six pairs for $25.) The point of this policy is to charge a high price per kilogram to those buyers who buy only a small quantity (and who therefore

A P P L I C A T I O N

THE COSTS AND BENEFITS OF USER CHARGES

For many years, Canadians have prided themselves on the fact that many of our public services have been provided on a "universal" basis—that is, these services have been available free of charge (on a per-use basis) for everyone, whatever their income. Let's examine this policy, and take as our example garbage disposal services.

All of us generate a lot of garbage. For some of this material, the benefit we get from being able to remove it from our homes and our children is very high; for other items that we throw away, the additional benefits we receive from its disposal through the municipal garbage system are trivial. The diagram shows the marginal utility curve for garbage disposal services that is consistent with these facts. Because *some* garbage disposal is essential to life, the left-hand end of the marginal utility curve never actually touches the vertical axis. This means that the area under the

marginal utility curve for garbage disposal is infinite. Because services such as this one are of such great importance to an individual, many take the view that it should be provided free (that is, at a zero user charge at the individual level).

But the notion that garbage disposal should be free because it is so important to people confuses total utility with marginal utility. Beyond a certain amount—say, distance OA — further garbage disposal through the municipal collection system is of very little use to an individual. The cost of other options such as composting and reusing containers is very low. But if the cost we are charged per item is even lower, individuals will expand their use of garbage disposal services until the marginal utility is essentially zero. Hence, if a very small user charge were imposed for garbage disposal—say, equal to distance OP — we could save a tremendous quantity of resources without reducing individuals' utility very much at all.

With the user charge, individuals will choose quantity OA, so their loss of utility is equal to the gold, triangular-shaped area, ABC. This is a trivial proportion of the overall area under the marginal utility curve (which approaches infinity). Thus, the charge brings a dramatic saving in resources (distance OA is much shorter than OB) for a very small proportionate loss in total utility. Given that governments are desperately looking for ways to save resources in areas that involve goods or services provided through the public sector, they should find even rather small user charges tempting. However, some people cannot afford even a small user fee, and many policy-makers want to avoid having one rule

(continued)

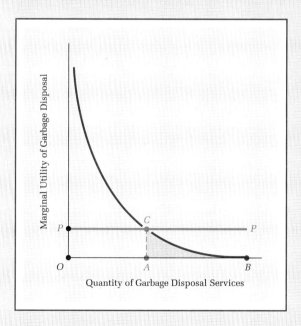

Quantity of Garbage Disposal Services

(continued)

for the poor (a zero user fee) and another for everyone else. Hence, user fees are often rejected on equity grounds, even though this decision involves a large cost on efficiency grounds, as this analysis has shown. In Chapter 15, we discuss a comprehensive approach to addressing the poverty issue. If this approach were followed, the reason why many people are lukewarm to the idea of user charges could be eliminated.

Even without this, user charges are starting to become more popular. For example, in 1993, the Ontario government announced plans for an experimental use of tolls on new highway 407, north of Toronto. An automated vehicle identification system, involving a card attached to each car's windshield, would be used to bill motorists for their use of the road. Also, the city of Toronto started a plan in 1990 to convert all homes to a meter system for water use. Since most homes are still on the old system (of paying a flat rate no matter how much water is consumed), it is not surprising that Torontonians use about twice as much water as do the citizens in European cities that have had meters (that is, user charges) for some time.

Also in 1993, Canadians were debating the value of user charges for medical care. In this field, the evidence shows that user fees are of limited value, since the consumer (patient) is so dependent on the seller (doctor) for knowledge concerning whether he or she wants or needs more service. Doctors can just shift the demand curve for their own services to the right to eliminate any decrease in quantity demanded that would otherwise follow from a higher user fee. A modified form of a user fee that is more appropriate for the medical field is discussed in a boxed insert in Chapter 30 (on pages 979–80).

have a high marginal utility) and to offer the lower price only to those who buy a large quantity. This strategy allows the firm to acquire some of what would otherwise be consumer surplus (if all individuals were permitted to buy the item at the lower price).

The Dutch auction is the classic example of a pricing policy designed to extract consumer surplus from buyers. At the beginning of such an auction, an item is offered for sale at a very high price. The auctioneer keeps lowering the price until someone bids, and the good is then sold at that price to that bidder. To guard against the chance that some other individual may get the item, each individual is tempted to make a bid equal to his or her full willingness to pay. This is not so true of the kind of auctions common in Canada, which start with a low price and allow an indefinite number of bids, a system that gives many chances to each individual.

The concept of consumer surplus allows us to be quite explicit about one of our twelve Ideas for Beyond the Final Exam. It used to be thought that neither party to a fair exchange could make a net gain, because each must pay the other just what the good is worth. But this view made no sense. If neither party could make any net gain from a trade, why would either take the time and trouble to carry out the transaction? Economists recognized several centuries ago that where an exchange is entirely voluntary and there is no cheating or misrepresentation, there must be a net gain for *both* parties—there must be mutual gains from trade.

The same must be true when a consumer makes a purchase from a supermarket or an appliance store: The consumer must expect a net gain from the transaction, or else he or she will simply not bother to buy. Even if the seller "overcharges" (by whatever standard that is judged), the size of the consumer's net gain may be reduced but it will not be eliminated altogether. If the seller is so greedy as to charge a price that does wipe out the net gain altogether, the punishment will fit the crime: The consumer will refuse to buy, and the greedy seller's would-be gain will never materialize.

As we have already noted, the net gain that the consumer obtains from a purchase is called consumer surplus. Numerous current policy issues can be better understood by appreciating this concept, as the boxed insert on pages 109–10 illustrates.

MORE ADVANCED TOPICS IN THE THEORY OF CONSUMER DEMAND

PRICES, INCOME, AND QUANTITY DEMANDED

Our study of marginal analysis has enabled us to examine the relationship between the price of a commodity and the quantity that will be purchased. But the quantity of a good demanded by a consumer also depends on the consumer's income. Let us first consider briefly how a change in income affects quantity purchased. Then we will use this information to learn more about the effects of a price change.

THE DEMAND CONSEQUENCES OF A CHANGE IN INCOME

A consumer's purchase of commodity X depends on both his income and the price of X. Let us consider what happens to the amount of X that a consumer will buy when his real income rises. It may seem almost certain that he will buy more X than before, but that is not necessarily so. A rise in real income can either increase or decrease the quantity of X purchased.

Why might it do the latter? People buy some goods and services only because they cannot afford any better. They eat bologna three days a week and filet mignon twice a year, but they would rather have it the other way around, or they purchase most of their clothing second-hand. If their real income rises, they may then buy more filet mignon and less bologna, more new shirts and fewer second-hand shirts. Thus, a rise in real income will reduce the quantities of bologna and second-hand shirts demanded. Economists have given the rather descriptive name **inferior goods** to the class of commodities for which quantity demanded falls when income rises.

The upshot of this discussion is that we cannot draw definite conclusions about the effects of a rise in consumer incomes on quantity

An **INFERIOR GOOD** is a commodity whose quantity demanded falls when the purchaser's real income rises, all other things remaining equal.

demanded. For most commodities, if incomes rise and prices do not change, there will be an increase in quantity demanded. (Such items are often called *normal goods*.) But for the inferior goods, there will be a decrease in quantity demanded.

THE TWO EFFECTS OF A CHANGE IN PRICE

A fall in the price of some good — say, heating oil — has two consequences. First, it makes fuel oil cheaper relative to electricity, gas, or coal. We say, then, that the *relative price* of fuel oil has fallen. Second, this price decrease leaves home-owners with more money to spend on movie admissions, soft drinks, or clothing. In other words, the decrease in the price of fuel oil increases the consumer's real income—his or her power to purchase other goods.

While a fall in the price of a commodity always produces these two effects simultaneously, our analysis will be easier if we study them separately.

The **INCOME EFFECT** is a portion of the change in quantity of a good demanded when its price changes. A rise in price cuts the consumer's purchasing power (real income), which leads to a change in the quantity demanded of that commodity. That change is the income effect.

1. ***The income effect of a change in price.*** As we have just noted, a fall in the price of a commodity leads to a rise in the consumer's *real income*—the amount that his or her wages will purchase. The consequent effect on quantity demanded is called the **income effect** of the price fall.

   The income effect caused by a fall in a commodity's price is similar to the effect that would have resulted if the consumer's wages had risen: The consumer will buy more of any commodity that is not an inferior good. The process producing the income effect has three stages: (1) the price of the good falls, causing (2) an increase in the consumer's real income, which leads to (3) a change in quantity demanded. Of course, if the price of a good rises, it will produce the same effect in reverse. The consumer's real income will decline, leading to the opposite change in quantity demanded.

The **SUBSTITUTION EFFECT** is the change in quantity demanded of a good resulting from a change in its relative price, exclusive of whatever change in quantity demanded may be attributable to the associated change in real income.

2. ***The substitution effect of a change in price.*** A change in the price of a commodity produces another effect on quantity demanded that is rather different from the income effect. This is the **substitution effect**, which is the effect on quantity demanded attributable to the fact that the new price is now higher or lower than before, relative to the prices of *other goods*. The substitution effect of a price change is the portion of the change in quantity demanded that can be attributed exclusively to the resulting change in relative prices rather than to the associated change in real income.

   There is nothing mysterious or surprising about the effect of a change in relative prices when a consumer's real income remains unchanged. Whenever it is possible for the consumer to switch between two commodities, he or she can be expected to buy more of the good whose relative price has fallen and less of the good whose relative price has risen. For example, some years ago, the telephone company instituted sharp reductions in the prices of evening long-distance telephone calls relative to daytime calls. The big decrease in the relative price of evening calls brought about a large increase in calling during the evening hours and a decrease in daytime calling, just as the telephone company had hoped. Similarly, a fall in the relative price of fuel oil will induce more of the people who are building new homes to install oil heat instead of electric heat.

When the price of a commodity, X, rises relative to the price of some other commodity, Y, a consumer whose real income has remained unchanged can be expected to buy less X and more Y than before. Thus, if we consider the substitution effect alone, a decline in price always increases quantity demanded, and a rise in price always reduces quantity demanded.

These two concepts, the income effect and the substitution effect, which many beginning economics students think were invented to torture them, are really quite useful. Let us consider an example of how economists use them. Suppose the price of hamburgers declines while the price of cheese remains unchanged. The substitution effect clearly induces the consumer to buy more hamburgers in place of grilled cheese sandwiches, because hamburgers are now comparatively cheaper. What of the income effect? Unless hamburger is an inferior good, the income effect leads to the same decision. The fall in price makes consumers richer, which induces them to increase their purchases of all but inferior goods. This example alerts us to two general points:

If a good is not inferior, it must have a downward-sloping demand curve, since income and substitution effects reinforce each other. However, an inferior good may violate this pattern of demand behaviour because the income effect of a decline in price leads consumers to buy less.

Do *all* inferior goods, then, have upward-sloping demand curves? Certainly not, for we have the substitution effect to reckon with, and the substitution effect always favours a downward-sloping demand curve. Thus, we have a kind of tug-of-war in the case of an inferior good. If the income effect predominates, the demand curve slopes upward; if the substitution effect prevails, the demand curve slopes downward.

Economists have concluded that the substitution effect generally wins out; so, while there are many examples of inferior goods, there are few examples of upward-sloping demand curves. When might the income effect prevail over the substitution effect? Certainly not when the good in question is a very small fraction of the consumer's budget, for then a fall in price makes the consumer only slightly "richer" and therefore creates a very small income effect. But the demand curve could slope upward if an inferior good constitutes a substantial portion of the consumer's budget.

We conclude this discussion of income and substitution effects with a warning against an error that is frequently made. Many students mistak-

FURTHER DETAIL

THE THEORY OF CONSUMER CHOICE AND WHITE RATS

"Boy have I got this guy conditioned! Every time I press the bar down he drops in a piece of food."

Some years ago, a team of economists and psychologists studied whether the theory of consumer choice that we have just outlined — including the different income and substitution effects of a price change —applies to animal species other than *Homo sapiens*. According to their research, it does.*

In one experiment, standard laboratory rats were placed in experimental chambers equipped with two levers; pressing one lever rewarded them with a prescribed amount of commodity A (say, water) while pressing the other rewarded them with a prescribed amount of commodity B (say, food). The rats were given a limited "budget," in that they could press the levers only a fixed number of times per day. Once they had exhausted their "income" by pressing the levers, say, 250 times, the lights above the levers would go out, signalling the rats that their presses would no longer result in rewards. Apparently, the little creatures learned the meaning of the lights quite quickly.

In this controlled environment, income effects could be observed by varying the permitted number of lever presses per day. The results showed clearly that when more lever presses were allowed, rats chose to consume more of both goods. Apparently, none of the goods, such as food, water, root beer, and Tom Collins mix, was an inferior good from the rats' point of view.

Measuring substitution effects was a bit trickier since, as we have stressed, a price change sets in motion both an income effect and a substitution effect. In the experiment, the "price" of each commodity was controlled by varying the amount of food or liquid produced by each lever press. Substitution effects were measured, for example, by raising the "price" of food (that is, reducing the amount of food yielded by each press), while at the same time allowing the rat enough additional lever presses to compensate him for his loss of purchasing power. As the analysis of this chapter has suggested, the rats responded to this change in their environment by "buying" less food.

Putting the two effects together, then, a higher price of food led to less consumption of food via the income effect and also to less consumption of food via the substitution effect. The demand curves of these rats were indeed negatively sloped.

---

*John H. Kagel, Raymond C. Battalio, Howard Rachlin, and Leonard Green, "Demand Curves for Animal Consumers," *Quarterly Journal of Economics*, vol. 96, February 1981, pages 1–16.

enly close their books thinking that price changes cause substitution effects while income changes cause income effects. This is incorrect. The foregoing example of hamburgers made the following point clear:

Any change in price sets in motion both a substitution effect and an income effect, both of which affect quantity demanded.

INDIFFERENCE CURVE ANALYSIS

Our analysis of consumer demand, while correct as far as it goes, has one shortcoming: By treating the consumer's decision about the purchase of each commodity as an isolated event, it conceals the necessity of choice imposed on the consumer by his or her limited budget. It does not indicate explicitly the hard choice behind every purchase decision—the sacrifice of some goods to obtain others. The idea, of course, is implicit because the purchase of a commodity involves a trade-off between that good and money. If you spend more money on rent, you have less to spend on entertainment. If you buy more clothing, you have less money for food. But to represent the consumer's choice problem explicitly, economists have invented two geometric devices, the *budget line* and the *indifference curve*, which we now describe.

GEOMETRY OF THE AVAILABLE CHOICES: THE BUDGET LINE

Suppose, for simplicity, that there were only two commodities produced in the world, cheese and audio tapes. The decision problem of any household then would be to determine the allocation of its income between these two goods. Clearly, the more it spends on one, the less it can have of the other. But just what is the trade-off? A numerical example will answer this question and also introduce the graphical device that economists use to portray the trade-off.

Suppose that cheese costs $2 per kilogram, tapes sell at $3 each, and our consumer has $12 at her disposal. She obviously has a variety of choices—as displayed in Table 4-3. For example, if she buys no tapes, she can go home with six kilograms of cheese, and so on. Each of the

TABLE 4-3
ALTERNATIVE PURCHASE COMBINATIONS FOR A $12 BUDGET

Number of Tapes (at $3 each)	Expenditure on Tapes (in dollars)	Remaining Funds (in dollars)	Kilograms of Cheese (at $2 per kg)	Label in Figure 4-3
0	0	12	6.0	A
1	3	9	4.5	B
2	6	6	3.0	C
3	9	3	1.5	D
4	12	0	0.0	E

FIGURE 4-3

A BUDGET LINE

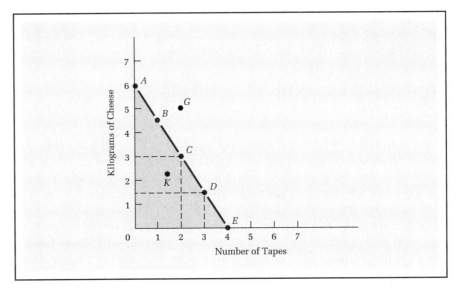

This budget line shows the different combinations of cheese and tapes the consumer can buy with $12 if cheese costs $2 per kilogram and tapes cost $3 each. At point *A*, the consumer buys six kilograms of cheese and has nothing left over for tapes. At point *E*, she spends the entire budget on tapes. At intermediate points (such as *C*) on the budget line, the consumer buys some of both goods (two tapes and three kilograms of cheese).

combinations of cheese and tapes that the consumer can afford can be shown in a diagram in which the axes measure the quantities of each commodity that are purchased. In Figure 4-3, kilograms of cheese are measured along the vertical axis, number of tapes is measured along the horizontal axis, and each of the combinations enumerated in Table 4-3 is represented by a labelled point. For example, point *A* corresponds to spending everything on cheese, point *E* corresponds to spending everything on tapes, and point *C* corresponds to buying two tapes and three kilograms of cheese.

If we connect points *A* through *E* by a straight line, the red line in the diagram, we can trace all the possible ways to divide the $12 between the two goods. For example, point *D* tells us that if the consumer buys three tapes, there will be only enough money left to purchase one and a half kilograms of cheese. We can readily see that this is correct by referring to Table 4-3. Line *AE* is therefore called the **budget line**.

The **BUDGET LINE** for a household represents graphically all the possible combinations of two commodities that it can purchase, given the prices of the commodities and some fixed amount of money at its disposal.

PROPERTIES OF THE BUDGET LINE

Let us now use t to represent the number of tapes purchased by our consumer and c to indicate the amount of cheese she acquires. Thus, at $2 per kilogram, she spends on cheese a total of 2 × (number of kilograms of cheese bought) = $2c$ dollars. Similarly, she spends $3t$ dollars on tapes, making a total of $2c + 3t = 12$, if the entire $12 is spent on the two commodities. This is the equation of the budget line. It is also the equation of the straight line drawn in the diagram.[3]

We note also that the budget line represents the *maximal* amounts of the commodities that the consumer can afford. Thus, for any given purchase of tapes, it tells us the greatest amount of cheese her money can buy. If our consumer wants to be thrifty, she can choose to end up at a point below the budget line, such as *K*. Clearly, then, the choices she has available include not only those points on budget line *AE*, but also any point in the shaded triangle formed by budget line *AE* and the two axes. By contrast, points above the budget line, such as *G*, are not available to the consumer, given her limited budget. A package consisting of five kilograms of cheese and two tapes would cost $16, which is more than she has to spend.

The position of the budget line is determined by two types of data: the prices of the commodities purchased and the income at the buyer's disposal. We can complete our discussion of the graphics of the budget line by examining briefly how a change in either of these magnitudes affects its location.

Obviously, any increase in the income of the household increases the range of options available to it. Specifically, increases in income produce parallel shifts in the budget line, as shown in Figure 4-4(a). The reason is simply that an increase of, say, 50 percent in available income, if entirely spent on the two goods in question, would permit the family to purchase exactly 50 percent more of either commodity. Point *A* in Figure 4-3 would shift upward by 50 percent of its distance from the origin, while point *E* would move to the right by 50 percent.[4] Figure 4-4(a) shows three such budget lines corresponding to incomes of $9, $12, and $18, respectively.

Finally, we can ask what happens to the budget line when there is a change in the price of some commodity. In Figure 4-4(b), we see that when the price of tapes decreases, the budget line moves outward, but the move is no longer parallel because the point on the cheese axis remains fixed. Once again, the reason is fairly straightforward. A 50 percent reduction in the price of tapes permits the family's $12 to buy twice as many tapes as before; point *E* is moved rightward to point *H*, at which eight tapes are shown as obtainable. However, since the price of cheese

---

3. The reader may have noticed one problem that arises in this formulation. If every point on budget line *AE* is a possible way for the consumer to spend her money, there must be some manner in which she can buy fractional tapes. Perhaps the purchase of one and a half tapes can be interpreted to include a down payment of $1.50 on a tape on her next shopping trip! Throughout this book, it is convenient to assume that commodities are available in fractional quantities when drawing diagrams. This makes the graphs clearer and does not really affect the analysis.

4. An algebraic proof is simple. Let *M* (which is initially $12) be the amount of money available to our household. The equation of the budget line can be solved for *c*, obtaining

$$c + -(3/2)t = M/2$$

This is the equation of a straight line with a slope of -3/2 and with a vertical intercept of *M*/2. A change in *M*, the quantity of money available, will not change the *slope* of the budget line; it will lead only to parallel shifts in that line.

FIGURE 4-4

THE EFFECT OF INCOME AND PRICE CHANGES ON THE BUDGET LINE

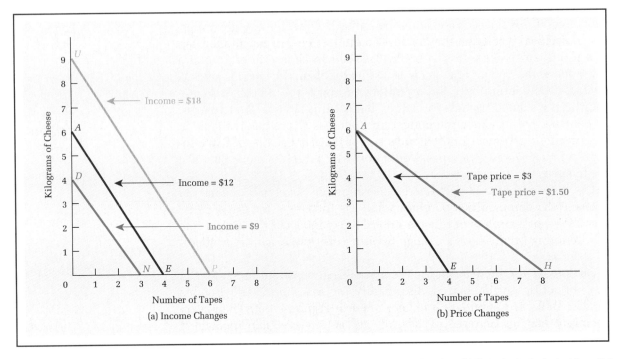

A change in the amount of money in the consumer's budget causes a parallel shift in the budget line (panel (a)). A rise in the budget from $12 to $18 raises the budget line from *AE* to *UP*. A fall from $12 to $9 lowers the budget line from *AE* to *DN*. On the other hand, a fall in the price of tapes causes the end of the budget line on the tapes axis to swing away from the origin (part (b)). A fall in tape price from $3 to $1.50 swings the price line from *AE* to *AH*. This happens because at the higher price, $12 buys only four tapes, but at the lower price, it buys eight tapes.

has not changed, point *A*, the amount of cheese that can be bought for $12, is unaffected. Thus, we have the general result that a reduction in the price of one of the two commodities swings the budget line outward along the axis representing the quantity of that item, while leaving the location of the other end of the line unchanged.

WHAT THE CONSUMER PREFERS: THE INDIFFERENCE CURVE

The budget line tells us what choices are *available* to the consumer, given the size of her income and the commodity prices fixed by the market. We next must examine the consumer's *preferences* in order to determine which of these possibilities she will want to choose.

After much investigation, economists have determined what they believe to be the minimum amount of information they need about a purchaser in order to analyze his or her choices. This information consists of the consumer's ranking of the alternative packages of commodities that are available. Suppose, for instance, that the consumer is offered a choice between two packages of goods—package *W*, which contains three tapes and one kilogram of cheese, and package *T*, which contains two tapes and three kilograms of cheese. The economist wants to know only whether the consumer prefers W to T, T to W, or whether she is indifferent about which one she gets. Note that the analysis requires no information about *degree* of preference — whether the consumer is wildly more enthusiastic about one of the packages or just prefers it slightly.

Graphically, the preference information is provided by a group of curves called **indifference curves** (Figure 4-5)—lines connecting all combinations of the commodities in question that are equally desirable to the consumer. But before we examine these curves, let us see how such a curve is interpreted. A single point on an indifference curve tells us nothing about preferences. For example, point R on curve I_a simply represents the bundle of goods composed of four tapes and one-half kilogram of cheese. It does *not* suggest that the consumer is indifferent between one-half kilogram of cheese and four tapes. For the curve to tell us anything, we must consider at least two of its points, for example, points S and W. Since they represent two different combinations that are on the same indifference curve, they are equally desirable to our consumer.

An **INDIFFERENCE CURVE** is a line connecting all combinations of the commodities in question that are equally desirable to the consumer.

PROPERTIES OF INDIFFERENCE CURVES

We do not know yet which package our consumer prefers among all the packages she can afford; we know only that a choice between certain packages will lead to indifference. So, before we can use an indifference

FIGURE 4-5

THREE INDIFFERENCE CURVES FOR CHEESE AND TAPES

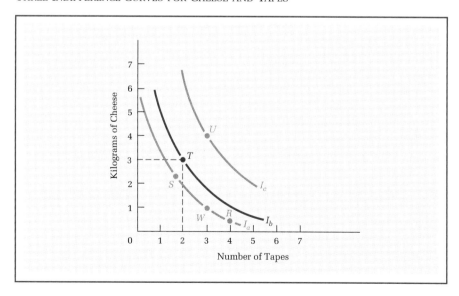

Any point in the diagram represents a combination of cheese and tapes (for example, T represents two tapes and three kilograms of cheese). Any two points on the same indifference curve (for example, S and W) represent two combinations of the goods that the consumer likes equally well. If two points, such as T and W, lie on different indifference curves, the one on the higher indifference curve is preferred by the consumer.

curve to analyze the consumer's choice, we must examine a few of its properties. Most important for us is the following:

As long as the consumer desires more of each of the goods in question, *every* point on a higher indifference curve (that is, a curve farther from the origin in the graph) will be preferred to *any* point on a lower indifference curve.

In other words, among indifference curves, higher is better. The reason is obvious. Given two indifference curves—say, I_b and I_c in Figure 4-5— the higher curve will contain points lying above and to the right of some points on the lower curve. Thus, point U on curve I_c lies above and to the right of point T on curve I_b. This means that at U the consumer gets more tapes *and* more cheese than at T. Assuming that she desires both commodities, our consumer must prefer U to T. Since every point on curve I_c is, by definition, equal in preference to point U, and the same relation holds for point T and all other points along curve I_b, every point on curve I_c will be preferred to any point on curve I_b.

This at once implies a second property of indifference curves: They never intersect. This is so because if an indifference curve, I_b, is anywhere above another, I_a, then I_b must be above I_a everywhere, since every point on I_b will be preferred to every point on I_a.

Another property that characterizes the indifference curve is its negative slope. Again, this holds only if the consumer wants more of both commodities. Consider two points, such as S and R, on the same indifference curve. If the consumer is indifferent between them, one cannot contain more of both commodities than the other. Since point S contains more cheese than does point R, R must offer more tapes than S does, or the consumer would not be indifferent about which she gets. This means that if, say, we move toward the one with the larger number of tapes, the quantity of cheese must decrease. The curve will always slope downhill toward the right, a negative slope.

A final property of indifference curves is the nature of their curvature —the way they round toward the axes. As drawn, they are "bowed in" —they flatten out (their slopes decrease in absolute value) as they extend from left to right. To understand why this is so, we must first examine the economic interpretation of the slope of an indifference curve.

THE SLOPES OF AN INDIFFERENCE CURVE AND A BUDGET LINE

In Figure 4-6, the average slope of the indifference curve between points M and N is represented by RM/RN. RM is the quantity of cheese the consumer gives up in moving from M to N. Similarly, RN is the increased number of tapes acquired in this move. Since the consumer is indifferent between packages M and N, the gain of RN tapes must just suffice to compensate her for the loss of RM kilograms of cheese. Thus, the ratio RM/RN represents the terms on which the consumer is just willing— according to her own preferences—to trade one good for the other. If RM/RN equals 2, the consumer is willing to give up (no more than) two kilo-

FIGURE 4-6

SLOPES OF A BUDGET LINE AND AN INDIFFERENCE CURVE

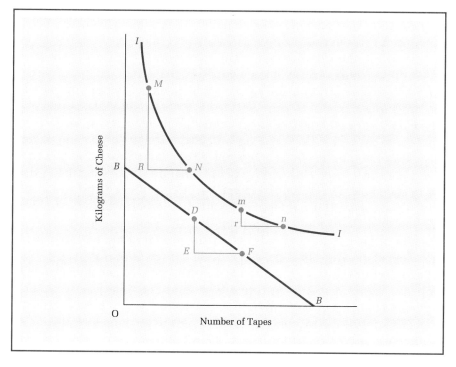

The slope of the budget line shows how many kilograms of cheese, *ED*, can be exchanged for *EF* tapes. The slope of the indifference curve shows how many kilograms of cheese, *RM*, the consumer is just willing to exchange for *RN* tapes. When the consumer has more tapes and less cheese (point *m* as compared with *M*), the slope of the indifference curve decreases, meaning that the consumer is willing to give up only *rm* kilograms of cheese for *rn* tapes.

grams of cheese for one additional tape. The slope of an indifference curve, then, referred to as the **marginal rate of substitution** between the commodities involved, represents the maximum amount of one commodity the consumer is willing to give up in exchange for one more unit of another commodity.

The slope of budget line *BB* in Figure 4-6 is also a rate of exchange between cheese and tapes. But it no longer reflects the consumer's subjective willingness to trade. Rather, the slope represents the rate of exchange the *market* offers to the consumer when she gives up cheese in exchange for tapes. Recall that the budget line represents all commodity combinations that a consumer can get by spending a fixed amount of money. The budget line is thus a constant expenditure. At current prices, if the consumer reduces her purchase of cheese by amount *DE* in Figure 4-6, she will save just enough money to buy an additional amount, *EF*, of tapes, since at points *D* and *F*, she is spending the same total number of dollars. The slope of a budget line, then, is the amount of one commodity that the market requires an individual to give up in order to

The **MARGINAL RATE OF SUBSTITUTION** between two commodities is the maximum amount of one commodity that the consumer is willing to give up in exchange for one more unit of the other commodity. Geometrically, it is represented by the slope of an indifference curve.

obtain one additional unit of another commodity without any change in the amount of money spent.

As you can see, the slopes of the two types of curves are perfectly analogous in their meaning. The slope of the indifference curve tells us the terms on which the *consumer* is willing to trade one commodity for another, while the slope of the budget line reports the *market* terms on which the consumer can trade one good for another.

It is useful to carry our interpretation of the slope of the budget line one step further. Common sense tells us that the market's rate of exchange between cheese and tapes would be related to their prices, p_c and p_t, and it is easy to show that this is so. Specifically, the slope of the budget line is equal to the ratio of the prices of the two commodities. The reason is straightforward. If the consumer gives up one tape, she has p_t more dollars to spend on cheese. But the lower the price of cheese, the greater the quantity of cheese this money will enable her to buy. Purchasing power will be inversely related to its price. Since the price of cheese is p_c per kilogram, these additional funds, p_t dollars, permit her to buy p_t/p_c more kilograms of cheese. Thus, the slope of the budget line is p_t/p_c.

Before returning to our main subject, the study of consumer choice, we pause briefly and use our interpretation of the slope of the indifference curve to discuss the third of the properties of the indifference curve —its characteristic curvature—which we left unexplained earlier. With indifference curves being the shape shown, the slope decreases as we move from left to right. We can see in Figure 4-6 that at point m, toward the right of the diagram, the consumer is willing to give up far less cheese for one more tape (quantity rm) than she is willing to trade at point M, toward the left. This is because at M, she initially has a large quantity of cheese and few tapes, while at m her initial stock of cheese is low and she has many tapes. In general terms, the curvature premise on which indifference curves are usually drawn asserts that consumers are relatively eager to trade away a commodity of which they have a large amount but are more reluctant to trade goods of which they hold small quantities. This psychological premise is what is implied in the curvature of the indifference curve.

THE CONSUMER'S CHOICE

We can now use our indifference curve apparatus to analyze how the consumer chooses among the combinations she can afford to buy; that is, the combinations of tapes and cheese shown by the budget line. Figure 4-7 brings together in the same diagram the budget line from Figure 4-3 and the indifference curves from Figure 4-5.

Since, according to the first of the properties of indifference curves, the consumer prefers higher to lower curves, she will go to the point on the budget line that lies on the highest indifference curve attainable. This will be point T on indifference curve I_b. She can afford no other point that she likes as well. For example, neither point K below the budget line

FIGURE 4-7

OPTIMAL CONSUMER CHOICE

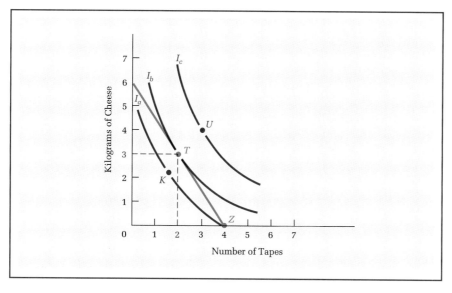

Point T is the combination of tapes and cheese that gives the consumer the greatest benefit for her money. I_b is the highest indifference curve that can be reached from the budget line. T is the point of tangency between the budget line and I_b.

nor point Z on the budget line gets her on as high an indifference curve, and any point on an indifference curve above I_b, such as point U, is out of the question because it lies beyond her financial means. We end up with a simple rule of consumer choice:

Consumers will select the most desired combination of goods obtainable for their money. The choice will be that point on the budget line at which the budget line is tangent to an indifference curve.

We can see why no point except the point of tangency, T (two tapes and three kilograms of cheese), will give the consumer the largest utility that her money can buy. Suppose the consumer were instead to consider buying four tapes and no cheese. This would put her at point Z on the budget line and on indifference curve I_a. But then, by buying fewer tapes and more cheese (a move to the left on the budget line), she could get to an indifference curve that was higher and hence more desirable without spending any more money. It clearly does not pay to end up at Z. Only at the point of tangency, T, is there no room for improvement.

At a point of tangency where the consumer's benefits from purchasing cheese and tapes are maximized, the slope of the budget line equals the slope of the indifference curve. This is true by the definition of a point of tangency. We have just seen that the slope of the budget line is the ratio of the prices of tapes and cheese. We can therefore restate the requirement for the optimal division of the consumer's money between the two commodities in slightly more technical language:

Consumers will get the most benefit from their money by choosing a combination of commodities with a marginal rate of substitution equal to the ratio of their prices.

It is worth reviewing the logic behind this conclusion. Why is it not advisable for the consumer to stop at a point like Z, where the marginal rate of substitution (slope of the indifference curve) is less than the price ratio (slope of the budget line)? Because by moving upward and to the left along her budget line, she can take advantage of market opportunities to obtain a commodity package that she likes better. This will always be the case if the rate at which the consumer is personally willing to exchange cheese for tapes (her marginal rate of substitution) differs from the rate of exchange offered on the market (the slope of the budget line).

CONSEQUENCES OF INCOME CHANGES: INFERIOR GOODS

Next, consider what happens to the consumer's purchases when there is a rise in income. We know that a rise in income produces a parallel outward shift in the budget line, such as the shift from BB to CC in Figure 4-8(a). This moves the consumer's equilibrium from tangency point P to tangency point F on a higher indifference curve.

A rise in income may or may not increase the demand for a commodity. In the case shown in Figure 4-8(a), the rise in income does lead the consumer to buy more cheese *and* more tapes. But her indifference curves need not always be positioned in a way that yields this sort of result. In Figure 4-8(b), we see that as the consumer's budget line rises from BB to CC, the tangency point moves leftward from H to G, so that when her income rises, she actually buys fewer tapes. In this case, we infer that tapes are an inferior good.

CONSEQUENCES OF PRICE CHANGES: DERIVING THE DEMAND CURVE

Finally, we come to the main question underlying demand curves: How does our consumer's choice change if the price of one good changes? We learned earlier that a reduction in the price of a tape causes the budget line to swing outward along the horizontal axis while leaving its vertical intercept unchanged. In Figure 4-9, on page 126, we depict the effect of a decline in the price of tapes on the quantity of tapes demanded. As the price of tapes falls, the budget line swings from BC to BD. The tangency points, T and E, also move in a corresponding direction, causing the quantity demanded to rise from two to three. The price of tapes has fallen, and the quantity demanded has risen: The demand curve for tapes is negatively sloped.

The demand curve for tapes can be constructed directly from Figure 4-9. Point T tells us that two tapes will be bought when the price of a

FIGURE 4-8

EFFECTS OF A RISE IN INCOME: INFERIOR GOODS

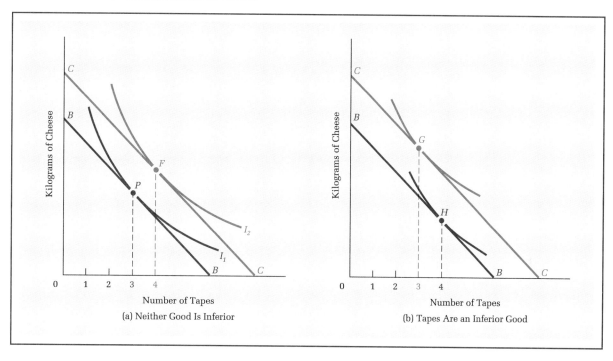

When neither good is inferior (panel (a)), the rise in income causes a parallel shift in the budget line from *BB* to *CC*. The quantity of tapes demanded rises from three to four, and the quantity demanded of cheese also increases. When tapes are an inferior good (part (b)), the upward shift in the budget line from *BB* to *CC* causes the quantity of tapes demanded to fall from four (point *H*) to three (point *G*).

tape is $3. Point *E* tells us that when the price of a tape falls to $1.50, quantity demanded rises to three tapes. (How do we know that the price of tapes corresponding to budget line *BD* is $1.50? Since the $12 total budget will purchase at most eight tapes (point *D*), the price per tape must be $12 ÷ 8 = $1.50.) These two pieces of information are shown in Figure 4-10 as points *t* and *e* on the demand curve for tapes. By examining the effects of other possible prices for tapes (other budget lines emanating from point *B* in Figure 4-9), we can find all the other points on the demand curve in exactly the same way.

The indifference curve diagram also brings out an important point that the demand curve diagram does not show. A change in the price of tapes also has consequences for the quantity of cheese demanded because it affects the amount of money left for cheese purchases. In the example illustrated in Figure 4-9, the decrease in the price of tapes increases the demand for cheese from three to three and three-quarters kilograms.

CONCLUSION

This completes our discussion of the logic behind consumer choice. In the next chapter, we will use this analysis as a base upon which to build

FIGURE 4-9

CONSEQUENCES OF PRICE CHANGES

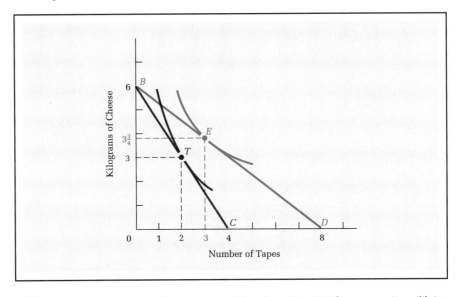

A fall in tape price swings the budget line outward from line *BC* to *BD*. The consumer's equilibrium point (the point of tangency between the budget line and an indifference curve) moves from *T* to *E*. The desired purchase of tapes increases from two to three, and the desired purchase of cheese increases from three kilograms to three and three-quarters kilograms.

FIGURE 4-10

DERIVING THE DEMAND CURVE FOR TAPES

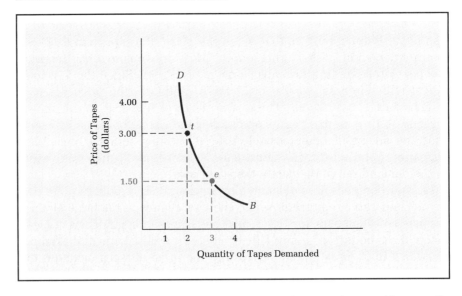

The demand curve is derived from the indifference curve diagram by varying the price of the commodity in question. Specifically, when the price is $3 per tape, we know from Figure 4-9 that the optimal purchase is two tapes (point *T*). This information is recorded here as point *t*. Similarly, the optimal purchase is three tapes when the price of tapes is $1.50 (point *E* in Figure 4-9). This is shown here as point *e*.

a theory of demand, thereby taking our first major step toward under-standing how the market system operates. Meanwhile, in this chapter, we have laid the foundation for an evaluation of the virtues and shortcomings of the market mechanism as an instrument to serve the consumer's wishes effectively. Tools such as the marginal utility of a purchase and the consumer surplus that this purchase gives to the buyer are instruments used by economists to analyze and evaluate the performance of the market mechanism.

SUMMARY

1. Economists distinguish between total utility and marginal utility. Total utility, or the benefit a consumer derives from a purchase, is measured by the maximum amount of money he or she would give up in order to have the good in question. Rational consumers seek to maximize total utility.

2. Marginal utility is the maximum amount of money a consumer is willing to pay for an additional unit of a commodity. Marginal utility is useful in calculating what set of purchases maximizes total utility.

3. The "law" of diminishing marginal utility is a psychological hypothesis stating that as a consumer acquires more and more of a commodity, the marginal utility of additional units of the commodity will decrease.

4. To maximize the total utility obtained by spending money on some commodity, X, given the fact that the other goods can be purchased only with the money that remains after buying X, the consumer must purchase a quantity of X such that the price is equal to the commodity's marginal utility (in money terms).

5. If a consumer acts to maximize utility and if his or her marginal utility of some good declines when larger quantities are purchased, then the consumer's demand curve for the good will have a negative slope. A reduction in price will induce the pur-chase of more units, leading to a lower marginal utility.

6. Abundant goods tend to have a low price and low marginal utility regardless of whether their total utility is high or low. That is why water can have a low price despite its high total utility.

7. As long as consumers have only to pay a price that equals the marginal utility of the last unit consumed for all units of the item they purchase, they receive a bonus. Economists use the term consumer surplus for this excess of willingness to pay over what is actually paid.

8. User charges may be needed to control the costs of providing some government services.

(Summary points 9 through 16 concern the more advanced material, which begins on page 111.)

9. An inferior good, such as second-hand clothing, is a commodity consumers buy less of when they get richer, all other things held equal.

10. A rise in the price of a commodity has two effects on quantity demanded: (a) a substitution effect, which makes the good less attractive because it has become more expensive than it was previously, and (b) an income effect, which decreases the consum-

er's total utility because higher prices cut his or her purchasing power.

11. Any increase in the price of a good always has a negative substitution effect; that is, considering only the substitution effect, a rise in price must reduce the quantity demanded.

12. The income effect of a rise in price may, however, push quantity demanded up or down. For normal goods, the income effect of a higher price (which makes consumers poorer) reduces quantity demanded; for inferior goods, the income effect of higher prices actually increases quantity demanded.

13. Indifference curve analysis permits us to study the interrelationships of the demands for two (or more) commodities. The basic tools of indifference curve analysis are the consumer's budget line and indifference curves.

14. A budget line shows all combinations of two commodities that the consumer can afford, given the prices of the commodities and the amount of money the consumer has available to spend. The budget line is a straight line whose slope equals the ratio of the prices of the commodities. A change in price changes the slope of the budget line. A change in the consumer's income causes a parallel shift in the budget line.

15. Two points on an indifference curve represent two combinations of commodities such that the consumer does not prefer one of the combinations over the other. Indifference curves normally have negative slopes and are "bowed in" toward the origin. The slope of an indifference curve indicates how much of one commodity the consumer is willing to give up in order to get an additional unit of the other commodity.

16. A consumer will choose the point on his or her budget line that gets him or her to the highest attainable indifference curve. Normally, this will occur at the point of tangency between the two curves. This choice indicates the combination of commodities that gives the consumer the greatest benefits for the amount of money he or she has available to spend. The consumer's demand curve can be derived from his or her indifference curve.

CONCEPTS FOR REVIEW

BASIC CONCEPTS

Diamond–water paradox
Marginal analysis
Total utility

Marginal utility
"Law" of diminishing marginal
    utility

Optimal purchase rule
    ($P = $ MU)
Scarcity and marginal utility
Consumer surplus

ADVANCED CONCEPTS

Inferior goods
Income effect

Substitution effect
Budget line

Indifference curves
Marginal rate of substitution

QUESTIONS FOR DISCUSSION

1. Describe some of the different things you do with water. Which would you give up if the price of water rose a little? If it rose by a fairly large amount? If it rose by a very large amount?

2. Which is greater: your total utility from twelve litres of water per day or your total utility from eighteen litres per day? Why?

3. Which is greater: your marginal utility at twelve litres per day or your marginal utility at eighteen litres per day? Why?

4. Some people who do not understand the optimal purchase rule argue that if a consumer buys so much of a good that its price equals its marginal utility, he could not possibly be behaving optimally. Rather, they say, he would be better off quitting when ahead, that is, buying a quantity such that marginal utility is much greater than price. What is wrong with this argument? (*Hint:* What opportunity does the consumer then miss? Is it maximization of marginal or total utility that serves the consumer's interests?)

5. According to Table 4-1, what is Jennifer's loss in consumer surplus if price rises from 72¢ to 88¢ per kilogram of bananas?

6. What inferior goods do you purchase? Why do you buy them? Do you think you will continue to buy them when your income is higher?

7. Which of the following items are likely to be normal goods to a typical consumer? Which are likely to be inferior goods?
   a. Expensive perfume
   b. Paper napkins
   c. Second-hand clothing
   d. Overseas trips

8. Suppose gasoline and safety pins each rise in price by 20 percent. Which will have the larger income effect on the purchases of a typical consumer? Why?

9. Around 1850, Sir Robert Giffen observed that Irish peasants actually consumed more potatoes as the price of potatoes increased. Use the concepts of income and substitution effects to explain this phenomenon.

10. John Q. Public spends all his income on cheap wine and hot dogs. Draw his budget line when
    a. His income is $80 and the cost of one bottle of wine and one hot dog is $1.60 each.
    b. His income is $120 and the two prices are as in (a).
    c. His income is $80 and hot dogs cost $1.60 each and wine costs $1.20 per bottle.

11. Draw some hypothetical indifference curves for John Q. Public on a diagram identical to the one you constructed for part (a) of Question 10.
    a. Approximately how much wine and how many hot dogs will Public buy?
    b. How will these choices change if his income increases to $120, as in part (b) of Question 10? Is either good an inferior good?
    c. How will these choices change if wine prices fall to $1.20 per bottle, as in part (c) of Question 10?

12. Explain what information the slope of an indifference curve conveys about a consumer's preferences. Use this to explain the typical U-shaped curvature of indifference curves.

CHAPTER 5

MARKET DEMAND
AND ELASTICITY

Economists who work for business firms are frequently assigned the task of studying consumer demand for the products their companies produce. Business managers count the results of such studies among the most important information they get. Government agencies also gather information about demand, which they use to study a wide variety of issues, such as general business conditions and receipts from sales taxes.

The quantity demanded in any market depends on many things: the incomes of consumers, the price of the good, the prices of other goods, the volume and effectiveness of advertising, and so on. Demand analysis deals with all these influences, but it has traditionally focussed on the price of the good in question. The reason is that the market price of a commodity plays a crucial role in influencing both quantity supplied and quantity demanded, and, in equilibrium, price is set at the level that makes these two quantities equal. We studied this role of price in Chapter 3, and we will return to it time and again throughout the book.

We begin this chapter by showing how the market-demand curve for a product is derived from the individual-demand curves of the individual consumers. Next, we pose a question: Who pays for the sales taxes levied on a product—consumers or producers? The important concept of elasticity is introduced as a way to measure the responsiveness of quantity demanded to price, and it is then used to answer this question and to explain why governments tax some goods more than others. Then, we turn to variables other than price that influence quantity demanded. Finally, we explain the importance of the time period to which a demand curve applies and, in an appendix, describe how this can create problems in obtaining demand information from statistical data. Near the end of the chapter, we also provide some examples of how knowledge of elasticity can illuminate important policy issues, such as the farm-income problem and the legal battles that are waged between companies.

There was a time when a fool and his money were soon parted, but now it happens to everybody.

ADLAI STEVENSON

FROM INDIVIDUAL-DEMAND CURVES TO MARKET-DEMAND CURVES

In Chapter 4, we studied how individual-demand curves are derived from the logic of consumer choice. Each consumer seeks to attain the highest total utility permitted by his or her limited budget and, in the process, will typically react to a higher price by reducing his or her quantity demanded. But to understand how the market system works, we must derive the relationship between price and quantity demanded in the market as a whole—the **market-demand curve**.

A **MARKET-DEMAND CURVE** shows how the total quantity demanded of some product during a specified period of time changes as the price of that product changes, holding other things constant.

If each individual pays no attention to other people's purchase decisions when making his or her own, deriving the market-demand curve from the customers' individual-demand curves is straightforward. We simply add the negatively sloping individual-demand curves *horizontally*, as shown in Figure 5-1. There we see three schedules: individual-demand curves *DD* and *BB* for two people, David and Brian, and total (market-) demand curve *MM*.

Specifically, this market-demand curve is constructed as follows. *Step 1:* Pick any relevant price, say $10. *Step 2:* At that price, determine David's quantity demanded (9 units) from David's demand curve in part (a) of Figure 5-1 and Brian's quantity demanded (6 units) from Brian's demand curve in part (b). Note that these quantities are indicated by line segment *AA* for David and line segment *RR* for Brian. *Step 3:* Add Brian's

FIGURE 5-1

THE RELATIONSHIP BETWEEN TOTAL MARKET DEMAND AND THE DEMANDS OF INDIVIDUAL CONSUMERS WITHIN THAT MARKET

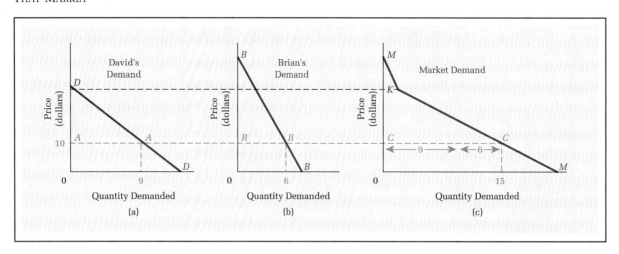

If David and Brian are the customers for a product, and at a price of $10 David demands 9 units (line *AA* in part (a)) and Brian demands 6 units (line *RR* in part (b)), then total quantity demanded by the market at that price is 9 + 6 = 15 (line *CC* in part (c)). In other words, we obtain the market-demand curve by adding horizontally all points on each consumer's demand curve at each given price. Thus, at a $10 price we have length *CC* on the market-demand curve, which is equal to *AA* + *RR* on the individual-demand curves. (The sharp angle at point *K* on the market curve occurs because it corresponds to the price at which David, whose demand pattern is different from Brian's, first enters the market. At any higher price, only Brian is willing to buy anything.)

and David's quantities demanded at the \$10 price (segment *AA* + segment *RR* = 9 + 6 = 15) to yield the total quantity demanded by the market at that price (line segment *CC*, with total quantity demanded equal to 15 units, in part (c)). Now repeat the process for all alternative prices to obtain other points on the market-demand curve until the shape of the entire curve, *MM*, is indicated. That is all there is to the adding-up process.

THE "LAW" OF DEMAND

A formal definition of the demand curve for an entire market was given in Chapter 3 and again in the margin of the previous page. We shall pay much attention in this chapter to the "other things" referred to in this definition. But for now, let us focus on price, and note that the total quantity demanded by the market normally moves in the opposite direction from price. Economists call this relationship the **"law" of demand.**

Notice that we have put the word *law* in quotation marks. By now you will have observed that economic laws are not always obeyed, and we shall see in a moment that the law of demand is not without its exceptions. But first, let us see why the law usually holds.

In Chapter 4, we learned that individual-demand curves are usually downward sloping because of the "law" of diminishing marginal utility. If individual-demand curves slope downward, then we see from the preceding discussion of the adding-up process that the market-demand curve must also slope downward. This is just common sense: If every consumer in the market buys fewer bananas when the price of bananas rises, the total quantity demanded in the market must surely fall.

But market-demand curves may slope downward even when individual-demand curves do not, because not all consumers are alike. For example, if a bookstore reduces the price of a popular novel, it may draw many new customers, but few customers will be induced to buy two copies. Similarly, people differ in their fondness for bananas. True devotees may maintain their purchases of bananas even at exorbitant prices, while others will not eat a banana even if it is offered free of charge. As the price of bananas rises, the less enthusiastic banana-eaters drop out of the market entirely, leaving the expensive fruit to the more devoted consumers. Thus, the quantity demanded declines as price rises simply because higher prices induce more people to kick the banana habit. Indeed, for many commodities, it is the appearance of new customers in the market when prices are lower, rather than the negative slope of individual-demand curves, that accounts for the law of demand.

This point is also illustrated in Figure 5-1, where we see that at a price higher than 0*D*, only Brian will buy the product. However, at a price below 0*D*, David is also induced to make some purchases. Hence, below point *K*, the market-demand curve lies farther to the right than it would have if David had not been induced to enter the market. To put the point another way, a rise in price from a level below *D* to a level above *D* will

The **"LAW" OF DEMAND** states that a lower price generally increases the amount of a commodity that people in a market are willing to buy. So, for most goods, demand curves have a negative slope.

cut quantity demanded for two reasons: first, because Brian's demand curve has a negative slope; and second, because it drives David out of the market.

We conclude, therefore, that the law of demand stands on fairly solid ground. If individual-demand curves are downward sloping, the market-demand curve surely will be as well. Also, the market-demand curve may slope downward even when individual-demand curves do not.

Nevertheless, exceptions to the law of demand have been noted. One common exception occurs when quality is judged on the basis of price —the more expensive a product, the better it is believed to be. For example, many people buy brand-name aspirin, even if right next to it on the drugstore shelf there is a "generic" aspirin, with an identical chemical formula, sold at half the price. The consumers who buy brand-name aspirin may well use comparative price to judge the relative qualities of different brands. They may prefer brand X to brand Y because X is slightly more expensive. If brand X were to reduce its price below that of Y, consumers might assume that it was no longer superior and actually reduce their purchases of it.

Another possible cause of an upward-sloping demand curve is snob appeal. If part of the reason for purchasing a Rolls Royce is to advertise one's wealth, a decrease in the car's price may actually reduce sales, even if the quality of the car is unchanged. Other types of exceptions have also been noted by economists, but, for most commodities, it seems quite reasonable to assume that demand curves have a negative slope, an assumption that is supported by the data.

APPLICATION: WHO PAYS AN EXCISE TAX?

An **EXCISE TAX** is a tax levied as a fixed amount of money per unit of product sold or as a fixed percentage of the purchase price.

The law of demand has many applications. Suppose, for example, that 18 million pocket books are sold per year, and the government considers placing a $4 tax on each book sold (called an **excise tax**), hoping to collect $72 million in revenue per year ($4 per book times 18 million books). The law of demand tells us that the government will collect less than $72 million. Why? Because the excise tax will push up the price and that will reduce quantity demanded below 18 million.

Knowing that revenues will rise by less than $72 million is useful, but it is not enough. If quantity demanded is highly responsive to price, a rise in price will cause consumers to cut back more sharply on book purchases—and the government will get less money from its tax—than if consumers are less sensitive to price in their demand for this item. So, to determine its tax receipts, the government needs to estimate how much the price will rise and how much quantity demanded will fall. For this purpose, the government needs a *quantitative measure* of the responsiveness of quantity demanded to price. Such a measure is the main subject of this chapter. But, to see how tax revenues can be estimated, we must detour briefly. In the process, we will also learn who really pays the excise tax.

Table 5-1 presents hypothetical supply and demand schedules for books in a format that is familiar from Chapter 3. You can see that the equilibrium price is $6 per book and the equilibrium quantity is 18 million books per year (point *A* in Figure 5-2(a)). Now, what happens if the government imposes a $4 per book excise tax? To find the answer, we must first determine what a $4 excise tax does to the supply curve.

THE EFFECT OF THE TAX ON THE SUPPLY CURVE

We do this by answering a series of hypothetical questions about how sellers would react to the tax at different levels of market price.

TABLE 5-1
DEMAND AND SUPPLY SCHEDULES FOR POCKET BOOKS

Price (dollars)	Quantity Supplied (millions of books per year)	Quantity Demanded
10	30	0
9	27	1
8	24	3
7	21	9
6	18	18
5	15	27
4	12	36
3	9	45

FIGURE 5-2
WHO PAYS AN EXCISE TAX?

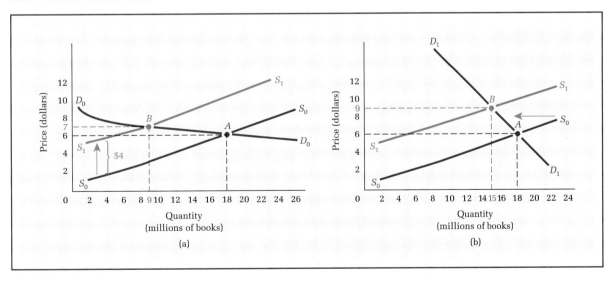

A $4 excise tax shifts the supply curve vertically upward by $4—from $S_0 S_0$ to $S_1 S_1$. The market equilibrium therefore shifts from point *A* to point *B*. In part (a), demand curve $D_0 D_0$ is rather flat, so the price rises only $1 (from $6 to $7), while the quantity falls dramatically (from 18 million to 9 million). Producers pay most of the tax. In part (b), demand curve $D_1 D_1$ is much steeper, so the price rises by $3 and quantity falls by much less (only 3 million books). Consumers pay most of the tax.

First, if books sell for $12, including the tax, how many will be supplied? The key point here is that suppliers will receive only $8 per book —$12 minus the $4 tax. Therefore, the tax-free supply schedule in Table 5-1 (third line) tells us that quantity supplied will be 24 million books per year. Thus, at a price to customers of $12 each, quantity supplied is 24 million books. This information is recorded in the top row of Table 5-2.

The rest of the supply schedule in Table 5-2 is constructed similarly. For example, a $10 price nets the seller $6, which, according to Table 5-1, leads to a quantity supplied of 18 million books.

A pattern is apparent in Table 5-2. At any given price, suppliers will provide the same quantity after the tax as they previously provided at a price $4 lower. Thus, we can draw the following conclusion:

An excise tax shifts the supply curve upward by the amount of the tax.

This conclusion is just common sense. After all, suppliers care about the price they receive, not about the price buyers pay. Graphically, our conclusion is depicted in part (a) of Figure 5-2, which shows demand curve D_0D_0 and the two supply curves—S_0S_0 before tax and S_1S_1 after tax. The two supply curves are parallel and $4 apart.

THE ROLE OF THE SHAPE OF THE DEMAND CURVE

Now we can answer the questions of interest: How much will the market price rise as a result of the tax? How much will the quantity fall? How much revenue will the government collect?

The answers depend on the responsiveness of quantity demanded to price changes—that is, on the shape of the demand curve. We start with a case in which demand is relatively responsive (part (a) of Figure 5-2); that is, a small (vertical) change in price leads to a large (horizontal) change in quantity, making the demand curve rather flat.

TABLE 5-2

EFFECT ON THE BOOK MARKET OF A $4 EXCISE TAX

Price Including Tax (dollars)	Price Received by Suppliers (dollars)	Quantity Supplied	Quantity Demanded
		(millions of books per year)	
12	8	24	0
11	7	21	0
10	6	18	0
9	5	15	1
8	4	12	3
7	3	9	9
6	2	6	18
5	1	3	27

Figure 5-2(a) shows that, in this case, the $4 excise tax raises the equilibrium price from $6 per book (point *A*) to $7 (point *B*). Because this lowers the quantity sold from 18 million to 9 million books per year, the government will collect only $36 million ($4 times 9 million) rather than $72 million.

In this example, the price rises by only one-fourth as much as the tax (from $6 to $7), so consumers wind up paying only one-fourth of the tax. The other $3 of tax is paid by businesses, which now collect only $3 per book ($7 less $4 tax) instead of $6. But consumers do not always pay such a small fraction of an excise tax. The way the tax burden is shared depends on how responsive quantity demanded is to price. In this example, quantity demanded responds very strongly. (The distribution of the tax burden also depends on the responsiveness of quantity *supplied* to price, but we are concentrating on demand here.)

Part (b) of Figure 5-2 shows that things work out quite differently if quantity demanded is much less responsive to price. Demand curve D_1D_1 is much steeper than demand curve D_0D_0, meaning that a given change in price elicits a much smaller quantity response. (The reader should verify that a fall in price from $7 to $6 per book raises quantity demanded by 9 million books in part (a) but only by about 1 million books in part (b).) As a result, the equilibrium price rises by much more ($3 instead of $1), and the quantity demanded falls by much less (only 3 million instead of 9 million).

With the unresponsive demand curve D_1D_1, consumers pay three-quarters of the tax and firms pay only one-quarter. Further, since the decline in quantity is much smaller in part (b) than in part (a), the government collects more revenue—$60 million per year ($4 times 15 million) in part (b) rather than the $36 million in part (a). The quantity of tax collected and the shape of the demand curve are related for a simple reason: The more responsive the demand curve is, the more the tax will cause quantity demanded to fall, and so the less tax revenues will rise. Thus, we conclude that *responsiveness* is the key influence here.

The less responsive consumer demand is to a change in price, the larger is the share of any excise tax that is paid by consumers and the more total tax revenue the government collects, other things being equal.

CANADIAN APPLICATIONS

Consumer demand tends to be relatively unresponsive to changes in the price of goods that are considered necessities (as we explain in greater detail later in the chapter). Is it any wonder, then, that the highest excise taxes in Canada are on gasoline (generally considered a necessity) and on alcohol and tobacco (considered a necessity by a devoted group of consumers)? For example, the tax rate on gasoline is slightly higher than 50 percent, and two-thirds of the price of a bottle of liquor is tax. Clearly, the government taxes most heavily those goods that people are most likely to keep buying despite the higher price caused by the tax. The government tries to avoid taxing goods for which people can find substitutes. Sometimes the government miscalculates how easily consumers can find alternatives. The whole issue of cross-border shopping has made it clear that when some Canadians feel that prices have increased too much, they find periodic shopping trips to the United States an appealing option. This tax-induced shift toward American products is becoming particularly acute with cigarettes. In late 1992, Canadian cigarette taxes were almost six times those levied in the United States. At that time, the estimated tax losses to Canadian governments that followed the shift to smuggled cigarettes was estimated at over $1 billion dollars annually.

To go beyond making broad observations of this sort, we need to develop a good way to measure demand responsiveness to price changes —a subject to which we turn next.

ELASTICITY: THE MEASURE OF RESPONSIVENESS

It is not only governments that need a way to measure the responsiveness of quantity demanded to price. So do other users of demand information, such as business firms, which need it for decisions on pricing of products, on whether to develop new models of their products, and so on. Economists measure this responsiveness by means of a concept they call "elasticity." A demand curve indicating that consumers respond sharply to a change in price is said to be "elastic" (or "highly elastic"). A demand curve involving a relatively small or insignificant response by consumers to a given price change is called "inelastic."

The precise measure used for this purpose is called the **price elasticity of demand**, or sometimes simply the **elasticity of demand**, and it is defined as the ratio of the percentage change in quantity demanded to the associated percentage change in price.

The **(PRICE) ELASTICITY OF DEMAND** is the ratio of the percentage change in quantity demanded to the percentage change in price that brings about the change in quantity demanded.

$$\text{Elasticity of demand} = \frac{\%\ \text{change in quantity demanded}}{\%\ \text{change in price}}$$

Thus, demand is called "elastic" if, say, a 10 percent rise in price leads to a reduction in quantity demanded greater than 10 percent. The demand is called "inelastic" if such a price rise reduces quantity demanded by any amount less than 10 percent.

Let us now consider how these definitions can be used to analyze a demand curve. At first, it may seem that the *slope* of the demand curve conveys the information we need: Since curve D_1D_1 is much steeper than curve D_0D_0 in Figure 5-3, any given change in price corresponds to a much larger change in quantity demanded in part (a) than in part (b), and thus it is tempting to call the curve in part (a) "more elastic." But slope will not do the job because the slope of any curve depends on the units of measurement, as we saw in the appendix to Chapter 1, and in economics there are no standardized units of measurement. Cloth output

FIGURE 5-3

THE SENSITIVITY OF SLOPE TO UNITS OF MEASUREMENT

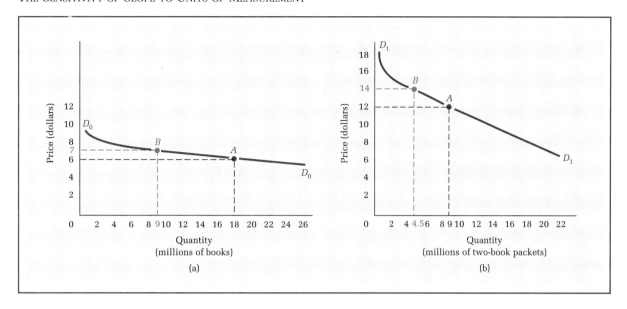

The slope of a curve changes whenever we change units of measurement. Part (a) repeats Figure 5-2(a); the demand curve looks very flat. In part (b), we measure quantity in two-book packets, so all the quantities are cut in half and all the prices are doubled. As a result, the demand curve looks rather steep. But the two demand curves present exactly the same information.

may be measured in metres or yards, milk in litres or quarts, and coal in kilograms or tonnes.[1]

It is because of this problem that economists use the elasticity measure, which is based on *percentage* changes in price and quantity rather than on absolute changes. The elasticity formula solves the units problem because percentages are unaffected by units of measurement. For example, if your height doubles between ages 5 and 15, it goes up 100 percent, whether measured in inches or in centimetres.[2]

In the formula that is actually used to measure price elasticity of demand, then, both the change in quantity demanded and the change in

---

1. An example will illustrate the problem. Figure 5-3(a) repeats demand curve D_0D_0 from Figure 5-2(a). It looks flat. Specifically, its slope between points A and B is

$$\text{Slope} = \frac{\text{change in price}}{\text{change in quantity demanded}} = \frac{\$1.00}{9} = 0.11$$

But suppose we measure quantity in millions of two-book packets, instead of in millions of single books. This is done in Figure 5-3(b), and here the demand curve looks very steep. Between points A and B, price changes by $2 per packet (that is, $1 per book) and quantity demanded changes by 4.5 million packets (9 million books). So the slope is now

$$\text{Slope} = \frac{\text{change in price}}{\text{change in quantity demanded}} = \frac{\$2.00}{4.5} = 0.44$$

This is quite a change in slope, but nothing has really changed. Points A and B represent exactly the same quantities and prices in both figures. Only the units of measurement have changed.

2. Applying the elasticity formula given above to our example illustrates that it really does solve the units problem. In moving from point A to point B in either version of Figure 5-3, quantity demanded

price are expressed as percentages. In addition to using percentages, the elasticity formula usually used in practice has a second important attribute: The change in quantity is not calculated either as a percentage of the initial quantity or as a percentage of the subsequent quantity, but as a percentage of the average of the two quantities. Similarly, the change in price is expressed as a percentage of the average of the two prices in question. To see why the issue arises, consider, as an example, the demand information presented in Table 5-1 (page 135). At a price of $6, quantity demanded is 18 million books; at a price of $7, quantity demanded is 9 million books. Suppose that a book company is deciding whether to price its product at $6 or $7. The difference in sales volume is 18 million − 9 million = 9 million. This difference in sales of 9 million units is 50 percent of 18 million but 100 percent of 9 million. Which is the correct figure to use as the percentage change in quantity?

This problem is always with us because any given change in quantity must involve some larger quantity, Q_L (18 million in our example), and some smaller quantity, Q_S (9 million), so that a given change in quantity must be a relatively small percentage of Q_L and a relatively large percentage of Q_S. Obviously, neither of these can claim to be the right percentage change in quantity. We therefore use what appears to be a compromise—the average of the two quantities. In terms of our example, we use the average of 18 million and 9 million—that is, 13.5 million—in our calculation of the percentage change in quantity.

Percentage change in quantity = 9 million as a percentage of 13.5 million
= 66⅔ percent

Similarly, in calculating the percentage change in price, we take the $1 change in price as a percentage of the average of $7 and $6, giving us $1/$6.50, or 15.4 percent, approximately.

Recall that, by the law of demand, when price increases, quantity demanded will normally decrease, and vice versa. That is, when the percentage change in price is positive, the percentage change in quantity demanded will be negative, and vice versa. So our elasticity formula would normally produce a negative number. In calculating elasticity, it is customary to disregard the minus sign to make the elasticity a positive number. That way, a *larger* elasticity number means that demand is *more* responsive to price.

To summarize, the elasticity formula has two basic attributes:
1. It deals only in percentages.
2. It calculates percentage change in terms of the average value of the quantities or prices at issue.

---

declines by 50 percent—from 18 million to 9 million in part (a), or from 9 million to 4.5 million in part (b). Similarly, the percentage rise in price from $6 to $7 in part (a), or from $12 to $14 in part (b), is 16.67 percent whether we use dollars, dimes, or pennies.

Mathematically, the reason is straightforward. If H_a and H_b represent height at age 5 and age 15, respectively, the formula for the percentage rise in height is $(H_b − H_a)/H_a$. Since an inch is about 2.5 centimetres, if we switch from inches to centimetres, in this formula both the numerator and the denominator are multiplied by 2.5. These 2.5s then cancel out, leaving the percentage figure unaffected by the switch from inches to centimetres.

In addition, the formula usually omits all minus signs.

We can now state the formula for price elasticity of demand. Keeping in mind all these features of the formula, we have the following:

$$\text{Price elasticity of demand} =$$

$$\frac{\text{Change in quantity as \% of average of the two quantities}}{\text{Change in price as \% of average of the two prices}}$$

so that in our example,

$$\text{Elasticity} = \frac{9 \text{ million as \% of } (18 \text{ million} + 9 \text{ million})/2}{\$1 \text{ as \% of } (\$7 + \$6)/2}$$

$$= \frac{66.67\%}{15.38\%}$$

$$= 4.33$$

For easy reference, the elasticity calculation for an additional example (for a demand curve that we have not drawn) is given in compact form in Table 5-3. For this demand curve, when P is 12, Q is 17, and when P is 8, Q is 23. The change in P is $12 - 8 = 4$, and average P is $(12 + 8)/2 = 10$, so the change in P is 4 as a percentage of 10, or 40 percent. Similarly, the change in Q is $23 - 17 = 6$, and average Q is $(23 + 17)/2 = 20$, so the change in Q is 6 as a percentage of 20, or 30 percent. Hence,

$$\text{Elasticity} = \frac{30}{40} = 0.75$$

ELASTICITY AND THE SHAPE OF DEMAND CURVES

Figure 5-4 shows how elasticity of demand is related to the shape of the demand curve. We begin with two extreme but important cases. Part (a) depicts a demand curve that is simply a vertical line. This curve is said to

TABLE 5-3

CALCULATION OF PRICE ELASTICITY OF DEMAND

	Price	Quantity
Situation 1	$P_1 = 12$	$Q_1 = 17$
Situation 2	$P_2 = 8$	$Q_2 = 23$
Change	$P_1 - P_2 = 12 - 8 = 4$	$Q_2 - Q_1 = 23 - 17 = 6$
Average	$(P_1 + P_2)/2 = 20/2 = 10$	$(Q_2 + Q_1)/2 = 40/2 = 20$
% change	4 as % of 10 = 40%	6 as % of 20 = 30%

Elasticity = % change in quantity/% change in price = 30/40 = 0.75

FIGURE 5-4

DEMAND CURVES WITH DIFFERENT ELASTICITIES

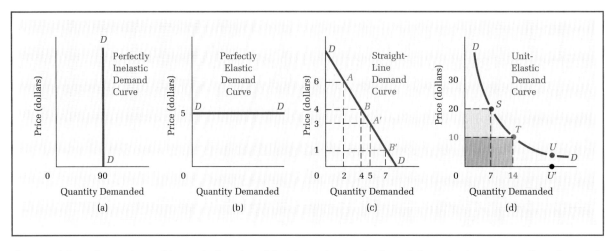

The vertical demand curve in part (a) is *perfectly inelastic* (elasticity = 0)—quantity demanded remains the same regardless of price. The horizontal demand curve in part (b) is *perfectly elastic*—at any price above $5, quantity demanded falls to zero. Part (c) shows a *straight-line demand curve*. Its slope is constant, but its elasticity is not. Part (d) depicts a *unit-elastic* demand curve with constant elasticity of 1.0 throughout. A change in price pushes quantity demanded in the opposite direction but does not affect total expenditure. When price equals $20, total expenditure is price times quantity, or $20 × 7 = $140; when price equals $10, expenditure equals $10 × 14 = $140.

be *perfectly inelastic* throughout because its elasticity is zero. This means that consumer purchases do not respond at all to any change in price. That is, quantity demanded remains at 90 units no matter what the price; thus, the percentage change in quantity is always zero and hence the elasticity is zero. Such a demand curve is quite unusual. It may perhaps be expected when the price range being considered already involves very low prices from the consumer's point of view. It does occur when the item (for example, insulin) is considered absolutely essential by the consumer.

Part (b) of Figure 5-4 shows the opposite extreme: a horizontal demand curve. It is said to be *perfectly elastic* (or *infinitely elastic*). If there is the slightest rise in price, quantity demanded will drop to zero; that is, the percentage change in quantity demanded will be infinitely large. This may be expected to occur where a rival product that is just as good in the consumer's view is available at the going price ($5 in our diagram). In cases where no one will pay more than the going price, the seller will lose all of his or her customers if the seller raises the price of the item by even one penny.

Part (c) depicts a case between these two extremes: a *straight-line* demand curve, which is neither vertical nor horizontal. Although the slope of a straight-line demand curve is constant throughout its length, its elasticity is not.

As we move down a straight-line demand curve, a given numerical change in quantity constitutes an ever smaller percentage change in quantity, while a given numerical change in price constitutes an ever larger percentage change in price. Since elasticity is defined as the percentage change in quantity divided by the percentage change in price, the numerator of the elasticity fraction gets smaller and the denominator gets larger as we move down a straight-line demand curve. Consequently, the following results:

Along a straight-line demand curve, the price elasticity of demand grows steadily smaller as we move from left to right. This is so because the quantity keeps getting larger, so that a given numerical change in quantity becomes an ever smaller percentage change, while the price keeps going lower so that a given numerical change in price becomes an ever larger percentage change.

Example: The elasticity of demand between points *A* and *B* in Figure 5-4(c) is:

$$\frac{\text{Change in } Q \text{ as \% of average } Q}{\text{Change in } P \text{ as \% of average } P} = \frac{2 \text{ as \% of } (2+4)/2}{2 \text{ as of \% of } (4+6)/2}$$

$$= \frac{\frac{2}{3}}{\frac{2}{5}} = \frac{66\frac{2}{3}\%}{40\%}$$

$$= 1.67 \text{ (approx.)}$$

But the elasticity of demand between points *A'* and *B'* is:

$$\frac{2 \text{ as \% of } (5+7)/2}{2 \text{ as \% of } (3+1)/2} = \frac{\frac{2}{6}}{\frac{2}{2}} = \frac{33\frac{1}{3}\%}{100\%} = 0.33 \text{ (approx.)}$$

If the elasticity of a straight-line demand curve varies from one part of the curve to another, what is the appearance of a demand curve with the same elasticity throughout its length? For reasons given in the next section, it looks like the curve in Figure 5-4(d), which is a curve with elasticity equal to 1 throughout (a *unit-elastic* demand curve). That is, a unit-elastic demand curve bends in the middle toward the origin of the graph and, at either end, moves closer and closer to the axes but never touches or crosses the axes.

As we have seen, it is conventional to speak of a curve whose elasticity is greater than 1 (the percentage change in quantity is greater than the percentage change in price) as an *elastic* demand curve and of one whose elasticity is less than 1 (the percentage change in price) as an *inelastic* curve. When elasticity is exactly 1, we say the curve is *unit-elastic.* This terminology is convenient for discussing the last important property of the elasticity measure, to which we turn in the next section.

ELASTICITY AND TOTAL EXPENDITURE

The elasticity of demand conveys useful information about the effect of a price change on a buyer's total expenditure. In particular, the following can be shown:

If demand is elastic, a fall in price will increase total expenditure. If demand is unit-elastic, a change in price will leave total expenditure unaffected. If demand is inelastic, a fall in price will reduce total expenditure. The opposite outcomes will occur when price rises.

These relationships hold because total expenditure equals price times quantity demanded, $P \times Q$, and a fall in price has two opposing effects on $P \times Q$. It decreases P and, if the demand curve is negatively sloped, it increases Q.

That is, a price decrease has two effects on expenditure: (1) the *price effect*, which decreases expenditure by cutting the amount of money a consumer spends on each unit of the good; and (2) the *quantity effect*, which increases the consumer's total expenditure on the good by raising the number of units of the good that he or she buys. The net consequence for expenditure depends on the elasticity. If price goes down 10 percent and quantity demanded increases 10 percent (a case of unit elasticity), the two effects will cancel out: $P \times Q$ will remain constant. On the other hand, if price goes down 10 percent and quantity demanded rises 15 percent (a case of elastic demand), $P \times Q$ will increase. Finally, if a 10 percent price fall leads to a 5 percent rise in quantity demanded (an inelastic case), $P \times Q$ will fall.

The connection between elasticity and total expenditure is easily seen in a graph. First we note the following:

The total expenditure represented by any point on a demand curve (any price–quantity combination), such as point S in Figure 5-5, is equal to the area of the rectangle under that point (the area of rectangle $0RST$ in the figure). This is so because the area of a rectangle equals height times width = $0R$ times $0T$ = price times quantity, and, by definition, price times quantity equals total expenditure.

To illustrate the connection between elasticity and consumer expenditure, Figure 5-5 shows an elastic portion of a demand curve, *DD*. At a price of $6 per unit, the quantity sold is four units, so total expenditure is $4 \times \$6 = \$24$. This is represented by the shaded gold rectangle, because the formula for the area of a rectangle is height $\times$ width, which in this case is $4 \times \$6 = \$24$. When price falls to $5 per unit, 12 units are bought. Consequently, the new expenditure ($\$60 = \$5 \times 12$), now measured by the shaded blue rectangle, will be larger than the old. In contrast, Figure 5-4(d), the unit-elastic demand curve, shows a case in which expenditure remains constant even though selling price changes. Total spending is $140 whether the price is $20 and 7 units are sold (point S) or the price is $10 and 14 units are sold (point T).

This discussion also indicates why a unit-elastic demand curve must have the shape depicted in Figure 5-4(d), hugging the axes more and more closely but never touching or crossing them. We have seen that when demand is unit-elastic, total expenditure must be the same at every point on the curve; it must be the same ($140) at points S and T and U. Suppose that at point U' (or some other point) the demand curve were to touch

FIGURE 5-5

AN ELASTIC DEMAND CURVE

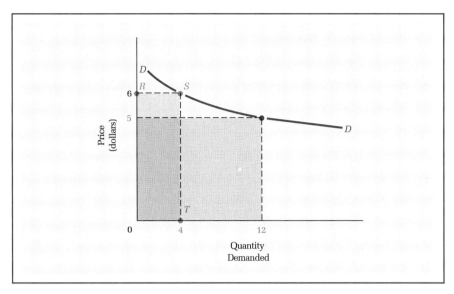

When price falls, quantity demanded rises by a greater percentage, increasing the total expenditure. Thus, when price falls from $6 to $5, quantity demanded rises from 4 to 12, and total expenditure rises from $6 × 4 = $24 to $5 × 12 = $60.

the horizontal axis. We will see now that this is impossible if expenditure at this point is to remain $140, because if U' lies on the axis, the price at that point must be zero. Therefore, at that point we must have total expenditure = $P \times Q = 0 \times Q$ = zero. We conclude that if the demand curve is unit-elastic throughout, it can never cross the horizontal axis (where $P = 0$) or the vertical axis (where $Q = 0$). Since the slope of the demand curve is negative, the curve simply must get closer and closer to the axes as one moves away from its middle points. That is why a unit-elastic demand curve must always have the shape illustrated in Figure 5-4(d).

All of this indicates why elasticity of demand is so important for business decisions. A firm should not jump to the most obvious conclusion — that an increase in price will add to its profits — for it may find that consumers take their revenge by cutting back on their purchases. In fact, if the demand curve is elastic, the firm will end up selling so many fewer units that its total revenue must actually fall, even though it makes more money than before on each unit it sells. In sum, whether a price rise or a price cut will be the better strategic move for a business firm depends very much on the elasticity of demand for its product.

WHAT DETERMINES ELASTICITY OF DEMAND?

What kinds of goods have elastic demand curves, meaning that quantity demanded responds strongly to price? What kinds of goods have inelastic demand curves? Several considerations are relevant.

Nature of the Goods

Necessities, such as basic foodstuffs, have very inelastic demand curves. The quantity of bread or potatoes demanded does not decline very much when the price of bread or potatoes rises. In contrast, many luxury goods, such as restaurant meals, have rather elastic demand curves. Statistical estimates of various elasticities confirm this principle. For example, consider the following elasticities, which have been estimated from postwar data: aluminum, 0.4; newspapers, 0.5; purchased meals, 1.1; pleasure boats, 2.4; china and tableware, 8.8.

Availability of Close Substitutes

If consumers can easily get a very good substitute, Y, for a product, X, they will switch readily to Y if the price of X rises sharply. Thus, the closer the substitutes for X that are available, the more elastic the demand for X will be. This factor is a critical determinant of elasticity. The demand for gasoline is inelastic because it is not easy to run a car without it. But the demand for any particular brand of gasoline is quite elastic, because another company's product will work just as well. This example suggests a general principle: The demand for narrowly defined commodities (like iceberg lettuce) is more elastic than the demand for more broadly defined commodities (like vegetables).

Fraction of Income Absorbed

The fraction of income absorbed by a particular item is also important. Who will buy less salt if its price rises? But many families will resist buying a second or third car if auto prices go up.

Passage of Time

This factor is relevant because the demand for many products is more elastic in the long run than in the short run. For example, when the price of home heating oil rose in the 1970s, some home-owners switched from oil heat to gas heat. But, at first, very few home-owners switched, so the demand for oil was quite inelastic. It gradually became more elastic as time passed and more home-owners switched, having had the opportunity to purchase and install new equipment and having made up their minds to do so because it became clear that the price change would last more than a very brief period.

ELASTICITY IS A GENERAL CONCEPT

We have spent much time studying the price elasticity of demand. But since elasticity is a very general measure of the responsiveness of one economic variable to another, we now consider other common and similar elasticity measures.

It is clear from what we have said that a firm will be very interested in the price elasticity of the demand curve for its product. But this is not where its interest in demand ends, for, as we have noted, quantity demanded depends on other things besides price, such as the consumer's income. The firm's management will want to know how much a change in consumers' income will affect the demand for its product. Fortunately, the elasticity measure can be helpful here too.

An increase in consumer incomes clearly raises the quantity demanded of most goods. To measure the response, we use the *income elasticity of demand*, defined as the ratio of the percentage change in quantity demanded to the percentage change in income.

Economists also use elasticity to measure other analogous responses. For example, to measure the response of quantity supplied to a change in the price of a product, economists use the *price elasticity of supply*, defined as the ratio of the percentage change in quantity supplied to the percentage change in price. The logic and analysis of all such elasticity concepts are, of course, perfectly analogous to those for price elasticity of demand.

CROSS ELASTICITY OF DEMAND: SUBSTITUTES AND COMPLEMENTS

The quantities demanded of many products depend on the quantities and prices of other products. Certain goods make one another *more* desirable. For example, cream and sugar can increase the desirability of coffee, and vice versa. The same is true of mustard or ketchup and hamburgers. In some extreme cases, neither of two products ordinarily has any use without the other—an automobile and tires, a pair of shoes and shoelaces, and so on. Such goods, each of which makes the other more valuable, are called **complements**.

Two goods are called COM-PLEMENTS if an increase in the price of one reduces the quantity demanded of the other, all other things remaining constant.

The demand curves of complements are interrelated, meaning that a rise in the price of coffee is likely to affect the quantity of sugar demanded. Why? When coffee prices rise, less coffee will be consumed and therefore less sugar will be demanded. The opposite will be true of a fall in coffee prices. A similar relationship holds for other complementary goods.

At the other extreme, some goods make one another *less* valuable. These are called **substitutes**. Ownership of a motorcycle, for example, may decrease the desire for a bicycle. If your pantry is stocked with cans of tuna, you are less likely to rush out and buy cans of salmon. As you might expect, demand curves for substitutes are also interrelated, but in the opposite direction. When the price of motorcycles falls, people may demand fewer bicycles, so the quantity demanded falls. When the price of coffee goes up, people drink less coffee and instead consume more tea or juice.

Two goods are called SUB-STITUTES if an increase in the price of one raises the quantity demanded of the other, all other things remaining constant.

Another elasticity measure can be used in determining whether two products are substitutes or complements: their **cross elasticity of demand**. This measure is defined much like the ordinary price elasticity of demand, only instead of measuring the responsiveness of the quantity demanded of, say, coffee to a change in the price of coffee, cross elasticity of demand measures the responsiveness of the quantity demanded of coffee to a change in the price of, say, sugar. For example, if a 20 percent rise in the price of sugar reduces the quantity of coffee demanded by

The CROSS ELASTICITY OF DEMAND for product X to a change in the price of another product, Y, is the ratio of the percentage change in quantity demanded of product X to the percentage change in the price of product Y that brings about the change in quantity demanded.

ELASTICITY IN PRACTICE: LEGAL CASES

We have already seen (on pages 137–38) how our government uses knowledge of the price elasticities of demand to make sure that it levies the highest rates of excise tax on the commodities with the most inelastic demands. But the judiciary also relies on elasticity estimates.

The case of Polaroid v. Kodak in the United States provides an example. Kodak had been found guilty of patent infringement when it began to sell instant cameras and film in 1976, and in 1989, a lengthy trial took place to determine just how much Kodak owed Polaroid in damages. The key issue was the estimation of how much profit Polaroid had lost as a result of Kodak's entry into the market. The concepts of price elasticity of demand and cross elasticity of demand both played crucial roles in the presentations of the two sides.

Price elasticity of demand was important in determining whether the explosive growth in instant-camera sales from 1976 to 1979 was in large part attributable to the fall in price resulting from competition by Kodak, or to the increased interest in the product among consumers that was brought about by Kodak's reputation and its access to additional retail outlets. In the latter case, Polaroid might actually have benefited residually from Kodak's entry into the market, rather than losing profit as a result of it.

After 1980, sales of instant cameras and film began to drop sharply. Cross elasticity was crucial in the explanation of the development because, at the same time, the prices of 35 millimetre cameras, film, developing, and printing had all begun to fall significantly. If it could be proved that this was the cause of the decline in Polaroid's overall sales, Kodak's instant-photography activity could not be held responsible, and the amount that Kodak would be required to pay to Polaroid would be significantly smaller. If, on the other hand, the cross elasticity of demand between conventional-photography prices and the demand for instant cameras and film proved to be low, then the cause of the decline in Polaroid's sales might have been Kodak's patent-infringing activity, adding to the damage payments to which Polaroid would be entitled.

The third elasticity issue in the case (an issue raised at the beginning of the chapter) was whether, and by how much, Polaroid's total revenue would have been increased by the rise in film price that Polaroid claimed it would have adopted had Kodak not been illegally competing with it. You now know that the crucial matter here was the price elasticity of demand for instant-camera film. Polaroid hoped to show that this elasticity figure was small because, if so, the rise in price would have raised its revenues greatly — meaning that Kodak had damaged it quite severely. Kodak, on the other hand, argued that the statistical evidence suggested that the elasticity

(continued)

(continued)
of demand for instant film was large. For, if so, a rise in price would have generated little additional revenue and might possibly have even reduced it.

On the basis of Polaroid's calculation of all of the elasticities it deemed relevant, Polaroid at one point claimed that Kodak was obligated to pay it $9 billion or more. Kodak claimed that it owed Polaroid only (!) something in the neighbourhood of $450 million. Obviously, much was at stake. The judge arrived at a total for damages very close to Kodak's figure.

5 percent (a change of minus 5 percent in quantity demanded), the cross elasticity of demand will be

$$\frac{\%\ \text{change in quantity of coffee demanded}}{\%\ \text{change in sugar price}} = \frac{-5\%}{20\%} = -0.25$$

Obviously, the producers of breakfast cereal X, for example, care a great deal about the cross elasticity of demand for product X with respect to the price of rival cereal Y.

Using the cross elasticity of demand measure, we come to the following rule about complements and substitutes:

If two goods are substitutes, a rise in the price of one of them raises the quantity demanded of the other; thus, their cross elasticities of demand will normally be positive. If two goods are complements, a rise in the price of one of them tends to decrease the quantity demanded of the other; thus, their cross elasticities will normally be negative. Because cross elasticities can be positive or negative, it is *not* customary to drop minus signs as we do when calculating ordinary price elasticity of demand.

This result is really a matter of common sense. If the price of a good goes up and there is a substitute available, people will tend to switch to the substitute. If the price of Japanese cameras goes up and the price of North American cameras does not, at least some people will switch to North American cameras. Thus, a rise in the price of Japanese cameras causes a rise in the quantity of North American cameras demanded. Both percentage changes are positive numbers and so their ratio, the cross elasticity of demand, is also positive.

On the other hand, if two goods are complements, a rise in the price of one will discourage not only its own use, but also the use of the complementary good. Automobiles and car radios are obviously complements. A large increase in the price of cars will depress the sale of cars, and this will in turn reduce the sale of car radios. Thus, a positive percentage change in the price of cars leads to a negative percentage change in the quantity of car radios demanded. The ratio of these numbers, the cross elasticity of demand for cars and radios, is therefore negative.

It should be clear from our discussion of substitute goods that if a rise in the price of firm X causes consumers of its product to switch in droves to competitive product Y, the cross elasticity of demand for product Y with

APPLICATION

ELASTICITY IN PRACTICE: THE FARM-INCOME PROBLEM*

In recent years, the real price of wheat has fallen dramatically. The resulting squeeze on farm profits has forced many farmers into bankruptcy, and prairie grain bins have been overflowing. A particularly tragic outcome has been that the world's hungry do not have access to much of this surplus. Why do things seem to get so out of balance in this and a number of other markets for basic commodities?

The proximate answer to this question is that many of the world's farmers receive massive subsidies, which stimulate very large levels of production. The existence of the subsidies is, however, symptomatic. We must appreciate why they were introduced in the first place if we are to come to a deeper understanding of current farm problems.

The key facts are as follows:

1. Technological improvements (new seeds, fertilizers, farming methods, and so on) have increased productivity in agriculture dramatically.

2. People's incomes have grown, but the income elasticity of food demand is low.

3. The price elasticity of food demand is low.

Fact 1 means that the supply curve for most agricultural products has shifted to the right very significantly, but, because of Fact 2, the demand curve has not shifted nearly as much. The general implications for farm revenues can be appreciated by considering what happens when the supply curve shifts to the right while the demand curve is stationary. Fact 3 means that the total-revenue rectangle must be getting smaller, so farm incomes are squeezed. To relieve this problem for farmers, governments have both offered subsidies and embarked on government purchase schemes.

These shifts and policies are illustrated in the accompanying diagram. Before the shift in technology, the equilibrium point is G, and farm revenues are represented by rectangle OCGD. After the supply-curve shift, the new free-market equilibrium is point H, and farm revenues equal OBHE. Since the demand curve is price-inelastic, area OBHE is smaller than OCGD; farmers' incomes are endangered. Thus, the government introduces some version of an income-support policy.

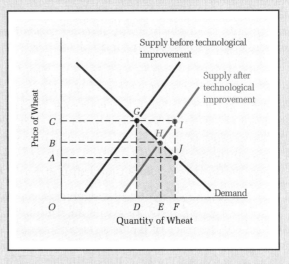

One scheme involves the government's buying and stockpiling grain; for example, if the government purchases quantity DF (equals GI) of wheat, the price will return to level OC, and farm revenues will total OCIF (of which DGIF is paid by the government). Only quantity OD of the wheat is actually consumed.

In an alternative scheme, the government lets the price fall but pays farmers the difference between the new market price and the pre-existing price, OC. If the government
(continued)

(continued)

guarantees a total price of *OC* to the farmers, they will produce amount *OF*. This entire quantity will be consumed, and consumers will pay a price of *OA* (equals *FJ*). The government must pay the difference between the old and new consumer prices — that is, amount *AC* (equals *JI*) per unit. The total cost to the government of this second policy is amount *ACIJ*. Since the demand curve is price-inelastic, this amount must exceed *DGIF*, the cost of the first policy.

Our knowledge of elasticity suggests that it is not surprising that governments often resort to purchase-and-storage schemes in an attempt to maintain farm incomes. But our analysis shows that this preference for the purchase-and-storage policy over the subsidy scheme is based on a narrow view of costs. It is true that the direct cost to government revenues is less with the purchase policy, but a more general view would acknowledge that people do not really care *how* they pay farmers—whether directly when buying the product, or indirectly through their taxes to fund either program. In either case, *OCIF* is paid to farmers. The only real difference is that, under the subsidy scheme, *all* of the product is enjoyed. Since the demand curve represents the aggregate marginal utility curve, and since the area under the marginal utility curve represents total utility, the value of the output that is *not* wasted under the subsidy policy is the gold trapezoid area, *DGJF*. By choosing the purchase-and-storage policy over the subsidy scheme, as we often do, we are throwing away an amount of material welfare equal to the gold trapezoid every period —a wasteful choice. This is not just a transfer from one group to another—it is an annual amount of satisfaction that is lost to everyone.

*For another boxed insert on farm-income problems (specifically, on agricultural marketing boards), see Chapter 16, pages 530–31.

---

respect to the price of *X* is high. That, in turn, means that competition is really powerful enough to prevent firm *X* from raising its price arbitrarily. This is why the concept of cross elasticity is so often cited in litigation before courts or hearings before government regulatory agencies when the degree of competition in an industry is an important aspect of the case.

Practical examples illustrating the importance of various elasticity concepts are provided in the two boxed inserts in this section.

SHIFTS IN DEMAND CURVES

Demand is obviously a complex phenomenon. We have studied in detail the dependence of quantity on price, and we have seen that quantity demanded depends on other variables such as incomes, the prices of substitutes and complements, and factors such as advertising. Because of these other variables, demand curves often do not retain the same shape and position as time passes. Instead, they shift about. Also, as we learned in Chapter 3, shifts in demand curves have predictable consequences for both quantity and price. But in public or business discussions, one often hears vague references to a "change in demand." By itself, this expression does not really mean anything. Remember from our discussion in Chapter 3 that it is vital to distinguish between a response to a price change (which is a *movement along* the demand curve) and a change in the relationship between price and quantity demanded (which is a *shift in* the demand curve).

When price falls, quantity demanded generally responds by rising. This is a movement along the demand curve. On the other hand, an effective advertising campaign may mean that more goods will be bought at any given price. This would be a rightward shift in the demand curve. In fact, such a shift can be caused by a change in the value of any of the variables, other than price, affecting quantity demanded.

In summary, a demand curve is expected to shift to the right (outward) if consumer incomes rise, if tastes change in favour of the product, if substitute goods become more expensive, or if complementary goods become cheaper. A demand curve is expected to shift to the left (inward) if any of these factors goes in the opposite direction.

THE TIME DIMENSION OF THE DEMAND CURVE AND DECISION MAKING

There is one more feature of a demand curve that does not show up on a graph but that is very important nevertheless. A demand curve indicates, at each possible price, the quantity of the good that is demanded during a particular period of time. That is, all the alternative prices considered in a demand curve must refer to the same time period. We do not compare a price of $10 for January with a price of $8 for September. This feature imparts a peculiar character to the demand curve and makes statistical estimates more difficult than might be supposed, because the available statistics usually give different prices and quantities only for different dates. Why, then, do economists adopt this apparently peculiar approach? The answer is that the time dimension of the demand curve is dictated inescapably by the logic of decision making.

When a business undertakes to find the best price for one of its products for, say, the next six months, it must consider the range of alternative prices available to it for that six-month period and the consequences of each possible choice. For example, if management is reasonably certain that the best price lies somewhere between $3.50 and $5.00, it should perhaps consider each of four possibilities, $3.50, $4.00, $4.50, and $5.00, and estimate how much it can expect to sell at each of these potential prices during the six-month period in question. The result of these estimates may appear in a format similar to that shown in the table below.

Potential price	$3.50	$4.00	$4.50	$5.00
Expected quantity demanded	75 000	73 000	70 000	60 000

This table, which supplies management with what it needs to know to make a pricing decision, also contains precisely the information an economist uses to draw a demand curve.

The demand curve describes a set of hypothetical responses to a set of potential prices, only one of which can actually be charged. All of the points on the demand curve refer to alternative possibilities for the *same* period of time—the period for which the decision is to be made.

Thus, the demand curve as just described is no abstract notion that is useful primarily in academic discussion. Rather, it offers precisely the information that businesses need for rational decision making. However, as already noted, the fact that all points on the demand curve are hypothetical possibilities, all for the same period of time, causes problems for statistical evaluation of demand curves. These problems are discussed in the appendix to this chapter.

SUMMARY

1. A market-demand curve for a product can be obtained by summing horizontally the demand curves of each individual in the market; that is, by adding up at each price the quantities demanded by each consumer.

2. The "law" of demand says that demand curves normally have a negative slope, meaning that a rise in price reduces quantity demanded.

3. To measure the responsiveness of quantity demanded to price, we use the elasticity of demand, which is defined as the percentage change in quantity demanded divided by the percentage change in price.

4. If demand is elastic (elasticity greater than 1), a rise in price will reduce total expenditure. If demand is unit-elastic (elasticity equal to 1), a rise in price will not change total expenditure. If demand is inelastic (elasticity less than 1), a rise in price will increase total expenditure.

5. The more inelastic is the demand for a commodity, other things being equal, the higher is the share of any excise tax that is paid by consumers, and the higher is the tax revenue collected by the government.

6. Demand is not a fixed number. Rather, it is a relationship showing how quantity demanded is affected by price and other pertinent influences. If one or more of these other variables change, the demand curve will shift.

7. Goods that make each other more desirable (hot dogs and mustard, wristwatches and watch straps) are called *complements*. Goods such that if we have more of one we usually want less of another (steaks and hamburgers, Coke and Pepsi) are called *substitutes*.

8. Cross elasticity of demand is defined as the percentage change in the quantity demanded of one good divided by the percentage change in the price of the other good. Two substitute products normally have a positive cross elasticity of demand. Two complementary products normally have a negative cross elasticity of demand.

9. A rise in the price of one of two substitute commodities can be expected to shift the other's demand curve to the right. A rise in the price of one of two complementary goods is apt to shift the other's demand curve to the left.

10. All points on a demand curve refer to the same time period—the time during which the price will be in effect.

CONCEPTS FOR REVIEW

Market-demand curve
"Law" of demand
Excise tax

(Price) elasticity of demand
Elastic, inelastic, and unit-
    elastic demand curves
Complements

Substitutes
Cross elasticity of demand
Shift in a demand curve

QUESTIONS FOR DISCUSSION

1. What variables besides price and advertising are likely to affect the quantity of a product that is demanded?

2. Describe the probable shifts in the demand curves for
   a. Airplane trips when there is an improvement in the airlines' on-time performance.
   b. Automobiles when air fares rise.
   c. Automobiles when gasoline prices rise.
   d. Electricity when average temperature in Canada rises during a particular year. (*Note:* The demand curve for electricity in Ontario and the demand curve for electricity in the Yukon should respond in different ways. Why?)

3. Which of the following goods may conceivably have positively sloping demand curves? Why?
   a. Diamonds
   b. Copper
   c. Milk
   d. Shoelaces

4. Explain why elasticity of demand is measured in percentages.

5. Give examples of commodities whose demand you expect to be elastic and some whose demand you expect to be inelastic.

6. Explain why the elasticity of a straight-line demand curve varies from one part of the curve to another.

7. Calculate the price elasticity of demand when price falls from $6 to $5 in Table 5-1.

8. If the price elasticity of demand for gasoline is 0.20 and the current price is 50¢ per litre, what rise in the price of gasoline will reduce its consumption by 10 percent?

9. A rise in the price of a product that has elastic demand will reduce the total revenue of the firm. Explain.

10. Which of the following product pairs would you expect to be substitutes and which would you expect to be complements?
    a. Shoes and shoelaces
    b. Gasoline and big cars
    c. Bread and crackers
    d. Butter and margarine

11. For each of the previous product pairs, what would you guess about their cross elasticity of demand?
    a. Do you expect it to be positive or negative?
    b. Do you expect it to be a large or small number? Why?

12. Explain why the following statement is true: "A firm with a demand curve that is inelastic at its current output level can always increase its profits by raising its price and selling less." (*Hint:* Refer back to the discussion of elasticity and total expenditure on pages 143–45.)

13. Analysts have concluded that public-transit use is in decline. To change this, we could either lower the price of public transit or raise the cost of driving a private car. (Car users are currently not charged directly for

driving on expressways or for the pollution and congestion costs that they impose.) Analysts have estimated that the cross elasticity of demand is higher than the price elasticity of demand for public transit. What is your advice as an economic adviser?

14. Assume there are two goods, X and Y, with prices P_x and P_y. The demand functions for each commodity are

$$X = 5 - 0.5P_x$$

$$Y = 8 - P_y$$

Assume that both goods can be purchased from the rest of the world at a constant price:

$P_x = 3$ and $P_y = 2$. What quantity of each good is consumed and what is the price elasticity of demand in that range of the demand curve for each good? Suppose the government needs to raise tax revenue equal to 5, and to do so, imposes an excise tax (which could be called a tariff in this case) on one good or the other. What is the loss of consumer surplus in each case? Which commodity should be taxed if the goal is to minimize the loss of consumer surplus for buyers, while still raising the necessary revenue? What have you learned about how the elasticity of demand determines which good should be taxed?

APPENDIX TO CHAPTER 5

STATISTICAL ANALYSIS OF DEMAND RELATIONSHIPS

The peculiar time dimension of the demand curve, in conjunction with the fact that many variables other than price can influence quantity demanded, makes it surprisingly hard to discover the shape of the demand curve from statistical data. It can be done, but the task is full of booby traps and can usually be carried out successfully only by using advanced statistical methods. Let us see why these two characteristics of demand curves cause problems.

The most obvious way to go about estimating a demand curve statistically is to collect a set of figures on prices and quantities sold in different periods, like those given in Table 5-4. These points can then be plotted on a diagram with price and quantity on the axes, as shown in Figure 5-6. One can then proceed to draw in a line (the dotted line, *TT*) that connects these points reasonably well and that appears to be the demand curve. Unfortunately, line *TT*, which summarizes the historical data, may bear no relationship to the demand curve we are after.

You may notice at once that the prices and quantities represented by the historical points in Figure 5-6 refer to different periods of time, and that they all have been actual, not hypothetical, prices and quantities at some time. This distinction is significant. Over the period covered by the historical data, the true demand curve, which is what we really want, may well have shifted because of changes in some of the other variables affecting quantity demanded.

What actually happened may be as shown in Figure 5-7. Here we see that in January the

demand curve was given by *JJ*, but by February the curve had shifted to *FF*, by March to *MM*, and so on. That is, there was a separate and distinct demand curve for each of the relevant months, and none of them need resemble the plot of historical data, *TT*.

In fact, the slope of the historical plot curve, *TT*, can be very different from the slopes of the true underlying demand curves, as is the case in Figure 5-7. This means that the decision-maker can be seriously misled if he selects his price on the basis of the historical data. He may, for example, think that demand is quite insensitive to changes in price (as line *TT* in the diagram seems to indicate), and so he may reject the possibility of a price reduction when, in fact, the true demand curves show that a price reduction will increase quantity demanded substantially. For example, if in February he charged a price of $7.80 rather than $8.00, the historical plot would suggest to him a rise in quantity demanded

TABLE 5-4

HISTORICAL DATA ON PRICE AND QUANTITY

	Price (dollars)	Quantity Sold
January	7.20	95 000
February	8.00	91 500
March	7.70	95 000
April	8.00	90 000
May	8.20	91 000

FIGURE 5-6

PLOT OF HISTORICAL DATA ON PRICE AND QUANTITY

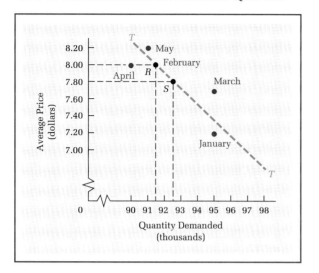

The dots labelled January, February, and so on represent actual prices and quantities sold in the months indicated. The blue line, *TT*, is drawn to approximate the dots as closely as possible.

FIGURE 5-7

PLOT OF HISTORICAL DATA AND TRUE DEMAND CURVES

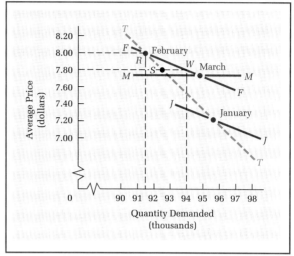

An analytical demand curve shows how quantity demanded in a particular month is affected by the different prices considered during that month. In the case shown, the true demand curves are much flatter (more elastic) than is the line plotting historical data. This means that a cut in price will induce a far greater increase in quantity demanded than the historical data suggest.

of only 1000 units. (Compare point *R*, with sales of 91 500 units, and point *S*, with sales of 92 500 units, in Figure 5-6.) However, as can be seen in Figure 5-7, the true demand curve for February (line *FF* in Figure 5-7) promises him an increment in sales of 2500 units (from point *R*, with sales of 91 500, to point *W*, with sales of 94 000) if he reduces February's price from $8.00 to $7.80. A manager who based his decision on the historical plot, rather than on the true demand curve, might be led into serious error.

In the light of this discussion, it is astonishing how often in practice one encounters demand studies that use apparently sophisticated techniques to arrive at no more than a graph of historical data. One must not allow oneself to be misled by the apparent complexity of the procedures employed to fit a curve to historical data. If these merely plot historical quantities against historical prices, the true underlying demand curve is not likely to be found.

AN ILLUSTRATION: DID THE ADVERTISING PROGRAM WORK?

A few years ago, one of the world's largest producers of packaged foods conducted a statistical study to determine the effectiveness of its advertising expenditures, which amounted to nearly $100 million a year. A company statistician collected year-by-year figures on company sales and advertising outlays and discovered, to his delight, that they showed a remarkably close relationship to one another: Quantity demanded rose as advertising rose. The trouble was that the relationship seemed just too perfect. In economics, data about demand and any one of the elements that influence it almost never make such a neat pattern. Human tastes and other pertinent influences are just too variable to permit such regularity.

Suspicious company executives asked one of the authors of this book to examine the analysis.

A little thought showed that the suspiciously close statistical relationship between sales and advertising expenditure resulted from a disregard for the principles just presented. The investigator had in fact constructed a graph of historical data on sales and advertising expenditure, analogous to *TT* in Figures 5-6 and 5-7 and therefore not necessarily similar to the truly relevant relationship.

The stability of the relationship actually arose from the fact that, in the past, the economy had based its advertising outlays on its sales, automatically allocating a fixed percentage of its sales revenues to advertising. The historical advertising–demand relationship therefore described only the company's budgeting practices, not the effectiveness of its advertising program. If management had used this curve in planning its advertising campaigns, it might have made some regrettable decisions. *Moral:* Avoid the use of historical curves like *TT* in making economic decisions.

INPUT DECISIONS AND PRODUCTION COSTS

Just as the consumer must decide what combination of products to buy and how much of each to purchase, the producer must decide how much to produce (the size of the firm's *output*) and what combination of inputs (labour, raw materials, machinery, and so on) to buy. Further, just as the key concept of the consumer's utility or preferences is crucial for the analysis of the buyer's behaviour, a fundamental phenomenon—production cost—underlies the analysis of the seller's decision.

Because a firm's decision on how much output to produce depends on costs, to understand the choice of output level, one must first analyze how costs are determined. This chapter therefore considers the logic of a firm's input decisions, while the next chapter will analyze its output choices.

For teaching purposes, the chapter is divided into two parts. In the first part, we begin with the simple case in which a firm varies the quantity of only a single input. This will vastly simplify the analysis and enable us to see more easily how to analyze the three key issues of this chapter: how the quantity of input used affects production, how the firm selects the optimal quantity of an input, and how the production relation between inputs and outputs gives the producer the cost information needed to determine output and price.

The second part of the chapter goes over the same territory—production, optimal input use, and the determination of a firm's cost curves—but deals with the more realistic case in which several input quantities can be changed.[1] Many new insights emerge from the multi-input analysis. Throughout the chapter, we assume that the price of each input is fixed by the market and is beyond the control of the firm that buys it.

A PRACTICAL APPLICATION: TESTING WHETHER A LARGER FIRM IS MORE EFFICIENT

Economies of large-scale production are thought to be a pervasive feature of modern industrial society. Automation, assembly lines, and sophisti-

---

1. *NOTE TO INSTRUCTORS:* You may prefer to postpone this part until later in the course.

cated machinery are widely believed to reduce production costs dramatically. But if this equipment has enormous capacity and requires a very large investment, small companies will not be able to benefit much from these products of modern technology. In this case, only large-scale production can offer the associated savings in costs. Where such *economies of scale*, as economists call them, exist, production costs per unit will decline as output expands.

But this favourable relationship between low costs and large size does not characterize every industry. When a court is called upon to decide whether a giant firm is operating against consumers' interests, officials need to know whether the industry has significant economies of scale. Those who want to break up large firms argue that industrial giants concentrate economic power, which is something these individuals wish to avoid. Those who oppose such breakups point out that if significant economies of scale are present, large firms will be much more efficient producers than will a number of small firms. It is crucial, therefore, to be able to decide whether economies of scale are present. What kind of evidence will speak to this issue?

Court cases of this sort have occurred and data like those shown in Figure 6-1 are sometimes offered to the courts. These figures, provided by AT&T in the United States, indicate that since 1942, as the volume of messages rose, the capital cost of long-distance communication by telephone dropped enormously. Yet economists maintain that while this graph may be valid evidence of efficiency, innovation, and perhaps other virtues of the telecommunications industry, it does not constitute legiti-

FIGURE 6-1

HISTORICAL COSTS FOR LONG-DISTANCE TELEPHONE TRANSMISSION

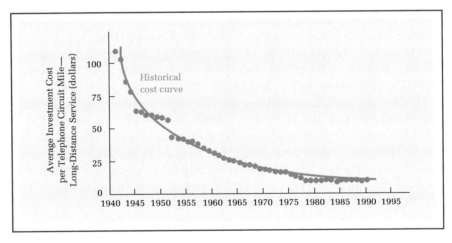

By the early 1990s, the dollar cost per circuit mile in the United States had fallen below 8 percent of what it was in 1942. Because prices had more than tripled in that period, the decline in *real* cost was even more sensational. Yet this diagram of historical costs is not legitimate evidence one way or the other about economies of scale in telecommunications.

SOURCE: AT&T, recent data estimated. Reprinted with the permission of AT&T.

mate evidence, one way or another, about the presence of economies of scale. Specifically, although this information shows that costs fell as the telephone company's volume of business grew, it does not show that a large firm is more efficient than a small one. At the end of this chapter, we will see precisely what is wrong with such evidence and what sort of evidence really is required to determine whether production by a very large firm is indeed more efficient.

PRODUCTION, INPUT CHOICE, AND COST WITH ONE VARIABLE INPUT

We begin our discussion with the single-variable input case. While a business firm uses many different inputs, we will assume for simplicity that it can change the quantity of only one of them. We are trying to replicate in our theoretical analysis what a physicist or a biologist does in the laboratory when conducting a controlled experiment in which only one variable is permitted to change at a time, to study the influence of that variable alone.

PRODUCTION: AN INPUT'S TOTAL, AVERAGE, AND MARGINAL PHYSICAL PRODUCTS

Consider, as an example of a firm, farmer Phil Pfister, who grows corn by himself on a 40-hectare plot of land. Ultimately, he can vary all his input quantities: He can hire many or few farmhands, buy more land, or sell some of the land he owns. But suppose for the moment that his only choice is how much fertilizer to apply to his land.

Farmer Pfister has studied the relationship between his **input** of fertilizer and his **output** of corn, and he has concluded that, at least up to a point, more fertilizer leads to more output. The relevant data are displayed in Table 6-1. We can see that the land has been worked so much that nothing will grow on the 40 hectares if no fertilizer is applied. But the application of more and more fertilizer yields additional output; for instance, with 4 tonnes of fertilizer, output is 1200 bushels. Eventually, however, a saturation point is reached beyond which additional fertilizer actually reduces the corn crop (any amount beyond 8 tonnes). These data are portrayed graphically in what we call a **total physical product (TPP)** curve in Figure 6-2. This curve shows how much corn Farmer Pfister can produce on 40 hectares of land when different quantities of fertilizer are used.

Two other physical product concepts are added in Table 6-2. **Average physical product (APP)** is simply the total physical product divided by the quantity of variable input used. It is the measure of output per unit of input. In our example, it is total corn output divided by number of tonnes of fertilizer used. APP is shown in the fourth column of Table 6-2,

An **INPUT** is any item that the firm uses in its production process. Labour, fuel, raw materials, machinery, and factories are all examples of inputs. The firm's **OUTPUT** is the good or service it produces. Sometimes the word "output" is used to mean the *quantity* of the good or service that the firm produces.

The firm's **TOTAL PHYSICAL PRODUCT (TPP) CURVE** shows what happens to the quantity of the firm's output as one changes the quantity of one of the firm's inputs while holding the quantities of all other inputs unchanged.

The **AVERAGE PHYSICAL PRODUCT (APP)** is the total physical product (TPP) divided by the quantity of input used. Thus, APP = TPP/Q_i, where Q_i is the quantity of input.

TABLE 6-1

FARMER PFISTER'S TOTAL PHYSICAL PRODUCT SCHEDULE*

Corresponding Label in Figure 6-2	Fertilizer Input (tonnes)	Corn Output (bushels)
A	0	0
B	1	250
C	2	550
D	3	900
E	4	1200
F	5	1450
G	6	1600
H	7	1650
I	8	1650
J	9	1600

*Data of the sort provided in this table do not represent the farmer's subjective opinion. They are *objective* information of the sort a soil scientist could supply from experimental evidence. It must be understood that the data refer to some particular time interval, such as one year.

in which the TPP schedule is reproduced. For example, since 4 tonnes of fertilizer yield 1200 bushels of corn, the APP of 4 tonnes of fertilizer is 1200/4 = 300 bushels per tonne. (For a real example, see the boxed insert opposite.)

If Farmer Pfister is to decide how much fertilizer to use, he must know how much *additional* corn output he can expect from each *additional*

FIGURE 6-2

TOTAL PHYSICAL PRODUCT WITH DIFFERENT QUANTITIES OF FERTILIZER

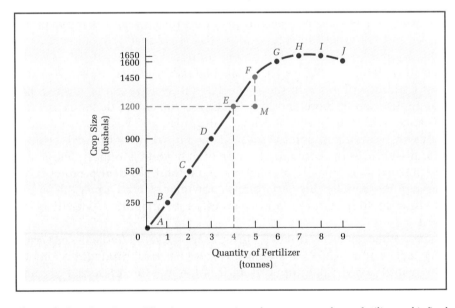

This graph shows how Farmer Pfister's corn crop varies as he uses more and more fertilizer on his fixed plot of land. (Other inputs, such as labour, are also held constant in this graph.)

FURTHER DETAIL

THE CANADIAN PRODUCTIVITY PROBLEM AND AVERAGE PHYSICAL PRODUCT

In recent years, there has been increasing concern in North America that the productivity of Japanese and other Asian workers is outstripping the productivity of Canadian and American workers. (See Chapter 32 on productivity for further discussion of these issues.) For example, statistics for two auto plants suggest that a Japanese auto worker, on the average, turns out nine engines per day, while his or her North American counterpart turns out only two. Thus, the productivity of labour in the auto industry is widely measured as the number of units of output produced per hour of labour.

But you will now recognize that the number of engines produced divided by the number of labour hours expended is exactly the same as the average physical product of an hour of labour in auto engine production. In other words, when you read the newspapers about trends in the productivity of Canadian labour or comparisons between that productivity and productivity in other countries, you will know that the report refers to the average physical product, which we discuss in this chapter.

tonne of fertilizer. This concept is known as **marginal physical product (MPP)**. Thus, the marginal physical product of, for example, the fourth tonne of fertilizer is the total output of corn when 4 tonnes of fertilizer are used *minus* the total output when 3 tonnes are used.

The marginal physical product schedule of fertilizer on Farmer Pfister's land is given in the third column of Table 6-2. For example, since 3 tonnes of fertilizer yield 900 bushels of corn and 4 tonnes yield 1200 bushels, the MPP of the fourth tonne is 1200 − 900 = 300 bushels.

The MARGINAL PHYSICAL PRODUCT (MPP) of an input is the increase in total output that results from a one-unit increase in the input, holding the amounts of all other inputs constant. Geometrically, it is the slope of the TPP curve. In symbols, MPP $= \Delta TPP/\Delta Q_i$.

TABLE 6-2

FARMER PFISTER'S SCHEDULES FOR TOTAL, AVERAGE, AND MARGINAL PHYSICAL PRODUCT AND MARGINAL REVENUE PRODUCT

Fertilizer Input (tonnes)	Total Physical Product (corn output in bushels)	Marginal Physical Product (bushels per tonne)	Average Physical Product (bushels per tonne)	Marginal Revenue Product (dollars)
0	0		—	—
1	250	250	250	500
2	550	300	275	600
3	900	350	300	700
4	1200	300	300	600
5	1450	250	290	500
6	1600	150	266.7	300
7	1650	50	235.7	100
8	1650	0	206.3	0
9	1600	−50	177.8	−100

The other MPP entries in Table 6-2 are calculated from the total product data in the same way. Figure 6-3(a) displays these numbers graphically in a *marginal physical product curve.*

The APP and MPP curves are shown together in Figure 6-3(b). The same information about the production process is contained in either of these curves. The APP curve is important since it reflects the way that productivity data are discussed in news reports. The MPP curve is useful for the firm in deciding the optimal level of an input to be used (as we will see presently).

THE "LAW" OF DIMINISHING MARGINAL RETURNS

The marginal physical product curve in Figure 6-3 shows a pattern that will prove significant for our analysis. Until 3 tonnes of fertilizer are used, the marginal physical product of fertilizer is increasing; between 3 tonnes and 8 tonnes, it is decreasing, but still positive; and beyond 8 tonnes, the MPP of fertilizer actually becomes negative. The graph has been divided into three zones to illustrate these three cases. The left zone is called the region of *increasing marginal returns*; the middle zone, the region of *diminishing marginal returns*; and the right zone, the region of *negative marginal returns.* In this graph, the marginal returns to fertilizer increase at first and then diminish. This is a typical pattern.

In the increasing marginal returns zone, each additional tonne of fertilizer adds more to TPP than the previous tonne added. In Figure 6-2, this corresponds to output levels 1–3, where the curve is rising with increasing rapidity. In the diminishing returns area, each additional tonne of fertilizer adds less to TPP than the previous tonne added. In Figure 6-2, this corresponds to output levels 4–7, where the TPP curve is still rising but at a diminishing rate. Finally, in the zone of negative marginal returns (outputs greater than 7), additional fertilizer actually reduces production (by damaging the plants).

The **"law" of diminishing marginal returns**, which has played a key role in economics for two centuries,[2] asserts that when we increase the amount of any one input, holding the amounts of all others constant, the marginal returns to the expanding input ultimately begin to diminish. The so-called law is no more than an empirical regularity based on some observation of the facts; it is not a theorem deduced analytically.

The reason why returns to a single input are usually diminishing is straightforward. As we increase the quantity of one input while holding all others constant, the input that we are increasing in quantity gradually becomes more and more abundant compared with the others. As the

2. The "law" is generally credited to Anne Robert Jacques Turgot (1727–81), one of the great comptrollers-general of France before the Revolution, whose liberal policies are said to have represented the old regime's last chance to save itself. But, with characteristic foresight, the king fired him.

FIGURE 6-3

FARMER PFISTER'S MPP AND APP

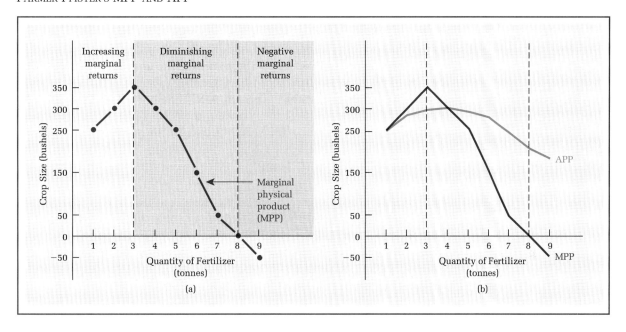

In part (a), the graph of marginal physical product (MPP) shows how much additional corn Farmer Pfister gets from each application of an additional tonne of fertilizer. The relation between the MPP curve and the total product curve in Figure 6-2 is simple and direct: The MPP curve at each level of input shows the slope of the corresponding total product curve. To see why, suppose we want to know what happens when Farmer Pfister increases fertilizer usage from 4 tonnes to 5 tonnes; that is, we want to determine the MPP of the fifth tonne. In Figure 6-2, this takes us from point *E* to point *F* on the total product curve, so that output increases from 1200 bushels to 1450 bushels. The difference, 250 bushels, is the marginal physical product of the fifth tonne of fertilizer. It is measured by the slope of the total product curve between points *E* and *F* because it corresponds to the rise in the curve (distance *MF*) resulting from a move to the right by one unit (distance *EM*)— which is precisely the definition of slope. Both MPP and APP curves are shown in part (b). The APP curve at each level of input shows (as a height) the slope of a ray joining the origin of the graph to each point on the TPP curve in Figure 6-2. This is because APP = TPP/*Q*. The APP and MPP curves intersect at the level of input use where the tangent to the TPP curve and the ray to the origin are the same line. *Note:* This makes MPP cut APP at its maximum point.

farmer uses more and more fertilizer with the fixed plot of land, the soil gradually becomes so well fertilized that adding yet more fertilizer does little good. Eventually, the plants are absorbing so much fertilizer that any further increase in fertilizer will actually harm them. At this point, the marginal physical product of fertilizer becomes *negative.*

THE OPTIMAL QUANTITY OF AN INPUT

We now have all the tools we need to see how the firm can decide on the quantity of input that is consistent with maximization of its profits. For this purpose, let us refer back to the first and third columns of Table 6-2, which show Farmer Pfister's marginal physical product schedule. Suppose fertilizer costs $350 per tonne, the farmer's product is worth $2 per bushel, and he is using 3 tonnes of fertilizer. Is this optimal for him? The answer is no, because the marginal physical product of the fourth tonne is 300 bushels (fourth entry in the marginal physical product column of Table 6-2). This means that, although a fourth tonne of fertilizer would cost $350, it would yield an additional 300 bushels, which at the price of $2 would add $600 to his revenue. Thus, he would come out $600 − $350 = $250 ahead if he added a fourth tonne.

It is convenient to have a specific name for the additional revenue that accrues to a firm when it increases the quantity of some input by one unit; we call it **marginal revenue product (MRP)**. So if Farmer Pfister's crop sells at a fixed price (say, $2 per bushel), the MRP of the input equals its marginal physical product (MPP) multiplied by the price of the product:

$$\text{MRP} = \text{MPP} \times \text{Price of output}$$

For example, we have just seen that the marginal revenue product of the fourth tonne of fertilizer to Farmer Pfister is $600, which we obtained by multiplying the MPP of 300 bushels by the price of $2 per bushel. The other entries in the last column of Table 6-2 are obtained in precisely the same way. The concept of MRP enables us to formulate a simple **rule for the optimal use of any input**:

When the marginal revenue product of an input exceeds its price, it pays the producer to expand its use of that input. Similarly, when the marginal revenue product of the input is less than its price, it pays the producer to use less of that input.

Let us test this rule in the case of Farmer Pfister. We have observed that 3 tonnes of fertilizer cannot be enough because the MRP of the fourth tonne ($600) exceeds its price ($350). What about the fifth tonne? Table 6-2 tells us that the MRP of the fifth tonne ($500) also exceeds its price; thus, stopping at 4 tonnes cannot be optimal. The same cannot be said of the sixth tonne, however. A sixth tonne is not a good idea, since its MRP is only $300, which is less than its $350 cost.

Notice the crucial role of diminishing returns in this analysis. Because the law of diminishing marginal returns holds true for Pfister's farm, the marginal *physical* product of fertilizer eventually begins to decline. Therefore, the marginal *revenue* product also begins to decline. At the point where MRP falls below the price of fertilizer, it is appropriate for Pfister to stop increasing his purchases. In sum, it always pays the producer to expand input use until diminishing returns set in and reduce the MRP to the price of the input.

A common expression suggests that it does not pay to continue doing something "beyond the point of diminishing returns." As we see from this analysis, the reality is quite to the contrary: It normally pays to do so! Only when the marginal revenue product of an input has been reduced (by diminishing returns) to the level of the input's price has the proper amount of the input been employed. Thus, the optimal quantity of an input is that at which the MRP is equal to its price (*P*). In symbols,

$$\text{MRP} = P \text{ of input}$$

The **MARGINAL REVENUE PRODUCT (MRP)** of an input is the additional revenue the producer is able to earn as a result of increased sales when he or she uses an additional unit of the input. MRP = MPP × price of product.

This analysis of the firm's input decisions now enables us to proceed to the derivation of the firm's cost curves, which play such a crucial role in its output decisions—the topic of our next chapter.

THE FIRM'S THREE COST CURVES

Costs are determined by the production relations that we have just studied and by the prices of the inputs. We can now use our two basic assumptions—that the price of fertilizer is beyond the control of the firm and that the quantities of all inputs other than fertilizer are somehow given—to deduce the firm's costs from the physical product schedules in Table 6-1 and Figure 6-2. We need simply to record, for each quantity of output, the amount of fertilizer required to produce it, multiply that quantity of fertilizer by its price, and add this to the cost of the other inputs whose quantities we are holding constant. It is critical to recognize that these must include the opportunity costs of any inputs the farmer contributes himself—his labour or his capital, which he could instead have used elsewhere to earn wages or interest.

Suppose that fertilizer costs $350 per tonne and that the cost of the fixed inputs (capital, labour, and land) is $1000. Then, from Table 6-1, we have the table of total costs shown in Table 6-3. For example, to produce 900 bushels of corn (fourth row), we know from Table 6-1 that it requires 3 tonnes of fertilizer at $350 per tonne, which when added to the $1000 cost of other inputs gives us the total cost, $2050.

The point of this exercise is as follows:

The total-product curve tells us the input quantities needed to produce any given output. From those input quantities and the price of the inputs, we can determine the *total cost* of producing any level of output. This is the amount the firm spends on the inputs needed to produce the output, plus any opportunity costs that arise in that production activity. Thus, the relation of total cost to output is determined by the technological production relations between inputs and outputs and by input prices.

TABLE 6-3
A PORTION OF FARMER PFISTER'S TOTAL-COST SCHEDULE

Output of Corn (bushels)	Total Cost (dollars)
0	$1000
250	$1000 + $350 = $1350
550	$1000 + 2 × $350 = $1700
900	$1000 + 3 × $350 = $2050
1200	$1000 + 4 × $350 = $2400
1450	$1000 + 5 × $350 = $2750
1600	$1000 + 6 × $350 = $3100
1650	$1000 + 7 × $350 = $3450

SOURCE: Obtained from the production data in Table 6-1, assuming fertilizer is the only variable input.

The behaviour of the firm's costs as output changes is obviously critical for output decisions. There are three interrelated cost curves that contain the pertinent information: the **total-cost curve**, the **average-cost curve**, and the **marginal-cost curve**, where marginal cost is a concept analogous to marginal physical product. As we shall see shortly, average and marginal costs are obtained directly from total costs (which we have just determined).

Total cost (TC) was just explained. But it is worth stressing that TC is not quite the same as the total expenditure of the firm. Expenditure and cost are not equal because, to an economist, "cost" must include the opportunity costs of inputs provided by owners of the firm—even though the owners do not explicitly "charge" for those inputs. Thus, if to produce 1600 bushels of corn, Farmer Pfister must purchase $2100 of fertilizer, and $200 of other inputs, and in addition he himself provides labour time, capital, and land with an opportunity cost of $800 (that is, those inputs could have earned $800 elsewhere), then the total cost of the 1600 bushels equals $2300 in input expenditures plus $800 in opportunity cost, or $3100.

Average cost (AC), also called *unit cost*, is simply total cost divided by output; that is,

$$\text{Average cost} = \frac{\text{Total cost}}{\text{Quantity of output}}$$

or in symbols,

$$AC = \frac{TC}{Q}$$

A firm's **TOTAL-COST (TC) CURVE** shows, for each possible quantity of output, the total amount that the firm must spend for its inputs to produce that amount of output plus any opportunity cost incurred in the process.

A firm's **AVERAGE-COST (AC) CURVE** shows, for each output, the cost per unit, that is, total cost divided by output.

A firm's **MARGINAL-COST (MC) CURVE** shows, for each output, the increase in the firm's total cost required if it increases its output by an additional unit. Geometrically, MC is the slope of the TC curve. In symbols, MC = $\Delta TC/\Delta Q$.

To determine the *marginal cost* (MC), we must know what would happen to TC if output were to increase by one unit. For example, the marginal cost of a fifth unit of output, MC_5, is the amount that production of this unit increases total cost. That is, it is equal to the excess of the total cost of the fifth unit, TC_5, over the total cost of the fourth unit, TC_4. Thus, $MC_5 = TC_5 - TC_4$. More generally,

$$MC = \frac{\Delta TC}{\Delta Q}$$

Table 6-4 presents the calculation for marginal cost systematically. For variety, we deal this time with the number of houses built per month by a construction firm that turns out standardized homes. We assume that the firm's total costs have already been determined from the relation between its inputs and its outputs, just as we did in the case of Farmer Pfister. For example, the coloured entries show that the total cost of four houses is $360 000 and the total cost of five houses is $425 000.

From the TC data, we can next obtain the AC figure for each output. For example, we see that the AC of four houses is $360 000/4 = $90 000.

TABLE 6-4
HYPOTHETICAL TOTAL, AVERAGE, AND MARGINAL COSTS OF A HOME-CONSTRUCTION FIRM

Houses Built per Period	Total Cost (thousands of dollars)	Marginal Cost (thousands of dollars)	Average Cost (thousands of dollars)
0	60		—
1	210	150	210
2	270	60	135
3	306	36	102
4	360	54	90
5	425	65	85
6	516	91	86
7	700	184	100

We can also obtain the MC figures from the TC numbers. For example, by subtracting the TC of four houses from the TC of five houses, we see that the MC of producing the fifth house is $425 000 − $360 000 = $65 000.

Generally, once we know a firm's total costs for its various outputs, we can calculate its average costs and its marginal costs from the same information.[3]

Figure 6-4 plots the numbers in this table and thus shows the total-, average-, and marginal-cost curves for the construction firm. The shapes of the curves depicted here are considered typical. The TC curve is generally assumed to rise fairly steadily as the firm's output increases. After all, one cannot expect to produce three houses at a lower total cost than two houses. The AC curve and the MC curve are both shown to be shaped roughly like the letter U—first going downhill then gradually turning uphill again. To explain these characteristic shapes, we must first distinguish between two important types of costs.

FIXED COSTS AND VARIABLE COSTS

Total, average, and marginal costs are often divided into two components: **fixed costs** and **variable costs**. A *fixed cost* is the cost of the indivisible outputs that the firm needs to produce any output at all. The total cost of such inputs does not change when the firm changes its outputs by an amount that does not exceed the inputs' production capacity. Any other cost of the firm's operation is called *variable* because the total amount of that cost will increase when the firm's output rises.

FIXED COSTS are unavoidable overhead costs that do not vary when the firm's output level changes. Any other cost of the firm is called a VARIABLE COST

---

3. The process also works the other way. If we know AC, we can work backwards to find TC from the formula TC = AC × Q. Similarly, if we know all the firm's marginal costs, we can work backwards to find its total costs.

FIGURE 6-4

TOTAL, AVERAGE, AND MARGINAL COSTS

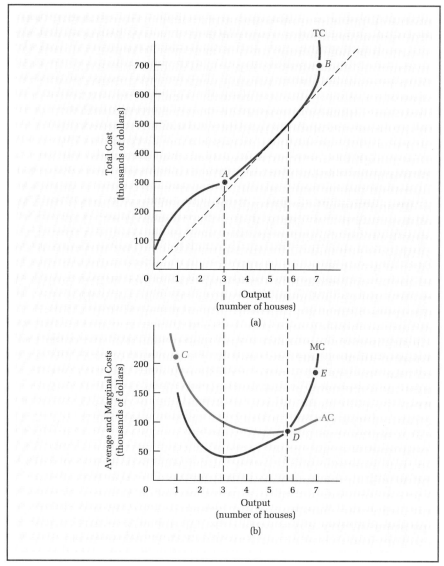

These cost curves of a hypothetical home-construction firm are based on figures presented in Table 6-4. These curves show how the firm's total, average, and marginal costs behave when the firm changes its decision on how many houses to produce. For any quantity of output, the AC curve in the lower panel shows, as a height, the slope of the ray joining the point on the TC curve for that quantity to the origin (upper panel), and the MC curve shows, as a height, the slope of the tangent to the TC curve at the same quantity. At the quantity level indicated by point *D*, this ray and this tangent are one and the same line; that is why the MC and the AC curves intersect here.

The difference between fixed costs and variable costs can be illustrated by comparing the cost of a railway's fuel with that of its track construction. To operate between Winnipeg and Regina, a railway must lay a set of tracks. It cannot lay half a set of tracks or a quarter of a set of tracks. We therefore call such an input "indivisible." The construction cost of the railway's tracks will be the same whether one train per month or five trains per day travel the route. (Note, however, that an increase in traffic will increase annual maintenance and replacement costs, so that replacement and maintenance are variable costs. Note also that opportunity costs can be fixed, variable, or a combination of the two.) In any event, up to a point, track-construction cost is not affected by output size, that is, by volume of traffic. On the other hand, the more trains that pass over those tracks, the higher the railway's total fuel bill will be. We therefore say that fuel costs are variable.

Although variable costs are only part of overall costs (fixed plus variable costs), the variable costs of a firm exhibit patterns of behaviour like those already shown in Table 6-4 and Figure 6-4. However, curves of *total fixed costs* (TFC) and *average fixed costs* (AFC) have very special patterns, which are illustrated in Table 6-5 and Figure 6-5. We see that TFC remains the same, whether the firm produces a lot or a little. (Here we assume that the fixed costs are also what economists call *sunk costs*, meaning that the firm has already spent the money in question or signed a contract to do so. Consequently, if it decides to go out of business (produce zero output), it must still spend the money. Sunk costs are further discussed later in this chapter.) As a result, any TFC curve, like the one in Figure 6-5(a), is horizontal—it has the same height at every output.

Average fixed cost, however, gets smaller and smaller as output increases because with TFC constant, AFC = TFC/Q gets smaller and smaller as output (the denominator) increases. Put another way, any increase in output permits the fixed cost to be spread among more units, leaving less and less of it to be carried by any one unit. For example, when only one house is built, the entire \$120 000 of the firm's fixed cost must be borne by that one house. But if the firm constructs two homes, each of them need cover only half the total—\$60 000.

However, AFC can never reach zero because even if the firm were to produce, say, a million houses, each would have to bear, on the average, one-millionth of the TFC, which is still a positive number, albeit a very small one. It follows that the AFC curve goes lower and lower as output increases, moving closer and closer to the horizontal axis but never crossing it. This is the pattern shown in Figure 6-5(b).

Table 6-5

Hypothetical Fixed Costs of a Home-Construction Firm

Houses Built per Period	Total Fixed Cost (thousands of dollars)	Average Fixed Cost (thousands of dollars)
0	120	—
1	120	120
2	120	60
3	120	40
4	120	30
5	120	24
6	120	20

FIGURE 6-5

FIXED-COST CURVES: TOTAL AND AVERAGE

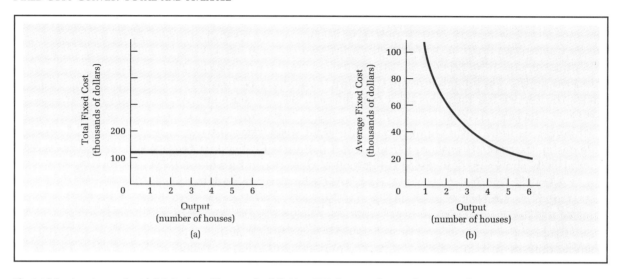

The total-fixed-cost curve (part (a)) is horizontal because, by definition, TFC does not change when output changes. AFC in part (b) decreases steadily as the TFC is spread among more and more units of output, but because AFC never reaches zero, the AFC curve never crosses the horizontal axis.

Since we have simply divided costs into two parts, fixed costs (FC) and variable costs (VC), we also have the rules

$$TC = TFC + TVC \qquad AC = AFC + AVC$$

The total-fixed-cost curve is always horizontal because, by definition, total fixed cost does not change when output changes. The average-fixed-cost curve declines when output increases, getting closer and closer to the horizontal axis but never crossing it.

SHAPES OF THE AVERAGE-COST AND TOTAL-COST CURVES

The preceding discussion of fixed and variable costs enables us to complete our investigation of the shapes of the total-, average-, and marginal-cost curves. Since the cost curves depend on the physical product curves, these technological relationships should serve to explain the shapes of the cost curves. We will next discuss what they imply about the shapes of the AC and TC curves.

We have drawn the AC curve to be U-shaped in the lower panel of Figure 6-4: The leftward portion of the curve is downward sloping, and the rightward portion is upward sloping. Why should we expect AC to decline when output increases in the leftward portion of the AC curve? Part of the answer is that production technology often exhibits increasing returns in that "start-up" range of output levels, and increasing returns mean decreasing costs. But fixed costs are a major element in the answer too. As we have seen in Figure 6-5(b), the average-*fixed*-cost curve always falls as output increases, and it falls very sharply at the leftward end of the AFC curve. But AC = AFC + AVC, so that the AC curve of virtually any product contains a fixed-cost portion, AFC, which falls when output increases. That is the main reason we can expect the AC curve for any product to have a downward-sloping portion such as *CD* in the lower panel of Figure 6-4—a portion that is said to be characterized by decreasing average cost. By decreasing average cost, we mean that when quantity goes up, say, 10 percent, total cost goes up by less than 10 percent, so that average cost, which is the ratio TC/*Q*, will fall.

The range between *D* and *E* in the same figure is the zone of increasing average costs—a given percentage rise in output requires a greater percentage rise in TC, so that AC = TC/*Q* must rise. Buy why does the portion of the AC curve with decreasing average cost come to an end? There are two reasons: (1) the law of diminishing returns, and (2) the administrative (bureaucratic) problems of large organizations.

The first of these phenomena is crucial for our present discussion, in which we are expanding one input (quantity of fertilizer) while holding all other input quantities constant. In that case, we can be sure that the law of diminishing returns will work to increase marginal (and average) costs, for reasons we have already considered. Moreover, in reality, where firms can and do vary more than one input quantity, the law of diminishing returns also works to raise MC and AC because a firm may not be able to expand all of its inputs in proportion as its output increases. For example, it may not be able to expand the time the very top management of the company devotes to its operation because there are limits to the number of hours the president can put in. Even if all other inputs double, the president may not be able to double the amount of time he or she puts in. With some inputs not expanding while others are, diminishing returns to the expanding inputs can be expected because the expanding inputs will grow less and less efficient, and that will tend to raise average costs.

The second source of increasing average cost in practice stems from sheer size. Large firms tend to be relatively bureaucratic, impersonal, and costly to manage. As the personal touch of top management is lost and the firm becomes very large, costs will ultimately rise disproportionately, and average costs will ultimately be driven upward.

The point at which average cost begins to rise varies from industry to industry. It occurs at a much larger volume of output in automobile production than in farming—which is why no farms are as big as even the smallest of automobile producers. A large part of the reason is that the fixed costs of automobile production are far greater than those in farming, so the resulting spread of fixed costs over the increasing number of units of output keeps AC falling in auto production for a far larger range of output than it does in farming. Thus, although firms in both industries may have U-shaped AC curves, the bottom of the U occurs at a far larger output in auto production than in farming.

The typical AC curve of a firm is U-shaped. Its downward-sloping segment is largely attributable to the fact that the firm's fixed costs are spread over larger and larger outputs. The upward-sloping segment is attributable to diminishing returns and the disproportionate rise in administrative cost that occurs as the firm grows larger. The output at which decreasing average cost ends or at which increasing average cost begins varies across industries. The greater the relative size of fixed costs, the higher will tend to be the output at which the switchover occurs.

This, then, indicates the basis for economists' conclusion that AC curves tend to be U-shaped. (Empirical evidence confirms this view, although it suggests that the bottom of the U is often long and flat. That is to say, there is often a considerable range of outputs between the regions of falling unit costs and rising unit costs.)

Going back to Figure 6-4 (upper panel), we see that between points 0 and A the TC curve is rising, but at a declining rate (its slope keeps falling). Roughly speaking, this means that in this region, TC goes up less rapidly than Q. Farther to the right, however, TC rises at an increasing rate, so that TC goes up more rapidly than Q. Since marginal cost is the increase in total costs divided by the increase in output, $MC = \Delta TC / \Delta Q$, marginal cost at any level of output is just the slope of the total-cost curve at that point. Thus, portion $0A$ of the TC curve in the upper panel of Figure 6-4 corresponds to the falling portion of the MC curve in the lower panel. On the other hand, region AB of the TC curve is the portion of the TC curve corresponding to the rising portion of the MC curve. Thus, the shape of the $0A$ region of the TC curve corresponds to that of the negatively sloped region of the MC curve—both reflect the spreading of fixed costs over an increasing output. Similarly, diminishing returns and disproportionate increases in administrative costs can account for segment AB of the TC curve, just as they help explain the rising portion of the MC curve.

LONG-RUN VERSUS SHORT-RUN COSTS

A **SUNK COST** is a cost to which a firm is precommitted for some limited period, either because the firm has signed a contract to make the payments or because it has already paid for some durable item (such as a machine or a factory) and cannot get its money back.

The cost to the firm of a change in its output depends very much on the period of time under consideration. The reason is that, at any point in time, many input choices are *precommitted* by past decisions. If, for example, a firm purchased machinery a year ago, it is committed to that decision for the remainder of the machine's economic life, unless the company is willing to take the loss involved in getting rid of it sooner. A precommitted cost is said to be a **sunk cost**.

The **SHORT RUN** is a period of time briefer than the long run, so that some, but not all, of the firm's sunk commitments will have ended.

An input to which the firm is committed for a short period of time, however, is not a fixed commitment when a longer planning horizon is considered. For example, a two-year-old machine with a nine-year economic life is a fixed commitment for the next seven years, but it is not a fixed commitment in plans that extend beyond the seven years. Economists summarize this notion by speaking of two different "runs" for decision making—the short run and the long run.

The **LONG RUN** is a period of time long enough for all of the firm's sunk commitments to come to an end.

These terms will recur time and again in this book. They interest us now because of their relationship to the shape of the cost curve. In the short run, there is relatively little opportunity for a firm to adapt its production processes to the size of its current output because the size of its plant has largely been predetermined by its past decisions. Over the long run, however, all inputs, including the size of the plant, become adjustable.

Consider the example of Farmer Pfister. Once the crop is planted, he has little discretion over how much of the various inputs to use. Over a somewhat longer planning horizon, he can decide how much labour to employ and how much seed to use. Over a still longer period, he can acquire new equipment and increase or decrease the size of his farm. Much the same is true of big industrial firms. In the short run, management has little control over the production technique. But with some advance planning, different types of machines using different amounts of labour and energy can be acquired, factories can be redesigned, and other choices can be made. Indeed, over the longest run, no inputs remain committed; all of them can be varied in both quantity and design.

It should be noted that the short and long runs do not refer to the same period of time for all firms; rather, they vary in length depending on the nature of the firm's sunk commitments. If, for example, the firm can change its work force every week, its machines every two years, and its factory every twenty years, then twenty years will be the long run, and any period shorter than twenty years will constitute the short run.

THE AVERAGE-COST CURVE IN THE SHORT AND LONG RUNS

As we just observed, which inputs can be varied and which are precommitted depends on the time horizon under consideration. Therefore, we can draw these conclusions:

The average- (and total-) cost curve depends on the firm's planning horizon. The average- (and total-) cost curve pertinent to the long run differs from that for the short run because more inputs become variable.

We can, in fact, be much more specific about the relationships between short-run and long-run average-cost (AC) curves. Consider, as an example, the publisher of a small newspaper. In the short run, the firm can choose only the number of typesetters and printers and the quantity of paper and ink it uses, but in the long run, it can also choose between two different sizes of printing press. If the firm purchases the smaller press, the AC curve looks like curve SL in Figure 6-6. That means that if the paper is pleasantly surprised and its circulation grows to 50 000 copies per day, its cost will be 12 cents per copy (point V). It may then wish it had purchased the bigger press (whose AC curve is shown as BG), which would have enabled the firm to cut unit cost to 9 cents per copy (point W). However, in the short run, nothing can be done about this decision; the AC curve remains SL. Similarly, had it bought the larger press, its short-run AC curve would have been BG and it would have been committed to this cost curve even if business were to decline sharply.

FIGURE 6-6

SHORT- AND LONG-RUN AVERAGE-COST CURVES FOR A NEWSPAPER

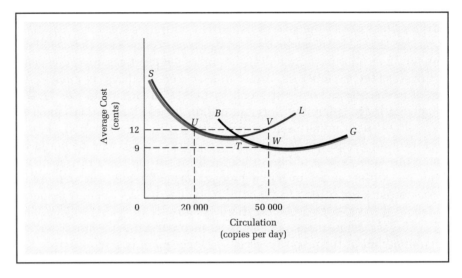

The publisher has a choice of two printing presses, a small one with AC curve *SL*, and a big one with AC curve *BG*. These are the short-run curves that apply as long as the newspaper is stuck with its chosen press. But in the long run, when it has its choice of press size, it can pick any point on the blue lower boundary of these curves. This lower boundary, *STG*, is the long-run average-cost curve.

In the long run, however, the machine must be replaced, and management has its choice once again. If it expects a circulation of 50 000 copies, it will purchase the larger press and its cost will be 9 cents per copy. Similarly, if management expects sales of only 20 000 copies, it will arrange for the smaller press and for average costs of 12 cents per copy (point *U*). In sum, in the long run, the firm will select the press size (that is, the short-run AC curve) that is most economical for the output level it expects to produce. The long-run average-cost curve, then, consists of all the lower segments of the short-run AC curves. In Figure 6-6, this composite curve is the blue curve, *STG*. If many different press sizes are possible, the long-run AC curve is a smooth locus that is tangent to all the short-run AC curves.

MULTIPLE INPUT DECISIONS: THE CHOICE OF INPUT COMBINATIONS[3]

Casual observation of industrial processes deludes many people into thinking that management really has very little discretion in choosing its inputs. Technological considerations alone, it would appear, dictate such

---

3. *NOTE TO INSTRUCTORS*: You may want to teach this part of the chapter (up to page 187) now or prefer to wait until you come to Chapter 14 on the determination of wages, interest rates, profit, and rent.

choices. A particular type of furniture-cutting machine may require two operators working for an hour on a certain amount of wood to make five desks, no more and no less. But this is an overly narrow view of the matter; whoever first declared that there are many ways to skin a cat saw things more clearly.

The furniture manufacturer may have several alternative production processes for making desks. For example, there may be simpler and cheaper machines that can change the same pile of wood into five desks using more than two hours of labour. Or still more workers could eventually do the job with simple hand tools, using no machinery at all. The firm will seek the least costly method of production. In advanced industrial societies, where labour is expensive and machinery is cheap, it may pay to use the most automated process; in less developed societies, where machinery is scarce and labour is abundant, making desks by hand may be the most economical solution. In other words, one input can generally be substituted for another.

Next we describe a method of analysis that a business firm can use to select the least costly production process. But you should know at the outset that the analysis is applicable well beyond the confines of business enterprises. Non-profit organizations, like your own university, are interested in finding the least costly ways to accomplish a variety of tasks (for example, maintaining the grounds and buildings). Government agencies are concerned with meeting their objectives at minimum costs. Even in the household, there are many "cats" that can be "skinned" in different ways. Thus, our present analysis of cost minimization is widely applicable.

THE MARGINAL RULE FOR OPTIMAL INPUT PROPORTIONS: AN INTRODUCTION

The second main topic of this chapter is the optimal choice of input quantities. Common sense guides the principles that can be used to determine what input proportions will minimize the cost of producing a given output. To bring out the logic of those principles, suppose Farmer Pfister is considering whether to use more fertilizer and less pesticide, or vice versa, in producing his contractually required 1600-bushel output of corn. Suppose also that fertilizer costs $350 per tonne, as in our earlier example, while an additional spraying of his land with pesticide costs exactly four times as much—$1400. If the marginal physical product of a tonne of fertilizer is 250 bushels, but the marginal physical product of an additional pesticide spraying is 750 bushels, what should Pfister do?

A little thought indicates the answer: Farmer Pfister should cut down on spraying and increase his use of fertilizer. Why? Because the pesticide costs four times as much as the fertilizer, but yields only three times as much corn; that is, the ratio of the marginal product of pesticide to the marginal product of fertilizer is less than the ratio of the price of pesticide to the price of fertilizer.

Let us examine the reasoning a bit more closely. Given the ratios in our example, it must pay the farmer to spend less on pesticide and more on fertilizer, because in doing so he will end up producing the same 1600 bushels of corn, but at a lower input cost. Suppose, for example, that Pfister decides to spend $1400 less on pesticide, thus cutting back one spraying of his land. This reduces his output by 750 bushels (the marginal product of pesticide). How much more fertilizer does he need to undo this output reduction? The answer is that with the MPP of fertilizer equal to 250 bushels, it will take about three additional tonnes of fertilizer to make up the shortfall. But, at a price of $350 per tonne, the three tonnes of fertilizer will cost the farmer just $1050. Thus, by trading one pesticide spraying for three tonnes of fertilizer, the farmer ends up saving $1400 − $1050 = $350 and producing the same output.

Such a move will always work out in this way. By switching from the input with the lower marginal product per dollar and buying sufficiently more of the input with the higher marginal product per dollar, the firm can reduce the money it spends on inputs without any reduction in output. This gives us the first basic rule for attaining the most economical input proportion for the production of a given output quantity:

A firm can reduce the cost of producing a given output quantity by using less of some input, A, and making up for it by using more of another input, B, whenever the ratio of the price of input A to the price of input B exceeds the ratio of the marginal physical product of A to the marginal physical product of B. That is, whenever

$$\frac{P_a}{P_b} > \frac{\mathrm{MPP}_a}{\mathrm{MPP}_b}$$

costs can be reduced by reducing the proportion of input A to input B used.

Obviously, the opposite will be true if the relative price of A is lower than its relative marginal product. In other words, input proportions cannot be optimal if the ratio of the prices of two inputs is not equal to the ratio of their marginal products. That is,

The proportions of any two inputs, A and B, used by the firm can be optimal only if

$$\frac{P_a}{P_b} = \frac{\mathrm{MPP}_a}{\mathrm{MPP}_b}$$

This rule also makes common sense. If a unit of input A has a marginal product that is, for example, three times as big as that of input B, the firm should be willing to pay exactly three times as much money for an additional unit of A as it does for an additional unit of B, no more and no less.

But what if the market happens to set input prices so that this doesn't work? Suppose the market price of A happens to be four times as large as that of *B*, as in our corn-growing example. What can the farmer do about it? We have seen that, in this case, the farmer will buy less of *A* (pesticide) and more of *B* (fertilizer). That will not change the market prices of fertilizer and pesticide, but it will change the *marginal physical products* of the two inputs because of the effects of the law of diminishing returns. As Farmer Pfister buys more fertilizer relative to pesticide, the marginal product of fertilizer will ultimately go down, as indicated in Table 6-2 and Figure 6-3(a). For exactly the same reason, as pesticide use falls and it becomes relatively scarce, its marginal product will rise. When the farmer has gone far enough in switching money from pesticide to fertilizer, the ratio of their marginal products will rise from 3:1 to 4:1. It will then equal the ratio of the prices of the two inputs, so the rule for cost minimization will be satisfied.

CHANGES IN INPUT PRICES AND OPTIMAL INPUT PROPORTIONS

The common-sense reasoning behind the rule for optimal input proportions leads to an important conclusion. Suppose the price of fertilizer rises while the price of pesticide remains the same. The rule

$$\frac{P \text{ of fertilizer}}{P \text{ of pesticide}} = \frac{\text{MPP of fertilizer}}{\text{MPP of pesticide}}$$

tells us that the optimal use of fertilizer now requires that the MPP of fertilizer must be higher than before. By the law of diminishing returns, the MPP of fertilizer is higher only when *less* fertilizer is used. Thus, a rise in the price of fertilizer leads the farmer to use less fertilizer and, if he still wants to produce 1600 bushels of output, use *more* pesticide.

Generally, as any one input becomes more costly relative to other competing inputs, a firm is likely to substitute one input for another—that is, to reduce its use of the input that has become more expensive and to increase its use of competing inputs.

This general principle of input substitution applies in industry just as it does on Farmer Pfister's farm. For some applications of the analysis, see the box on the following page.

THE PRODUCTION FUNCTION

To help select the combination of inputs that can produce the desired output most cheaply, economists have invented a concept they call the **production function**. The production function summarizes the technical and engineering information about the relationship between inputs and output in a given firm, taking all the firm's inputs into account. It indicates, for example, just how much output Farmer Pfister can produce if he has given amounts of land, labour, fertilizer, and so on.

The **PRODUCTION FUNCTION** indicates the maximum amount of product that can be obtained from any specified combination of inputs, given the current state of knowledge. That is, it shows the largest quantity of goods that any particular collection of inputs is capable of producing.

INPUT SUBSTITUTION ON THE RANGE

When fuel prices soared in the 1970s, newspapers carried a story about ranchers in the southwestern United States who were reportedly hiring additional cowhands to drive cattle on foot instead of carrying them on trucks. In other words, the rising price of oil had led ranchers to substitute the work of cowhands for the gasoline formerly used in driving cattle-carrying trucks. This is no scenario from a Wild West movie, but an illustration of the way in which life follows the analytical principles described in the text, substituting inputs whose relative prices have not risen for inputs whose relative prices have risen.

There are many other illustrations of this phenomenon. It helps to explain the disappearance, in half a century, of personal servants, who were once commonplace in the homes of middle-class families (in the 1920s, almost every such home had at least a full-time maid), and the substitution of washing machines, clothes dryers, and dishwashers as real wages rose. It also helps to account for the disappearance of wooden houses in England as forests disappeared and wood became increasingly expensive compared with other building materials. You can easily come up with other examples.

When there are only two inputs—which are enough to illustrate the basic principles involved—a production function can be represented graphically (which we do in the appendix to this chapter) or by a simple table. Table 6-6 indicates Farmer Pfister's production function for the use of two inputs, labour and fertilizer, to produce corn on his farm. To make the table easier to read, most of the numbers that normally would be entered (but that are irrelevant for our purposes) have been replaced by dashes.

The table is read like a city-to-city distance chart. So, to see how much can be produced with two tonnes of fertilizer and three months of labour, we locate the 2 in the column of numbers on the left, which indicates the quantity of fertilizer, and the 3 in the row of numbers across the top, which represents the quantity (in months) of labour. Then, in the spot horizontally to the right of the 2 and vertically below the 3, we find the number 1600, meaning that this input combination can produce 1600 bushels of output per month. Similarly, you should be able to verify that

TABLE 6-6

A PRODUCTION FUNCTION

		Quantity of Labour (months)				
	0	1	2	3	4	5
1		250	900	1400	1600	—
2		550	1250	1600	1800	—
3		900	1450	1750	—	—
4		1200	1600	—	2400	—
5		1450	2000	—	—	—
6		1600	—	—	3900	—
7		1650	—	—	—	—
8		1650	2700	3600	4400	5000
9		1600	—	—	—	—

Quantity of Fertilizer (tonnes) labels rows 1–9.

with eight tonnes of fertilizer and three months of labour, 3600 bushels per month can be produced.

The first column of Table 6-6, which corresponds to alternative amounts of fertilizer used in combination with one month of labour, is familiar to us already—it is just the total physical product schedule that we have been using for Farmer Pfister working alone with various amounts of fertilizer. The other columns represent alternative production arrangements in which Pfister hires one or more farmhands to help him.

How much labour and fertilizer should Farmer Pfister use if he wants to grow 1600 bushels of corn? The production-function table shows us that there are several alternatives available to him. He can, for example, work alone and use six tonnes of fertilizer. Or he can hire a second worker and use only four tonnes. The coloured entries in Table 6-6 indicate all the different ways in which Farmer Pfister can conceivably meet his 1600-bushel production target.

Which will he choose? Naturally, the one that costs him the least. Table 6-7 shows Farmer Pfister's cost calculations. It is assumed here that fertilizer costs $350 per tonne, that farm labour costs $500 per month, and that Pfister's sunk costs on such items as land and machinery amount to $800 per month. Thus, for example, the first line tells us that Pfister can produce 1600 bushels using only his own labour (which costs $500), six tonnes of fertilizer (which cost $2100), and land and machinery that cost $800 per month, for a total cost of $500 + $2100 + $800 = $3400. The other lines in Table 6-7 can be read the same way. We see that the cheapest way to produce 1600 bushels of corn is by using three months of labour and two tonnes of fertilizer, for a total cost of $3000, which is less than the cost of any other alternative.

Notice that two types of information are relevant to Farmer Pfister's decision. The *technological information* embodied in the production function tells Pfister all the possible ways that 1600 bushels can be produced; that is, it tells him about the possibilities for factor substitution.

TABLE 6-7

PRODUCTION COSTS UNDER ALTERNATIVE INPUT COMBINATIONS CAPABLE OF PRODUCING 1600 BUSHELS

Quantity of Labour (months)	Cost of Labour (at $500 per month)	Quantity of Fertilizer (tonnes)	Cost of Fertilizer (at $350 per tonne)	Fixed Costs (for land, machinery, etc.)	Total Cost
1	$ 500	6	$2100	$800	$3400
2	1000	4	1400	800	3200
3	1500	2	700	800	3000
4	2000	1	350	800	3150

Then, *financial information* — about the prices of the two inputs — is needed to tell him which alternative is the least costly. As we saw from our analysis in the preceding section, if either set of data changes, Farmer Pfister's decision on input combinations is likely to change as well. For example, if fertilizer gets much more expensive, he might switch to an alternative that uses more labour and less fertilizer. (*EXERCISE:* Suppose that fertilizer rises in price to $600 per tonne. Construct a new version of Table 6-7 and use it to show that it will be optimal to reduce fertilizer use from two tonnes to zero and to increase the use of labour from three months to five months.)

THE FIRM'S COST CURVES

Earlier, we calculated the firm's cost curves in the special case where the quantity of only one input—fertilizer—was selected by the firm. Now we can see how the cost curves can be determined in the more realistic case of choices about the quantities of several inputs.

In deciding on the quantity of output that serves its objectives best, the firm must consider alternative production levels and compare their costs. In the present example, an output of 1600 bushels is not likely to be the only possible production level that Farmer Pfister is considering. He might wonder, for example, about the least costly way to produce 1100 bushels or 2100 bushels.

By the same procedures as those outlined in Table 6-7, Farmer Pfister can compute the minimum cost of producing any quantity of output, using the logic of the requirement that, in such a cost-minimizing decision, the relative marginal physical products of any two inputs must equal their relative prices.

Let us suppose that Farmer Pfister has calculated the minimum total costs for alternative production levels displayed in Table 6-8. Here we have the numbers Pfister needs to plot three different points on his total-cost curve, which is the curve shown in Figure 6-7. Point *A* shows the $2700 total cost of 1200 bushels of output, point *B* shows the $3000 total cost of 1600 bushels, and point *C* shows the $3550 total cost of 2000 bushels. As before, by dividing the total cost for each output by the quantity of the output, we obtain the corresponding *average cost*; that is, the

TABLE 6-8
DATA FOR PFISTER'S TOTAL-COST CURVE

Output Level (bushels)	Total Cost (TC) (dollars)
1200	2700
1600	3000
2000	3550

cost per unit of output. For example, when output is 1600 bushels, total cost is $3000; so average cost is $3000/1600, or $1.88. Similarly, we can deduce the marginal-cost curve from the total-cost figures, just as we did before.

ECONOMIES OF SCALE

We are now beginning to put together the apparatus we need to address the question posed at the start of this chapter: How can we tell if a firm has substantial **economies of scale**? We are now in a position to give a definition of this concept.

Production is said to involve ECONOMIES OF SCALE, also referred to as INCREASING RETURNS TO SCALE, if, when all input quantities are doubled, the quantity of output is more than doubled.

FIGURE 6-7
TOTAL-COST CURVE

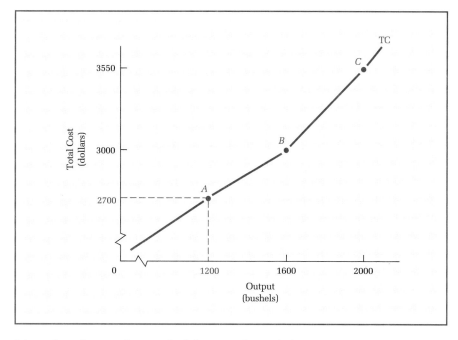

Point *A* shows that to produce 1200 bushels per month, a total of $2700 in cost must be incurred, just as Table 6-8 indicates.

The scale of operation of a business enterprise is defined by the quantities of the various inputs it uses. To see what happens when the firm doubles its scale of operations, we inquire about the effect on output of a doubling of each and every one of the firm's input quantities. As an example of economies of scale, turn back to the production function for Farmer Pfister in Table 6-6 (on page 181) and assume that labour and fertilizer are the only two inputs. (This assumption is necessary because the table deals with only two inputs and the definition requires that all inputs be doubled simultaneously. So, to be true to the definition, because labour, fertilizer, land, and machinery were all used by the farmer, their quantities would all have to be doubled.) Notice that with two months of labour and four tonnes of fertilizer, output is 1600 bushels. What happens if we double both inputs—to four months of labour and eight tonnes of fertilizer? The table shows us that output rises to 4400—that is, it more than doubles. Thus, Farmer Pfister's production function, at least in this range, is said to display **increasing returns to scale** (economies of scale).

Economies of scale seem to be present in many modern industries. Where they are present, they foster large firm size because then large firms have a cost advantage over small ones. Automobile production and telecommunications are examples commonly cited.

The reasons for the scale economies are technological—that is, the technical nature of an economic activity determines whether or not it is characterized by scale economies. Consider warehouse space as an example of one such type of technical relationship. Imagine that there are two warehouses, each shaped like a perfect cube, but that warehouse A has length, width, and height equal to 100 feet, while in warehouse B those dimensions are equal to 200 feet. Because the area of a square floor or a square wall is equal to the square of its length, the amount of land and building material (bricks, and so on) of warehouse B will be four times as great as that of warehouse A. However, since the area of a cube equals length times width times height—that is, its area equals the cube of its length—warehouse B will have $2^3 = 8$ times as much storage space as warehouse A. Thus, multiplying each input (roughly) by 4 yields 8 times the storage space. This example is, of course, oversimplified, and omits such complications as the need for stronger supports in taller buildings, the increased difficulty of moving goods in and out of higher storeys, and the like. Still, the basic idea is correct and shows why, up to a point, the very nature of warehousing creates technological relationships that lead to economies of scale.

We can relate our definition of economies of scale to the shape of the long-run average-cost curve instead of the production function. Notice that the definition requires a doubling of *every* input to bring about more than a doubling of output. If all input quantities are doubled, total cost must double. But if output more than doubles as a result, cost per unit (average cost) must decline.

Production functions with economies of scale lead to long-run average-cost curves that decline as output expands.

An example will clarify the arithmetic behind this rule. We saw earlier (Table 6-7) that it costs $3200 to produce 1600 bushels of corn with two months of labour and four tonnes of fertilizer. The average cost is thus

$2.00 per bushel. If, as the production function states, doubling all inputs (and thus doubling costs to $6400) leads to production of 4400 bushels, cost per unit will become $6400/4400, or approximately $1.45. Economies of scale in the production function thus lead to *decreasing* average cost as output expands; in this case, average cost decreases by 55¢—from $2.00 to $1.45.

A decreasing average-cost curve is depicted in Figure 6-8(a). But this is only one of three possible shapes the long-run average-cost curve can take. A second possibility is shown in part (b) of the figure. In this case, we have an example of **constant returns to scale**, where both total cost (TC) and quantity of output (Q) double, so average cost (AC = TC/Q) remains constant. Finally, it is possible that output less than doubles when all inputs double. This would be a case of **decreasing returns to scale**, which leads to a rising long-run average-cost curve like the one depicted in Figure 6-8(c). Thus, an association exists between the slope of the AC curve and the nature of the firm's return to scale; the correspondence is precise if the firm does find it efficient to carry out any changes in its output by means of proportionate changes in all of its inputs.

It should be pointed out that the same production function can display increasing returns to scale in some ranges, constant returns to scale in others, and decreasing returns to scale in yet others. Farmer Pfister's production function in Table 6-6 provides an illustration of this. We have already seen that it displays increasing returns to scale when inputs are doubled from two months of labour and four tonnes of fertilizer to four months of labour and eight tonnes of fertilizer. But, looking back at Table 6-6 (page 181), we can see that there are constant returns to scale when inputs double from two months of labour and one tonne of fertilizer (900 bushels of output) to four months of labour and two tonnes of fer-

FIGURE 6-8

THREE POSSIBLE SHAPES FOR THE LONG-RUN AVERAGE-COST CURVE

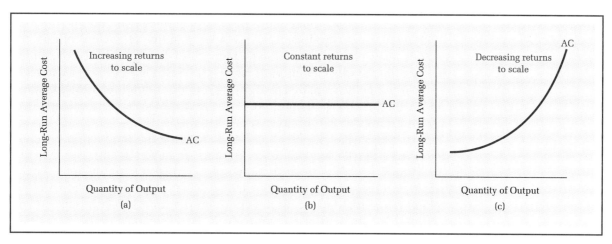

In part (a), long-run average costs are decreasing as output expands because the firm has significant economies of scale (increasing returns to scale). In part (b), constant returns to scale lead to a long-run AC curve that is flat; costs per unit are the same for any level of output. In part (c), which pertains to a firm with decreasing returns to scale, long-run average costs rise as output expands.

tilizer (1800 bushels). We can also find a region of decreasing returns to scale. Notice that with two months of labour and two tonnes of fertilizer, the yield is 1250 bushels, while with double those inputs—four months of labour and four tonnes of fertilizer—the yield is only 2400 bushels.

DIMINISHING RETURNS AND RETURNS TO SCALE

Earlier in this chapter, we discussed the "law" of diminishing marginal returns. Is there any relationship between economies of scale and the phenomenon of diminishing returns? It may seem at first that the two are contradictory. After all, if a producer gets diminishing returns from inputs as he or she uses more of each of them, doesn't it follow that by using more of every input, the producer cannot obtain economies of scale? The answer is that there is no contradiction, for the two principles deal with fundamentally different issues.

1. ***Returns to a single input.*** Here we must ask the question, How much can output expand if we increase the quantity of just *one* input, holding all other input quantities unchanged?

2. ***Returns to scale.*** Here the question is, How much can output expand if *all* inputs are increased simultaneously by the same percentage?

The law of diminishing returns provides an answer to the first question, while economies of scale pertain to the second.

Table 6-6 shows us that Farmer Pfister's production function satisfies the law of diminishing returns to a single input. To see this, we must hold the quantity of one input constant while letting the other vary. The row corresponding to eight tonnes of fertilizer will serve as an example, since an entry is provided for every quantity of labour. Reading across the row, we see from the second entry that the use of one month of labour and eight tonnes of fertilizer yields 1650 bushels of corn. The next entry shows that the same eight tonnes of fertilizer plus one additional month of labour produces a marginal product of 1050 bushels (that is, the total of 2700 bushels produced by the two months of labour minus the 1650 bushels obtained from the first month's labour). In the third column, we find that another month of labour (still holding fertilizer use at eight tonnes) brings in a smaller marginal product of 900 (3600 total bushels minus the 2700 bushels produced by the first two months' labour). The law of diminishing returns is clearly satisfied.

Returns to scale, on the other hand, describe the production response to a proportionate increase in *all* inputs. We have already seen that this production function displays increasing returns to scale in some ranges, constant returns to scale in others, and decreasing returns to scale in yet others. Thus, the law of diminishing returns (to a single input) is compatible with any sort of returns to scale. Let's summarize:

Returns to scale and returns to a single input (holding all other input quantities constant) refer to two distinct aspects of a firm's technology.

A production function that displays diminishing returns to a *single* input may show diminishing, constant, or increasing returns when *all* input quantities are increased proportionately.

HISTORICAL COSTS VERSUS ANALYTICAL COST CURVES

In the appendix to the previous chapter, we made much of the fact that all points on a demand curve pertain to the same period of time, and that a plot of historical data on prices and quantities is normally *not* the demand curve that the decision-maker needs. A similar point relating to cost curves will resolve the problem posed at the beginning of the chapter regarding whether declining historical costs are evidence of economies of scale.

All points on any of the cost curves used in economic analysis refer to the same period of time.

One point on the cost curve of an auto manufacturer tells us, for example, how much it costs to produce 2.5 million cars during 1994. Another point on the curve tells us what happens to the firm's costs if instead it produces, say, 3 million cars in 1994. Such a curve is called an **analytical cost curve** or, when there is no possibility of confusion, simply a **cost curve**. This curve must be distinguished from a diagram of **historical costs**, which shows how costs have changed from year to year.

The different points on an analytical cost curve represent alternative possibilities, all for the same time period. In 1994, the car manufacturer will produce either 2.5 or 3 million cars (or some other amount), but certainly not both. Thus, at most, only one point on this cost curve will ever be observed. The company may indeed produce 2.5 million in 1994 and 3 million in 1995, but the latter is not relevant to the 1994 cost curve. By the time 1995 comes around, the cost curve may well have shifted, so the 1994 cost figure will not apply to the 1995 cost curve. We can, of course, draw a different sort of graph that indicates, year by year, how costs and outputs have varied. Such a graph, which gathers the statistics for a number of different periods, is not, however, a *cost curve* as that term is used by economists. An example of such a diagram of historical costs was given at the beginning of the chapter in Figure 6-1.

But why do economists rarely use historical cost diagrams and instead deal primarily with analytical cost curves, which are much more difficult to explain and to obtain statistically? The answer is that analysis of real policy problems—such as the desirability of having a single supplier of telephone services—leaves no choice in the matter. Rational decisions require analytical cost curves. Let us see why.

RESOLVING THE ECONOMIES-OF-SCALE PUZZLE

Since the 1940s, there has been great technical progress in the telephone industry. From ordinary open wire, the industry has gone to microwave systems, telecommunications satellites, and coaxial cables of enormous capacity, and new techniques using laser beams are on the way. Innovations in switching techniques and in the use of computers to send messages along uncrowded routes are equally impressive. All of this means that the entire analytical cost curve of telecommunications must have shifted downward quite dramatically from year to year. Innovation must have reduced not only the cost of large-scale operations but also the cost of smaller-scale operations.

Now, if we are to determine whether in 1994 a single supplier can provide telephone service more cheaply than a number of smaller firms, we must compare the costs of both large- and small-scale production in 1994. It does no good to compare the cost of a large supplier in 1994 with its own costs as a smaller firm back in 1942, because that cannot possibly give us the information we need. The cost situation in 1942 is irrelevant for today's decision between large and small suppliers because no small firm today would use the obsolete techniques of 1942. Until we compare the costs of the large and small supplier *today*, we cannot make a rational choice between single-firm and multi-firm production. It is the analytical cost curve, all of whose points refer to the same period, that by definition supplies this information.

Figures 6-9 and 6-10 show two extreme hypothetical cases, one in which economies of scale are present and one in which they are not. Yet both of them are based on the same historical cost data (in blue) with their very sharply declining costs. (This curve is reproduced from Figure 6-1.) They also show (in red) two possible average-cost curves, one for 1942 and one for 1994. In Figure 6-9, the analytical AC curve has shifted

FIGURE 6-9

DECLINING HISTORICAL COST CURVE WITH THE ANALYTICAL AVERAGE-COST CURVE ALSO DECLINING IN EACH YEAR

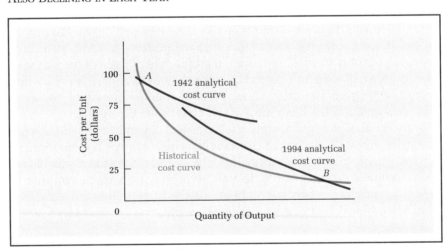

The two analytical cost curves shown indicate how the corresponding points (*A* and *B*) on the historical cost curve are generated by that year's analytical curve. The analytical cost curves are declining, so we know that there are economies of scale in the production activity whose costs are shown.

FIGURE 6-10

DECLINING HISTORICAL COST CURVE WITH U-SHAPED ANALYTICAL COST CURVES IN EACH YEAR

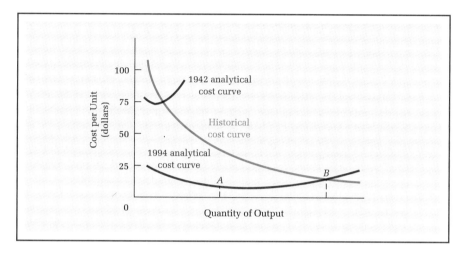

Here, the shape of the analytical average-cost curves does not show economies of scale.

downward very sharply from 1942 to 1994, as technological change has reduced all costs. Moreover, both of the AC curves slope downward to the right, meaning that, in either year, the larger the firm the lower its average costs. Thus, the situation shown in Figure 6-9 really does represent a case in which there are economies of large-scale production so that one firm can produce at lower cost than many.

But now look at Figure 6-10, which shows exactly the same historical costs as Figure 6-9. Here, both analytical AC curves are U-shaped. In particular, we note that the 1994 AC curve has its minimum point at an output level, *A*, that is less than one-half the current output, *B*, of the large supplier. This means that in the situation shown in Figure 6-10, despite the sharp downward trend of historical costs, a smaller company can produce more cheaply than a large one. In this case, one cannot justify domination of the market by a single large firm on the grounds that its costs are lower. In sum, the behaviour of historical costs tells us nothing about the cost advantages or disadvantages of a single large firm.

Because a diagram of historical costs does not compare the costs of large and small firms at the same point in time, it cannot be used to determine whether there are economies of large-scale production. Only the analytical cost curve can supply this information.

COST MINIMIZATION IN THEORY AND PRACTICE

Lest you be tempted to run out and open a business, confident that you now understand how to minimize costs, we should point out that decision making in business is a good deal harder than we have indicated here. Most business executives do not know for sure what their production function looks like, or the exact shapes of their marginal revenue product schedules, or the precise nature of their cost curves. No one can provide a cookbook for instant success in business. What we have presented here is a set of principles that constitutes a guide to good decision making.

Business management has been described as the art of making critical decisions on the basis of inadequate information, and in our complex and ever-changing world, there is often no alternative to an educated guess. Actual business decisions will at best approximate the cost-minimizing ideal outlined in this chapter. Certainly, there will be mistakes. But when management does its job well and the market system functions smoothly, the approximation may prove amazingly good. While no system is perfect, inducing firms to produce at the lowest possible cost is undoubtedly one of the jobs the market system does best.

SUMMARY

1. A firm's total-cost (TC) curve shows the lowest possible cost for producing any given level of output. It is derived from the input combination used to produce any given output and the prices of the inputs.

2. A firm's average-cost (AC) curve shows the lowest possible cost per unit at which it is possible to produce any given level of output. It is derived from the TC curve by simple arithmetic: AC = TC/Q.

3. A firm's marginal-cost (MC) curve shows for each output level the increase in total cost resulting from a one-unit increase in output.

4. The long run is a period sufficiently long for the firm's plant to require replacement and for all of its current contractual commitments to expire. The short run is any period briefer than that.

5. Fixed costs are costs whose total amounts do not vary when output increases. All other costs are called *variable*. In the short run, fixed costs are *sunk*.

6. At all outputs, the total-fixed-cost (TFC) curve is horizontal, and the average-fixed-cost (AFC) curve declines toward the horizontal axis but never crosses it.

7.
$$TC = TFC + TVC$$
$$AC = AFC + AVC$$
$$MC = \frac{\Delta TC}{\Delta Q} = \frac{\Delta TVC}{\Delta Q}$$

8. It is normally possible to produce the same quantity of output in a variety of ways by substituting more of one input for less of another. Firms normally seek the least costly way to produce any given output.

9. The marginal physical product of an input is the increase in total output resulting from a one-unit increase in the use of that input, holding the quantities of all other inputs constant.

10. The "law" of diminishing marginal returns states that if we increase the amount of one input (holding all other input quantities constant), the marginal physical product of the expanding input will eventually begin to decline.

11. Profit maximization requires the firm to purchase that quantity of any input at which the

input's marginal revenue product is equal to its price.

12. A firm that wants to minimize costs will use those quantities of any two inputs at which the ratio of their marginal physical products is equal to the ratio of the prices of those two inputs.

13. The production function shows the relationship between inputs and output. It indicates the maximum quantity of output obtainable from any given combination of inputs.

14. If a doubling of all of a firm's inputs *just* permits it to double its output, the firm is said to have constant returns to scale. If with doubled inputs it can *more than* double its output, it has increasing returns to scale (or economies of scale). If a doubling of inputs produces *less than* double the output, the firm has decreasing returns to scale.

15. With increasing returns to scale, the firm's long-run average costs are decreasing; constant returns to scale are associated with constant long-run average costs.

16. We cannot tell if there are economies of scale (increasing returns to scale) simply by inspecting a diagram of historical cost data. Only the underlying analytical cost curve can supply this information.

CONCEPTS FOR REVIEW

Total physical product (TPP)
Average physical product (APP)
Marginal physical product (MPP)
"Law" of diminishing marginal returns
Marginal revenue product (MRP)

Rule for optimal input use
Total-cost (TC) curve
Average-cost (AC) curve
Marginal-cost (MC) curve
Fixed cost
Variable cost
Sunk cost
Short and long runs
Substitutability of inputs

Production function
Economies of scale (increasing returns to scale)
Constant returns to scale
Decreasing returns to scale
Historical versus analytical cost relationships

QUESTIONS FOR DISCUSSION

1. A firm's total fixed cost is $44 000. Construct a table of total and average fixed costs for this firm for output levels varying from 0 to 6 units. Draw the corresponding TFC and AFC curves.

2. With the data in the accompanying table, calculate the firm's AVC and MVC and draw the graphs for TVC, AVC, and MVC.

Quantity	Total Variable Costs (thousands of dollars)
1	40
2	80
3	120
4	176
5	240
6	360

3. From the figures in Questions 1 and 2, calculate TC, AC, and MC for each of the output levels from 1 to 6, and draw the three graphs.

4. If a firm's commitments in 1994 include machinery that will need replacement in five years, a factory building rented for ten years, and a two-year union contract specifying how many workers it must employ, when, from its point of view in 1994, does the firm's long run begin?

5. If the marginal revenue product of a kilowatt hour of electric power is 8 cents and the cost of a kilowatt hour is 12 cents, what can a firm do to increase its profits?

6. A firm hires two workers and rents fifteen hectares of land for a season. It produces 150 000 bushels of crop. If it had doubled its land and labour, production would have been 280 000 bushels. Does it have constant, diminishing, or increasing returns to scale?

7. Suppose wages are $25 000 per season and land rent per hectare is $4000. Calculate the average cost of 150 000 bushels and the average cost of 280 000 bushels, using the figures in Question 6. (Note that average costs diminish when output increases.) What connection do these figures have with the firm's returns to scale?

8. Farmer Pfister has bought a great deal of fertilizer. Suppose he now buys more land, but not more fertilizer, and spreads the fertilizer evenly over all his land. What may happen to the marginal physical product of fertilizer? What is the role of input proportions in the determination of marginal physical product?

9. Labour costs $10 per hour. Nine workers produce 180 bushels of product per hour. Ten workers produce 196 bushels. Land rents for $1000 per hectare per year. With ten hectares worked by nine workers, the marginal physical product of a hectare of land is 1400 bushels per year. Does the farmer minimize costs by hiring nine workers and renting ten hectares of land? If not, which input should he use in larger relative quantity?

10. A firm finds there is a sudden increase in the demand for its product. In the short run, it must operate longer hours and pay higher overtime wage rates. In the long run, however, the firm will profit by installing more machines and operating them for shorter hours. Which do you think will be lower, the short-run or the long-run average cost of the increased output? How is your answer affected by the fact that the long-run average cost includes the new machines the firm buys, while the short-run average cost includes no machine purchases?

APPENDIX TO CHAPTER 6

A GRAPHIC ANALYSIS OF INPUT DECISIONS

To describe a production function—that is, the relationship between input combinations and size of total output — we can use a graphic device called an **isoquant** instead of the sort of numerical information described in Table 6-6 in the chapter.

An *isoquant* is a curve in a graph showing quantities of inputs on its axes. Each isoquant indicates *all* combinations of input quantities capable of producing a given quantity of output efficiently; thus, there must be a separate isoquant for each quantity of output.

If you have read the final sections of Chapter 4 on indifference curves and consumer choice, you will recognize a close analogy in logic (and in geometric shape) between consumers' indifference curves and producers' isoquants. Figure 6-11 represents different quantities of labour and land capable of producing given amounts of wheat. The isoquant labelled 220 000 bushels indicates that an output of 220 000 bushels of wheat can be obtained with the aid of *any one* of the combinations of inputs represented by points on the curve. For example, it can be produced by 10 years of labour and 200 hectares of land (point *A*) or, instead, it can be produced by the labour–land combination shown by point *B* on the same curve. Because point *A* lies considerably below and to the right of point *B*, it represents a productive process that uses more labour and less land than shown at point *B*.

The isoquants in a diagram such as Figure 6-11 constitute a complete description of the

production function. For each combination of inputs, they show how much output can be produced. Since the diagram is drawn in two dimensions, it can deal with only two inputs at a time. In more realistic situations, there may be more than two inputs, in which case an algebraic analysis must be used. But all the principles we need to analyze such a situation can be derived from the two-variable case.

FIGURE 6-11

AN ISOQUANT MAP

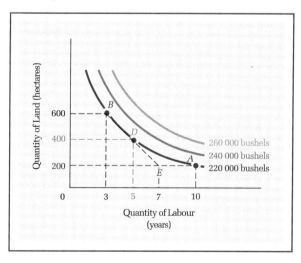

The figure shows three isoquants, one for the production of 220 000 bushels of wheat, one for 240 000 bushels, and one for 260 000 bushels. For example, the lowest curve shows all combinations of land and labour capable of producing 220 000 bushels of wheat. Point *A* on that curve shows that 10 years of labour and 200 hectares of land are enough to do the job.

CHARACTERISTICS OF ISOQUANTS

Before discussing input pricing and quantity decisions, we first examine what is known about the shapes of isoquants. The main characteristics are straightforward and entirely analogous to the properties of consumer-indifference curves discussed in Chapter 4.

Characteristic 1: Higher curves correspond to larger outputs. Points on a higher isoquant represent larger quantities of *both* inputs than the corresponding points on a lower curve. Thus, the higher the curve, the larger the output it represents.

Characteristic 2: The isoquant will generally have a negative slope. It goes downhill as we move toward the right. This means that if we reduce the quantity of one input used and we do not want to cut production, we must use more of another input. For example, if we want to use less land to produce 220 000 bushels of wheat, we will have to hire more labour to make up for the reduced land input.

Characteristic 3: The curves are typically assumed to curve inward toward the origin near their "middle." This is a reflection of the law of diminishing returns to a single input. For example, in Figure 6-11, points *B*, *D*, and *A* represent three different input combinations capable of producing the same quantity of output. At point *B*, a large amount of land and relatively little labour is used, while the opposite is true at point *A*. Point *D* falls between the two. Indeed, point *D* is chosen so that its use of land is exactly halfway between the amounts of land used at *A* and *B*.

Now consider the choice among these input combinations. As the farmer considers first the input combination at *B*, then the one at *D*, and finally the one at *A*, he is considering the use of less and less land, making up for it by the use of more and more labour so that he can continue to produce the same output. But the trade-off does not proceed at a constant rate because of diminishing returns in the substitution of labour for land.

When the farmer considers moving from point *B* to point *D*, he gives up 200 hectares of land and instead hires two additional years of labour. Similarly, the move from *D* to *A* involves giving up another 200 hectares of land. But this time, hiring an additional two years of labour does not make up for the reduced use of land. Diminishing returns to labour as he hires more and more workers to replace more and more land mean that now a much larger quantity of additional labour, five years rather than two, is needed to make up for the reduction in the use of land. If there had been no such diminishing returns, the isoquant would have been a straight line, *DE*. The curvature of the isoquant through points *D* and *A* reflects diminishing returns to substitution of inputs.

THE CHOICE OF INPUT COMBINATIONS

An isoquant describes only what input combinations *can* produce a given output; it indicates the technological possibilities. A business cannot decide which of the available options suits its purposes best without the corresponding cost information, that is, the relative prices of the inputs.

Just as we did for the consumer in Chapter 4, we can construct a **budget line** — a representation of equally costly input combinations — for the firm. For example, if farmhands are paid $9000 a year and land rents for $1000 per hectare a year, then a farmer who spends $360 000 can hire 40 farmhands but rent no land (point *K* in Figure 6-12), or he can rent 360 hectares but have no money left for farmhands (point *J*). But it is undoubtedly more sensible for him to pick some intermediate point on his budget line, *JK*, at which he divides the $360 000 between the two inputs.

There is an important difference, however, in how this budget line is used. The consumer had

FIGURE 6-12

A BUDGET LINE

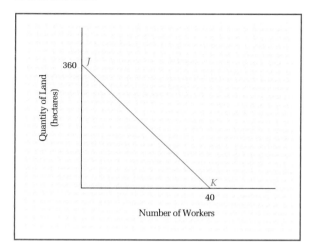

The firm's budget line, *JK*, shows all the combinations of inputs it can purchase with a fixed amount of money—in this case, $360 000.

a fixed budget and sought the highest indifference curve attainable with these limited funds. The firm's problem in minimizing costs is just the reverse. Its budget is not fixed. Instead, it wants to produce a given quantity of output (say, 240 000 bushels) with the smallest possible budget.

A way to find the minimum budget capable of producing 240 000 bushels of wheat is illustrated in Figure 6-13, which combines the isoquant for 240 000 bushels from Figure 6-11 with a variety of budget lines similar to *JK* in Figure 6-12. The firm's problem is to find the lowest budget line that will allow it to reach the 240 000-bushel isoquant. Clearly, an expenditure of $270 000 is too little; there is no point on budget line *AB* that permits production of 240 000 bushels. Similarly, an expenditure of $450 000 is too much, because the firm can produce its target level of output more cheaply. The solution is at point *T*, meaning that 15 workers and 225 hectares of land are used to produce the 240 000 bushels of wheat.

The least costly way to produce any given level of output is indicated by the point of tangency between a budget line and the isoquant corresponding to that level of output.

COST MINIMIZATION, EXPANSION PATH, AND COST CURVES

Figure 6-13 shows how to determine the input combination that minimizes the cost of producing 240 000 bushels of output. We can repeat this procedure exactly for any other output quantity, such as 200 000 bushels or 300 000 bushels. In each case, we draw the corresponding isoquant and find the lowest budget line that permits it to be produced. For example, in Figure 6-14, budget line *BB* is tangent to the isoquant for 200 000 units of output and budget line *B'B'* is tangent to the isoquant for 300 000 units of output. In this way, we obtain three tangency points: *S*, which gives us the input combination that produces a 200 000-bushel output at lowest cost; *T*, which gives the same information for a 240 000-bushel output; and *S'*, which indicates the cost-minimizing input combination for the production of 300 000 bushels.

FIGURE 6-13

COST MINIMIZATION

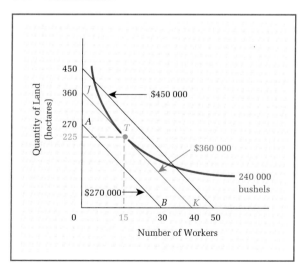

The least costly way to produce 240 000 bushels of wheat is shown by point *T*, where the isoquant is tangent to budget line *JK*. Here the farmer is employing 15 workers and using 225 hectares of land. It is not possible to produce 240 000 bushels on a smaller budget, and any larger budget would be wasteful.

FIGURE 6-14
THE FIRM'S EXPANSION PATH

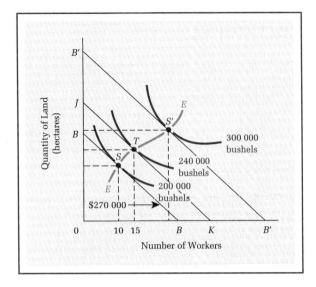

Each point of tangency, such as *S*, between an isoquant and a budget line shows the combination of inputs that can produce the output corresponding to that isoquant at lowest cost. The locus of all such tangency points is *EE*, the firm's expansion path.

see that output is 200 000 units and total cost is $270 000.

This is precisely the sort of information we need to find the firm's total-cost curve; that is, it is just the sort of information contained in Table 6-4, from which we first calculated the total-cost curve and then the average- and marginal-cost curves in Figure 6-4. Thus, we see the following:

The **points of tangency** between a firm's isoquants and its budget lines yield its expansion path. The expansion path shows the firm's cost-minimizing input combination for each pertinent output level. This information also yields the output and total cost for each point on the expansion path, which is just what we need to draw the firm's cost curves.

EFFECTS OF CHANGES IN INPUT PRICES

Suppose now that the cost of renting land increases and the wage rate of labour decreases. This means that the budget lines will differ from those depicted in Figure 6-13. Specifically, with land now more expensive, any given sum of money will rent fewer hectares, so the intercept of each budget line on the vertical (land) axis will shift downward. Conversely, with labour cheaper, any given sum of money will buy more labour, so the intercept of the budget line on the horizontal (labour) axis will shift to the right. A series of budget lines corresponding to a rental rate of $1500 per hectare for land and a $6000 annual wage for labour is depicted in Figure 6-15. We see that these budget lines are less steep than those shown in Figure 6-13 and that the least costly way to produce 240 000 bushels of wheat is now given by point *E*.

To assist you in seeing how things change, Figure 6-16 combines in a single graph budget line *JK* and tangency point *T* from Figure 6-13 and budget line *WV* and tangency point *E* from Figure 6-15. Notice that point *E* lies below and to the right of *T*, meaning that as wages decrease and rents increase, the firm will hire more

This process can be repeated for as many other levels of output as we like. For each such output, we draw the corresponding isoquant and find its point of tangency with a budget line. That tangency point will show the input combination that produces the output in question at lowest cost.

Curve *EE* in Figure 6-14 connects all these cost-minimizing points; that is, it is the locus of *S*, *T*, and *S'*, and all the other points of tangency between an isoquant and a budget line. Curve *EE* is called the firm's **expansion path**, which is defined as the locus of the firm's cost-minimizing input combinations for all relevant output levels.

In Figure 6-13, we were able to determine for tangency point *T* the quantity of output (from the isoquant through that point) and the total cost (from the tangent budget line). Similarly, once the data concerning the output level that corresponds to each isoquant are added to the diagram, we can determine the output and total cost for every other point on the expansion path, *EE*, in Figure 6-14. For example, at point *S*, we

FIGURE 6-15

OPTIMAL INPUT CHOICE AT A DIFFERENT SET OF INPUT PRICES

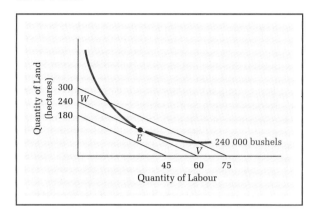

If input prices change, the combination of inputs that minimizes costs will normally change too. In this diagram, land rents for $1500 per hectare (more than in Figure 6-13) while labour costs $6000 per year (less than in Figure 6-13). As a result, the least costly way to produce 240 000 bushels of wheat shifts from point *T* in Figure 6-13 to point *E* here.

labour and rent less land. As common sense suggests, when the price of one input rises in comparison with that of others, it will pay the firm to hire less of this input and more of other inputs to make up for its reduced use of the more expensive input.

FIGURE 6-16

HOW CHANGES IN INPUT PRICES AFFECT INPUT PROPORTIONS

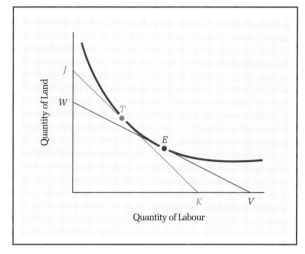

When land becomes more expensive and labour becomes cheaper, the budget lines (such as *JK*) become less steep than they were previously (see *WV*). As a result, the least costly way to produce 240 000 bushels shifts from point *T* to point *E*. The firm uses more labour and less land.

In addition to this substitution of one input for another, a change in the price of an input may induce the firm to alter the level of output that it decides to produce. But this is the subject of the next chapter.

SUMMARY

1. A production function can be fully described by a family of isoquants, each of which shows all the input combinations capable of producing a specified amount of output.

2. As long as each input has a positive marginal physical product, isoquants will have a negative slope and the higher curves will represent larger amounts of output than the lower curves. Because of diminishing returns, these curves characteristically bend toward the origin near their middle.

3. The optimal input combination for any given level of output is indicated by the point of tangency between a budget line and the appropriate isoquant.

4. A firm's expansion path shows, for each of the firm's possible output levels, the combination of input quantities that minimizes the cost of producing that output.

5. From the isoquants and the budget lines tangent to them along the expansion path, one can find the total cost for each output level.

From these figures, one can determine a firm's total-cost, average-cost, and marginal-cost curves.

6. When input prices change, firms will normally use more of the input that becomes relatively less expensive and less of the input that becomes relatively more expensive.

CONCEPTS FOR REVIEW

Isoquant
Budget line

Expansion path

Point of tangency between
   budget line and
   corresponding isoquant

QUESTIONS FOR DISCUSSION

---

1. Typical Manufacturing Corporation (TMC) produces gadgets with the aid of two inputs: labour and glue. If labour costs $5 per hour and glue costs $5 per litre, draw TMC's budget line for a total expenditure of $100 000. In this same diagram, sketch an isoquant indicating that TMC can produce no more than 1000 gadgets with this expenditure.

2. With respect to Question 1, suppose that wages rise to $10 per hour and glue prices rise to $6 per litre. How are TMC's optimal input proportions likely to change? (Use a diagram to explain your answer.)

3. What happens to the expansion path of the firm in Question 2?

OUTPUT–PRICE DECISIONS AND MARGINAL ANALYSIS

When computer companies introduce ever more powerful notebook computers, they have to decide on the price at which each model should be offered and the number of each to produce. These are clearly among the most crucial decisions a firm makes. These decisions have a vital influence on its labour requirements, on the reception given the product by consumers, and, indeed, on the very survival of the company.

This chapter describes the tools that firms can use to make decisions on outputs and prices—tools that are equally useful to government agencies and non-profit organizations in making analogous decisions. We begin the chapter by examining the relationship between a firm's price decisions and the quantity of product it sells. We then discuss the assumption of profit maximization before turning to the techniques firms can use to achieve the largest possible profit. We will explore—in words, with numerical examples, and with graphs—several methods of finding the level of output that maximizes profits. Each of these methods teaches us something about the nature of the firm's decision-making process and provides some general lessons about the use of marginal analysis. The analysis will also yield two conclusions that may be somewhat surprising and show that unaided common sense can sometimes be misleading in business decisions. Specifically, we will show that a change in fixed costs does not change the levels of price and output that maximize a firm's profits and that it may be possible for a firm to make a profit by increasing the amount it sells at a price that is, apparently, below cost.

Annual income twenty pounds, annual expenditure nineteen nineteen six, result happiness. Annual income twenty pounds, annual expenditure twenty pounds ought and six, result misery.

CHARLES DICKENS

TWO ILLUSTRATIVE CASES[1]

Price and output decisions can perplex even the most experienced business people, as the following real-life illustrations show. At the end of

---

1. The figures in these examples are doctored to help preserve the confidentiality of the information and to simplify the calculations. The cases, however, are real.

the chapter, we will see how the tools described in it helped in solving the problems.

CASE 1: PRICING A SIX-PACK

The managers of one of America's largest manufacturers of soft drinks became concerned when a rival company introduced a cheaper substitute for one of its leading products. As a result, some of the firm's managers advocated a reduction in the price of a six-pack from $1.50 to $1.35. This stimulated a heated debate. It was agreed that the price should be cut if doing so was not likely to reduce the company's profits. Although some of the managers maintained that the cut made sense because of the demand it would stimulate, others held that the price cut would hurt the company by cutting profit per unit of output. The company had reliable information about costs but knew little about its consumers' responsiveness to price changes. At this point, consultants were called in to offer their suggestions. We will see how economic analysis enabled them to solve the problem even though the vital demand elasticity figures were unavailable.

CASE 2: MAKING PROFITS BY SELLING BELOW COSTS

In a recent legal battle between two manufacturers of pocket calculators, which we will call Company A and Company B, the latter accused the former of selling 10 million sophisticated calculators at a price of $12.00, "which [A] knew was too low to cover its costs." B claimed that A was doing this "only to drive [B] out of the business." Company A's records, which were revealed to the court, appeared at first glance to confirm B's accusation. The cost of materials, labour, fuel, direct advertising of the calculator during the dispute, and other such direct costs came to $10.30 per calculator. Company A's accountants also assigned to this product its share of the company's annual expenditure on administration, research, advertising, and the like (which were referred to collectively as "overhead")—a total of $4.25 per calculator. The $12.00 price clearly did not cover the $14.55 cost attributed to each calculator sold. Yet, economists representing Company A were able to convince the court that manufacture of the calculator was a profitable activity for Company A, so that there was no basis on which to conclude that its only purpose was to destroy B. At the end of the chapter, we will explain just how this was possible.

PRICE AND QUANTITY: ONE DECISION, NOT TWO

This chapter is about how firms, like those in the preceding cases, select a *price* and a *quantity* of output that best serve their financial interests. While it would seem that firms must choose two numbers, in fact they can pick only one. Once they have selected the price, the quantity they will sell is up to consumers. Alternatively, firms may decide how much they want to sell, but then they must leave it to the market to determine the price at which this quantity can be sold.

Management gets its two numbers by making only one decision because the firm's demand curve tells it, for any quantity it may decide to market, the highest possible price its product can fetch. For purposes of illustration, consider a hypothetical firm, Computron, Inc., which produces giant computers. Computron's demand curve, *DD* in Figure 7-1, shows that if the company decides to charge the relatively high price of $15 million per computer (point *a* on the curve), it can sell only one unit per year. On the other hand, if it wants to sell as many as six computers per year, it can do so only by offering its product at the low price of $8 million (point *f*).

Each point on the demand curve represents a price–quantity pair. The firm can pick any such pair. But it can never pick the price corresponding to one point on the demand curve and the quantity corresponding to another point, since such an output would never be sold at the selected price.

Throughout this chapter, then, we will not discuss price and output decisions separately, for they are merely two different aspects of the same decision. To analyze this decision, we will make a strong assumption about the behaviour of business firms, which, while not literally correct,

FIGURE 7-1

<small>COMPUTRON'S DEMAND CURVE</small>

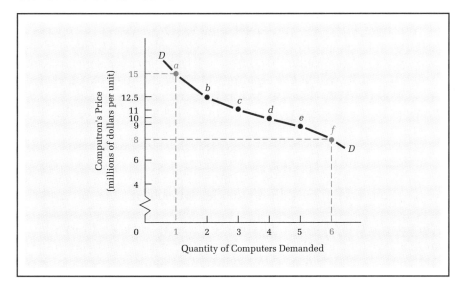

This graph shows the quantity of product demanded at each price. For example, the curve shows that at a price of $8 million (point *f*), 6 units will be demanded.

seems to be a useful simplification of a much more complex reality—the assumption that firms strive for the largest possible total profit.

DO FIRMS REALLY MAXIMIZE PROFITS?

Naturally, many people have questioned whether firms really try to maximize profits, to the exclusion of all other goals. Business people are like other human beings: Their motives are varied and complex. Given the choice, many executives might prefer to control the largest firm rather than the most profitable one. Some may be influenced by envy, others by a desire to "do good." Different managers within the same firm may not always agree with one another. Thus, any attempt to summarize a firm's objectives in terms of a single number (profit) is bound to be an oversimplification.

In addition, the exacting requirements for maximizing profits are tough to satisfy. In practice, the required calculations are rarely carried out fully. In deciding on how much to invest, on what price to set for a product, or on how much to allocate to the advertising budget, the firm's managers face an enormous range of available alternatives. Further, information about each alternative is often expensive and difficult to acquire. As a result, when a firm's management decides on an $18 million construction budget, it rarely compares the consequences of that decision in any detail with the consequences of all the possible alternatives—such as budgets of $17 million or $19 million. But unless all the available possibilities are compared, there is no way management can be sure it has chosen the one that will generate the highest possible profits.

Often management studies with care only the likely effects of the proposed decision itself: What sort of plant will it obtain for the money? How costly will it be to operate the plant? How much revenue is it likely to obtain from the sale of the plant's output? Management's concern is whether the decision will produce results that satisfy the firm's standard of acceptability — whether its risks will not be unacceptably great, whether its profits will not be unacceptably low, and so on. Such analysis does not necessarily lead to the maximum possible profit because, although the decision may be good, some of the alternatives that have not been investigated may be better.

Decision making that seeks only acceptable solutions has been called **satisficing** to contrast with optimizing. Some analysts, such as Carnegie-Mellon University's Nobel Prize winner Herbert Simon, have concluded that decision making in industry and government is often of the satisficing variety.

But even if this is true, it does not necessarily make profit maximization a bad assumption. Recall our discussion of abstraction and model-building in Chapter 1. A map of Montreal that omits thousands of roads is no doubt "wrong" if interpreted as a literal description of the city. Nonetheless, by capturing the most important elements of reality, it may help us understand the city better than a map that is cluttered with too much detail. Similarly, we can learn much about the behaviour of business firms by assuming that they try to maximize profits, even though we know that all of them do not act this way all of the time.

We will therefore assume throughout this and the next few chapters that a firm has only one objective: It wants to make its total profit as large as possible. Our analytic strategy will be to determine what output level (or price) achieves this goal.

TOTAL PROFIT: KEEP YOUR EYE ON THE GOAL

Total profit, then, is assumed to be the goal of profit-maximizing firms. It is, by definition, the difference between what a firm earns in the form of sales revenue and what it pays out in the form of costs:

$$\text{Total profit} = \text{Total revenue} - \text{Total costs}$$

Total profit defined in this way is called **economic profit**, to distinguish it from the accountant's definition of profit. The two concepts of profit differ because total cost, in the economist's definition, includes the opportunity cost of any capital, labour, or other inputs supplied by the owner of the firm. Thus, if a small business earns just enough to pay the owner the normal fee for her labour and the use of her capital—say, $50 000 a year—and not a penny more, an economist will say she is earning zero economic profit (she is just covering all her costs) while most accountants will say her profit is $50 000.

To analyze how total profit depends on output, we must study the behaviour of total profit's two components: **total revenue (TR)** and **total cost (TC)**. We know from preceding chapters that both total revenue and total cost depend on the output–price combination the firm selects.

Total revenue can be calculated directly from the demand curve, since by definition it is the product of price times the quantity that will be bought at that price:

$$\text{TR} = P \times Q$$

Table 7-1 shows how the total-revenue schedule is derived from the demand schedule for our illustrative firm, Computron. The first two columns simply express the demand curve of Figure 7-1 in tabular form. The third column gives, for each quantity, the product of price times quantity. For example, if Computron markets 3 computers per year at a price of $11 million per computer, its annual sales revenue will be 3 × $11 million = $33 million.

Figure 7-2 displays Computron's total-revenue schedule in graphical form as the red TR curve. This graph shows precisely the same information as the demand curve in Figure 7-1, but in a somewhat different form. For example, point d on the demand curve in Figure 7-1, which shows a price–quantity combination of $P = $10 million and $Q = 4$ computers, appears as point D in Figure 7-2 as a total revenue of $40 million

TABLE 7-1

DEMAND SCHEDULE AND TOTAL- AND MARGINAL-REVENUE SCHEDULES FOR COMPUTRON, INC.

Number of Computers (per year)	Price = Average Revenue (millions of dollars per computer)	Total Revenue (millions of dollars per year)	Marginal Revenue (millions of dollars per computer)
0	—	0	—
1	15	15	15
2	12.5	25	10
3	11	33	8
4	10	40	7
5	9	45	5
6	8	48	3

($10 million price per unit times 4 units) corresponding to a quantity of 4 computers. Similarly, each point on the TR curve in Figure 7-2 corresponds to the similarly labelled point in Figure 7-1.

The relationship between the demand curve and the TR curve can be rephrased in a slightly different way. Since the price of the product is the revenue *per unit* that the firm receives, we can view the demand curve as the curve of **average revenue**. Average revenue (AR) and total revenue (TR) are related to one another in the same way as average cost and total cost. (See the appendix to this chapter for a general discussion of the relationship between totals and averages.) Specifically, since

AVERAGE REVENUE (AR) is total revenue (TR) divided by quantity.

FIGURE 7-2

COMPUTRON'S TOTAL-REVENUE CURVE

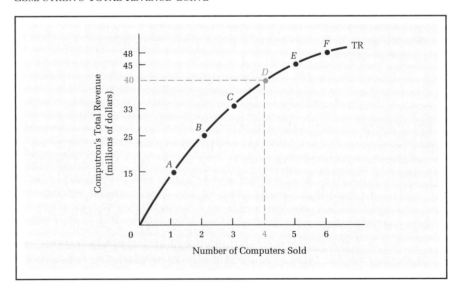

The total-revenue curve for Computron, Inc., is derived directly from the demand curve, since total revenue is the product of price times quantity. Points *A, B, C, D, E,* and *F* in this diagram correspond to points *a, b, c, d, e,* and *f*, respectively, in Figure 7-1.

$$AR = \frac{TR}{Q} = \frac{P \times Q}{Q} = P$$

average revenue and price are two names for the same thing.

Finally, the last column of Table 7-1 shows the **marginal revenue** for each level of output, that is, the addition to total revenue resulting from the addition of 1 unit to total output. Its definition and calculation are precisely analogous to those of marginal cost, which were described at length in Chapter 6 (pages 168–69). Thus, in Table 7-1, we see that when output rises from 2 to 3 units, total revenue goes up from \$25 million to \$33 million, so that marginal revenue is \$33 million − \$25 million = \$8 million.

The revenue side is, of course, only half of the profit picture. We must turn to the cost side for the other half. The last chapter explained how the total-cost (TC), average-cost (AC), and marginal-cost (MC) schedules are determined by the firm's production techniques and the prices of the inputs it buys. Rather than repeat this analysis, we simply list the total-, average-, and marginal-cost schedules for Computron in Table 7-2. Figure 7-3 depicts the total-cost curve as the red TC curve.

Notice that total costs at zero output are not zero, because Computron incurs **fixed costs** of \$2 million per year even if it produces nothing. For example, Computron will have to pay the rent for its factory and the salary of its president whether it produces 1 computer, 5 computers, or 10 computers.

To study how total profit depends on output, we bring together in Table 7-3 (on page 206) the total-revenue and total-cost schedules. The last column in Table 7-3, total profit, is just the difference between total revenue and total cost for each level of output. Remembering that Computron's assumed objective is to maximize profits, it is a simple matter to determine the level of production it will choose. By producing and selling 3 computers per year, Computron achieves the highest level of profits it is capable of achieving—some \$12 million per year. Any higher or lower rate of production would lead to lower profits. For example, profits would drop to \$8 million if output were expanded to 4 units.

MARGINAL REVENUE, often abbreviated MR, is the addition to total revenue resulting from the addition of one more unit to total output. Geometrically, marginal revenue is the slope of the total-revenue curve. The formula is $MR = \Delta TR / \Delta Q$.

TABLE 7-2

TOTAL, AVERAGE, AND MARGINAL COSTS FOR COMPUTRON, INC.

Number of Computers (per year)	Total Cost (millions of dollars)	Marginal Cost (millions of dollars per computer)	Average Cost (millions of dollars per computer)
0	2		—
1	9	7	9
2	14	5	7
3	21	7	7
4	32	11	8
5	45	13	9
6	60	15	10

FIGURE 7-3

COMPUTRON'S TOTAL-COST CURVE

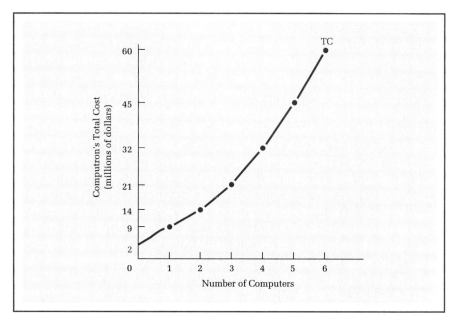

The graph shows, for each possible level of output, Computron's total costs. Because Computron has some fixed costs, the level of total cost at zero output is $2 million, not zero.

PROFIT MAXIMIZATION: A GRAPHICAL INTERPRETATION

Precisely the same analysis can be presented graphically. In Figure 7-4, we bring together into a single diagram the total-revenue curve from Figure 7-2 and total-cost curve from Figure 7-3. Total profit, which is the difference between total revenue and total cost, appears in the diagram as the *vertical* distance between the TR and TC curves. For example,

TABLE 7-3

TOTAL REVENUES, COSTS, AND PROFIT FOR COMPUTRON, INC.

Number of Computers (per year)	Total Revenue	Total Cost	Total Profit
		(millions of dollars per year)	
0	0	2	−2
1	15	9	6
2	25	14	11
3	33	21	12
4	40	32	8
5	45	45	0
6	48	60	−12

FIGURE 7-4

PROFIT MAXIMIZATION: A GRAPHICAL INTERPRETATION

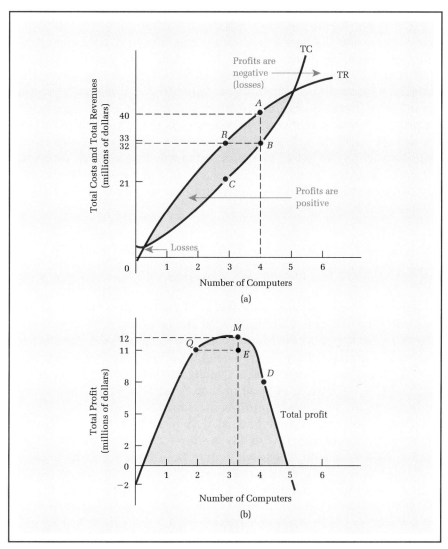

Computron's profits are maximized when the vertical distance between its total-revenue curve, TR, and its total-cost curve, TC, is at its maximum. In the diagram, this occurs at an output of 3 units per year, total profits are *CR*, or $12 million. The total-profit curve is shown in the lower portion of the figure. Naturally, it reaches its maximum value ($12 million) at 3 units (point *M*).

when output is 4 units, total revenue is $40 million (point *A*), total cost is $32 million (point *B*), and total profit is the distance between points *A* and *B*, or $8 million.

In this graphical view of the problem, Computron wants to maximize total profit, which is the vertical distance between the TR and TC curves. The curve of total profit is drawn in the lower portion of Figure 7-4. We see that it reaches its maximum value, $12 million, at an output level of approximately 3 units per year. This is, naturally, the same conclusion we reached with the aid of Table 7-3.

The total-profit curve in Figure 7-4 is shaped like a hill. Although such a shape is not inevitable, we expect a hill shape to be typical for the following reason. If a firm produces nothing, it certainly earns no profit, and it will probably incur a loss if it has an idle factory on its hands and must spend money to guard it and keep it from deteriorating. At the other extreme, a firm can produce so much output that it swamps the market, forcing price down so low that it again loses money. Only at intermediate levels of output — something between zero and the amount that floods the market — will the company earn a positive profit. Consequently, the total-profit curve will rise from zero (or negative) levels at a very small output to positive levels in between and fall to negative levels when output gets too large. Thus, the total-profit curve will normally be a hill like the one shown in Figure 7-4.

MARGINAL ANALYSIS AND MAXIMIZATION OF *TOTAL* PROFIT

We see that there may be many levels of output that yield a positive profit. But the firm is not aiming for just any level of profit—it wants the largest profit that is obtainable. The profit graph shows that the hill reaches its summit ($12 million) when output quantity is approximately $Q = 3$. If the firm produces only 2 units, it earns only $11 million in profit. If $Q = 4$, profit falls to $8 million. Thus, the firm's goal is to get to the top of the hill, where profit is maximized.

If management really knew the exact shape of its profit hill, choosing the optimal level of output would be a simple task indeed. It would only have to locate the point corresponding to M in Figure 7-4, the top of its profit hill. However, management rarely if ever has its information in such a simple form, so a different technique for finding the optimum is required. That technique is **marginal analysis**—the same set of tools that we used in our analysis of consumers maximizing utility in Chapter 4 and a firm minimizing costs in Chapter 6.

MARGINAL PROFIT is the addition to total profit resulting from one more unit of output.

To see how marginal analysis helps solve Computron's problem, we introduce an expository concept: **marginal profit**. Referring back to Table 7-3, for example, we see that an increase in Computron's annual output from 2 to 3 computers would raise total profit from $11 million to $12 million. That is, it would generate $1 million in *additional* profits, which we call the marginal profit resulting from the addition of the third unit. Similarly, marginal profit from the fourth unit would be

$$\frac{\text{Total profit}}{\text{from 4 units}} - \frac{\text{Total profit}}{\text{from 3 units}} = \$8 \text{ million} - \$12 \text{ million} = -\$4 \text{ million}$$

The marginal rule for finding the optimal level of output is easy to understand:

If the marginal profit from increasing output by one unit is positive, output should be increased. If the marginal profit from increasing output by one unit is negative, output should be decreased. Thus, an output level can maximize total profit only if marginal profit equals zero at that output.

In the Computron example, the marginal profit from the third unit is +$1 million (going from the second to the third unit *adds* $1 million to profit), so it pays to produce the third unit. But marginal profit from the fourth unit is −$4 million (going from the third unit to the fourth *reduces* total profit by $4 million), so the firm should not produce the fourth unit. Since Computron is dealing in whole numbers—for example, it cannot produce 3.12 computers—it cannot achieve a marginal profit of exactly zero. But by producing 3 units per year, it comes quite close.

The profit hill in Figure 7-4 gives us a graphical interpretation of the "marginal profit equals zero" condition. Marginal profit is defined as the additional profit that accrues to a firm when output rises by 1 unit. Thus, when output is increased, say, from 2 units to 3 units (distance *QE* in Figure 7-4), total profit rises by $1 million (distance *EM*) and the marginal profit is therefore *EM/QE*. This is precisely the definition of the slope of the total-profit curve between points *Q* and *M*.

Marginal profit is the slope of the total-profit curve.

With this geometric interpretation in hand, we can easily understand the logic of the marginal-profit rule. At a point such as *Q*, where the total-profit curve is rising, marginal profit (= slope) is positive. Profits cannot be maximal at such a point, because we can increase profits by moving farther to the right. If the firm decided to stick to point *Q*, it would be wasting the opportunity to increase profits by increasing output. Similarly, the firm cannot be maximizing profits at a point like *D*, where the slope of the curve is negative, because there marginal profit (= slope) is negative. If it finds itself at a point like *D*, the firm can raise its profit by decreasing its output.

Only at a point such as *M*, where the total-profit curve is neither rising nor falling, can the firm possibly be at the top of the profit hill rather than on one of the sides of the hill. Note also that point *M* is precisely where the slope of the curve—and hence the marginal profit—is zero. An output decision cannot be optimal unless the corresponding marginal profit is zero.

The firm is not interested in marginal profit for its own sake, but rather for what it implies about *total* profit. Marginal profit is like the needle on the pressure gauge of a boiler: The needle itself is of no concern to anyone, but if one fails to watch it, the consequences may be quite dramatic.

One common misunderstanding that arises in discussions of the marginal criterion of optimality is the idea that it seems foolish to go to a point where marginal profit is zero. "Isn't it better to earn a positive marginal profit?'' This notion springs from a confusion between the quantity one is seeking to maximize (*total* profit) and the gauge that indicates whether such a maximum has in fact been attained (*marginal* profit). Of course it is better to have a positive total profit than zero total profit. But a zero value on the marginal-profit gauge merely indicates that all is apparently well, that total profit may be at its maximum.

MARGINAL REVENUE AND MARGINAL COST: GUIDES TO AN OPTIMUM

A more conventional version of the marginal analysis of profit maximization proceeds directly in terms of the cost and revenue components of profit. For this purpose, refer back to Figure 7-4, where the profit hill was constructed from the total-revenue (TR) and total-cost (TC) curves. Observe that there is another way of finding the profit-maximizing solution. We want to maximize the vertical distance between the TR and TC curves. This distance, we see, is not maximal at an output level such as 2 units, because there are two curves growing farther apart. If we move farther to the right, the vertical distance between them (which is total profit) will increase. Conversely, we have not maximized the vertical distance between TR and TC at an output level such as 4 units, because there the two curves are coming closer together. We can add to profits by moving farther to the left (reducing output).

The conclusion from the graph, then, is that total profit (the vertical distance between TR and TC) is maximized only when the two curves are neither growing farther apart nor coming closer together, that is, when their slopes are equal. While this conclusion is rather mechanical, we can breathe some life into it by interpreting the slopes of the two curves as **marginal revenue** and **marginal cost**. These concepts, which have already been defined and illustrated, permit us to restate the geometric conclusion we have just reached in an economically significant way:

Profit can be maximized only at an output level at which marginal revenue is (approximately) equal to marginal cost. In symbols,

$$MR = MC$$

The logic of the MR = MC rule for profit maximization is straightforward.[2] When MR is not equal to MC, profits cannot possibly be maximized because the firm can increase its profits either by raising its output or by reducing it. For example, if MR = $16 million and MC = $12 million, the firm can increase its net profit by $4 million by producing and selling 1 more unit. If MC exceeds MR—say, MR = $7 million and MC = $10 million—the firm loses $3 million on its marginal unit, so it can add $3 million to its profit by reducing output by 1 unit. Only

2. You may have surmised by now that just as total profit = total revenue − total cost, it must be true that marginal profit = marginal revenue − marginal cost. This is in fact correct. It also shows that when marginal profit = 0, we must have MR = MC.

when MR = MC is it impossible for the firm to add to its profit by changing its output level.

Table 7-4 (on page 212) reproduces marginal-revenue and marginal-cost data for Computron, Inc., from Tables 7-1 and 7-2. The table confirms that the MR = MC rule leads us to the same conclusion as did Figure 7-4 and Table 7-3: Computron should produce and sell 3 computers per year.

The marginal revenue of the third computer is $8 million ($33 million from selling 3 computers less $25 million from selling 2) while the marginal cost is only $7 million ($21 million minus $14 million). Thus, the firm should produce the third unit. But the fourth computer brings in only $7 million in marginal revenue while its marginal cost is $11 million —clearly a losing proposition.

Because the graphs of marginal analysis will prove so useful in the following chapters, Figure 7-5(a) shows the MR = MC condition for profit maximization graphically. The red curve labelled MR in the figure is the marginal-revenue schedule from Table 7-4. The curve labelled MC is the marginal-cost schedule. They intersect at point *E*, which is therefore the point where marginal revenue and marginal cost are equal. The optimal output for Computron is 3 units.[3] Figures 7-5(b) and 7-5(c), respectively, are reproductions of the TR and TC curves from the upper part of Figure 7-4 and the total-profit curve from the lower part of that figure. Note how MC and MR intersect at the same output at which the distance of TR above TC is greatest, which is the output at which the profit hill reaches its summit.

APPLICATIONS

(1) FIXED COST AND THE PROFIT-MAXIMIZING PRICE

Our analytic apparatus can now be used to offer a surprising insight. Suppose there is a rise in the firm's fixed cost; say, the rental cost of an indispensable air-filtering machine doubles. What will happen to the profit-maximizing price and output? Should price go up to cover the increased cost? Should the firm push for a larger output (even if that requires a fall in price)? The answer is neither.

When a firm's fixed cost increases, its profit-maximizing price and output remain completely unchanged, so long as it pays the firm to stay in business.

In other words, the firm's management can do nothing to offset the effect of the rise in fixed cost. It must just lie back and take it.

Why is this so? Remember that, by definition, a fixed cost is a cost that does not change when output changes. Computron's air-filtering cost

---

3. One qualification must be stated. Sometimes, marginal-revenue and marginal-cost curves do not have the streamlined shapes depicted in Figure 7-5(a), and they may intersect more than once. In such cases, while it remains true that MC = MR at the output level that maximizes profits, there may be other output levels at which MC is also equal to MR but at which profits are not maximized.

TABLE 7-4

MARGINAL REVENUE AND MARGINAL COST FOR COMPUTRON, INC.

Number of Computers (per year)	Marginal Revenue	Marginal Cost
	(millions of dollars per year)	
0	—	—
1	15	7
2	10	5
3	8	7
4	7	11
5	5	13
6	3	15

increase is the same whether business is slow or booming, whether production is 2 or 6 computers. This is illustrated in Table 7-5, which also reproduces Computron's total profits from Table 7-3. The third column of the table shows that total fixed cost has risen by $2 million per year, no matter what the firm's output. As a result, for each possible output of the firm, total profit is $2 million less than what it would have been otherwise. For example, when output is 4 units, we see that total profit must fall from $8 million (second column) to $6 million (last column).

Now, because profit is reduced by the same amount at each and every output level, the output level that was most profitable to the firm before the rent increase must still be the output that yields the highest profit. In Table 7-5, we see that $10 million is the largest entry in the last column, which shows profits after the rise in fixed cost. The highest profit is attained, as it was before, when output equals 3 units. Given the firm's demand curve (Figure 7-1), this, of course, means that the profit-maximizing price will remain at $11 million—the price at which it sells 3 units (point c on the demand curve).

TABLE 7-5

TOTAL PROFIT BEFORE AND AFTER A RISE IN FIXED COST

Number of Computers (per year)	Total Profit before Fixed-Cost Increase	Increase in Fixed-Cost Payment	Total Profit after Fixed-Cost Increase
	(millions of dollars per year)		
0	−2	2	−4
1	6	2	4
2	11	2	9
3	12	2	10
4	8	2	6
5	0	2	−2
6	−12	2	−14

FIGURE 7-5

PROFIT MAXIMIZATION: ANOTHER GRAPHICAL INTERPRETATION

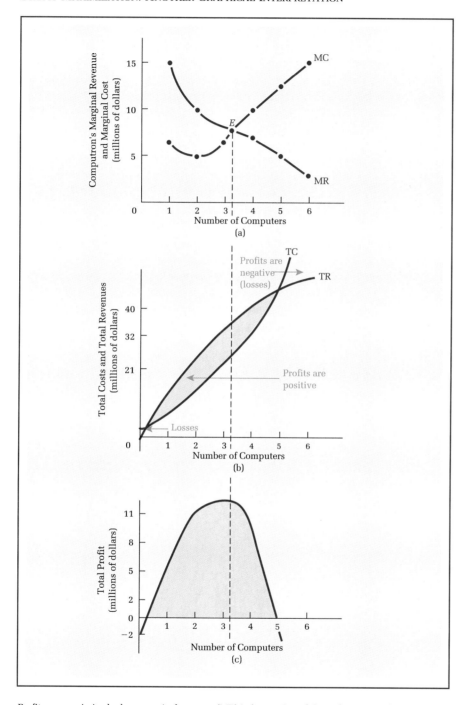

Profits are maximized where marginal revenue (MR) is (approximately) equal to marginal cost (MC), for only at such a point will marginal profit be zero. Part (a) shows the MR = MC condition for profit maximization graphically as point *E*, where output is close to 3 computers. Since Computron does not produce fractions of computers, the best it can do is to produce 3 of them. The diagram also reproduces from Figure 7-4 the TR and TC curves (part (b)) and the total-profit curve (part (c)), showing how all three agree that the profit-maximizing output is a bit larger than 3 units.

All of this is also shown in Figure 7-6, which shows the firm's total profit hill before and after the rise in fixed cost (reproducing Computron's initial profit hill from Figure 7-4). We see that the cost increase simply moves the profit hill straight downward by $2 million, so that the highest point on the hill is just lowered from point *M* to point *N*. But the top of the hill is shifted neither toward the left nor toward the right. It remains at the 3-unit output level. Just as we saw before, the profit-maximizing output level remains unchanged when fixed costs rise.

(2) TAXES AND THE PROFIT-MAXIMIZING PRICE

The result we have just described, which applies only to fixed costs and not to variable costs, is important for government policy regarding the taxing of firms. If the government levies an excise tax (a certain amount per unit of the good that the firm produces and sells), the firm's marginal costs will be increased (the MC curve will shift up). This rise will reduce the profit-maximizing level of output, so one can predict that the firm will pass on some of the excise tax by raising the selling price and lowering the level of inputs (say, by laying off workers). But if the government levies a *licence fee*, that is, an amount a firm must pay to be in business at all, only fixed costs are increased. Consequently, as we have just seen, such a levy will not be passed on in higher prices or cause the firm to lay off any inputs.

The choice between the two types of taxes will depend on the goals of the government. If the tax is meant to reduce profits and to redistribute

FIGURE 7-6

FIXED COST DOES NOT AFFECT PROFIT-MAXIMIZING OUTPUT

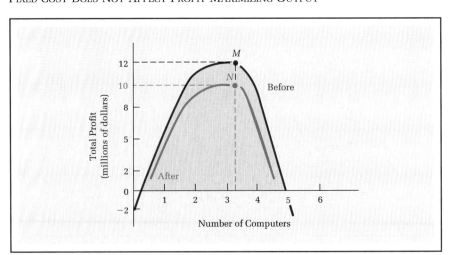

The graph reproduces Computron's initial profit hill from Figure 7-4 (the red curve labelled "before"). A $2 million increase in fixed cost shifts the profit hill downward to the blue curve marked "after." But the original point of maximum profit (point *M*) and the new one (point *N*) are at the same output level. This is so because the cost increase pushes the profit hill straight downward.

the resulting incomes to others, the licence fee is appealing because it involves no unfortunate side effects in terms of higher prices or layoffs. If, on the other hand, the tax is meant to increase a product's price so that, for example, the price more properly reflects the costs of pollution that are involved in its production, the excise tax will be the more appealing option. In this case, because the government is seeking to reduce consumption of the item, higher prices and less production are desirable outcomes.

MARGINAL ANALYSIS IN REAL DECISION PROBLEMS

We can now put the marginal analysis of profit determination to work to unravel the puzzles with which we began this chapter. It should be noted that neither example involves a mechanical application of the MC = MR rule. Both examples are drawn from reality, and reality never works as neatly as a textbook illustration. However, as these cases show, the reasoning taught in the text does help to deal with real problems.

CASE 1: THE SOFT-DRINK-PRICING PROBLEM

Our first problem dealt with a firm's choice between keeping the price of a brand of soft drink at $1.50 per six-pack or reducing it to $1.35 when a competitor entered the market. The trouble was that to know what to do, the firm needed to know its demand curve (and hence its marginal-revenue curve). However, the firm did not have enough data to determine the shape of its demand curve. How, then, could a rational decision be made?

As we indicated, the debate among the firm's managers finally reached agreement on one point: The price should be cut if, as a result, profits were not likely to decline, that is, if marginal profit were not negative. Fortunately, the data needed to determine whether marginal profit was positive were obtainable. Initial annual sales were 10 million units, and the firm's engineers maintained emphatically that marginal costs were very close to constant at $1.20 per six-pack over the output range in question. Instead of trying to determine the *actual* increase in sales that would result from the price cut, the team of consultants decided to try to determine the *minimum necessary* increase in quantity demand required to avoid a decrease in profits.

It was clear that the firm needed additional revenue at least as great as the additional cost of supplying the added volume, if profits were not to decline. The consultants knew that sales at the initial price of $1.50 per six-pack were $15 million ($1.50 per unit times 10 million units). Letting Q represent the (unknown) quantity of six-packs that would be sold at the proposed new price of $1.35, the economists compared the added revenue with the added cost of providing the Q new units. Since MC was constant at $1.20 per unit, the added cost amounted to

$$\text{Added cost} = \$1.20 \times (Q - 10 \text{ million})$$

This was to be compared with the added revenue:

$$\text{Added revenue} = \text{New revenue} - \text{Old revenue}$$
$$= \$1.35Q - \$15 \text{ million}$$

No loss would result from the price change if the added revenue was greater than or equal to the added cost. The minimum Q necessary to avoid a loss, therefore, was that at which added revenue equalled added cost, or

$$1.35Q - 15 \text{ million} = 1.2Q - 12 \text{ million}$$

or

$$0.15Q = 3 \text{ million}$$

This would be true if, and only if, Q, the quantity sold at the lower price, would be

$$Q = 20 \text{ million units}$$

In other words, this calculation showed that the firm could break even from the 15¢ price reduction only if the quantity of its product demanded rose at least 100 percent (from 10 to 20 million units). Since past experience indicated that such a rise in quantity demanded was hardly possible, the price reduction proposal was quickly abandoned. Thus, the logic of the MC = MR rule, plus a little ingenuity, enabled the consultants to deal with a problem that at first seemed baffling—even though they had no estimate of marginal revenue.

CASE 2: THE "UNPROFITABLE" CALCULATOR

Our second case study concerned a firm that was apparently losing money on its calculator sales because its $12 price was less than the $14.55 average cost that the company's accountants assigned to the product. This $14.55 included $10.30 of costs arising directly from the manufacture and marketing of the calculators, plus a $4.25 per-calculator share of the company's overall general expenses ("overhead"). Accused of deliberately selling below cost in order to drive a competitor out of business, the company was able to use marginal analysis to show that this was not true and that the price at which the calculators were sold was in fact profitable.

To demonstrate this, the company's witness explained that, if the sales were really unprofitable, the company would have been able to raise its net earnings by ceasing production and sale of the calculators. A moment's consideration shows, however, that the opposite would have happened—that profits would have decreased if the company had given up its annual sale of $10 million calculators. The company's revenues would have been reduced by the (marginal) figure of $12 on each of its 10 million units sold—a revenue reduction of $120 million. But how much cost would it have saved? The answer is that the cost saving would equal only the cost outlay actually *caused* by the production of the calculator—the $10.30 per unit in direct cost. None of the company's overhead would have been saved by ending calculator production — the company president would not have been fired if the product had been discontinued, and the company would probably even have had to increase general expenditure on new product research. Rather, the (marginal) saving would have been the direct cost of $10.30 per calculator times the output of 10 million calculators—a total saving of $103 million. Thus, elimination of the product would have reduced total company profit by $17 million per year—the $103 million cost saving minus the $120 million in revenue foregone. In other words, continued production of the calculators was not causing losses; on the contrary, it was contributing $17 million in profits every year. The court concluded that this reasoning was correct, and used this conclusion in its decision.

This case illustrates a point that is encountered frequently. The calculator producer was selling a product at a price that *appeared* not to cover costs, but really did. The same sort of issue frequently faces firms considering the introduction of a new product or the opening of a new branch office. In many such cases, the new operation may not cover average costs as measured by standard accounting methods. Yet following the apparent implications of those cost figures would amount to throwing away a valuable opportunity to add to the net earnings of the firm and, perhaps, to contribute to the welfare of the economy. Only marginal analysis can reveal whether the contemplated action is really worthwhile.

CONCLUSION: THE FUNDAMENTAL ROLE OF MARGINAL ANALYSIS

In Chapter 4, we saw how marginal analysis helps us to understand the consumer's purchase decisions. In Chapter 6, it helped us to understand the firm's input choices, and in this chapter, it enabled us to examine output decisions. The logic of marginal analysis applies not only to economic decisions by consumers and firms but also to those of governments, universities, hospitals, and other organizations. In short, the analysis can be used by any individual or group making economic choices for the use of scarce resources. Thus, one of the most important conclusions that can be drawn from the last four chapters, a conclusion brought out vividly by the two examples we have discussed, concerns the importance of marginal analysis.

The Importance of Marginal Analysis

In any decision about whether to expand an activity, marginal cost and marginal revenue are always the relevant factors. A calculation based on *average* figures is likely to lead the decision-maker to miss all sorts of opportunities, some of them critical.

More generally, if one wants to make optimal decisions, marginal analysis should be used in the planning calculations. This is true whether the decision applies to a business firm seeking to maximize profit or minimize cost, to a consumer trying to maximize utility, or to a less-developed country striving to maximize per-capita output. It applies as much to decisions on input proportions and advertising as it does to decisions about output levels and prices. Indeed, this is such a general principle of economics that it is one of the twelve Ideas for Beyond the Final Exam.

A LOOK BACK AND A LOOK FORWARD

We have now completed four chapters describing how consumers and business managers can make optimal decisions. Will you find executives in head offices calculating marginal cost and marginal revenue in order to decide how much to produce? Hardly. Not any more than you will find consumers in stores computing their marginal utilities in order to decide what to buy. Like consumers, successful business people often rely heavily on intuition and "hunches" that cannot be described by any set of rules.

However, we have not sought a literal *description* of consumer and business behaviour but rather a *model* to help us analyze and predict this behaviour. Just as astronomers construct models of the behaviour of objects that do not think at all, economists construct models of consumers and business people who do think, but whose thought processes may be rather different from those of economists. In the chapters that follow, we will use these models to serve the purposes for which they were designed: to analyze the functioning of a market economy and to see what things it does well and what things it does poorly.

SUMMARY

1. A firm can choose the quantity of its product it wants to sell or the price it wants to charge. But it cannot choose both because price affects the quantity demanded.

2. In economic theory, it is usually assumed that firms seek to maximize profits. This should not be taken literally, but interpreted as a useful simplification of reality.

3. Marginal revenue is the additional revenue earned by increasing sales by one unit. Marginal cost is the additional cost incurred by increasing production by one unit.

4. Maximum profit requires a firm to choose the level of output at which marginal revenue is equal to marginal cost.

5. Geometrically, the profit-maximizing output level occurs at the highest point of the total-profit curve. There, the slope of the total-profit curve is zero, meaning that marginal profit is zero.

6. A change in fixed cost will not change the profit-maximizing level of output.

7. It may pay a firm to expand its output if it is selling at a price greater than marginal cost, even if that price happens to be below average cost.

8. Optimal decisions must be made on the basis of marginal-cost and marginal-revenue figures, not average-cost and average-revenue figures. This is one of the twelve Ideas for Beyond the Final Exam.

CONCEPTS FOR REVIEW

Profit maximization
Satisficing
Total profit
Economic profit

Total revenue and cost
Average revenue and cost
Marginal revenue and cost

Fixed cost
Marginal analysis
Marginal profit

QUESTIONS FOR DISCUSSION

1. "It may be rational for a firm not to try to maximize profits." Discuss the circumstances under which this statement may be true.

2. Suppose the firm's demand curve indicates that at a price of $9 per unit, customers will demand 2 million units of its product. Suppose management decides to pick both price and output, produces 3 million units of its product, and prices it at $14. What will happen?

3. Suppose a firm's management would be pleased to increase its share of the market, but if it expands its production, the price of its product will fall and so its profits will decline somewhat. What choices are available to this firm? What would you do if you were president of this company?

4. Why does it make sense for a firm to seek to maximize total profit, rather than to maximize marginal profit?

5. A firm's marginal revenue is $41 and its marginal cost is $19. What amount of profit does the firm fail to generate by refusing to increase output by one unit?

6. Calculate average revenue (AR) and average cost (AC) in Table 7-3. How much profit does the firm earn at the output at which AC = AR? Why?

7. A firm's total cost is $200 if it produces one unit, $350 if it produces two units, and $450 if it produces three units of output. Draw up a table of total, average, and marginal costs for this firm.

8. Draw average- and marginal-cost curves for the firm in Question 7. Describe the relationship between the two curves.

9. A firm with no fixed costs has the demand and total-cost schedules given in the table below. If it wants to maximize profits, how much output should it produce?

Quantity	Price (dollars)	Total Cost (dollars)
1	6	1
2	5	2.5
3	4	4
4	3	7
5	2	11

10. Review the concept of fixed cost in Chapter 6. Suppose Computron's total costs increased by $10 million per year. Show in Table 7-2 how this affects Computron's total, marginal, and average costs.

11. Why does it make sense for a change in a firm's fixed cost not to change the output level that maximizes its profit?

12. Consider a firm whose demand curve is $Q = 6 - 0.5P$, where P and Q stand for price and quantity. The firm must pay rent of 6 per period for its premises and a constant cost of 2 per unit in production costs. What price will this firm charge? What will be the firm's response if the government imposes a price ceiling of 4 per unit? Explain your answers fully.

APPENDIX TO CHAPTER 7

THE RELATIONSHIPS AMONG TOTAL, AVERAGE, AND MARGINAL DATA

By now you will have noticed that there is a close connection between the average-revenue and average-cost curves and the corresponding marginal-revenue and marginal-cost curves. After all, we deduced our total-revenue figures from the average revenue and then calculated our marginal-revenue figures from the total revenues; a similar chain of deduction applied to costs.

Marginal, average, and total figures are inextricably bound together. From any one of the three, the other two can be calculated. Total, average, and marginal figures bear relationships to one another that hold for any variable—such as revenue, cost, or profit — that is affected by the number of units in question.

To illustrate and emphasize the wide applicability of marginal analysis, we switch our example from profits, revenues, and costs to a non-economic variable, cooking weights. We do so because calculation of weights is more familiar to most people than calculation of profits, revenues, or costs, and we can use this example to illustrate several fundamental relationships between average and marginal figures. A not-so-expert hamburger-maker is shaping patties and piling them on a platter balanced on a kitchen scale. The data on what he produces are in Table 7-6. (Note that in this illustration, "number of patties" is analogous to units of output, "total weight" to total revenue or cost, and so on.)

He begins with an empty scale (the total weight of the patties is equal to zero). The first patty he makes weighs exactly 100 grams; marginal and average weight are both 100 grams. If the next patty weighs 140 grams (the marginal weight equals 140 grams), the average weight rises to 120 grams (240 ÷ 2), and so on.

The way to calculate average weight from total weight is quite clear. When, for example, the scale holds 4 patties with a total weight of 500 grams, the average weight must be 500 ÷ 4 = 125 grams, as shown in the corresponding entry of the third column. In general, the rule for converting totals to averages, and vice versa, is

Rule 1a. Average weight equals total weight divided by number of items.

TABLE 7-6
WEIGHTS OF HAMBURGER PATTIES

Number of Patties on Scale	Total Weight (grams)	Average Weight (grams)	Marginal Weight (grams)
0	0	—	—
1	100	100	100
2	240	120	140
3	375	125	135
4	500	125	125
5	600	120	100
6	660	110	60

Rule 1b. Total weight equals average weights times number of items.

This rule naturally applies equally well to cost, revenue, profit, or any other variable of interest.

Calculation of marginal weight from total weight follows the subtraction process we have already encountered in the calculation of marginal utility, marginal cost, and marginal revenue.

Rule 2a. The marginal weight of, say, the third item equals the total weight of three items minus the total weight of two items.

For example, when the fourth patty is placed on the scale, total weight rises from 375 grams to 500 grams, and hence the corresponding marginal weight is $500 - 375 = 125$ grams, as is shown in the last column of Table 7-6. We can also go in the opposite direction — from marginal to total—by the reverse, addition, process:

Rule 2b. The total weight of, say, three items equals the marginal weight of the first item plus the marginal weight of the second item plus the marginal weight of the third item.

Rule 2b can be checked by referring to Table 7-6. There we see that the total weight of three items, 375 grams, is indeed equal to $100 + 140 + 135$ grams, the sum of the preceding marginal weights. A similar relation holds for any other total weight figure in the table, as you should verify.[4]

In addition to these familiar arithmetic relationships, there are two other useful relationships. The first of these may be stated as follows:

Rule 3. In the absence of fixed weight (costs), the marginal, average, and total figures for the first item must all be equal.

This rule holds because when the scale holds only one item, the weight of which is X grams, the average weight will obviously be X, the total weight must be X, and the marginal weight must also be X (since the total must have risen from 0 to X grams). Put another way, when the marginal item is alone, it is obviously also the average item, and also represents the totality of all relevant items.

Now for a final, very important relationship:

Rule 4. If marginal weight is lower than average weight, average weight must fall when the number of items increases. If marginal weight exceeds average weight, average weight must rise when the number of items increases. If marginal and average weight are equal, average weight must remain constant when the number of items increases.

These three possibilities are all illustrated in Table 7-6. Notice, for example, that when the third patty is placed on the scale, the average weight rises from 120 to 125 grams. That is because this patty's (marginal) weight is 135 grams, which is above the average, as Rule 4 requires. Similarly, when someone asks for a small hamburger and a 60-gram patty is added to the pile, the average falls from 120 to 110 grams because marginal weight, 60 grams, is below average weight.

The reason Rule 4 works is easily explained with the aid of our example. When the third patty is added, we see that the average rises. At once, we know that this patty must be above average weight, for otherwise its addition would not have pulled up the average. Similarly, the average will be pulled down by the addition of a patty whose weight is below the average (marginal weight is less than average weight). Further, the addition of a patty of average weight (marginal equals average weight) will leave the existing average figure unchanged. That is all there is to the matter.

It is essential to avoid a common misunderstanding of this rule: It does *not* state, for exam-

---

4. There is an exception in the case of costs. Summing marginal-cost figures as in Rule 2b leads to total *variable* cost. If there are *fixed* costs, they must be added in to arrive at total (variable plus fixed) costs.

ple, that if the average figure is rising, the marginal figure must be rising. When the average rises, the marginal figure may rise, fall, or remain unchanged. The addition of two patties both well above average will push the average up in two successive steps, even if the second new one is lighter than the first. We see such a case in Table 7-6, where the arithmetic shows that while average weight rises successively from 100 to 120 to 125 grams, the marginal weight falls from 140 to 135 to 125 grams.

GRAPHIC REPRESENTATION OF MARGINAL AND AVERAGE CURVES

We have shown how, from a curve of total profit (or total cost or total anything else), one can determine the corresponding marginal figure. We noted several times in the chapter that the marginal value at any particular point is equal to the slope of the corresponding total curve at that point. But, for some purposes, it is convenient to use a graph that records marginal and average values directly rather than deriving them from the curve of totals.

We can obtain such a graph by plotting the data in a table of average and marginal figures, such as Table 7-6. The result looks like the graph shown in Figure 7-7. Here we have indicated the number of hamburger patties in the pile on the horizontal axis and the corresponding average and marginal weight figures on the vertical axis. The solid dots represent average weights; the circles represent marginal weights. Thus, for example, point *A* shows that when two patties are on the scale, their average weight is 120 grams, as was reported on the third line of Table 7-6. Similarly, point *B* on the graph represents information provided in the next column of the table: the marginal weight of the third patty is 125 grams. For visual convenience, these points have been connected into a marginal curve and average curve, represented respectively by the solid and the broken curves in the diagram. This

is the representation of marginal and average values that economists most frequently use.

Figure 7-7 illustrates two of our rules. Rule 3 says that, for the first unit, the marginal and average values will be the same. That is precisely why the two curves start out together at point *C*. When there is only one patty on the scale, marginal and average weight *must* be the same. The graph also obeys Rule 4: Between points *C* and *E*, where the average curve is rising, the marginal curve lies *above* the average. (Notice, however, that over part of this range, the marginal curve falls even though the average curve is rising—Rule 4 says nothing about the rise or fall of the marginal curve.) We see also that over range *EF*, where the average curve is falling, the marginal curve is below the average curve, again in accord with Rule 4. Finally, at point *E*, where the average curve is neither rising nor falling, the marginal curve meets the average curve: Average and marginal weights are equal at that point.

FIGURE 7-7

THE RELATIONSHIP BETWEEN MARGINAL AND AVERAGE CURVES

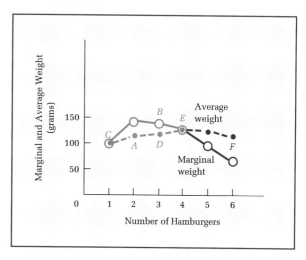

If the marginal curve is above the average curve, the average curve will be pulled upward. Thus, wherever the marginal curve is above the average curve, the average curve must be going upward (blue segment of curves). The opposite is true where the marginal curve is below the average curve.

QUESTIONS FOR DISCUSSION

1. Suppose the following is your record of exam grades in Principles of Economics:

Exam Date	Grade	Comment
September 30	65	A slow start.
October 28	75	A big improvement.
December 13	90	Congratulations!
January 30	85	Slipped a little.
March 1	95	Well done!

Use these data to make up a table of total, average, and marginal grades for the five exams.

2. From the data in your table, illustrate each of the rules mentioned in this appendix. Be sure to point out an instance where marginal grade falls but average grade rises.

PART 3

THE MARKET SYSTEM: VIRTUES AND VICES

Besides the consumer demands and the business costs that we studied in the last four chapters, the decisions of firms also depend on the number, size, and behaviour of the other firms in the industry. The strength of the competition faced by a company can profoundly affect its pricing, its output decisions, and its input purchases. Strong competitive pressures, sometimes taking subtle forms, can severely limit management's freedom of choice in setting prices and can, in the process, protect the interests of consumers. Giant corporations may also find themselves under this sort of pressure, even where there are few rival domestic firms. In recent years, for example, many Canadian companies have found themselves facing stiffening competition from foreign firms. This part of the book analyzes some of the forms that competition — or its absence — can take, and examines some of the implications for general welfare.

Again, to provide motivation in the introduction to each part of this book, we give advance notice about four key insights that are contained in the coming chapters. Each of the four propositions listed at right is intended to make you better informed on election issues.

Taxes on emissions and subsidies for emission reduction both induce firms to cut pollution. But unlike taxes, subsidies can lead to an *increase* in total emissions. (pages 248–49)

A larger portion of a sales tax is passed on to consumers in a perfectly competitive industry than in a monopoly. (pages 305–307)

If trade must be restricted, tariffs are better than quotas. (pages 379–80)

Free trade with the United States will eventually give Canadians a stream of benefits with a present value equal to more than one year's entire national output— enough to compensate those who lose from the agreement. But the income redistributions needed to ensure compensation have not been made. (pages 385–86)

CHAPTER 8

THE FIRM AND THE INDUSTRY UNDER PERFECT COMPETITION

Industries differ dramatically in the number of firms that populate them and in the typical size of those firms. Some industries, like the fishing industry, have a great many very small firms; others, like the automobile industry, are composed of a few industrial giants. This chapter deals with a particular type of market structure — called *perfect competition* — in which firms are numerous and small. We begin by comparing alternative market forms and defining perfect competition precisely. We then use the tools we acquired in Chapter 7 to analyze the behaviour of the perfectly competitive firm and derive its supply curve. Next, we consider the supply curve of *all* the firms in an industry — the *industry supply curve* — and investigate how developments in the industry affect the individual firms.

APPLICATION: POLLUTION POLICY

As usual, before delving into the analysis, we begin with a puzzling but important application. By the end of the chapter, the analysis will have supplemented your common sense sufficiently to supply the required insights to the problem.

Many economists and others who are concerned with the environment believe that cleaner air and water can be achieved cheaply and effectively when polluters are required to pay for the damages they cause. If a polluting firm can avoid the emissions charge by emitting less, that will provide the required incentive. (See Chapter 17 for more details.)

Yet such charges are often viewed as taxes, and that can make them political poison. Some politicians have reasoned that a donkey can be made to move as effectively by means of a carrot as by a stick. Consequently, some have proposed rewards for firms that cut down their emissions of pollutants. Instead of charging the firms money for every unit of pollutant they emit, the government would give them money for every unit by which they cut their emissions.

This system of bribes (or subsidies) does work, at least up to a point. Polluting firms will, indeed, respond by cutting pollution. But, ultimately, society will end up with more pollution than before! Payments to the firms actually worsen the pollution problem. How can it be that each firm pollutes less, yet total pollution is worse? By the end of this chapter, we will be able to answer this question.

VARIETIES OF MARKET STRUCTURE: A SNEAK PREVIEW

A **MARKET** refers to the set of all sale and purchase transactions that affect the price of some commodity.

It will be helpful to open our discussion by explaining clearly what is meant by the word **market**. Economists do not reserve the term to denote only an organized exchange operating in a well-defined physical location. In its more general and abstract usage, market refers to a set of sellers and buyers whose activities affect the price at which a particular commodity is sold. For example, two separate sales of Canadian Pacific shares in different parts of the country may be considered as taking place in the same market, while the sale of bread and carrots in neighbouring stalls of a market square may, in our sense, occur in totally different markets.

So far, this book has not distinguished among firms in terms of the sort of market in which they operate. We have talked only about firms in general. But in this chapter and the next few, we will see that market form makes a great deal of difference to the way in which firms can and do behave. Under some market forms, for example, the firm has no control over price. In others, the firm has the power to adjust price in a way that adds to its profits and that, in the opinion of some people, constitutes exploitation of consumers. Economists distinguish among different kinds of markets according to (1) how many firms they include, (2) whether the products of the different firms are identical or somewhat different, and (3) how easy it is for new firms to enter the market. Table 8-1 summarizes the main features of the four market structures we will study in this and subsequent chapters. It is provided here as a kind of road map of where we are going. **Perfect competition** is obviously at one extreme (many small firms selling an identical product) while **pure monopoly** (a single firm) is at the other. In between are hybrid forms—called **monopolistic competition** (many small firms each selling products slightly different from the others') and **oligopoly** (a few large rival firms)—that share some of the characteristics of perfect competition and some of the characteristics of monopoly.

Perfect competition is not the typical market form in the Canadian economy. Indeed, it is quite rare. Some farming and fishing industries approximate perfect competition, as do some financial markets. Pure monopoly—literally one firm—is also infrequent. Most of the products you buy are no doubt supplied by oligopolies or monopolistic competitors—terms we will be defining precisely in Chapter 11.

TABLE 8-1

VARIETIES OF MARKET STRUCTURE

Type of Market Structure	Number of Sellers	Definition Nature of the Product	Barriers to Entry	Where to Find It In the Canadian Economy	In This Textbook
Perfect competition	Many	All firms produce identical products (example: wheat)	None	Some agricultural markets and parts of retailing come close	Chapter 8
Monopolistic competition	Many	Different firms produce somewhat different products (example: restaurant meals)	Minor	Most of the retailing sector, textiles, and restaurants	Chapter 11
Oligopoly	Few	Firms may produce identical or differentiated products (example: brands of toothpaste)	May be considerable	Much of the manufacturing sector, especially autos, steel, and cigarettes	Chapter 11
Pure monopoly	One	Unique product	May be considerable	Public utilities	Chapter 10

PERFECT COMPETITION DEFINED

You will appreciate just how special perfect competition is once we provide a comprehensive definition. A market is said to operate under perfect competition when the following four conditions are satisfied:

1. ***Numerous participants.*** Each seller and purchaser constitutes so small a portion of the market that the firm's decisions have no effect on the price. This requirement rules out trade associations or other collusive arrangements strong enough to affect price.

2. ***Homogeneity of product.*** The product offered by any seller is identical to that supplied by any other seller. (*Example:* Wheat of a given grade is a homogeneous product; different brands of toothpaste are not.) Because the product is homogeneous, consumers do not care from which firm they buy.

3. ***Freedom of entry and exit.*** New firms desiring to enter the market face no special impediments that the existing firms can avoid. Similarly, if production and sale of the good proves unprofitable, there are no barriers preventing firms from leaving the market.

4. ***Perfect information.*** Each firm and each customer is well informed about the available products and their prices. They know whether one supplier's price is lower than another's price.

These are obviously exacting requirements that are met infrequently in practice. One example might be a market for common shares: There are literally thousands of buyers and sellers of Bell Canada stock; all of the shares are exactly alike; anyone who wishes can enter the market easily; and most of the relevant information is readily available in the daily newspaper. But other examples are hard to find. Our interest in perfect competition is surely not for its descriptive realism.

Why, then, do we spend time studying perfect competition? The answer takes us back to the central theme of this book. It is under perfect competition that the market mechanism performs best in allocating society's resources. Therefore, if we want to learn what markets do well, we can put the market's best foot forward by beginning with perfect competition.

As Adam Smith suggested some two centuries ago, perfectly competitive firms use society's scarce resources with maximum efficiency. Further, as Friedrich Engels suggested in the opening quotation of this chapter, perfectly competitive firms serve consumers' tastes effectively. Thus, by studying perfect competition, we can learn just how much an ideally functioning market system might accomplish. This is the topic of the present chapter and the next one. Then, in Chapters 10 and 11, we will consider other market forms and see how they deviate from the perfectly competitive ideal. Still later chapters (especially Chapter 12 and those in Part 4) will examine many important tasks that the market does not perform at all well, even under perfect competition. These chapters combined should provide a balanced assessment of the virtues and vices of the market mechanism.

THE COMPETITIVE FIRM AND ITS DEMAND CURVE

To discover what happens in a market in which perfect competition prevails, we must deal separately with the behaviour of *individual firms* and the behaviour of the *industry* that is constituted by those firms. One basic difference between the firm and the industry under competition relates to pricing:

Under perfect competition, the firm is a **price taker**. It has no choice but to accept the price that has been determined in the market.

The fact that a firm in a perfectly competitive market has no control over the price it charges follows from the definition of perfect competition. The presence of a vast number of competitors, each offering identical products, forces each firm to meet but not exceed the price charged by the others. Like a shareholder with 100 shares of Bell Canada, the firm simply finds out the prevailing price on the market and either accepts that price or refuses to sell. But while the individual firm has no influence over price under perfect competition, the industry does. This influence is not conscious or planned—it happens spontaneously through the impersonal forces of supply and demand, as we observed in Chapter 3.

With two important exceptions, the analysis of the behaviour of the firm under perfect competition is exactly the same as that pertaining to any other firm, so the tools developed in Chapters 6 and 7 can be applied directly. The two exceptions are (1) the special shape of the competitive firm's demand curve and (2) the effects on the firm's profits that stem from the freedom of entry and exit. We will consider them in turn, beginning with the demand curve.

In Chapter 7, we assumed that the firm's demand curve always slopes downward; if a firm wished to sell more (without increasing its advertising or changing its product specifications), it had to reduce the price of its product. The competitive firm is an exception to this general principle.

A perfectly competitive firm has a **horizontal demand curve**. This means it can double or triple its sales without any reduction in the price of its product.

How is this possible? The answer is that the competitive firm is so insignificant relative to the market as a whole that it has absolutely no influence over price. The farmer who sells his barley through the exchange in Winnipeg must accept the current quotation his broker reports to him. Because there are thousands of farmers, the Winnipeg price per tonne will not budge because Farmer Jones decides he doesn't like the price and holds back a truckload for storage. Thus, the demand curve for Farmer Jones's barley is as shown in Figure 8-1; the price he is paid in Winnipeg will be $80 per tonne whether he sells one truckload (point *A*) or two (point *B*) or three (point *C*). This is so because price is

FIGURE 8-1

DEMAND CURVE FOR A FIRM UNDER PERFECT COMPETITION

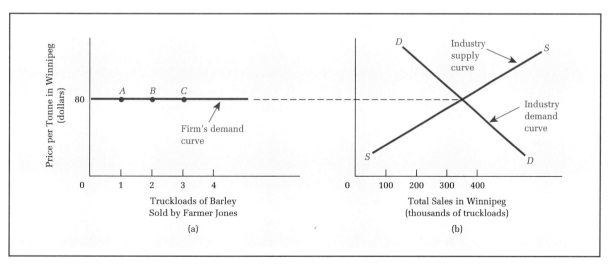

Under perfect competition, the size of the output of a firm is so small a portion of the total industry output that it cannot affect the market price of the product. Even if the firm's output increases many times, market price remains $80, where it is set by industry supply and demand.

determined by the *industry's* supply and demand curves, shown in the right-hand portion of the graph.

SHORT-RUN EQUILIBRIUM OF THE PERFECTLY COMPETITIVE FIRM

We have pointed out that economists consider the short run to be a period so brief that some relevant arrangements cannot be changed. For example, if a firm has signed a five-year rental lease, that firm's long run must be a period greater than five years. Another critical element that does not change in the short run is the number of firms in the industry. Even if an industry is making profits sufficiently high to induce newcomers to open up for business, entrance usually takes time. For the short run, then, we can ignore the possibility of entry or exit and study the decisions of the firms already in the industry. We already have sufficient background to analyze how the competitive firm decides how much to produce. To begin, recall from Chapter 7 that profit maximization requires the firm to pick an output level that makes its marginal cost equal to its marginal revenue: MC = MR. The only feature that distinguishes the profit-maximizing equilibrium of the competitive firm from that of any other type of firm is its horizontal demand curve.

Because the demand curve is horizontal, the competitive firm's marginal-revenue curve is a horizontal straight line that coincides with its demand curve; hence, MR = price (*P*). It is easy to see why this is so. If the price does not depend on how much the firm sells (which is what a horizontal demand curve means), then each additional unit sold brings in an amount of revenue (the *marginal* revenue) exactly equal to the market price. Thus, marginal revenue always equals price under perfect competition; the demand curve and the MR curve coincide because the firm is a price taker.

Once we know the shape and position of a firm's marginal-revenue curve, we can use this information and the marginal-cost curve to determine its optimal output and profit, as shown in Figure 8-2. As usual, the profit-maximizing output is that at which MC = MR (point *B*). This competitive firm produces 5000 tonnes per year—the output level at which MC and MR are both equal to the market price, $80.

Because a firm in a perfectly competitive market is a price taker, its marginal-revenue schedule coincides with the going market-price line. Thus, the equilibrium of a profit-maximizing firm in a perfectly competitive market must occur at an output level at which marginal cost is equal to price, or in symbols,

$$MC = P$$

The same information is shown in Table 8-2, which gives the firm's total revenue, total cost, and profit for different output quantities. We see

FIGURE 8-2

SMALL-RUN EQUILIBRIUM OF THE COMPETITIVE FIRM

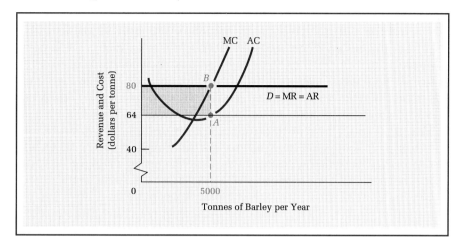

The profit-maximizing firm will select the output (5000 tonnes per year) at which marginal cost equals marginal revenue (point *B*). The demand curve, *D*, is horizontal because the firm's output is too small to affect market price; thus, it is also the marginal-revenue curve. In the short run, demand may be either high or low in relation to cost. Therefore, each unit it sells may return a profit (*AB*) or a loss.

from the last column that total profit is maximized at an output of either 4000 or 5000 tonnes, where total profit is $80 000. Table 8-2 also gives marginal costs and marginal revenues. We see that an increase in output from 4000 tonnes to 5000 tonnes incurs a marginal cost ($80 000) that is equal to the corresponding marginal revenue ($80 000), confirming that 5000 tonnes is the profit-maximizing level of output.[1]

---

1. The MC = MR rule yields the conclusion that the firm should produce exactly 5000 tonnes, while the profit column in Table 8-2 suggests that the firm should be indifferent between operating at 4000 or 5000 tonnes. The source of this slight inconsistency is essentially a measurement error. To calculate marginal costs and marginal revenues accurately, we should increase output 1 tonne at a time, instead of proceeding in leaps of 1000 tonnes. But that would require too much space!

TABLE 8-2

REVENUES, COSTS, AND PROFITS OF A COMPETITIVE FIRM

Quantity (thousands of tonnes)	Total Revenue	Marginal Revenue	Total Cost	Marginal Cost	Total Profit
		(thousands of dollars)			
0	0				
1	80	80	80	0	
2	160	80	140	60	20
3	240	80	180	40	60
4	320	80	240	60	80
5	400	80	320	80	80
6	480	80	440	120	40
7	560	80	640	200	−80

SHORT-RUN PROFIT: GRAPHIC REPRESENTATION

The analysis so far tells us how the firm can pick the output that maximizes profit. But even if it succeeds in doing so, the firm may conceivably find itself in trouble. If the demand for the firm's product is weak or its costs are high, even the most profitable option may lead to a loss. To determine whether the firm is making a profit or incurring a loss, we must compare total revenue (TR = $P \times Q$) with total cost (TC = AC $\times Q$). Since Q is common to both of these, we need only compare P and AC.

The firm's profit is shown in Figure 8-2. By definition, profit per unit of output is revenue per units minus cost per unit. To enable us to represent profit per unit graphically, we have included in Figure 8-2 the firm's average-cost (AC) curve, which was explained in Chapter 6. We see in the figure that average cost at 5000 tonnes per year is only $64 per tonne (point A). Since the price, or average revenue (AR), is $80 per tonne (point B), the firm is making a profit of AR − AC = $16 per tonne. This profit margin appears in the graph as the vertical distance between points A and B.

Notice that in addition to showing the profit per unit, the graph can be used to show the firm's *total profit*. Total profit is the profit per unit ($16 in this example) times the number of units (5000 per year). Therefore, total profit is represented as the area of the shaded rectangle whose height is the profit per unit ($16) and whose width is the number of units (5000). (Recall that the formula for the area of a rectangle is area = height $\times$ width.) That is, total profit at any output is the area of the rectangle whose base equals the level of output and whose height equals AR − AC. Thus, in this case, profits are $80 000 per year.

The MC = P condition gives us the output that maximizes the perfectly competitive firm's profit. It does not tell us whether the firm is making a profit or a loss. To determine this, we must compare price with average cost.

THE CASE OF SHORT-TERM LOSSES

The market is obviously treating the farmer in the graph rather nicely. But what if the market is not so generous in its rewards? What if, for example, the market price is only $40 per tonne instead of $80? Figure 8-3 shows the equilibrium of the firm under these circumstances. The firm still maximizes profits by producing the level of output at which marginal cost is equal to price—point B in the diagram. But this time, "maximizing" profits really means keeping the loss as small as possible.

At the optimal level of output (3000 tonnes per year), average cost is $60 per tonne (point A), which exceeds the $40 per tonne price (point B). The firm is therefore running a loss of $20 per tonne times 3000 tonnes, or $60 000 per year. This loss, which is represented by the area of the shaded rectangle in Figure 8-3, is the best the firm can do. If it selected any other output level, its loss would be even greater.

FIGURE 8-3

SHORT-RUN EQUILIBRIUM OF THE COMPETITIVE FIRM WITH A LOWER PRICE

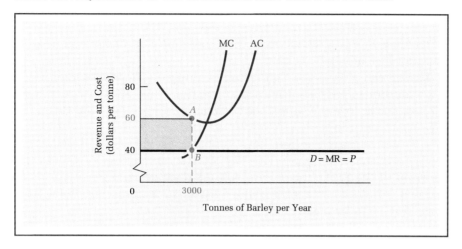

In this diagram, the cost curves are the same as in Figure 8-2, but the demand curve (D) has shifted down to a market price of $40 per tonne. The firm still does the best it can by setting MC = P (point B). But since its average cost at 3000 tonnes per year is $60 per tonne, it runs a loss (shown by the shaded rectangle).

The price-taking firm will always equate MC and P, but in the short run, it may wind up with either a profit or a loss.

SHUT-DOWN AND BREAK-EVEN ANALYSIS

There is, however, a limit to the amount of loss a firm can be forced to accept. If losses get too big, the firm can simply shut down. To understand the logic of the decision between shutting down and remaining in operation, we must return to the distinction between costs that are sunk (the fixed costs) and costs that are variable in the short run. Recall from the discussion in Chapter 6 that costs are sunk if the firm cannot escape them in the short run, either because of a contract (say, with a landlord or a union) or because it has already bought an item (say, a machine), and can get its money back only by operating that item as long as it lasts.

If the firm stops producing, its revenue will fall to zero. Its escapable or variable costs will also fall to zero. But its sunk or fixed costs—such as rent—will remain to plague it. If the firm is losing money, sometimes it will be better off continuing to operate until its obligations to pay sunk costs expire, but sometimes it will do better by shutting down. Two rules govern the decision:

Rule 1.   The firm will not lose money if total revenue (TR) exceeds total cost (TC). In that case, it should not plan to shut down in either the short run or the long run.

Rule 2.   The firm should not shut down in the short run if TR exceeds total escapable or variable cost (TVC). It should, nevertheless, plan to close in the long run if TR is less than TC.

The first rule is obvious. If the firm's revenues cover its total costs, it does not lose money.

The second rule is a bit more subtle. Suppose TR is less than TC. If our unfortunate firm continues in operation, how much will it lose? Clearly, it will lose the difference between total cost and total revenue:

$$\text{Loss if the firm stays in business} = \text{TC} - \text{TR}$$

However, if the firm shuts down, both its revenues and its escapable or variable costs become zero, leaving only its sunk costs—the total fixed costs (TFC)—to be paid:

$$\text{Loss if the firm shuts down} = \text{TFC}$$

Rule 2 is illustrated by the two cases in Table 8-3.[2] Case A deals with a firm that loses money but is better off staying in business in the short run. If it closes down, it will lose its $60 000 fixed cost. But if it continues in operation, it will lose only $40 000 because TR ($100 000) exceeds TVC ($80 000) by $20 000, so that its operation contributes $20 000 toward meeting its sunk costs. In Case B, on the other hand, continued operation only adds to its losses. If the firm operates, it will lose $90 000 (last entry in Table 8-3), whereas if it shuts down, it will lose only the $60 000 in sunk costs that it must pay in any case, whether it operates or not.

The shut-down decision can also be analyzed graphically. In Figure 8-4, the firm will run a loss whether the price is P_1, P_2, or P_3, because

---

2. More generally, we see that the firm will find it advisable to shut down if it is better to lose TFC than to lose TC − TR (that is, if TC − TR > TFC or TC − TFC > TR). Finally, since TC = TFC + TVC, we can express this condition as TVC > TR, which is Rule 2.

TABLE 8-3
THE SHUT-DOWN DECISION

	Case A	Case B
	(thousands of dollars)	
Total revenue (TR)	100	100
Total variable cost (TVC)	80	130
Total fixed cost (TFC)	60	60
Total cost (TC)	140	190
Loss if firm shuts down (TFC)	60	60
Loss if firm does not shut down (TC − TR)	40	90

none of these prices is high enough to reach the minimum level of average cost (AC). The lowest price that keeps the firm from shutting down can be shown in the graph by introducing one more curve: the **average variable cost (AVC)** curve mentioned in Chapter 6. Why is this curve relevant? Because, as we have just seen, it pays the firm to remain in operation if its total revenue (TR) exceeds its **total variable cost (TVC)**. If we divide both TR and TVC by quantity (Q), we get TR/Q = P and TVC/Q = AVC, so this condition may be stated equivalently as the requirement that price exceed AVC. The conclusion is as follows:

The firm will produce nothing unless price lies above the minimum point on the AVC curve.

Figure 8-4 illustrates this principle by showing an MC curve, an AVC curve, and several alternative demand curves corresponding to different possible prices. Price P_1 is below the minimum average variable cost. With this price, the firm cannot even cover its variable costs and is better off shutting down (producing zero output). Price P_3 is higher. While the firm still runs a loss if it sets MC = P at point A (because AC exceeds P_3), it is at least covering its escapable or variable costs, and so it pays to keep operating in the short run. Price P_2 is the borderline case. If the price is P_2, the firm is indifferent between shutting down and staying in business and producing at a level where MC = P (point B). P_2 is thus the lowest price at which the firm will produce anything. As we see from the graph, P_2 corresponds to the minimum point on the AVC curve.

FIGURE 8-4

SHUT-DOWN ANALYSIS

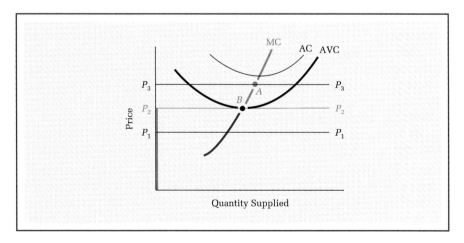

At a price as low as P_1, the firm cannot even cover its average variable costs; it is better off shutting down entirely. At a price as high as P_3, the firm selects point A but operates at a loss (because P_3 is below AC). However, it is more than covering its average variable costs (since P_3 exceeds AVC), so it pays to keep producing. Price P_2 is the borderline case. With this price, the firm selects point B and is indifferent between shutting down and staying open.

THE SHORT-RUN SUPPLY CURVE OF THE COMPETITIVE FIRM

Without realizing it, we have now derived the **supply curve of the competitive firm** in the short run. Why? Recall that a supply curve summarizes the answers to such questions as, If the price is so and so, how much will the firm produce? We have now discovered that there are two possibilities, as indicated by the thick gold lines in Figure 8-4.

1. If the price exceeds the minimum AVC, in the short run it pays a competitive firm to produce the level of output that equates MC and P. Thus, for any price above point B, we can read the corresponding quantity supplied from the firm's MC curve.

2. If the price falls below the minimum AVC, it pays the firm to produce nothing. Quantity supplied falls to zero.

Putting these two observations together, we conclude as follows:

The short-run supply curve of the perfectly competitive firm is its marginal-cost curve above the point where it intersects the average variable-cost curve, that is, above the minimum level of AVC. If price falls below this level, the firm's quantity supplied drops to zero.

THE SHORT-RUN SUPPLY CURVE OF THE COMPETITIVE INDUSTRY

Having completed the analysis of the competitive firm's supply decision, we turn our attention next to the competitive *industry*. Again, we need to distinguish between the short run and long run, but the distinction is different here. The short run for the industry is defined as a period of time too brief for new firms to enter the industry or for old firms to leave, so the number of firms is fixed. By contrast, the long run for the industry is a period of time long enough for any firm that so desires to enter (or leave). In addition, the long run must be a period protracted sufficiently to permit each firm in the industry to adjust its output to its own long-run costs. We begin our analysis of industry equilibrium in the short run.

With the number of firms fixed, it is a simple matter to derive the **supply curve of the competitive industry** from those of the individual firms. At any given price, we simply add up the quantities supplied by each of the firms to arrive at the industry-wide quantity supplied. For example, if each of 1000 identical firms in the barley industry supplies 4000 tonnes when the price is $60 per tonne, the quantity supplied by the industry at a $60 price will be 4000 tonnes per firm × 1000 firms = 4 million tonnes.

This process of deriving the *market* supply curve from the *individual* supply curves of firms is perfectly analogous to the way we derived the market demand curve from the individual demand curves of consumers in Chapter 5. Graphically, we are summing the individual supply curves

FIGURE 8-5

DERIVATION OF THE INDUSTRY SUPPLY CURVE FROM THE SUPPLY CURVES OF THE INDIVIDUAL FIRMS

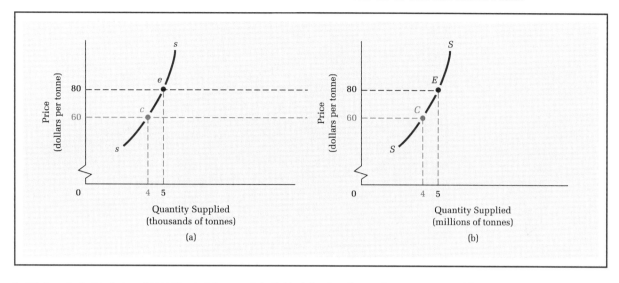

In this hypothetical industry of 1000 identical firms, each individual firm has the supply curve *ss* in part (a). For example, quantity supplied is 4000 tonnes when the price is $60 per unit (point *c*). By adding up the quantities supplied by each firm at each possible price, we arrive at the industry supply curve *SS* in part (b). For example, at a unit price of $60, total quantity supplied by the industry is 4 million units (point *C*).

horizontally, as illustrated in Figure 8-5. At a price of $60, each of the 1000 firms in the industry supplies 4000 tonnes (point *c* in part (a)), so the industry supplies 4 million tonnes (point *C* in part (b)). At a price of $80, each firm supplies 5000 tonnes (point *e* in part (a)), and so the industry supplies 5 million tonnes (point *E* in part (b)). Similar calculations can be done for any other price. This indicates, incidentally, that the supply curve of the industry will shift to the right whenever a new firm enters the industry.

The supply curve of the competitive industry in the short run is derived by horizontally summing the supply curves of all the firms in the industry.

Notice that if the short-run supply curves of individual firms are upward sloping, the short-run supply curve of the competitive industry will be upward sloping, too. We have seen that the firm's supply curve is its marginal-cost curve (above the level of minimum average variable cost), so it follows that rising marginal costs lead to an upward-sloping *industry* supply curve.

INDUSTRY EQUILIBRIUM IN THE SHORT RUN

Now that we have derived the industry supply curve, we need only add a market demand curve to determine the price and quantity that will emerge. This is done for our illustrative barley industry in Figure 8-6,

FIGURE 8-6

SUPPLY–DEMAND EQUILIBRIUM OF A COMPETITIVE INDUSTRY

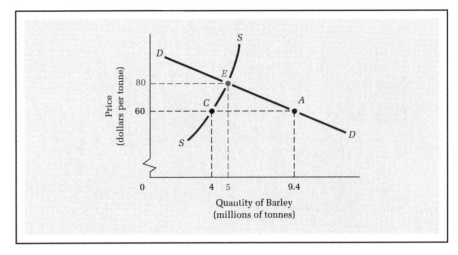

The only equilibrium combination of price and quantity is a price of $80 and a quantity of 5 million tonnes, at which supply curve SS and demand curve DD intersect (point E). At a lower price, such as $60, quantity demanded (9.4 million tonnes, as shown by point A on the demand curve) will be higher than the 4-million-tonne quantity supplied (point C). Thus, the price will be driven back up toward the $80 equilibrium. The opposite will happen at a price such as $100, which is above equilibrium.

where the industry supply curve (carried over from Figure 8-5(b)) is SS and the demand curve is DD. Note that for the competitive industry, unlike the competitive firm, the demand curve is normally downward sloping. Why? Each firm by itself is so small that if it alone were to double its output, the effect would hardly be noticeable. But if *every* firm in the industry were to expand its output, that would make a substantial difference. Customers can be induced to buy the additional quantities arriving at the market only if the price of the good falls.

Point E is the equilibrium point for the competitive industry, because only at the combination of a price of $80 and a quantity of 5 million tonnes are neither purchasers nor sellers motivated to upset matters. At a price of $80, sellers are willing to offer exactly the amount consumers want to purchase.

Should we expect price actually to reach, or at least to approximate, this equilibrium level? The answer is yes. To see why, we must consider what happens when price is not at its equilibrium level. Suppose it takes a lower value, such as $60. The low price will stimulate customers to buy more, and it will also lead firms to produce less than at a price of $80. Our diagram confirms that at a price of $60, quantity supplied (4 million tonnes) is lower than quantity demanded (9.4 million tonnes). Thus, unsatisfied buyers will probably offer to pay higher prices, which will force price upward in the direction of its equilibrium value, $80.

Similarly, if we begin with a price higher than the equilibrium price, we may readily verify that quantity supplied will exceed quantity demanded. Under these circumstances, frustrated sellers are likely to reduce their prices, so price will be forced downward. In the circumstances depicted in Figure 8-6, then, there is in effect a magnet at the equilibrium price of $80 that will pull the actual price in its direction if for some reason the actual price starts out at some other level.

In practice, there are few cases in which competitive markets, over a long period of time, have not apparently moved toward equilibrium prices. Matters eventually seem to work out as depicted in Figure 8-6. Of course, numerous transitory influences—a strike that cuts production, a sudden change in consumer tastes, and so on—can jolt any real-world market away from its equilibrium point. There also have been periods, sometimes of distressingly long duration, when the "bottom has dropped out" of some nearly competitive markets, such as stock exchanges. During such market "crashes," it certainly did not seem that prices were moving toward equilibrium.

Yet, as we have just seen, powerful forces do push prices back toward equilibrium—toward the level at which the supply and demand curves intersect. These forces are of fundamental importance for economic analysis, for without such forces, prices in the real world would bear little resemblance to equilibrium prices, and there would be little reason to study supply–demand analysis. Fortunately, the required equilibrating forces do exist.

INDUSTRY AND FIRM EQUILIBRIUM IN THE LONG RUN

The equilibrium of a competitive industry in the long run may differ from the short-run equilibrium that we have just studied. There are two reasons. First, in the long run, the number of firms in the industry is not fixed. Second, as we saw in Chapter 6 (pages 174–75), in the long run the firm can vary its plant size and make other changes that had been prevented by temporary commitments. Hence, the firm's (and the industry's) long-run cost curves are not the same as its short-run cost curves.

What will lure new firms into the industry or repel old ones? Profits. Remember that when a firm selects its optimal level of output by setting MC = P, it may wind up with either a profit or a loss. Such profits or losses must be *temporary* for a competitive firm, because the freedom of new firms to enter the industry or of old firms to leave it will, in the long run, eliminate them.

Suppose very high profits accrue to firms in the industry. Then new companies will find it attractive to enter the business, and expanded production will force the market price to fall from its initial level. Why? Recall that the industry supply curve is the horizontal sum of the supply curves of individual firms. Under perfect competition, new firms can enter the industry on the same terms as existing firms. This means that new entrants will have the same individual supply curves as old firms. If the market price did not fall, entry of new firms would lead to an increased number of firms with no change in output *per firm*. Consequently, the total quantity supplied on the market would be higher and would exceed quantity demanded. But, of course, this means that in a free market, entry of new firms *must* push the price down.

Figure 8-7 shows how the entry process works. In this diagram, the demand curve, *DD*, and the original (short-run) supply curve, S_0S_0, are carried over from Figure 8-6. The entry of new firms (each farm is a firm) seeking high profits shifts the short-run supply curve outward to the right, to S_1S_1. The new market equilibrium is at point *A* (rather than at point *E*), where price is $70 per tonne and 7.2 million tonnes are produced and consumed. Entry of new firms reduces price and raises total output. (Had the price not fallen, quantity supplied after entry would have been 8 million tonnes—point *F*.) Why must the price fall? Because the demand curve for the industry is downward sloping—an increase in output will be purchased by consumers only if the price is reduced.

To see where the entry process stops, we must consider how the entry of new firms affects the behaviour of old firms. At first, this may seem to contradict the notion of perfect competition; perfectly competitive firms are not supposed to care what their competitors are doing. Indeed, these barley farmers do not care. But they do care very much about the market price of barley, and, as we have just seen, the entry of new firms into the barley-farming industry lowers the price of barley.

FIGURE 8-7

A SHIFT IN THE INDUSTRY SUPPLY CURVE CAUSED BY THE ENTRY OF NEW FIRMS

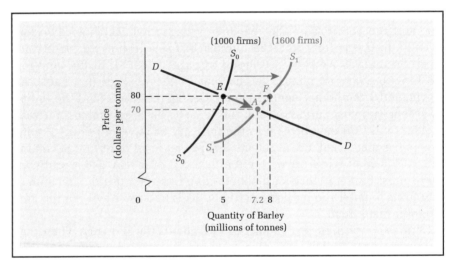

This diagram shows what happens to the industry equilibrium where new firms enter the industry. Quantity supplied at any given price increases; that is, the supply curve shifts to the right, from S_0S_0 to S_1S_1 in the figure. As a result, the market price falls (from $80 to $70) and the quantity increases (from 5 million tonnes to 7.2 million tonnes).

In Figure 8-8, we have juxtaposed the diagram of the equilibrium of the competitive firm (Figure 8-2 on page 233) and the diagram of the equilibrium of the competitive industry (Figure 8-7). Before entry, the market price was $80 (point E in Figure 8-8(b)) and each of the 1000 firms was producing 5000 tonnes—the point where marginal cost and price were equal (point e in Figure 8-8(a)). The demand curve facing each firm was horizontal line D_0 in Figure 8-8(a). There were profits because average costs (AC) at 5000 tonnes per firm were less than price.

Now suppose 600 new firms are attracted by these high profits and enter the industry. Each has the cost structure indicated by the AC and MC curves in Figure 8-8(a). As we have noted, the industry supply curve in Figure 8-8(b) shifts to the right, and price falls to $70 per tonne. Firms in the industry cannot fail to notice this lower price. As we see in Figure 8-8(a), each firm reduces its output to 4500 tonnes in reaction to the lower price (point a). But now there are 1600 firms, so total industry output is 4500 × 1600 = 7.2 million tonnes (point A in Figure 8-8(b)).

At point a in Figure 8-8(a), there are still profits to be made because the $70 price exceeds average cost. Thus, the entry process is not yet complete. When will it end? Only when all profits have been competed away. Only when entry shifts the industry supply curve so far to the right (S_2S_2 in Figure 8-9(b)) that the demand curve facing individual firms falls

FIGURE 8-8

THE COMPETITIVE FIRM AND THE COMPETITIVE INDUSTRY

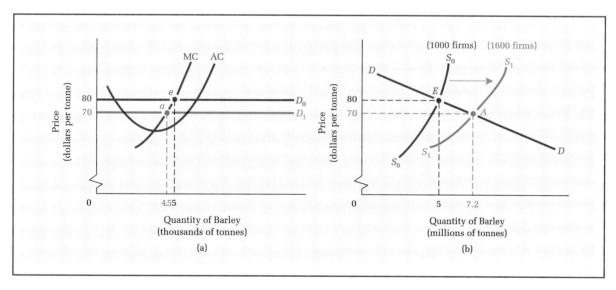

Here we show the interaction between developments at the industry level (in part (b)) and developments at the firm level (in part (a)). An outward shift in the industry supply curve from S_0S_0 to S_1S_1 in part (b) lowers the market price from $80 to $70. In part (a), we see that a profit-maximizing competitive firm reacts to this decline in price by curtailing output. When the demand curve of the firm is D_0 ($80), it produces 5000 tonnes (point e). When the firm's demand curve falls to D_1 ($70), its output declines to 4500 tonnes (point a). However, there are now 1600 firms rather than 1000, so total industry output has expanded from 5 million tonnes to 7.2 million tonnes (part (b)). Entry has reduced profits. But since P still exceeds AC at an output of 4500 tonnes per firm in part (a), some profits remain.

FIGURE 8-9

LONG-RUN EQUILIBRIUM OF THE COMPETITIVE FIRM AND INDUSTRY

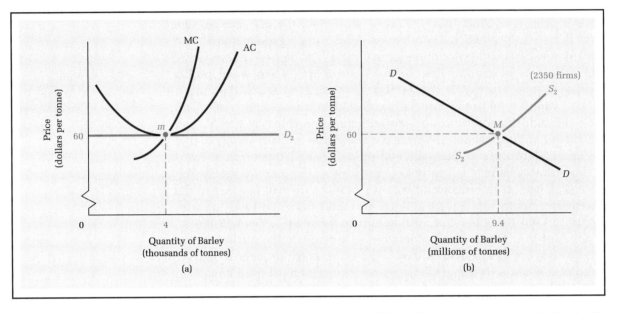

By the time 2350 firms have entered the industry, the industry supply curve is S_2S_2 and the market price is $60 per tonne. At this price, the horizontal demand curve facing each firm is D_2 in part (a), so the profit-maximizing level of output is 4000 tonnes (point m). Here, since average cost and price are equal, there is no economic profit.

to the level of minimum average cost (point m in Figure 8-9(a)) will all profits be eradicated and entry cease.

The two panels of Figure 8-9 show the competitive firm and the competitive industry in long-run equilibrium.[3] Notice that at the equilibrium point (m in part (a)), each firm picks its own output level so as to maximize its profit. This means that, for every firm, P = MC. But free entry forces P to be equal to AC in the long run (point M in part (b)), for if P were not equal to AC, firms would either earn profits or suffer losses.

When a perfectly competitive industry is in long-run equilibrium, firms maximize profits so that P = MC and entry forces the price down until it is tangent to the average-cost curve (P = AC). As a result, in long-run competitive equilibrium, it is true that

$$P = MC = AC$$

Thus, even though every firm earns zero economic profit, profits are at the maximum that is attainable.

_____

3. If the original short-run equilibrium had involved losses instead of profits, firms would have exited from the industry, shifting the industry supply curve inward, until all losses were eradicated; we would have ended up in a position exactly like Figure 8-9. *EXERCISE:* To test your understanding, draw the version of Figure 8-8 that corresponds to this case.

THE LONG-RUN INDUSTRY SUPPLY CURVE

In the numerical example just presented to explain this long-run efficiency point, we have implicitly assumed that the long-run industry supply curve is horizontal. We made this assumption just to simplify the exposition. Let us now clarify where it crept in. When new firms entered the industry, we did not adjust the position of the cost curves for the representative firm. Thus, even though we were discussing a long-run time horizon, we assumed that the new firms built plants just like the old ones and that the old firms chose not to install different sizes or kinds of plants. If instead we had assumed, for example, the use of more efficient (lower average cost) techniques, both the MC and the AC curves would have been lower, resulting in an industry supply curve that was negatively sloped. Thus, if increasing returns to scale are possible for each firm, the long-run industry supply curve will be downward sloping.

This possibility is not the only one. Suppose each individual firm has constant returns to scale, but as the industry expands, the demand by the entire industry forces up the price of one of the inputs. This would raise the position of each firm's MC and AC curves, and the long-run industry supply curve would be positively sloped. It is this long-run industry supply curve, whatever its slope, that is relevant to determination of long-run equilibrium price and quantity in the standard supply–demand diagram. This long-run supply curve of the industry coincides with the industry's long-run average-cost curve.

ZERO ECONOMIC PROFIT: THE OPPORTUNITY COST OF CAPITAL

In our discussion of the long run, something may be troubling you. Why would there be any firms in the industry at all if there were no profits to be made? What sense does it make to call a position of zero profit a "long-run equilibrium"? The answer is that the zero-profit concept used in economics does not mean the same thing it does in ordinary usage.

As we have noted repeatedly, when economists measure average cost, they include the cost of *all* the firm's inputs, including the **opportunity cost** of the capital or any other input, such as labour, provided by the firm's owners. Since the firm may not make explicit payments to those who provide it with capital, this element of cost may not be picked up by the firm's accountants. Thus, what economists call *zero economic profit* may correspond to some positive amount of profit as measured by conventional accounting techniques.

For example, if investors can earn 15 percent by lending their funds elsewhere, the firm must earn a 15 percent rate of return to cover its opportunity cost of capital. Because economists consider this 15 percent opportunity cost to be the cost of the firm's capital, they include it in the AC curve. If the firm cannot earn at least 15 percent on its capital, funds

ECONOMIC PROFIT equals net earnings, in the accountant's sense, minus the firm's opportunity cost of capital.

will not be made available to it because investors can earn greater returns elsewhere. Thus, in the economist's language, in order to break even—earn zero **economic profit**—a firm must earn enough to cover not only the cost of labour, fuel, and raw materials, but also the cost of its funds, including the opportunity cost of any funds supplied by the owners of the firm.

To illustrate the difference between economic profits and accounting profits, suppose Canadian government bonds pay 15 percent and the owner of a small shop earns 10 percent on her business investment. The shopkeeper might say she is making a 10 percent profit, but an economist would say she is *losing* 5 percent on every dollar she has invested in her business. The reason is that by keeping her money tied up in the firm, she gives up the chance to buy government bonds and receive a 15 percent return. With this explanation of economic profit, we can now understand the logic behind the zero-profit condition for the long-run industry equilibrium.

Zero profit in the economic sense simply means that firms are earning the normal economy-wide rate of profit in the accounting sense. This condition is guaranteed by freedom of entry and exit.

Freedom of entry guarantees that those who invest in a competitive industry will receive a rate of return on their capital *no greater than* the return that capital could earn elsewhere in the economy. If economic profits are being earned in some industry, capital will be attracted into it. The new capital will shift the industry supply curve to the right, which will drive down prices and profits. This process will continue until the return on capital in this industry is reduced to the return that capital could earn elsewhere—its opportunity cost.

Similarly, freedom of exit of capital guarantees that in the long run, once capital has had a chance to move, no industry will provide a rate of return *lower than* the opportunity cost of capital. This results because, if returns in one industry are particularly low, resources will flow out of it. Plant and equipment will not be replaced as they wear out. As a result, the industry supply curve will shift to the left, and prices and profits will rise toward their opportunity-cost level.

PERFECT COMPETITION AND ECONOMIC EFFICIENCY

We have now completed our discussion of the long-run equilibrium of the industry. What about the firm? We have already implicitly answered that in Figure 8-9(a). We see there that in equilibrium, the firm's horizontal demand curve, D_2D_2, must be just tangent to its long-run AC curve. Why? If the AC curve lay below D_2D_2, the firm could make a profit by producing an output at which P is greater than AC (as in Figure 8-8(a)). If AC were everywhere above D_2D_2, the firm would suffer a loss because

P would be smaller than AC—no matter what output the firm produces. We know that neither situation is compatible with competitive equilibrium because positive profits induce entry and losses cause exit. We conclude as follows:

Long-run competitive equilibrium of a firm will occur at the lowest point on the firm's long-run AC curve where that curve is tangent to the firm's horizontal demand curve. Thus, the outputs of competitive industries are produced at the lowest possible cost to society.

Why is it always most efficient if each firm in a competitive industry produces at the point where AC is as small as possible? Our example will illustrate the point. Suppose the industry is in long-run equilibrium with 9.4 million tonnes of barley being produced by the 2350 firms (each farm producing 4000 tonnes). This total amount can also be produced by 4700 farms each producing 2000 tonnes or by 1800 farms each producing 5000 tonnes. This is so since $2000 \times 4700 = 4000 \times 2350 = 5000 \times 1880 = 9.4$ million. (Of course, the job can be done by other numbers of farms, but for simplicity, let us consider only these three possibilities.) The AC figures for the farms are as shown in Table 8-4. An output of 4000 tonnes corresponds to the lowest point on the AC curve, with an AC of $60 per tonne. Which is the cheapest way for the industry to produce its output of 9.4 million tonnes? That is, what is the cost-minimizing number of firms for the job? Looking at the last column of Table 8-4, we see that the output of 9.4 million tonnes is produced at the least total cost if it is done by 2350 firms each producing the cost-minimizing output of 4000 tonnes.

Why is this so? The answer is not difficult to see. For a given industry output, it is obvious that total industry cost will be as small as possible if and only if AC for each firm is as small as possible; that is, if the number of firms doing the job is such that each is producing the output at which AC is as low as possible.

That this kind of cost efficiency characterizes perfect competition in the long run can be seen in Figures 8-8 and 8-9. Before full long-run equilibrium is reached (Figure 8-8), firms may not be producing in the least costly way. For example, the 5 million tonnes being produced by 1000 firms at points e and E in Figures 8-8(a) and (b) could be produced

TABLE 8-4
AVERAGE COST FOR THE FIRM AND TOTAL COST FOR THE INDUSTRY

Firm's Output (thousands of tonnes)	Firm's Average Cost (thousands of dollars)	Number of Firms	Industry Output (millions of tonnes)	Total Industry Cost (millions of dollars)
2	70	4700	9.4	658.0
4	60	2350	9.4	564.0
5	64	1880	9.4	601.6

more cheaply by more firms, each producing a smaller volume, because the point of minimum average cost lies to the left of point *e* in Figure 8-8(a). This problem is rectified, however, in the long run by entry of new firms seeking profit. We see in Figure 8-9 that after the entry process is complete, every firm is producing at its most efficient (lowest AC) level—4000 tonnes. As Adam Smith might have put it, even though each farmer cares only about his or her own profits, the barley-farming industry as a whole is guided by an "invisible hand" to produce the amount of barley that society wants at the lowest possible cost.

CUTTING POLLUTION: THE CARROT OR THE STICK?

We end the chapter by returning to the puzzle with which it began, because we now have all the tools needed to resolve it. We had discussed two pollution-curbing proposals: Should polluters be taxed on their emissions, or should they, instead, be offered a subsidy to cut emissions? Such a subsidy would indeed induce firms to cut their emissions. Nevertheless, we stated early in the chapter that the paradoxical net result would likely be an increase in total pollution.

This paradox is readily illustrated with the help of a standard supply–demand diagram for a competitive industry. We see in Figure 8-10 that a tax on polluting output will raise the cost of the industry and hence raise the price of whatever quantity it supplies. Thus, a tax will shift the supply curve upward to the curve labelled "Supply after tax." Similarly, the subsidy will reduce dollar costs to the industry and so will shift the supply curve downward to the curve labelled "Supply after subsidy." Thus, under a tax on emissions, the equilibrium point will move from point *E* to point *T*, reducing the output of the polluting product from *e* to *t*. But the subsidy, which moves the supply–demand equilibrium point from *E* to *S*, will actually *increase* the output of the polluting industry, from *e* to *s*. Thus, contrary to intuition, and despite the fact that each firm emits less, the industry must pollute more!

What explains this paradox? The answer is *entry*. The subsidy will initially bring economic profits to the polluters, and that will attract even more polluters into the industry. In essence, a subsidy is a bribe for more polluters to open up for business. But our graph takes us one step beyond this simple observation. It is true that we end up with more polluting firms, but each will be polluting less than before. Thus, we have one influence leading to increased pollution and one pushing in the opposite direction. Which of these forces will win out? The graph tells us that if a rise in the polluting good's output always increases pollution, then when a subsidy is the policy instrument used, increased pollution will prevail.

FIGURE 8-10

SUBSIDY FOR REDUCED EMISSIONS INCREASES POLLUTION BUT EMISSION CHARGES
DECREASE POLLUTION

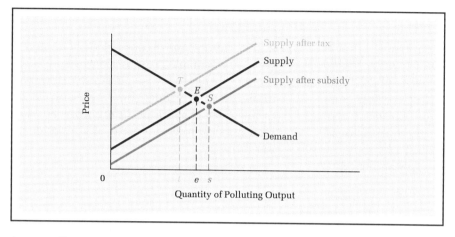

Quantity of Polluting Output

A tax on pollution raises costs and so shifts the supply curve upward; that is, a higher price is needed
to elicit a given quantity supplied. This causes equilibrium output to fall from *e* to *t* and succeeds in its
purpose—reducing pollution. But a subsidy to those who decrease their polluting output reduces costs
and shifts the supply curve downward. By reducing costs, it attracts more firms into the industry. Paradoxically, output of the polluting product must actually increase from *e* to *s*.

SUMMARY

1. Markets are classified into several types
depending on the number of firms in the
industry, the degree of similarity of their
products, and the possibility of impediments to entry.

2. The four main market structures are monopoly (single-firm production), oligopoly (production by a few firms), monopolistic
competition (production by many firms with
somewhat different products), and perfect
competition (production by many firms with
identical products and free entry and exit).

3. Few industries satisfy the conditions of perfect competition exactly, although some
come close. We study perfect competition
because it is easy to analyze and because it
is useful as a yardstick for measuring the
performance of other market forms.

4. The demand curve of a perfectly competitive
firm is horizontal because its output is such
a small share of the industry's production
that it cannot affect price. With a horizontal
demand curve, price, average revenue, and
marginal revenue are all equal.

5. The short-run equilibrium of a perfectly
competitive firm is at the level of output that
maximizes profits, that is, where MC equals
MR equals price. This equilibrium may
involve either a profit or a loss.

6. The short-run supply curve of a perfectly
competitive firm is the portion of its marginal-cost curve that lies above its average
variable cost (AVC) curve.

7. An industry's short-run supply curve under
perfect competition is the horizontal sum of
the supply curves of all of its firms.

8. In the long run, freedom of entry forces a perfectly competitive firm to earn zero economic profit; that is, it earns no more than the firm's capital could earn elsewhere (the opportunity cost of the capital).

9. Industry equilibrium under perfect competition is at the point of intersection of the industry's supply and demand curves.

10. In long-run equilibrium under perfect competition, a firm's output is chosen so that average cost, marginal cost, and price are all equal. Output is at the point of minimum average cost, and the firm's demand curve is tangent to its average-cost curve at its minimum point.

11. A competitive industry's long-run supply curve coincides with its long-run average-cost curve.

12. Both a tax on emission of pollutants and a subsidy payment for reduction in emissions induce firms to cut emissions. However, under perfect competition, a subsidy leads to the entry of more polluting firms and the likelihood of a net increase in emissions by the industry.

CONCEPTS FOR REVIEW

Market
Perfect competition
Pure monopoly
Monopolistic competition
Oligopoly

Price taker
Horizontal demand curve
Short-run equilibrium
Average variable cost (AVC)
Total variable cost (TVC)

Supply curve of the firm
Supply curve of the industry
Long-run equilibrium
Opportunity cost
Economic profit

QUESTIONS FOR DISCUSSION

1. Explain why a perfectly competitive firm does not expand its sales without limit if its horizontal demand curve means that it can sell as much as it wants to at the current market price.

2. Explain why a demand curve is also a curve of average revenue. Recalling that when an average-revenue curve is neither rising nor falling, marginal revenue must equal average revenue, explain why it is always true that $P = MR = AR$ for a perfectly competitive firm.

3. Explain why in the short-run equilibrium of a perfectly competitive firm, P = MC, while in long-run equilibrium, $P = MC = AC$.

4. Which of the four attributes of perfect competition (many small firms, freedom of entry, standardized product, perfect information) are primarily responsible for the fact that the demand curve of a perfectly competitive firm is horizontal?

5. Which of the four attributes of perfect competition is primarily responsible for a firm's zero economic profit in long-run equilibrium?

6. The text indicates (pages 237–38) that the MC curve cuts the AVC curve at the minimum point of the latter. Explain why this must be so. (*Hint:* Since marginal costs are, by definition, all variable costs, the MC

curve can be considered the curve of marginal variable costs. Apply the general relationships between marginals and averages explained in Chapter 7).

7. Explain why it is not sensible to close a business firm if it earns zero economic profit.

8. If a perfectly competitive firm's lowest average cost is $12 and the corresponding average variable cost is $6, what does it pay the firm to do if
   a. the market price is $11?
   b. the price is $7?
   c. the price is $4?

9. If the market price in a competitive industry is above its equilibrium level, what do you expect to happen?

10. A few years ago when oil prices were very high, it was proposed to mix alcohol distilled from grain with gasoline to make "gasohol." This obviously would have caused an upward shift in the demand for grain. Use Figure 8-9 to analyze the effects on barley-growing profit and output
    a. in the short run.
    b. in the long run.

11. In this chapter, we asserted that a firm's MC curve goes through the lowest point of its AC curve as well as through the lowest point of its AVC curve. Since the AVC curve lies below the AC curve, how can both these statements be true?

CHAPTER 9

THE PRICE SYSTEM: LAISSEZ FAIRE VERSUS ECONOMIC PLANNING

Early in the book, we posed a two-part question that provides an organizing framework for our study of microeconomics: What does the market do well, and what does it do poorly? Given what we have learned about demand in Chapters 4 and 5 and about supply in Chapters 6 to 8, we can now offer a fairly comprehensive answer to the first part of this question: What does the market do well?

We begin by returning to two important themes raised in Chapters 2 and 3: first, that because all resources are scarce, it is critical to use them efficiently; second, that an economy must have some way to co-ordinate the actions of many individual consumers and producers. Specifically, we emphasize that society must somehow choose how much of each good to produce, what input quantities to use in the production process, and how to distribute the resulting outputs among consumers.

As the opening quotations suggest, these tasks are exceedingly difficult for central planners to accomplish effectively. But they are rather simple for a market system, which is why observers with philosophies as diverse as those of Adam Smith and Leon Trotsky have been admirers of the market. But this chapter should not be misinterpreted as a salute to the market system, for that is not its purpose.

We have organized this textbook in a way that allows us to give a full account of both the strengths and the weaknesses of the market. Now that we have completed our discussion of perfect competition, it makes sense to explain the market's advantages fully in this chapter and, hence, to make clear why economists view perfect competition as the standard by which to compare other market structures. In the following two chapters, we discuss various forms of monopoly, then devote an entire chapter to cataloguing the market's major shortcomings.

We have divided this chapter into two parts. The first part, like the last several chapters, is analytical; it explains how economic efficiency can be obtained through the operation of *de*centralized markets under conditions of perfect competition. The second part is institutional and

If there existed the universal mind that ... would register simultaneously all the processes of nature and of society, that could forecast the results of their interreactions, such a mind ... could ... draw up a faultless and an exhaustive economic plan. ... In truth, the bureaucracy often conceives that just such a mind is at its disposal; that is why it so easily frees itself from the control of the market.

LEON TROTSKY (a leader of the Russian Revolution)

There is no worthy alternative to the market mechanism as the method for co-ordinating economic activities.

LEONID ABALKIN (deputy prime minister of the Soviet Union, 1989)

historical; it explains the experiences of several countries that have relied on varying degrees of central planning instead of (or in addition to) the market. The two parts of the chapter can be read independently of each other. Your instructor may choose to help you through the first part, but leave you to read the second part (on the countries of Eastern Europe, China, and Japan) on your own. The chapter closes with an appendix, which extends the analytical material of the first part of the chapter, and which is optional in shorter courses.

EFFICIENCY AND FREE MARKETS

The version of the price system we shall study here is an idealized one in which every good is produced under the exacting conditions of perfect competition. While, as we have seen, a few industries are reasonable approximations of perfect competition, other industries in our economy are as different from this idealized world as the physical world is from a frictionless vacuum tube. But just as the physicist uses the vacuum tube to illustrate the laws of gravity with a clarity that is otherwise unattainable, the economist uses the theoretical concept of a perfectly competitive economy to illustrate the virtues of the market. There will be plenty of time in later chapters to study its vices. Indeed, the next three chapters, as we noted above, discuss the weaknesses of the market, and the whole of Part 4 investigates areas in which many regard the market to operate imperfectly—areas such as income distribution, monopoly, and pollution.

EFFICIENT RESOURCE ALLOCATION: THE CONCEPT

The fundamental fact of scarcity limits the volume of goods and services that any economic system can produce. In Chapter 2, we illustrated the concept of scarcity with a graphical device called a *production possibilities frontier*, which we repeat here for convenience as Figure 9-1. The frontier, curve *BC*, depicts all combinations of manufactured goods and clean air that this society can produce given the limited resources at its disposal. For example, if it decides to use pollution-control devices to maintain an air quality level of 20 on the pollution index, it will have enough resources left over to produce *no more than* $500 billion of manufactured goods (point *D*). Of course, it is always possible to produce less than $500 billion of manufactured goods—at a point, such as *G*, below the production possibilities frontier. But if society does this, it is wasting some of its productive potential; that is, it is not operating efficiently.

In Chapter 2, we defined efficiency rather loosely as the absence of waste. Since the main subject of this chapter is how a competitive market economy allocates resources efficiently, we now need a more precise definition. It is easiest to define an **efficient allocation of resources** by saying what it is not. Suppose it were possible to rearrange things so that some people would have more of the things they want and no one would have to give up anything. Then, failure to change the allocation of resources to take advantage of this opportunity would surely be wasteful—that is, *inefficient*. When there are no such possibilities for reallocating resources to make some people better off without making anyone else worse off, we say that the allocation of resources is *efficient*.

Figure 9-1 illustrates the idea. Points below the frontier, such as *G*, are inefficient because, if we start at *G*, we can make both clean-air lovers and material-consumption lovers better off by moving to a point *on* the frontier, like *E*. Thus, no point below the frontier can represent an efficient allocation of resources. By contrast, *every* point on the frontier is efficient because, no matter where on the frontier we start, it is impossible to get more of one good without giving up some of the other.

This example brings out two important features of the concept of efficiency. First, it is strictly a technical concept; there are no value judgements stated or implied, and tastes are not questioned. An economy is

An **EFFICIENT ALLOCA-TION OF RESOURCES** is one that takes advantage of every opportunity to make some individuals better off, in their own estimation, while not worsening the lot of anyone else.

FIGURE 9-1

THE PRODUCTION POSSIBILITIES FRONTIER AND EFFICIENCY

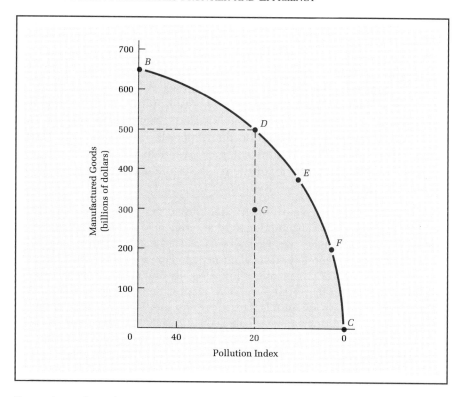

Every point on the production possibilities frontier, *BC*, represents an efficient allocation of resources, because it is impossible to get more of one item without giving up some of the other. Any point below the frontier, such as *G*, is inefficient, since it wastes the opportunity to obtain more of both goods.

judged efficient if it is good at producing whatever people want. Thus, the economy in the example is just as efficient when it produces only manufactured goods at point *B* as when it produces only pollution-control devices at point *C*.

Second, there are normally many efficient allocations of resources; in the example, every point on frontier *BC* is efficient. As a rule, the concept of efficiency does not permit us to tell which allocation is "best" for society. In fact, the most amazing thing about the concept of efficiency is that it gets us anywhere at all. At first blush, the criterion seems vacuous. It seems to assert, in effect, that anything agreed to unanimously is desirable. If some people are made better off in their own estimation and none are harmed, society is certainly better off by anyone's definition. Yet, as we shall see in this chapter, the concept of efficiency can be used to formulate surprisingly detailed rules to steer us away from situations in which resources are being wasted.

EFFICIENCY AND THE PUBLIC INTEREST

Let us now consider the meaning of efficiency and its connection with pricing. We can start off by indicating that prices can sometimes be *too low* to serve the public interest. This statement raises a point that people untrained in economics always find difficult to accept: low prices may not always be in the public interest. The reason is clear enough. If a price is set too low (for example, the price of using a crowded airport or the price of oil), consumers will receive the wrong signals. They will be encouraged to crowd the airport even more or to consume more oil, thereby squandering society's precious resources. A historical illustration is perhaps the most striking way to convey the point. In 1834, some ten years before the great potato famine caused unspeakable misery and death by starvation and brought so many people from Ireland to North America, a professor of economics named Mountifort Longfield lectured at the University of Dublin about the price system. He offered the following remarkable illustration of his point:

> Suppose the crop of potatoes in Ireland was to fall short in some year one-sixth of the usual consumption. If [there were no] increase of price, the whole . . . supply of the year would be exhausted in ten months, and for the remaining two months a scene of misery and famine beyond description would ensue. . . . But when prices [increase] the sufferers [often believe] that it is not caused by scarcity. . . . They suppose that there are provisions enough, but that the distress is caused by the insatiable rapacity of the possessors . . . [and] they have generally succeeded in obtaining laws against [the price increases] . . . which alone can prevent the provisions from being entirely consumed long before a new supply can be obtained.[1]

---

1. Mountifort Longfield, *Lectures on Political Economy* (Dublin, 1834), pages 53–56.

Longfield's reasoning can usefully be rephrased. If the crop fails, potatoes become scarcer. If society is to use its very scarce resources efficiently, it must cut back on the consumption of potatoes—which is just what rising prices would do automatically if the market mechanism were left to its own devices. However, if the price is held artificially low, consumers will be using society's resources inefficiently. In this case, the inefficiency results in famine and suffering when the year's crop is consumed months before the next crop arrives.

It is not easy to accept the notion that higher prices can serve the public interest better than lower ones. Politicians who voice this view are put in the position of a parent who, before spanking his or her child, announces, "This is going to hurt me much more than it hurts you!" Since advocacy of higher prices courts political disaster, the political system often rejects the market solution when resources suddenly become more scarce.

The pricing of oil in Canada in the 1970s provided an excellent example. For years after the OPEC oil cartel drastically raised prices, legislation in Canada held domestic oil prices below free-market levels. The consequence, as economists were quick to point out, was that Canadian consumers faced a market price for oil that was below the true marginal cost of oil to society. Consumers and producers were therefore encouraged to use too much oil, so Canadian industry lagged behind its competitors in shifting to less energy-intensive methods of production. Suggestions to end the price controls were rebuffed by policy-makers, who feared the political consequences.

Interferences with the "Law" of Supply and Demand

Recall from Chapter 3 that one of the twelve Ideas for Beyond the Final Exam states that interfering with free markets by preventing price increases can sometimes serve the public very badly. In extreme cases, it can even create havoc — undermining production and causing extreme shortages of vitally needed products. The reason is that prohibiting price increases in situations of true scarcity prevents the market mechanism from reallocating resources to help cut down the shortage efficiently. The invisible hand is not permitted to do its work.

Of course, there are cases in which it is appropriate to resist price increases — where unrestrained monopoly would otherwise succeed in gouging the public and where rising prices fall so heavily on the poor that rationing becomes the more acceptable option. But it is important to recognize that artificial restrictions on prices can produce serious and even tragic consequences — consequences that should be taken into account before deciding to tamper with the market mechanism.

SCARCITY AND THE NEED TO CO-ORDINATE ECONOMIC DECISIONS

Efficiency becomes a particularly critical issue for the general welfare when we concern ourselves with the workings of the economy as a whole rather than with a narrower topic such as the setting of one price (for potatoes or even oil). An economy may be thought of as a complex machine with literally millions of component parts. If this machine is to function efficiently, some way must be found to make the parts work in harmony.

A consumer in Calgary may decide to purchase two dozen eggs, and on the same day similar decisions are made by thousands of shoppers throughout the country. None of these purchasers knows or cares about the decisions of the others. Yet scarcity requires that these demands must somehow be co-ordinated with the production process so that the total quantity of eggs demanded does not exceed the total quantity supplied. The supermarkets, wholesalers, shippers, and chicken farmers must somehow arrive at consistent decisions, for otherwise the economic process will deteriorate into chaos. Many other such decisions must be co-ordinated. One cannot run machines that are completed except for a few parts that have not been delivered. Planes and cars cannot be used unless there is an adequate supply of fuel.

In an economy that is planned and centrally directed, it is easy to imagine how such co-ordination takes place — although the implementation turns out to be far more difficult than the idea. Central planners set production targets for firms and may even tell firms how to meet these targets. In extreme cases, consumers may even be told, rather than asked, what they want to consume.

In a market system, prices are used to co-ordinate economic activity instead. High prices discourage consumption of the resources that are most scarce, while low prices encourage consumption of the resources that are comparatively abundant. For example, if supplies of oil begin to run out while enormous reserves of coal remain, the price of oil can be expected to rise in comparison with the price of coal. As the price of oil rises, only those for whom oil offers the greatest benefits will continue to buy it. Firms or individuals that can get along almost equally well with coal or gas will switch to these more economical fuels. Some business firms will transform their equipment, and new homes will be built with heating systems that use gas. Only those who find alternative fuels a poor or unacceptable substitute for oil will continue to use oil despite its higher price. In this way, prices are the instrument used by Adam Smith's invisible hand to organize the economy's production.

The invisible hand has an astonishing capacity to handle a co-ordination problem of truly enormous proportions — one that will remain beyond the capabilities of computers at least for the foreseeable future. It is true that, like any mechanism, this one has its imperfections, some

APPLICATION

PRICING TO PROMOTE EFFICIENCY: AN EXAMPLE

To consider the connection between pricing and efficiency, let us use a real-life example — the prices that are charged to use Canada's airports.

Congested airports have caused some of the most bitter squabbles about resource use. For example, Montreal's Dorval Airport has long been congested at peak times (such as 5:00 P.M. on Fridays) but not at other times (such as the middle of Thursday afternoons). Because of the crowding that sometimes occurred, the federal government built the extremely underused Mirabel Airport. No one denies the dramatic wastage of resources that was involved.

Most of this waste has followed from the presumption that airport congestion must be approached from a purely technical point of view. Officials simply do not question the assumption that more runways, more parking and terminal facilities, and more efficient methods of refuelling and loading are the answers.

The problem is that all of these aspects of the issue involve resources that are not currently priced on any market. Transport Canada issues a complete book to airport administrations entitled *Air Service Fee Regulations*. In it, the charges for landings, take-offs, plane parking, bridges (the structures used for passengers to enter the planes), and various aspects of terminal use are listed.

These charges depend on all kinds of things, such as whether the flight is domestic, trans-border, or trans-ocean; the type of engine on the airplane; and the gross take-off weight of the aircraft. However, *none* of the fees depends at all on the economic value of the use of the airport. Consequently, a very few passengers in a small private aircraft can pay a trivial landing fee and significantly add to congestion at peak times.

To an economist, the problem of peak-load congestion at airports is an obvious outcome of improper pricing. Airport charges for services should differ among airports and among times of the week and year. There should be low prices during those hours when space is abundant, and higher prices during rush hours, when space is scarce. Such a variable price structure would provide the incentive for those who can conveniently change times or location (for example, use the airport at Hamilton instead of Toronto) to do so. As a result, use of the airport could be switched away from the congested periods with the least total sacrifice. This flexibility is precluded by the current rigid price structure. The result is much wastage, including airport lands that could have been (or were) used for farms, homes, parks, productive industries, or simply open space near the cities.

of them rather serious. But without understanding the nature of the overall task performed by the market system, it is all too easy to lose sight of the tremendously demanding task that it constantly accomplishes — unnoticed, undirected, and at least in some respects, amazingly well. Let us, then, examine in more detail the nature of this co-ordination problem.

THREE CO-ORDINATION TASKS IN THE ECONOMY

We noted in Chapter 2 that any economic system, whether planned or unplanned, must find answers to three basic questions of resource allocation:

1. ***Output selection.*** How much of each commodity should be produced?

2. ***Production planning.*** What quantities of each of the available inputs should be used to produce each good?

3. ***Distribution.*** How should the resulting goods be divided among the consumers?

These co-ordination tasks may at first appear tailor-made for a regime of governmental central planning. Yet experience has shown that these are the tasks that central planning performs most poorly and, paradoxically, that the free market, with its utter lack of conscious planning and central direction, is at its best when coping with them. To understand how the unguided market manages the miracle of producing co-ordination out of what might otherwise have been chaos, let us look at how each of these questions is answered by a system of free and unfettered markets, the method of economic organization that the eighteenth-century French economists named **laissez faire**. Under laissez faire, the government would prevent crime, enforce contracts, and build roads and other types of public works, but it would not set prices and would interfere as little as possible with the operation of free markets. How does such an unmanaged economy solve the three co-ordination problems?

LAISSEZ FAIRE refers to a program of minimal interference with the workings of the market system. The term means that people should be left alone in carrying out their economic affairs.

OUTPUT SELECTION

In a free market system, the price mechanism decides what to produce via what we have called the "law" of supply and demand. Where there is a *shortage*—that is, where quantity demanded exceeds quantity supplied—the market mechanism pushes the price up, thereby encouraging more production and less consumption of the commodity in short supply. Where there is a *surplus*—that is, where quantity supplied exceeds quantity demanded—the same mechanism works in reverse: the price falls, which discourages production and stimulates consumption.

   We can make these abstract ideas more concrete by looking at a particular example. Suppose millions of people wake up one morning with a craving for omelettes. For the moment, the quantity of eggs demanded exceeds the quantity supplied. But within days, the market mechanism swings into action to meet this sudden change in demand. The price of eggs rises, which stimulates the production of eggs. In the first instance, farmers simply bring more eggs to market by taking them out of storage. Over a somewhat longer period of time, chickens that otherwise would have been sold for meat are kept in the chicken coops laying eggs. Finally, if the high price of eggs persists, farmers begin to increase their flocks, build more cages, and so on. Thus, a shift in consumer demand leads to a shift in society's resources; more eggs are wanted, and so the market mechanism sees to it that more of society's resources are devoted to the production of eggs. Some characterize this process as being driven by **consumer sovereignty**.

Similar reactions follow if a technological breakthrough reduces the input quantities needed to produce some item. Electronic calculators are a perfect example. Just 25 years ago, calculators were so expensive that they could be found only in business firms and scientific laboratories. Then, advances in science and engineering reduced their cost dramatically, and the market went to work. With costs sharply reduced, prices plummeted and the quantity demanded skyrocketed. Electronics firms flocked into the industry to meet this demand: in other words, more of society's resources were devoted to producing the calculators that were suddenly in such great demand. These examples lead us to the following conclusion:

Under laissez faire, the allocation of society's resources among different products depends on two basic influences: consumer preferences and the relative difficulty of producing the goods, that is, their production costs. Prices vary so as to bring the quantity of each commodity produced into line with the quantity demanded.

Notice that no bureaucrat or central planner arranges the allocation of resources. Instead, allocation is guided by an unseen force—the lure of profits, which is the invisible hand that guides chicken farmers to increase their flocks when eggs are in greater demand and guides electronics firms to build new factories when the cost of electronic products falls.

CONSUMER SOVEREIGNTY means that consumer preferences determine what goods shall be produced, and in what amounts.

PRODUCTION PLANNING

Once the composition of output has been decided, the next co-ordination task is to determine just how those goods are going to be produced. The production-planning problem includes, among other things, the assignment of inputs to enterprises—that is, which farm or factory will get how much of which materials. These decisions can be crucial. If a factory runs short of an essential input, the entire production process may grind to a halt.

In reality, inputs and outputs cannot be selected separately. The inputs assigned to the growing of coffee rather than of bananas determine the quantities of coffee and bananas that can be obtained. However, it is simpler to think of these decisions as if they occurred one at a time.

Once again, under laissez faire it is the price system that apportions fuels and other raw materials among the different industries in accord with those industries' requirements. The firm that needs a piece of equipment most urgently will be the last to drop out of the market for that product when prices rise. If more grain is demanded by millers than is currently available, the price will rise and bring quantity demanded back into line with quantity supplied, always giving priority to those users who are willing to pay the most for grain.

In a free market, inputs are assigned to the firms that can make the most productive (most profitable) use of them. Firms that cannot make a sufficiently productive use of some input will be priced out of the market for that item.

This task, which sounds so simple, is actually almost unimaginably complex. Many centrally planned systems have floundered trying to accomplish it. We will return to this task shortly, as an illustration of how difficult it is to replace the market with a central-planning bureau. But first let us consider the third of our co-ordination problems.

DISTRIBUTION OF PRODUCTS AMONG CONSUMERS

The third task of any economy is to decide which consumer gets each of the goods that have been produced. The objective is to distribute the available supplies so as to match the differing preferences of consumers as well as possible. Coffee lovers must not be flooded with tea while tea drinkers are showered with coffee.

The price mechanism solves this problem by assigning the highest prices to the goods in greatest demand and then letting individual consumers pursue their own self-interests. Consider our example of the rising price of eggs. As the price of eggs rises, those whose craving for omelettes is not terribly strong will begin to buy fewer eggs. In effect, the price acts as a rationing device, apportioning the available eggs among the consumers who are willing to pay the most for them.

But the price mechanism has one important advantage over other rationing devices: It is able to pay attention to consumer preferences. If eggs are rationed by the most obvious and usual means (say, two to a person), everyone ends up with the same quantity—one consumer might think of eggs as the most unpleasant component of his breakfast, while another might value them as the ingredients of the soufflé for which she has pined all day long. The price system, on the other hand, permits each consumer to set his or her own priorities. If you just barely tolerate eggs, a rise in their price quickly induces you to get your protein from some other source. But the egg lover is not induced to switch so readily.

The price system carries out the distribution process by rationing goods on the basis of preferences *and relative incomes*.

Notice the last three words. This rationing process does favour the rich, and this is a problem that market economies must confront. Each dollar gets a vote in the market. However, we may still want to think twice before declaring ourselves opposed to the price system. If equality is our goal, might not a more reasonable solution be to use the tax system to equalize incomes, and then let the market mechanism distribute goods in accord with preferences?

We have just seen, in broad outline, how a laissez faire economy addresses the three basic issues of resource allocation: what to produce, how to produce it, and how to distribute the resulting products. Since it performs these tasks quietly, without central direction and with no apparent concern for the public interest, many radical critics have predicted that such an unplanned system must degenerate into chaos. Yet that does not seem to happen. Unplanned the market may be, but its results are far from chaotic. In fact, quite ironically, it is the centrally planned economies that often find themselves in economic chaos. Perhaps the best way to appreciate the accomplishments of the market is to consider how a centrally planned system copes with the three co-ordination problems we have just outlined. For this purpose, we will concentrate on just one of them: production planning.

INPUT–OUTPUT ANALYSIS: THE VIRTUAL IMPOSSIBILITY OF PERFECT CENTRAL PLANNING

Of the three co-ordination tasks of any economy, the assignment of inputs to specific industries and firms has claimed the most attention of central planners. The reason is this: Because the production processes of the various industries are interdependent, the whole economy can grind to a halt if the production-planning problem is not solved satisfactorily.

Let's take a simple example. Gasoline is used both by consumers to run cars and by the trucking industry. Unless the planners allocate enough gasoline to trucking, products will not get to market, and unless they allocate enough trucks to haul the gasoline to gas stations, consumers will not be able to get to the market to buy the products. Thus, trucking activity depends on gasoline production but the latter also depends on the former. We seem to be caught in a circle. Although it turns out not to be a vicious circle, both problems must be dealt with together, not separately.

Because the output required from any one industry depends on the output desired from every other industry, planners can be sure that the production of the various outputs is sufficient to meet both consumer and industrial demands only by taking explicit account of the interdependence among industries. If they change the output target for one industry, every other industry's output target must also be adjusted.

For example, if planners decide to provide consumers with more electricity, more steel must be produced for more electric generators. But an increase in steel output requires more coal to be mined. More mining in turn means that still more electricity is needed to light the mines, to run the elevators, and perhaps even to run some of the trains that carry the coal, and so on. Any single change in production sets off a chain of adjustments throughout the economy that require still further adjustments.

To decide how much of each output an economy must produce, a planner must use statistics to form a set of equations, one equation for each product, and then solve those equations *simultaneously*. (The simultaneous solution process prevents the circularity of the analysis—electricity output depends on steel production but steel output depends on electricity production—from becoming a vicious circle.) The technique used to solve these complicated equations—**input–output analysis**—was invented by economist Wassily Leontief, and it won him the Nobel Prize in 1973.

The equations of input–output analysis, which are illustrated in the boxed insert on the opposite page, take account of the interdependence among industries by describing precisely how each industry's target output depends on every other industry's target. Only by solving these equations simultaneously for the required outputs of electricity, steel, coal, and so on can one be sure of a consistent solution that produces the required amounts of each product—including the amount of each product needed to produce every other product.

The example of input–output analysis that appears in the box is not provided so that you can learn how to apply the technique yourself. Its real purpose is to illustrate the very complicated nature of the problem that faces a real central planner, for such a problem, while analogous to the one in the box, is enormously more complex. In any real economy, the number of commodities is far greater than the three outputs in the example. In Canada, some large manufacturing companies individually deal in hundreds of items and keep thousands of different items in inventory. In planning, it is ultimately necessary to make calculations for each such item. It is not enough to plan the right number of bolts in total; we must make sure that the required number of *each size* is produced. (Try to put five million large bolts into five million small nuts.) Thus, to be sure our plans will really work, we need a separate equation for every size of bolt and one for every size and type of nut. But then, to replicate the analysis described in the boxed insert, we will have to solve simultaneously several million equations!

This problem of computation has two dimensions. The first is the sheer size of the matrices that must be inverted to solve such a vast number of simultaneous equations. The second concerns the functional form of the millions of equations involved. For such a large system to be solved, the equations must be linear, but real-world technological relationships are not linear: Because of diminishing returns, production functions are curved relationships. Thus, even with the aid of a powerful computer, the standard input–output analysis explained in the boxed insert could supply, at best, only an approximation of the actual solution. (It might

FURTHER DETAIL

INPUT–OUTPUT EQUATIONS: AN EXAMPLE

Imagine an economy with only three outputs — electricity, steel, and coal — and let E, S, and C represent the dollar value of their respective outputs. Suppose that for every dollar's worth of steel, $0.20 worth of electricity is used up, so that the total electricity demand of steel manufacturers is $0.2S$. Similarly, assume the coal manufacturers use up $0.30 of electricity in producing $1 worth of coal, or a total of $0.3C$ units of electricity. Since E dollars of electricity are produced in total, the amount left over for consumers, after subtraction of industrial demands for fuel, will be

$$E \quad - \quad 0.2S \quad - \quad 0.3C$$
(available   (use in steel   (use in coal
electricity)   production)   production)

Suppose further that the central planners have decided to supply $15 million worth of electricity to consumers. We end up with the following electricity output equation:

$$E - 0.2S - 0.3C = 15$$

The planner will also need such an equation for each of the two other industries, specifying for each of them the net amounts intended to be left for consumers after the industrial uses of these products. The full set of equations might then be

$$E - 0.20S - 0.30C = 15$$

$$S - 0.10E - 0.06C = 7$$

$$C - 0.15E - 0.40S = 10$$

The planner can now solve these equations to determine the values of E, S, and C that will just meet all needs. These are typical equations in an input–output analysis. However, in practice, a typical analysis has hundreds and sometimes thousands of equations with corresponding numbers of unknowns. This, then, is the logic of input–output analysis.

be interesting to note here that by the early 1990s, computer technology had progressed to the point where it could just begin to handle computations of this magnitude—suggesting that, at least from the mathematical perspective, central planning might one day become feasible. Ironically, it was at this time that countries all over the world were moving away from planning and toward a decentralized, market approach.)

Worse still is the data problem. Each of the three equations in our boxed insert requires three pieces of statistical information, making 3×3, or 9, numbers in total. This is because the equation for electricity must indicate on the basis of statistical information how much electricity is needed in steel production, how much is needed in coal production, and how much is demanded by consumers. In a five-industry analysis, 5×5, or 25, pieces of data are needed; a 100-industry analysis requires 100^2, or 10 000, numbers; and a 1-million-item input–output study would need 1 *trillion* pieces of information. The data-gathering problems are therefore no easy task, to put it mildly. There are still other complications, but we have seen enough to conclude as follows:

A full, rigorous central-planning solution to the production problem is a tremendous task, requiring an overwhelming quantity of information and some incredibly difficult calculations. Yet this very difficult job is carried out automatically and unobtrusively by the price mechanism in a free-market economy.

HOW PERFECT COMPETITION ACHIEVES EFFICIENCY: WHAT TO PRODUCE

Earlier in the chapter, we indicated how the market mechanism solves the three basic co-ordination problems of any economy — what to produce, how to produce, and how to distribute the goods to consumers. Further, we suggested that these same tasks pose almost insurmountable difficulties for central planners. One critical question remains: Is the allocation of resources that the market mechanism selects *efficient*, according to the precise definition of efficiency presented earlier in this chapter? The answer is that, under the idealized circumstances of perfect competition, it is. Since a detailed proof of this assertion for all three co-ordination tasks would be long and time-consuming, we will present the proof only for the first of the three tasks — output selection. The corresponding analyses for the production-planning and distribution problems are quite similar and are reserved for the appendix to this chapter.

Our question is this: Given the output combination selected by the market mechanism, is it possible to improve matters by producing more of one good and less of another? Might it be "better," for example, if society produced more beef and less lamb? We shall answer this question in the negative, thus showing that, at least in theory, perfect competition does guarantee efficiency in production.

We will do this in two steps. First, we will derive a criterion for efficient output selection, that is, a test telling us whether or not production is being carried out efficiently. Second, we will examine why that test is automatically passed by the prices that emerge from the market mechanism under perfect competition.

STEP 1: RULE FOR EFFICIENT OUTPUT SELECTION

We begin by stating the rule for efficient output selection:

Efficiency in the choice of output quantities requires that, for each of the economy's outputs, the marginal cost (MC) of the last unit produced be equal to the marginal utility (MU) of the last unit consumed.[2] In symbols,

$$MC = MU$$

---

2. Recall from Chapter 4 that we measure marginal utility in money terms, that is, as the amount of money that a consumer is willing to give up for an additional unit of the commodity. Economists usually call this the marginal rate of substitution between the commodity and money.

Let us use an example to see why this rule must be satisfied for the allocation of resources to be efficient. Suppose the marginal utility of an additional kilogram of beef to consumers is $8, while its marginal cost is only $5. Then the value of the resources that would have to be used up to produce one more kilogram of beef (its MC) would be $3 less than the consumers' willingness to pay for that additional kilogram (its MU). In a sense, society could get more (the MU) out of the economic production process than it was putting in (the MC) by increasing the output of beef by one kilogram. It follows that the output at which MU > MC cannot be optimal, since society would be made better off by an increase in that output level.

The opposite is true if the MC of beef exceeds the MU of beef. In that case, the last kilogram of beef must have used up more value (MC) than it produced (MU). It would therefore be better to have less beef and more of something else.

We have therefore shown that, if there is *any* product for which MU is not equal to MC, the economy must be wasting an opportunity to produce a net improvement in consumers' welfare. This is exactly what we mean by using resources inefficiently. Just as was true at point G in Figure 9-1, if MC $\neq$ MU for any commodity, it is possible to rearrange things so as to make some people better off while harming no one. It follows that efficiency in the choice of outputs is achieved only when MC = MU for *every* good.[3]

Step 2: The Critical Role of the Price System

The next step in the argument is to show that, under perfect competition, the price system *automatically* leads buyers and sellers to behave in a way that makes MU and MC equal. To see this, recall from the last chapter that, under perfect competition, it is most profitable for each beef-producing firm to produce the quantity of beef at which the marginal cost of the beef is equal to the price of beef:

$$MC = P$$

This must be so because, if the marginal cost of beef were less than the price, the farmer could add to his profits by increasing the size of his herd (or the amount of grain that he feeds his animals), and the reverse would be true if the marginal cost of beef were greater than its price.

---

3. Warning: We will find in Chapter 12 that one reason markets sometimes perform imperfectly is the fact that the marginal cost to the individual decision-maker (this is called *marginal private cost*) is not the same as the marginal cost to society (*marginal social cost*). This situation occurs when the individual whose actions cause the cost is able to escape paying it and instead lets someone else bear the burden. For example, Firm X's production causes pollution emissions that increase the laundry bills of households in the neighbourhood. In such a case, the efficiency rule requires that MU = marginal social cost. That rule will obviously be violated—and inefficiency will result—if the behaviour of the market makes MU = marginal private cost.

Thus, under perfect competition, the lure of profits leads each producer of beef (and of every other product) to supply the quantity that makes MC = P.

We also learned, in Chapter 4, that it is in the interest of each consumer to purchase the quantity of beef at which the marginal utility of beef in terms of money is equal to the price of beef:

$$MU = P$$

If the consumer did not do this, we saw, either an increase or a decrease in his or her purchase of beef would leave the consumer better off.

Putting these last two equations together, we see that the invisible hand enforces the following string of equalities:

$$MC = P = MU$$

But if both the MC of beef and the MU of beef are equal to the same price, P, they must surely be equal to each other. That is, it must be true that the quantity of beef produced and consumed in a perfectly competitive market satisfies the equation

$$MC = MU$$

which is precisely our rule for efficient output selection. Since the same must be true of every other product supplied by a competitive industry, we conclude as follows:

Under perfect competition, the unco-ordinated decisions of producers and consumers can be expected to produce *automatically* a quantity of each good that satisfies the MC = MU rule for efficiency in deciding what to produce. That is, under the idealized conditions of perfect competition, the market mechanism, without any government intervention, is capable of allocating society's scarce resources efficiently.

THE INVISIBLE HAND AT WORK

This is truly a remarkable result. How can the price mechanism automatically satisfy all the exacting requirements for efficiency — requirements that no central planner can hope to handle because of the masses of statistics and the enormous calculations they require? The conclusion seems analogous to the rabbit that is suddenly pulled from the magician's hat. But, as always, rabbits come out of hats only if they were hidden there in the first place. What really is the machinery by which our act of magic works?

The secret is that the price system lets consumers and producers pursue their own best interests—something they are probably very good at doing. Prices are the dollar costs of commodities to consumers. Thus, in pursuing their own best interests, consumers will buy the commodities that give them the most satisfaction *per dollar*. As we learned in Chapter 4, this means that each consumer will continue to buy beef until the marginal utility of beef is equal to the market price. Since every consumer pays the same price in a perfectly competitive market, the market mechanism ensures that every consumer's MU will be equal to this common price.

Turning next to the producers, we know from Chapter 8 that competition equates prices with marginal costs. Once again, since every producer faces the same market price, the force of competition will bring the MC of every producer into equality with this common price. Since MC measures the resource cost (in every firm) of producing one more unit of the good and MU measures the money value (to every consumer) of consuming one more unit, then when MC = MU, the cost of the good to society is exactly equal to the value that consumers place on it. Therefore, we conclude as follows:

When all prices are set equal to marginal costs, the price system is giving the correct cost signals to consumers. It has set prices at levels that induce consumers to use the resources of society with the same care they devote to watching their own money.

This is the magic of the invisible hand. Unlike central planners, consumers need not know how difficult it is to manufacture a certain product or how scarce are the inputs required by the production process. Everything the consumer needs to know to make his or her decision is embodied in the market price, which, under perfect competition, accurately reflects marginal costs.

A GRAPHIC EXPOSITION OF EFFICIENCY

Figure 9-2 illustrates the logic behind the MU = MC rule for determining society's efficient level of production. It shows the demand and supply curves for a particular commodity that is produced competitively. Remember that the demand curve represents households' marginal utility schedule for this commodity, while the supply curve represents the producing firms' marginal cost. Assume that initially in this market, the price is not free to adjust; it is fixed at an amount given by distance *OF* by a law stipulating that amount as the maximum price allowed. We now examine how this law creates inefficiency for the economy.

Initially, the quantity produced is *OJ*, and there is an unsatisfied demand equal to *JL*. The MU = MC rule for efficiency in output selection is not satisfied, since marginal utility is *JB*, which is greater than marginal cost (*JG*).

Now consider what happens if the maximum price law is removed. Price will rise to level *OC*, and quantity will increase to level *OK*. Marginal utility and marginal cost will then be equal, at a value of *OC*. Let us now explicitly calculate the gain to society of moving to the level of output at which MU = MC.

FIGURE 9-2

EFFICIENCY IN OUTPUT SELECTION (MU = MC RULE)

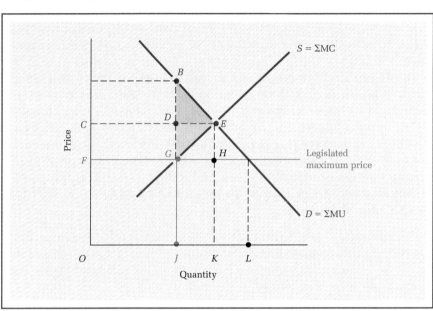

When the price ceiling, distance *OF*, is removed, the price level rises to *OC*, and quantity produced rises from *OJ* to *OK*, the level of output at which marginal utility equals marginal cost. The additional benefit to society at this efficient output level is equal to the shaded area, *GEB*.

By being able to consume the *JK* additional units of the commodity, consumers have a gain in total satisfaction (as measured by their willingness to pay) equal to area *JKEB*. But households must make an additional payment to firms for this extra amount of the good; this additional payment is equal to area *JKED*. After subtracting this additional payment to firms, the net gain in consumer surplus (which comes from the consumption of the additional *JK* units) is area *BDE*.

As just noted, firms receive extra revenue equal to area *JKED* for the sale of the additional *JK* units of the good. But firms had to incur additional costs to produce this extra output; these additional costs are equal to area *JKEG*. After subtracting these costs, we see that the additional profit (producer surplus) is area *GDE*. The additional benefit to society as a whole is equal to the sum of the consumers' net gain (*BDE*) and the producers' net gain (*GDE*)—a total of area *GEB*. The initial level of output, *OJ*, was not optimal, since when output increases to level *OK*, the gain in utility exceeds the additional costs to society by amount *GEB*.

Now consider the *OJ* units that were produced in the first place. They are still being purchased by consumers but, without the maximum price law, households now pay area *OJDC*, not just *OJGF*, for these units. Thus, consumers lose area *FGDC* from what was previously consumer surplus. This amount is now producer surplus; it is simply transferred to firms, not lost to society as a whole. That is why area *GEB* remains the correct measure of what the society loses overall by producing at a level for which MU does not equal MC.

Of course, in addition to the efficiency problem, there is a distributional issue at stake here. As we have just explained, the total amount of material welfare to be had by everyone, taken together, increases when the maximum price law is removed (by amount *GEB*). This is the efficiency point. But to obtain this aggregate gain, there is a transfer from consumers to producers of amount *FGDC*, which many regard as an undesirable distribution effect. One of our twelve Ideas for Beyond the Final Exam focusses on the trade-off between efficiency and equality, and this trade-off is at the heart of the issue of whether prices should be set by a planner or allowed to be determined by market forces. In Part 4, we consider how income can be redistributed toward low-income earners in ways that minimize the degree of interference with the goal of efficiency.

OTHER ROLES OF PRICES: INCOME DISTRIBUTION AND FAIRNESS

So far, we have stressed the role of prices most emphasized by economists: Prices guide the allocation of resources. But, as we have just noted, a different role of prices often commands the spotlight in public discussions: Prices influence the distribution of income between buyers and sellers. A concrete example of this issue is high rents, which often make tenants poorer and landlords richer, and lead to the implementation of rent controls.

This rather obvious role of prices draws the most attention from the public, politicians, and regulators, and we should not lose sight of it. Markets serve only those demands that are backed up by consumers' desire *and ability* to pay. Although the market system may do well in serving a poor family, giving that family more food and clothing than a less efficient economy would provide, it offers far more to the family of a millionaire. Many observers object that such an arrangement represents a great injustice, however efficient it may be.

Often, recommendations made by economists for improving the economy's efficiency are opposed on the grounds that they are unfair. For example, economists frequently advocate higher prices for transportation facilities at the time of day when they are most crowded. They propose a pricing arrangement called *peak/off-peak pricing*, under which prices for public transportation are higher during rush hours than during other hours.

The rationale for this proposal should be clear from our discussion of efficiency and from the boxed example about airport congestion earlier in this chapter (page 259). A seat on a train is a much scarcer resource during rush hours than during other times of the day, when the trains run fairly empty. Thus, according to the principles of efficiency outlined in this chapter, seats should be more expensive during rush hours to discourage consumers from using the trains during peak periods. The same notion applies to other services. Charges for nighttime long-distance telephone calls are lower than those in the daytime and, in some places, electricity is sold more cheaply at night, when demand does not strain the supplier's generating capacity.

Yet the proposal that higher fares should be charged for public transportation during peak hours—say, from 8:00 A.M. to 9:30 A.M. and from 4:30 P.M. to 6:00 P.M.—often runs into stiff opposition on the grounds that most of the burden will fall on lower-income working people, who have no choice about the timing of their trips. In this case, people simply find the efficient solution unfair and so refuse to adopt it. (It must be noted, however, that in many other cases, it seems that proposals promoting efficiency are rejected simply because people do not understand the concept—witness the cartoon on this page!)

Economics alone cannot decide the appropriate trade-off between equity and efficiency. It cannot even pretend to judge which pricing arrangements are fair and which are unfair. But it can and should indicate whether a particular pricing decision, proposed because it is considered fair, will impose heavy inefficiency costs upon the community. Economic analysis also can and should indicate how to evaluate these costs, so that the issues can be decided on the basis of an understanding of the facts.

Sometimes it is possible to design policies that, as a package, promote both efficiency and equity simultaneously. We return to the trade-off between the objectives of equity and efficiency in Chapter 13, and then again in Part 4 of this book.

"They should move Christmas to January — everything's cheaper."

TOWARD ASSESSMENT OF THE PRICE MECHANISM

Our analysis of the case for laissez faire is not meant to imply that the free-enterprise system is an ideal of perfection, without flaw or room for improvement. In fact, it has a number of serious shortcomings, which we will examine in subsequent chapters. But recognition of these imperfections should not conceal the enormous accomplishments of the price mechanism.

We have shown that, given the proper circumstances, this mechanism is capable of meeting the most exacting requirements of allocative efficiency, requirements that go well beyond the capacity of any central-planning bureau. The market mechanism has provided an abundance of goods unprecedented in human history. No one has invented an instrument for directing the economy that can replace the price mechanism, which no one ever designed or planned for, but which simply grew by itself, a child of the processes of history. Even centrally planned economies have started to turn to the market in recent years. We shall now discuss the experience of some of these economies in greater detail.

ECONOMIC PLANNING

ALTERNATIVE ECONOMIC SYSTEMS: WHAT ARE THE CHOICES?

No one will ever forget 1989, the year the Berlin Wall crumbled—both literally and figuratively. For decades, the rivalry between western **capitalism** and Soviet-style **socialism** dominated the world's geopolitical scene. This competition had important military and ideological dimensions; for example, the yearning for individual freedom surely played a major role in the breakup of the Soviet empire. However, the miserable performance of the Soviet economic system was certainly a decisive factor.

The economic and political transformations now taking place in Eastern Europe and the former Soviet republics dramatize the importance of choosing the right economic system. And there *are* choices to be made. Here in North America, we tend to take economic institutions as given and immutable. But they are not. In fact, there are many ways to practise capitalism, as the differing economic structures of Japan and Western Europe illustrate. A century ago, our country had no social welfare system, no income tax, no central bank, no competition laws, and hardly any labour unions. More than likely, the structure of the Canadian economy will change at least as much in the next century as it did in the last. But in which directions?

In this part of the chapter, we examine how a society might choose among alternative economic systems, and describe some of the actual choices that have been made in the contemporary world. We consider the evolving economic structures of Russia and the People's Republic of China, two nations in which serious economic problems have precipitated major institutional shifts away from their socialist backgrounds. Then we turn to a notable example of a successful capitalist country that does things rather differently than we do: Japan.

CAPITALISM is a method of economic organization in which private individuals own the means of production, either directly or indirectly through corporations.

SOCIALISM is a method of economic organization in which the state owns the means of production.

THE RUSSIAN ECONOMY

Joseph Stalin's strategy called for single-minded application of Soviet resources to the goal of rapid industrial development with emphasis on heavy industry, particularly armaments. To achieve such rapid growth and industrialization, it was necessary to limit consumption severely; the Soviet consumer was forced to make major sacrifices. To feed the urban labourers needed for industrial expansion, the Soviet Union's backward agricultural peasants were forced—at extremely high human and economic costs—onto collective farms, where they were required to sell their food at low prices and to work for pitifully low wages. This rigorous system of central planning that worked in Stalin's day, when the economic goals were simple and well defined, seems ill-suited to more sophisticated modern economies with complex and diverse goals.

FURTHER DETAIL

PROBLEMS OF CENTRAL PLANNING

In 1986, before *perestroika* was officially formulated, Gosplan, the highest planning commission in the Soviet Union, issued two thousand sets of instructions for major "product groups," such as construction materials, metals, and automotive vehicles. Gossnab, the State Material and Technical Supply Commission, then divided these product groups into fifteen thousand categories—lumber, copper, and trucks, for instance — and the various ministries in charge of the categories in turn subdivided them into fifty thousand more finely detailed products (shingles, beams, laths, boards) and then into specific products in each category (large, medium, and small shingles). These plans then percolated down through the hierarchy of production, receiving emendations or protests as they reached the level of plant managers and engineers, and thereafter travelled back up to the ministerial level. In this Byzantine process, perhaps the most difficult single step was to establish "success indicators"—desired performance targets—for enterprises. For many years, targets were given in physical terms—so many yards of cloth or tons of nails—but that led to obvious difficulties. If cloth was rewarded by the yard, it was woven loosely to make the yarn yield more yards. If the output of nails was determined by their number, factories produced huge numbers of pinlike nails; if by weight, smaller numbers of very heavy nails. The satiric magazine *Krokodil* once ran a cartoon of a factory manager proudly displaying his record output, a single gigantic nail suspended from a crane.

The difficulty, of course, was that the inevitable mismatches and mistakes could not be set to rights by the decisions of platoon sergeants or regimental commanders who were able to see that the campaign was not going as expected. [Nikolai] Shmelev and [Vladimir] Popov [two very well known Soviet economists, whose recently published "The Turning Point" gives a scathing account of Russian economic problems] tell of the Kurgan Bus Factory, to which the Gorky Automotive Factory shipped chassis assemblies. These assemblies had extra parts attached to them, suitable for the trucks that the Gorky factory produced but not for the buses that the Kurgan plant produced. The Kurgan workers then took sledgehammers and converted the truck chassis into bus chassis. "It is much harder to change GOST [State All-Union Standards] than to swing a sledgehammer," the authors comment.

SOURCE: Excerpted from Robert Heilbroner, "Reflections: After Communism," *The New Yorker*, September 10, 1990, pages 91–100. © 1990 Robert Heilbroner. Used with the permission of *The New Yorker*.

One perennial problem experienced by the Soviets was the tremendous burden of information transmission required by the central-planning apparatus. Many millions of pieces of information had to pass up and down the hierarchy each year. As a result, Soviet planners were often overwhelmed or misinformed, and made correspondingly incorrect decisions.

A second, and related, problem was that enterprises strove to obtain low production quotas that were easy to meet or surpass. Why? Because their success was measured not by profits or sales, but by their ability to meet the quotas. Thus, plant managers deliberately misled their superiors and understated their productive capacity—which, of course, made the information problem that much worse.

The system of production targets based on physical quantities rather than on profits or sales often led to huge stockpiles of unwanted and inferior goods and equally huge waiting lines for other goods, as the boxed insert opposite makes clear. As you are no doubt aware, a major move toward reliance on markets is now taking place in Russia and various countries in Eastern Europe.

This transition is very difficult to accomplish quickly. After all, decentralized trading requires well-established private property rights and a legal system to enforce those property rights. Without private property, there is no profit, and without that incentive to change and innovate, one of the fundamental features of the market system is missing. It is very difficult to move from a system of state ownership to private ownership, because people argue about what is "fair." The western economies never worried about this when they developed. In feudal times, our economies were run on a mixture of command and tradition, with only a very small proportion of economic activity taking place through markets (usually in the form of infrequent gatherings that took place when itinerant traders passed through). It took hundreds of years for us to develop gradually institutions to cope with the increased reliance on private markets and the growing acceptance of the profit motive. As noted, there was no presumption that these institutions had to be fair. Much of history is about people rebelling against what they perceived as the injustice of these early institutional arrangements. Thus, the former socialist countries are trying to accomplish something that is far more difficult than what the western economies have ever attempted.

Even though the planned economies involved a command system, they did not have well-developed tax systems that could be easily adapted to a market environment. The governments simply collected the "profits" from the state enterprises, or covered the "losses" incurred by other enterprises by printing money. A strict system of price controls kept the excess money-printing from causing inflation, and the excess demand showed up instead in the form of long queues. In the early 1990s, the planning system was abandoned, and the trading agreement among east bloc countries fell apart. The result was a loss in demand for the output of many state enterprises. Much money was printed to keep the workers employed, but with price controls lifted, prices began to soar. In the final months of 1992, inflation was running at a rate of 1300 percent per year in Russia.

Another problem is that state shops are limited by law to a price markup of no more than 25 percent. This means that many enterprising individuals became busy as third parties — buying goods at the state shops and selling them at scalper's prices on the new free markets. With-

PUBLIC CONTROVERSY

CAPITALISM OR BUST

The following small example of one of the problems Poland has had in moving toward a market economy illustrates how difficult this process is. The Polish government allowed individual firms to operate on their own in the 1980s, but the government did not abandon price controls at the same time. One result of this policy was that Poland became an exporter of semi-tropical flowers by the end of the decade. The reason for this was that the government had fixed the price of energy at a small fraction of the world price, so that it cost private firms almost nothing to heat their greenhouses. From a private point of view, the business made sense (given the local prices that firms faced). But from a social point of view, the Poles were actually subsidizing the citizens throughout the rest of the world who were buying these flowers. This example shows how things can go wrong when only one part of a distorted economic system is reformed, while other problems are left unreformed.

Another problem stems from the distortions that exist in the financial sector of the Eastern economies. Under central planning, the central banks printed money and made transfer payments to the operators of state enterprises whenever they were deemed to have "lost money." Even when these enterprises are turned into privately-owned com-

panies that compete with firms in the rest of the world, there is a big inflation problem if central-bank behaviour has not been reformed at the same time. To avoid massive unemployment, Eastern central banks have tended to continue making cash payments to firms to cover losses. Knowing that such bailouts are possible, the individual firms have every reason to offer almost any price to acquire the foreign exchange they need to buy important inputs. The result of all this printing of domestic money is a dramatic fall in the international value of the country's currency, and rampant inflation.

The moral of this experience is that to embrace a market system, a country must adopt what advisors have called the "big bang" approach. Countries must reform on three fronts — all at the same time and in a very thorough fashion. The country must privatize state enterprises, eliminate price controls, and create a private banking system that cares about its own profitability (so that bailouts of losing enterprises are not automatically forthcoming by direct money printing). It is a monumental task for these countries— to have major institutional change on all these fronts at once. While the long-term benefits that follow from this effort are large, the adjustment costs that are incurred in getting to that long run are large as well.

out private property rights set up for the inputs to the production process (land, factories, and raw materials), entrepreneurs had no option but to operate as nonproductive "rent-seekers" in the markets for the goods that were already produced by others. (Rent-seeking behaviour is discussed in several later chapters; perhaps reading the boxed insert on page 429 would be useful at this point.) The boxed insert on this page describes more of the difficulties being encountered as countries move toward the market system.

THE CHINESE ECONOMY

The People's Republic of China makes a good case study for this chapter because the Chinese have spent much of the last 45 years groping to find an economic model that suits them. In the process, they have squarely confronted the fundamental question of this chapter—decentralized markets or central planning?—and have come up with different answers at different times.

After the Communist takeover in 1949, the Chinese economy was patterned on the Soviet model and developed with Soviet economic aid and technical expertise. In particular, the Chinese economy was very much a command economy, perhaps even more so than the Soviet. Also, China's emphasis on rapid economic growth, particularly industrial growth, was similar to that of the Soviet Union.

But there were also important differences stemming in part from ideology and in part from the fact that the Soviet model was not quite suitable to China. Probably the most important of these differences was the decision by Mao Tse-tung *not* to rely on material incentives to motivate the work force. Mao and the Chinese leadership looked with disdain at this "bourgeois" practice and preferred to motivate Chinese workers by exhortation, appeals to patriotism, and, where necessary, force. The Soviets bent their socialist doctrine somewhat to accommodate human nature. But Chinese communism for many years seemed determined to bend human nature to accommodate Maoist doctrine—to create "the new man in the new China," an effort that has now been abandoned.

A second, less important, difference is that Chinese planning has always been less centralized than Soviet planning. Local and industrial authorities have more power and discretion than they did in the Soviet Union. This decentralization was probably dictated by China's immense size and economic backwardness in 1949. Without modern communications (and perhaps even with them), there was no way for planners in Beijing to hope to control economic activity in the outlying provinces. Even today, this remains a problem for Beijing.

Chinese economic growth under the Communist regime has proceeded in fits and starts, not least as a result of Mao's abrupt changes of mind regarding the emphasis he placed on ideology as opposed to technical planning. Although it was not the first major reversal of policy, the Great Proletarian Cultural Revolution (1965–69) is a dramatic example. During this period, Mao decided that the ideologically pure "Reds" were in and the technocratic "experts" were out as never before. The infamous Red Guards (later assisted by the army) were sent out to purge rightist elements from Chinese society, organize revolutionary cadres, and spread the teachings of Chairman Mao. If anyone worried about economic productivity in this environment, it did not show. By the summer of 1967, the Chinese economy and other elements of Chinese society were in utter disarray. National output fell substantially.

Things began to change again in the 1970s. The period until Mao's death in 1976 was one of consolidation and economic growth. The Chinese revolutionary fever receded, and the "experts" were rehabilitated. There was a restoration of material incentives and of rational economic calculation—both of which had been considered reactionary during the Cultural Revolution. In general, politics and ideology were de-emphasized, and economic growth was promoted.

Since the death of Mao, the Chinese economic system has continued to change rapidly. The leaders who succeeded Mao have shown themselves to be far less interested in doctrine and far more interested in results.

The technicians and scientists who fell into disgrace during Mao's Cultural Revolution were restored to positions of influence. In a startling reversal, it was Mao and the revolutionaries whose wisdom was now being questioned.

In the late 1970s, the Chinese began a series of reforms that eventually amounted to adopting important features of the market economy. These trends accelerated in the early 1980s, as market forces were allowed increasingly to supplement central planning. Farmers were given land to do with as they pleased—once they paid a fixed amount of produce to the state. Markets, and even limited amounts of local entrepreneurship, were allowed to flourish in the form of private shops and other small businesses. Foreign companies were invited to set up operations in China, and the Chinese seemed eager to learn the ways of western business.

In the late 1980s, however, two problems arose. While allowing markets to gradually replace planning, the government failed to implement sound macroeconomic management. Consequently, China experienced high inflation for the first time since the Communist takeover. At about the same time, the Chinese people began to demand political freedoms to accompany their new-found economic freedoms. A struggle within the Chinese leadership ensued, which hard-liner Li Peng and his supporters won after having brutally suppressed a massive popular revolt in Tiananmen Square in June 1989.

The fundamental dilemma facing the current leaders is that the individual freedom they refuse to grant their people (for political reasons) is necessary to facilitate the desired market-oriented reforms and more rapid economic growth.

THE AMAZING JAPANESE ECONOMY

People all over the world today view Japan the way they once viewed the United States—with a mixture of awe and resentment. The Japanese are admired as producers and feared as competitors. Their efficiency seems matchless; their ability to export, boundless. How do the Japanese do it? is a question frequently asked, with barely concealed wonderment.

The reality is somewhat different. We will learn in Chapter 32, for example, that economy-wide productivity in Japan is still below that in North America. Average standards of living lag even further behind our own, in part because so many Japanese live in tiny dwellings. Also, Japan's retail and service industries are such marvels of inefficiency that many Japanese goods cost more in Tokyo than they do in New York!

Yet the Japanese economy is certainly *the* most outstanding success story of the period since World War II. From 1955 (when Japan began its productivity-enhancement campaign) to 1989, real gross national product (GNP) in Japan rose by an astounding 836 percent. (GNP measures the total income generated by an entire economy in a particular year.) The corresponding expansion of the U.S. economy—the usual world standard —was only 177 percent. Japan's automobile, electronics, and semiconductor industries, to name just a few, lead the world in technological and manufacturing prowess. Its banks and other financial institutions are the world's largest. As an economic power, Japan has truly come of age.

But how? Many say that Japan succeeded by adopting free-market capitalism—but it must be acknowledged that both free markets and capitalism look quite different in Japan than they do in North America.

Export-Led Growth

Japan is a crowded island nation, far removed from the world's major markets. Almost totally devoid of natural resources, it must import large amounts of raw materials, energy, and foodstuffs just to survive. Yet, by concentrating on manufacturing and exporting, it has managed not just to prosper, but to propel itself into the forefront of nations.

One of the secrets of Japan's economic success has certainly been its emphasis on both high levels of investment and **export-led growth**. From 1955 to 1989, Japanese exports grew by an astounding 3227 percent in real terms. How has Japan done it? There is no simple answer. High levels of investment have certainly facilitated the adoption of the latest technology. Also, Japanese industry is clearly outward-looking in a way that North American industry is not. Many organizations, such as the fabled Ministry of International Trade and Industry (MITI) and the Japan External Trade Organization, work to promote exports. Japanese business has also shown a remarkable ability to adapt to changing world markets. As one industry (say, shipbuilding) declines, the Japanese shift rapidly into another (say, consumer electronics), whose star is rising. Above all, the major Japanese companies seek always to grow — and that means exporting.

EXPORT-LED GROWTH refers to the strategy of emphasizing the production of goods for export.

"Japan, Inc."

Japan has no tradition of enforcing competition laws. Indeed, at times, the Japanese government has seemed to promote rather than oppose bigness, perhaps as a way to catch up to the West. Consequently, Japanese industry is far more concentrated than American industry. Industrial concentration, barriers to imports, and inefficient retailing combine to keep domestic prices of consumer goods high. The cozy relationship between the big Japanese corporations (*kaisha*) and the Japanese government has prompted the nickname "Japan, Inc.," suggestive of an economic policy geared more to the interests of producers than of consumers.

Japanese industrial organization also looks different from inside the corporation. An industrial giant like Toyota may be surrounded by satellite companies that supply parts and help it operate its famous "just-in-time" inventory system (*kanban*)—a highly efficient way of organizing the factory floor to minimize delays. These smaller companies live at the mercy of the large *kaisha* and act as shock absorbers when demand declines.

In addition, members of Japan's manufacturing combines (*keiretsu*) own chunks of one another's stock and forge tight links with the world's largest banks. This gives Japanese industry access to cheap, "patient" capital—funds from lending institutions that are willing to wait for a return on their investment. Japanese managers pay scant attention to daily movements of the stock market and never worry about hostile takeovers. All this helps Japanese industry maintain its long-run focus.

JAPAN'S SYSTEM OF LABOUR–MANAGEMENT RELATIONS

Japan also differs from North America in the way that its work force is organized and paid. For one thing, many employees of large Japanese corporations have lifetime-employment guarantees that protect them from being laid off. Such features help align the interests of labour and management, build loyalty to the company, and make Japanese workers less resistant to change than are their North American counterparts. For example, if a Japanese plant introduces automation, most employees know they will not only keep their jobs but share in any gains automation may bring.

The workplace is less hierarchical in Japan than in North America. Pay differentials between executives and workers are much smaller there, and the distribution of income is consequently much more equal. Managers eat in the same cafeterias, drink in the same bars, and sometimes even wear the same uniforms as blue-collar workers. Japanese workers are also consulted closely on how the factory is to be run. Decision making is by consensus—even if consensus takes a long time to develop. North American management, by contrast, exercises more "top-down" control.

For these reasons, and perhaps also because of strong conformist tendencies within Japanese society, labour–management relations are less adversarial and more co-operative in Japan than they are in North America.

IS JAPAN A PLANNED ECONOMY?

All this did not happen by means of the invisible hand alone. The system was consciously designed to raise industrial productivity, keep it growing, and turn Japan into an industrial powerhouse that would equal the western nations. Many Japanese innovations, such as *kanban*, originated in the private sector. But the government—through the Japan Productivity Center, the Economic Planning Agency, the powerful Ministry of Finance, and MITI—played an active role in promoting what it saw as good ideas, discouraging those it considered bad, and, in general, lending a helping and guiding hand.

The role of the government, and especially of MITI, in Japan's economic success is highly controversial. Ardent free-marketeers downplay its contribution and point to episodes in which MITI clearly got in the way (one such episode was its ill-conceived attempt to drive several companies out of the automobile business in the 1960s). Protectionists seeking to limit Japanese imports exaggerate the role of MITI and portray "Japan, Inc." as a monolith (which it certainly is not). In their eyes, Japan's industrial policy is the key to its success. (Industrial policy, or industrial strategy, will be discussed in Chapter 32, page 1038.)

It is somewhat difficult to strike a balanced view of the matter, especially since few westerners can fathom the cliquish ways of Japanese businesses. But a few things seem clear. First, the Ministry of Finance and the Bank of Japan (the central bank) have exercised a more comprehensive control over their financial system than is the custom here. Second, Japanese industrial policy, while far from infallible, seems to have had considerable success in assisting winners and shutting down losers. Third, Japanese industry benefits enormously from a work force that may be the best educated and most co-operative in the world; this is certainly a substantial achievement of government.

Many people believe that the most important things we can learn from the Japanese are not the latest innovations in robotics or chip manufacturing, but rather their ways of organizing and motivating people—from their education system, which has virtually eradicated illiteracy, to their unique labour-relations system, to *kanban* and other management techniques.

Some observers predict that, as the Japanese get richer, their behaviour will come to resemble that of North Americans more closely. Already, for example, there are signs that Japanese households are saving less and that Japanese workers are changing jobs more frequently than in the past. Other observers, however, stress that basic cultural differences are likely to militate against rapid change, if not preclude significant change altogether.

A more general, and more controversial, hypothesis is that the Japanese "corporatist" style of doing business is better suited to the modern world of international competition than is the American "individualist" style. The two brands of capitalism are indeed different. Is the Japanese brand the wave of the future and the American a thing of the past? Only time will tell.

POSTSCRIPT

This chapter should be viewed as the answer to the first half of the two-part question, "What does the market do well, and what does it do poorly?" Many observers underestimate the very real contribution market forces can make to achieving high levels of material welfare. In an attempt to counter that view, we have stressed in this chapter that it is almost impossible to overstate the advantages of the market for achieving economic efficiency. Our brief review of countries that have suppressed market forces supports the analytical material. But this is only half the story. In the next two chapters, we analyze various forms of monopoly, then devote Chapter 12 to an account of the negative half of the story. Reserve judgement in your own evaluation of the market mechanism until then.

SUMMARY

1. Resource allocation is considered inefficient if it wastes opportunities to change the use of the economy's resources in any way that would make consumers better off. Conversely, it is called efficient if there are no such wasted opportunities.

2. Resource allocation involves three basic co-ordination tasks: (a) How much of each good to produce, (b) What quantities of the available inputs to use in producing the different goods, and (c) How to distribute the goods among different consumers.

3. Under perfect competition, the free-market mechanism adjusts prices so that the resulting resource allocation is efficient. It induces firms to buy and use inputs in ways that yield the most valuable outputs per unit of input; it distributes products among consumers in ways that match individual preferences; and it produces commodities whose value to consumers exceeds the cost of producing them.

4. Efficient decisions about what goods to produce require that the marginal cost (MC) of producing each good be equated to its marginal utility (MU) to consumers. If the MC of any good differs from its MU, society can improve resource allocation by changing the level of production.

5. Because the market system induces firms to set MC equal to price and induces consumers to set MU equal to price, it automatically guarantees that the MC = MU condition is satisfied.

6. Sometimes, improvements in efficiency require some prices to increase in order to stimulate supply or to prevent waste in consumption. This is why price increases can sometimes be beneficial to consumers.

7. In addition to allocating resources, prices also influence the distribution of income between buyers and sellers.

8. The workings of the price mechanism can be criticized on the grounds that it is unfair because of the preferential treatment it accords wealthy consumers. The most direct answer to this criticism is to redistribute income rather than to restrict the workings of the price mechanism. By doing so, we can avoid both the inefficiencies of central planning and the undesirable income-distribution effects of the market.

9. Free markets seem to do a good job of selecting the bill of goods and services to be produced and at choosing the most efficient techniques for producing these goods and services. Planned systems have difficulties with both these choices, as well as with

stimulating inventiveness in the absence of the profit motive.

10. Market economies, however, do not guarantee an equitable distribution of income and are often plagued by business fluctuations. In these two areas, planning seems to have the advantage.

11. Planning in the Soviet Union was bureaucratic and hierarchical. It encountered monumental difficulties in transmitting accurate information, equating supply and demand for the various inputs, and motivating both workers and managers.

12. Currently, the former Soviet republics are moving away from central planning toward a more market-oriented economy in which private ownership of capital is permitted and prices are determined by supply and demand. No one knows how far or how fast this liberalization will go.

13. The Chinese economic system has changed several times since the Communist takeover in 1949, passing through several periods of intense revolutionary fervour and little economic progress. Planning there has been somewhat less centralized than it was in the Soviet Union.

14. Since the late 1970s, the Chinese have introduced important aspects of the market economy into their economic system.

15. Japan has used export-led growth to propel itself to the forefront of nations; but lately, its single-minded concentration on exporting has been a source of international tension.

16. Compared with the United States in particular, Japan has more industrial concentration, a less adversarial system of labour–management relations, tighter links between manufacturing companies and banks, and more active co-operation between government and industry. Observers disagree about the relative importance of each of these influences in accounting for Japan's industrial success.

CONCEPTS FOR REVIEW

Efficient allocation of resources
Co-ordination tasks: output selection, production planning, distribution of goods

Laissez faire
Consumer sovereignty
Input–output analysis
MC = P (requirement of perfect competition)

MC = MU (efficiency requirement)
Capitalism
Socialism
Planning
Export-led growth

QUESTIONS FOR DISCUSSION

1. What are the possible social advantages of price increases in each of the two following cases?

a. Charging higher prices for electrical power on very hot days when many people use air conditioners.

b. Raising water prices in drought-stricken areas.

2. Discuss the fairness of the two preceding proposals.

3. Discuss the nature of the inefficiency in each of the following cases:

   a. An arrangement that makes available relatively little coffee and much tea to people who prefer coffee and that accomplishes the reverse for tea lovers.

   b. An arrangement in which skilled mechanics are assigned to ditch-digging and unskilled labourers to repairing cars.

   c. An arrangement that produces a large quantity of trucks and few cars, assuming that both cost about the same to produce and to run but that most people in the community prefer cars to trucks.

4. In reality, which of the following circumstances might give rise to each of the preceding problem situations?

   a. Regulation of output quantities by a government.

   b. Rationing of commodities.

   c. Assignment of soldiers to different jobs in an army.

5. We have said that the economy's three co-ordination tasks are output selection, production planning, and product distribution. Which of these is done badly in the case described in Question 3(a)? in 3(b)? in 3(c)?

6. In a free market, how will the price mechanism deal with each inefficiency described in Question 3?

7. Suppose a given set of resources can be used to make either one handbag or two wallets, and the MC of a handbag is $23 while the MC of a wallet is $9. If the MU of a wallet is $9 and the MU of a handbag is $30, what can be done to improve resource allocation? What can you say about the gain to consumers?

8. If you were the leader of a small, developing country, what are some of the factors that would weigh heavily in your choice of an economic system?

9. If you were a plant manager under old-style Soviet planning, what are some of the things you might do to make your life easier and more successful? (Use your imagination. Soviet plant managers did!)

10. What are some special problems encountered when a country tries to make the transition from central planning to markets? (*Hint:* What kinds of difficulties can arise when some markets are tightly controlled while others are free?)

11. Many formerly communist countries are now taking the path toward markets and capitalism. Some are trying a gradual approach. Others are trying to make the leap all at once. What are some of the pros and cons of gradualism versus the "big bang" approach?

12. Do you think the Canadian government should take a more active role in guiding industry? Do you consider Japan to be a good or a poor model? Explain your answer.

APPENDIX TO CHAPTER 9

THE INVISIBLE HAND IN THE DISTRIBUTION OF GOODS AND IN PRODUCTION PLANNING

On pages 266–69, we offered a glimpse of the way economists analyze the workings of the invisible hand by showing how the market handles the problem of efficiency in one of the three tasks of resource allocation: the selection of outputs. We explained the MC = MU rule that must be followed for a set of outputs to be efficient and showed how a free market can induce people to act in a way that satisfies that rule. In this appendix, we complete the story, examining how the price mechanism handles the two other tasks of resource allocation: the distribution of goods among consumers and the planning of production.

EFFICIENT DISTRIBUTION OF COMMODITIES: WHO GETS WHAT?

While decisions about distribution among consumers depend critically on value judgements, a surprising amount can be said purely on grounds of efficiency. For example, consumers' desires are not being served efficiently if large quantities of milk are given to someone who prefers apple cider, while numerous litres of cider are assigned to a milk lover. Deciding how much of which commodity goes to whom is a matter that requires delicate calculation. It causes great difficulties during wartime when planners must ration goods. They generally end up using a crude egalitarianism: the same amount of butter to everyone, the same amount of coffee to everyone, and so on. This may be justified, to paraphrase the statement of a high-ranking official in another country, by an unwillingness to pander to acquired tastes, but it is easy to see that such fixed rations are unlikely to produce an efficient result.

The analysis of the efficient distribution of the economy's different products among its many consumers turns out to be quite similar to our previous analysis of efficient output selection. Suppose there are two individuals, Mr. Steaker and Ms. Chop, and that Steaker wants lots of beef and little lamb, while the opposite is true of Chop. Suppose each is getting one kilogram of lamb and one kilogram of beef per week. It is then possible to make *both* people better off without increasing their total consumption of two kilograms of beef and two kilograms of lamb if Steaker trades some of his lamb to Chop in return for some beef. The initial distribution of goods was not efficient because it left room for trades that would yield mutual gains.

It is easy enough to think of allocations of commodities among consumers that are inefficient—simply assign to each person only what he or she does not like. But how does one recognize an allocation that is efficient? After all, there are many of us whose preferences have much in common. If two individuals both like beef and lamb, how shall the available amounts of the two commodities be divided between them? We will now show that, as in the analysis of efficient output selection, there is a simple rule that must be satisfied by any efficient distribution of products among consumers. Consider any two commodities in the economy, such as beef and lamb, and any two consumers, like Steaker and Chop, each of whom likes to eat some of each type of meat. Therefore, the basic rules for the efficient distribution of beef and lamb between Steaker and Chop are that

Steaker's MU of beef = Chop's MU of beef

and

Steaker's MU of lamb = Chop's MU of lamb

Analogous equations must be satisfied for every other pair of individuals, and for every other pair of products.

Why are these equalities required for efficiency? Recall that a distribution of commodities among consumers can be efficient only if it has taken advantage of every potential gain from trade. That is, if two people can trade in a way that makes them both better off, the distribution cannot be efficient. We can show that if *either* of the previous equations is not satisfied, such trades are possible.

Suppose, for example, that the following are the relevant marginal utilities:

Steaker's MU of beef = $40
Chop's MU of beef = $20
Steaker's MU of lamb = $10
Chop's MU of lamb = $10

In such a case, a mutually beneficial exchange of beef and lamb can be arranged. For example, if Steaker gives Chop three kilograms of lamb in return for one kilogram of beef, they will both be better off. Steaker loses three kilograms of lamb, which are worth $30 to him, and gets a kilogram of beef, which is worth $40 to him. Thus, he winds up $10 ahead. Similarly, Chop

gives up one kilogram of beef, which is worth $20 to her, and gets in return three kilograms of lamb, worth $30 to her. Thus, she also gains $10. Such a mutually beneficial exchange is possible here because the two consumers have different marginal utilities for beef. Each can benefit by giving up what he or she considers less valuable in exchange for something valued more highly. The initial position in which the two equations were not both satisfied was therefore not efficient because without any increase in the total amounts of beef and lamb available to them, both could be made better off. The lesson of this example is quite general:

Any time that two persons have unequal MUs for any commodity, the welfare of both parties can be increased by an exchange of commodities. Efficiency requires that any two individuals have the same MUs for any pair of goods.

The great virtue of the price system is that it induces people to carry out *voluntarily* all opportunities for mutually beneficial swaps. Without the price system, Steaker and Chop might not make the trade because they do not know each other. But the price system enables them to trade with each other by trading with the market. Remember from our discussion of consumer choice in Chapter 4 that it pays any consumer to buy any commodity up to the point where the good's money marginal utility is just equal to its price. In other words, in equilibrium,

$$\text{Steaker's MU of beef} = \text{Price of beef} = \text{Chop's MU of beef}$$

This is so because, if, say, Steaker's MU of beef were greater than the price of beef, he could improve his lot by exchanging more of his money for beef. The reverse could be true if Steaker's MU of beef fell short of the price of beef. For the same reason, since the price of lamb is the same for both individuals, each will choose voluntarily to buy quantities of lamb at which

$$\text{Steaker's MU of lamb} = \text{Price of lamb} = \text{Chop's MU of lamb}$$

Thus, we see that as long as both consumers face the same prices for lamb and beef, their independent decisions *must* satisfy our criteria for efficient distribution of beef and lamb between them:

Steaker's MU of beef = Chop's MU of beef

Steaker's MU of lamb = Chop's MU of lamb

Given any prices for two commodities, each consumer, acting only in accord with his or her preferences and with no necessary consideration of the effects on the other person, will automatically make the purchases that efficiently serve the mutual interests of both purchasers.

This time, where have we sneaked the rabbit into our price system argument? The answer is that the market acts as an intermediary between any pair of consumers. Given the prices offered by the market, each consumer will use his or her dollars in a way that exhausts all opportunities for gains from trade *with the market.* Steaker and Chop each take advantage of every such opportunity to gain by trading with the market, and in the process, they automatically take advantage of every opportunity for advantageous trades between themselves.

EFFICIENT PRODUCTION PLANNING: ALLOCATION OF INPUTS

Finally, we note briefly that a similar analysis shows how the price system leads to an efficient allocation of inputs among the different production processes — the third of our allocative issues. For precisely the same reasons as in the case of the distribution of products among consumers, the following can be said of production:

Efficient use of two inputs (say, labour and fertilizer) in the production of two goods (say, wheat and corn) requires that

$$\frac{\text{MPP}_{\text{wheat, fertilizer}}}{\text{MPP}_{\text{wheat, labour}}} = \frac{\text{MPP}_{\text{corn, fertilizer}}}{\text{MPP}_{\text{corn, labour}}}$$

where, for example, "$\text{MPP}_{\text{wheat, fertilizer}}$" means the marginal physical product of fertilizer when it is employed in wheat production.

By the same logic as before, we can show that if these equations do not hold, it is possible to produce more corn and more wheat without using more labour and fertilizer than before merely by redistributing the quantities of the two inputs between the two crops. (See Discussion Question 2 at the end of this appendix.) But we learned in Chapter 6 that maximum profits require wheat farmers to hire so much labour and so much fertilizer that the ratio of their marginal physical products equals the ratio of their prices. That is,

$$\frac{\text{MPP}_{\text{wheat, fertilizer}}}{\text{MPP}_{\text{wheat, labour}}} = \frac{P_{\text{fertilizer}}}{P_{\text{labour}}}$$

(where, for example, "$P_{\text{fertilizer}}$" means price of fertilizer). The same relationship must also hold true for every profit-maximizing corn producer:

$$\frac{\text{MPP}_{\text{corn, fertilizer}}}{\text{MPP}_{\text{corn, labour}}} = \frac{P_{\text{fertilizer}}}{P_{\text{labour}}}$$

Since, in a competitive industry such as agriculture, wheat farmers and corn farmers must pay the same prices for each of their inputs such as labour and fertilizer, it follows that the ratio of the marginal physical product of fertilizer and labour must be the same in wheat growing, corn growing, and in every other competitive industry that uses these two inputs, just as the formula for efficient production planning requires.

Thus, we conclude that by making the independent choices that maximize their own profits, and without necessarily considering the effects on anyone else, each farmer (firm) will automatically act in a way that satisfies the efficiency condition for the allocation of inputs among different products.

SUMMARY

1. The condition for efficient distribution of commodities among consumers is that every consumer have the same marginal utility (MU) for every product. If this condition is not met, two consumers can arrange a swap that makes both of them better off.

2. In a free market, all consumers pay the same price. Thus, if they pursue their own self-interest by setting MU = P, they automatically satisfy the condition for efficient distribution of commodities.

3. The condition for efficient allocation of inputs to the various production processes is that the ratio of the marginal physical products (MPP) of any pair of inputs be the same in every industry.

4. Since all producers pay the same prices for inputs under perfect competition, if each firm pursues its own self-interest by setting the ratio of the marginal physical products of any two of its inputs equal to the ratio of the prices of these inputs, the condition for efficient production planning will be satisfied automatically.

QUESTIONS FOR DISCUSSION

1. Show that commodities are not being distributed efficiently if Olson's marginal utilities of a kilogram of tomatoes and a kilogram of potatoes are, respectively, 80¢ and 40¢, while Johnson's are, respectively, 60¢ and 50¢.

2. Suppose the marginal revenue product of a litre of petroleum in the trucking industry is 50¢ while the marginal revenue product of petroleum in the auto-racing industry is 28¢. Show that petroleum inputs are being allocated inefficiently. How would a market system tend to prevent this situation from occurring?

MONOPOLY

The price of monopoly is upon every occasion the highest which can be got.

ADAM SMITH[1]

In Chapters 8 and 9, we described an idealized market system in which all industries are perfectly competitive, and we extolled the beauty of that system. In this chapter, we turn to one of the blemishes—the possibility that some industries may be monopolized—and to the consequences of such monopolization.

We begin by defining *monopoly* precisely and investigating some of the reasons for its existence. Then, using the tools of Chapter 7, we consider the monopolist's choice of an optimal price–output combination. As we shall see, while it is possible to analyze how much a monopolist will choose to produce, a monopolist has no "supply curve" in the usual sense. This and other features of monopolized markets require basic modification of our supply–demand analysis of the market mechanism. That modification leads us to the central message of this chapter—that monopolized markets do not match the ideal performance of perfectly competitive ones. In particular, we will see that in the presence of monopoly, the market mechanism no longer allocates society's resources efficiently. This observation opens up the possibility that government actions to constrain monopoly may actually improve the workings of the market—a possibility we will study in detail in Chapter 16.

APPLICATION: MONOPOLY AND POLLUTION CHARGES

We begin, as usual, with a real-life problem. Chapter 1 noted that most economists want to control pollution by charging polluters heavily, making them pay more money the more pollution they emit. Making it sufficiently expensive for firms to pollute, it is said, will force them to cut their emissions. (Details on this method of pollution control are provided in Chapter 17.)

A common objection to this proposal is that it simply will not work when the polluter is a monopolist: The monopoly firm, so the thinking goes, can just raise the price of its product, pass the pollution charge on

---

1. But Adam Smith's statement is incorrect! See Discussion Question 7 at the end of the chapter.

to its customers, and go on polluting as before, with total impunity. After all, if a firm is a monopoly, what is to stop it from raising its price when it is hit by a pollution charge?

Yet observation of the behaviour of firms threatened with pollution charges suggests that there is something wrong with this objection. If the polluting firm could escape the penalty completely, we would expect it to acquiesce or to put up only token opposition. Yet wherever charges on the emission of pollutants have been proposed, the outcries have been enormous, even from firms with no important rivals. Lobbyists are dispatched at once to do their best to stop the legislation. In fact, rather than agree to being charged for their emissions, firms usually indicate a preference for direct controls that force them to adopt specific processes that are less polluting than the ones they are using—that is, the firms seem to prefer having government tell them what they must do!

In this chapter, we will see how to analyze the issue and learn why monopolies cannot make their customers pay the pollution charge—or at least not all of it.

MONOPOLY DEFINED

A **PURE MONOPOLY** is an industry in which there is only one supplier of a product for which there are no close substitutes, and in which it is very hard or impossible for another firm to co-exist.

Pure monopoly was defined in Table 8-1 on page 229, and the definition is quite stringent. First, there must be only one firm in the industry—the monopolist must be "the only supplier in town." Second, there must be no close substitute for the monopolist's product. Thus, even the sole provider of natural gas in a city would not be considered a pure monopoly, since other firms offer close substitutes like heating oil and coal. Third, there must be some reason why survival of a potential competitor is extremely unlikely, for otherwise monopolistic behaviour and its excessive profits could not persist.

These rigid requirements make pure monopoly a rarity in the real world. The local telephone company and the post office are good examples of one-firm industries that face little or no effective competition. But most firms face competition from substitute products. Even if only one airline serves a particular town, it must compete with bus lines, trucking companies, and railways. Similarly, the producer of a particular brand of beer may be the only supplier of that specific product, but is not a monopolist by our definition. Since many other beers are close substitutes for its product, the company will lose much of its business if it tries to raise its price much above the prices of other brands.

There is one other reason why the unrestrained pure monopoly of economic theory is rarely encountered in practice. We will learn in this chapter that pure monopoly can have a number of undesirable features. As a consequence, in markets where pure monopoly might otherwise prevail, government has intervened to prevent monopolization or to limit the discretion of the monopolist to set its price.

If we do not study pure monopoly for its descriptive realism, why do we study it? Because, like perfect competition, pure monopoly is a market form that is easier to analyze than the more common market structures that we will consider in the next chapter. Thus, pure monopoly is a stepping stone toward models of greater reality. Also, the "evils" of monopoly stand out most clearly when we consider monopoly in its purest form, and this greater clarity will help us understand why governments have rarely allowed unfettered monopoly to exist.

CAUSES OF MONOPOLY: BARRIERS TO ENTRY AND COST ADVANTAGES

The key element in preserving a monopoly is keeping potential rivals out of the market. In some cases, a specific impediment prevents the establishment of a new firm in the industry. Economists call such impediments **barriers to entry**. Some examples are as follows:

1. ***Legal restrictions.***   Canada Post has a monopoly position because Parliament has given it one. Private companies that might want to compete with the post office are prohibited from doing so by law. Local monopolies of various kinds are sometimes established either because government grants some special privilege to a single firm (for example, the right to operate a food concession in a municipal stadium) or prevents other firms from entering the industry (for instance, by licensing only a single local radio station).

2. ***Patents.***   A special, but very important, legal impediment to entry is the **patent**. To encourage inventiveness, the government gives exclusive production rights for a period of time to the inventor of certain products. As long as the patent is in effect, the firm has a protected position and is a monopoly. For example, Xerox had for many years (but no longer has) a monopoly in plain-paper copying.

3. ***Control of a scarce resource or input.***   If a certain commodity can be produced only by using a rare input, a company that gains control of the source of that input can establish a monopoly position for itself.

4. ***Deliberately erected entry barriers.***   A firm may deliberately attempt to make entry difficult for others. One way to do so is to start costly lawsuits against new rivals, sometimes on trumped-up charges. Another is to spend exorbitant amounts on advertising, thus forcing any potential entrant to match that expenditure.

Obviously, such barriers can keep rivals out and ensure that an industry is monopolized, but monopoly can also occur in the absence of barriers to entry if a single firm has important cost advantages over its potential rivals. Two examples of this are as follows:

5. ***Technical superiority.***   A firm whose technological expertise vastly exceeds that of potential competitors can, for a period of time, maintain a monopoly position. For example, IBM for many years had very little competition in the computer business mainly because of its technological virtuosity. Eventually, however, competitors caught up.

6. ***Economies of scale.***   If mere size gives a large firm a cost advantage over a smaller rival, it is likely to be impossible for anyone to compete with the largest firm in the industry.

NATURAL MONOPOLY

This last type of cost advantage is important enough to merit special attention. In some industries, economies of large-scale production or economies from simultaneous production of a large number of items (for example, car motors and bodies, truck parts, and so on) are so extreme that the industry's output can be produced at far lower cost by a single firm than by a number of smaller firms. In such cases, we say there is a **natural monopoly**, because once a firm gets large enough relative to the size of the market for its product, its natural cost advantage may well drive the competition out of business, whether or not anyone in the relatively large firm has evil intentions.

A monopoly need not be a large firm if the market is small enough. What matters is the size of a single firm relative to the total market demand for the product. Thus, a small bank in a rural town or a gasoline station at a lightly travelled intersection may both be natural monopolies even though they are very small firms.

Figure 10-1 shows the sort of average-cost (AC) curve that leads to natural monopoly. Suppose that any firm producing widgets would have this AC curve and that, initially, the industry has two firms, one large and one small. Suppose also that the large firm is producing 2 million widgets at an average cost of $2.50, and the small firm is producing 1 million widgets at an average cost of $3.00. Clearly, the large firm can drive the small firm out of business by offering its output for sale at a price below $3.00 (so the small firm can match the price only by running a loss) but above $2.50 (so the large firm can still make a profit). The managers of the large firm will be smart enough to realize this possibility, and hence a monopoly will arise "naturally" even in the absence of barriers to entry. Once the monopoly is established (producing, say, 2.5 million widgets) the economies of scale act as a very effective deterrent to entry because no new entrant can hope to match the low average cost ($2.00) of the existing monopoly firm. Of course, the public interest may be well served if the firm with a natural monopoly uses its low cost to keep its prices low. The danger, however, is that the firm may raise its price once rivals have left the industry.

Many public utilities are permitted to operate as *regulated* monopoly suppliers for exactly such reasons. It is believed that the technology of

A **NATURAL MONOPOLY** is an industry in which the advantages of large-scale production make it possible for a single firm to produce the entire output of the market at lower average cost than could a number of firms each producing a smaller quantity.

FIGURE 10-1

NATURAL MONOPOLY

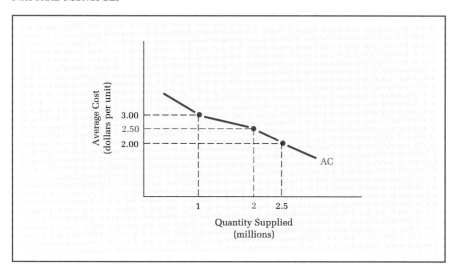

When the average-cost curve of a firm is declining, as depicted here, natural monopoly may result. A firm producing 2 million widgets will have average costs of $2.50, which are well below those of a smaller competitor producing 1 million widgets (average cost = $3.00). The larger firm can cut its price to a level (lower than $3.00) that its competitor cannot match and thereby drive the competitor out of business.

producing or distributing their output enables them to achieve substantial cost reductions when they produce large quantities. It is therefore often considered desirable to permit these firms to obtain the lower costs they achieve by having the entire market to themselves and to subject them to regulatory supervision, rather than break them up into a number of competing firms. The issue of regulating natural monopolies will be examined in detail in Chapter 16. We can summarize this discussion as follows:

There are two basic reasons why a monopoly may exist: barriers to entry, such as legal restrictions and patents, and cost advantages of large-scale operation that lead to natural monopoly. It is generally considered undesirable to break up a large firm whose costs are low as a result of scale economies. In contrast, barriers to entry are usually considered contrary to the public interest unless, as in the case of patents, they are believed to offer offsetting advantages.

The rest of this chapter will analyze how a monopoly can be expected to behave if its freedom of action is not limited by government.

THE MONOPOLIST'S SUPPLY DECISION

A monopoly firm does not have a "supply curve," as we usually define the term. It does not just observe the market price of a product and then decide what quantity to produce. Unlike a perfect competitor, a monopoly is not at the mercy of the market; the firm does not have to take the market price as given and react to it. Instead, it has the power to set the price, or rather to select the price–quantity combination on the demand curve that suits its interests best.

Put differently, a monopolist is not a price taker who must simply adapt to whatever price the forces of supply and demand decree. Rather, the monopolist is a *price maker* who can, if so inclined, raise the product's price. For any price that the monopolist might choose, the demand curve for the product indicates how much consumers will buy. Thus, the standard supply-demand analysis described in Chapter 3 does not apply to the determination of price or output in a monopolized industry.

The monopolist's demand curve, unlike that of a perfect competitor, is normally downward sloping, not horizontal. This means that a price rise will not cause the monopoly to lose all its customers. But any increase will cost it *some* business. The higher the price, the less the monopolist can expect to sell.

It is because of the downward-sloping demand curve that the sky is not the limit in pricing by a monopolist. Some price increases are not profitable. In deciding what price best serves the firm's interests, the monopolist must consider whether profits can be increased by raising or lowering the product's price.

In our analysis, we shall assume that the monopolist wants to maximize profits. We note two things about that. First, even a monopoly firm is not guaranteed a positive profit. If the demand for its product is low or the firm is inefficient, it may lose money and may eventually be forced to go out of business. Second, if a monopoly firm does earn a positive profit, it may be able to keep on doing so even in the long run if entry of new competitors on profitable terms is difficult or impossible. This is so because absence of entry can permit the monopoly firm to keep its price well above its average cost.

The methods of Chapter 7 can be used to determine which price the profit-maximizing monopolist will prefer. To maximize profits, the monopolist must compare marginal revenue (the addition to total revenue resulting from a one-unit rise in output) with marginal cost (the addition to total cost resulting from that additional unit). For this purpose, a marginal-cost (MC) curve and a marginal-revenue (MR) curve for a typical monopolist are drawn in Figure 10-2, which also contains the monopolist's demand curve (*DD*).

THE MONOPOLIST'S PRICE AND MARGINAL REVENUE

Notice that the marginal-revenue curve is always *below* the demand curve, meaning that MR is always less than price (*P*). This is an important fact and is easy to explain. A monopoly normally must charge the same price to all of its customers. Thus, if the monopoly firm wants to increase

FIGURE 10-2

PROFIT-MAXIMIZING EQUILIBRIUM FOR A MONOPOLIST

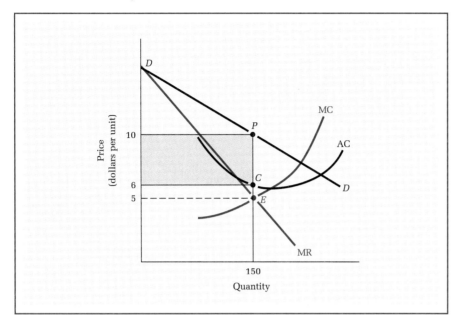

This monopoly has the cost structure indicated by the black average-cost (AC) curve and the red marginal-cost (MC) curve. Its demand curve is the black line labelled *DD*, and its marginal-revenue curve is the red line labelled MR. The monopoly maximizes profits by producing 150 units, because at this level of production, MC = MR (point *E*). The price the monopoly charges is $10 per unit (as given by point *P* on the demand curve). Since the average cost per unit ($6) is given by point *C* on the AC curve, the monopoly's total profit is indicated by the shaded rectangle.

sales by one unit, it must lower its price somewhat to *all* of its customers. When the price is cut to attract new sales, all previous customers also benefit. Thus, the additional revenue that the monopoly firm takes in when sales increased by one unit (marginal revenue) is the price the firm collects from the new customer *minus* the revenue it loses by cutting the price paid by all of its old customers. This means that MR is necessarily less than price; graphically, it implies that the MR curve is below the demand curve, as in Figure 10-2.

Figure 10-3 illustrates the relationship between price and marginal revenue in a specific example. Suppose a monopoly is initially selling 15 units at a price of $2.10 per unit (point *A*), and the monopolist wishes to increase sales by 1 unit. The demand curve indicates that in order to sell the 16th unit, the firm must reduce the price to $2.00 (point *B*). How much revenue will be gained from this increase in sales; that is, how large is the monopolist's marginal revenue?

As we know, total revenue at point *A* is the area of the rectangle whose upper right-hand corner is point *A*, or $2.10 × 15 = $31.50. Similarly, total revenue at point *B* is the area of the rectangle whose upper right-

FIGURE 10-3

THE RELATIONSHIP BETWEEN MARGINAL REVENUE AND PRICE

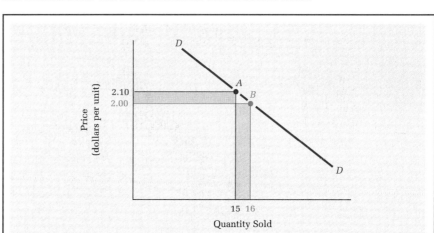

Line *DD* is the demand curve of a monopoly. In order to raise sales from 15 to 16 units, the firm must cut its price from $2.10 (point *A*) to $2.00 (point *B*). If it does this, its revenues *go up* by the $2.00 price it charges the buyer of the 16th unit (the area of the tall gold rectangle) but *go down* by the 10¢ price reduction it offers to its previous customers (the area of the flat blue rectangle). The monopoly's marginal revenue, therefore, is the difference between these two areas. Since the price is the area of the gold rectangle, it follows that marginal revenue is less than price for a monopolist.

hand corner is point *B*, or $2.00 × 16 = $32. The marginal revenue of the 16th unit is, by definition, total revenue when 16 units are sold minus total revenue when 15 units are sold, or $32 − $31.50 = $0.50.

In Figure 10-3, marginal revenue appears as the area of the tall gold rectangle ($2.00) minus the area of the flat blue rectangle ($1.50). We can see that MR is less than price by observing that the price is shown in the diagram by the area of the gold rectangle. (Because the width of this rectangle is 1 unit, its area is height × width = $2.00 per unit × 1 unit = $2.00.) Clearly, the price (area of the gold rectangle) must exceed the marginal revenue (area of the gold rectangle minus area of the blue rectangle), as was claimed.[1]

DETERMINING THE PROFIT-MAXIMIZING OUTPUT

We return now to the supply decision of the monopolist depicted in Figure 10-2. Like any other firm, the monopoly maximizes its profits by setting marginal revenue (MR) equal to marginal cost (MC). It selects

---

1. There is another way to arrive at this conclusion. Recall that the demand curve is the curve of average revenue. Since the average revenue is declining as we move to the right, it follows from one of the rules relating marginals and averages (see the appendix to Chapter 7) that the marginal-revenue curve must always be below the average.

point *E* in the diagram, where output is 150 units. But point *E* does not tell us the monopoly price because, as we have just seen, price exceeds MR for a monopolist. To learn what price the monopolist charges, we must use the demand curve to find the price at which consumers are willing to purchase 150 units. The answer, we see, is given by point *P*. The monopoly price is $10 per unit, which naturally exceeds both MR and MC (which are equal at $5).

The monopoly firm depicted in Figure 10-2 is earning a tidy profit. This profit is shown in the graph by the shaded rectangle, whose height is the difference between price (point *P*) and average cost (point *C*) and whose width is the quantity produced (150 units). In the example, profits are $4 per unit, or $600. The monopolist has the power to raise price above $10 per unit, but chooses not to, since doing so would lower profits.

To study the decisions of a profit-maximizing monopolist, we must

1. Find the output at which MR = MC, to select the profit-maximizing output level.

2. Find the height of the demand curve at that level of output, to determine the corresponding price.

3. Compare the height of the demand curve with that of the AC curve at that output to see whether the net result is a profit or a loss.

A monopolist's profit-maximization calculation can also be shown numerically. In Table 10-1, the first two columns show the price and quantity figures that constitute a monopolist's demand curve. Column 3 shows total revenue (TR), which is the product of price and quantity, for each output. Thus, for 3 units of output, we have TR = $92 × 3 = $276. Column 4 shows marginal revenue (MR). For example, when output rises from 3 to 4 units, TR increases from $276 to $320, so MR is $320 − $276 = $44. Column 5 gives the monopolist's total costs for each level of output. Column 6 derives marginal cost (MC) from total cost (TC) in the

TABLE 10-1

A PROFIT-MAXIMIZING MONOPOLIST'S PRICE–OUTPUT DECISION

Demand Curve		Revenue		Cost		Total Profit
(1)	(2)	(3)	(4)	(5)	(6)	(7)
Q	*P*	TR = *P* × *Q*	MR	TC	MC	TR − TC
0	—	$ 0		$ 10		$−10
1	$140	140	$140	73	$63	67
2	107	214	74	123	50	91
3	92	276	62	166	43	110
4	80	320	44	210	44	110
5	66	330	10	265	55	65
6	50	300	−30	348	83	−48

usual way. Finally, by subtracting TC from TR for each level of output, we derive total profit in column 7.

This table brings out a number of important points. We note first (columns 2 and 3) that a cut in price sometimes raises total revenue. For example, when output rises from 1 to 2, P falls from $140 to $107 and TR rises from $140 to $214. But sometimes a fall in P reduces TR; when (between 5 and 6 units of output) P falls from $66 to $50, TR falls from $330 to $300. Next, by comparing columns 2 and 4, we observe that, after the first unit, price always exceeds marginal revenue. Finally, from columns 4 and 6, we see that MC = MR = $44 when Q is 4 units, indicating that this is the level of output that maximizes the monopolist's total profit. This is confirmed in the last column of the table, which shows that at that output, profit reaches its highest level, $110, for any of the output quantities considered in the table.

COMPARISON OF MONOPOLY AND PERFECT COMPETITION

This completes our analysis of the monopolist's price–output decision. At this point, it is natural to wonder whether there is anything distinctive about monopoly, and whether its consequences are desirable or undesirable. For the purpose of finding out, we need a standard of comparison. Perfect competition provides this standard because, as we learned in Chapters 8 and 9, it is a benchmark of ideal performance against which other market structures can be judged. By comparing the results of monopoly with those of perfect competition, we will see why economists since Adam Smith have condemned monopoly as inefficient.

Monopoly Profit Persists

The first difference between competition and monopoly is a direct consequence of the absence of barriers to entry in the former. Profits such as those shown in Figure 10-2 would be competed away by free entry in a competitive market. In the long run, a competitive firm must earn zero economic profit; that is, it can earn only enough to cover its costs, including the opportunity cost of the owner's capital and labour. But higher profits can persist under monopoly — if the monopoly is protected by barriers to entry. The fates can be kind to a monopolist firm and allow it to grow wealthy at the expense of the consumer. Because people find such accumulations of wealth objectionable, monopoly is widely condemned and, when monopolies are regulated by government, limitations are usually placed on the profits monopolies can earn.

Monopoly Restricts Output to Raise Price

Excess monopoly profits may be a problem, but the second difference between competition and monopoly is even more worrisome in the opinion of economists:

Compared with the perfectly competitive ideal, the monopolist restricts output and charges a higher price.

To see that this is so, let us conduct the following thought experiment. The operation of a competitive industry is shown in Figure 10-4. For the moment, ignore everything except the demand and supply curves. We see that these industry demand and supply curves intersect at point *A*. Since the industry supply curve is the horizontal summation of all the marginal-cost curves of the individual factories (above minimum average variable costs) and since point *A* is on that supply curve, price equals marginal cost at point *A*.

   Now suppose one firm takes over the industry and operates the same set of plants, so that cost curves are not affected. Holding a monopoly, this firm will now calculate the marginal-revenue curve that is associated with the industry demand curve, and operate at the output level given by point *B*, since this is where marginal revenue equals marginal cost. The corresponding point on the demand curve, and hence the price the monopolist will charge, is therefore *C*. By comparing points *A* and *C*, we can clearly see that the monopolist sells a smaller quantity of the good to buyers and charges a higher price per unit than does the corresponding competitive industry. Excess profits are earned (indefinitely, given

FIGURE 10-4

COMPARISON OF A MONOPOLY AND A COMPETITIVE INDUSTRY

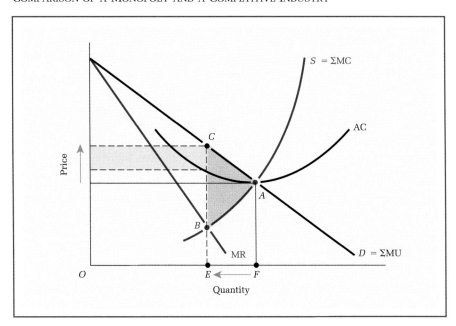

The monopoly price–output combination is point *C* (at which MC = MR), while that of the competitive industry is point *A* (where *P* = MC, and AC is at the minimum level possible). The *net* loss to society as a result of losing output amount *EF* is equal to area *ABC* in every period during which a monopoly prevails.

barriers to entry), and inefficiency exists, as we can see, since the unit cost of production (that is, average cost) is no longer minimized. Thus, the detrimental effects of monopoly involve dimensions of both equity and efficiency.

MONOPOLY LEADS TO INEFFICIENT RESOURCE ALLOCATION

We conclude, then, that a monopoly will charge a higher price and produce a smaller output than will a competitive industry with the same demand and cost conditions. Why do economists find this situation so objectionable? Because, as you will recall from Chapter 9, a competitive industry devotes just the right amount of society's scarce resources to the production of its particular commodity. Therefore, if a monopoly produces less than a competitive industry, it must be producing too little.

Remember from Chapter 9 that efficiency in resource allocation requires that the marginal utility (MU) of each commodity be equal to its marginal cost, and that perfect competition guarantees that

$$MU = P \quad \text{and} \quad MC = P, \quad \text{so} \quad MU = MC$$

Under monopoly, consumers continue to maximize their own welfare by setting MU equal to P. But the monopoly producer, we have just learned, sets MC equal to MR. Since MR is *below* the market price, P, we conclude that in a monopolized industry,

$$MU = P \quad \text{and} \quad MC = MR < P, \quad \text{so} \quad MU > MC$$

Because MU exceeds MC, too small a share of society's resources are being used to produce the monopolized commodity. Adam Smith's invisible hand is sending out the wrong signals. Consumers are willing to pay an amount for an additional unit of the good (its MU) that exceeds what it costs to produce that unit (its MC). But the monopoly refuses to increase production, for if it raises output by one unit, the revenue it will collect (the MR) will be less than the price the consumer will pay for the additional unit (P). Thus, the monopolist does not increase production and resources are allocated inefficiently. Let's summarize:

Because it is protected from the entry of other firms, a monopoly firm may earn profits in excess of the opportunity cost of capital. At the same time, monopoly breeds inefficiency in resource allocation by producing too little output and charging too high a price. For these reasons, some virtues of laissez faire evaporate if an industry becomes monopolized.

The inefficiency caused by monopoly can actually be measured from Figure 10-4. How much would it cost society to increase the output of this industry from the monopoly level, amount *OE*, to the competitive level, amount *OF*? The answer is given by the area under the marginal-cost curve within the range of additional production (*EF*), that is, area *EFAB*. This is so because we can get the overall increase in cost by adding together all the marginal costs of each unit as output is increased from *OE* to *OF*.

How much does society gain if output is increased in this way? The answer can be had by considering people's overall willingness to pay for this extra output, which is reflected by the area under the demand curve within the range of the additional purchases (*EF*), that is, by area *EFAC*. This is so because we get the overall increase in utility by adding together all the marginal utilities of each unit as output is increased from *OE* to *OF*. The demand curve is the summation of all individuals' marginal utility schedules.

The excess of benefits over costs is the difference between the two areas, *EFAB* and *EFAC*. The net benefit of moving back to the competitive outcome is therefore area *ABC*—the shaded blue triangle in Figure 10-4. Once these curves have been estimated with actual data in particular cases, economists directly measure areas such as *ABC* to calculate the loss to society that is incurred in *every* period during which a monopoly prevails.

Actually, the inefficiency caused by monopoly can be greater than the amount indicated by the blue triangle in each period. The reason for this is that individuals may fight over who owns the monopoly, with a view to acquiring the right to receive the stream of positive economic profits (equal to the gold area in Figure 10-4) in each period. (This process is called **rent-seeking**. For further discussion of rent-seeking behaviour, see pages 348 and 429.) Many resources are spent on the talents of accountants, lawyers, and others as various individuals and companies make takeover bids for companies that generate excess profits of this sort. Competition among these would-be owners forces the expenditures that are made by the successful bidder up to an amount that is approximately equal to the prize itself—the gold area. Thus, while at first glance we must interpret the blue triangle as the efficiency cost of monopoly and the gold rectangle as the equity dimension of monopoly, we see that much of the gold rectangle can become truly wasted resources as well. Many observers have used precisely this reasoning to conclude that the wave of takeovers in the 1980s was very costly. The resources used in the takeover battles had a high opportunity cost.

RENT-SEEKING refers to unproductive activity in the pursuit of economic profit, that is, profit in excess of competitive earnings.

But this whole discussion has assumed that after the takeover, the monopolist will still operate every plant. This may be a bad assumption, since the monopolist may be able to effect some cost savings by consolidating the operations, as we will see below.

CAN ANYTHING GOOD BE SAID ABOUT MONOPOLY?

Except for the case of natural monopoly, where a single firm offers important cost advantages, or the case of a monopoly obtained through an inventor's patent, which is designed to encourage innovation, it is not easy to find arguments in favour of monopoly. But the comparison between monopoly and perfect competition in the real world is not quite as simple as it is in our example.

MONOPOLY MAY SHIFT DEMAND

For one thing, we have assumed that the market-demand curve is the same whether the industry is competitive or monopolized. But is this necessarily so? The demand curve will be the same if the monopoly firm does nothing to expand its market, but that hardly seems likely.

Under perfect competition, purchasers consider the products of all suppliers in an industry to be identical, and so no single supplier has any reason to advertise. A farmer who sells apples through one of the major markets has absolutely no motivation to spend money on advertising because he can sell all the apples he wants to at the going price.

When a monopoly firm takes over, however, it may very well pay to advertise. If management believes that advertising can make consumers' hearts beat faster as they rush to the market to purchase the apples whose virtues have been extolled on television, the firm will allocate a substantial sum of money to accomplish this feat. This should shift the demand curve outward; after all, that is the purpose of these expenditures. The monopoly's demand curve and that of the competitive industry will then no longer be the same. The higher demand curve for the monopoly's product will perhaps induce it to expand its volume of production and to reduce the difference between the competitive and the monopolist output levels indicated in Figure 10-4. It may also, however, make it possible for the monopoly firm to charge even higher prices, so the increased output may not constitute a net gain for consumers.

MONOPOLY MAY SHIFT COST CURVES

Similarly, the advent of a monopoly may produce shifts in the average- and marginal-cost curves. One reason for higher costs is the advertising we have just been discussing. Another is that the sheer size of the monopolist's organization may lead to bureaucratic inefficiencies, co-ordination problems, and the like. On the other hand, the monopolist may be able to eliminate certain types of duplication that are unavoidable for a number of small independent firms: One purchasing agent may do the job where many buyers were needed before, and a few large machines may replace many small items of equipment in the hands of the competitive firms. In addition, the large scale of the monopoly firm's input purchases may permit it to take advantage of quantity discounts not available to small competitive firms.

If the unification achieved by monopoly does succeed in producing a downward shift in the marginal-cost curve, monopoly output will thereby tend to move up closer to the competitive level, and the monopoly price will tend to move down closer to the competitive price.

MONOPOLY MAY AID INNOVATION

In addition, some economists, most notably Joseph Schumpeter, have argued that it is potentially misleading to compare the cost curves of a monopoly and a competitive industry at a single point in time. Because a monopoly is protected from rivals and therefore sure to capture the benefits from any cost savings it can devise, it has a particularly strong motivation to invest in research, these economists argue. If this research bears fruit, the monopolist's costs will be lower than those of a competitive industry in the long run, even if they are higher in the short run. Monopoly, according to this view, may be the handmaiden of innovation. While the argument is an old one, it remains controversial. The statistical evidence is decidedly mixed.

NATURAL MONOPOLY: WHERE SINGLE-FIRM PRODUCTION IS CHEAPEST

Finally, we must remember that the monopoly depicted in Figure 10-4 is not a natural monopoly. But some of the monopolies you find in the real world are. Where the monopoly is natural, costs of production would, by definition, be higher and possibly much higher if the single large firm were broken up into many smaller firms. In such cases, it may be in society's best interest to allow the monopoly to exist so that consumers can benefit from the economies of large-scale production. But then it may be appropriate to place legal limitations on the monopolist's ability to set a price; that is, it may be appropriate to *regulate* the monopoly. Regulation of business will occupy our attention in Chapter 16.

MONOPOLY POLICY

Monopoly raises both an efficiency issue (since, with a monopolist, MU > MC) and an equity issue (since positive economic profits persist indefinitely). Often, the use of a single policy instrument improves one problem but exacerbates the other. For example, if a monopoly firm is hit with an excise tax, its profit will be reduced. But the tax will shift its marginal-cost curve up, causing it to reduce its output level even further below what it would obtain in a competitive environment. Thus, the excise tax compounds the efficiency problem.

Since there are two dimensions to the monopoly problem, two policy instruments are needed. One policy package that can help solve the problem involves increasing fixed costs by levying a licence fee (thereby decreasing profits without causing any change in price or output) and, at the same time, decreasing variable cost by paying a per-unit-of-output subsidy (thereby shifting the marginal-cost curve down and, as a result, increasing output and lowering price). As long as the licence fee is high enough, profits will be reduced despite the subsidy. The effects of this policy package are shown in Figure 10-5. Initially, the monopolist is producing output level *OA* and earning profits *CD*. The per-unit subsidy pivots the total-cost curve down, and the licence fee shifts the total-cost curve up in a parallel fashion. If the two effects are combined perfectly, as shown in Figure 10-5, the monopolist could be pushed to point *E*— offering more output to the market but earning no economic profit.

One problem with this policy package is that a large licence fee adds to the barriers to entry. If only small barriers to entry exist in the first place, the licence fee is not an appealing option. But if the barriers are already large, the package can, at least in principle, solve both the equity and the efficiency aspects of the monopoly problem.

In later chapters, we consider the following three policy approaches to the monopoly problem: (1) regulation, (2) laws and their enforcement through the courts, and (3) the discipline of the market. The idea behind this third alternative is to make more substitutes for the monopolist's product available to the public (say, by decreasing tariffs and forcing the firm into competition with foreign suppliers). To make this last point more explicit, it is useful at this stage to derive the formula for a monopolist's price "markup." This derivation follows from a manipulation of the MR = MC condition for profit maximization.

Recall that, by definition, marginal revenue equals $\Delta TR/\Delta Q$. Now, since total revenue equals price times quantity, *PQ*, and since $\Delta(PQ) = P\Delta Q + Q\Delta P$,

FIGURE 10-5

TACKLING BOTH THE EQUITY AND EFFICIENCY PROBLEMS OF MONOPOLY

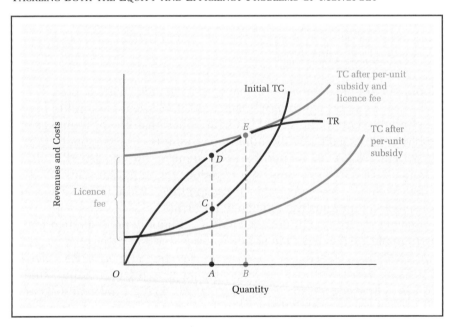

Without any tax or subsidy, the monopolist chooses output *OA*. A per-unit subsidy pivots TC down (leading to higher output and lower price), and a licence fee shifts TC up in a parallel fashion (since it represents an increase in fixed costs). The licence fee drives profits down (to zero at point *E* in this diagram) without driving the price up or causing output to decline.

$$\text{MR} = \frac{\Delta \text{TR}}{\Delta Q} = \frac{\Delta PQ}{\Delta Q} = \frac{P\Delta Q}{\Delta Q} + \frac{Q\Delta P}{\Delta Q} = P\left(1 + \frac{Q\Delta P}{P\Delta Q}\right)$$

But the elasticity of demand, E, equals $- (\Delta Q/Q)/(\Delta P/P)$. When this definition is substituted into the expression for marginal revenue, it becomes

$$\text{MR} = P(1 - 1/E)$$

For profit maximization, MR = MC, so this equation becomes

$$\text{MC} = P(1 - 1/E)$$

Finally, by cross-division, we arrive at the monopolist's price markup formula:

$$\frac{P}{\text{MC}} = \frac{1}{1 - 1/E}$$

Clearly, the closer an industry comes to perfect competition—that is, as the elasticity of demand facing each individual firm approaches infinity, making E very high—the more the markup shrinks toward zero. In this case, the markup formula reduces to $P = \text{MC}$. Economists believe that anything that can be done to raise demand elasticities is a good anti-monopoly policy. Raising the availability of substitutes is the most obvious way of accomplishing this objective, and this is one of the appealing aspects of free trade.

MONOPOLY AND THE SHIFTING OF POLLUTION CHARGES

We conclude our discussion of monopoly by returning to the application that began this chapter—the effectiveness of pollution charges as a means of reducing emissions. Recall that the question is whether a monopoly can raise its price enough to cover any pollution fees, thus shifting these charges entirely to its customers and evading them altogether.

The answer is that any firm or industry can usually shift part of the pollution charge to its customers. Economists argue that this shifting is a proper part of a pollution-control program since it induces consumers to redirect their purchases from goods that are highly polluting to goods that are not. For example, a significant increase in taxes on leaded gasoline with, perhaps, a simultaneous decrease in the tax on unleaded gasoline will send more motorists to the unleaded-gas pumps, and that will reduce dangerous lead emissions.

But more important for our discussion here is the other side of the matter. While some part of a pollution charge is usually paid by the consumer, the seller will usually be stuck with some part of the charge, even if the seller is a monopolist. Why? Because of the negative slope of the demand curve. If the monopoly firm raises the price of its product, it will lose customers, and that will eat into its profits. The monopoly firm will therefore do better by absorbing *some* of the charge itself rather than trying to pass all of it on to its customers.

This is illustrated in Figure 10-6. In part (a), we show the monopolist's demand, marginal-revenue, and marginal-cost curves. As in Figure 10-2, equilibrium output is 150 units—the point at which marginal revenue (MR) equals marginal cost (MC). Price is again $10—the point on the demand curve corresponding to 150 units of output (point *A*).

Now, put a charge of $5 per unit on the firm's polluting output, shifting the marginal-cost curve up uniformly to the curve labelled "MC plus fee" in Figure 10-6(b). Then the profit-maximizing output falls to 100 units (point *F*), for here, MR = MC + pollution fee. The new output, 100 units, is lower than the precharge output, 150 units. Thus, the charge leads the monopoly firm to restrict its polluting output. The price of its product rises to $12 (point *B*), the point on the demand curve corresponding to 100 units of output. But the rise in price from $10 to $12 is less than half the $5 pollution charge per unit. Thus, we can conclude as follows:

FIGURE 10-6
MONOPOLY PRICE AND OUTPUT WITH AND WITHOUT A POLLUTION CHARGE

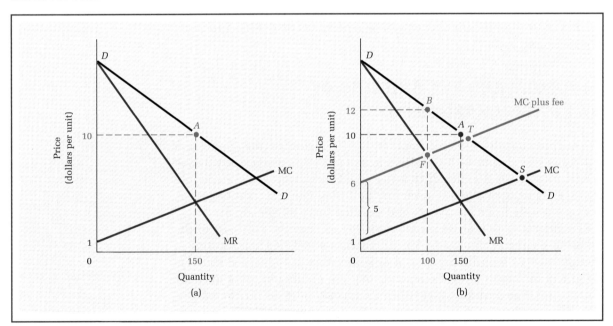

Part (a) shows the monopoly equilibrium without a pollution charge, with price equal to $10 and quantity equal to 150 units. In part (b), a $5 fee is levied on each unit of polluting output. This raises the marginal-cost curve by the amount of the fee, from the red to the blue line. As a result, the output at which MC = MR falls from 150 to 100 units. Price rises from $10 to $12. Note that this $2 price rise is less than the $5 pollution fee, so the monopolist will be stuck with the remaining $3 of the charge.

The pollution charge *does* hurt the polluter even if the polluter is a profit-maximizing monopolist, and it *does* force the monopoly to cut its polluting outputs.

No wonder the polluters' lobbyists fight so vehemently! Polluters realize that they will often be far better off with direct controls that impose a financial penalty *only* if they are caught in a violation, prosecuted, and convicted—and even then the fines are often negligible, as we will see in Chapter 17.

It is interesting to compare the reaction of a monopolist to a pollution fee with that of a competitive industry in the short run. Using Figure 10-6(b) to represent a situation of perfect competition with the same demand and cost conditions, we see that the industry outcome point moves from point *S* before the fee to point *T* after the fee. By comparing the gap between points *S* and *T* and the gap between points *A* and *B*, we see that the pollution fee can cut back output more in the competitive case, since more of the charge is passed on through higher prices in the competitive case. Since an emission charge is just a specific form of a sales tax, we see that a larger portion of any sales tax is passed on by the firms in a competitive industry. Most individuals who are untrained in economics just presume that taxes are passed on more by monopolists.

We may note, finally, that any rise in a monopoly's costs will hurt its profits. The reason is exactly the same as in the case of a pollution charge. Even though the firm is a monopoly, it cannot simply raise its price and make up for any cost increase, because consumers can and will respond by buying less of the monopoly's commodity. After all, that is what the negative slope of the demand curve means.

If a monopoly already charges the price that maximizes its profits, a rise in cost will always hurt because any attempt to offset it by a price increase must reduce profit. The monopolist cannot pass on the entire burden of the cost increase to consumers.

SUMMARY

1. A pure monopoly is a one-firm industry producing a product for which there are no close substitutes.

2. Monopoly can persist only if there are important cost advantages to single-firm operation or barriers to free entry. These barriers may be legal impediments (patents, licensing), some unique advantage the monopoly acquires for itself (control of a scarce resource), or the result of "dirty tricks" designed to make things tough for an entrant.

3. One important case of cost advantages is natural monopoly: instances where only one firm can survive because of important economies of large-scale production.

4. A monopoly has no supply curve. It maximizes its profit by producing an output at which its marginal revenue equals its mar-

ginal cost. Its price is given by the point on its demand curve corresponding to that output.

5. In a monopolistic industry, if demand and cost curves are the same as those of a competitive industry and if the demand curve has a negative slope and the supply curve a positive slope, output will be lower and monopoly price will be higher than those of the competitive industry. Economists regard this as an undesirable inefficiency.

6. Advertising may enable a monopoly to shift its demand curve above that of a comparable competitive industry; also, through econo-

mies such as large-scale input purchases, it may be able to shift its cost curves below those of a competitive industry.

7. If a pollution charge is imposed on the product of a profit-maximizing monopoly, that monopoly will raise its price, but normally not by the full amount of the charge. That is, the monopolist will end up paying part of the pollution fee.

8. Any rise in costs generally hurts a monopolist. Because of the negatively sloping demand curve, a monopolist cannot simply pass the increase on to consumers.

CONCEPTS FOR REVIEW

Pure monopoly
Barriers to entry
Patents

Natural monopoly
Monopoly profits
Inefficiency of monopoly

Rent-seeking
P/MC (markup formula)
Shifting of pollution charges

QUESTIONS FOR DISCUSSION

1. Which of the following industries are pure monopolies?
   a. The only supplier of water in an isolated desert town.
   b. The only supplier of Esso gas in town.
   c. The only supplier of instant cameras.
   Explain your answers.

2. Suppose a monopoly industry produces less output than a similar competitive industry. Discuss why this may be considered "socially undesirable."

3. If a competitive firm earns zero economic profits, explain why anyone would invest money in it. (*Hint:* What is the role of the opportunity cost of capital in economic profit?)

4. The following are the demand and total-cost schedules for Company Town Water Company, a local monopoly.

Output (litres)	Price (dollars per litre)	Total Cost (dollars)
50 000	0.14	3 000
100 000	0.13	6 500
150 000	0.11	11 000
190 000	0.10	16 000
250 000	0.08	23 000
300 000	0.06	32 000

How much output will Company Town produce, and what price will it charge? Will it earn a profit? How much? (*Hint:* You will first have to compute its MR and MC schedules.)

5. Show from the preceding table that for the water company, marginal revenue (per 50 000-litre unit) is always less than price.

6. Suppose a tax of $12 is levied on each item sold by a monopolist firm, and as a result, it decides to raise its price by exactly $12. Why may this decision be against the firm's own best interest?

7. Use Figure 10-2 to show that Adam Smith was wrong when he claimed that the price a monopoly charges is always "the highest which can be got."

8. Explain fully why you either agree or disagree with each of the following propositions. When necessary, assume constant returns to scale.
   a. An increase in fixed costs will raise prices in a competitive industry, but not in a monopoly.
   b. A larger portion of an excise tax is passed on to consumers in a perfectly competitive industry than in a monopoly.
   c. It does not matter whether it is the buyers or the seller(s) that are hit with an excise tax—the real burden is the same for each group in either case. This statement is true for both perfect competition and monopoly.

9. Each team in the NHL has a monopoly in its own region for selling tickets to its games. Assume that the demand curve for tickets is a downward-sloping straight line and that the marginal cost of catering to another ticket buyer is zero. Assuming that only one ticket price can be set, how should that price be determined to maximize profits? Does it make sense to keep the price so high that some seats remain empty? Suppose there is an increase in the players' salaries. How would this change your answer to the preceding questions?

BETWEEN COMPETITION AND MONOPOLY

Most productive activity in Canada, as in any advanced industrial society, can be found between the two theoretical poles considered so far: perfect competition and pure monopoly. Thus, if we want to understand the workings of the market mechanism in a real, modern economy, we must look between competition and monopoly, at the hybrid market structures first mentioned in Chapter 8: *monopolistic competition* and *oligopoly*.

Monopolistic competition is a market structure characterized by many small firms selling somewhat different products. Each firm's output is so small relative to the economy's total output of closely related and, hence, rival products that it does not expect its rivals to respond to or even to notice changes in its own behaviour. Monopolistic competition or something close to it is widespread in the retail sector of our economy; shoe stores, restaurants, and gasoline stations are good examples. We will use the theory of the firm described in Chapter 7 to analyze the output–price decision of a monopolistically competitive firm, and then consider industry-wide adjustments, as we did in Chapter 8.

Oligopoly is a market structure in which a few large firms dominate the market. Industries like steel, automobiles, and tobacco are good examples of oligopoly in our economy. The critical feature distinguishing an oligopolist from either a monopolist or a perfect competitor is that the oligopolist cares very much about what other firms in that industry do. The resulting interdependence of decisions, we will see, makes oligopoly very hard to analyze. Consequently, economic theory contains not one but many models of oligopoly (some of which will be reviewed in this chapter), and it is often hard to know which model to apply in any particular situation. But we can say that the case for laissez faire is weakened by the existence of either monopolistic competition or oligopoly.

SOME PUZZLING OBSERVATIONS

It is easy to see that we need to study the hybrid market structures considered in this chapter, for many things we observe in the real world defy understanding within the framework of either perfect competition or pure monopoly. Here are two examples:

1. ***Advertising.***   While some advertising is primarily informative (for example, help-wanted ads), much of the advertising that bombards us on TV and in magazines is part of a competitive struggle for our business. Many big companies use advertising as the principal weapon in their battle for customers, and advertising budgets can constitute a very large share of their expenditures. Yet oligopolistic industries containing a few giant firms are often accused of being "uncompetitive," while farming is considered as close to perfect competition as any industry in our economy, even though most individual farmers spend nothing at all on advertising. (But farmers' associations and agricultural marketing boards do spend money on advertising. Furthermore, where marketing boards and similar agencies exist and impose price controls or production quotas, competition among farmers is reduced.) Why do the allegedly uncompetitive oligopolists and marketing boards make such heavy use of advertising while very competitive farmers operating without marketing boards do not?

2. ***Excessive number of firms.***   We have all seen intersections with three or four gasoline stations in close proximity. Often, two or three of them have no cars waiting to be served and the attendants are unoccupied. There seem to be more gas stations than the available amount of traffic warrants, with a corresponding waste of labour time, equipment, and other resources. Why do they all stay in business?

Among other things, this chapter will offer some answers to these two questions.

MONOPOLISTIC COMPETITION

For years, most economic theorists dealt with only two workable models of the behaviour of firms: the monopoly model and the perfectly competitive model. This gap was partially filled, and the realism of economic theory was thereby greatly increased, by the work of Edward Chamberlin of Harvard University and Joan Robinson of Cambridge University during the 1930s. The market structure they analyzed is called **monopolistic competition**.

A market is said to operate under conditions of monopolistic competition if it satisfies four conditions, three of which are the same as those that define perfect competition: (1) numerous participants — that is, many buyers and sellers, all of whom are small; (2) freedom of exit and entry; (3) perfect information; and (4) heterogeneity of products—as far as the buyer is concerned, each seller's product is at least somewhat different from every other's.

Notice that monopolistic competition differs from perfect competition in only one respect (item 4 in the definition). While all products are identical under perfect competition, under monopolistic competition, products differ from seller to seller—in quality, in packaging, or in supplementary services offered (for example, length of the guarantee, car-window washing by a gas station, and so on). The factors that serve to differentiate products need not be "real" in any objective or scientific sense. For example, differences in packaging or in associated services can and do distinguish products that are otherwise identical. On the other hand, two products may perform quite differently in quality tests, but if consumers know nothing about this difference, it is irrelevant for the market outcome.

Since products under monopolistic competition are not identical, there is no reason to expect the price of any firm's product to remain unchanged when the quantity supplied varies. Each seller, in effect, deals in a market slightly separated from the others and caters to a set of customers who vary in their loyalty to the particular product. If one firm raises its price somewhat, it will drive some but not all of its customers into the arms of its competitors. If it lowers its price, it may expect to attract some trade from its rivals. But since the firm's product is not a perfect substitute for its rivals' products, if the firm undercuts them slightly, it will not attract away *all* of their business as it would in the perfectly competitive case.

Thus, if Harriet's Hot Dog House reduces its price slightly, it will attract those customers of Sam's Sausage Shop who were nearly indifferent between the two. A bigger price cut by Harriet will bring in some customers who have a slightly greater preference for Sam's product. But even a big cut in Harriet's price will not bring her the hard-core sausage lovers who hate hot dogs. Thus, the monopolistic competitor's demand curve is negatively sloped, like that of a monopolist, rather than horizontal, like that of a perfect competitor.

Since each product is distinguished from all others, a monopolistically competitive firm appears to have something akin to a small monopoly. Can we therefore expect it to earn more than zero economic profit? As with a perfect competitor, perhaps this is possible in the short run. But in the long run, high economic profits will attract new entrants into a monopolistically competitive market—not entrants with products identical to an existing firm's, but those with products sufficiently similar to hurt.

If one ice cream parlour's location enables it to do a thriving business, it can confidently expect another, selling a different brand, to open nearby. When one seller adopts a new, attractive package, rivals will soon follow suit, with a slightly different design and colour of their own. In this way, freedom of entry ensures that the monopolistically competitive firm earns no higher return on its capital in the long run than it could earn elsewhere. Just as under perfect competition, price will be driven to the level of average cost, including the opportunity cost of capital. In this sense, although its product is somewhat different from that of everyone else, the firm under monopolistic competition has no more monopoly power than does a firm operating under perfect competition.

Let us now examine the process that assures that economic profits will be driven to zero in the long run, even under monopolistic competition.

PRICE AND OUTPUT DETERMINATION UNDER MONOPOLISTIC COMPETITION

The short-run equilibrium of the firm under monopolistic competition differs little from the case of monopoly. Since the firm faces a downward-sloping demand curve (labelled *D* in Figure 11-1), its marginal-revenue (MR) curve will lie below its demand curve. Profits are maximized at the output level at which marginal revenue and marginal cost (MC) are equal. In Figure 11-1, the profit-maximizing output for a hypothetical gasoline station is 20 000 litres per week, and it sells this output at a price of 50¢ per litre (point *P* on the demand curve).

This diagram, you will note, looks much like Figure 10-2 (page 295) for a monopoly. The only difference is that the demand curve of a monopolistic competitor is likely to be much flatter than the pure monopolist's because there are many close substitutes for the monopolistic competitor's product. If our gas station raises its price to 60¢ per litre, most of

FIGURE 11-1

SHORT-RUN EQUILIBRIUM OF THE FIRM UNDER MONOPOLISTIC COMPETITION

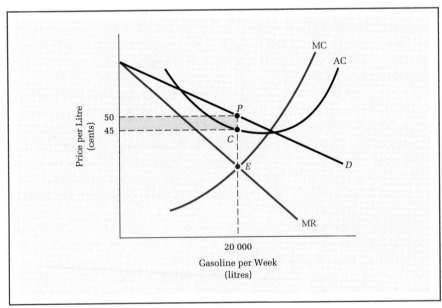

Like any firm, a monopolistic competitor maximizes profits by equating marginal cost (MC) and marginal revenue (MR). In this example, the profit-maximizing output level is 20 000 litres per week and the profit-maximizing price is 50¢ per litre. The firm is making a profit of 5¢ per litre, which is depicted by the vertical distance from *C* to *P*.

its customers will go across the street. If it lowers its price to 40¢ per litre, it will have long lines at its pumps.

The gas station depicted in Figure 11-1 is making economic profits. Since average cost at 20 000 litres per week is only 45¢ per litre (point *C*), the station is making a profit on gasoline sales of 5¢ per litre, or $1000 per week in total (the shaded rectangle). Under monopoly, such profits can persist. But under monopolistic competition, they cannot, because new firms will be attracted into the market. While the new stations will not offer the identical product, they will offer products that are close enough to take away some business from our firm (for example, they may sell Sunoco or Shell gasoline instead of Esso).

When more firms share the market, the demand curve facing any individual firm must fall. But how far? The answer is basically the same as it was under perfect competition: until the most that the profit-maximizing firm can earn is zero economic profit, for only then will entry cease.

Figure 11-2 depicts the same monopolistically competitive firm as in Figure 11-1 *after* the adjustment to the long run is complete. The demand curve has been pushed down so far that when the firm equates MC and MR in order to maximize profits (point *E*), it simultaneously equates price (*P*) and average cost (AC) so that profits are zero (point *P*). Compared with the short-run equilibrium depicted in Figure 11-1, the long-run equilibrium involves lower price (47¢ per litre versus 50¢ per litre), more

FIGURE 11-2

LONG-RUN EQUILIBRIUM OF THE FIRM UNDER MONOPOLISTIC COMPETITION

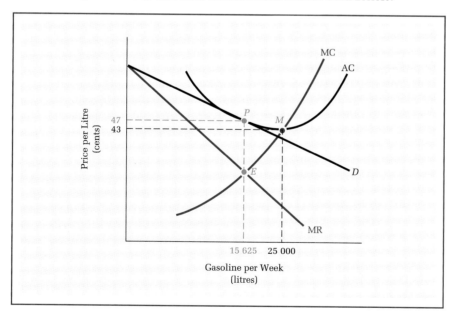

In this diagram, the cost curves are identical to those of Figure 11-1, but the demand curve (and hence also the MR curve) has been depressed by the entry of new competitors. When the firm maximizes profits by equating marginal revenue and marginal cost (point *E*), its average cost is equal to its price (47¢), so economic profits are zero. For this reason, the diagram depicts a *long-run* equilibrium position.

firms in the industry, and smaller output by each firm (15 625 litres versus 20 000 litres) at a higher average cost per litre (47¢ versus 45¢).

Long-run equilibrium under monopolistic competition generally requires that the firm's demand curve be tangent to its average-cost curve.

Why? Because if the two curves intersected, there would be output levels at which price exceeded average cost, which means that economic profits could be earned and there would be an influx of new substitute products. Similarly, if the average-cost curve failed to touch the demand curve altogether, the firm would be unable to obtain returns equal to those that its capital could get elsewhere, and firms would leave the industry.

This analysis of entry is quite similar to that of the perfectly competitive case. Moreover, the notion that firms under monopolistic competition earn exactly zero economic profits seems to correspond fairly well to what we see in the real world. Filling-station operators, whose market has the characteristics of monopolistic competition, do not earn notably higher profits than do small farmers, who operate under conditions closer to those of perfect competition.

THE EXCESS-CAPACITY THEOREM AND RESOURCE ALLOCATION

But there is one important difference between perfect and monopolistic competition. Look at Figure 11-2 again. The tangency point between the average-cost and demand curves, point *P*, occurs along the negatively sloping portion of the average-cost curve, since only there does the AC curve have the same (negative) slope as the demand curve. If the AC curve is U-shaped, the tangency point must therefore lie above and to the left of the minimum point on the average-cost curve, point *M*. By contrast, under perfect competition, the firm's demand curve is horizontal, so tangency must take place *at* the minimum point on the average-cost curve, as is easily confirmed by referring back to Figure 8-9(a) on page 244. This observation leads to the following important conclusion:

Under monopolistic competition, the firm in the long run will tend to produce an output lower than that which minimizes its unit costs, and hence unit costs of the monopolistic competitor will be higher than is necessary. Since the level of output corresponding to minimum average cost is naturally considered to be the firm's optimal capacity, this result has been called the **excess-capacity theorem of monopolistic competition**.

It follows that if every firm under monopolistic competition were to expand its output, cost per unit of output would be reduced. But we must be careful about jumping to policy conclusions from that observation. It does not follow that every monopolistically competitive firm *should* produce more. After all, such an overall increase in industry output would mean that a smaller portion of the economy's resources would be available for other uses, and from the information at hand, we have no way of knowing whether that would leave us ahead or behind in terms of social benefits.

Yet the situation represented in Figure 11-2 can still be interpreted to represent a substantial inefficiency. While it is not clear that society would gain if every firm were to achieve lower costs by expanding its production, society *can* save resources if firms combine into a smaller number of larger companies that produce the same total output. For example, suppose that in the situation shown in Figure 11-2 there are 32 monopolistically competitive firms each selling 15 625 litres of gas per week. The total cost of this output, according to the figures given in the diagram, would be

$$(\text{Number of firms}) \times (\text{Output per firm}) \times (\text{Cost per unit})$$
$$= 32 \times 15\ 625 \times \$0.47 = \$235\ 000$$

If, instead, the number of stations were cut to 20, and each sold 25 000 litres, total production would be unchanged. But total costs would fall to $20 \times 25\ 000 \times \$0.43 = \$215\ 000$, a net saving of \$20 000 for the *same total output*.

This result is not dependent on the particular numbers used in our illustration. It follows directly from the observation that lowering the cost per unit must always reduce the total cost of producing any given industry output. The excess-capacity theorem explains one of the puzzles mentioned at the start of this chapter. The intersection with four filling stations, where two could serve the available customers with little increase in delays and at lower costs, is a practical example of excess capacity.

The excess-capacity theorem seems to imply that there are too many sellers in monopolistically competitive markets and that society would benefit from a reduction in their numbers. However, such a conclusion would be a bit hasty. Even if a smaller number of larger firms could reduce costs, society may not benefit from the change because it would leave consumers a smaller range of choice. Since all products are at least slightly different under monopolistic competition, a reduction in the number of firms means that the number of different products falls as well. We achieve greater efficiency at the cost of greater standardization. In some cases, consumers may agree that this trade-off represents a net gain, particularly where the variety of products available was initially so great that it served only to confuse them. But for some products, many consumers might argue that the diversity of choice is worth the extra cost involved. After all, we would probably save money on clothing if every student were forced to wear the same uniform. But since the uniform is likely to be too hot for Student A, too cool for Student B, and aesthetically displeasing to everyone, would the cost saving really be a net benefit?

OLIGOPOLY

In terms of the dollar value of all manufactured goods produced in our economy, first place must be assigned to our final market form — **oligopoly**. An oligopoly is a market dominated by a few sellers, at least several of which are large enough relative to the total market to be able to influence the market price.

In highly developed economies, it is not monopoly, but oligopoly, that is virtually synonymous with "big business." Any oligopolistic industry includes a group of giant firms, each of which keeps a watchful eye on the actions of the others. (Notice that nothing is said in the definition about the degree of product differentiation. Some oligopolies sell products that are essentially identical [such as steel plate from different steel-makers], while others sell products that are quite different in the eyes of consumers [for example, Chevrolets, Fords, and Plymouths].) It is under oligopoly that rivalry among firms takes its most direct and active form. Here one encounters such actions and reactions as the frequent introduction of new products, free samples, and aggressive—if not downright nasty—advertising campaigns. One firm's price decision is likely to elicit a cry of pain from its rivals, and firms engage in a continuing battle in which strategies are planned day by day and each major decision can be expected to induce a direct response.

A manager of a large oligopolistic firm who has occasion to study economics is somewhat taken aback by the notion of perfect competition, because it is devoid of all harsh competitive activity as he or she knows it. Remember that under perfect competition, the managers of firms make no price decisions — they simply accept the price dictated by market forces and adjust their output accordingly. As we observed at the beginning of the chapter, a competitive firm does not advertise; it adopts no sales gimmicks; it does not even know who most of its competitors are. But since oligopolists are not as dependent on market forces, they do not enjoy such luxuries. They worry about prices, spend fortunes on advertising, and try to understand their rivals' behaviour patterns.

The reasons for such divergent behaviour should be clear. First, a perfectly competitive firm can sell all it wants at the current market price. Thus, why should it waste money on advertising? By contrast, Ford and Chrysler cannot sell all the cars they want at the current price. Since their demand curves are negatively sloped, if they want to sell more, they must either reduce prices or advertise more (to shift their demand curves outward).

Second, since the public believes that the products supplied by firms in a perfectly competitive industry are identical, if Firm A advertises its product, the advertisement is just as likely to bring customers to Firm B. Under oligopoly, however, products are usually not identical. Ford advertises to try to convince consumers that its automobiles are better than General Motors' or Toyota's. If the advertising campaign succeeds, GM and Toyota will be hurt and probably will respond with more advertising of their own. Thus, it is the firm in an oligopoly with differentiated products that is forced to compete via advertising, while the perfectly competitive firm gains little or nothing by doing so.

WHY OLIGOPOLISTIC BEHAVIOUR IS SO HARD TO ANALYZE

The relative freedom of choice in pricing of at least the largest firms in an oligopolistic industry and the necessity for them to take direct account of their rivals' responses are potentially troublesome. Producers that are able to influence the market price may find it expedient to adjust their outputs to secure more favourable prices. As in the case of monopoly, such actions are likely to be at the expense of the consumer and detrimental to the economy's efficient use of resources.

It is not easy, however, to reach definite conclusions about resource allocation under oligopoly. The reason is that oligopoly is much more difficult to analyze than the other forms of economic organization. The difficulty arises from the interdependent nature of oligopolistic decisions. For example, Ford's management knows that its actions will probably lead to reactions by GM, which in turn may require a readjustment in Ford's plans, thereby producing a modification in GM's response, and so on. Where such a sequence of moves and countermoves may lead is difficult enough to ascertain. But the fact that Ford executives know all this in advance and may take it into account in making their initial decision makes even that first step difficult, if not impossible, to analyze and predict.

The truth is that almost anything can happen under oligopoly, and sometimes does. Early American railway barons went so far as to employ gangs of hoodlums who engaged in pitched battles to try to prevent the operation of rival lines. At the other extreme, overt or more subtle forms of collusion have been employed to avoid rivalry altogether—to transform an oligopolistic industry, at least temporarily, into a monopolistic one. Arrangements designed to make it possible for the firms to live and let live have also been used: Price leadership (see page 321) is one example; an agreement allocating geographic areas among firms is another.

Because of this rich variety of behaviour patterns, it is not surprising that economists have been unable to agree on a single, widely accepted model of oligopoly behaviour. Nor should they. Since oligopolies in the real world are so diverse, oligopoly models in the theoretical world should also come in various shapes and sizes. The theory of oligopoly contains some remarkable pieces of economic analysis, some of which we will review in the following sections.

A SHOPPING LIST

An introductory course cannot hope to explain all the different models of oligopoly; nor would that serve any purpose but to confuse you. Since economists differ in their opinions about which approaches to oligopoly theory are the most interesting and promising, we offer in this section a quick catalogue of some models of oligopoly behaviour. Then, in the remainder of the chapter, we will describe in greater detail a few other models.

IGNORE INTERDEPENDENCE

One simple approach to the problem of **oligopolistic interdependence** is to assume that the oligopolists themselves ignore it: that they behave as if their actions will not elicit reactions from their rivals. It *is* possible that an oligopolist, finding the "if they think that we think that they think" chain of reasoning too complex, will decide to ignore rivals' behaviour. The firm may then just maximize profits on the assumption that its decisions will not affect those of its rivals. In this case, the analysis of oligopoly is identical to the analysis of monopoly in the previous chapter.

STRATEGIC INTERACTION

While it is possible that some oligopolies ignore interdependence some of the time, it is very unlikely that such models offer a general explanation for the behaviour of most oligopoly behaviour most of the time. The reason is quite simple. Because, for example, the makers of Brand X and Brand Y detergents operate in the same market, their price and output decisions really are interdependent. Suppose that the management of Brand X, Inc., decides to cut its price to $1.05 per box (on the assumption that Brand Y, Inc., will continue to charge $1.12 per box), to manufacture 5 million boxes per year, and to spend $1 million per year on advertising. It may find itself surprised when Brand Y, Inc., cuts its price to $1 per box, raises production to 8 million boxes per year, and sponsors the Stanley Cup playoffs. If so, Brand X's profits will suffer, and the company will wish it had not cut its price. Most important for our purposes here, it will learn not to ignore interdependence in the future. For many oligopolies, then, competition resembles military operations involving tactics, strategies, moves, and countermoves. Thus, it seems imperative to consider models that deal explicitly with oligopolistic interdependence. We will study several such models, probably the most notable of them being those provided by the theory of games.

CARTELS

The opposite end of the spectrum from ignoring interdependence is for all the firms in an oligopoly to collude overtly with one another, thereby transforming the industry into a giant monopoly—a **cartel**.

A CARTEL is a group of sellers of a product who have joined together to control its production, sale, and price in the hope of obtaining the advantages of monopoly.

A notable example of the formation of a cartel is the Organization of Petroleum Exporting Countries (OPEC), which first began to make decisions in unison in 1973. For a while, OPEC was one of the most spectacularly successful cartels in history. By restricting output, the member nations managed to quadruple the price of oil in 1973–74. Then, unlike most cartels, which come apart because of internal bickering or for other reasons, OPEC held together through two worldwide recessions and a variety of unsettling political events, and struck again with huge price increases in 1979–80; only in the mid-1980s did it run into trouble.

But the story of OPEC is not the norm. Cartels are not easy to organize and are even more difficult to preserve. Firms find it hard to agree on such things as the amount by which each will reduce its output in order to help push up the price. Yet for a cartel to survive, each member must agree to produce no more than some level of output that has been assigned to it by the group of colluding firms. Once price is driven up and profitability increased, however, it becomes tempting for each seller to offer secret discounts in order to lure some of the profitable business away from other members of the cartel. Indeed, some of this happened to OPEC in the early 1980s. When this happens or is even suspected by cartel members, it is often the beginning of the end of the collusive arrangement. Each member begins suspecting the others and is tempted to cut price first, before the others beat it to the punch.

Therefore, cartels usually adopt elaborate policing arrangements, in effect spying on each member firm to make sure it does not sell more than it is supposed to or at a price lower than that chosen by the cartel. This means that cartels are unlikely to succeed or to last very long if the firms sell many varied products the prices of which are difficult to compare and the outputs of which are difficult to monitor. In addition, if prices are often negotiated customer by customer and special discounts are frequent, a cartel may be almost impossible to arrange.

Many economists consider cartels to be one of the least desirable forms of market organization. If a cartel is successful, it may end up charging the monopoly price and obtaining monopoly profits. But because the firms do not actually combine their operations but continue to produce separately, the cartel offers the public no offsetting benefits in the form of economies of large-scale production. For these and other reasons, open collusion among firms is illegal in Canada, as we will see in Chapter 16, and outright cartel arrangements are rarely found. There are some exceptions: firms are allowed to collude in making export arrangements, and collusion is in some cases essentially enforced through the government regulation process. In many other countries, though, cartels are common.

PRICE LEADERSHIP AND TACIT COLLUSION

Though overt collusion is quite rare, some observers think that tacit collusion is quite common among oligopolists in our economy. Oligopolists who do not want to rock what amounts to a very profitable boat may seek to develop some indirect way of communicating with one another and signalling their intentions. Each tacitly colluding firm hopes that if it behaves in a way that does not make things too difficult for its competitors, its rivals will return the favour.

One common example of tacit collusion is **price leadership**, an arrangement in which one firm in the industry is, in effect, assigned the task of making pricing decisions for the entire group. It is expected that

Under PRICE LEADERSHIP, one firm sets the price for the industry and the others follow.

other firms will adopt the prices set by the price leader, even though there is no explicit agreement, only tacit consent. Often, the price leader will be the largest firm in the industry. But in some price-leadership arrangements, the role of leader may rotate among firms.

Price leadership *does* overcome the problem of oligopolistic interdependence, although it is not the only possible way of doing so. If Brand X, Inc., is the price leader for the detergent industry, it can predict how Brand Y, Inc., will react to any price increases it announces. (Brand Y will match the increases.) Similarly, Brand Z executives will be able to predict Brand Y's behaviour as long as the price-leadership arrangement holds up.

But one problem besetting price leadership is that, while the oligopolists as a group may benefit by avoiding a damaging **price war**, one of them may benefit more than the others. The firm that is the price leader is clearly in a better position to maximize its own profits than are any of the rival firms, which must simply fall in line. It is therefore the responsibility of the price leader to take into account its rivals' welfare when making its price decision—or else it may find itself dethroned! For this reason, a price-leadership arrangement, if effective, can lead to the same sort of price and production decisions as would a cartel. Alternatively, leadership can break down entirely.

SALES MAXIMIZATION

Early in our analysis of the theory of the firm, we discussed the hypothesis that firms try to maximize profits and noted that other objectives are possible (see page 202). Among these alternative goals, the one that has achieved the most attention is **sales maximization**.

Modern industrial firms are managed and owned by entirely different groups of people. The managers are paid executives who work for the company on a full-time basis and may grow to identify their own welfare with that of the company. The owners may be a large and diffuse group of shareholders, most of whom own only a tiny fraction of the outstanding stock, take little interest in the operations of the company, and do not feel that the company is "theirs" in any real sense. In such a situation, it is not entirely implausible that the company's decisions will be influenced more heavily by management's goals than by the goal of the owners (which is, presumably, to maximize profit).

There is some statistical evidence, for example, that managers' salaries and prestige may be tied more directly to the company's *size*, as measured by its dollar sales volume, than to its profits. Therefore, the firm's managers may select an output–price combination that maximizes sales rather than profits. But does sales-revenue maximization lead to different decisions than does profit maximization? We shall see now that the answer is yes.

Figure 11-3 is a diagram that should be familiar by now. It shows the marginal-cost (MC) and average-cost (AC) curves for a firm—in this case,

In a **PRICE WAR**, each competing firm is determined to sell at a price that is lower than the prices of its rivals, usually regardless of whether that price covers the pertinent cost. Typically, in such a price war, firm A cuts its price below firm B's; then firm B retaliates by undercutting firm A, and so on until one or more of the firms surrender and let themselves be undersold.

FIGURE 11-3

SALES-MAXIMIZATION EQUILIBRIUM

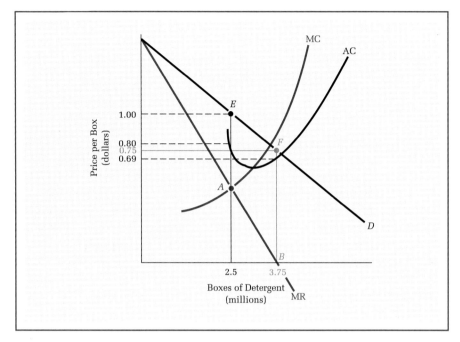

A firm that wishes to maximize sales revenue will expand output until marginal revenue (MR) is zero
—point *B* in the diagram, where output is 3.75 million boxes per year. This is a greater output level than
it would choose if it were interested in maximizing profits. In that case, it would select point *A*, where
MC = MR, and produce only 2.5 million boxes. Since the demand curve is downward sloping, the price
corresponding to point *B* (75¢) must be less than the price corresponding to point *A* ($1.00).

Brand X, Inc. — along with its demand and marginal-revenue (MR)
curves. We have used such diagrams before and know that if the company
wants to maximize profits, it will select point *A*, where MC = MR. This
means that it will produce 2.5 million boxes of detergent per year and
sell them at a price of $1 each (point *E*). Since average cost at this level
of output is only 80¢ per box, profit per unit is 20¢. Total profits are
therefore $0.20 × 2 500 000 = $500 000 per year. This is the highest
attainable profit level for Brand X, Inc.

Now what if Brand X wants to maximize sales revenue instead? In this
case, it will want to keep producing until MR is depressed to zero; that
is, it will select point *B*. Why? By definition, MR is the *additional* revenue obtained by raising output by one unit. If the firm wishes to maximize revenue, then any time it finds that MR is positive, it will want to
increase output further, and any time it finds that MR is negative, it will
want to decrease output. Only when MR = 0 can the maximum sales
revenue have possibly been achieved. (The logic here is exactly the same
as the logic that led to the conclusion that a firm maximizes profits by
setting marginal profit equal to zero.)

Thus, if Brand X, Inc., is a sales maximizer, it will produce 3.75 million
boxes of detergent per year (point *B*), and charge 75¢ per box (point *F*).

Since average costs at this level of production are only 69¢ per box, profit per unit is 6¢ and, with 3.75 million units sold, total profit is $225 000. Naturally, this level of profit is less than what the firm can achieve if it reduces output to the profit-maximizing level. But that is not the firm's goal. Its sales revenue at point *B* is 75¢ per unit times 3.75 million units, or $2 812 500, whereas at point *A*, it was only $2 500 000 (2.5 million units at $1 each). We conclude, then, as follows:

If a firm is maximizing sales revenue, it will produce more output and charge a lower price than it would if it were maximizing profits.

We see clearly in Figure 11-3 that this result holds for Brand X, Inc. But does it always hold? The answer is yes. Look again at Figure 11-3, but ignore the numbers on the axes. At point *A*, where MR = MC, marginal revenue must be positive because it is equal to marginal cost (which, we may assume, is always positive). At point *B*, MR is equal to zero. Since the marginal-revenue curve is negatively sloped, the point where it reaches zero (point *B*) must necessarily correspond to a higher level of output than the point where it cuts the marginal-cost curve (point *A*). Thus, sales-maximizing firms always produce more than profit-maximizing firms and, to sell this greater volume of output, they must charge a lower price.

There are other differences between sales-revenue-maximizing firms and profit-maximizing firms; for example, they can react differently when confronted by certain taxes. Question 5 at the end of this chapter will lead you to appreciate some of the implications of these differences for tax policy.

GAME THEORY

Game theory, contributed in 1944 by mathematician John von Neumann (1903–57) and economist Oskar Morgenstern (1902–77), adopts a more imaginative approach than any other analysis of oligopoly. It attacks the issue of interdependence directly by assuming that each firm's managers proceed on the assumption that their rivals are extremely ingenious decision-makers. In this model, each oligopolist is seen as a competing player in a game of strategy. Since managers believe that their opponents will always adopt the most profitable countermove to any move they make, they seek the optimal defensive strategy.

Two fundamental concepts of game theory are the *strategy* and the *payoff matrix*. A strategy represents an operational plan for one of the participants. In its simplest form, it may refer to just one of a participant's possible decisions—for example, "I will add to my product line a car with a TV set that the driver can watch," or "I will cut the price of my car to $9500." Since much of the game-theoretic analysis of oligopoly has focussed on an oligopoly of two firms—a *duopoly*—we illustrate the payoff matrix for a two-person game in Table 11-1.

AT THE FRONTIER

GAME THEORY AND ENTRY DETERRENCE

Game theory has moved toward domination of research on the theory of oligopoly. An example is the game-theory model of strategic decisions by firms already inside an industry ("old firms") whose primary purpose is to prevent the entry of new rivals ("new firms"). One way in which an old firm can do this is by building a bigger factory than it would want to construct otherwise, in the belief that the output of the excessive factory capacity will force prices down and, in the process, make entry unprofitable. The old firm recognizes that it is giving up some profit in comparison to what it would earn if no new firm even threatened to enter. However, it hopes that it will be better off than if entry did occur.

Some hypothetical numbers and a graph typical of those used in game theory will make the story clear. The old firm has two options: to build a small factory or a big one. The potential new firm also has two options: to open for business (that is, to enter) or not to enter. The accompanying graph shows the four possible combinations of decisions and the consequent profits or losses the two firms may expect in each case.

The graph shows (fourth line) that the best arrangement of all for the old firm is one in which it builds a small factory and the new firm decides not to enter. In that case, the old firm will earn $6 million while the new firm (since it never starts up) will earn nothing. However, if the old firm does decide to build a small factory (third line), it can be pretty sure the new firm *will* open up for business because then that new firm will earn $2 million (rather than zero), and in the process, it will reduce the old firm's profits to $2 million.

(continued)

Possible Choices of Old Firm	Possible Choices of New Firm	Profits	
		Old Firm	New Firm
Big Factory — Enter		−2	−2
Big Factory — Don't Enter		4	0
Small Factory — Enter		2	2
Small Factory — Don't Enter		6	0

This graph shows the possible choices of an old firm and the possible responses of a potential entrant. If the old firm builds a big factory, the entrant will avoid $2 million in losses by staying out, leaving the old firm with $4 million in profit (asterisk lines). On the other hand, if the old firm builds a small factory, the new firm will enter (dashed lines), so the old firm would be worse off, with only $2 million in profit.

(continued)

On the other hand, if the old firm selects its other option and builds a big factory, the increased output will depress prices and profits. The old firm will now earn only $4 million even if the new firm stays out (second line), while each firm will *lose* $2 million (first line) if the new firm enters. Obviously, if the old firm builds a big factory, the new firm will be better off staying out of the business rather than subjecting itself to a $2 million loss.

What size factory, then, will it pay the old firm to build? When one considers the matter, it becomes clear that it will be profitable for the old firm to build the large factory with its excessive capacity. Then it can expect the new firm to stay out, and the big factory will enable the old firm to earn $4 million. In contrast, if a small factory is built, the new firm will open for business and reduce the old firm's profit to $2 million.

Thus, taking the new firm's strategic choices into account, it is obvious that it pays the old firm to build the oversized factory and take the $4 million in profits it will thereby earn by deterring the other firm from entering. *Moral:* Wasting money on excess capacity may not be wasteful in terms of the oligopolist's self-interest.

This matrix is a table of numbers reporting the profits that each of two rival firms, the Atlantic (A) and Pacific (P) companies, can expect to earn, depending on the pricing strategy that each adopts (not knowing the secret price the other is offering customers). This table is read like a distance chart. For example, the upper left-hand cell indicates that, if both firms decide to charge high prices, both A and P will earn $10 million.

The choice open to each firm is to charge either a "high price" or a "low price," and the payoff matrix reports the profits each of the firms can expect to earn, given its own pricing choice and that of its rival. We see that, if either firm succeeds in charging a low price when the other does not, the price cutter will actually raise its profit to $12 million (presumably by capturing enough of the market) and drive its rival to a $2 million loss. However, if *both* firms offer low prices, each will be left with a modest $3 million profit.

How does game theory analyze optimal strategy choice? We may envision the management of, say, firm A reasoning as follows: "If I choose a

Table 11-1

A Payoff Matrix

		Pacific's Strategy			
		High Price		Low Price	
Atlantic's Strategy	High Price	A gets 10	P gets 10	A gets −2	P gets 12
	Low Price	A gets 12	P gets −2	A gets 3	P gets 3

high-price strategy, the worst that can happen to me is that my competitor will select the low-price counter-strategy, which will cut my return to minus $2 million. Similarly, if I select a low-price strategy, the worst outcome for which I must be prepared is a $3 million profit."

How can the management of firm A best protect itself from trouble in these circumstances? Game theory suggests that firm A should select among strategies on the basis of the *minimum* payoff of each, just as described above. It should pick the strategy whose minimum payoff is higher than that of any other strategy. This is called the **maximin criterion**: one seeks the *maxi*mum of the *mini*mum payoffs of the various available strategies. In this case, the maximin strategy for each firm is to offer a low price and earn a profit of $3 million.

Notice that, in this case, fear of what its rival will do virtually forces each firm to offer a low price and to forego the high ($10 million) profit each could earn if it could trust the other to stick to a high price. This example illustrates why many observers conclude that, particularly where the number of firms is small, firms should not be permitted to confer about or exchange information on prices. The same sort of analysis also helps to explain how competition limits profits and benefits consumers, and why price-cartel arrangements are fragile.

The **MAXIMIN CRITERION** means selecting the strategy that yields the maximum payoff, on the assumption that your competitor will do as much damage to you as it can.

A payoff matrix with a pattern like that in Table 11-1 has many other interesting applications. It is used to show how people make each other (and themselves) worse off by driving polluting cars in the absence of laws requiring emission controls. Each does so because he or she does not trust other drivers to install emission controls voluntarily, and this is the analytical basis for making emission controls compulsory.

There is still another interpretation, one that gave this matrix the name by which it is known to game theorists: "the prisoners' dilemma." Here, instead of a two-firm industry, the underlying scenario is that of a pair of burglars captured by the police and taken for interrogation into two separate rooms. Each has two strategy options: to deny the charge or to confess. If both deny it, both go free, for the police have no other evidence. But if one confesses and the other does not, the silent partner can expect the key to his cell to be thrown away. The maximin solution, then, is for both to confess and receive the moderate sentence that this option would bring.

There is, of course, a great deal more to game theory than we have been able to suggest in a few paragraphs. We have sought only to suggest a little of its flavour. Game theory provides, for example, an illuminating analysis of coalitions, indicating, for cases involving more than two firms, which firms would do well to align themselves together against which others. The theory of games has also been used to analyze a variety of complicated problems outside the realm of oligopoly theory. It has been employed in management-training programs and by a number of government agencies. It is used in political science and in formulating military strategy. It has been presented here to offer the reader a glimpse of the type of work that is taking place on the frontiers of economic analysis and to suggest how economists think about complex analytical problems.

FURTHER DETAIL

GAME THEORY: THE MINIMUM-DIFFERENTIATION PRINCIPLE

Sometimes competition among just a very few sellers can result in a less efficient outcome than what results with a complete monopoly. To understand this possibility, consider two sellers of cold drinks along a stretch of beach that is 400 metres long. If the two sellers were both employed by one monopolist, they would probably be located at the 100-metre and the 300-metre marks along the beach, so that the users of the beach would have the shortest distance to go to reach one of the sellers.

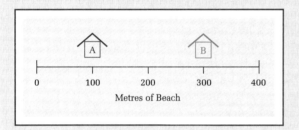

Metres of Beach

Now suppose the monopolist sells off the two cold drinks facilities, one to each of the previous sellers, and then leaves these two to conduct business on their own. Assuming that swimmers and sunbathers will always go to the nearest of the two sellers, will the individual vendors remain at the one-quarter and three-quarter marks along the beach? The answer is likely not.

Each seller can see that it is profitable for her, and therefore for her competitor, to move closer to the centre of the beach. For example, if seller B in the graph moves over just to the right of seller A, seller B will get all the sales

to her right and half the sales derived from those occupying that bit of the beach between the two sellers. Clearly, seller A must move to the right of B, if B does move near her in this way. This leap-frogging would continue until both sellers were right beside each other at the halfway point along the beach.

This is a "prisoners' dilemma" outcome. Total sales to be shared by the two sellers are less in this competitive outcome, since fewer swimmers and sunbathers will purchase cold drinks when (on average) they must walk farther to reach a cold drinks stall.

We can certainly see this minimum-differentiation principle at work in the political arena. In an attempt to capture as much of the "market" as possible, to get elected, each political party tries to appeal to the other's "customers" as best it can. The result is often a "competition" between mainstream parties that offer much the same approach on the issues. Many voters have become cynical of politicians who constantly regale them about how outrageous the other parties are, when it is obvious to these voters that there are sometimes very few substantive differences between the parties' positions. But perhaps an understanding of the logic behind the minimum-differentiation principle can lead us to temper our cynicism. This principle implies that it is in the very nature of the democratic process for successful political parties to become quite similar. This outcome does not imply that those who go into politics must be less sincere than the rest of us.

MONOPOLISTIC COMPETITION, OLIGOPOLY, AND PUBLIC WELFARE

How good or bad, from the viewpoint of the general welfare, is the performance of firms that are monopolistically competitive or oligopolistic?

We have seen that their performance *can* leave much to be desired. For example, the excess-capacity theorem showed us that monopolistic competition can lead to inefficiently high production costs. Similarly, because market forces may not be sufficiently powerful to restrain oligopolists' behaviour, their prices and outputs may differ substantially from those that are socially optimal. Moreover, some observers believe that misleading advertising by corporate giants often distorts the judgements of consumers, leading them to buy things they do not need and would otherwise not want. Others argue that much advertising simply cancels out advertising by rival brands. Thus, even if consumer choices are not significantly distorted, many resources may simply be wasted. It is also said that such corporate gains wield political power, economic power, and power over the minds of consumers—and that all of these undermine the beneficent workings of Smith's invisible hand. Finally, because many large firms in Canada are foreign owned, it is sometimes feared that the way in which they operate is even more likely to ignore the general welfare of this country.

Because oligopolistic behaviour is so varied, we cannot generalize with confidence. Since one oligopolist decides on price, output, and advertising in a manner very different from another, the implications for social welfare vary from case to case.

Yet, recent analysis has provided one theoretical case in which both the behaviour and the quality of performance of an oligopolistic or monopolistically competitive firm can be predicted and judged unambiguously. This is the case in which entry into or exit from the market is costless and unimpeded. In such a case, called a **perfectly contestable market** (see the boxed insert that ends the chapter), the constant threat of entry forces even the largest firm to behave well—to produce efficiently and never to overcharge. For if that firm is inefficient or sets its prices too high, it will be threatened with replacement by an entrant that offers to serve customers more inexpensively.

A market is **PERFECTLY CONTESTABLE** if entry and exit are costless and unimpeded.

Of course, no industry is perfectly contestable, and many are not even nearly so. But in those industries that are highly contestable—that is, in which entry and exit costs are fairly small—market forces can do a reasonably good job of forcing business to behave in the manner that most effectively promotes the public interest. Further, where an industry is not very contestable but there are ways to reduce entry and exit costs (for example, through the elimination of tariffs), the new theory of contestable markets suggests that this may sometimes be a more promising approach than any attempt by government to interfere with the behaviour of the oligopolistic firms in order to improve their performance.

AT THE FRONTIER

THE NEW THEORY OF CONTESTABLE MARKETS

Perfect competition has long been used as a standard for the structure and behaviour of an industry, although it is widely recognized to be unattainable in reality. Recently, some economists have tried to supplement this concept with the aid of a generalized criterion called a *perfectly contestable market*. Some markets that contain a few relatively large firms may be highly contestable, although they are certainly not perfectly competitive. Because perfect competition requires a large number of firms, all of them negligible in size relative to the size of the industry, no industry with economies of large-scale production can be perfectly competitive.

A market is defined as perfectly contestable if firms can enter it and, if they choose, exit without losing the money they invested. Note that the crucial issue is not the amount of capital that is required to enter the industry but whether or not an entrant firm can get its investment out if it wishes — whether that expenditure is a *sunk cost*. For example, if entry involves investing in highly mobile capital — such as airplanes, barges, or cars — the entrant may be able to exit quickly and cheaply. If a car rental agency enters the Vancouver market and finds business disappointing, it can easily transfer its cars to, say, Winnipeg.

A profitable market that is contestable is, therefore, attractive to *potential* entrants. Because of the absence of barriers to entry or exit, firms undertake little risk by going into such a market. If their entry turns out to have been a mistake, they can move to another market without significant loss.

Performance of Contestable Markets

The constant threat of entry elicits good performance by oligopolists, or even by monop-olists, in a perfectly contestable market. In particular, highly contestable markets have at least two desirable characteristics.

First, profits exceeding the opportunity cost of capital are eliminated in the long run by freedom of entry, just as they are in a perfectly competitive market. If the current opportunity cost of capital is 12 percent while the firms in a contestable market are earning a return of 18 percent, new firms will enter the market, expand the industry's outputs, and drive down the prices of its products to the point where all excess profit will have been removed. To avoid this outcome, established firms must expand to a level that precludes excess profit.

Second, inefficient enterprises cannot survive in a perfectly contestable industry because cost inefficiencies invite replacement of the incumbents by entrants who can provide the same outputs at lower cost and lower prices. Only firms operating at the lowest possible cost, using the most efficient techniques, can survive.

In sum, firms in a perfectly contestable market will be forced to operate as efficiently as possible and to charge prices as low as long-run financial survival permits. Soon after the contestable-market theory was first published, the idea became widely used by courts and government agencies concerned with the performance of business firms. This occurred because the theory provides workable guidelines for improved or acceptable behaviour in industries in which economies of scale mean that only a small number of firms can or should operate.

The concept is particularly relevant for Canada, if considered in the context of tariff policy. The government can ensure that many

(continued)

(continued)

markets within Canada become contestable if it lowers existing tariffs. Indeed, if the government established a record of behaviour along these lines, even the threat of tariff reduction might make other markets contestable.

SUMMARY

1. Under monopolistic competition, there are numerous small buyers and sellers; each firm's product is at least somewhat different from every other firm's product — that is, each firm has a partial "monopoly" of some product characteristics and thus a downward-sloping demand curve; there is freedom of entry and exit; and there is perfect information.

2. In long-run equilibrium under monopolistic competition, free entry eliminates economic profits by forcing the firm's demand curve into a position of tangency with its average-cost curve. Therefore, output will be below the point at which average cost is lowest. This is why monopolistic competitors are said to have "excess capacity."

3. An oligopolistic industry is composed of a few large firms selling similar products in the same market.

4. Under oligopoly, each firm carefully watches the major decisions of its rivals and will often plan counter-strategies. As a result, rivalry is often vigorous and direct, and the outcome is difficult to predict.

5. One model of oligopolistic behaviour assumes that the oligopolists ignore interdependence and simply maximize profits or sales revenue. A second assumes that they join together to form a cartel and thus act like a monopoly. A third possibility is price leadership, where one firm sets prices and the others follow suit. A fourth holds that each firm assumes that its rivals will adopt the optimal countermove to any move it makes.

6. A firm that maximizes sales revenue will continue producing up to the point where marginal revenue is driven down to zero. Consequently, a sales maximizer will produce more than a profit maximizer and will charge a lower price.

7. Game theory provides new tools for analyzing business strategies under conditions of oligopoly.

8. Monopolistic competition and oligopoly can be harmful to the general welfare. But these harmful effects can be limited if the market is contestable, that is, if entry and exit are not too costly. The threat of entry can lead to fairly small departures from optimal performance.

CONCEPTS FOR REVIEW

Monopolistic competition	Cartel	Game theory
Excess-capacity theorem	Price leadership	Maximin criterion
Oligopoly	Price war	Perfectly contestable markets
Oligopolistic interdependence	Sales maximization	

QUESTIONS FOR DISCUSSION

1. How many real industries can you name that are oligopolies? How many that operate under monopolistic competition? Perfect competition? Which of these is hardest to find in reality? Why do you think this is so?

2. Consider some of the products that are widely advertised on TV. By what kind of firm is each produced—a perfectly competitive firm, an oligopolistic firm, or what? How many major products can you think of that are *not* advertised on TV?

3. In what ways may the small retail sellers of the following products differentiate their goods from those of their rivals to make themselves monopolistic competitors: hamburgers, radios, cosmetics?

4. Discussion Question 4 at the end of Chapter 10 presented cost and demand data for a monopolist and asked you to find the profit-maximizing solution. Use these same data to find the sales-maximizing solution. Are the answers different? Explain.

5. Suppose that both the profit-maximizing firm and the sales-revenue-maximizing firm in the preceding question are hit with a licence fee of $1000. Explain how their responses will differ.

6. Explain why you either agree or disagree with the following statement: If a monopoly firm were found to be operating at a price–quantity combination on the *inelastic* portion of its demand curve, we would know that the firm must be a sales-revenue maximizer, not a profit maximizer.

7. Explain how the "prisoners' dilemma" concept can shed light on the issues of arms buildup and disarmament.

8. A new entrant, Bargain Airways, cuts air fares between Eastwich and Westwich by 20 percent. Biggie Airlines, which has been operating on this route, responds by cutting fares by 35 percent. What does Biggie hope to achieve?

9. If air transportation is perfectly contestable, why will Biggie fail to achieve the ultimate goal of its price cut?

10. If there were no regulation, which of the following industries would be most likely to be contestable?
    a. Aluminum production.
    b. Barge transportation.
    c. Automobile manufacturing.
    d. Air transportation.
    Explain your answers.

11. Some unions operate like sales-revenue maximizers—they demand a wage that maximizes the total income of their workers. If the demand for a union's labour is given by the function of $4 - w/3$, where w is the wage rate, what value of the wage maximizes total income?

CHAPTER 12

THE MARKET MECHANISM: SHORTCOMINGS AND REMEDIES

*When she was good
She was very, very good.
But when she was bad she was
horrid.*

HENRY WADSWORTH
LONGFELLOW

What does the market do well, and what does it do poorly? These questions constitute the central theme of our study of microeconomics, and we are by now well on our way toward getting some answers. We began in Chapters 8 and 9 by explaining and extolling the workings of Adam Smith's invisible hand — the mechanism by which a perfectly competitive economy allocates resources efficiently without any guidance from government. While the theoretical model studied there was an idealized one, observation of the real world confirms the accomplishments of the market mechanism. Free-market economies have achieved levels of output, productive efficiency, variety in available consumer goods, and general prosperity that are unprecedented in history and that are now the envy of economies that had once relied primarily on central planning.

Yet the market mechanism also displays some glaring weaknesses. One of these — the fact that large and powerful business firms can interfere with the invisible hand in a way that leads to both concentration of wealth and misallocation of resources — was the subject of Chapters 10 and 11. Now we take a more comprehensive view of the failures of the market and at some of the things that can be done to remedy these failures.

That the market cannot do everything we would like it to do is quite apparent. Amid the outpouring of goods and services, we find areas of depressing poverty, cities choked with traffic and pollution, and educational institutions and artistic organizations in serious financial trouble. Our economy, although capable of yielding an overwhelming abundance of material wealth, seems far less capable of eradicating social ills and controlling environmental damage. In this chapter, we will examine the reasons for the market's failings in these areas and indicate specifically why the price system *by itself* may be incapable of dealing with them.

WHAT DOES THE MARKET DO POORLY?

While it is probably impossible to come up with an exhaustive list of the imperfections of the market mechanism, we can identify seven major areas in which the market has been accused of failing:

1. Market economies suffer from severe business fluctuations.
2. The market distributes income rather unequally.
3. Where markets are monopolized, they allocate resources inefficiently.
4. The market deals poorly with the incidental side effects of many economic activities.
5. The market cannot provide public goods, such as national defence.
6. The market may do a poor job of allocating resources between the present and the future.
7. The market mechanism causes public and personal services to become increasingly expensive, often inducing the government to take countermeasures that can be socially detrimental.

The first two of these issues — business fluctuations and income inequality—will be discussed in detail in later chapters, and the third topic —monopoly—has already been discussed. The remaining four items constitute the subject matter of this chapter. Each of these, like monopoly, represents an instance in which the efficiency of the market mechanism is compromised. Therefore, to help us analyze these problems, we offer a brief review of the concept of efficient resource allocation, which was discussed in detail in Chapter 9.

EFFICIENT RESOURCE ALLOCATION: A REVIEW

The basic problem of resource allocation is deciding how much of each commodity the economy should produce. At first glance, it may seem that the solution is simple: the more the better, so we should produce as much of each good as we can. But careful thinking tells us that this is not necessarily the right decision.

Outputs are not created out of thin air. They are produced from the available supplies of labour, fuel, raw materials, and machinery. Further, if we use these scarce resources to produce, say, more handkerchiefs, we must take them away from some other product, such as hospital linens. Thus, to decide whether increasing the production of handkerchiefs is a good idea, we must compare the utility of that increase with the loss of utility caused by having to produce fewer hospital linens. The increased output will be a good thing only if society considers the additional handkerchiefs more valuable than the foregone hospital linens.

Opportunity Cost and Resource Allocation

Here it is worth remembering the concept of *opportunity cost*, one of our twelve Ideas for Beyond the Final Exam. The opportunity cost of an increase in the output of some product is the value of the other goods and services that must be foregone when inputs (resources) are taken away from their production in order to increase the output of the product in question. In our example, the opportunity cost of the increased handkerchief output is the decrease in output of hospital linens that results when resources are reallocated from the latter to the former. The general principle is that an increase in some output represents a *misallocation* of resources if the utility of that increased output is less than its opportunity cost.

To illustrate this idea, we repeat a graph encountered several times in earlier chapters—a *production possibilities frontier*—but we put it to a somewhat different use. Curve *ABC* in Figure 12-1 is a production possibilities frontier showing the alternative combinations of handkerchiefs and hospital linens that the economy can produce by allocating its resources to the production of one good or the other in varying proportions. For example, point *A* amounts to allocation of all the resources to handkerchief production, so that 100 million of these items and no hospital linens are produced. Point *C* represents the reverse situation, with all resources allocated to hospital linens and none to handkerchiefs. Point *B* represents an intermediate allocation, resulting in the production of 8 million metres of linen and 60 million handkerchiefs.

Suppose now that point *B* represents the optimal resource allocation —that is, the only combination of outputs that best satisfies the wants of society among all the possibilities that are attainable (given the technology and resources as represented by the production frontier). Two questions are pertinent to our discussion of the price system:

1. What prices will get the economy to select point *B*; that is, what prices will yield an *efficient* allocation of resources?

2. How can the wrong set of prices lead to a misallocation of resources?

The first question was discussed extensively in Chapter 9. There we concluded as follows:

An efficient allocation of resources requires that each product's price be equal to its marginal cost; that is,

$$P = \text{MC}$$

The reasoning, in brief, is as follows. In a free market, the price of any good reflects the money value to consumers of an additional unit, that

Figure 12-1

The Economy's Production Possibilities Frontier for the Production of Two Goods

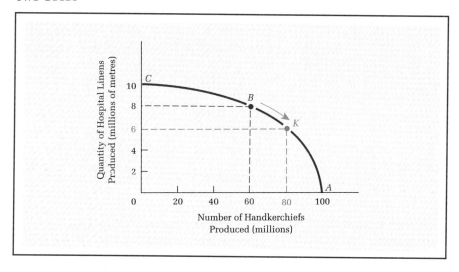

This graph shows all combinations of outputs of the two goods that the economy can produce with the resources available to it. If point *B* is the most desired output combination among those that are possible, it will correspond to a market equilibrium in which each good's price is equal to its marginal cost. If the price of linens is above their marginal cost, or the price of a handkerchief is below its marginal cost, then linen output will be inefficiently small and handkerchief output inefficiently large (point *K*).

is, its *marginal utility* (MU). Similarly, if the market mechanism is working well, the *marginal cost* (MC) measures the value (the opportunity cost) of the resources needed to produce an additional unit of the good. Hence, if prices are set equal to marginal costs, consumers, by using their own money in the most effective way to maximize their own satisfaction, will automatically be using *society's* resources in the most effective way. That is, as long as the market mechanism sets prices equal to marginal costs, it automatically satisfies the MC = MU rule for efficient resource allocation that we studied in Chapter 9. (If you need review, consult pages 266–67.) In terms of Figure 12-1, this means that if *P* = MC for both goods, the economy will automatically gravitate to point *B*, which we assumed to be the optimal point.

This chapter is devoted mainly to the second question: How can the "wrong" prices cause a *mis*allocation of resources? The answer is not too difficult, and we can use the case of monopoly as an illustration.

The "law" of demand tells us that a rise in the price of a commodity will normally reduce the quantity demanded. Suppose now that the linen industry is a monopoly, so the price of linens exceeds their marginal cost. (To review why price under monopoly may be expected to exceed marginal cost, you may want to reread pages 294–301.) This will decrease the quantity of linens demanded below the 8 million metres that we have assumed to be socially optimal (point *B* in Figure 12-1). Thus, the economy will move from point *B* to a point like *K*, where too few linens and too many handkerchiefs are being produced for maximal consumer satisfaction. By setting the "wrong" prices, then, the market fails to achieve the most efficient use of the economy's resources. With the prices being "wrong," the market is sending the wrong signals to individual consumers. Thus, while consumers still maximize their own individual satisfaction, this does not lead to the optimal resource allocation for society.

In sum, if the price of a commodity is above its marginal cost, the economy will tend to produce less of that item than would maximize consumer benefits. The opposite will occur if an item's price is below its marginal cost.

In the remainder of this chapter, we will encounter several other instances in which the market mechanism may set the "wrong" prices.

EXTERNALITIES

We come now to the fourth item on our list of market failures—one of the least obvious, yet one of the most consequential of the imperfections of the price system. Many economic activities provide incidental benefits to others for whom they are not specifically intended. For example, a home-owner who plants a beautiful garden in front of her house incidentally and unintentionally provides pleasure to her neighbours and to those who pass by—people from whom she receives no payment. We say then that her activity generates a **beneficial externality**.

Similarly, some activities indiscriminately impose costs on other people. For example, the operator of a motorcycle repair shop, from which all sorts of noise besiege the neighbourhood and for which the operator pays no compensation to others, is said to produce a **detrimental externality**. Pollution constitutes the classic illustration of a detrimental externality.

To see why the presence of externalities causes the price system to misallocate resources, we need only recall that the system achieves efficiency by rewarding producers who serve consumers well—that is, at as low a cost as possible. This argument breaks down, however, as soon as some of the costs and benefits of economic activities are left out of the profit calculation.

When a firm pollutes a river, it uses up some of society's resources just as surely as when it burns coal. However, if it pays for coal but not for the use of water, it is natural for management to be economical in its use of coal and wasteful in its use of water. Similarly, a firm that provides benefits to others for which it receives no payment is unlikely to be generous in allocating resources to the activity, no matter how socially desirable it may be.

In an important sense, the source of the difficulty is to be found in the definition of *property rights*. Coal mines are private property; their owners will not let anyone take coal without paying for it. Thus, coal is costly and so is not used wastefully. But waterways are not private property.

An activity is said to generate a BENEFICIAL or DETRIMENTAL EXTERNALITY if that activity causes incidental benefits or damages to others, and no corresponding compensation is provided to or paid by those who generate the externality.

Since they belong to everyone in general, they belong to no one in particular. They can therefore be used free of charge as dumping grounds for wastes by anyone who chooses to do so. Because no one pays for the use of the oxygen in a public waterway, that oxygen will be used wastefully. That is the source of detrimental externalities.

EXTERNALITIES AND INEFFICIENCY

Using these concepts, we can see precisely why an externality has undesirable effects on the allocation of resources. In discussing externalities, it is crucial to distinguish between *social* and *private* marginal cost. We define **marginal social cost** (MSC) as the sum of two components: (1) **marginal private cost** (MPC), which is the share of marginal cost caused by an activity that is paid for by the people who carry out the activity; and (2) *incidental cost*, which is the share of the marginal cost that is borne by others.

The **MARGINAL SOCIAL COST** of an activity is the sum of **MARGINAL PRIVATE COST** plus the incidental cost (positive or negative) that is borne by others.

If increased output by a firm increases the amount of smoke it emits, then, in addition to its direct private costs as recorded in the company accounts, expansion of its production imposes incidental costs on others in the form of increased laundry bills, medical expenditures, and outlays for air conditioning and electricity, as well as the unpleasantness of living in a cloud of noxious fumes. These are all part of the activity's marginal *social* cost.

Where the firm's activities generate detrimental externalities, the firm's marginal social cost will be greater than its marginal private cost. In symbols, MSC > MPC. This must be so because, in equilibrium, the market will yield an output at which consumers' marginal utility (MU) is equal to the firm's marginal private cost (MU = MPC). It follows that marginal utility is smaller than marginal social cost. Society would then necessarily benefit if output of that product were *reduced*: It would lose the marginal utility but save the marginal social cost. Further, since "MSC > MU" means that the production of the marginal unit of the good entails a cost to society larger than the benefit contributed by that unit, society would come out ahead. We conclude as follows:

Where a firm's activity causes detrimental externalities, free markets will leave us in a situation where marginal benefits are less than marginal social costs. Outputs smaller than those that maximize private profits will therefore be socially desirable.

We have already indicated why this is so. Private enterprise has no motivation to take into account costs that it creates for others but for which it does not have to pay. Thus, goods that cause such externalities will be produced in undesirably large amounts by private firms. For precisely analogous reasons, we can conclude as follows:

Where a firm's activity generates beneficial externalities, free markets will produce too little output. Society would be better off with larger output levels.

These principles can be illustrated with the aid of Figure 12-2. This diagram repeats the two basic curves needed for the analysis of the equilibrium of a firm: a marginal-revenue curve and a marginal-cost curve (see Chapter 7). These represent the *private* costs and revenues accruing to a particular firm (in this case, a paper mill). The mill's maximum profit is attained with 100 000 tonnes of output corresponding to the intersection of the marginal-cost and the marginal-revenue curves (point *A*).

Now suppose that the factory's wastes pollute a nearby waterway, so that its production creates a detrimental externality whose cost the ownership does not itself pay. Then, marginal social cost must be higher than marginal private cost, as shown in the diagram, and the socially desirable level of output (70 000 tonnes) is at point *B* rather than point *A*.

Notice that if instead of being able to impose the external costs on others, the mill's ownership were forced to pay the costs itself, its own private marginal-cost curve would correspond to the higher of the two curves shown. Ownership's output of the polluting commodity would then fall to 70 000 tonnes, corresponding to point *B*, the intersection between the marginal-revenue curve and the marginal-*social*-cost curve. But because the firm does not in fact pay for the pollution damage its output causes, it produces an output (100 000 tonnes) that is larger than the output it would produce if the cost imposed on the community were instead borne by the firm (70 000 tonnes).

FIGURE 12-2

EQUILIBRIUM OF A FIRM WHOSE OUTPUT PRODUCES DETRIMENTAL EXTERNALITIES (POLLUTION)

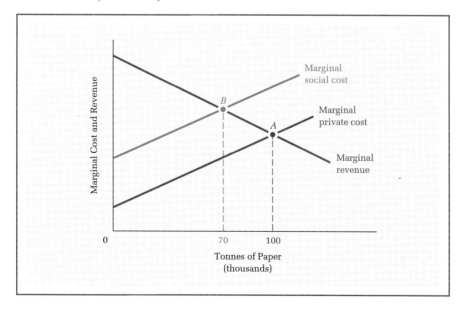

The firm's profit-maximizing output, at which its marginal private cost and its marginal private revenue are equal, is 100 000 tonnes. But if the firm paid all the social costs of its output instead of shifting some of them to others, its marginal-cost curve would be the curve labelled "marginal social cost." Then it would pay the firm to reduce its output to 70 000 tonnes, thereby reducing the pollution it causes.

The same sort of diagram can be used to show that the opposite relationship will hold when a firm's activity produces beneficial externalities. The firm will produce less of its beneficial output than it would if it were rewarded fully for the benefits that its activities yield. Beneficial externalities arise when the activities of Firm A create incidental benefits for Firm B or Individual C (and perhaps for many others as well) or when A's activities reduce the costs of others' activity. For example, Firm A's research laboratories, while making its own products better, may also incidentally discover new research techniques that reduce the research costs of other firms in the economy.

But these results can perhaps be seen more clearly with the help of a production possibilities frontier diagram similar to that in Figure 12-1. In Figure 12-3, we see the frontier for two industries: electricity generation, which causes air pollution (a detrimental externality), and tulip growing, which makes an area more attractive (a beneficial externality). We have just seen that detrimental externalities make marginal social cost greater than marginal private cost. Hence, if the electric company charges a price equal to its own marginal (private) cost, that price will be less than the true marginal (social) cost. Similarly, in tulip growing, a price equal to marginal private cost will be above the true marginal cost to society.

We saw earlier in the chapter that an industry that charges a price above marginal cost will reduce quantity demanded through this high

FIGURE 12-3

EXTERNALITIES, MARKET EQUILIBRIUM, AND EFFICIENT RESOURCE ALLOCATION

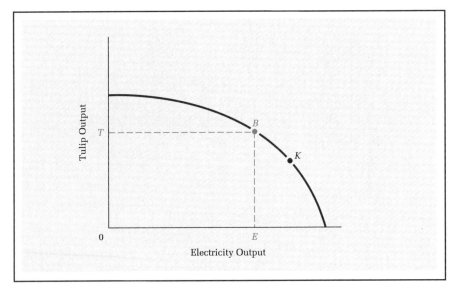

Because electricity producers emit smoke (a detrimental externality), they do not bear the true marginal social cost of their output. Thus, electricity price will be below marginal social cost, and electricity output will be inefficiently large (point *K*, not point *B*). The opposite is true of tulip production. Because they generate beneficial externalities, tulips will be priced above the marginal social cost and tulip output will be inefficiently small.

price, and so it will produce an output too small for an efficient allocation of resources. The opposite will be true for an industry that charges a price below marginal social cost. In terms of Figure 12-3, suppose point B again represents the efficient allocation of resources, involving the production of E kilowatt hours of electricity and T dozen tulips. Because the polluting electric company charges a price below marginal social cost, it will produce more than E kilowatt hours of electricity. Similarly, because tulip growers generate external benefits, and so charge a price above marginal social cost, they will produce less than T dozen tulips. The economy will end up with the resource allocation represented by point K rather than that represented by point B. There will be too much smoky electricity production and too little attractive tulip growing.

An industry that generates detrimental externalities will generally have a marginal social cost higher than its marginal private cost. If its price is equal to its own marginal private cost, that price will, therefore, be below the true marginal cost to society. The market mechanism thereby tends to encourage inefficiently large outputs of products that cause detrimental externalities. The opposite is true of products that cause beneficial externalities—private industry will provide inefficiently small quantities of these products.

EXTERNALITIES ARE UNIVERSAL

Externalities occur throughout the economy. Many are beneficial. A factory that hires unskilled or semiskilled labourers gives them on-the-job training and provides the external benefit of better workers to future employers. Benefits to others are also generated when firms produce useful but unpatentable products or even patentable products that can be imitated by others to some degree.

Detrimental externalities are also widespread. The emission of air and water pollutants by factories, cars, and airplanes is the source of some of our most pressing environmental problems. The abandonment of buildings causes the quality of a neighbourhood to deteriorate and is the source of serious externalities in some cities. Externality represents a common form of market failure simply because there are so many areas in which property rights are not clearly established.

Externalities

Externalities lie at the heart of some of society's most pressing problems: the problems of the environment, research policy, and a variety of other critical issues. For this reason, the concept of externalities is one of our twelve Ideas for Beyond the Final Exam. It is a subject that will recur again and again in this book as we discuss some of these problems in greater detail.

GOVERNMENT POLICY AND EXTERNALITIES

Because of the market's inability to cope with externalities, governments have found it appropriate to support activities that are felt to generate external benefits. Education is subsidized not only because it helps promote equal opportunity for all citizens, but also because it is believed to generate beneficial externalities. For example, educated people normally commit fewer crimes than uneducated people do, so the more we educate people, the less we will spend on crime prevention. Also, academic research that has been provided partly as a by-product of the educational system often benefits the entire population and has, indeed, been judged to be a major contributor to the nation's economic growth. We have consequently come to believe that if education were offered only by profit-making institutions, the output of these beneficial services would be provided at less than the optimal level.

Similarly, governments have recently begun to impose fines on companies that contribute heavily to air and water pollution. This approach to policy is in fact suggested by the economist's standard analysis of the effects of externalities on resource allocation. The basic problem is that, in the presence of externalities, the price system fails to allocate resources efficiently. Resources are used up without any price being charged for them, and benefits are supplied without financial compensation to the provider. As a result, the market will produce excessive quantities of outputs that pollute or create other detrimental externalities because these outputs are, in effect, produced at a bargain price that does not cover their entire marginal social cost.

One effective way to deal with externalities may be through the use of taxes and subsidies, making polluters pay for the costs they impose on society, and paying the generators of beneficial externalities for the incidental benefits of their activities (which can be considered an offset or deduction from the social cost of the activity).

For example, firms that generate beneficial externalities should be given a subsidy per unit of their output equal to the difference between their marginal social costs and their marginal private costs. Similarly, firms that generate detrimental externalities should be taxed at levels that effectively make them pay the entire marginal social cost. In terms of Figure 12-2, when the firm pays the tax, its marginal-private-cost curve shifts up until it coincides with the marginal-social-cost curve; the market price is then set in a manner consistent with efficient resource allocation.

While there is much to be said for this approach in principle, it is often difficult to implement. Social costs are rarely easy to estimate, partly because they are so widely diffused throughout the community (everyone in the area is affected by pollution) and partly because many of the costs and benefits (effects on health, unpleasantness of living in smog) are not readily assessed in monetary terms. The pros and cons of this approach and the alternative policies available for the control of externalities will be discussed in greater detail in Chapter 17, which considers environmental problems.

PUBLIC GOODS

Another area in which the market fails to perform adequately is in the provision of **public goods**. These are commodities that are valuable socially but whose provision, for reasons we will now explain, cannot be financed by private enterprise. Thus, government must pay for the public goods if they are to be provided at all. Standard examples range from national defence to the services of lighthouses.

It is easiest to explain the nature of public goods by contrasting them with **private goods**, commodities at the opposite end of the spectrum. Private goods are characterized by two important attributes. One can be called **depletability**. If you eat a steak or use a litre of gasoline, there is that much less beef or fuel in the world available for others to use. Your consumption depletes the supply available for other people, either temporarily or permanently.

But a pure public good is like the legendary widow's jar of oil, which always remained full no matter how many people used it. Once the snow has been removed from a street, the improved driving conditions are available to every driver who uses the street, whether 10 or 1000 cars pass that way. One passing car does not make the road less snow-free for another. The same is true of the spraying of swamps near a town to kill disease-bearing mosquitoes. The cost of the spraying is the same whether the town has a population of 10 000 or 20 000. A resident of the town who benefits from this service does not deplete its advantages to others.

The other property that characterizes private goods but not public goods is **excludability**, meaning that anyone who does not pay for the good can be excluded from enjoying its benefits. If you do not buy a ticket, you are excluded from the ball game. If you do not pay for an electric guitar, the storekeeper will not give it to you.

But some goods or services are such that, if they are provided to anyone, they automatically become available to many other persons, whom it is difficult, if not impossible, to exclude from the benefits. If a street is cleared of snow, everyone who uses the street benefits, regardless of who paid for the snowplough. If a country provides a strong military establishment, everyone receives its protection, even persons who do not happen to want it.

A public good is defined as a good that lacks depletability. Very often, it also lacks excludability. Notice two important implications.

First, since non-paying users usually cannot be excluded from enjoying a public good, suppliers of such goods will find it difficult or impossible to collect fees for the benefits they provide. This is the so-called "free rider" problem. How many people, for example, will voluntarily cough up $2000 a year to support our national defence establishment? Yet this is roughly what it costs per Canadian family. Services like national defence and public health, which are not depletable and with regard to which excludability is simply impossible, cannot be provided by private enterprise because no one will pay for something that can be

A **PUBLIC GOOD** is a commodity or service whose benefits are *not* depleted by an additional user and for which it is generally difficult or impossible to exclude people from its benefits, even if they are unwilling to pay for them. In contrast, a **PRIVATE GOOD** is characterized by both excludability and depletability.

A commodity is **DEPLETABLE** if it is used up when someone consumes it.

A commodity is **EXCLUDABLE** if someone who does not pay for it can be kept from enjoying it.

had for free. Since private firms are not in the business of giving services away, the supply of public goods must be left to government authorities and non-profit institutions.

The second thing we notice is that, since the supply of a public good is not depleted by an additional user, the marginal (opportunity) cost of serving an additional user is zero. With zero marginal cost, the basic principle of optimal resource allocation calls for provision of public goods and services to anyone who wants them at no charge. In a word, not only is it often impossible to charge a market price for a public good, it is often *undesirable* to do so as well. Any non-zero price would discourage some users from enjoying the public good; this would be inefficient, since one more person's enjoyment of the good costs society nothing. Let's summarize:

It is usually not possible to charge a price for a pure public good because people cannot be excluded from enjoying its benefits. It may also be undesirable to charge a price for it because that would discourage some people from using it even though using it does not deplete its supply. For both these reasons, we find government supplying many public goods. Without government intervention, public goods simply would not be provided.

Referring back to our example in Figure 12-1, if hospital linens were a public good and their production were left to private enterprise, the economy would end up at point *A* on the graph, with zero production of hospital linens and far more output of handkerchiefs than would be called for by efficient allocation (point *B*). Usually, communities have not been content to let that happen; today, a quite substantial proportion of government expenditure — indeed, the bulk of municipal budgets — is devoted to the financing of public goods or services believed to generate substantial external benefits. National defence, public health, police and fire protection, and research are among the services provided by governments because they offer beneficial externalities or because they are public goods.

ALLOCATION OF RESOURCES BETWEEN PRESENT AND FUTURE

When a society invests, more resources are devoted to building up a capacity to produce consumer goods in the future. But the inputs that go into building new plant and equipment are unavailable for consumption for the present. Fuel used to make steel for a factory cannot be used to heat homes or drive cars. Thus, the allocation of inputs between current consumption and investment—that is, their allocation between present and future—determines how fast the economy grows.

In principle, the market mechanism should be as efficient in allocating resources between present and future uses as it is in allocating resources among different outputs at any given time. If future demands for a particular commodity—say, computers for the home—are expected to be higher than they are today, it will pay manufacturers to plan now to build the necessary plant and equipment so they will be ready to turn out the computers when the expanded market materializes. More resources are thereby allocated to future consumption.

The allocation of resources between present and future can be analyzed with the aid of a production possibilities frontier diagram, such as that in Figure 12-1. Suppose the issue is how much labour and capital to devote to producing consumer goods and how much of those inputs to devote to the construction of factories that will produce output in the future. Instead of handkerchiefs and linens, the graph will show consumer goods and number of factories on its axes, but otherwise it will be exactly the same as Figure 12-1. Such a graph appears in Figure 12-4.

The profit motive directs the flow of resources between one time period and another just as it handles resource allocation among different industries in a given period. The lure of profits directs resources to products that command high prices *and* to time periods in which high prices promise to make output most profitable. But at least one feature of the process of allocation of resources among different time periods distinguishes it from the process of allocation among industries. This is the special role that the *interest rate* plays in allocation among time periods.

FIGURE 12-4

PRODUCTION POSSIBILITIES FRONTIER BETWEEN PRESENT AND FUTURE

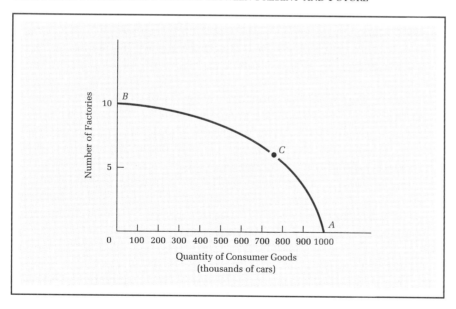

With a given quantity of resources, the economy can produce 1 million cars for immediate use and build no factories for the future (point *A*). Alternatively, at the opposite extreme (point *B*), it can build 10 factories where products will become available in the future, while producing no cars for current consumption. At points in between on the frontier, such as *C*, the economy will produce a combination of some cars for present consumption and some factories for future use.

If the receipt of a given amount of money is delayed until some time in the future, the recipient suffers an opportunity cost—the interest that the money could have earned if it had been received earlier and invested. For example, if the rate of interest is 9 percent and you can persuade someone who owes you money to make a $100 payment one year earlier than originally planned, you come out $9 ahead. Put the other way, if the rate of interest is 9 percent and the payment to you of $100 is postponed one year, you lose the opportunity to earn $9. Thus, the rate of interest determines the size of the opportunity cost to a recipient who gets money at some date in the future instead of now. For this reason, we can conclude as follows:

Low interest rates will persuade people to invest more now, since the future benefits of the investment are still attractive in view of the moderate opportunity cost involved. Thus, more resources will be devoted to the future if interest rates are low. Conversely, high interest rates make investment, with its benefits in the future, less attractive. Thus, high interest rates will tend to increase the use of resources for current output at the expense of reduced future outputs.

On the surface, it seems that the price system can allocate resources among different time periods in the way consumers prefer, because the supply of and the demand for loans, which determine the interest rate, reflect the public's preferences between present and future. Suppose, for example, that the public suddenly became more interested in future consumption (say, people wanted to save more for their retirement). The supply of funds available for borrowing would increase and interest rates would tend to fall. This would stimulate investment and add to the future output of goods at the expense of current consumption.

But several questions have been raised about the effectiveness, in practice, of the market mechanism's allocation of resources among different time periods.

One thing that makes economists uneasy is that the rate of interest, which is the price that controls allocation over time, is also used for a variety of other purposes. As we will see in Chapter 27, in large countries like the United States, the interest rate is manipulated by means of fiscal and monetary policy in an attempt to control business fluctuations. In the process, policy-makers seem to give little thought to the effects on the allocation of resources between present and future, and so one may well worry whether the resulting interest rates are the most appropriate ones. Also, for countries like Canada, whose bonds must compete in international financial markets to be sold, the level of interest rates is largely determined by conditions in the rest of the world.

Second, it has been suggested that even in the absence of government manipulation of interest rates, the market may devote too many resources to immediate consumption. One British economist, A.C. Pigou, argued simply that people suffer from "a defective telescopic faculty"—that they are too short-sighted to give adequate weight to the future. A "bird in the hand" point of view leads people to care so much about the present that they sacrifice the legitimate interests of the future. As a result, too much goes into today's consumption and too little into investment for tomorrow.

A third reason that the free market may not ensure efficient investment for the future is that investment projects, such as the construction of a new factory, are much greater risks to the investor than they are to the community. Even if a factory falls into someone else's hands through bankruptcy, it will probably go on turning out goods. But the profits will not go to the investors or their heirs. Therefore, the loss to the individual investor will be far greater than the loss to society. For this reason, individual investment for the future may fall short of the amounts that are socially optimal. Investments too risky to be worthwhile to any group of private individuals may nevertheless be advantageous to society as a whole.

Fourth, our economy shortchanges the future when it despoils irreplaceable natural resources, exterminates whole species of plants and animals, floods canyons, "develops" attractive areas into potential slums, and so on. Worst of all, industry, the government, and individuals bequeath a ticking time bomb to the future when they leave behind lethal and slow-acting residues, such as nuclear wastes, which may remain dangerous for hundreds or even thousands of years and whose disposal containers are likely to fall apart long before their contents lose their lethal properties.

Such actions are essentially *irreversible*. If a factory is not built this year, the deficiency in facilities provided for the future can be remedied by building it next year. But a canyon, once destroyed, can never be replaced.

Many economists believe that **irreversible decisions** have a very special significance and must not be left entirely in the hands of private firms and individuals.

However, some observers question the general conclusion that the free market cannot be relied upon to ensure sufficient investment for the future. They point out that the prosperity of our economy has grown fairly steadily from one decade to the next, and that there is every reason to expect future generations to have real incomes and an abundance of consumer goods far greater than our own. Pressures to increase investment for the future may, in their view, be akin to taking from the poor to give to the rich—a sort of backward Robin Hood redistribution of income.

SOME OTHER SOURCES OF MARKET FAILURE

With the exception of a special problem, which we examine later in the chapter, we have now completed our survey of the most important imperfections of the market mechanism. But our list is not complete, and it can never be. In this imperfect world, nothing ever works out ideally, and by examining anything with a sufficiently powerful microscope, one can always detect more blemishes. However, some of the items we have omitted from our lists are also important, and we now provide a brief description of three of them.

IMPERFECT INFORMATION

The analysis of the virtues of the market mechanism in Chapter 9 assumed that consumers and producers have all the information they need in order to make their decisions. But in reality, things are very different. When buying a house or a second-hand car, or when selecting a doctor, consumers are vividly reminded of how little they know about what they are purchasing. The old motto "Let the buyer beware" applies. Obviously, if participants in the market are ill-informed, they will not always make the optimal decisions described in our theoretical models.

Yet, not all economists agree that imperfect information is really a failure of the market mechanism. They point out that information, too, is a commodity that costs money to produce. Neither firms nor consumers have complete information because it would be irrational for them to spend the enormous amounts needed to get it. As always, the optimum is a compromise. One should, ideally, stop buying information at the point where the marginal utility of further information is no greater than its marginal cost. With this amount of information, the business executive or the consumer is able to make what have been referred to as "optimally imperfect" decisions.

RENT-SEEKING

An army of lawyers, expert witnesses, and business executives crowd our courtrooms and pile up enormous costs. Business firms seem to sue each other at the slightest provocation, wasting vast resources and delaying business decisions. Why? Because it is possible to make money by means of such unproductive activities—that is, by means of legal battles over profit-making opportunities.

Rent-seeking has become an important issue in takeover battles, where some outside group tries to gain control of a corporation by buying up a large percentage of its shares. Since the new owners are likely to fire the firm's current management, the latter group may fight hard to prevent the takeover, even if the new arrangement would benefit the company's shareholders.

In general, any source of unusual profit, such as that which exists under monopoly, is a temptation for firms to waste economic resources in an effort to obtain control of the source of profits. This process, called **rent-seeking** by economists (meaning that the firms hope to obtain earnings without contributing to production), has been judged by some observers to be a major source of inefficiency in our economy. (Takeovers will be discussed in Chapter 24, pages 811–12. For a more detailed discussion of rent-seeking, see Chapter 14, pages 421–29.) For example, measured as a proportion of the population, the number of lawyers in

RENT-SEEKING refers to unproductive activity in the pursuit of economic profit, that is, profit in excess of competitive earnings.

Canada has almost tripled in the last fifteen years. This is one rough indicator that the rent-seeking problem may be getting bigger.

MORAL HAZARD

Another widely discussed problem of the market mechanism is associated with insurance. Insurance—the provision of protection against risk—is viewed by economists as a useful commodity like shoes or the provision of information. But it also creates a problem by encouraging the very risks against which it provides protection. For example, if an individual has valuables that are fully insured against theft, she has little motivation to take steps to protect them against burglars. She may, for example, fail to lock them up in a safety deposit box, and this failure makes burglary a more attractive and lucrative profession. This problem—the tendency of insurance to encourage the source of risk—is called **moral hazard**, and it constrains private profit-seeking insurance firms from providing the socially optimal amount of insurance. Critics of our bank-deposit insurance system (see pages 842–43) and our unemployment insurance system (see page 636) are referring to this concept when they argue that these systems increase the number of bankruptcies among trust companies and raise the unemployment rate above the level it would be otherwise.

HERMAN®

"I need as much fire insurance as I can get by next Friday night."

MORAL HAZARD refers to the tendency of insurance to discourage policyholders from protecting themselves from risk.

MARKET FAILURE AND GOVERNMENT FAILURE

Having pointed out some of the most noteworthy failures of the invisible hand, we seem forced to conclude that a market economy, if left entirely to itself, is likely to produce results that are, at least in some respects, far from ideal. In our discussion, we have noted either directly or by implication some of the things government can do to correct these deficiencies. But the fact that government often *can* intervene constructively in the operation of the economy does not always mean that it will actually succeed in doing so. The fact is that governments cannot be relied upon to behave ideally any more than business firms can.

It is apparently hard to make this point in a way that is suitably balanced. Commentators too often stake out one extreme position or the other. Those who think the market mechanism is inherently unfair and biased by the greed of those who run its enterprises seem to think of government as the saviour that can cure all economic ills. Those who deplore government intervention are prone to consider the public sector as the home of every sort of inefficiency, graft, and bureaucratic stultification. The truth, as usual, lies somewhere in between.

Governments are inherently imperfect, like the humans who constitute them. The political process leads to compromises that sometimes bear little resemblance to rational decisions—for example, the prolonged use of rent controls (see Chapter 3). Yet the problems engendered by an unfettered economy are often too serious to be left to the free market. The

AT THE FRONTIER

ASYMMETRIC INFORMATION, LEMONS, AND AGENTS

Have you ever wondered why a six-month-old car sells for so much less than a new one? One explanation is offered by economists, who have recently intensified their study of the effects of imperfect information on markets.

The problem is that some small proportion of automobiles are "lemons"; that is, they are constantly subject to mechanical troubles. The new-car dealer must sell *all* his cars, and, in any event, he probably knows no more than the buyer whether a particular car is a lemon. The two parties, therefore, have *symmetric* information, and the chances that a car purchased from a new-car dealer will turn out to be a lemon are relatively small. In the second-hand market, however, information is *asymmetric*. The seller knows whether the car is a lemon, but the buyer does not. Moreover, a seller who wants to get rid of a fairly new car is likely to be doing so only because it is a lemon. Potential buyers realize that. Hence, if someone is forced to sell a good new car because of an unexpected need for cash, she too will be stuck with a low price because she cannot prove that her car is in fact reliable. The moral is that asymmetric information tends to harm not only buyers, but honest sellers as well.

Economists have also examined the implications of asymmetric information in labour kets, and the result is an increased understanding of why unemployment exists. After all, when there is an excess supply of labour (unemployment), why don't wages simply fall to eliminate the excess supply? One reason is that some workers are "lemons" — they shirk while on the job. In a complicated production environment, it is very difficult for supervisors to know which workers are putting forth a low effort on the job, since only group output is objectively measurable. That is, there is asymmetric information — only the worker knows whether he or she is shirking; the employer does not. If firms allow wages to fall enough to employ all the lemons, the "good" workers will not be satisfied, and they will leave for other jobs. It is therefore in the profit interest of firms to offer wages above the market-clearing level, to ensure that it is not their best workers that leave. Also, with a supply of would-be workers ready to take the place of existing employees (at the going wage) if they are fired, there is an increased incentive for the lemons not to shirk.

This application of asymmetric information analysis is called the *efficiency wage theory*. It is widely accepted as one of the reasons why unemployment exists, even in full equilibrium. Unemployment exists because there is only one market price (the wage rate) and there are two markets that require an adjustment in that price to reach equilibrium: There in the market for individuals wanting work and the market in the amount of effort devoted by each worker while on the job. The *(continued)*

(continued)

asymmetric nature of the information forces firms to rely on the wage to "clear" the effort-per-worker market, so the wage is not available for clearing the workers' market.

Problems relating to asymmetric information pervade most economic relationships. They lead to what are called *principal–agent problems*, the analysis of which has been a major concern of recent economic research. The issue arises from the necessity of delegating many critical tasks to others. Shareholders in a corporation delegate the running of the firm to its management team; Canadian citizens delegate lawmaking to their federal Parliament and provincial legislatures; union members delegate many decisions to their union leadership. In such cases, the people who give away part of their decision-making powers are called *principals*, and those who exercise those powers are called *agents*. In effect, the principals hire agents to do the jobs in question.

Asymmetric information is crucial here. The principals know only imperfectly whether their agents are serving their interests faithfully and efficiently or are instead neglecting or even acting against their interests to pursue selfish interests of their own. Misuse of principals' property, embezzlement, and political corruption are extreme examples of such dereliction of duty by agents, but, unfortunately, they seem to occur with increasing regularity. Among other things, economic analysis studies ways of remedying or at least alleviating such problems through forms of compensation for agents that bring the agents' interests more closely into line with those of the principals. For example, if the salaries of corporate managers depend heavily on company profits or on the market value of company shares, then managers can make themselves better off only by promoting the welfare of shareholders. Also, the shareholders, even though they know only imperfectly what the management team is doing, can have a fair degree of confidence that this team will try to serve their interests well.

problems of inflation, environmental decay, and the provision of public goods are cases in point. In such instances, government intervention is likely to yield substantial benefits to the general public. However, even when it is fairly clear that some government action is warranted, it may be difficult (if not impossible) to calculate the optimal degree of government intervention. There is a danger of intervention so excessive that society might have been better off without it.

But in other areas, the market mechanism is likely to work reasonably well, and the small imperfections that are present do not constitute sufficient justification for intervention. In any event, even where government intervention is appropriate, it is essential to consider marketlike instruments as the means to correct the deficiencies in the workings of the market mechanism. The tax incentives described in our discussion of externalities are an outstanding example of what we have in mind, and that is why we devote most of an entire chapter (Chapter 17) to this issue. An editorial in a recent issue of Britain's *The Economist* pleaded for a balanced approach to economic policy generally, involving government initiatives that try to *take advantage* of the incentive mechanism that is the core of the market system, rather than to ignore or override it. (See the boxed insert on pages 352–53.)

PUBLIC CONTROVERSY

THE CASE FOR CENTRAL PLANNING

Conservative thinking has ruled economic policy for the past decade. It is no coincidence that the 1980s were a time of diminishing public investment in infrastructure. Governments railed against public spending of most sorts—and, by and large, rightly so. But they sometimes failed to distinguish between useful spending programmes and wasteful ones, and then went on to shrink the former and boost the latter. The inter-connected parts of a country's economic infrastructure—roads, railways, airports and so on—are especially easy to starve of resources, because the costs of neglect mount slowly. But the price, in the end, can be great.

Congestion has become an increasingly punishing tax on business and leisure across the industrialised world. In the cities of some developing countries, it threatens to throttle growth altogether. The problem is likely to worsen. Because the supply of infrastructure has failed to keep pace with the demands placed upon it, the capacity of each system has come under greater strain. Ever-increasing efforts to maintain and repair each system are required; and each of those efforts is itself, while under way, a cause of ever-greater disruption. Tackling this problem properly calls for something that is rather difficult to arrange: an intelligent alliance of state and market.

Roads to Prosperity

As pot-holes grow deeper, traffic-queues and travel-times longer, and complaints from voters and businesses louder, it is unsurprising that infrastructure has become a hot political topic. In America, for instance, Bill Clinton promises, if elected president, to spend $80 billion on renovating the country's roads, creating a new high-speed rail network linking America's major cities and developing new technologies to expand the capacity of the existing infrastructure.

America is not the only country where the left seems to have the biggest and brightest ideas about infrastructure—while conservatives maintain an embarrassed silence on the subject, broken only by the occasional weary platitude about "getting the private sector involved". Often, in fact, both sides are almost equally wrong — the left because it underestimates the role that market economics should indeed play in the provision and efficient use of infrastructure, the right because it fondly hopes that governments need not trouble themselves.

Consider the over-crowded infrastructure that the industrial countries already have. How might this be better used? At present, a congested road is rationed among would-be travellers in the least efficient way known to economics: by queueing. Rationing by price would work much better. It calls for a change in attitudes—but one not so dramatic as you might think. (Shoppers in the West readily saw the absurdity of the Soviet economy, which only took the West's method of allocating road space and applied it to life in general.) It also calls for clever technology — which promises to make efficient road-pricing acceptable as well as feasible.

With in-car computers and detectors under the road, it is already possible to log a vehicle's use of that road—and to use the information either to send the owner a bill, or to deduct units from a card (available at your

(continued)

(continued)

local petrol station) placed in the vehicle's computer. Schemes of this sort have been tested in Dallas, New Orleans and Hong Kong. The virtue of such technology is that pricing can vary: charges are highest at times when the strain on the system is greatest. This flattens the peaks of frustration, reduces travel times and makes better use of roads during the course of each day. It also raises revenue, which can be spent on maintenance and on new investment in infrastructure — or on lower taxes.

Though such an approach relies on the price mechanism (and will thus offend many on the left) it also requires governments to take the lead (and will thus dismay many on the right). Governments will have to stimulate development of the necessary technology, for unless they declare an interest in pricing the use of roads they already "own", private firms are unlikely to try hard to improve the means to do so. Then they will need to invest in the widespread installation of the systems. After that they will need to set, or at any rate regulate, the prices charged. That much is necessary for any utility with monopolistic power. But in the pricing of roads and other transport infrastructure, where the balance of costs and benefits to the economy depends so heavily on "externalities" (one man's short-cut causes another's misery), it is especially important that the judgment be made by a policy-maker who takes, and can be held accountable for, an overview of the entire transport system — a planner, in other words.

What about investment in new or bigger roads, or in other additions to infrastructure? Again, the government's role is pivotal. Big infrastructure projects are immensely disruptive to local communities. Projects within cities, especially, call for compulsory purchase of thousands of houses and large tracts of land; this coercion is often bitterly opposed by the owners. Only a government, accountable to an electorate, can be allowed to wield such power. As before, pervasive externalities call for a weighing of social, rather than private costs and benefits. And the riskiness and distant time-horizons of projects of this sort nearly always call, in practice, for explicit or implicit government financing. For all these reasons, governments should lead, and be seen to be leading, big investment projects in new infrastructure.

That is hard for the right to swallow. But those on the left, who favour more public investment as the solution to any problem, also need to vet their prejudices. Without road-use pricing and other quasi-market ways of using existing infrastructure better, it is hard to know whether more capacity is really needed, let alone how much. Also, the very progress in technology that is making road-pricing feasible is allowing firms and businesses to reduce the costs of congestion in ways of their own devising. And road-pricing and other technologies will soon enable private enterprise to operate, as well as build, new roads — recovering at least some of the cost from their own revenues rather than from the public purse. In short, it is daft merely to call for more public spending.

Adequate infrastructure, well used, undoubtedly promotes economic growth. To get those benefits in full, governments must take charge — always making as much use of market forces and private enterprise as possible, but never seeking to shirk their responsibility as chief executive. Policy on infrastructure will be one of the biggest challenges facing governments in the rest of this decade — all the more formidable because the ideological certainties of the 1980s shed so little light on it.

SOURCE: *The Economist*, September 12, 1992, page 13. © 1992 The Economist Newspaper Group, Inc. Reprinted with permission.

THE COST DISEASE OF THE SERVICE SECTOR

The last problem to be considered in this chapter is *not* a failure of the market mechanism. However, in this case, the market's behaviour creates that illusion and therefore often leads to ill-advised government action that does not in fact serve the general welfare. The problem is this: While private standards of living have increased and material possessions have grown, the community has simultaneously been forced to cope with deterioration in a variety of services, both public and private.

Throughout the world, streets and subways have grown increasingly dirty. Public safety has declined as crimes of violence have become more commonplace in almost every major city. Public transit and railway services have been reduced. In the mid-nineteenth century in suburban London, there were twelve mail deliveries per day on weekdays and one on Sundays. We all know what has happened to postal services since then.

There have been parallel cutbacks in the quality of private services. Doctors have become increasingly reluctant to visit patients at home; in many areas, the house call has become something that occurs only in a life-and-death emergency, if even then. Another example, though undoubtedly a matter of lesser concern, is what has happened to restaurants. Although they are reluctant to publicize the fact, a great number of restaurants, including some of the most elegant and expensive, serve preprepared, frozen, and reheated meals. They charge high prices for what amount to little more than TV dinners.

There is no single explanation for all these matters. It would be naïve to offer a cut-and-dried hypothesis that purports to account for phenomena as diverse as the rise in crime and violence throughout western society and the deterioration in postal services. Yet at least one common influence underlies all these problems of deterioration in service quality —an influence that is economic in character and that may be expected to grow more serious with the passage of time. The issue has been called the **cost disease of the personal services**, in reference to the fact that the costs of all basic services such as health care and education have risen so dramatically in recent decades.

But what accounts for these ever-increasing costs? Are they attributable to inefficiencies in government management? Perhaps, in part. But there is another reason—one that could not be avoided by any administration, no matter what its integrity and efficiency, and that affects private industry just as severely as it does the public sector.

The problem stems from the basic nature of services. Many services require direct contact between those who consume the service and those who provide it. Firefighters, teachers, and librarians are all engaged in activities that require direct person-to-person contact. Moreover, the quality of the service deteriorates if firefighters, teachers, and librarians provide less time to each user of their services.

In contrast, the buyer of an automobile usually has no idea who worked on it, and, provided it operates well, could not care less how

much labour time went into its production. A labour-saving innovation in auto production need not imply a reduction in product quality. As a result, it has proved far easier for technological change to save labour in manufacturing than in providing services. While output per hour of labour in manufacturing and agriculture went up in the period after World War II at an average rate of close to 3 percent a year, the number of teacher hours per pupil actually increased because classes became smaller.

These disparate performances in productivity have grave consequences for prices. If both wages and productivity in manufacturing rise 3 percent, the cost of manufactured products is not affected because increased productivity makes up for the rise in wages. But the nature of services makes it very difficult to introduce labour-saving devices in the service sector. Thus, a 3 percent rise in the wages of teachers or police officers is not offset by higher productivity and must lead to an equivalent rise in government budgets. Similarly, a 3 percent rise in the wages of hairdressers must lead beauty salons to raise their prices.

The Cost Disease of the Personal Services

In the long run, wages and salaries throughout the economy tend to go up and down together; otherwise, an activity whose wage rate fell seriously behind would tend to lose its labour force. Thus, auto workers and police officers will see their wages rise at roughly the same rate in the long run. But if productivity on the assembly line advances while productivity in the patrol car does not, police protection must grow ever more expensive as time goes on.

This phenomenon is another of our twelve Ideas for Beyond the Final Exam. Because productivity improvements are very difficult to achieve in most services, the cost of services can be expected to rise faster, year in, year out, than does the cost of manufactured goods. Over a period of several decades, this difference in the growth rates of the two sectors' costs compounds to make services enormously more expensive relative to manufactured goods.

If services continue to grow ever more expensive in comparison with goods, the implications for life in the future are profound indeed. This analysis portends a world in which the typical home, while containing luxuries and furnishings that we can hardly imagine, is surrounded by garbage and perhaps by violence. It portends a future in which the services of doctors, teachers, and police are limited and impersonal, and in which arts and crafts are supplied largely by amateurs because the cost of professional work in these fields has become too high.

If this is the shape of the economy a hundred years from now, it will be significantly different from our own, and some people will undoubtedly question whether the quality of life has increased commensurately with the increased material prosperity. Some may even ask whether it has increased at all.

Is this future inevitable? Is there anything that can be done to escape it? The answer is that it is by no means inevitable. To see why, we must first recognize that the source of the problem, paradoxically, is the growth in productivity of our economy — or rather, the *unevenness* of that growth. Garbage-removal costs go up not because garbage collectors become less efficient, but because labour in car manufacturing becomes *more* efficient, thus enhancing the sanitation workers' potential value as employees on the automotive assembly line. Their wages must go up to keep them at their job of garbage removal.

But increasing productivity can never make a nation poorer. It can never make it unable to afford things it was able to afford in the past. Increasing productivity means that we can afford more of *all* things — medical care and education as well as TV sets and electric toothbrushes.

The role of services in our future depends on how we order our priorities. If we value services sufficiently, we can have more and better services — at some sacrifice in the rate of growth of manufactured goods. Whether that is a good choice for society is not for economists to say. But it is important to recognize that society *does* have a choice, and that if it fails to exercise it, matters are very likely to proceed relentlessly in the direction they are now headed — toward a world in which there is an enormous abundance of material goods and a great scarcity of many of the things that most people now consider primary requisites for a high quality of life.

How does the cost disease relate to the central topic of this chapter—the performance of the market and its implications for the economic role of government? Here the problem is the reverse of those discussed earlier in the chapter. The cost disease is a case in which the market *does* give the appropriate price signals, but they are likely to be misunderstood by government and to lead to decisions that do not promote the public interest most effectively.

Health care is a suggestive example. The cost disease is capable of causing the costs of health care (say, per patient day) to rise faster than the economy's rate of inflation because hospital care cannot be standardized enough to permit the productivity gains offered by automation and assembly lines. Thus, to prevent standards of care from falling, it is not enough to allow hospital budgets to grow at the same rate as the economy's rate of inflation. Those budgets must actually grow faster to prevent quality from declining. For example, when the inflation rate is 2 percent per year, it may be necessary to raise hospital budgets by 5 percent annually.

In these circumstances, something will surely seem amiss to a provincial government that increases the budget of its hospitals 4 percent per year. Responsible legislators will doubtless be disturbed by the fact that the budget is growing steadily in real terms and yet standards of quality are constantly slipping. If the legislators do not realize that the cost disease is the cause of the problem, they can be expected to look for villains—greedy doctors, hospital administrators who are inefficient, and so on. The net result, all too often, is a set of wasteful rules that hamper the freedom of action of hospitals and doctors inappropriately or that tighten hospital budgets below the level that demands and costs would require if they were determined by the market mechanism rather than by government.

In sum, the cost disease is not a case of poor market performance. But it is a case in which the market *appears* to misbehave by singling out particular sectors for exceptionally large cost increases. Further, because the market seems to be working badly, it is likely to lead to government reaction that can be highly detrimental to the public interest. (Governments have also been induced to intervene in the operation of some private sectors affected by the cost disease. For example, they control the prices of automobile insurance policies, which pay for such things as medical care of accident victims and repair of damaged automobiles, both of which are susceptible to the disease.)

EVALUATIVE COMMENTS

This chapter, like Chapter 9, has offered a rather unbalanced assessment of the market mechanism. We spent Chapter 9 extolling the market's virtues, and this chapter cataloguing its vices. We come out, as in the nursery rhyme, concluding that the market is either very, very good, or horrid.

There seems to be nothing moderate about the performance of a market system. As a means of achieving efficiency in the production of ordinary consumer goods and responding to changes in consumer preferences, it is unparalleled. It is, in fact, difficult to overstate the accomplishments of the price system in these areas.

On the other hand, it has proven itself unable to cope with business fluctuations, income inequality, and the consequences of monopoly. It has proven to be a very poor allocator of resources among outputs that generate external costs and external benefits, and it has shown itself completely incapable of arranging for the provision of public goods. Some of the most urgent problems that plague our society—the despoliation of our atmosphere, the social unrest attributable to poverty—can be ascribed in part to one or another of these shortcomings of the market system.

Most economists conclude from these observations that while the market mechanism is virtually irreplaceable, considerable modifications in the way it works are required. Proposals designed to deal directly with the problems of poverty, monopoly, and resource allocation over time abound in the economic literature. All of them call for government to intervene in the economy, either by supplying directly those goods and services that, it is believed, private enterprise does not supply in adequate amounts, or by seeking to influence the workings of the economy more indirectly through regulation or other policies. Many of these programs have been discussed in earlier chapters; others will be encountered in chapters to come.

SUMMARY

1. There are at least seven major imperfections associated with the workings of the market mechanism: inequality of income distribution, fluctuations in economic activity (inflation and unemployment), monopolistic output restrictions, beneficial and detrimental externalities, inadequate provision of public goods, misallocation of resources between present and future, and finally, deteriorating quality and rising costs of services.

2. Efficient resource allocation is basically a matter of balancing the benefits of producing more of one good against the benefits of devoting the required inputs to the production of some other good.

3. A detrimental externality occurs when an economic activity incidentally does harm to others; a beneficial externality occurs when an economic activity incidentally creates benefits for others.

4. When an activity causes a detrimental externality, the marginal social cost of the activity (including the harm it does to others) must be greater than the marginal private cost to those who conduct the activity. The opposite will be true for a beneficial externality.

5. If manufacture of a product causes detrimental externalities, its price will generally not include all the marginal social cost it causes, since part of the cost will be borne by others. The opposite is true for beneficial externalities.

6. The market will therefore tend to overallocate resources to the production of goods that cause detrimental externalities and underallocate resources to the production of goods that create beneficial externalities. This is one of the twelve Ideas for Beyond the Final Exam.

7. A public good is defined by economists as a commodity that (like clean air) is not depleted by additional users and from whose use it is difficult to exclude anyone, even those who refuse to pay for it. A private good, in contrast, is characterized by both excludability and depletability.

8. Free-enterprise firms generally will not produce a public good even if it is extremely useful to the community, because they cannot charge money for the use of the good.

9. Many observers feel that the market often short-changes the future, particularly when it makes irreversible decisions that destroy natural resources.

10. Because personal services—such as education, medical care, and police protection—are not amenable to labour-saving innovations, they suffer from a "cost disease": Their costs tend to rise considerably faster than do costs in the economy as a whole. This can lead to a distortion in the supply of such services by government because their rising cost is misinterpreted as the result of mismanagement and waste. The cost disease of the service sector is another of our twelve Ideas for Beyond the Final Exam.

CONCEPTS FOR REVIEW

Opportunity cost
Resource misallocation
Production possibilities
  frontier
Price above or below marginal
  cost
Externalities (detrimental and
  beneficial)

Marginal social cost and
  marginal private cost
Public goods
Private goods
Depletability
Excludability
Irreversible decisions

Rent-seeking
Moral hazard
Asymmetric information
Principals and agents
Cost disease of the personal
  services

QUESTIONS FOR DISCUSSION

1. Specifically, what is the opportunity cost to society of a chair? Why may the price of that chair not adequately represent that opportunity cost?

2. Suppose that because of a new disease that attacks coffee plants, far more labour and other inputs are required to raise a pound of coffee than were required before. How might that affect the efficient allocation of resources between tea and coffee? Why? How would the prices of coffee and tea react in a free market?

3. Give some examples of goods whose production causes detrimental externalities and some examples of goods that create beneficial externalities.

4. Compare cleaning an office building with cleaning the atmosphere of a city. Which is a public good and which is a private good? Why?

5. Give some other examples of public goods, and discuss in each case why additional users do not deplete them and why it is difficult to exclude people from using them.

6. Think about the goods and services that your local government provides. Which of these are "public goods" as economists use the term?

7. Explain why the services of a lighthouse are considered an example of a public good.

8. Explain why education is not a very satisfactory example of a public good.

9. In recent decades, university tuition costs have risen faster than the general price level even though the salaries of professors have failed to keep pace with the price level. Can you explain why?

10. A firm holds a patent that is estimated to be worth $20 million. The patent is repeatedly challenged in the courts by a large number of (rent-seeking) firms, each hoping to grab away the patent. In what sense may the rent-seekers be "competing perfectly" for the patent? In that sense, how much will end up being spent in the legal battles? (*Hint:* Under perfect competition, should firms expect to earn any economic profit?)

13

COMPARATIVE ADVANTAGE: THE QUESTION OF FREE TRADE

Which document will shape Canada's economy into the 21st century?
a. NAFTA
b. GATT
c. IOU

RICK GREEN AND
ANDREW GREEN
(1992 year-end quiz,
The Globe and Mail)

For many years, Canada's strategy for economic development has involved the use of tariff barriers, and this has fostered the growth of various industries within the country. But as a result of Canada's tariff barriers and those imposed by other countries against our manufactured goods, Canadian producers have had to limit the scale of their operations to the small domestic market. This has meant operating at relatively low volume, with relatively high unit costs and just a few firms in each industry. We have tried to control monopoly practices through direct regulation and competition laws. But as we shall see in Chapter 16, these policies have met with only limited success, and many economists argue that we should rely instead on the discipline of the market. This discipline can be enforced by exposing firms that operate in Canada to more competition with firms already existing elsewhere in the world. As Canada cuts its tariffs, our producers are forced to expand operations (in order to reduce unit costs) and to sell a significant part of their output on world markets, or to get out of business.

The benefits of a tariff-reduction policy are rather obvious: Canadian consumers are able to buy a host of products at reduced prices, since the increased competition forces producers to approximate more closely the efficiency gains that exist in a perfectly competitive economy. To many people, however, especially Canadian workers, the costs of this policy are equally obvious. They fear that our producers are not able to compete with the low prices charged by those employing "cheap foreign labour." These opponents of tariff cuts think that many business failures and a large increase in unemployment follow any cut in tariffs. Thus, they argue that we simply cannot afford to lower our trade barriers unilaterally. Many economists disagree, and we explain why in this chapter.

To be complete, our investigation into the benefits and costs of tariff cuts must take a rather circuitous route. First, we explain the purpose of foreign trade and the ways in which governments seek to influence or limit it. Second, we study the crucial *law of comparative advantage*, which determines what commodities a country finds advantageous to export and what commodities it finds advantageous to import. This principle shows that even if there are *no* economies of large-scale production, both trading countries benefit from increased international exchange. Third, we see how the prices of goods traded between countries are determined by supply and demand. Finally, we examine the pros and cons of tariffs and other devices designed to protect a country's industries from foreign competition, and we discuss Canada's Free Trade Agreement with the United States in this context. In the end, we will have exposed the fallacy behind the view that "cheap foreign labour" necessitates tariff barriers.

At the close of this chapter, in the section entitled Microeconomic Policy: A Review and a Preview, we return to the theme of equality versus efficiency—one of our twelve Ideas for Beyond the Final Exam. This final section of the chapter serves as a link between Part 3, which has focussed on the pros and cons of a decentralized market system, and Part 4, which concerns itself with the problems of income distribution, economic power, pollution, and resource depletion. Free trade is the issue around which competing views on economic efficiency and unfair distributional effects have been most heatedly debated in recent years. For this reason, it is an ideal subject through which to focus once again on the equity–efficiency trade-off, before proceeding to Part 4.

ISSUE: THE COMPETITION OF "CHEAP FOREIGN LABOUR"

When analyzing international trade, common sense can be extremely valuable; indeed, there is no substitute for it. Yet, in the absence of factual confirmation and careful analysis, conclusions based on common sense can be misleading.

One important example is the argument that buying products made by cheap foreign labour is unfair and destructive to domestic interests. Some Canadian business people and most union leaders argue that imports take bread out of the mouths of Canadian workers and depress standards of living in this country. According to this view, cheap foreign goods cause job losses and put pressure on Canadian businesses to lower wages. As this book goes to press, this very concern is frequently expressed in the news media with regard to NAFTA, the North American Free Trade Agreement, which proposes to add Mexico to the existing Canada–U.S. Free Trade Agreement. Union leaders have been vocal about the damage that imports produced by cheap Mexican labour would inflict on Canadian industries and workers.

But the facts are not consistent with this scenario. Many of Canada's imports come from Western Europe and Japan. Since the early 1960s, wages have risen far more dramatically in these other countries than they have here, yet we continue to import such items as Volvos, Hondas, and

Toyotas in large numbers. More important, the rise in these foreign wages relative to Canadian wages has not strengthened Canada's position in the international marketplace. Conversely, back in the 1950s, when European and Japanese wages were far below those in Canada, we had no trouble marketing our products abroad. Clearly, cheap foreign labour does not necessarily create a crucial obstacle to Canadian sales abroad, as a "common-sense" view of the matter suggests. In this chapter, we will see what is wrong with that view.

WHY TRADE?

The main reason that countries trade with one another rather than try to run completely independent economies is that the earth's resources are not equally distributed across its surface. Canada has an abundant supply of forests and fresh water, resources that are quite scarce in most of the rest of the world. Saudi Arabia has very little land that is suitable for farming, but it sits atop a huge pool of oil. Because of this seemingly whimsical distribution of vital resources, every nation must trade with others to acquire what it lacks. In general, the more varied the endowment of a particular country, the less it will have to depend on others to make up for its deficiencies.

Even if countries had all the resources they needed, other differences in natural endowments—such as climate, terrain, and so on—would lead them to engage in trade. Canadians *could*, with great difficulty, grow their own banana trees and coffee shrubs in hothouses, but these items are much more efficiently grown in such places as Honduras and Brazil, where the climate is appropriate. On the other hand, wheat grows in Canada with little difficulty, while mountainous Switzerland is not a good place to grow either bananas or wheat.

The skills of a country's labour force also play a role. If New Zealand has a large group of efficient farmers but few workers with industrial experience while the opposite is true in Great Britain, it makes sense for New Zealand to specialize in agriculture and for Great Britain to concentrate on manufacturing.

This last point suggests a very important reason why countries choose to trade—the many advantages of **specialization**. If one country were to try to produce everything, it would end up with a number of industries whose scale of operation was too small to permit the use of mass production techniques, specialized training facilities, and other arrangements that give a cost advantage to large-scale operations. Even now, despite the considerable volume of world trade, this problem seems to arise for some countries, whose operation of their own international airlines or their own steel mills, for example, seems explainable only in political rather than economic terms. Inevitably, small nations that insist on operating in industries that are economical only when their scale of operation is large find that these enterprises can survive only with the aid of large government subsidies. Let's summarize:

SPECIALIZATION means that a country devotes its energies and resources to only a small proportion of the world's productive activities.

International trade is essential for the prosperity of the trading nations for at least three reasons: (1) every country lacks some vital resources that it can get only by trading with others; (2) each country's climate, labour force, and other endowments make it a relatively efficient producer of some goods and an inefficient producer of other goods; and (3) specialization permits larger outputs and can therefore offer economies of large-scale production.

MUTUAL GAINS FROM TRADE

Many people believe that one nation can gain from trade only at the expense of another. Centuries ago, early writers on international trade argued that because nothing is produced by the act of trading, the total collection of goods in the hands of the two parties at the end of an exchange is no greater than it was before the exchange took place. Therefore, they concluded (fallaciously), if one country gains from a swap, the other country must necessarily lose.

One of the consequences of this mistaken view was a policy prescription calling for each country, in the interests of its citizens, to do its best to act to the disadvantage of its trading partners—in Adam Smith's terms, to "beggar its neighbours." The idea that one nation's gain must be another's loss means that a country can promote its own welfare only by harming others.

Yet, as Adam Smith and others after him emphasized, in any *voluntary exchange*, unless there is misunderstanding or misrepresentation of the facts, both parties *must* gain (or at least expect to gain) something from the transaction. Otherwise, why would both parties agree to the exchange?

But how can mere exchange, in which no production takes place, actually leave both parties better off? The answer is that although trade does not increase the quantity of goods available, it does allow each party to acquire items better suited to its needs and tastes. Suppose Brian has four sandwiches and nothing to drink, while David has four cartons of milk and nothing to eat. A trade of two of Brian's sandwiches for two of David's cartons of milk does not increase the total supply of either food or beverages, but it clearly produces a net increase in the welfare of both boys. By exactly the same logic, both Canada and the United States must be better off if Canada voluntarily ships timber to the United States in return for chemicals.

Mutual Gains from Voluntary Exchange

Both parties must expect to gain from any voluntary exchange. Trade brings about mutual gains by redistributing products in such a way that both participants end up holding a combination of goods that is better adapted to their preferences than the goods they held before. This principle, which is one of our twelve Ideas for Beyond the Final Exam, applies to nations just as it does to individuals.

COMPARATIVE ADVANTAGE: THE FUNDAMENTAL PRINCIPLE OF SPECIALIZATION

Some of the reasons trade can be beneficial to both parties are obvious. We now turn to an important source of mutual benefit that is far from obvious.

We know that coffee can be produced in Colombia using less labour and smaller quantities of other inputs than would be needed to grow it in Canada. Further, we know that Canada can produce passenger aircraft at a lower resource cost than can Colombia. We say then that Colombia has an **absolute advantage** over Canada in coffee production, and Canada has an absolute advantage over Colombia in aircraft production.

A numerical example will illustrate the idea. According to Table 13-1, one year of labour time in Canada can produce either 50 kilograms of coffee or $1/20$ of an airplane. By contrast, one year of labour time in Colombia can produce 300 kilograms of coffee or $1/100$ of an airplane. Thus, six years of labour input would be required to produce 300 kilograms of coffee in Canada, whereas Colombia could do the job with only one year's worth of labour. On the other hand, it would take Colombia 100 years of labour to produce an airplane, a job Canada could do in only 20 years.

Obviously, if Canada wants coffee and Colombia wants airplanes, each can save resources by specializing in what it does best and trading with the other. Each exports the good in which it has an absolute advantage.

Suppose, however, that one country is more efficient than another in producing *every* item. Can they still gain by trading? The surprising answer is definitely yes, and a simple parable will help explain why.

The work of a highly paid business consultant frequently requires computer analysis. Suppose the consultant began her career as a computer operator doing her own data entry and was extremely good at it. In her current position, she may grow impatient with the slow, sloppy work of some of the low-paid support staff who work for her and at times be tempted to do all the work herself. Good judgement tells her, however, that although she is better *both* at giving business advice *and* at data entry than are her employees, it is foolish to devote any of her valuable time to the low-skilled job. This is because the opportunity cost of an hour devoted to data entry is an hour less devoted to business consulting—a far more lucrative activity.

This is an example of **comparative advantage** at work. The consultant specializes in business advice despite her absolute advantage in data

One country is said to have an **ABSOLUTE ADVANTAGE** over another in the production of a particular good if it can produce that good using smaller quantities of resources than can the other country.

One country is said to have a **COMPARATIVE ADVANTAGE** over another in the production of a particular good relative to other goods it can produce if it produces that good least inefficiently in comparison with the other country.

TABLE 13-1

ALTERNATIVE OUTPUTS FROM ONE YEAR OF LABOUR INPUT

	In Canada	In Colombia
Coffee (kilograms)	50	300
Airplanes	1/20	1/100

entry because she has a greater absolute advantage in her role as a business consultant. She suffers some direct loss by not doing her own data entry, but that loss is more than compensated for by what she earns by selling her consulting services to clients.

Our example brings out the fundamental principle that underlies the economic analysis of patterns of specialization and exchange among different nations. This principle is called the *law of comparative advantage*, and it is one of our twelve Ideas for Beyond the Final Exam. It was discovered by David Ricardo, one of the giants in the history of economic analysis.

The Law of Comparative Advantage

Even if one country is at an absolute disadvantage relative to another country in the production of every good, it is said to have a *comparative advantage* in making the good in the production of which it is *least inefficient* in comparison with the other country.

Ricardo's basic finding was that two countries can still gain by trading even if one country is more efficient than another in the production of *every* commodity (that is, it has an absolute advantage in every commodity).

In determining the most efficient patterns of production, what matters is *comparative* advantage, not absolute advantage. Thus, one country will often gain by importing a certain good even if that good can be produced at home more efficiently than it can be produced abroad. Such imports will be profitable if the country is even more efficient at producing the goods that it exports in exchange.

THE ARITHMETIC OF COMPARATIVE ADVANTAGE

Let's see precisely how this works using numbers based on Ricardo's original example. Suppose labour is the only input used to produce wine and cloth in two countries, England and Portugal. Suppose further that Portugal has an absolute advantage in both goods, as indicated in Table 13-2. In this example, a week's worth of labour can produce either 12 metres of cloth or 6 barrels of wine in Portugal, but only 10 metres of cloth or 1 barrel of wine in England. Thus, Portugal is the more efficient producer of both goods. Nonetheless, as our example of the multitalented consultant suggests, it pays for Portugal to specialize in wine production and to trade with England.

We verify that this is so in two steps. First, we note that Portugal has a comparative advantage in wine while England has a comparative advantage in cloth. Second, we show that both countries can gain if Portugal specializes in producing wine, England specializes in producing cloth, and the two countries trade with one another.

TABLE 13-2

ALTERNATIVE OUTPUTS FROM ONE WEEK OF LABOUR INPUT

	In England	In Portugal
Cloth (metres)	10	12
Wine (barrels)	1	6

According to the numbers in Table 13-2, Portugal is 20 percent more efficient than England in producing cloth; it can produce 12 metres with a week's labour, whereas England can produce only 10 metres. However, Portugal is six times as efficient as England in producing wine; it can produce 6 barrels per week rather than 1. Thus, Portugal's competitive edge is far greater in wine than in cloth. That is precisely what we mean by saying that Portugal has a competitive advantage in wine. From the British perspective, these same numbers indicate that England is only slightly less efficient than Portugal in cloth production but drastically less efficient in wine production. Thus, England's comparative advantage is in cloth. According to Ricardo's law of comparative advantage, the two countries can benefit if Portuguese wine is traded for English cloth.

Let us check that this is true. Suppose Portugal transfers 1 million weeks of labour out of the textile industry and into winemaking. According to the figures in Table 13-2, its cloth output falls by 12 million metres while its wine output rises by 6 million barrels. (See Table 13-3.) Suppose, at the same time, England transfers 2 million weeks of labour out of winemaking (thereby losing 2 million barrels of wine) and into cloth-making (thereby gaining 20 million metres of cloth). Table 13-3 shows us that these transfers of resources in the two countries increase the total world production of both outputs!

Together, the two countries now have 4 million additional barrels of wine and 8 million additional metres of cloth—surely a nice outcome. But there seems to be some sleight of hand here. All that has taken place is an exchange; yet somehow Portugal and England have gained both cloth and wine. How can such gains in physical output be possible?

The explanation is that the trade process we have just described involves more than just a swap of a fixed bundle of commodities. It is also a change in the *production arrangements*, with some of England's wine production taken over by the more efficient Portuguese wine producers and with some of Portugal's cloth production taken over by Eng-

TABLE 13-3

EXAMPLE OF THE GAINS FROM TRADE

	England	Portugal	Total
Cloth (millions of metres)	+20	−12	+8
Wine (millions of barrels)	−2	+6	+4

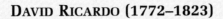

BIOGRAPHICAL NOTE

DAVID RICARDO (1772–1823)

David Ricardo was born four years before publication of Adam Smith's *Wealth of Nations*. Descended from a wealthy Jewish family of Portuguese origins, he had twenty brothers and sisters. Ricardo's formal education ended at the age of 13, so he was largely self-educated. He began his career by working in his father's brokerage firm in London. At age 21, Ricardo married a Quaker woman and decided to become a Unitarian, a sect then considered "little better than atheist." By Jewish custom, Ricardo's father formally broke off relations with him, although apparently the two remained friendly.

Ricardo then decided to go into the brokerage business on his own and was enormously successful. During the Napoleonic Wars, he regularly scored business coups over leading British and foreign financiers, including the Rothschilds. After gaining a huge profit on government securities that he had bought just before the Battle of Waterloo, Ricardo decided to retire from business when he was just over 40 years old.

He purchased a country estate, Gatcomb (now owned by the royal family), where a brilliant group of intellectuals met regularly. Particularly remarkable for the period was the number of women included in the circle, among them Maria Edgeworth, the novelist (who wrote of Ricardo's mind with extravagant praise), and Jane Marcet, an author of textbooks, one of which was probably the first textbook in economics. Ricardo's close friends included economists T.R. Malthus and James Mill, father of John Stuart Mill, the noted philosopher–economist. Malthus remained a close friend of Ricardo even though they disagreed on many subjects and continued their arguments in personal correspondence and in their published works.

James Mill persuaded Ricardo to go into Parliament. As was then customary, Ricardo purchased his seat by buying a piece of land that entitled its owner to a seat in Parliament. There he proved to be a noteworthy advocate of many causes that were against his personal interests.

James Mill also helped persuade Ricardo to write his masterpiece, *The Principles of Political Economy and Taxation*, which may have been the first book of pure economic theory ever published. It is noteworthy that Ricardo, the most practical of practical men, had little patience with empirical economics and preferred to rest his analysis explicitly and exclusively on theory. This book made considerable contributions to the analysis of pricing, wage determination, and the effects of various types of taxes, among many other subjects. It also gave us the law of comparative advantage. In addition, the book described what has come to be called the Ricardian rent theory—even though Ricardo did not discover the analysis and explicitly denied having done so.

Ricardo died in 1823 at the age of 51. He seems to have been a wholly admirable person—honest, charming, witty, conscientious, brilliant—almost too good to be true.

lish weavers, who are *less inefficient* at producing cloth than English vintners are at producing wine.

When every country does what it can do best, all countries can benefit because more of every commodity can be produced without increasing the amounts of labour used.

If this result still seems a bit mysterious, the concept of *opportunity cost* will help clarify it. If the two countries do not trade, Table 13-2 shows that England can acquire a barrel of wine on its own only by giving up 10 metres of cloth. Thus, the opportunity cost of a barrel of wine in England is 10 metres of cloth. But in Portugal, the opportunity cost of a barrel of wine is only 2 metres of cloth (again, see Table 13-2). Thus, in terms of real resources foregone, it is cheaper—for either country—to acquire wine in Portugal. By a similar line of reasoning, the opportunity cost of cloth is higher in Portugal than in England, so it makes sense for both countries to acquire their cloth in England.

THE GRAPHICS OF COMPARATIVE ADVANTAGE

The gains from trade can also be displayed graphically, and doing so helps us understand how these gains arise.

The lines *UK* and *PG* in Figure 13-1 are the *production possibilities frontiers* of the two countries, drawn on the assumption that each country has 6 million weeks of labour available. (For simplicity in this numerical example, we assume no diminishing returns in either economy.) For example, Table 13-2 tells us that with 6 million weeks of labour, England can produce 6 million barrels of wine and no cloth (point *K*), 60 million metres of cloth and no wine (point *U*), or any combination in between (line *UK*). Similar reasoning shows that *PG* is Portugal's production possibilities frontier.

Note that Portugal's production possibilities frontier lies *above* England's throughout the diagram. That is because Portugal is the more efficient producer of *both* commodities. With the same amount of labour, it can obtain more wine and more cloth than England can. Thus, the higher position of Portugal's frontier is the graph's way of showing Portugal's absolute advantage in both wine and cloth.

Portugal's comparative advantage in wine production and England's comparative advantage in cloth production are shown in a different way —by the relative slopes of the two production possibilities frontiers. Portugal's frontier is not only higher than England's; it is also flatter. What does this mean economically? One way of looking at the difference is to remember that while Portugal can produce six times as much wine as England (compare points *P* and *K*), it can produce only 20 percent more cloth than England (compare points *G* and *U*). England is, relatively speaking, much better at cloth production than at wine production. That is what we mean when we say it has a comparative advantage in the former.

FIGURE 13-1

ABSOLUTE AND COMPARATIVE ADVANTAGE SHOWN BY TWO COUNTRIES'
PRODUCTION POSSIBILITIES FRONTIERS

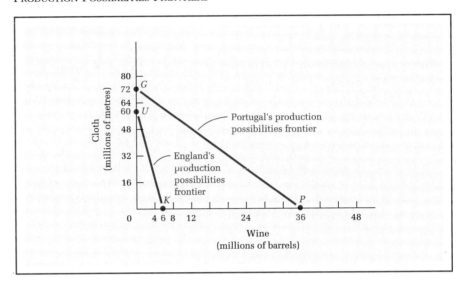

Portugal's absolute advantage is shown by its ability to produce more of every commodity using the same quantity of labour as does England. Therefore, Portugal's production possibilities frontier, *PG*, is higher than England's *UK*. But Portugal has a comparative advantage in wine production, in which it is six times as productive as England. It can produce 36 million barrels (point *P*), compared with England's 6 million barrels (point *K*). On the other hand, Portugal is only 20 percent more productive in cloth production (point *G*) than England (Point *U*). Thus, England is *less inefficient* in producing cloth, where it consequently has a comparative advantage.

We can express this difference more directly in terms of the slopes of the two lines. The slope of Portugal's production possibilities frontier is $0G/0P = 72/36 = 2$. This means that if Portugal reduces its wine production by 1 barrel, it will obtain 2 metres of cloth. Thus, the opportunity cost of a barrel of wine in Portugal is 2 metres of cloth, as we observed earlier.

Now turning to the case of England, the slope of the production possibilities frontier is $0U/0K = 60/6 = 10$. That is, if England reduces wine production by 1 barrel, it gets 10 additional metres of cloth. Thus, in England, the opportunity cost of a barrel of wine is 10 metres of cloth.

One country's absolute advantage in production over another country is shown by its having a higher production possibilities frontier. The difference in the comparative advantage of the two countries is shown by the difference in the slopes of their frontiers.

Because opportunity costs differ in two countries, gains from trade are possible. How these gains are divided between the two countries depends on the prices for wine and cloth that emerge from world trade, which is the subject of the next section. But we already know enough to see that world trade must leave a barrel of wine costing less than 10 metres of cloth and more than 2 metres. Why? Because if a barrel of wine cost more than 10 metres of cloth (its opportunity cost in England), England would be better off producing its own wine rather than trading with Portugal. Similarly, if a barrel of wine fetched less than 2 metres of cloth (its opportunity cost in Portugal), Portugal would prefer to produce its own cloth rather than trade with England.

We conclude, therefore, that if both countries are to benefit from trade, the rate of exchange between cloth and wine must be somewhere between 10 to 1 and 2 to 1. To illustrate the gains from trade in a concrete example, suppose the world price ratio settles at 4 to 1; that is, 1 barrel of wine costs 4 metres of cloth. How much, precisely, do England and Portugal gain from world trade?

Figure 13-2 is designed to help us see the answer. Production possibilities frontiers *UK* in part (a) and *PG* in part (b) are the same as in Figure 13-1. But England can do better than *UK*. Specifically, with a world price ratio of 4 to 1, England can buy a barrel of wine by giving up only 4 metres of cloth rather than 10 metres (which is the opportunity cost of wine in England). Hence, if England produces only cloth (point *U* in

FIGURE 13-2

THE GAINS FROM TRADE

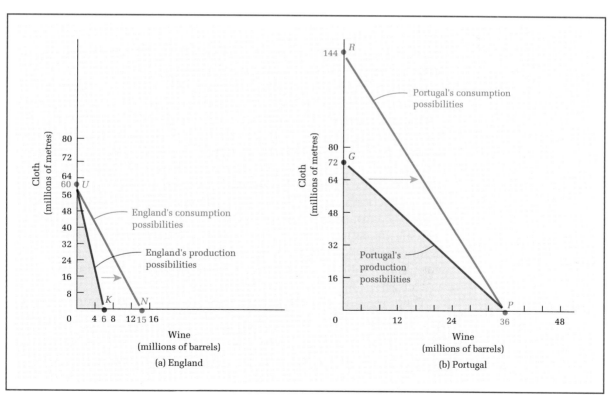

(a) England

(b) Portugal

In this diagram, we suppose that trade opens up between England and Portugal and that the world price of wine is four times the world price of cloth. Now England's consumption possibilities are all the points on line *UN* (which starts at *U* and has a slope of 4), rather than just the points on its own production possibilities frontier, *UK*. Similarly, Portugal can choose any point on line *PR* (which begins at *P* and has a slope of 4), rather than just points on *PG*. Thus, both nations gain from trade.

Figure 13-2(a)) and buys its wine from Portugal, England's *consumption possibilities* will be as indicated by the blue line that begins at point *U* and has a slope of 4—indicating that each additional barrel of wine costs England 4 metres of cloth. Since trade allows England to choose a point on *UN* rather than on *UK*, trade opens up consumption possibilities that were simply not available before.

The story is similar for Portugal. If the Portuguese produce only wine (point *P* in Figure 13-2(b)), they can acquire 4 metres of cloth from England for each barrel of wine they give up as they move along the blue line, PR (the slope of which is 4). This is better than they can do on their own, since a sacrifice of 1 barrel of wine yields only 2 metres of cloth in Portugal. Hence, world trade enlarges Portugal's consumption possibilities from *PG* to *PR*.

Figure 13-2 shows graphically that gains from trade arise to the extent that world prices (4 to 1 in our example) differ from domestic opportunity costs (10 to 1 and 2 to 1 in our example). Thus, it is a matter of some importance to understand how prices in international trade are established. Supply and demand is a natural place to start.

SUPPLY–DEMAND EQUILIBRIUM AND PRICING IN FOREIGN TRADE

When applied to international trade, the supply–demand model runs into several complications we have not encountered before. First, it involves at least two demand curves: that of the exporting country and that of the importing country. Second, it may also involve two supply curves, since the importing country may produce some part of what it consumes. The third and final complication is that equilibrium does not occur at the intersection point of *either* pair of supply–demand curves. Why? Because if there is any trade, the exporting country's quantity supplied must be *greater* than its quantity demanded, while the quantity supplied by the importing country must be *less* than its quantity demanded.

These complications are illustrated in Figure 13-3, where we show, in part (a), the supply and demand curves of a country that exports wine and, in part (b), the supply and demand curves of a country that imports wine. For simplicity, we assume that these countries do not deal in wine with anyone else.

Where will the two-country wine market reach equilibrium? Ignoring transport costs, the equilibrium price in a free market must satisfy two requirements:

1. The price of wine must be the same in both countries.

2. The quantity of wine exported (the excess of the exporting country's quantity supplied over its quantity demanded) must equal the quantity of wine imported (the excess of the importing country's quantity demanded over its quantity supplied).

FIGURE 13-3

SUPPLY–DEMAND EQUILIBRIUM IN THE INTERNATIONAL WINE TRADE

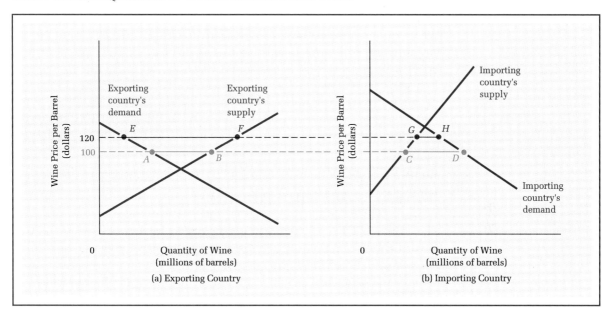

(a) Exporting Country

(b) Importing Country

Equilibrium requires that net exports, *AB* (that is, the exporting country's quantity supplied, *B*, minus its quantity demanded, *A*), exactly balance imports, *CD*, by the importing country. At $100 per barrel of wine, there is equilibrium. But at a higher price, say $120, there is disequilibrium because net export supply, *EF*, exceeds net import demand, *GH*.

In Figure 13-3, this happens at a price of $100 per barrel. At that price, distance *AB* between what the exporting country produces (point *B*) and what it consumes (point *A*) equals distance *CD* between the quantity demanded of the importing country (point *D*) and its quantity supplied (point *C*). At a price of $100 per barrel, the amount the exporting country has available to sell abroad is exactly equal to the amount the importer wants to buy. Thus, matters are in balance, and $100 per barrel is the market price.

At any price higher than $100, producers in both countries will want to sell more and consumers in both countries will want to buy less. For example, if the price rises to $120 per barrel, the exporting country's quantity supplied will rise from *B* to *F*, and its quantity demanded will fall from *A* to *E*, as shown in Figure 13-3(a). As a result, there will be a rise in the amount available for export, from *AB* to *EF*. For exactly the same reason, the price increase will cause higher production and lower sales in the importing country, leading to a shrinkage in the amount the importing country wants to import — from *CD* to *GH* in part (b). This means that the new price, $120 per barrel, cannot be sustained if the international market is free and competitive. With export supply *EF* far greater than import demand *GH*, there must be a downward pressure on price and a move back toward the $100 equilibrium price. Similar reasoning shows that prices of less than $100 also cannot be sustained.

We can now see the straightforward role of supply–demand equilibrium in international trade:

In international trade, the equilibrium price must be at a level at which the amount the exporting country wants to export is exactly equal to the amount the importing country wants to import. Equilibrium will thus occur at a price at which horizontal distance *AB* in Figure 13-3(a) (the excess of the exporter's quantity supplied over its quantity demanded) equals horizontal distance *CD* in Figure 13-3(b) (the excess of the importer's quantity demanded over its quantity supplied). At this price, the *world's* quantity demanded is equal to the *world's* quantity supplied.

COMPARATIVE ADVANTAGE AND COMPETITION OF "CHEAP FOREIGN LABOUR"

The principle of comparative advantage takes us a good part of the way toward an explanation of the fallacy in the "cheap foreign labour" argument described earlier in the chapter. Given the assumed productive efficiency of Portuguese labour and the inefficiency of British labour in Ricardo's example, we would expect wages to be much higher in Portugal than in England. Under these circumstances, one can expect Portuguese workers to be apprehensive about an agreement to permit trade between the countries — "How can we hope to meet the unfair competition of those underpaid British workers?" British labourers are also likely to be concerned—"How can we hope to meet the competition of those Portuguese, who are so efficient in producing everything?"

The principle of comparative advantage shows us that both fears are unjustified. As we have just seen, when trade is opened up between Portugal and England, workers in *both* countries will be able to earn higher real wages than they did before because of the increased productivity that comes about through specialization.

Figure 13-2 shows this fact directly. We have seen from our illustration that, with trade, England can end up with more wine and more cloth than it had before, and so the living standards of its workers can rise even though they have been left vulnerable to the competition of the super-efficient Portuguese. Portugal can also end up with more wine and more cloth, so the living standards of its workers can rise even though they have been exposed to the competition of cheap British labour. These higher living standards should be reflected in higher real wages earned by workers in both countries. The lesson to be learned here is that nothing helps raise standards of living more than does a greater abundance of goods.

TARIFFS, QUOTAS, AND OTHER INTERFERENCES WITH TRADE

Despite the mutual gains obtainable, international trade has historically been subjected to unrelenting pressure for government interference. In fact, until the rise of a free trade movement in England at the end of the eighteenth and the beginning of the nineteenth centuries (with such economists as Adam Smith and David Ricardo at its vanguard), it was taken for granted that one of the essential tasks of government was the imposition of regulations to impede trade, presumably in the national interest. This view has been extremely durable in Canada, as is made clear in the articles by two Canadian journalists that are reprinted in the following boxed insert (pages 376–77).

Many people take the view that a nation's wealth consists of the amount of gold or other moneys at its command. Consequently, the proper aim of government policy is to do everything it can to promote exports (in order to increase the amount foreigners owe to it) and to discourage imports (in order to decrease the amount the country owes to foreigners).

Obviously, there are limits to carrying out this policy. A country *must* import vital foodstuffs or critical raw materials that it cannot supply for itself; if it does not, it must suffer a severe fall in living standards. Moreover, it is mathematically impossible for *every* country to sell more than it buys—one country's exports must be some other country's imports. If everyone competes in this game and cuts imports to the bone, obviously exports must go the same way. As a result, everyone will be deprived of the mutual gains that trade can provide.

In more recent times, notably in the United States during the first three decades of the twentieth century, there was a return to an active policy to reduce competition from foreign imports. Since then, however, western countries have attempted to promote freedom of trade, and barriers have gradually been reduced, although, during the 1980s, there was some pressure to move back the other way. In the United States, a combination of high unemployment rates and a deterioration of the country's competitive position led to strong political pressures to reduce imports.

Modern governments use three main devices to control trade: tariffs, quotas, and export subsidies. A **tariff** is simply a tax on imports. An importer of wine, for example, may be charged $10 for each barrel of wine it brings into the country. A **quota** is a legal limit on the amount of a good that may be imported. For example, the government might allow no more than 5 million barrels of wine to be imported in a year. In some cases, governments ban the importation of certain goods outright, in effect imposing a quota of zero. An **export subsidy** is a payment by the government to an exporter. By reducing exporters' costs, such subsidies permit them to lower their selling prices and compete more effectively in world trade. Export subsidies are used extensively by some foreign governments to assist their industries—a practice that provokes Canadian manufacturers to complain bitterly about "unfair competition." American manufacturers voice similar complaints about Canadian practices. Since we have more generous government-funded social policies than do the Americans, and since these policies indirectly lower labour costs for Canadian firms, Americans regard programs such as our unemployment insurance scheme and our provincial health plans as export subsidies— that is, as "unfair trade practices."

A TARIFF is a tax on imports.

A QUOTA specifies the maximum amount of a good that is permitted into the country from abroad per unit of time.

An EXPORT SUBSIDY is a payment by the government to exporters to permit them to reduce the selling price of their goods so they can compete more efficiently in foreign markets.

PUBLIC CONTROVERSY

CANADIAN SOVEREIGNTY AND THE TARIFF

Most countries need myths, and Canada is no exception. Our mythology relies heavily on the idea of economic independence. That's why, when trade issues are discussed, we grow exceptionally emotional.

Americans worry about trade only when jobs are threatened. But Canadians believe that a change in trading arrangements can destroy our culture and our way of life.

Many of us learned in school that Sir John A. Macdonald's National Policy of 1878 was the rock on which Canada rested. Without this tariff on manufactured products, we were instructed, there would be no manufacturing in Canada at all, and no reason to have a country.

Thank God our first prime minister, the founder of Canada, was far-sighted enough to erect the tariff wall that made Canada possible. Otherwise, we would all have been Americans.

In the 1940s we learned to sing, in the words of what was then our national anthem, "God Save Our Gracious King," but our history teachers made it clear that it would have been even more appropriate to sing God Save Our Gracious Tariff.

They also taught us to respect—indeed, be profoundly grateful for—the voters of 1911 who saved us from continental economic union. In that epochal election the Liberal prime minister, Sir Wilfrid Laurier, was a free trader and the Conservatives were protectionists. The Conservatives won, and the Liberals' reciprocity treaty with the Americans died.

The line on which the Conservatives rode to victory, "No truck nor trade with the Yankees," is almost the only political slogan from the past that most Canadians can quote. That was, as political scientists now say, a "defining moment" in our history.

There are two crucial points about 1911 that historians only occasionally mention. The first is that the Conservative slogan, if meant at all seriously, was madness. Sharing a continent with the Americans, we would have been foolish indeed if we declined to sell them our products and buy theirs. But trade, even then, was so potent a symbol of nationhood that this obvious truth was buried beneath anti-American and pro-British propaganda.

The other point about 1911 is far more important: it settled nothing. It did not, as our history books told us, and as many journalists and politicians repeated during the controversy of 1988, dictate the course of U.S.–Canada relations. All to the contrary.

After the dust of 1911 settled, Canadians and Americans continued the process of continental economic integration that geography made inevitable. Each year Canada traded a little less with Britain and a little more with the United States. In the 1920s the United States replaced Britain as our main trading partner.

But 1911 did change something: it taught politicians how dangerous the issue was. So they stopped talking about it. Certainly the word "reciprocity" never again emerged from the mouth of a prime minister.

If tariffs had to be lowered, as frequently they did, then this was best accomplished by stealth. Changes were presented as mere technical adjustments, not at all the sort of thing that would interest a voter.

Over the three-quarters of a century separating 1911 from 1988 we grew steadily closer, economically, to the Americans. In 1965 we integrated the auto industries of the two countries in a way that greatly benefited

(continued)

(continued)

Canada, particularly Southern Ontario. Yet we imagined something else was happening, and children—particularly in Ontario—were still taught that our very existence as a nation depended on the tariff.

We lived a kind of fiction, and we cherished this story that we told each other. The more that reality eroded the truth of it, the more committed to it we became. When the General Agreement on Tariffs and Trade made the ancient National Policy impossible as well as obsolete, our belief still remained unshaken.

But no one knew, until the trauma of 1988, how deeply this myth was rooted in the Canadian soul. When the free-trade agreement was first announced, a good many citizens reacted with genuine astonishment as well as shock.

The government was proposing to move forward (and perhaps put on a more rational basis) a process that had been under way since the time of Queen Victoria. But the words "free trade," which Prime Minister Brian Mulroney decided to use in an uncharacteristic moment of frankness, triggered confusion and fear.

The words "sellout" and "treason" suggested the extent to which our sense of patriotism depended on trade barriers that barely existed. It was as if we had been jerked out of a dream. Today we speak of 1911 and 1988 in the same breath, as watershed elections, which no doubt they were. But they were far more important for what they revealed about our mass psychology than for their effect on this continental economy.

Jeffrey Simpson has stressed that the policies of deregulation and free trade have generated a tension among Canadians between their role as consumers and their role as workers.

In the age of huge government deficits and global economic pressures, the role of government in Canada is changing.

Paradoxically, . . . deregulation has both enhanced the choices of all citizens as consumers and increased the apprehensions of some citizens as workers and members of the body politic.

This has led to an increase in the bystander role of government, and a feeling of helplessness among ordinary citizens at the loss of control over their lives.

The greater the sense of helplessness, the greater the demand that government act—and the greater the gap between what governments are asked to do and what they can actually accomplish.

As this gap grows between demand and delivery, so does the public's disillusionment with political leaders, who find themselves trapped between running hugely indebted governments and responding to demands from citizens who already feel themselves overtaxed.

These are among the political consequences of a combination of the shackled world of government and the unshackled corporate world of the global economy.

SOURCE: Robert Fulford, "God Save Our Gracious Tariff," *The Globe and Mail*, September 24, 1992, page C7. Reprinted with the permission of *The Globe and Mail*.

SOURCE: Jeffrey Simpson, "Shackled Government in an Unshackled Corporate World," *The Globe and Mail*, January 22, 1993, page A20. Reprinted with the permission of *The Globe and Mail*.

HOW TARIFFS AND QUOTAS WORK

Both tariffs and quotas restrict supplies coming from abroad and drive up prices. A tariff works by raising prices and hence cutting the demand for imports, while the sequence associated with a quota goes the other way—restriction in supply forces prices up.

Let us use our international trade diagrams to see what a quota does. The supply and demand curves in Figure 13-4 are like those in Figure 13-3. Just as in Figure 13-3, equilibrium in a free international market occurs at a price of $100 per barrel of wine (in both countries). At this price, the exporting country produces 10 million barrels (point *B* in part (a)) and consumes 5 million barrels (point *A*), so that exports are 5 million barrels—distance *AB*. Similarly, the importing country consumes 8 million barrels (point *D* in part (b)) and produces only 3 million (point *C*), so that imports are also 5 million barrels (distance *CD*).

Now suppose the government of the importing nation imposes an import quota of (no more than) 3 million barrels. The free trade equilibrium is no longer possible. Instead, the market must reach equilibrium at a point where both exports and imports are 3 million barrels. As Figure 13-4 indicates, this requires different prices in the two countries.

Imports in part (b) will be 3 million—distance *QT*—only when the price of wine in the importing nation is $110 per barrel, because only at

FIGURE 13-4
QUOTAS AND TARIFFS IN INTERNATIONAL TRADE

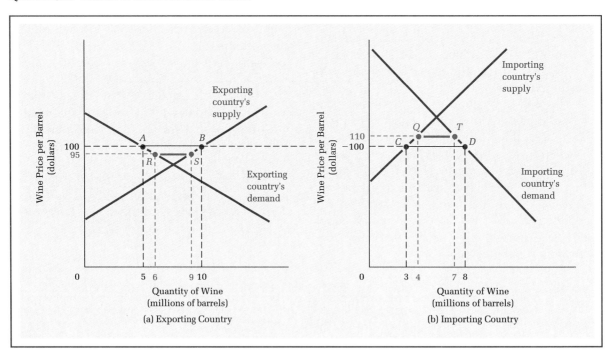

Under free trade, the equilibrium price of wine is $100 per barrel. The exporting country, in part (a), sends *AB*, or 5 million barrels, to the importing country (distance *CD*). If the importing country imposes a quota of 3 million barrels, these two distances must shrink to 3 million barrels. The solution is shown by distance *RS* for exports and distance *QT* for imports. Exports and imports are equal, as must be the case, but the quota forces prices to be unequal in the two countries. Wine sells for $110 per barrel in the importing country but only $95 per barrel in the exporting country. A tariff achieves the same result differently. It *requires* that the prices in the two countries be $15 apart. This, as the graph shows, dictates that exports (= imports) will be equal at 3 million barrels.

this price will quantity demanded exceed domestic quantity supplied by 3 million barrels. Similarly, exports in part (a) will be 3 million barrels —distance *RS*—only when the price in the exporting country is $95 per barrel. At this price, quantity supplied exceeds domestic quantity demanded by 3 million barrels in the exporting country. Thus, the quota raises the price in the importing country to $110 and lowers the price in the exporting country to $95.

An import quota on a product will normally reduce the trade volume of that product, raise its price in the importing country, and reduce its price in the exporting country.

The same restriction of trade can be accomplished through a tariff. In the example we have just completed, a quota of 3 million barrels resulted in a price that was $15 higher in the importing country than in the exporting country ($110 − $95). Suppose that, instead of a quota, the importing nation posts a tariff of $15 per barrel. International trade equilibrium then must satisfy the following two requirements:

1. The price that consumers in the importing country pay for wine must exceed the price that suppliers in the exporting country receive by $15 (the amount of the tariff).

2. The quantity of wine exported must equal the quantity of wine imported.

By consulting the graphs in Figure 13-4, you can see exactly where these two requirements are satisfied. If the exporter produces at *S* and consumes at *R*, while the importer produces at *Q* and consumes at *T*, then exports and imports are equal (at 3 million barrels) and the two domestic prices differ by exactly $15. (They are $100 and $95.) What we have just discovered is a very general result of international trade theory:

Any restriction of imports that is accomplished by a quota can normally also be accomplished by a tariff.

In this case, the tariff corresponding to an import quota of 3 million barrels is $15 per barrel.

TARIFFS VERSUS QUOTAS

Although tariffs and quotas can accomplish the same reduction in international trade and lead to the same domestic prices in the two countries, there are some important differences between the two types of restrictions.

First, under a quota, profits from the price increases in the importing country usually go into the pockets of the foreign and domestic sellers of the product. Because supplies are limited by quotas, customers in the importing country must pay more for the product. Thus, the suppliers, be they foreign or domestic, receive more for every unit they sell. For example, the Canadian quota on imports of Japanese automobiles has raised the profit margins of both Canadian and Japanese automakers.

On the other hand, when trade is restricted by a tariff, the profits from the resulting price increase go to the *government* of the importing country as tax revenues. In effect, the government increases its tax revenues partly at the expense of its citizens and partly at the expense of foreign exporters, who must accept a reduced price because of the resulting decrease in quantity demanded in the importing country. (Domestic producers again benefit, because they are exempt from the tariff.) In this respect, a tariff is certainly a better proposition than a quota from the viewpoint of the country that enacts it.

Another important distinction between the two measures is the difference in their applications for productive efficiency and long-run prices. A tariff handicaps all foreign suppliers equally. It still awards sales to the firms and nations that are most efficient and can therefore supply the goods most cheaply. A quota, on the other hand, necessarily awards its import licences more or less capriciously—perhaps on a first-come, first-served basis; in proportion to past sales; by some other arbitrary standard; or even on the basis of political criteria. There is not the slightest reason to expect the most efficient and least costly suppliers to get the important permits. In the long run, the population of the importing country is likely to end up with significantly higher prices, poorer products, or both.

The Canadian quota on Japanese cars illustrates all of these effects. Japanese automakers responded to the limit on the number of small cars by shipping bigger models equipped with more "optional" equipment. The newer, smaller Japanese automakers—like Subaru—found it difficult to compete in the Canadian market because their quotas were so much smaller than those of Toyota, Nissan, and Honda.

One interesting example that concerns the distribution of revenues created by trade impediments is provided by the dispute that occurred in the late 1980s between Canada and the United States over softwood lumber products. The Americans wanted to raise employment and profits in their lumber industry by making the Canadian products more expensive to buy in the United States. They felt that Canadian softwood lumber was priced "unfairly" low because Canadian provinces did not charge Canadian firms much tax to cut timber on provincial government lands. Interpreting these low taxes as "subsidies" to the Canadian lumber firms, the Americans threatened to place a large tariff on softwood lumber imports. Canada tried to stop this action. But once it was clear that this attempt would fail, Canada gave up and satisfied the Americans by increasing the domestic taxes imposed on producers. The Canadian government decided that since the Canadian producers were going to lose sales (by being forced to charge higher prices south of the border), Canadians—instead of Americans — might just as well collect the extra revenue involved. (This tax was eventually lowered after the Canada–U.S. Free Trade Agreement was signed.)

If trade restrictions must be used, there are two important reasons for preferring tariffs over quotas: (1) some of the resulting financial gains from tariffs go to the government, rather than to foreign and domestic producers; and (2) unlike quotas, tariffs offer no special benefits to inefficient exporters.

WHY INHIBIT TRADE?

To state that tariffs are a better way to inhibit international trade than quotas leaves open a far more basic question: Why limit trade in the first place? There are two primary reasons for adopting measures that restrict trade. First, they may help the importing country get more advantageous prices for its goods, and second, they protect particular industries from foreign competition.

SHIFTING PRICES IN YOUR FAVOUR

How can a tariff make prices more advantageous for the importing country if it raises consumer prices there? The answer is that it forces foreign exporters to sell more cheaply. Because their market is restricted by the tariff, they will be left with unsold goods unless they cut their prices. Suppose, as in Figure 13-4(b), that a $15 tariff on wine raises the price of wine in the importing country represented by the length of the black line, CD to the smaller amount represented by the blue line, QT. To the exporting country, this means an equal reduction in exports (see the change from AB to RS in Figure 13-4(a)).

As a result, the price at which the exporting country can sell its wine is driven down (from $100 to $95 in the example), while producers in the importing country—being exempt from the tariff—can charge $110 per barrel. In effect, such a tariff amounts to government intervention to rig prices in favour of domestic producers and to exploit foreign sellers by forcing them to sell more cheaply than they otherwise would.

This technique works, however, only as long as foreigners accept tariff exploitation passively. They rarely do. Instead, they retaliate, usually by imposing tariffs or quotas of their own on their imports from the country that began the tariff game. This can easily lead to a trade war in which no one gains in terms of more favourable prices and everyone loses in terms of the resulting reductions in overall trade. Something like this happened to the world economy in the 1930s and helped prolong worldwide depression.

Even if there is no retaliation, the tariff or quota can rig prices in favour of domestic producers only if the country imposing the tariff is a significant part of the world demand for that commodity. This requirement is not satisfied in Canada's case. Indeed, we often represent an insignificant portion of world demand for many of our imports. As a result, Canada is essentially in the same position as an individual firm in a perfectly competitive industry. We are a price taker on the world market for our imports.

With this realistic simplification, our analysis of tariffs can be accomplished without the two-part diagram used above. In Figure 13-5, the demand curve and the supply curve of the importing country are shown precisely as they were in Figure 13-4(b). Also, the world supply curve of this commodity (wine) to the small economy is shown as the horizontal line at the price of $100 per barrel. The world supply curve is perfectly elastic at the going world price, since a small country can purchase whatever quantity it desires and have no effect on the world price.

In our example, before any tariff is levied, the country produces 3 million barrels of wine, consumes 8 million barrels, and imports 5 million barrels (as indicated by distance *CD* in Figure 13-5). If world suppliers must pay a tariff of $15 per barrel to sell within this economy, the world supply curve shifts up to the $115 point on the price axis. Just as before, equilibrium requires a gap of $15 per barrel between the going world price and the price of wine in the country that levies the tariff. However, when the importing country is small, its price rises by the *full*

FIGURE 13-5

QUOTAS AND TARIFFS WHEN THE IMPORTING COUNTRY IS SMALL

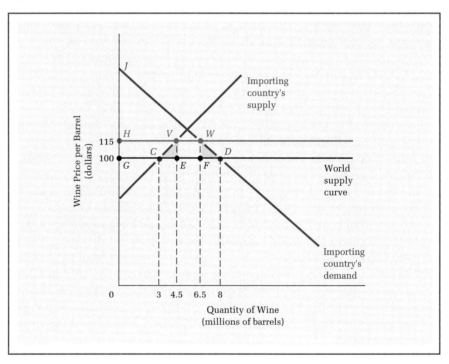

Canada is too small to affect the world price of wine, which is $100 per barrel in this example. Under free trade, Canada produces 3 million barrels, consumes 8 million barrels, and imports 8 − 3 = 5 million barrels (distance *CD*). This amount is an insignificant portion of world production. If a tariff of $15 per barrel is imposed in Canada, our price rises by the full amount, from $100 to $115 per barrel. Price is unaffected in the rest of the world. Domestic production increases to 4.5 million barrels, consumption falls to 6.5 million barrels, and imports fall to 6.5 − 4.5 = 2 million barrels (distance *VW*). Consumer surplus falls by area *GDWH*, the profits of domestic firms rise by *GCVH*, and government revenue rises by *EFWV*. The net losses to the nation as a whole are shown by the areas of the two gold triangles.

amount of the tariff, and the world price is not forced down at all. This is shown in Figure 13-5, since, after the tariff, domestic production increases to 4.5 million barrels, purchases fall to 6.5 million barrels, and imports fall to 2.0 million barrels (given by distance *VW* in the diagram). Our analysis simply verifies the common-sense notion that a small country cannot rig world prices in its favour.

We conclude that ours is too small a country to shift world prices of imports in our favour. Thus, even without considering retaliation, we can state that the price-setting argument for tariffs and quotas is inapplicable to Canada.

We must note, however, that a tariff that fails to rig world prices in our favour not only results in our losing out on a possible benefit, but also causes a greater loss to the nation, which can be calculated as follows. In our wine example, Canadians were consuming 8 million barrels each period before the tariff. Since the demand curve represents the marginal utility schedule for this wine, we know that, in Figure 13-5, the total utility that Canadians derive from the 8 million barrels of wine is the area under this demand curve, up to point *D*. But since Canadians were able to purchase this wine for only $100 per barrel, the amount paid was less than the total utility obtained. The difference is given by area *GDJ*. In Chapter 4 (pages 107–11), we called this free benefit *consumer surplus*. By focussing on this concept here, we can appreciate the costs of a tariff for Canada.

In our example, after the tariff is imposed, Canadians pay $115 per barrel for the decreased quantity of 6.5 million barrels. Consumer surplus is now reduced to area *HWJ*. Thus, the buyers of wine lose area *GDWH* in consumer surplus. Some of this loss is a transfer to domestic firms, and some is a transfer to the government. Domestic firms receive more than they did before the tariff, but their costs have increased as well. The net increase for domestic firms (that is, the increase in their profits) is given by the area *above* their marginal-cost curve (that is, above the domestic supply curve). This is shown by area *GCVH* (the portion of the area between the old and the new price lines that is above the cost curve). The government's revenue is given by area *EFWV* (since the tariff is $15 per barrel times the 2 million barrels imported). The difference between the loss to wine consumers and the gains to domestic producers and the government is the sum of the two triangles that are shown in gold in Figure 13-5. In this example, the sum is $22.5 million. Thus, the nation as a whole loses this amount *in every period* as a result of the tariff.

Incidentally, because economists have estimated the elasticities of demand and supply for most traded commodities, we can estimate the sum of the net-loss triangles for all the commodities for which Canada restricts imports. Using this method, and estimating the benefits following from certain economies of scale, the *annual* gains to Canada of free trade with the United States have been estimated to be an amount equal to about 3 percent of our economy's entire output in one year; that is, 3 percent of our gross domestic product (GDP). These little triangles add up.

PROTECTING PARTICULAR INDUSTRIES

The second and probably more common reason that countries restrict trade is to protect particular industries from foreign competition. If foreigners can produce steel or watches or shoes more cheaply, domestic business and unions in these industries are quick to demand protection, and their government is often reluctant to deny it to them. It is here that the argument regarding cheap foreign labour is most likely to be invoked.

The fact is, however, that firms unable to compete in the market are the ones whose relative inefficiency does not permit them to beat foreign exporters at their own game. In Ricardo's example of comparative advantage, one can well imagine the complaints from Portuguese clothmakers as the opening of trade leads to increased importation of English cloth. At the same time, the English grape growers would likely express equal concern over the flood of imported wine from Portugal. Protective tariffs and quotas are designed to undercut harsh competition coming from abroad, yet it is precisely this competition that gives consumers the benefits of international specialization.

When an industry feels threatened by foreign competition, it usually argues that some form of protection against imports is needed to prevent loss of jobs. But we will see in our discussion of macroeconomics in Part 6 that there are better ways to stimulate employment. Yet it must be admitted that any program that limits foreign competition will, in the short run, preserve jobs in the protected industry. It will work, but often at a very considerable cost to consumers (in the form of higher prices) and to the economy (in the form of inefficient use of resources). For example, several American studies have estimated that tariffs and import quotas cost consumers in the United States about $750 000 for each job saved in the steel industry, $105 000 for each job saved in the automobile industry, $100 000 for each job saved in the book manufacturing industry, and $42 000 for each job saved in the textile industry.[1] Similarly, each job in Canadian agriculture that is preserved by means of such trade restrictions costs our government $100 000.

Nevertheless, union complaints over proposals to reduce a tariff or a quota are justified unless something is done to ease the cost to individual workers of switching to those lines of production that trade has now made profitable.

The argument for free trade between countries cannot be considered airtight if there is no adequate program to assist the minority of citizens in each country who will be harmed whenever patterns of production change drastically, as would happen, for example, if tariff and quota barriers were suddenly brought down.

Owners of wineries in Britain and of textile mills in Portugal might see heavy investments suddenly rendered unprofitable, as would workers

---

1. Gary C. Hufbauer, Diane T. Berliner, and Kimberly Ann Elliott, *Trade Protection in the United States: 31 Case Studies* (Washington, D.C.: Institute for International Economic Studies, 1986), Table 1.2.

who invested in acquiring special skills and training that were no longer marketable. Nor are the costs to displaced workers only monetary. Often, they have to move to new locations as well as to new industries, uprooting their families, losing old friends and neighbours, and so on. That the *majority* of citizens will undoubtedly gain from free trade is no consolation to those who are its victims. To help alleviate this problem, it is often argued that Canada should expand its **trade adjustment assistance** programs to help workers who have lost jobs because of the changing patterns of world trade.

TRADE ADJUSTMENT ASSISTANCE provides special unemployment benefits, loans, retraining programs, or other aid to workers and firms that are harmed by foreign competition.

Sometimes, however, these policies provide too much assistance and actually hinder adjustment when governments simply prop up uneconomic operations through subsidies. A more productive policy in the long run is to let the workers be laid off, then subsidize their retraining and relocation so that they can obtain jobs in other industries that will last — without ongoing government support. There was discussion that this kind of adjustment assistance might be part of the Canada–U.S. Free Trade Agreement signed in 1988, but such policies were not introduced. This fact alone may go a long way toward explaining the unpopularity of the deal.

Some argue that the benefits of free trade are too small to let us afford to pay much adjustment assistance. The following rough calculations suggest that this view is incorrect. To see that even large adjustment costs can be afforded, let's assume that without adjustment assistance, a full 10 percent of workers will be completely unemployed for five years following a free trade agreement. This would result in a decrease in national output of roughly 10 percent for five years.

To calculate the *present value* of this stream of costs, we must have data about the annual growth rate of national output and the average after-tax, net-of-inflation interest rate. A representative value for the average annual growth rate of national output is 2.25 percent. A plausible value for the after-tax real interest rate is 3.25 percent. Using these representative values for this illustration, we can calculate the present value of the costs of a free trade agreement as

$$(0.10) \times \begin{matrix} \text{current} \\ \text{national} \\ \text{output} \end{matrix} \times \left[1 + \frac{1.025}{1.035} + \left(\frac{1.025}{1.035}\right)^2 + \left(\frac{1.025}{1.035}\right)^3 + \left(\frac{1.025}{1.035}\right)^4 \right]$$

The first two terms in this formula represent the one-tenth of national output that is lost in the first year following the free trade deal, because of the layoffs in the declining industries. The four other terms in the summation reflect the fact that we are assuming similar losses in the next four years. The present value of these losses is larger because national output is larger in the future (the formula accounts for this by having the numerator of each subsequent term growing at the compound rate of 2.25 percent). But the present value of these losses is smaller because of the usual discount factor involved in compound interest — the growing denominators in the formula. (For a review of the concept of discounting in present value calculations, see the appendix to this chapter.)

Against these costs, we must compare the benefits of free trade. For this example calculation, we will assume that *no* benefits occur until after the initial five-year period of adjustment. From the sixth year on, we will assume that national output would be 3 percent higher (recall the estimates reported above, in the discussion of the little gold net-benefit triangles). The present value of this stream of benefits can be calculated as

$$(0.03) \times \begin{matrix} \text{current} \\ \text{national} \\ \text{output} \end{matrix} \times \left[\left(\frac{1.025}{1.035}\right)^5 + \dots \left(\frac{1.025}{1.035}\right)^\infty \right]$$

In any one year, these benefits are smaller than the costs that were incurred in any one of the first five years (since 10 percent exceeds 3 percent). But the stream of benefits is an ongoing annuity while the stream of costs lasts only for five years. After working out these formulas, the present value of the *excess* of benefits over cost is

$$\text{Initial national output} \times [(0.3)(98.4) - (0.10)(4.9)]$$
$$= \text{initial national output} \times 2.5$$

What have we learned from this illustrative calculation? Even after we allow for generous compensation (a full 10 percent of national output for five years) for the losers (those who are unemployed for those five years), the rest of the citizens receive a stream of benefits that is equivalent to 2.5 times one whole year's worth of the entire output of the Canadian economy. That's a lot of material welfare that can be put toward health care, education, or anything that is deemed in short supply.

These sorts of calculations convince most economists that we *can* afford to make generous adjustment assistance policies available, and still have significant gains from trade left over.

OTHER ARGUMENTS FOR PROTECTION

NATIONAL DEFENCE AND OTHER NON-ECONOMIC CONSIDERATIONS

There are times when a tariff or some other measure to interfere with trade may be justified on non-economic grounds. If a country considers itself vulnerable to military attack, it may be perfectly rational to keep alive industries whose outputs can be obtained more cheaply abroad but whose supplies might be cut off during an emergency. For example, airplane production by small countries makes sense only on these grounds.

The danger is that many industries, even those with the most peripheral relationship to defence, are likely to invoke this argument on their own behalf. For instance, the U.S. watchmaking industry claimed protection for itself for many years on the grounds that its skilled workers would be invaluable during wartime. Perhaps so, but a technicians' training program probably could have done the job more cheaply and even more effectively by teaching exactly the skills needed for military purposes.

THE INFANT-INDUSTRY ARGUMENT

Another common argument for protectionism is the so-called **infant-industry argument**. Promising new industries often need breathing room to flourish and grow; if we expose these infants to the rigours of international competition too soon, the argument goes, they may never develop to the point of being able to survive on their own in the international marketplace.

The argument, while valid in certain instances, is less defensible than it may at first appear. It makes sense only if the industry's prospective future gains are sufficient to repay the social losses incurred while it is being protected. But if the industry is likely to be so profitable in the future, why doesn't private capital rush in to take advantage of the prospective net profits? The annals of business are full of cases in which a new product or a new firm lost money at first but profited handsomely later. Only where funds are not available for some reason to a particular industry, despite its glowing profit prospects, does the infant-industry argument for protection stand up to scrutiny. Even then, it may make more sense to provide a government loan than to provide trade protection.

It is hard to think of examples where the infant-industry argument applies. But even in cases where it is a legitimate argument, another real danger exists—namely, that the industry might remain in diapers forever. Too often, the time to withdraw the protection awarded to an industry never arrives. The Canadian textile industry comes to mind. In the late 1980s, Canada signed 30 bilateral trade-restraint agreements with foreign textile suppliers—arrangements that would raise every Canadian family's clothing costs by about $60 per year. Afterwards, government officials said that the policy was not designed to shield Canadian industry from imports! Rather, they claimed, the aim was to give more security to the Canadian industry while it modernized—in other words, while it grew up. We must be wary of infant industries that *never* grow up.

STRATEGIC TRADE POLICY

Another argument for protectionism has become popular in recent years. Advocates of this argument agree that free trade for all is the best system. But they point out that we live in an imperfect world in which many nations refuse to play by the rules of the free trade game. Further, they fear that a nation that pursues free trade in a protectionist world is likely to lose out. It therefore makes sense, they argue, to threaten to protect your markets unless other nations agree to open theirs.

Economists have trouble dealing with this argument. While it accepts the superiority of free trade, it argues that threatening protectionism is the best way to establish free trade. Such a strategy might work, but it clearly involves great risks. If threats that Canada will turn protectionist induce other countries to scrap existing protectionist policies, the gamble will have succeeded. But if the gamble fails, the world ends up with even more protection than before. As we have already noted, however, if Canada were to make such threats, they would probably have little effect on other countries, so this is not a compelling argument with regard to Canadian tariffs. For the United States, on the other hand, it could be a worthwhile strategy.

There is a rather obvious analogy here to arms negotiation in the Cold War era. Suppose, for example, that the Americans had threatened to install new missiles unless the Soviets agreed to dismantle some of theirs. If the Soviets had agreed, the world would have been a safer place and everyone would have been better off. But, if they had not, the arms race would have accelerated and everyone would have been worse off. Would the American threat to build new missiles therefore have been a wise or a foolish policy? There is no agreement on this question, so we should not expect agreement on the advisability of using protectionist measures in a strategic way.

TRADE VERSUS THE ENVIRONMENT

Recently, protectionists have argued that free trade agreements limit a country's ability to pursue policies designed to help the environment. For example, Americans are upset by Mexican tuna fishers. Since tuna congregate under shoals of dolphins, the tuna fishers trap many dolphins while catching the tuna. The rules of GATT (the General Agreement on Tariffs and Trade) prevent the United States from blocking tuna imports from Mexico. Environmental groups in the United States obtained a court order forcing their government to impose such an import embargo, but Mexico successfully sought a GATT ruling to lift this embargo. Environmentalists are unimpressed; their list of grievances about free trade are summarized in the boxed insert opposite.

THE DEVELOPMENT OF TRADE POLICY

In the late 1870s, Sir John A. Macdonald devised a policy of high tariffs for Canada with the aim of stimulating the growth of the manufacturing sector. Although the policy was meant to unify the country, it turned out to be divisive: It alienated both the western and the Maritime provinces, which had to share in paying the costs of the high tariffs, even though there was little chance that their own manufacturing industries would develop as a result. By 1890, the average tariff rate in Canada was about 21 percent; a century later, it had dropped to about 5 percent. The average tariff rate declined reasonably steadily throughout the century, although it did increase somewhat during the depression years of the 1930s.

In 1947, Canada was one of 23 countries that signed the General Agreement on Tariffs and Trade (GATT), which established an organization

P U B L I C   C O N T R O V E R S Y

GATT VS ENVIRONMENTALISTS

Environmentalists object to GATT procedures and regulations for a number of reasons:

- Free trade stimulates economic growth and environmentalists feel that growth is bad for the environment.

- Trade agreements limit sovereignty and so limit a country's ability to impose independent pollution standards.

- GATT rules out the possibility of a country imposing import restrictions on another country that has lax environmental standards.

- GATT rules makes it impossible for countries to impose export bans (and environmentalists want their governments to preclude the export to developing countries of pesticides that are prohibited in the developed countries).

- GATT resolves disputes in a fairly secretive fashion, which limits the role environmentalists can take in these proceedings.

GATT officials have responded to some of these complaints. For one thing, they note that GATT rules do allow individual countries to impose whatever environmental standards they want; they only insist that the legislation apply equally to both imports and domestic producers. Another point raised by GATT officials is that growth may not, in fact, be bad for the environment. Evidence shows, for example, that while air pollution in cities rises with national income up to a level of about $5000 per head per year, pollution amounts fall as incomes rise above that level. Since GATT officials think that trade sanctions against poor countries will simply keep them poor, they see sanctions as making it impossible for incomes in the developing countries to grow enough for those individuals to afford to be environmentally conscious.

---

dedicated to arranging for member nations to legislate reductions in tariffs. All observers agree that this co-operation stimulated much world trade and, therefore, employment growth. But the co-operation has been breaking down in recent years.

The earliest exceptions to GATT's rules were made in the areas of agriculture and textiles. Now, trade arrangements for these items, as well as for steel, are handled largely outside GATT. For the textiles trade, for example, Canada is an active participant in the Multi-Fibre Arrangement, a now-permanent feature of international policy involving discriminatory restraints that completely contradict GATT rules. Canada is also involved in many arrangements pertaining to agricultural commodities as well as voluntary export deals pertaining to automobiles that also go beyond GATT.

For an example of how such trade restraints escalate, consider what happened when Spain and Portugal joined the European Community

(EC) in March 1986. These countries were obliged to switch to EC member nations for many of their imports and to bring their own trade restrictions in line with those of other EC countries. For example, Spain had to replace its 20 percent tariff on corn and sorghum with the common EC levy of more than 100 percent. The United States filed a complaint, claiming compensation for its lost exports; when that was denied, the Americans set out to produce a comparable loss of trade by erecting equivalent barriers to EC exports. For more on this problem, see the boxed insert opposite.

In recent years, there have been some signs that trade restrictions on agricultural commodities may once again be negotiated on a worldwide basis, but concrete arrangements have yet to be signed. All western nations now offer their farmers subsidies in an attempt to make them competitive internationally. To this end, as of 1991, some $300 billion was being spent annually by the major western countries, and most of these expenditures served only to cancel out some of the effects of the other countries' subsidies. In 1991, Canadian farmers received 45 percent of their income in the form of subsidies. The subsidy percentages for their counterparts in other countries were the EC (average), 49; Switzerland, 80; the United States, 30; and Japan, 66. Across all the countries involved in the agricultural subsidy wars, the economic losses generated by the resulting inefficiencies are estimated to total $100 billion each year.

During the 1980s, Canada faced new tariffs or quotas imposed by the United States in all of the following areas: sugars and syrups, carbons and certain steel-alloy products, specialty steel products, dried salted codfish, raspberries, hogs and pork, sewer grates and construction castings, cedar shakes and shingles, Atlantic groundfish, gas- and oil-well steel products, salmon and herring fisheries, softwood lumber, carnations, brass sheets and strips, potash, and natural gas. Then, in 1988, the U.S. Congress passed what has become known as the Omnibus Trade Bill, which enshrines in legislative form the American practice of identifying countries that are believed to be restricting imports from the United States. The legislation stipulates that a **countervailing duty** should be applied on the corresponding exports from such countries to the United States. This trade bill had serious repercussions for Canada, since 80 percent of Canadian exports go to the United States.

A **COUNTERVAILING DUTY** is a tariff levied on imports to offset the effects of what are perceived as unrealistically low prices set by producers in the exporting country.

THE CANADA–U.S. FREE TRADE AGREEMENT

THE BENEFITS

The Free Trade Agreement (FTA), which Canada signed with the United States on January 1, 1989, in many ways represents a defensive policy on Canada's part. Since we export more than one-quarter of our national product, and since 80 percent of that trade is with the United States, our economy is vulnerable to fundamental disruption by American protectionist policies. It was hoped that the FTA would safeguard us against such policies.

FURTHER DETAIL

THE TROUBLE WITH REGIONALISM

What is a believer in free trade to make of regional free trade arrangements like the North American Free Trade Agreement?

They are to be welcomed if they serve as a stepping stone to worldwide free trade, and if they create more trade than they divert. But some analysts doubt whether these provisos are always satisfied.

Consider a situation in which a country like Canada was importing an item from Asia before NAFTA. Because it was more efficient in the production of this item, the Asian company was able to keep Mexican companies from entering the Canadian market. Then, after NAFTA comes into effect, Canada has dropped its tariff against Mexico, but not against Asian countries. If Canada ends up importing this item from Mexico, Canadians will be getting the product from a source that is not the most efficient. Instead of the principle of comparative advantage being sup-

ported, it would be denied in this situation. To avoid this outcome, regional free trade arrangements need to be policed by some agency like GATT, to ensure that informal measures that are designed to divert trade in this fashion are not too widespread.

Sceptics concerning regional free trade areas also point out that governments will find it increasingly difficult to resist the arguments of protectionists. The bigger the regional free trade area, the more compelling is the argument that the market is already "big enough" to secure the economies of large scale operations. Since we already can observe that big countries are more inward-looking than small ones, there is probably some truth to this conjecture. As a result, it is possible for a believer in worldwide free trade to be against particular regional free trade deals.

A second rationale for the FTA was Canada's need for secure access to a larger market, which would justify longer production runs and provide the gains in productive efficiency that come only with the increased degree of specialization facilitated by large-scale operations. How could Canadian producers, who were supplying a large variety of products for a domestic market of fewer than 28 million people, hope to compete with the United States, Japan, and the EC, with their much larger domestic (and therefore tariff-free) markets? (The EC, for example, represents a combined domestic market of over 320 million people.) A similar reaction to the problems created by small domestic markets is evident among the six countries that constitute the European Free Trade Association (EFTA) — Austria, Finland, Iceland, Norway, Sweden, and Switzerland. This group, with a combined population only one-tenth that of the EC, has never been part of the EC; rather, it has long been the EC's largest single trading partner (just as Canada has been in relation to the United States). The EFTA countries are now arranging for membership within the EC.

To gain full free access to one of the world's largest markets, Canada has had to accept the costs of cutting its own tariffs—namely, the important adjustment costs that must be paid by formerly protected workers and firms. Conversely, however, benefits come to Canadians from the Americans' cutting their tariffs on *our* exports. As we noted earlier, these benefits flow from three sources—comparative advantage, the increased specialization resulting from larger-scale operations, and lower monopoly markups—and have been estimated to equal about 3 percent of GDP every year. This ongoing flow of benefits is what Canada would have thrown away had we not signed the FTA.

The largest share of these estimated benefits is expected to come from the cost reductions that accompany large-scale production. For these gains to materialize, however, firms operating within Canada must make major investments to reorient their operations. Some critics of the FTA doubt that sufficient investment will occur, because, even with the FTA, such investments are risky: Because either side can abrogate the agreement with only six months' notice, large investments in plant and equipment in Canada could suddenly become worth very little. However, the threat of possible abrogation seems to have waned over time, and the necessary investment expenditures will probably be forthcoming.

Some evidence is already in, as this book goes to press. In the 1989–92 period, 19 of the 22 industry groups in Statistics Canada data registered an increase in their share of the U.S. market. Exports to the United States of those goods that have involved tariff reductions have increased by 16 percent, while exports of those same goods to other countries have not increased. No other G7 country has matched Canada's increase in export sales to the United States since 1989. It is true that many jobs were lost in our manufacturing industries during the 1989–92 period. But there were other causes for many of these job losses, including a worldwide recession and a high value for the Canadian dollar. (We discuss Canada's exchange-rate policy, and how it complicated life for Canadian exporters in the early years of the FTA, in Chapter 28). Opponents of free trade like to blame all the job losses on the FTA. But this cannot be right. After all, California has an economy that is slightly larger than Canada's. California did not enter any new trade deal with the rest of the United States in 1989 and it lost many more manufacturing jobs than did Canada during the 1989–92 period. Major restructuring is proceeding throughout the world.

THE COSTS

Let us now consider some of the costs that must be incurred to acquire the higher standard of living that free trade promises. Critics often raise the concern that the FTA will strip Canada's exports down to raw materials alone because, they argue, our manufacturing and processing industries will be forced to contract as a result of free trade. Two responses to this concern are in order. First, if our comparative advantage is in the area of natural resources, why would we wish to have lower incomes just to keep factory jobs? Second, we must remember that the FTA removes both Canadian *and* American tariffs. Thus, while the removal of our tariffs does hurt some Canadian manufacturers, the removal of U.S. tariffs helps other Canadian manufacturers. In other words, it is not at all clear that, on balance, our manufacturing industries will have to contract. Indeed, many firms in southern Ontario, for example, are better situated to serve the important markets in the northeastern United States than are many U.S. manufacturers.

As noted above, during the first years after the FTA was signed, it seemed that every plant closure in Canada was blamed on free trade. It is important to remember, however, that job losses make news stories, while new investments by manufacturing firms tend to be ignored. This imbalance in media coverage is due in part to the fact that it takes longer to expand a plant or to build a new one that it does to close one. It should also be recognized that Canada's job losses in the early 1990s were due largely to the recession. This recession was caused by a slowdown in the United States, as well as by the record-high levels of both real interest rates and the Canadian dollar that prevailed during that period. Since the unemployment rate rose by no more than the amount one would expect in a recession of this magnitude, its rise cannot reasonably be attributed to the FTA. In other words, if free trade caused job losses, it must have been generating a similar number of new jobs at the same time. Otherwise, the unemployment rate would have to have been significantly higher.

Another issue of concern regarding the FTA is adjustment costs: Critics stress how painful it is for workers to shift from industries that decline as a result of free trade to those that promise to expand. These costs are real, and there is no question that affected workers should receive assistance. Nonetheless, the magnitude of adjustment costs is often exaggerated. The FTA is being phased in gradually over ten years, and much of the necessary adjustment may well occur as part of the ongoing pattern of job changing that is already taking place. Many people are surprised to learn that, on average, almost one out of every five Canadian workers changes jobs every year. Also, it is interesting to note how quickly the adjustments took place when other free trade areas were created. The Treaty of Rome created the European Economic Community in 1958; two years later, those involved were so pleased with the low level of actual adjustment costs that the plan's implementation speed was tripled.

HOW ARE DISPUTES SETTLED?

A third criticism of the FTA is that it could lead to a loss in the degree of Canada's political independence, in that our domestic policies could be sacrificed for the survival of the agreement. Critics fear, for example, that if a domestic policy were deemed by the United States to constitute an "unfair subsidy," our government might be compelled to alter the policy. It is difficult to respond to this concern, since we do not yet know how the so-called unfair subsidies (which must be assumed to exist within both countries) will be formally defined. (The agreement requires that a clear definition be established by 1996). We must also bear in mind that American countervailing duties had forced Canada to alter domestic policies even before the FTA was signed (recall our example of softwood lumber on page 380). If the dispute-settlement mechanism that is finally negotiated by the two countries actually lessens the United States' ability to impose its protectionist desires on Canada, we will have gained some independence. But many expect that it may in fact provide the Americans with a greater power to dictate which domestic policies within Canada are or are not acceptable to them.

Some analysts also expect pressure for an erosion of Canada's social and medical assistance programs, which are more comprehensive, and therefore more expensive, than their counterparts in the United States. The argument is that increased competition with American firms, which pay much less to help finance such programs than do Canadian firms, will cause Canadian firms to lobby for a reduction in the amounts that are collected from them. Thus, according to this argument, our social programs could be forced down to the level of those in the United States. But historical evidence does not seem to support this argument. After all, most of our social programs were developed during the years when our tariffs were being significantly *reduced*. Furthermore, there is a notice-able range in the scope of social programs across the different states south of the border (and, from the perspective of the individual states, their own country is in effect a free trade area). Similarly, there are significant differences among the social policies of various countries within the EC.

Nonetheless, as we noted earlier, the dispute-settlement mechanism associated with the FTA will remain unsatisfactory until a sensible def-inition of unfair trade practices is developed. (The existing dispute-set-tlement scheme requires only that each country satisfy an independent five-person tribunal that its *own* existing trade laws are being applied properly). Furthermore, our bargaining power in the dispute-settlement negotiations is admittedly small, given the much larger size of our partner in these negotiations. Also, unlike member countries of the EC, we have no other small partners to whom we can appeal for support. Indeed, our bargaining power could shrink even further over time, because the more resources our industries invest in their adjustment to free trade, the more costly the consequences of abrogation will be for the country. Again, although the same principle would hold for the United States, the relative impact of the costs involved would be much smaller because the U.S. economy is so much larger than ours.

Despite these concerns, it is noteworthy that at the time of writing this text (spring 1993), Canada has won *all* disputes taken to the panels that are part of the existing FTA. For example, the ruling on wheat in February 1993 went in Canada's favour despite the fact that Americans made up the majority of the panel. Clearly, when Canada has a good case, we can win, so the FTA *does* limit the Americans' ability to pursue trade policies that would be detrimental to Canada.

NAFTA

In 1992, the executive branches of the Canadian, American, and Mexican governments signed an agreement for a three-country free trade area. As this book goes to press, the Canadian Parliament has passed NAFTA, but the legislatures of the other two countries have not yet done so. The debate has already involved the "cheap foreign labour" argument. Indeed, wages for many Mexican workers are ten times lower than Canadian wages. But it is important to note that 85 percent of Mexican exports to Canada enter tariff-free already (and the rest bear an average tariff of only 10 percent). If wage differentials were all that mattered, firms should have already moved to Mexico long ago. Clearly, productivity differences matter too, as does the availability of raw materials. Since Canada has many raw materials, an effective policy is to invest in the education and skills of our workforce, so that firms continue to see Canada as a good place to invest despite high wages. Ultimately, goods, machines, and raw materials are all tradable. The least mobile item internationally seems to be labour, since most people develop an allegiance to the area where they have lived. Thus, of all the investments a country can make, an investment in the skills of its population stands the least chance of being devalued by developments in other countries.

THE ETHICS OF COMPETITION

Proponents of the FTA are frustrated by the fact that many Canadians see the issue as one that pits materialism against moral justice. For example, in 1988, Canada's major Christian churches submitted a joint statement to the parliamentary committee that was considering the FTA. This statement claimed that free trade was "morally unacceptable" because it would "require a number of human sacrifices on the altar of the almighty dollar." Many economists, concerned with the alarming extent of poverty in the less developed countries, disagree. They see the development of free trade throughout the world as the only possible hope for limiting human suffering in those countries. Foreign-aid programs have proved not to be a viable option, because they typically have so many strings attached that the receiving nations are kept in a position of dependence. The experience of the newly industrialized countries in Asia (such as Taiwan and Korea) shows that foreign trade can lead to a vast reduction in poverty, *without* creating an ongoing relationship of dependence. Hence, it seems that if one is genuinely concerned about worldwide poverty, there is no better option than to support freer trade.

WHAT IMPORT PRICES BENEFIT A COUNTRY?

One of the most curious features of the protectionist position is the fear of low prices charged by foreign sellers. Countries that subsidize exports are accused of **dumping**—of getting rid of their goods at unconscionably

DUMPING means selling goods in a foreign market at lower prices than those charged in the home market.

PUBLIC CONTROVERSY

UNFAIR FOREIGN COMPETITION

Satire and ridicule are often more persuasive than logic and statistics. Exasperated by the spread of protectionism to so many industries under the prevailing Mercantilist philosophy, French economist Frédéric Bastiat decided to take the protectionist argument to its logical conclusion. His fictitious petition of the French candlemakers to the Chamber of Deputies, written in 1845 and excerpted below, has become a classic in the battle for free trade.

We are subject to the intolerable competition of a foreign rival, who enjoys, it would seem, such superior facilities for the production of light, that he is enabled to *inundate* our *national market* at so exceedingly reduced a price, that, the moment he makes his appearance, he draws off all custom for us; and thus an important branch of French industry, with all its innumerable ramifications, is suddenly reduced to a state of complete stagnation. This rival is no other than the sun.

Our petition is, that it would please your honorable body to pass a law whereby shall be directed the shutting up of all windows, dormers, skylights, shutters, curtains, in a word, all openings, holes, chinks, and fissures through which the light of the sun is used to penetrate our dwellings, to the prejudice of the profitable manufactures which we flatter ourselves we have been enabled to bestow upon the country. . . .

We foresee your objections, gentlemen; but there is not one that you can oppose to us . . . which is not equally opposed to your own practice and the principle which guides your policy. . . .

Labor and nature concur in different proportions, according to country and climate, in every article of production. . . . If a Lisbon orange can be sold at half the price of a Parisian one, it is because a natural and gratuitous heat does for the one what the other only obtains from an artificial and consequently expensive one. . . .

Does it not argue the greatest inconsistency to check as you do the importation of coal, iron, cheese, and goods of foreign manufacture, merely because and even in proportion as their price approaches *zero*, while at the same time you freely admit, and without limitation, the light of the sun, whose price is during the whole day at *zero*?

SOURCE: F. Bastiat, *Economic Sophisms* (New York: G.P. Putnam's Sons, 1922).

Within our economy, people usually rejoice when competition leads one company to sell a product at a price below its competitors'. No one wants laws to preclude this. But in the field of international trade, such beneficial outcomes for consumers are ruled out by anti-dumping laws, since selling goods more cheaply to foreigners is known as "dumping." A recent editorial in The Globe and Mail *used satire in an attempt to awaken Canadians to the folly involved.*

Time to Dump the Anti-Dumping Laws

Anti-dumping law is a kind of reverse Zellers policy: where the highest price is the law. If domestic producers, responding to sluggish demand, want to lower their prices, they can. Foreign competitors, however, are not allowed to match them — not if that means charging less than they do back home. The second definition, selling below cost, is

(continued)

(continued)

applied just as unevenly: one man's dumping is another man's loss leader. If these are such crimes, you'd think it would not matter who committed them. The premise behind the ban on dumping is that otherwise benign business practices mysteriously turn harmful when carried out by foreigners.

This is nutty enough on its own. It's double-nuts for two countries sharing a free trade area, and triple-nuts in as continentally integrated an industry as steel. That both countries should be suing each other for dumping at the same time only confirms the absurdity. Apparently, each country's industry is selling steel for less than the other. We are living in an M.C. Escher print. So each countries' consumers will now pay to make steel more expensive in either country than it is in the other.

SOURCE: Editorial, *The Globe and Mail*, January 30, 1993, page D6. Reprinted with the permission of *The Globe and Mail*.

low prices. For example, the Americans accused the Canadian steel industry of dumping in 1993 (see the accompanying boxed insert).

A moment's thought should indicate why this fear must be considered curious. As a nation of consumers, we should be indignant when foreigners charge us *high* prices, not low ones. That is the common-sense rule that guides every consumer, and the consumers of imported commodities should be no exception. Only from the topsy-turvy viewpoint of an industry seeking protection from competition are high prices seen as being in the public interest.

Ultimately, it must be in the best interest of a country to get its imports as cheaply as possible. It would be ideal for Canada if the rest of the world were willing to provide its exports to us free or virtually free. We could then live in luxury at the expense of the rest of the world.

The notion that low import prices are bad for a country is a fitting companion to the idea—so often heard—that it is good for a country to export much more than it imports. True, this means that foreigners will end up owing us a good deal of money. But it also means that we will have given them large quantities of our products and have received relatively little in foreign products in return. That surely is not an ideal way for a country to reap gains from international trade.

Our gains from trade do not consist of accumulations of gold or of heavy debts owed us by foreigners. Rather, our gains are composed of the goods and services that others provide minus the goods and services we must provide them in return.

The preceding discussion should indicate the fundamental fallacy in the argument that Canadian workers have to fear cheap foreign labour. If workers in other countries are willing to supply their products to us with little compensation, this must ultimately *raise* the standard of living of the average Canadian worker. As long as the government's monetary and fiscal policies succeed in maintaining high levels of employment at home, how can we lose by getting the products of the world at bargain prices?

There are, however, some important qualifications to this prognosis. First, our employment policy may not be effective. If Canadian workers who are displaced by foreign competition cannot find jobs in other industries, they will indeed suffer from international trade. But that is a shortcoming of the government's employment program, not of its international trade policies.

Second, we have noted that an abrupt stiffening of foreign competition, resulting, say, from a major innovation in another country or from a discovery of a new and better source of raw materials or from a sharp increase in export subsidies by a foreign country, *can* hurt Canadian workers by not giving them an adequate chance to adapt gradually to the new conditions. The more rapid the change, the more painful it will be. If change occurs fairly gradually, workers can retrain and move on to the industries that now require their services. If the change is even more gradual, no one may have to move. People who retire or leave the threatened industry for other reasons simply need not be replaced. But competition that inflicts its damage overnight is certain to impose very real costs on the affected workers, costs that are no less painful for being temporary.

But these are, after all, minor qualifications to an overwhelming argument. They call for intelligent monetary and fiscal policies and for transitional assistance to unemployed workers, not for abandonment of free trade and permission for monopoly power to flourish behind protection.

In the long run, labour will be "cheap" only where it is not very productive. Wages will tend to be highest in those countries in which high labour productivity keeps costs down and permits exporters to compete effectively despite high wages.

We note that in this matter it is absolute advantage, not comparative advantage, that counts. The country that is most efficient in every output can pay its workers more in every industry.

We started this chapter by noting that tariff cuts involve both benefits and costs. The benefits are that consumers acquire goods at lower prices and that the anticompetitive behaviour of firms can be limited without having to rely on regulations and attempted prosecutions. (These methods, which are used in an attempt to enforce competition policy, have met with quite limited success, as we explain in Chapter 16.) The costs of tariff cuts are the jobs that many expect would be lost to cheap foreign labour. This chapter has shown that these costs are very much exaggerated in popular discussion. This is because the principle of comparative advantage is not generally appreciated and because the problems associated with increased competition can be better solved by appropriate monetary, fiscal, and adjustment assistance policies.

MICROECONOMIC POLICY: A REVIEW AND A PREVIEW

THE PROPER ASSIGNMENT OF POLICIES TO GOALS

At many points throughout this book, we have stressed the unfortunate trade-off between two of the fundamental goals of economic policy: efficiency and equality. Indeed, this trade-off is one of our twelve Ideas for Beyond the Final Exam. It is useful at this stage to generalize the discussion of policy goals and instruments, in order to clarify how the terms of this trade-off can be kept as appealing as possible. After all, would it not be desirable to sacrifice as little efficiency as possible in our pursuit of equity—that is, of greater economic equality?

To start, let us group our major economic policy goals into three main categories:

Goal 1: Efficiency.   To achieve a high level of average income.

Goal 2: Equality.   To redistribute some income from the rich to the poor.

Goal 3: Stabilization.   To minimize the swings in unemployment and inflation caused by variations in the level of national output.

Once again, to facilitate our discussion, let us group into three broad categories the many policies that the government can either adopt or reject in its pursuit of our economic goals:

Policy A: Market Controls.   For example, tariffs, quotas, minimum-wage laws.

Policy B: An Egalitarian Tax/Transfer System.   A general income tax with significant tax relief for low-income earners and very few tax shelters for the rich.

Policy C: Macroeconomic and Adjustment-Assistance Policies.   For example, temporary variations in government spending, taxes, and the money supply or the exchange rate to limit recessions and inflationary periods; and the legislation of ongoing stabilizers, such as unemployment insurance and grants for retraining and relocation.

Our fundamental objective is to assign policy instruments to goals in a way that minimizes the trade-offs involved. Most economists are convinced that the optimal assignment is to pair

- Goal 1 with the rejection of Policy A;
- Goal 2 with the adoption of Policy B;
- Goal 3 with the adoption of Policy C.

In more specific terms, this assignment calls for rejecting market controls, such as tariffs, on the grounds that they impair the efficiency of the market system, which works well only when the necessary decentralized market signals are allowed to operate. If the goal of efficiency is not pursued, average income is lowered. As far as our objective of equality is concerned, we should redistribute income in ways that involve the fewest possible disincentive effects. For example, welfare programs that encourage people not to work (and therefore prevent them from acquiring skills through experience—see Chapter 15) and minimum-wage laws (which increase the unemployment rate for unskilled workers) are undesirable since they *lower* the overall level of income in the course of attempting to redistribute it. This is the rationale for pairing Goal 2 with the adoption of Policy B. It is true that our pursuit of efficiency can lead to more inequality if we accomplish that efficient outcome by rejecting such measures as tariffs and minimum-wage laws. But we can make up for this reduction in equality more effectively by having our general income tax system redistribute more income from the rich to the poor than by giving up the benefits of, for example, free trade indefinitely. In short, the adoption of Policy B has a comparative advantage in achieving the goal of equity, while the rejection of Policy A has a comparative advantage in achieving the goal of efficiency. If we assign policies to goals improperly —for example, by trying to use market controls for income redistribution and a plethora of taxes and subsidies to guide the allocation of resources —we end up scoring lower with respect to *both* equity and efficiency objectives.

A similar argument can help to explain why our stabilization objectives should be pursued through macroeconomic policy adjustment and the use of policies that increase labour mobility. For example, if we are attempting to relieve unemployment, it makes no sense to use a *permanent* tariff, which imposes permanent losses on all citizens, just to avoid a *temporary* disruption, which could be addressed with a more appropriate set of policy instruments.

Many individuals argue for the use of market controls to pursue both equity and stabilization objectives (Goals B and C). These individuals seem to regard economic efficiency (Goal A) as not particularly important. (The prevalence of the argument that free trade is bad because it involves some job losses attests to the popularity of this point of view.) Economists have two general responses to such arguments: First, if society has three broad goals in the economic arena, and three independent classes of policy options, it is counterproductive not to use all three kinds of policies in a co-ordinated way. To do otherwise—for example, to try to achieve more than one goal with only one policy instrument—will tend to maximize the trade-offs that we have to face. Second, much evidence suggests that the issue of efficiency matters more than many people think it does. As we shall see in Chapter 15, our gradual progress in reducing poverty in Canada was halted during the 1980s by a major recession. It is a simple fact of history that most people are unwilling to participate in a redistribution of income toward the poor if their own incomes are not showing signs of growth. In short, if we care about equality, we cannot afford not to care about efficiency.

SUMMARY

1. Countries trade because differences in their natural resources and other inputs create discrepancies in the efficiency with which they can produce different goods, and because specialization may offer them greater economies of large-scale production.

2. Voluntary trade will generally be advantageous to both parties in an exchange. This is one of our twelve Ideas for Beyond the Final Exam.

3. International trade is more complicated that trade within a nation because of political factors, different national currencies, and impediments to the movement of labour and capital across national borders.

4. Both countries will gain from trade if each one exports goods in which it has a comparative advantage. That is, even a country that is generally inefficient will benefit by exporting goods in the production of which it is least inefficient. This is another of the twelve Ideas for Beyond the Final Exam.

5. When countries specialize and trade, each can enjoy consumption possibilities that exceed its production possibilities.

6. The prices of goods traded between countries are determined by supply and demand, but one must consider explicitly the demand curve and the supply curve of *each* country involved. Thus, in international trade, the equilibrium price must occur where the excess of the exporting country's quantity supplied over its domestic quantity demanded is equal to the excess of the import-

ing country's quantity demanded over its quantity supplied.

7. The "cheap foreign labour" argument ignores the principle of comparative advantage, which shows that real wages can rise in both the importing and the exporting country as a result of specialization.

8. Tariffs and quotas are designed to protect a country's industries from foreign competition. Such protection may sometimes be advantageous to that country, but not if foreign countries adopt tariffs and quotas of their own as a means of retaliation, and not if the country constitutes a small share of the world market.

9. While a tariff and a quota can accomplish the same restriction of trade, tariffs offer at least two advantages to the country that imposes them: (1) some of the gains go to the government rather than to foreign producers, and (2) there is greater incentive for efficient production.

10. When a nation shifts from protection to free trade, some industries and their workers will lose out. Equity demands that these people and firms be compensated in some way. Adjustment assistance programs (rather than the rejection of free trade) offer the optimal solution to this problem.

11. Several arguments for protectionism, under the right circumstances, have some validity. These include the national-defence argument, the infant-industry argument, and the strategic-trade-policy argument. Unfortu-

nately, each of these rationales is frequently abused.

12. Since a reduction in tariffs is beneficial even if domestic industries are competitive (as illustrated by the principle of competitive advantage), it is doubly appealing if domestic industries are noncompetitive. Thus, tariff cuts represent a significant element in a country's competition policy.

13. Canada's Free Trade Agreement (FTA) with the United States is predicted to raise our average income level by an estimated 3 percent on an ongoing basis. Some studies forecast greater gains; others estimate smaller ones. This uncertainty exists because it is still unclear whether Canada will gain secure and full access to U.S. markets. An accurate assessment will be possible only when a definition of what constitutes an "unfair subsidy" has been agreed upon by the two countries.

14. We have three broad goals in economics— efficiency, equality, and stabilization. If we do not properly assign the three available policy instruments to these three goals, we are likely to face very severe trade-offs. Experience shows that the trade-offs are minimized when market controls such as tariffs are rejected as a means of promoting efficiency, and when the general income tax system is used to achieve the desired degree of economic equality. Finally, macroeconomic and labour mobility policies should be used to counter any short-term unemployment problems that may arise as a result of the removal of market controls.

CONCEPTS FOR REVIEW

Imports	Comparative advantage	Export subsidy
Exports	"Cheap foreign labour"	Trade adjustment assistance
Specialization	argument	Infant-industry argument
Mutual gains from trade	Tariff	Countervailing duty
Absolute advantage	Quota	Dumping

QUESTIONS FOR DISCUSSION

1. Country A has mild weather and plenty of rain, plentiful land, and an unskilled labour force. What sorts of products do you think it is likely to produce? What are the characteristics of countries with which you would expect it to trade?

2. In the eighteenth century, some writers argued that one party in a trade could be made better off only by gaining at the expense of the other. Explain the fallacy in this argument.

3. Upon removal of a quota on semiconductors, a Canadian manufacturer of semiconductors goes bankrupt. Discuss the pros and cons of the quota removal in the short run and in the long run.

4. The following table describes the number of red socks and the number of white socks that can be produced with an hour of labour in two different cities:

	In Boston	In Chicago
Red socks (pairs)	3	2
White socks (pairs)	3	1

    a. If there is no trade, what is the price of white socks relative to red socks in Boston?

    b. If there is no trade, what is the price of white socks relative to red socks in Chicago?

    c. Suppose each city has 1000 hours of labour available per year. Draw the production possibilities frontier for each city.

    d. Which city has an absolute advantage in the production of which good(s)? Which city has a comparative advantage in the production of which good(s)?

    e. If the cities start trading with each other, which city will specialize in, and export, which good?

    f. What can be said about the prices at which trade will take place?

5. Suppose that Canada and Mexico are the only two countries in the world. In Canada, a worker can produce 12 bushels of wheat *or* 1 barrel of oil a day. In Mexico, a worker can produce 2 bushels of wheat *or* 2 barrels of oil a day.

    a. What will be the price ratio between the two commodities (that is, the price of oil in terms of wheat) in each country if there is no trade?

    b. If free trade is allowed and there are no transportation costs, what commodity would Canada import? What about Mexico?

    c. In what range will the price ratio have to fall under free trade? Why?

    d. Picking one possible post-trade price ratio, show clearly how it is possible for both countries to benefit from free trade.

6. The table below presents the demand and supply curves for microcomputers in Japan and Canada.

    a. Draw the demand and supply curves for Canada on one diagram and those for Japan on another one.

    b. If there is no trade between Canada and Japan, what are the equilibrium price and quantity in the computer market in Canada? In Japan?

    c. Now suppose trade is opened up between the two countries. What will be the equilibrium price of computers in the world market? What has happened to the price of computers in Canada? In Japan?

    d. Which country will export computers? How many?

    e. When trade opens up, what happens to the quantity of computers produced, and therefore to employment, in the computer industry in Canada? In Japan? Who benefits and who loses *initially* from free trade?

Price per Computer (thousands of dollars)	Quantity Demanded in Canada (thousands)	Quantity Supplied in Canada (thousands)	Quantity Demanded in Japan (thousands)	Quantity Supplied in Japan (thousands)
0	100	0	100	0
1	90	10	90	25
2	80	20	80	50
3	70	30	70	70
4	60	40	60	80
5	50	50	50	90
6	40	60	40	100
7	30	70	30	110
8	20	80	20	120
9	10	90	10	130
10	0	100	0	140

7. Under current trade law, the president of the United States must report periodically to Congress on countries engaging in unfair trade practices that inhibit U.S. exports. How would you define an "unfair" trade practice? Suppose that Canada exported much more to the United States than it imported from that country, year after year. Would that constitute evidence that Canada's trade practices were unfair? What would constitute such evidence?

8. Suppose the United States finds Canada guilty of unfair trade practices and penalizes it with import quotas, so that Canada's exports to the United States fall. Further, suppose that Canada does not alter its trade practices in any way. Is the United States better or worse off? What about Canada?

APPENDIX TO CHAPTER 13

DISCOUNTING AND PRESENT VALUE

Frequently, in business and economic problems, it is necessary to compare sums of money received (or paid) at different dates. Consider, for example, the purchase of a machine that costs $11 000 and will yield a revenue of $14 520 two years from today. If the machine can be financed by a two-year loan bearing 10 percent interest, it will cost the firm $2200 in interest payments and $11 000 in principal repayment by the end of the second year (see the table below). Is the machine a good investment?

COSTS AND BENEFITS OF INVESTING IN A MACHINE

	End of Year 1	End of Year 2
Benefits		
Revenue derived from the machine	0	$14 520
Costs		
Interest	$1100	1 100
Repayment of principal on loan	0	11 000
Total	$1100	$12 100

The total costs of owning the machine over the two-year period ($1100 + $12 100 = $13 200) are less than the total benefits ($14 520). But this is clearly an invalid comparison, because the $14 520 in future benefits is not worth $14 520 in terms of today's money. Adding up dollars received (or paid) at different dates is a bit like adding apples and oranges. The process that has been invented for making these magnitudes comparable is called **discount-**ing, or **computing the present value** of a future sum of money.

To illustrate the concept of present value, let us ask how much $1 received a year from today is worth in terms of today's money. If the rate of interest is 10 percent, the answer is about 91¢. Why? Because if we invest 91¢ today at 10 percent interest, it will grow to 91¢ plus 9.1¢ in interest = 100.1¢ in a year. Similar considerations apply to any rate of interest.

If the rate of interest is i, the present value of $1 to be received in a year is

$$\frac{\$1}{(1 + i)}$$

This is so because in a year $\frac{\$1}{(1 + i)}$ will grow to

$$\frac{\$1}{(1 + i)} (1 + i) = \$1$$

What about money to be received two years from today? Using the same reasoning, $1 invested today will grow to $1 × (1.1) = $1.10 after one year and to $1 × (1.1) × (1.1) = $1 × $(1.1)^2$ = $1.21 after two years. Consequently, the present value of $1 to be received two years from today is

$$\frac{\$1}{(1.1)^2} = \frac{\$1}{1.21} = 82.64¢$$

A similar analysis applies to money received three years from today, four years from today, and so on.

The general formula for the present value of $1 to be received N years from today when the rate of interest is i is

$$\frac{\$1}{(1 + i)^N}$$

The present-value formula highlights the two variables that determine the present value of any future flow of money: the rate of interest (i) and how long you have to wait before you get it (N). Clearly, the higher the interest rate, the smaller the present value of any future sum. Often when firms invest in a machine, most of the costs are incurred immediately, while most of the revenues arrive well into the future. Thus, the higher the interest rate, the more likely it is that the present value of the revenue will not exceed the cost of the machine, and so overall investment spending by firms will be less. This inverse dependence of investment spending on the level of interest rates has been emphasized in the text.

Let us apply this analysis to the specific example that we used to start this appendix. The present value of the revenue is easy to calculate since it all comes two years from today. Since the rate of interest is assumed to be 10 percent ($i = 0.1$), we have the following:

$$\begin{aligned}
\text{Present value of revenues} &= \frac{\$14\,520}{(1.1)^2} \\
&= \frac{\$14\,520}{1.21} \\
&= \$12\,000
\end{aligned}$$

The present value of the costs is a bit trickier in this example, since they occur at two different dates. The present value of the first interest payment is

$$\frac{\$1100}{(1 + i)} = \frac{\$1100}{1.1} = \$1000$$

The present value of the final payment of interest plus principal is

$$\frac{\$12\,100}{(1 + i)^2} = \frac{\$12\,100}{(1.1)^2} = \frac{\$12\,100}{1.21} = \$10\,000$$

Now that we have expressed each sum in terms of its present value, it is permissible to add them up. Thus, the present value of all costs is

$$\begin{aligned}
\text{Present value of costs} &= \$1000 + \$10\,000 \\
&= \$11\,000
\end{aligned}$$

Comparing this to the $12 000 present value of the revenues clearly shows that the machine is a good investment. This same calculation procedure is applicable to all investment decisions.

SUMMARY

To determine whether a loss or a gain will result from a decision whose costs and returns will come at several different periods of time, the figures represented by these gains and losses must all be discounted to obtain their present value. For this, one uses the present value formula for X dollars receivable N years from now:

$$\text{Present value} = \frac{X}{(1 + i)^N}$$

One then adds together the present values of all the returns and all the costs. If the sum of the present values of the returns is greater than the sum of the present values of the costs, the decision to invest will promise a net gain.

CONCEPTS FOR REVIEW

Discounting   Present value

QUESTIONS FOR DISCUSSION

1. Compute the present value of $1000 to be received in four years if the rate of interest if 15 percent.

2. A government bond pays $100 in interest each year for three years and also returns the principal of $1000 in the third year. How much is it worth in terms of today's money if the rate of interest is 10 percent? If the rate of interest is 15 percent?

PART 4

MICROECONOMIC ISSUES

In our study of microeconomics thus far, we have stressed the concept of efficiency. We have seen that various policies such as tariffs and minimum-wage laws lead to inefficiency. It is not that the proponents of these policies do not value efficiency as a worthwhile goal; it is simply that they are so concerned about income distribution issues, they feel that some inefficiency must be tolerated in order to solve equity problems. In Part 4, we consider income distribution directly: how it is determined and how the government can use tax and competition policy to affect the income distribution in a way that minimizes unfortunate side effects. Thus, one of our twelve Ideas for Beyond the Final Exam, the trade-off between efficiency and equity, takes centre stage. Also, one dimension of the income distribution, that between current and future generations, is highlighted in our discussion of pollution and resource depletion. To whet your appetite, some of the specific issues we highlight at this stage are outlined in the margin at right.

Owners of capital bear none of the burden of a tax that is levied on their earnings. (pages 492–93)

A guaranteed annual income policy can provide income support for the disadvantaged without the unintended side effect of our current welfare policies (which tend to keep recipients in a poverty trap). (pages 503–506)

Agricultural marketing boards help only that subset of farmers who owned farms when the boards were first created. (pages 529–30)

More private ownership, not less, is required to tackle the problems of pollution and resource depletion. (pages 584–86, 602–605)

CHAPTER 14

PRICING THE FACTORS OF PRODUCTION: INCOME DISTRIBUTION

Masters are always and every-where in a sort of tacit, but constant and uniform combi-nation, not to raise the wages of labour.

ADAM SMITH

uch of this book is devoted to examining the things the free-market system does well and the things it does poorly. We mentioned in Chapter 12 that the market mechanism cannot be counted on to distribute income in accordance with ethical notions of "fairness" or "justice," and we listed this failing as one of the market's shortcomings. But there is much more to be said about how income is distributed in a market economy and about how governments alter this distribution process. These are the subjects of this and the next chapter.

The broad outlines of how the market mechanism distributes income are familiar to all of us. Each person owns some **factors of production—**the inputs used in the production process. Many of us have only our own labour, but some of us also have funds that we can lend, land that we can rent, or natural resources that we can sell. These factors are sold on markets at prices determined by supply and demand. Thus, the distribution of income in a market economy is determined by the level of employment of the factors of production and by their prices. For example, if wages are rather high and are fairly equal among workers and if unemployment is low, few people will be poor. But if wages are low and unequal and unemployment is high, many people will be poor.

For purposes of discussion, the factors of production may be grouped into five broad categories: labour, capital, land, exhaustible natural resources, and a rather mysterious input called entrepreneurship. Exhaustible natural resources will be studied in Chapter 17. In this chapter, we will study the payments made for the use of the other four factors: the wages paid to labour, the interest paid to capital, the rent of land, and the profits earned by entrepreneurs.

Since this chapter focusses on the *theories* of factor pricing, it may be useful first to look briefly at how much these inputs earn in reality. According to Canadian data on net domestic income at factor cost for 1991, interest payments accounted for about 11 percent of national income, land rents and non-corporate profits for a mere 8 percent, and corporate profits for about 6 percent. In total, the returns to these factors of production amounted to about 25 percent of national income. Where did the rest of it go? The answer is that about 75 percent of national income was composed of employee compensation—wages and salaries.

The distribution of income is perhaps the one area in economics in which any one individual's interests almost inevitably conflict with another's. By definition, if a larger share of the total income is distributed to me, a smaller share will be left for you. It is also a topic around which emotions run high, often causing the logic or the facts of the issues to be ignored. In this chapter, we will encounter several examples of people's misunderstandings of the facts and their unwillingness to face up to the undesirable consequences of income controls.

The chapter is divided into three main sections. The first explores marginal productivity theory, and notes a number of criticisms that have been levelled at that approach and at mainstream economics generally. This section covers the basic material that all students should read. The final two sections discuss, in greater detail, the determination of interest and profit incomes and the operation of labour markets, respectively. These two sections can be omitted in a brief course.

MARGINAL PRODUCTIVITY THEORY

THE PRINCIPLE OF MARGINAL PRODUCTIVITY

By now, it will not surprise you to learn that factor prices are analyzed in terms of supply and demand. The supply sides of the markets for the various factors differ enormously from one another, which is why each factor market must be considered separately. But one basic principle, the **principle of marginal productivity**, has been used to explain the demand for every input. Before restating the principle, we should recall two concepts that were introduced in Chapter 6: **marginal physical product** (MPP) and **marginal revenue product** (MRP). (To review these concepts, see Chapter 6, pages 163 and 166.)

Table 14-1 helps us review these two concepts by recalling the example of Farmer Pfister, who had to decide how much fertilizer to apply to his fixed plot of land. The marginal *physical* product column tells us how many additional bushels of corn each additional tonne of fertilizer yields. For example, according to the table, the fourth tonne increases the crop by 300 bushels. The marginal *revenue* product column tells us how many dollars this MPP is worth. In the example in the table, corn is assumed always to sell at $2 per bushel, so the MPP of the fourth tonne of fertilizer is $2 per bushel times 300 bushels, or $600. We can now state the marginal productivity principle formally:

The marginal productivity principle states that when factor markets are competitive, it always pays a profit-maximizing firm to hire that quantity

The **MARGINAL PHYSICAL PRODUCT (MPP)** of an input is the increase in output that results from a one-unit increase in the use of the input, holding the amounts of all other inputs constant.

The **MARGINAL REVENUE PRODUCT (MRP)** of an input is the additional sales revenue the firm takes in by selling the marginal physical product of that input.

TABLE 14-1

MARGINAL PHYSICAL PRODUCTS AND MARGINAL REVENUE PRODUCTS OF
FARMER PFISTER'S FERTILIZER

Fertilizer (tonnes)	Marginal Physical Product (bushels)	Marginal Revenue Product (dollars)
1	250	500
2	300	600
3	350	700
4	300	600
5	250	500
6	150	300
7	50	100
8	0	0
9	−50	−100

of any input at which the marginal revenue product is equal to the price of the input.

The basic logic behind the principle is both simple and powerful. If the input's MRP is, for example, greater than its price, it will pay the firm to hire more and more of it because an additional unit of input brings the firm (via the output it contributes) an addition to revenue that is greater than the cost of that unit of input. Consequently, if MRP is greater than the input price, the firm should expand the quantity of the input it purchases. It should increase the quantity purchased up to the amount at which diminishing returns reduce the MRP to the level of the input's price. Conversely, if MRP is less than price, the firm is using too much of the input. Let us use Table 14-1 to demonstrate how the marginal productivity principle works.

Suppose the firm is using 4 tonnes of fertilizer at a cost of $350 per tonne. Since the table tells us that a fifth tonne has an MRP of $500, the firm could obviously add $150 to its profits by buying a fifth tonne. Only when the firm has used so much fertilizer that (because of diminishing returns) the MRP of still another tonne is less than $350 does it pay to stop expanding the use of fertilizer. In this example, 5 tonnes is the optimal amount to use.

One corollary of the principle of marginal productivity is obvious: The quantity of the input demanded depends on its price. The lower the price of fertilizer, the more fertilizer it pays a firm to use. In the example of the previous paragraphs, it pays the firm to use 5 tonnes when the price of fertilizer is $350 per tonne. But if fertilizer were more expensive, say, $550 per tonne, that price would exceed the value of the marginal product of the fifth tonne. It would therefore pay the firm to stop after the fourth tonne. Thus, marginal productivity analysis shows that the quantity demanded of an input normally will decline as the price of the input rises. The "law" of demand applies to inputs just as it applies to consumer goods.

THE DERIVED DEMAND CURVE FOR AN INPUT

We can, in fact, be much more specific than this, for the marginal productivity principle tells us precisely how the demand curve for any input is derived from its MRP curve.

Figure 14-1 presents graphically the MRP schedule from Table 14-1. Recall that, according to the marginal productivity principle, the quantity demanded of the input is determined by setting MRP equal to the input's price. Figure 14-1 considers three different possible prices for a tonne of fertilizer: $600, $500, and $300. At a price of $600 per tonne, we see that the quantity demanded is 4 tonnes (point *A*) because, at that point, MRP equals price. Similarly, if the price of fertilizer drops to $500 per tonne, quantity demanded rises to 5 tonnes (point *B*). Finally, if the price falls all the way to $300 per tonne, the quantity demanded is 6 tonnes (point *C*). Points *A*, *B*, and *C* are therefore three points on the demand curve for fertilizer.

The demand curve for any input is the downward-sloping portion of its marginal revenue product curve.

Note that we restrict ourselves to the downward-sloping portion of the MRP curve. The logic of the marginal productivity principle dictates this. For example, if the price of fertilizer is $500 per tonne, there are two input quantities for which MRP is $500: 1 tonne (point *D*) and 5 tonnes (point *B*). But point *D* cannot be the optimal stopping point because the MRP of a second tonne ($600) is greater than the cost of the second tonne

FIGURE 14-1

A MARGINAL REVENUE PRODUCT CURVE

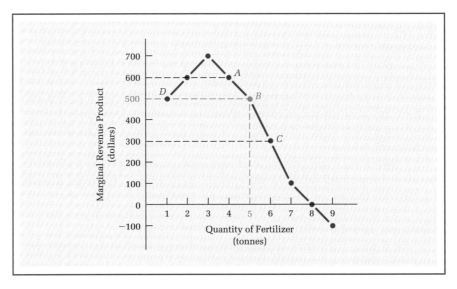

This diagram depicts the data in Table 14-1, which show how the marginal revenue product (MRP) of fertilizer first rises and then declines as more and more fertilizer is used. Since the optimal purchase rule is to keep applying fertilizer until MRP is reduced to the price of fertilizer, the *downward-sloping* portion of the MRP curve is Farmer Pfister's demand curve for fertilizer.

($500). The marginal productivity principle applies only in the range where returns are diminishing.

The demand for fertilizer (or for any other input) is called a **derived demand** because it is derived from the underlying demand for the final product (corn, in this case). For example, suppose that a surge in demand drove the price of corn to $4 per bushel. Then, at each level of fertilizer usage, the MRP would be twice as large as when corn fetched $2 per bushel. This is shown in Figure 14-2 as an *upward* shift of the (derived) demand curve for fertilizer, from $D_0 D_0$ to $D_1 D_1$. (To make the diagram easier to read, we have omitted the (irrelevant) upward-sloping portion of each curve.) We conclude, in general, as follows:

An outward shift in the demand curve for any commodity causes an outward shift of the derived demand curve for all factors used in the production of that commodity. Conversely, an inward shift in the demand curve for a commodity leads to inward shifts in the demand curves for factors used in producing that commodity.

FIGURE 14-2

A SHIFT IN THE DEMAND CURVE FOR FERTILIZER

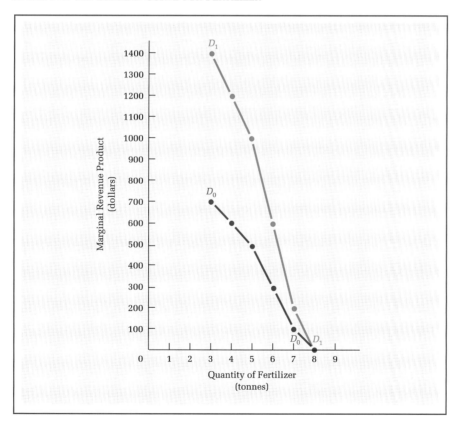

If the price of corn goes up, the marginal *revenue* product curve shifts upward—from $D_0 D_0$ to $D_1 D_1$ in the diagram—even though the marginal *physical* product curve has not changed. In this sense, a greater demand for corn leads to a greater *derived* demand for fertilizer.

We have almost completed our introductory discussion of the marginal productivity principle and how it serves as a general explanation of the demand for any and all inputs. We will now use this theory in our discussion of the determination of two rather different forms of income: wages paid for unskilled labour and rents received for scarce land. Applying the tools of demand *and* supply in these two areas will allow us to clarify the important principles of income determination and to outline the useful (and the less useful) methods available to the government for altering income distribution—the subject of our next chapter.

THE BASIC DETERMINANTS OF INCOME DISTRIBUTION

If we consider a factor of production that is very plentiful throughout the economy, we know that the supply curve for that factor in a supply and demand diagram must be drawn far over to the right. We also know that the supply curve will intersect the demand curve (the MRP curve) at a point where the MRP is very low, since if a large quantity of any factor is employed, diminishing returns have set in to a very great extent. This tells us that the payment received for the use of an abundant factor is likely to be very low. It follows logically that if a person owns only a small amount of that one abundant factor, that person will be poor. Similar reasoning leads to the conclusion that people who own factors of production that are very scarce will have high incomes (since the supply curves for scarce factors intersect their demand curves at very high levels of payment). Marginal productivity theory, then, leads us to this basic point:

High incomes go to the owners of scarce factors, and low incomes go to the owners of abundant factors.

This outcome suggests three ways in which governments can influence the distribution of income:

Option 1. By redefining who owns the various factors of production.

Option 2. By intervening in the market's determination of factor prices.

Option 3. By leaving factor ownership and market signals alone, but redistributing income according to the directives of the general tax system.

Option 1 has been the choice of revolutionary governments, and flows from the basic principles of Marxist economics. Also, the various affirmative-action programs that have been implemented in capitalist countries to counter discrimination against minority groups in the labour market are a very mild form of this sort of income-redistribution strategy. (We discuss discrimination and pay equity in Chapter 15.)

Generally, economists have a strong preference for Option 3 over Option 2. The main reason for this preference is the tendency of the market's invisible hand to fight back, producing a variety of undesirable outcomes, when market forces are tampered with (recall our discussion of Option 2 in Chapter 3). The more general the mechanism for income redistribution (such as progressive income taxation, with gradual increases in the tax rates and few tax shelters), the better are the chances that redistribution will occur without counterproductive disincentive effects.

We are now in a position to tackle the subjects of minimum-wage laws and the taxation of economic rents, which will allow us to clarify the issue of incentive effects. In the next chapter, we will discuss our overall tax and welfare systems with a view to explaining how our existing anti-poverty programs might be improved.

ISSUE: THE MINIMUM WAGE AND UNEMPLOYMENT

Unemployment is always higher among the young than it is in the labour force as a whole. Figure 14-3 shows the record. It indicates that whenever unemployment rates have gone down in the economy as a whole, they

FIGURE 14-3

THE YOUTH UNEMPLOYMENT PROBLEM

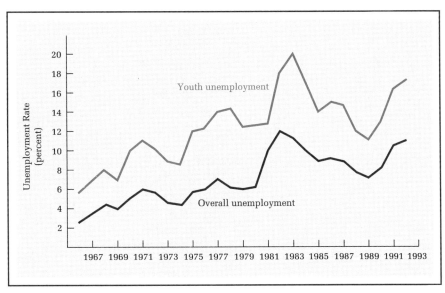

Youth unemployment rates have consistently been much higher than overall unemployment rates.

SOURCE: Compiled from data in Statistics Canada, *Canadian Economic Observer*, Historical Statistical Supplement, 1991/92, catalogue no. 11-210, page 38. Used with the permission of the Minister of Industry, Science and Technology, 1993.

have almost always decreased for the young. However, young workers have always suffered more from unemployment than has the average worker. When things are generally bad, things are much worse for the young.

Many economists are less surprised than other concerned people about the intractability of this problem. They maintain that despite all the legislation that has been adopted to improve the position of the young and inexperienced, there is a law on the books that, although apparently designed to protect low-skilled workers, is actually an impediment to any attempt to improve job opportunities for the young. As long as this law remains in effect, the young, the inexperienced, and those with educational disadvantages will continue to find themselves handicapped on the job market, and attempts to eliminate their more serious unemployment problems will stand only a limited chance of success.

What is the law? None other than the **minimum-wage law**. We will now explain the grounds on which many observers argue that this law has such pernicious—and presumably unintended—effects.

The labour market is really composed of many submarkets for labour of different types, each with its own supply and demand curves. To understand the possible effects of minimum-wage legislation, it suffices to consider two such markets, which we call for convenience "skilled" and "unskilled" labour and which are illustrated graphically in the two parts of Figure 14-4. As drawn, the demand curve for skilled workers is

FIGURE 14-4
POSSIBLE EFFECTS OF MINIMUM-WAGE LEGISLATION

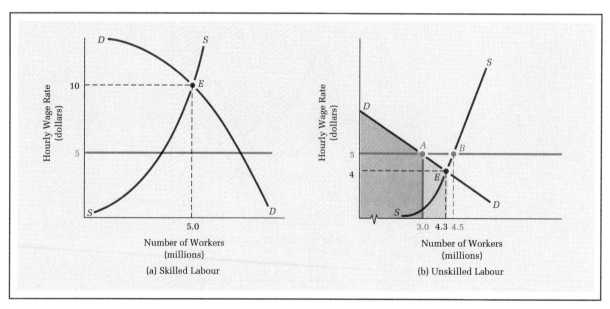

(a) Imposing a minimum wage of $5 per hour does not affect the market for skilled labour because the equilibrium wage there ($10 per hour) is well above the legal minimum. (b) However, the minimum-wage legislation does have important effects in the market for unskilled labour. There, the equilibrium wage ($4 per hour) is below the minimum, so the minimum wage makes the quantity supplied (4.5 million workers) exceed the quantity demanded (3.0 million workers). The result is unemployment of unskilled labour.

higher than that for unskilled workers. The reason is obvious: Skilled workers have higher productivity. Conversely, we have drawn the supply curve of skilled workers farther to the left than the supply curve of unskilled workers to reflect the greater scarcity of skilled workers. The consequence, as we can see in Figure 14-4, is that the equilibrium wage is much higher for skilled workers. In the example, the equilibrium wages are $10 per hour for skilled workers and $4 per hour for unskilled workers.

Now suppose the government, seeking to protect unskilled workers, imposes a legal minimum wage of $5 per hour (the heavy blue line in both parts of Figure 14-4). Turning first to part (a), we see that the minimum wage has no effect in the market for skilled workers (such as carpenters and electricians). Since wages in that market are well above $5 per hour, a law prohibiting the payment of wage rates below $5 cannot possibly matter.

But the effects of the minimum wage may be pronounced in the market for unskilled labour—and presumably quite different from those that the government intended. Figure 14-4(b) indicates that at the $5 minimum wage, firms want to employ only 3.0 million unskilled workers (point *A*) whereas employment of unskilled workers would have been 4.3 million (point *E*) in a free market. Although the 3.0 million unskilled workers lucky enough to retain their jobs do indeed earn a higher wage ($5 instead of $4 per hour) in this hypothetical example, 1.3 million of their compatriots earn no wage at all because they have been laid off. The job-losers will clearly be the workers whose productivity was lowest, since the minimum wage effectively bans the employment of workers whose marginal revenue product is less than $5 per hour.

Although the minimum wage leads to higher wages for those unskilled workers who retain their jobs, it also restricts employment opportunities for unskilled workers.

An additional point warrants emphasis. Before the minimum wage is introduced in this example, the total income generated by the employment of the 4.3 million unskilled workers is equal to the gold shaded area in Figure 14-4(b). This is because the *total* revenue generated by these workers' employment is equal to the area under their *marginal* revenue product curve (which is the demand curve for their services). The workers receive the wage bill (the gold rectangle below the $4 wage line) and their employers receive the amount represented by the triangular gold area above the $4 wage line. After the minimum wage of $5 is imposed and employment of unskilled workers drops to 3.0 million, the total revenue generated by employment in this sector is reduced to the blue shaded area in Figure 14-4(b). Proponents of minimum wages often argue that higher wages mean increased buying power for products, so employment should go up with such minimums in place. But this argument confuses workers' wage rates with their total income (which is wage rate times the number of workers employed). The argument also ignores non-labour (employers') income. As the diagram makes clear (compare

A P P L I C A T I O N

MINIMUM-WAGE LAW NO HELP TO UNSKILLED

One of the simplest methods of testing the effect of minimum-wage laws is by conducting a cross-province comparison. Such a study was reported in The Financial Post *in 1985, and we reprint an excerpt of that article here. More recently, a study commissioned by the Ontario Ministry of Labour confirmed these effects. That 1989 study found that a 10 percent increase in the minimum wage would eliminate 25 000 jobs.*

How can we test the economic principle that high minimum-wage levels lead to relatively increased unemployment rates for unskilled workers? One way is to calculate the unemployment rates of youthful Canadians as a percentage of those of the more highly productive adult employees in this nation, and then compare this figure with the minimum-wage levels which apply in each of the provinces. (We choose workers between 20 and 24 as our control because this is the youngest group subject to the "adult" minimum-wage law.)

The results are painfully obvious. Manitoba, with the highest minimum-wage level ($4.30) has the largest unemployment rate for its young workers, relative to the general population (289%). Saskatchewan, with the next greatest level ($4.25), weighs in with the second biggest relative unemployment rate for youth (257%). And at the bottom of the pack in terms of the disenfranchisment of their young people come B.C. and Alberta, with two of the country's lowest minimum-wage levels.

	Unemployment Rate for 20–24-Year-Olds Relative to Employees Aged 25+ (percent)	Provincial Minimum-Wage Level, 1985 (dollars)
Alberta	182	3.80
British Columbia	190	3.65
Newfoundland	204	4.00
Quebec	206	4.00
Nova Scotia	213	4.00
New Brunswick	237	3.80
Ontario	251	4.00
Saskatchewan	257	4.25
Manitoba	289	4.30
Prince Edward Island	n.a.	3.75

SOURCE: Walter Block, *The Financial Post*, August 17, 1985, reprinted in the *Fraser Forum*, August 1985, pages 4–5.

the gold and the blue areas), total income—that is, overall buying power—*must* fall with higher wages.[1]

Finally, minimum wages may have particularly pernicious effects on those who are the victims of discrimination. Because of the minimum

---

1. While it is total income that is relevant for the overall-buying-power argument, the diagram makes clear that the total-labour-income component *could* increase as a result of the minimum wage. This would occur if the income of the 3.0 million workers who are still employed increased by more than the loss of wages suffered by the 1.3 million who lost their jobs because of the minimum-wage law. But for such a significant wage increase to occur, the demand for unskilled labour would have to be inelastic—which it is not, since it is so easy to replace unskilled workers in the production process. In any event, we should not ignore the buying power of those receiving the income shown by the triangle above the wage line.

wage, as Figure 14-4(b) shows, employers of unskilled labour have more applicants than job openings. Consequently, they are able to pick and choose among the available applicants and may, for example, discriminate on the basis of sex, race, or ethnicity against groups whose members have been prevented by past discrimination from acquiring the skills required for admission to the higher-paid portion of the labour force.

For these reasons, many economists feel that the youth unemployment problem and especially the unemployment problem of minority groups will be very difficult to solve as long as the minimum wage remains in effect. Obviously, the minimum wage is not the only culprit. But statistical studies — and even analyses as simple as the one reported in the boxed insert opposite — support the conclusion that forced overpricing of unskilled labour contributes significantly to unemployment. It is analysis of this sort that induces most economists to reject attempts to repeal the laws of supply and demand in the aim of redistributing income. As we noted earlier, the preferred approach will be outlined in the next chapter.

THE DETERMINATION OF RENT

We turn our attention now to the market for land — the one factor of production whose quantity supplied is roughly the same at every possible price. Indeed, the classical economists used this notion as the working definition of land. And the definition seems to fit, at least approximately. Although people may accumulate landfill, clear land, drain its swamps, fertilize it, build on it, or convert it from one use (a farm) to another (a housing development), it is very difficult for human effort to make a great deal of change in the total supply of land.

What does this fact tell us about the determination of land rents? Figure 14-5 helps to provide an answer. The vertical supply curve, *SS*, represents the fact that no matter what the level of rents, there are still 1000 hectares of land in a small hamlet called Littletown. The demand curve, *DD*, is a typical marginal revenue product curve, predicated on the notion that the use of land, like everything else, is subject to diminishing returns. The free-market price is determined, as usual, by the intersection of the supply and demand curves. In this example, each hectare of land in Littletown rents for $2000 per year. Because quantity supplied is rigidly fixed at 1000 hectares whatever the price, the diagram displays an interesting feature:

The market level of rent is entirely determined by the demand side of the market.

If, for example, the relocation of a major university to Littletown attracts more people who want to live there, the *DD* curve will shift outward, as depicted in Figure 14-6. Equilibrium in the market will shift from point *E* to point *A*; there will still be only 1000 hectares of land, but now each hectare will command a rent of $2500. The landlords will collect more rent, though they themselves will have done nothing productive. Also,

FIGURE 14-5

DETERMINATION OF LAND RENT IN LITTLETOWN

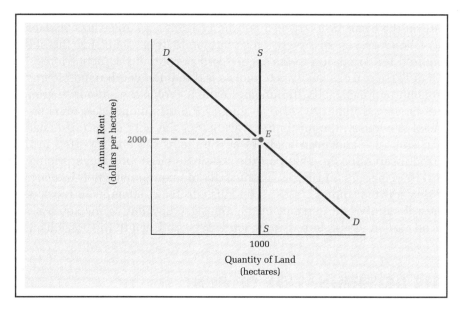

The supply curve of land, *SS*, is vertical, meaning that 1000 hectares are available in Littletown regardless of the level of rent. The demand curve for land slopes downward for the usual reasons. Equilibrium is established at point *E*, where the annual rental rate is $2000 per hectare.

FIGURE 14-6

A SHIFT IN DEMAND WITH A VERTICAL SUPPLY CURVE

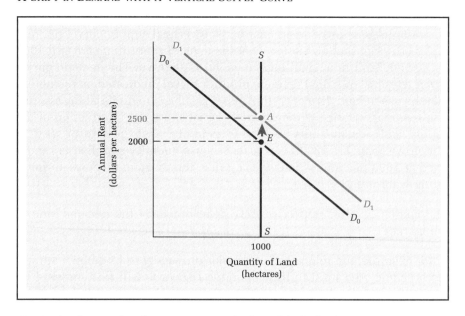

Now imagine that something happens to increase the demand for land — that is, to shift the demand curve from D_0D_0 to D_1D_1. Quantity supplied cannot change, but the rental rate can, and does. In this example, the annual rental for a hectare of land increases from $2000 to $2500.

society will obtain no additional land from the landlords in return for its additional rent payment.

The same process also works in reverse, however. If the university shuts its doors and the demand for land declines as a result, the landlords will suffer even though they will have in no way contributed to the decline in the demand for land. (To see this, simply reverse the logic of Figure 14-6. The demand curve begins at D_1D_1 and shifts to D_0D_0.)

This discussion shows the special feature of rent that leads economists to distinguish it from payments to other factors of production: An *economic rent* is a payment for a factor of production (such as land) that does not change the amount of that factor that is supplied.

If every parcel of land were of identical quality, there would be nothing more to the theory of land rent. But, of course, plots of land do differ—in quality of soil, in topography, in access to sun and water, in proximity to marketplaces, and in other ways. The classical economists realized this and took it into account in their analysis of rent determination — a remarkable piece of economic logic formulated late in the eighteenth century and still considered valid today.

The basic notion is that funds invested in any piece of land must yield the same return as funds invested in any other piece of land that is actually used. Why? If it were not so, capitalists would bid against one another for the more profitable pieces of land until the rents of these parcels were driven up to a point where their advantages over other parcels had been eliminated.

Suppose that on one piece of land a given crop is produced for $160 000 per year in labour, fertilizer, fuel, and other non-land costs, while the same crop is produced for $120 000 on a second piece of land. The rent on the second parcel must be *exactly* $40 000 per year higher than the rent on the first, because otherwise production would be cheaper on one plot than on the other. If, for example, the rent difference were only $30 000 per year, it would be $10 000 cheaper to produce on the second plot of land. No one would want to rent the first plot, and every grower would instead bid for the second plot. Obviously, rent on the first plot would be forced down by a lack of customers, and rent on the second would be driven up by eager bidders. These pressures would come to an end only when the rent difference reached $40 000, so that both plots became equally profitable.

At any given time, there are some pieces of land of such low quality that it does not pay to use them at all—remote deserts are a prime example. Any land that is exactly on the borderline of being used is called **marginal land**. By definition, marginal land earns no rent because if any rent were charged for it, there would be no takers.

Land that is just on the borderline of being used is called **MARGINAL LAND**

We now combine these two observations—that the difference between the costs of producing on any two pieces of land must equal the difference between their rents, and that zero rent is charged on marginal land —to conclude as follows:

Rent on any piece of land will equal the difference between the cost of producing the output on that land and the cost of producing it on marginal land.

That is, competition for the superior plots of land will permit the land-lords to charge prices that capture the full advantages of their superior parcels.

A useful feature of this analysis is that it helps us to understand more completely the effects of an outward shift in the demand curve for land. Suppose there is an increase in the demand for land because of a rise in population. Naturally, rents will rise, but we can be more specific. In response to an outward shift in the demand curve, two things will happen:

1. *It will now pay to employ some land whose use was formerly unprofitable.* The land that was previously on the zero-rent margin will no longer be on the borderline, and some land that is so poor that it was formerly not even worth considering will now just reach the borderline of profitability. The settling of the West illustrates this process quite forcefully. Land that once could not be given away is now quite valuable.

2. *People will begin more intensive use of the land that was already in use.* Farmers will use more labour and fertilizer to squeeze larger crops out of their land, as has happened in recent decades. Urban real estate on which two-storey buildings previously made most sense will now be used for highrises.

Rents will be increased in a predictable way by these two developments. Since the land that is marginal *after* the change must be inferior to the land that was marginal previously, rents must rise by the difference in yields between the old and the new marginal lands.

But there is a second factor pushing up land rents — the increased intensity of use of land that was already in cultivation. As farmers apply more fertilizer and labour to their land, the marginal productivity of land increases, just as factory workers become more productive when they are given better equipment. Once again, the landowner is able to capture this increase in productivity in the form of higher rents. (If you do not understand why, refer back to Figure 14-6 and remember that the demand curves are marginal revenue product curves.) Thus, we can summarize the classical theory of rent as follows:

As the use of land increases, landlords receive higher payments from two sources:

1. Increased demand leads the community to employ land previously not good enough to use; the advantage of previously used land over the new marginal land increases, and rents go up correspondingly.

2. Land is used more intensively; the marginal revenue product of land rises, thus increasing the ability of the producer who uses the land to pay rent.

As late as the end of the nineteenth century, this analysis still exerted a powerful influence beyond technical economic writings. An American journalist, Henry George, was nearly elected mayor of New York in 1886 by running on the platform that all government should be financed by "a single tax"—a tax on landlords, who, he said, are the only ones who earn incomes while contributing nothing to the productive process and who reap the fruits of economic growth without contributing to economic progress.

GENERALIZATION: WHAT DETERMINES MARIO LEMIEUX'S SALARY?

Land is not the only scarce input whose supply is fixed, at least in the short run. Toward the beginning of this century, some economists realized that the economic analysis of rent can be applied to inputs other than land. As we will see, this extension yielded some noteworthy insights.

Consider as an example the earnings of Mario Lemieux. Performers such as Lemieux might seem to have little in common with plots of land in downtown Toronto. Yet, to an economist, the same analysis—the theory of rent—explains the incomes of these two factors of production. To understand why, we first note that there is only one Mario Lemieux. That is, he is a scarce input whose supply is fixed just like the supply of land. Because he is in fixed supply, the price of his services must be determined in a way similar to the determination of land rents. Hence, economists arrived at a more general definition of **economic rent** as any payment made to a factor above the amount necessary to keep that factor in its present employment.

ECONOMIC RENT is said to be earned whenever a factor of production receives a reward that exceeds the minimum amount necessary to keep the factor in its present employment.

To understand the concept of economic rent, it is useful to divide the payment for any input into two parts. The first part is simply the minimum payment needed to acquire the input: the cost of equipment or the compensation for the unpleasantness, hard work, and loss of leisure involved in performing labour. The second part of the payment is a bonus that does not go to every input, but only to those that are of particularly high quality. Payments to workers with exceptional natural skills are a good example. These bonuses are like the extra payment for a better piece of land and so are called *economic rents*.

Notice that only the first part of the factor payment is essential to induce the owner to supply the input. If workers are not paid at least this first part, they will not supply their labour. But the additional payment —the economic rent—is pure gravy. The skilful worker is happy to have it as an extra, but it is not the deciding consideration in his or her choice of whether or not to work.

A moment's thought shows how this general notion of rent applies both to land and to Mario Lemieux. The total quantity of land available for use is the same whether rent is high, low, or zero; no payments to landlords are necessary to induce land to be supplied to the market. Thus, by definition, the payments to landholders for their land are entirely economic rent—payments that are not necessary to induce the provision of the land to the economy. Mario Lemieux is (almost) similar to land in this respect. He has hockey talents that are rare and that cannot be reproduced. What determines the income of such a factor? Since the quantity supplied of such a unique, non-reproducible factor is absolutely fixed, and therefore unresponsive to price, the analysis of rent determination summarized in Figure 14-5 applies. The position of the demand curve determines the price.

Figure 14-7 summarizes the "Mario Lemieux market." The numbers we use in this explanation are not intended to be accurate; our intention is simply to explain the principles involved. (Mario Lemieux's salary is revised upward much too frequently for us to keep this example completely accurate.) Vertical supply curve *SS* represents the fact that no matter what salary he is paid, there is only one Mario Lemieux. Demand curve *DD* is a marginal productivity curve of sorts, but not quite the kind we encountered earlier in the chapter. Since the question "What would be the value of a second unit of Mario Lemieux?" is nonsensical, the demand curve is constructed by considering only the portion of his time

FIGURE 14-7

HYPOTHETICAL MARKET FOR MARIO LEMIEUX'S SERVICES

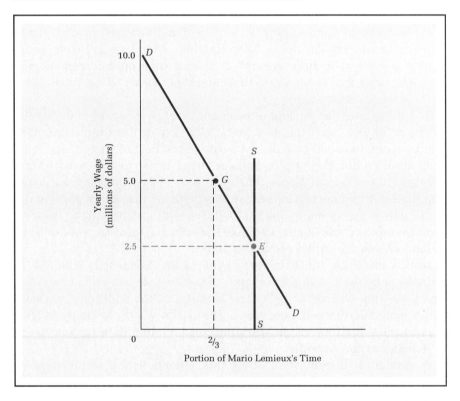

At an annual salary of $10.0 million or more, no one is willing to bid for his time. At a somewhat lower salary, $5.0 million, two-thirds of his time will be demanded (point *G*). Only at an annual salary no higher than $2.5 million will all of Lemieux's available time be demanded (point *E*).

demanded at various salary levels. The curve indicates that at an annual salary of $10.0 million, no employer can afford even a little bit of Mario Lemieux. At a lower salary of, say, $5.0 million per year, however, there are enough profitable uses to absorb two-thirds of his time. At $2.5 million per year, Lemieux's full time is demanded, and at lower salary rates, the demand for Lemieux's time exceeds the amount of it that is for sale.

Equilibrium is at point E in the diagram, where the supply of and the demand for Lemieux's time are equal. His annual salary in our numerical example is, then, $2.5 million. Now we can ask, How much of Mario Lemieux's salary is economic rent? According to the economic definition of rent, his entire $2.5 million salary is rent. Since, according to the vertical supply schedule, Lemieux's financial reward is unnecessary to get him to supply his services, every penny he earns is rent.

This is why we said that stars like Lemieux are *almost* good examples of pure rent. For, in fact, if his salary were low enough, Lemieux might well prefer to stay home rather than work. Suppose, for example, that $400 000 per year is the lowest salary at which Lemieux will offer even one minute of his services, and that his labour supply then increases with his pay up to an annual salary of $1.0 million, at which point he is willing to work full time. Then, while his equilibrium salary will still be $2.5 million per year, not all of it will be rent, because some of it, at least $400 000, is required to get him to supply any services at all.

This same analysis applies to any factor of production whose supply curve is not vertical, as in Figure 14-8. There, we see that at any price

FIGURE 14-8

RENT WHEN THE SUPPLY CURVE IS NOT VERTICAL

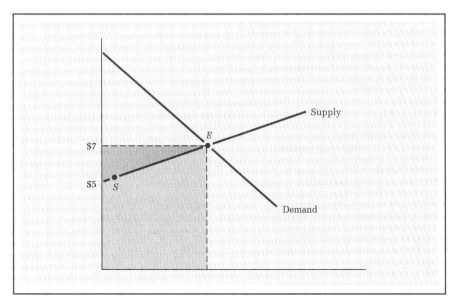

Some of the input would be supplied (point S) at a price of $5 (or a bit more), but the equilibrium price is $7, so the units of input to the left of the equilibrium amount must be earning a rent of up to $2. The total rent is represented by the blue triangle.

above $5, suppliers would be willing to provide some units of the input. Yet the supply–demand equilibrium point yields a price of $7 — well above the minimum price at which some input supply would be forthcoming. The difference must constitute a rent to suppliers of the input. The overall earnings of this factor of production are shown by the gold rectangle in Figure 14-8; the portion that is rent is shown by the blue shaded triangle. Any such factor earns some rent—or gets paid more than the minimum amount that would induce it to work. Almost all employees earn some rent. What sorts of factors earn no rent? Those that can be exactly reproduced by a number of producers at constant cost. No supplier of ball bearings will ever receive any rent on a ball bearing, at least in the long run, because any desired number of them can be produced at (roughly) constant cost. If one supplier tried to charge a price that included rent, another firm would undercut that supplier and take its customers away. That is, if it costs 50¢ to produce a ball bearing, no matter how many or how few are provided, none will be supplied at a price below 50¢, and competition will prevent the price from exceeding that figure, so the price will include no rent.

RENT CONTROLS: THE MISPLACED ANALOGY

Why is the analysis of economic rent important? Because only economic rent can be taxed away without reducing the quantity of the input supplied. Here, common English gets in the way of sound reasoning. Many people feel that the rent they pay to their landlord is economic rent. After all, their apartments will still be there if they pay $500 per month, or $300, or $100. This view, while true in the short run, is quite myopic.

Like the ball-bearing producer, the owner of a building cannot expect to earn *economic* rent because there are too many other potential owners whose costs of construction are roughly the same as her own. If she tried to charge a price that included some economic rent—that is, a price that exceeded her production costs plus the opportunity cost of her capital— other builders would undercut her. Thus, far from being in perfectly *inelastic* (vertical) supply, like raw land, buildings come rather close to being in perfectly *elastic* (horizontal) supply, like ball bearings. As we have learned from the theory of rent, this means that builders and owners of buildings cannot collect economic rent in the long run. Since apartment owners collect very little economic rent, the payments that tenants make in a free market must be just enough to keep those apartments on the market. (This is the definition of zero economic rent.) If rent controls push these prices down, the apartments will start to disappear from the market.[2]

---

2. None of this is meant to imply that temporary rent controls in certain locations cannot have salutory effects in the short run. In the short run, the supply of apartments and houses really is fixed, and large shifts in demand would hand windfall gains to landlords—gains that are true economic rents. Controls that eliminate such windfalls should not cause serious problems. But knowing when the "short run" fades into the "long run" can be a tricky matter. "Temporary" rent-control laws have a way of lasting for quite a time, as we saw in Chapter 3 (pages 79–81).

AT THE FRONTIER

RENT-SEEKING

Current research uses the rent concept to analyze such common phenomena as lobbying by industrial groups, lawsuits between rival firms, and battles over exclusive licences (as for a TV station). Such interfirm battles can waste economic resources, such as the time that is expended by executives, bureaucrats, judges, lawyers, and economists. Because this valuable time could have been used in production, such activities entail a large opportunity cost. The new analysis offers insights into the reasons for these battles, and provides a way to assess the quantity of resources that are wasted.

The opportunity to earn economic rent is extremely attractive to many individuals and firms. Consequently, when a rent-earning opportunity becomes available (a relatively common occurrence), a number of parties are usually prepared to fight over it. The search for such opportunities and the battles over them are called "rent-seeking." The theory of rent-seeking gives us some idea of the extent of society's resources that are wasted in such a process.

Consider a race for a monopoly cable TV licence, which, once awarded, will keep competitors out of the field. There is nothing to prevent competitors from entering the race to grab the licence. Anyone can hire the lobby-ists and the lawyers or offer the bribes needed in the battle. Thus, while the cable business itself is not competitive, the process of fighting for the licence is.

We know from the analysis of long-run equilibrium under perfect competition, however, that economic profit approximates zero —revenues just cover costs. Thus, if the cable licence is expected to yield, say, $900 million in rent over its life, rent-seekers are likely to waste something near that amount in the fight for the licence.

Why? Suppose there are ten bidders, each with an equal chance at the prize. To each bidder, that chance should be worth about $90 million. If the average bidder has so far spent only, say, $70 million on the battle, there will still be an expected economic profit of $90 million − $70 million = $20 million to the rent-seeking activity. This will tempt an eleventh bidder to enter and raise the ante to, say, $80 million in lobbying fees, hoping to grab the rent. For risk-neutral participants, this process stops only when a sum equal to the total expected economic rent to be gained from the cable licence has been wasted on the rent-seeking process. (Now might be a good time to review our earlier encounters with rent-seeking: Chapter 10, page 301, and Chapter 12, pages 348–49.)

CRITICISMS OF MARGINAL PRODUCTIVITY THEORY AND MAINSTREAM ECONOMICS

The theory of factor pricing described in this chapter is another example of supply–demand analysis. Its special feature is its heavy reliance on the principle of marginal productivity to derive the shape and position of the demand curve. For this reason, the analysis is often rather misleadingly called the *marginal productivity theory of income distribution*. Over the years, this analysis has been subject to attack on many grounds.

In general, those who criticize mainstream economics are often called "radical economists." They do not limit their criticism to marginal productivity theory; indeed, they maintain that, as a rule, mainstream economists are asking all the wrong questions and using the wrong set of tools (economic models) to provide the answers. In the sections that follow, we investigate some of these claims.

JUSTIFICATION OF THE STATUS QUO

One frequent accusation, which is largely (but not entirely) groundless, is as follows:

Marginal productivity theory is merely an attempt to justify the distribution of income that the capitalist system yields—that is, it is a piece of pro-capitalist propaganda.

According to this argument, when marginal productivity theory claims that each factor is paid exactly its marginal revenue product (MRP), this is only a sneaky way of asserting that each factor is paid exactly what it deserves. These critics claim that the theory legitimizes the gross inequities of the system—the poverty of many and the great wealth of the few.

The argument is straightforward but wrong. Payments are made *not* to factors of production but to the people who happen to own them. If land earns $2000 because that is its MRP, this does not mean the payment is *deserved* by the landlord, who may even have acquired it by fraud.

Second, an input's MRP depends not only on "how hard it works" but also on how much of it happens to be employed—for, according to the "law" of diminishing returns, the more that is employed, the lower its MRP. Thus, that factor's MRP is not (and cannot legitimately be interpreted as) a measure of the intensity of its "productive effort." In any event, what an input deserves may be taken to depend on more than what it does in the factory. A worker may be held to deserve funds because she is sick, because she has many children, or because of many reasons other than her productivity. On these and other grounds, no economist today claims that marginal productivity analysis shows that distribution under capitalism is either just or unjust. It is simply wrong to claim that marginal productivity theory is pro-capitalist propaganda. The marginal productivity principle is just as relevant to organizing production in a socialist society as it is in a capitalist one.

NARROWNESS OF FOCUS

One of the more general criticisms levelled by the radical economists against the mainstream approach can be stated as follows:

Conventional economists typically narrow their field of inquiry so much that they are incapable of addressing the important questions.

For one thing, in contrast to Marx's teachings, modern economics is *ahistorical*. It is very much based on the here and now, with scant attention paid to the origins of the current system or the directions in which it may be headed. Perhaps as a consequence of this narrow scope, mainstream economics accepts institutions as given and (tacitly) as immutable. Little attention is paid to how institutions change.

Amplifying the attack, the radicals chide conventional economists for their preoccupation with analysis of *marginal* changes, using the celebrated tools of marginal analysis that we have described in earlier chapters. This, they argue, makes economics incapable of dealing with the really big issues: the institution of private property, poverty and discrimination, unemployment, and alienation. For example, Professor John Gurley of Stanford University, who converted from conventional to radical economics many years ago, scoffed at a prominent economist who expressed the belief that reducing unemployment would do more good things for the distribution of income than any measure he could imagine:

> Well, any radical economist can imagine a direct measure that would do even better things—expropriation of the capitalist class and turning over of ownership of capital goods and land to all the people. That, of course, sounds wild—unimaginable—to anyone who does not question the existing system.[3]

The consequence of this disciplinary narrowness, radicals contend, is that economists become, whether deliberately or unwittingly, apologists for the present system, supporters of the propertied class, and defenders of the status quo.

Most economists are prepared to plead guilty to the charge of disciplinary narrowness. Yale's Nobel Prize winner James Tobin put it this way:

> Most contemporary economists feel ill at ease with respect to big topics— national economic organization, interpretation of economic history, relations of economic and political power, origins and functions of economic institutions. The terrain is unsuitable for our tools. We find it hard even to frame meaningful questions, much less to answer them.[4]

But mainstream economists tend to view their inadequacy in this area as a misdemeanour, not a felony. They point out, in their defence, that a narrow focus is imperative if progress in analysis is to be made. Further, they are quite proud of the achievements of economic science compared with those of the more diffuse social sciences, such as sociology and political science. They counter that radicals try to paint with such broad strokes that everything becomes necessarily superficial and imprecise. They argue also that the radicals, with their very clear political biases, are hardly in a position to question the objectivity of other economists.

ACCEPTANCE OF TASTES AND MOTIVATION AS GIVEN

Just as they do with institutions, conventional economists accept the tastes of consumers and the motivations of workers and managers as

---

3. J.G. Gurley, "The State of Political Economics," *American Economic Review* (May 1971), page 59.

4. J. Tobin, book review of Lindbeck's *The Political Economy of the New Left*, in *Journal of Economic Literature* (December 1972), page 1216.

given and unchangeable—"just human nature." Radicals, on the other hand, argue as follows:

Consumers are manipulated. Not only are they bombarded by advertising, they are also brainwashed in the school system, influenced by politicians, and subtly moulded by other social institutions.

This argument is broadened further by the assertion that the need for material incentives to motivate both workers and managers is culturally acquired rather than innate, a product of capitalism rather than a cause of it.

Naturally, mainstream economists do not really believe that tastes are God-given. Everyone realizes that they are acquired and influenced by many things. The question is, What are we to do about this? Lacking a theory of taste formation, basic economic analysis proceeds on the assumption that consumer tastes are to be respected *regardless* of how they became what they are. If we forsake this principle, we find ourselves on some dangerous ground: If consumers do not know what's good for them, who does? Still, most economists would willingly concede that more research into taste formation is desirable, and some have worked on this. The radicals have no doubt pushed the profession in a healthy direction.

OBSESSION WITH EFFICIENCY RATHER THAN EQUALITY

At several points in this book, we have emphasized the fundamental trade-off between efficiency and equality. All mainstream economists appreciate and understand this principle, and a great many—in their role as private citizens—advocate greater equality. However, the radicals have a legitimate complaint:

The preponderant majority of economic analysis and research is concerned with efficiency, not with equality.

Many conventional economists agree with this criticism.[5] But the radicals do not ask simply for a change in emphasis; they also want a change in the economist's tool kit. The marginal productivity theory of income distribution, they argue, is irrelevant. They maintain that to understand the distribution of income in contemporary market economies, we must first understand the distribution of *power*, which is largely determined by who controls the means of production.

Here the conventional and the radical economists part company. The conventional economist wants to know just how this "power" is measured. Are there statistical studies showing that power influences the distribution of income? In short, mainstream economics treats this approach to distribution theory as rhetoric, not as science.

---

5. Alice M. Rivlin, "Income Distribution—Can Economists Help?" *American Economic Review* (May 1975), pages 1–15; Robert Aaron Gordon, "Rigor and Relevance in a Changing Institutional Setting," *American Economic Review* (March 1976), pages 1–14.

MYOPIC CONCENTRATION ON QUANTITY
RATHER THAN QUALITY

The radical left is critical of mainstream economists' preoccupation with policies designed to increase the gross domestic product. They argue that a great deal of this output is no more than junk, and that using society's resources to produce such things is patently irrational. They also point to the spoliation of the environment caused by modern industrial production, although at least some radicals concede that conventional economics has some solutions to these problems (see Chapter 17). Further, they are dismayed that a system so adept at producing private consumer goods should be so pathetically inept at feeding the hungry, housing and clothing the poor, and providing public services of all kinds. Radicals add one more element to this indictment:

In addition to ruining the quality of the environment, capitalist production ruins human beings.

It makes them aggressive, competitive, even dehumanized, by forcing them into a rat race for material gain. In Marxian terms, workers have little voice in determining the nature of their productive activities and so become alienated from their work rather than proud of their accomplishments.

Are the outputs of the system really that bad? As Professor Robert Solow of the Massachusetts Institute of Technology notes, it is hard to disagree with the radicals' disparaging remarks about essentially unnecessary products, from pungent deodorants to ostentatiously useless gadgets, "without appearing boorish." Yet such products are not only part of the wasteful expenditures of the idle rich. It must be remembered that the median family income in Canada is not excessively high—it is currently less than $46 000 per year. By definition, fully half of Canadian families earn less than this. Are they squandering their money on frivolities, or are these the things that the Canadian people really want? Solow concludes as follows:

> [The radicals'] attitudes toward ordinary consumption remind one of the Duchess who, upon acquiring a full appreciation of sex, asked the Duke if it were perhaps too good for the common people.[6]

As for alienation, it is safe to say that conventional economists have never known what to make of the notion. If this is an important way in which capitalism has damaged the quality of life, then conventional economics surely has been blind to it. As with "power," however, no one has yet figured out a way to measure alienation. As for the alleged dehumanization of the labour force, this seems to be a side effect of modern industrial activity—whether that activity is conducted under capitalism or under socialism. The radicals, however, hope that we can reform the

---

6. Robert M. Solow, "The New Industrial State or Son of Affluence," *The Public Interest*, no. 9 (Fall 1967), page 108. © 1967 by National Affairs, Inc.

basic structure of society by arranging a *participatory* system in which workers have some real control over what they do and how they do it (not one in which orders flow only from the top down). These changes, radicals believe, would make workers both happier and more productive.

NAÏVE CONCEPTION OF THE STATE

Radical economists maintain that mainstream economists hold a naïve and sentimental view of the state. In this view, government is available to set things right when the market system fails (as in the case of income distribution or externalities, for example), and in so doing, allows its decisions to be dictated by the broad public interest. Note, however, the contrasting view:

> The State, in the radical view, operates ultimately to serve the interest of the controlling class in a class society. Since the "capitalist" class fundamentally controls capitalist societies, the state functions in capitalist societies to serve that class. It does so either directly, by providing services only to members of that class, or indirectly, and probably more frequently, by helping preserve and support the system of basic institutions which support and maintain the power of that class.[7]

This subservience of the state to the capitalists manifests itself in several ways. First, since capitalists are driven by competition to accumulate capital continually and to expand production, they must gain access to more and bigger markets in which to sell this bountiful output. As a result, capitalist nations turn to imperialist ventures to secure new markets. Second, in order to maintain domestic demand at high levels, the military–industrial complex promotes a *war economy*, which, if not actually at war, is continually spending inordinate sums on armaments. Third, according to this view, even reforms that appear to be pro-labour, such as minimum wages, social-welfare programs, unemployment insurance, and the like, are really intended to "buy off" the working class so that it will not rise up in revolt, as radical economists imply Marx had predicted. In this view, for example, the social and economic programs initiated as a result of the Great Depression were not motivated by a desire to help the working class, but rather by a desire to forestall the coming revolution.

Mainstream economists admit to a certain political naïvete. Yet most economists are unimpressed by the radicals' view of the state. Without denying that corporations often curry political favour and often succeed, mainstream economists wonder how the radical model can explain progressive income taxation, inheritance taxes, competition policy, antidiscrimination regulations, universal health insurance, the "baby bonus," and many, many more laws that most of the wealthy opposed bitterly at the time they were enacted. Furthermore, they point out, the policy pre-

---

7. D.M. Gordon, *Theories of Poverty and Underemployment* (Lexington, Mass.: D.C. Heath & Company, 1972), page 61.

scriptions that conventional economists offer to improve the functioning of markets are intended as just that—prescriptions for improvement, not predictions about what government will actually do. Economists are not *that* naïve.

This completes our presentation of the core material of this chapter. We have explained marginal productivity theory, used this theory to understand minimum-wage laws and the concept of economic rent, and discussed the radical critique of mainstream economists and its emphasis on marginal analysis. At this point in shorter courses, instructors may choose to move directly to Chapter 15 and its analysis of income redistribution by governments. The two remaining parts of this chapter provide further discussion of factor pricing, covering the determination of interest and profit incomes and the operation of the labour market in greater detail.

INTEREST AND PROFIT

THE ISSUE OF USURY LAWS: ARE INTEREST RATES TOO HIGH?

The rate of interest is the price at which funds can be rented (borrowed). Like other factor prices, the rate of interest is determined by supply and demand. However, this is one area in which many people have been dissatisfied with the outcome of the market process. Fears that interest rates, if left unregulated, would climb to exorbitant levels have made usury laws quite popular in many times and places. In a related development, in the late 1980s, some Canadian politicians called for limits on the amount that banks could charge on credit-card loans. However, this sort of intervention, and usury laws generally, interfere with the operation of supply and demand and are often harmful to economic efficiency.

Funds are loaned (rented to users) in many ways: home mortgages, corporate or government bonds, consumer credit, and so on. On the demand side of these credit markets are borrowers—people or institutions that, for one reason or another, wish to spend more than they currently have.

In business, loans are used primarily to finance investment. To the business executive who "rents" (borrows) funds in order to finance an **investment** and pays interest in return, the funds really represent an intermediate step toward the acquisition of the machines, buildings, inventories, and other forms of physical **capital** that the firm will purchase.

Although the words "investment" and "capital" are often used interchangeably in everyday parlance, it is important to keep the distinction in mind. The relation between investment and capital has an analogy in

INVESTMENT is the flow of resources into the production of new capital. It is the labour, steel, and other inputs devoted to the construction of factories, warehouses, railways, and other capital items during some period of time.

CAPITAL refers to an inventory (a stock) of plant, equipment, and other productive resources held by a business firm, an individual, or some other organization.

the filling of a bathtub: The accumulated water in the tub is analogous to the stock of capital, while the flow of water from the tap (which adds to the tub's water) is like the flow of investment. Just as the tap must be turned on in order for more water to accumulate, the capital stock increases only when there is investment. If investment ceases, the capital stock stops growing. Notice that when investment is zero, the capital stock remains constant; it does not fall to zero any more than a bathtub suddenly becomes empty when you turn off the tap.

The process of building up capital by investing, and then using this capital in production, can be divided into five steps:

Step 1.   The firm decides to enlarge its stock of capital.

Step 2.   It raises the funds with which to finance its expansion.

Step 3.   It uses these funds to hire the inputs, which are put to work building factories, warehouses, and the like. This step is the act of *investment*.

Step 4.   After the investment is completed, the firm ends up with a larger stock of *capital*.

Step 5.   The capital is used (along with other inputs) either to expand production or to reduce costs. At this point, the firm starts earning *returns* on its investment.

Notice that what investors put into the investment process is money, either their own or funds borrowed from others. The funds are then transformed, in a series of steps, into a physical input suitable for use in production. If the funds were borrowed, the investor will someday return them to the lender with some payment for their use. This payment is called **interest**, and it is calculated as a percentage per year of the amount borrowed. For example, if the interest rate is 12 percent per year and $1000 is borrowed, the annual interest payment is $120.

The marginal productivity principle governs the quantity of funds demanded just as it governs the quantity of fertilizer demanded:

Firms will demand the quantity of borrowed funds that makes the marginal revenue product of the investment financed by the funds just equal to the interest payment charged for borrowing.

Capital, however, has one noteworthy feature that distinguishes it from other inputs, like fertilizer. The fertilizer applied by Farmer Pfister is used once and then it is gone, but a blast furnace, which is part of a steel company's capital, normally lasts many years. The furnace is a *durable* good, and because it is durable, it contributes not only to today's production but also to future production. This fact makes calculating the marginal revenue product (MRP) more complex for a capital good than for other inputs.

INTEREST is the payment for the use of funds employed in the production of capital; it is measured as a percentage per year of the value of the funds tied up in the capital.

To determine whether the MRP of a capital good is greater than the cost of financing it (that is, to decide whether an investment is profitable), we need a way to compare money values received at different times. To make such comparisons, economists and business people use a calculation procedure called **discounting**. Discounting was explained in detail in the appendix to Chapter 13, but it is not important that you master this technique in an introductory course. For the present discussion, there are really only two important points to learn:

1. A sum of money received at a future date is worth less than a sum of money received today.

2. This difference in values between money today and money in the future is greater when the rate of interest is higher.

It is not difficult to understand why this is so. Consider what you could do with a dollar that you received today as opposed to one that you might receive a year from today. If the annual rate of interest is 10 percent, you could lend it out (for example, by putting it into a bank account) and receive $1.10 in a year's time—your original $1.00 plus 10¢ interest. For this reason, money received today is worth more than the same number of dollars received later. Specifically, at an interest rate of 10 percent per year, $1.10 to be received a year from today is equivalent to $1.00 of today's money. This illustrates the first of our two points.

Now suppose the annual rate of interest is 15 percent instead. In this case, $1.00 invested today would grow to $1.15 (rather than $1.10) in a year's time, which means that $1.15 (not $1.10) received a year from today would be equivalent to $1.00 received today, and that $1.10 one year in the future must be worth less than $1.00 today. This illustrates the second point.

THE MARKET DETERMINATION OF INTEREST RATES

Let us now return to the way in which interest rates are determined in the market. We are concerned about the level of interest rates because they play a crucial role in determining the economy's level of investment —that is, in selecting the amount of current consumption that consumers will forego in order to use resources to build machines and factories that can increase the output of consumers' goods in the future. Thus, the interest rate is crucial in determining the allocation of society's resources between present and future.

THE DOWNWARD-SLOPING DEMAND CURVE FOR FUNDS

The two attributes of discounting discussed in the previous section are all we need to explain why the quantity of funds demanded declines when the interest rate rises, or why the demand curve for funds has a negative slope.

Remember that the demand for borrowed funds is a *derived demand*, derived from the desire to invest in capital goods. But part, and perhaps all, of the MRP of a machine or a factory is received in the future. Hence, the value of this MRP in terms of *today's* money shrinks as the rate of interest rises. Why? Because future returns must be discounted more heavily when the interest rate rises. The consequence of this shrinkage is that a machine that appears to be a good investment when the rate of interest is 10 percent may look like a terrible investment when the rate of interest is 15 percent.

As the rate of interest on borrowing rises, more and more investments that previously looked profitable start to look unprofitable. The demand for borrowing for investment purposes, therefore, is lower at higher rates of interest.

An example of a derived demand schedule for borrowing is given in Figure 14-9 and is labelled *DD*. Its negative slope illustrates the conclusion we have just stated — the higher the interest rate, the less money people and firms will want to borrow to finance their investments.

FIGURE 14-9

EQUILIBRIUM IN THE MARKET FOR LOANS

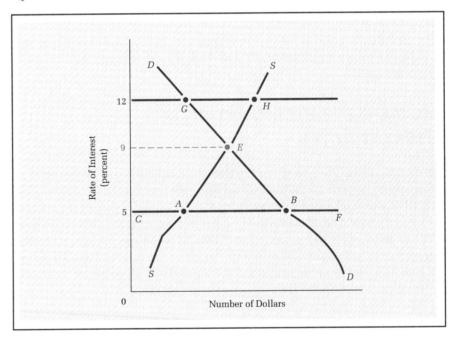

If there is no foreign lending, the free-market interest rate is 9 percent. At this interest rate, the quantity of loans supplied is equal to the quantity demanded. However, if an interest-rate ceiling is imposed at, say, 5 percent, the quantity of funds supplied (point *A*) will be smaller than the quantity demanded (point *B*).

THE SUPPLY OF FUNDS

Similar principles apply on the supply side of the market for funds — where the *lenders* are consumers, banks, and other types of business firms. Funds lent out are usually returned to the owner (with interest) only over a period of time. Loans will look better to lenders when they bear higher interest rates, so it is natural to think of the supply schedule for loans as being upward sloping — at higher rates of interest, lenders supply more funds — as shown by curve *SS* in Figure 14-9.

It is interesting to note, incidentally, that some lenders may have supply curves that do not slope uphill to the right the way curve *SS* does. Suppose, for example, that Jones is saving to buy a $10 000 boat in three years and that if he lends money out at interest in the interim, at current interest rates, he must save $3000 a year to reach his goal. If interest rates were higher, he could save less than $3000 each year and still reach his $10 000 goal. (The higher interest payments would, of course, contribute the difference.) Thus, his saving (and lending) might decline. But this argument applies only to savers like Jones who have a fixed accumulation goal.

Generally, we do expect the quantity of loans supplied from domestic sources to rise when the interest reward rises, so the domestic supply curve has a positive slope, like *SS* in Figure 14-9. The equilibrium rate of interest is at point *E*, where quantity supplied and quantity demanded are equal. Thus, if our loan market operates in isolation from the rest of the world, we conclude that the equilibrium interest rate on loans is 9 percent.

CEILINGS ON INTEREST RATES

Let us now assume that Figure 14-9 refers to the supply of loans by banks to consumers. Consider what happens if there is a usury law that prohibits interest of more than 5 percent per annum on consumer loans. At this interest rate, the quantity supplied (point *A*) falls short of the quantity demanded (point *B*). This means that many applicants for consumer loans are being turned down even though the banks consider them to be creditworthy.

Who generally gains and who loses as a result of this usury law? The gainers are easiest to identify: those lucky consumers who are able to get loans at 5 percent even though they would have been willing to pay 9 percent. The law represents a windfall gain for them. The losers are on both the supply side and the demand side. First, there are the consumers who would have been willing and able to get credit at 9 percent but who are not lucky enough to get it at 5 percent. Then there are the banks (or, more accurately, bank shareholders) who could have made profitable loans at rates of up to 9 percent if there had been no interest-rate ceiling.

This analysis helps explain the political popularity of usury laws. Few people sympathize with bank shareholders; indeed, the widespread feeling that banks are "gouging" their borrowers provides much of the impetus for usury laws. The consumers who get loans at lower rates will, naturally, be quite pleased with the result of the law. The others, who would like to borrow at 5 percent but cannot because quantity supplied is less than quantity demanded, are quite likely to blame the bank for refusing to lend, rather than blame the government for outlawing some mutually beneficial transactions.

This analysis has little good to say about usury ceilings, and economists generally oppose them. However, interest-rate ceilings can play a constructive role when there is a monopoly over credit. If there is a monopoly lender, the analysis of Chapter 10 leads us to expect that firm to restrict its "output" (the volume of loans) by raising its "price" (the interest rate). Under such circumstances, an interest-rate ceiling may conceivably make sense.[8] But *may* is not *will*. Most economists believe that, except for isolated instances, the credit market is far closer to the competitive model than it is to the monopoly model.

THE IMPORTANCE OF FOREIGN LENDING FOR INTEREST-RATE DETERMINATION

The existence of foreign lending makes the supply curve of loans horizontal at the height given by existing foreign interest rates. This case is most relevant for Canada, since our financial markets are so integrated with those in the rest of the Western world. In particular, Canadians regularly borrow in the United States, and the total of our borrowing is very small relative to the overall size of the American loan market. This makes Canadian sellers of bonds perfectly competitive sellers on the world bond market—they can sell whatever quantity they wish at the going price (that is, interest rate). Thus, the world demand curve for our bonds (which is the same as the foreign supply curve of loan funds to Canada) is horizontal at the interest-rate value observed in the United States.

Suppose the American interest rate is 5 percent. Since Canadian savers have the option of lending their funds in the United States at 5 percent, the Canadian supply of funds in Figure 14-9 is no longer *SS*. Only the part above 5 percent is relevant, so the supply curve becomes *CAE*. The foreign supply curve is *CF*. Given this foreign supply, domestic borrowers can obtain all the funds they want at 5 percent and so choose point *B*. In this case, point *A* indicates the proportion of loans that comes from domestic sources and the quantity of foreign borrowing that takes place (amount *AB*).

This analysis shows that a tax on foreign interest earnings in Canada and an increase in U.S. interest rates have exactly the same effects on Canadian interest rates. Both events raise the horizontal line indicating foreign willingness to lend in Canada. Suppose a tax or a hike in U.S. interest rates raises the horizontal line to *GH* in Figure 14-9. Canadian

---

8. Chapter 10 of the *Study Guide* that accompanies this book contains an exercise exploring the effects of a maximum price law on a monopolist. Review your answer to that question now; it provides a more precise version of the argument given here.

borrowing (demand for funds) will drop to the level indicated by point *G*, and Canadian savers will lend abroad an amount given by distance *GH*. Canadian interest rates will rise along with American rates, to 12 percent in this example. We can now appreciate why U.S. interest-rate increases are so unpopular in Canada, except among Canadians with money to lend. The analysis shows that our interest rates must rise along with U.S. rates, with the result that many of our firms' investment projects become unprofitable. This process contributes to lower employment in Canada. Perhaps the more surprising conclusion to follow from the analysis is that:

A tax on foreign interest income in Canada has the same effect as does a higher interest rate. Often, the politicians who express the most concern over high interest rates are the same ones who most favour increased taxes on foreigners who earn income in Canada!

ISSUE: ARE PROFITS TOO HIGH OR TOO LOW?

We turn next to business profits, a subject whose discussion seems to elicit more passion than logic. With the exception of some economists, almost no one thinks that the rate of profit is at about the right level. Critics on the left point accusingly at the billion-dollar profits of some giant corporations and argue that they are unconscionably high. They call for much stiffer taxes on profits. On the other hand, chambers of commerce, the Canadian Manufacturers' Association, and other business groups complain that regulations and "ruinous" competition keep profits too low, and they are constantly petitioning the government for tax relief.

The public has many misconceptions about the nature of the economy, but probably none is more severe than the popular view of the amount of profit that corporations earn. We suggest to you the following experiment. Ask five of your friends who have never had an economics course what fraction of our national income they imagine is accounted for by profits. The correct answer varies from year to year, but corporate profits represented only 12 percent of national income in 1989, and, as noted earlier in this chapter, just 6 percent in 1991. A comparable percentage of the prices you pay represents before-tax profit. Most people assume that this figure is much, much higher. (See the boxed insert at the top of the next page.)

As you have no doubt noticed by now, economists are reluctant to brand factor prices as "too low" or "too high" in some moral and ethical sense. Rather, they are likely to ask first, What is the market equilibrium price? Then they will ask whether there are any good reasons to interfere with the market solution. This analysis, however, is not so easy to apply to the case of profits, since it is hard to use supply and demand analysis when you do not know what factor of production earns profit.

In both a bookkeeping and an economic sense, profits are the residual: They are what remains from the selling price after all other factors have been paid.

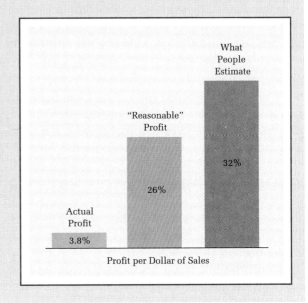

PUBLIC CONTROVERSY

PUBLIC OPINION ON PROFITS

Most people think corporate profits are much higher than they actually are. A recent public-opinion poll, for example, found that the average citizen thought that corporate profits *after* tax amounted to 32 percent of sales for the typical manufacturing company. The actual profit rate at the time was only 3.8 percent! Interestingly, when a previous poll asked how much profit was "reasonable," the response was 26 cents on every dollar of sales —more than six times as large as profits actually were.

SOURCE: "Public Attitudes Toward Corporate Profits," *Public Opinion Index*, Opinion Research Corporation, Princeton, N.J., August 1986.

But what factor of production receives this reward? What factor's marginal productivity constitutes the profit rate?

WHAT ACCOUNTS FOR PROFITS?

Economic profit, it will be recalled from Chapter 8, is the amount a firm earns over and above the payments for all other inputs, including the interest payments for the capital it uses and the opportunity cost of any capital provided by the owners of the firm. The profit rate and the interest rate are closely related. In an imaginary (and uninteresting) world in which everything was certain and unchanging, capitalists who invested money in firms would simply earn the market rate of interest on their funds. Profits beyond this level would be competed away. Profits below this level could not persist because capitalists would withdraw their funds from the firms and deposit them in banks. Capitalists in such a world would be mere moneylenders.

But the real world is not at all like this. Some capitalists are much more than moneylenders and the amounts they earn often exceed the interest rate by a considerable margin. Those activist capitalists who seek out or even create earnings opportunities are called **entrepreneurs**. They are the ones who are responsible for the constant change that character-

ENTREPRENEURSHIP is the act of starting new firms, introducing new products and technological innovations, and, in general, taking the risks that are necessary in seeking out business opportunities.

izes business firms and who prevent the operations of the firms from stagnating. Since they are always trying to do something new, it is difficult to provide a general description of their activities. However, we can list three primary ways in which entrepreneurs are able to drive profits above the level of interest rates.

Exercise of monopoly power.   If the entrepreneur can establish a monopoly over some or all of her products, even for a short while, she can use the monopoly power of her firm to earn monopoly profits. The nature of these monopoly earnings was analyzed in Chapter 10.

Risk-bearing.   The entrepreneur may engage in risky activities. For example, when a firm prospects for oil, it will drill an exploratory shaft hoping to find a pool of petroleum at the bottom. But a high proportion of such attempts produce only dry holes, and the cost of the operation is wasted. Of course, if the investor is lucky and does find oil, he may be rewarded handsomely. The income he obtains is a payment for bearing risk.

Obviously, a few lucky individuals make out well in this process, while most suffer heavy losses. How well can we expect risk-takers to fare on the average? If, on the average, one exploratory drilling out of ten pays off, do we expect its return to be exactly ten times as high as the interest rate, so that the *average* firm will earn exactly the normal rate of interest? The answer is that the payoff will be *more* than ten times the interest rate if investors dislike gambling, that is, if they prefer to avoid risk. Why? Because investors who dislike risk will be unwilling to put their money into a business in which nine firms out of ten lose out unless there is some compensation for the financial peril to which they expose themselves.

In reality, however, there is no certainty that things will always work out this way. Some people love to gamble, and these people tend to be overoptimistic about their chances of coming out ahead. They may plunge into projects to a degree unjustified by the odds. If there are enough such gamblers, the average payoff to risky undertakings may end up below the interest rate. The successful investor will still make a good profit, just like the lucky winner in Las Vegas. But the average participant will have to pay for the privilege of bearing risk.

Returns to innovation.   The third major source of profits is perhaps the most important of all from the point of view of social welfare. The entrepreneur who is first to market a desirable new product or to employ a new cost-saving machine or to innovate in some other way will receive a special profit as his reward. Innovation is different from invention. **Invention** is the act of generating a new idea; **innovation** is the next step, the act of putting the new idea into practical use. Business people are rarely inventors, but they are often innovators.

INVENTION is the act of generating a new idea. INNOVATION, the next step, is the act of putting the new idea into practical use.

When an entrepreneur innovates, even if her new product or her new process is not protected by patents, she will be one step ahead of her competitors. She will be able to capture much of the market either by offering customers a better product or by supplying the product more cheaply. In either case, she will temporarily find herself with some monopoly power left by the weakening of her competitors, and monopoly profit will be the reward for her initiative.

However, this monopoly profit, the reward for innovation, will only be temporary. As soon as the success of the idea has demonstrated itself to the world, other firms will find ways of imitating it. Even if they cannot turn out precisely the same product or use precisely the same process, they will have to find ways to supply close substitutes if they are to survive. In this way, new ideas are spread through the economy. In the process, the special profits of the innovator are brought to an end. The innovator can resume earning special profits only by finding still another promising idea.

Entrepreneurs are forced to keep searching for new ideas, to keep instituting innovations, and to keep imitating those that they have not been the first to put into operation. This process is at the heart of the growth of the capitalist system. It is one of the secrets of its extraordinary dynamism.

THE ISSUE OF PROFITS TAXATION

We have learned that profits in excess of the market rate of interest can be considered as the return on entrepreneurial talent. But this is not really very helpful, since no one can say exactly what entrepreneurial talent is. Certainly we cannot measure it, nor can we teach it in a college course (though business schools try!). Therefore, we do not know how the observed profit rate relates to the minimum reward necessary to attract entrepreneurial talent into the market—a relationship that is crucial for the contentious issue of profits taxation.

Consider a windfall profits tax on oil companies as an example. If oil company profit rates are well above this minimum necessary reward, they contain a large element of economic rent. In that case, we could tax away these excess profits (rents) without fear of reducing oil production. On the other hand, if the profits being earned by oil companies do not contain much economic rent, the windfall profits tax might seriously curtail exploration and production of oil.

This example illustrates the general problem of deciding how heavily profits should be taxed. Critics of big business who call for high profits taxes believe that profits are mostly economic rent. But if they are wrong, if most of the observed profits are necessary to attract people into entrepreneurial roles, a high profits tax can be dangerous. It can threaten the very lifeblood of the capitalist system. Business lobbyists predictably claim that this is the case. Unfortunately, neither group has offered much evidence for its conclusion.

THE LABOUR MARKET

THE SUPPLY OF LABOUR

The economic analysis of labour supply is based on the following simple observation: Given the fixed amount of time in a week, one's decision to *supply labour* to a firm is simultaneously a decision to *demand leisure* time for oneself. Assuming that after necessary time for eating and sleeping is deducted, a worker has 90 usable hours in a week, a decision to spend 40 of those hours working is simultaneously a decision to demand 50 of them for other purposes.

This suggests that we can analyze the supply of this particular input — labour — with the same tools we used in Chapter 4 to analyze the demand for commodities. In this case, the commodity is leisure. A consumer "buys" her own leisure time, just as she buys bananas, or backscratchers, or pizzas. In Chapter 4, we observed that any price change has two distinct effects on quantity demanded: an income effect and a substitution effect. Let us review these two effects and see how they operate in the context of the demand for leisure (that is, the supply of labour).

1. ***Income effect.*** Higher wages make consumers richer. We expect this increased wealth to raise the demand for most goods, leisure included.

   The income effect of higher wages probably leads most workers to want to work less.

2. ***Substitution effect.*** Consumers "purchase" their own leisure time by giving up their hourly wage, so the wage rate is the "price" of leisure. When the wage rate rises, leisure becomes more expensive relative to other commodities that consumers might buy. Thus, we expect a wage increase to induce them to buy less leisure time and more goods.

   The substitution effect of higher wages probably leads most workers to want to work more.

Putting these two effects together, we are led to conclude that some workers may react to an increase in their wage rate by working more, while others may react by working less. Still others will have little or no discretion over their hours of work. In terms of the market as a whole, therefore, higher wages could lead to either a larger or a smaller quantity of labour supplied.

Statistical studies of this issue have reached the conclusions that (a) the response of labour supply to wage changes is not very strong for most workers; (b) for low-wage workers, the substitution effect seems clearly dominant, so they work more when wages rise; and (c) for high-wage workers, the income effect just about offsets the substitution effect, so they do not work more when wages rise. Figure 14-10 depicts these approximate "facts." It shows labour supply rising (slightly) as wages rise to point *A*. Thereafter, labour supply is roughly constant as wages rise.

It is even possible that when wages are raised sufficiently high, further increases in wages will lead workers to purchase more leisure and therefore to work less. The supply curve of labour is then said to be "**backward-bending**," as illustrated by the broken portion of the curve above point *B*.

AN APPLICATION: THE LABOUR-SUPPLY PARADOX

Labour-supply analysis helps explain the following puzzling observation. Throughout the twentieth century, wages have generally been rising, both in number of dollars paid per hour and in the quantity of goods those dollars can buy. Yet labour has asked for and received reductions in the length of the work day and the work week. At the beginning of the century, a work week of 5½ days and a work day of 10 or more hours were standard, making for a work week of 50 to 60 hours (and there were virtually no vacations). Since then, labour hours have generally declined.

FIGURE 14-10

A TYPICAL LABOUR SUPPLY SCHEDULE

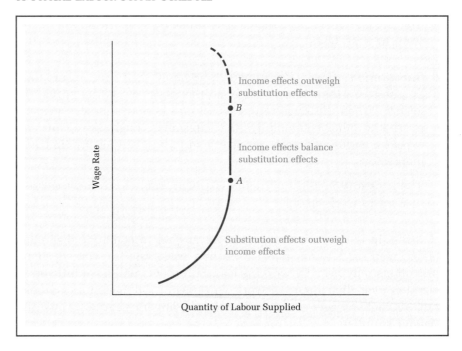

The labour supply schedule depicted here has a positive slope up to point *A*, as substitution effects outweigh income effects. At higher wages, however, income effects become just as important as substitution effects, and the curve becomes roughly vertical. At still higher wages (above point *B*), income effects might overwhelm substitution effects.

Today, the standard work week is down to 35 to 40 hours. Where has the common-sense view of the matter gone wrong? Why, as hourly wages have risen, have workers not sold more of the hours they have available instead of pressing for a shorter and shorter work week?

Part of the answer becomes clear when one recalls that any wage increase sets in motion both a substitution effect *and* an income effect. If only the substitution effect operated, rising wages would indeed cause people to work longer hours because the high price of leisure makes leisure less attractive. But this reasoning leaves out the income effect. As higher wages make workers richer, they will want to buy more of most commodities, including vacations and other leisure-time activities. Thus, the income effect of increasing wages induces workers to work fewer hours.

It is the strong income effect of rising wages that may account for the fact that labour supply has responded in the "wrong" direction, with workers working ever-shorter hours despite their rising real wages. If so, the long-run supply curve of labour is indeed backward-bending.

THE DEMAND FOR LABOUR AND THE DETERMINATION OF WAGES

Not much can be said about the demand for labour that has not already been said about the demand for other inputs. Like any factor of production, labour has a marginal revenue product curve from which a downward-sloping demand curve for labour is derived. If there are no interferences with the operation of a free market in labour—such as minimum wages (see pages 417–21), asymmetric information (pages 350–51 in Chapter 12), or unions (pages 452–60)—equilibrium will occur at the point where the supply and demand curves intersect (as we assumed in our discussion of minimum wages).

WHY WAGES DIFFER

But, of course, there is not one labour market but many—each with its own supply and demand curves and its own equilibrium wage. We all know that certain groups in our society (the young, the uneducated) earn relatively low wages, and that some of our most severe social ills (poverty, crime, drug addiction) are related to this fact. But why are some wages so low while others are so high?

Supply and demand analysis at once tells us everything and nothing about this question. It implies that wages are relatively high in markets where demand is great and supply is small, while wages are comparatively low in markets where demand is weak and supply is high. This can hardly be considered startling news. But to make the analysis useful, we need to breathe some life into the supply and demand curves.

We begin our discussion on the demand side. Why is the demand for labour greater in some markets than in others? The marginal productivity principle teaches us that there are two types of influences to be considered. Since a worker's marginal revenue product depends both on his marginal physical product *and* on the price of the product he produces, variables that influence either of these will influence his wage.

The determinants of the prices of commodities were discussed at some length in earlier chapters, and there is no need to repeat the analysis here. It is sufficient to remember that because the demand for labour is a derived demand, anything that raises or lowers the demand for a particular product will tend to raise or lower the wages of the workers who produce that product.

A worker's marginal physical product depends on several things, including, of course, his own abilities and degree of effort on the job. But sometimes these characteristics are less important than the other factors of production that he has to work with. Workers in Canadian industry are more productive than workers in many other countries because they have generous supplies of machinery, natural resources, and technical know-how to work with. As a consequence, they earn high wages.

Turning next to the supply of labour, it is clear that the size of the available working population relative to the magnitude of industrial activity in a given area is of major importance. This helps to explain why wages rose so high in the sparsely populated North when exploration for Arctic oil created many new jobs, and why wages have been and remain so low in Atlantic Canada, where industry is relatively dormant.

Also, it is clear that the non-monetary attractiveness of any job will also influence the supply of workers to it. (The monetary attractiveness is the wage itself, which governs movements *along* the supply curve.) Jobs that people find pleasant and satisfying will attract a large supply of labour and will consequently pay a relatively low wage. In contrast, a premium will have to be paid to attract workers to jobs that are onerous, disagreeable, or dangerous—such as washing the windows of skyscrapers.

Finally, the amount of ability and training needed to enter a particular job or profession is relevant to its supply of labour. Brain surgeons and professional baseball players earn generous incomes because there are few people as highly skilled as they are and because it is time consuming and expensive to acquire these skills even for those who have the ability.

In addition to all this, it is important to recognize that adjustments in the labour market are slow in comparison with those for other inputs or commodities. Workers are reluctant, for example to move their homes from a low-wage geographic area to a higher-wage area, so wage differentials may persist longer than price differentials do in other markets. In the labour markets, long-run equilibrium takes a long time to attain, particularly where substantial retraining and relocation are required to eliminate differences in wages among jobs.

ABILITY AND EARNINGS

In considering the effects of ability on earnings, it is useful to distinguish between skills that can be duplicated easily and skills that cannot. If

Jones has an ability that Smith cannot acquire even if he undergoes extensive training, the wages that Jones earns will contain an element of economic rent, just as in the case of Mario Lemieux. Virtually anyone with moderate athletic ability can be taught to shoot a hockey puck at a net. But in most cases, no amount of training will teach the player to play hockey the way Lemieux does. His high salary is a reward for his unique ability.

But many of the abilities that the market rewards generously—such as the skills of doctors and lawyers—clearly can be duplicated. Here, the theory of rent does not apply, and we need a different explanation for the high wages that these skilled professionals earn. Once again, however, part of our analysis from earlier in this chapter finds an immediate application because the acquisition of skills, through formal education and other forms of training, has much in common with business investment decisions. Why? Because the decision to undertake more education in the hope of increasing future earnings involves a sacrifice of *current* income for the sake of *future* gain—precisely the hallmark of an investment decision.

INVESTMENT IN HUMAN CAPITAL

That education is an investment is a concept familiar to most college and university students. You made a conscious decision to go to school rather than to enter the labour market, and you are probably acutely aware that this decision is now costing you money—lots of money. Your tuition payments may be only a minor part of the total cost of going to college or university. Think of a high-school friend who chose not to go on to postsecondary education and who is now working. The salary that he or she is earning could, perhaps, have been yours. You are deliberately giving up this possible income in order to acquire more education.

In this sense, your education can be thought of as an investment in yourself—a *human investment*. Like a firm that devotes some of its money to building a plant that will yield profits at some future date, you are investing in your own future, hoping that your postsecondary education will help you earn more than what your high-school-educated friend can earn or that it will enable you to find a more pleasant or prestigious job when you graduate. Economists call activities like obtaining a postsecondary degree **investments in human capital** because such activities give the human being many of the attributes of a capital investment.

Doctors and lawyers earn such high salaries partly because of their many years of training. That is, part of their wages can be construed as a return on their (educational) investments, rather than as economic rent. Unlike the case of Mario Lemieux, there are a number of people who conceivably could become surgeons if they found the job sufficiently attractive to endure the long years of training that are required. Few, however, are willing to make such a large investment of their own time, money, and energy. Consequently, the few who do become surgeons earn very generous incomes.

Economists have devoted much attention to the acquisition of skills through human investment. An entire branch of economic theory — called **human-capital theory**—analyzes an individual's decisions about education, training, and so on in exactly the same way as we have analyzed a firm's decision to buy a machine or build a factory. Although educational decisions can be influenced by love of learning, desire for prestige, and a variety of other preferences and emotions, human-capital theorists find it useful to analyze a schooling decision as though it had been made purely as a business plan. The optimal approach to education, from this point of view, is to stay in school until the marginal revenue (in the form of increased future income) of another year of schooling is exactly equal to the marginal cost.

One implication of human-capital theory is that postsecondary graduates should earn sufficiently more than high-school graduates to compensate them for their extra investments in schooling. Do they? Will your investment pay off? Many generations of college and university students have supposed that it would, and for years, studies of the incomes earned by graduates indicated that they were right. These studies showed that the income differentials earned by postsecondary graduates provided a good "return" on the tuition payments and sacrificed earnings that they had "invested" in their schooling. But education investments turned a bit sour in the 1970s. The reason was the obvious one: Relative to high-school graduates, the supply of college and university graduates expanded more rapidly than did the demand. More recently, the estimated returns on postsecondary education have returned to higher values.

Human-capital theory stresses that jobs that require more education must pay higher wages if they are to attract enough workers, because people insist on a financial return on their human investments. But the theory does not address the other side of the question: What is it about more-educated people that makes firms willing to pay them higher wages? To put the point differently, the theory explains why the quantity of educated people *supplied* is limited but does not explain why the quantity *demanded* is substantial even at high wages.

Most human-capital theorists complete their analyses by assuming that students in colleges and universities are acquiring particular skills that are productive in the marketplace. In this view, educational institutions are factories that take less-productive workers as their raw materials, apply doses of training, and produce more-productive workers as outputs. It is a view of what happens in schools that makes educators happy and accords well with common sense. However, a number of social scientists doubt that this is how schooling raises earning power.

EDUCATION AND EARNINGS: DISSENTING VIEWS

Just why is it that jobs with stiffer educational requirements typically offer higher wages? The common-sense view that educating people makes them more productive is not universally accepted.

CHAPTER 14 PRICING THE FACTORS OF PRODUCTION: INCOME DISTRIBUTION 451

Education as a sorting mechanism. One alternative view denies that the educational process teaches students anything directly relevant to their subsequent performance on the job. Rather, it holds that people differ in ability when they enter the school system and differ in more or less the same way when they leave. What the educational system does, according to this theory, is to sort individuals by ability. Skills like intelligence and self-discipline that lead to success in schools, it is argued, are closely related to the skills that lead to success in jobs. As a result, more-able individuals stay in school longer and perform better. Prospective employers know this and consequently seek to hire those whom the school system has suggested will be the most productive workers.

The radical view of education. Many radical economists question whether the educational system really sorts people according to ability. The rich, they note, are better situated to buy the best education and to keep their children in school regardless of ability. Thus, education may be one of the instruments by which a more-privileged family passes its economic position on to its heirs while making it appear that there is a legitimate reason for firms to give them higher earnings. As radicals see it, education sorts people according to their social class, not according to their ability.

Radicals also hold a different idea about what happens inside schools to make workers more "productive." They believe that, instead of serving primarily as instruments for the acquisition of knowledge and improved ability to think, schools primarily teach people discipline—how to show up five days a week at 9:00 A.M., how to speak in turn and respectfully, and so on. These characteristics, radicals claim, are what business firms prefer and what cause them to seek more-educated workers. They also suggest that the schools teach docility and acceptance of the capitalist status quo, and that this, too, makes schooling attractive to business.

The dual labour market theory. A third view of the linkages among education, ability, and earnings is part of a much broader theory of how the labour market operates—the theory of **dual labour markets**. Proponents of this theory suggest that there are two very different types of labour markets, with relatively little mobility between them.

The "primary labour market" is where most of the economy's "good jobs" are—jobs in computer programming, business management, and skilled crafts that are interesting and offer considerable possibilities for career advancement. The educational system helps decide which individuals get assigned to the primary labour market, and, for those who make it, greater educational achievement does indeed offer financial rewards.

The privileged workers who wind up in the primary labour market are offered opportunities for additional training on the job; they augment their skills by experience and by learning from their fellow workers, and they progress in successive steps to more-responsible, better-paying positions. Where jobs in the primary labour market are concerned, dual labour market theorists agree with human-capital theorists that education really is productive. But they agree with the radicals that admission to the primary labour market depends in part on social position and that firms probably care more about steady work habits and punctuality than about reading, writing, and arithmetic.

Everything is quite different in the "secondary labour market"—where we find all the "bad jobs." Jobs like domestic service and fast-food service offer low rates of pay, few fringe benefits, and virtually no training to improve the workers' skills. They are dead-end jobs offering little or no hope for promotion or advancement. As a result, lateness, absenteeism, and thievery are expected as a matter of course, so that workers in the secondary labour market tend to develop bad work habits that confirm the prejudices of those who assigned them to inferior jobs in the first place.

In the secondary labour market, increased education leads neither to higher wages nor to increased protection from unemployment—benefits that generally come with increased schooling elsewhere in the labour market. For this reason, workers in the secondary market have little incentive to invest in education.

In sum, we have a well-established fact—that people with more education generally earn higher wages—but very little agreement on the theory accounting for this fact. There is probably some truth to each of the proposed explanations, and each of them consequently has some relevance for the workings of the labour market in reality.

UNIONS AND COLLECTIVE BARGAINING

Thus far, our analysis of labour markets has ignored one rather important fact: The supply of labour is not at all competitive in many labour markets; instead, it is controlled by a labour monopoly, a **union**.

While unions are important, only about 30 percent of Canada's non-agricultural workers belong to unions. Union membership seems much more significant than this to the public because unions are large, and therefore newsworthy, institutions.

Unions are less prevalent in the United States, where only about 16 percent of the workers are unionized, but they are more prevalent in some other industrialized countries. For example, about 43 percent of British workers and about 90 percent of Swedish workers belong to unions.

THE DEVELOPMENT OF UZNIONISM IN CANADA

There is no doubt that industrial working conditions were terrible before unions were formed and these conditions created widespread support among workers for the labour movement. Just 50 years ago, working conditions remained poor (see the boxed insert on the next page), and management strongly resisted the organization of unions.

The original Canadian unions, which appeared in the early 1800s, were formed by workers in particular crafts or trades. These craft unions were the first to appear for two reasons: The relatively small number of members in each of the unions meant that organization costs were small, and there were few substitutes for the services offered by these skilled workers. This meant that the threat of a strike represented a much bigger problem for employers than would have been the case with easily replaced unskilled workers.

Early union history included a number of ugly incidents. Sometimes employers would hire men to intimidate union leaders or strike organizers, and often violent incidents were arranged to cast the labour leaders as the troublemakers. Another problem that limited union growth was the treatment of unions in the courts. Initially, the courts interpreted the withholding of services for higher wages as a form of restraint of trade.

In the late 1800s, the Canadian affiliate of the Knights of Labour, a powerful American union, attempted to organize Canada's less-skilled workers along industry rather than craft lines. The Knights of Labour stressed the broader political issues concerning the role of labour in society. As it turned out, however, the workers cared more about what they saw as bread-and-butter issues, and union membership began to decline after 1886. The Knights of Labour and some smaller Marxist-oriented unions in British Columbia continued to exert some influence until about 1930.

The first widely successful confederation of labour in Canada was the Trades and Labor Congress of Canada (TLC), founded in 1883, which became the Canadian affiliate of the American Federation of Labor (AFL). The TLC reverted to an emphasis on skilled workers, organizing them on a country-wide basis by craft. The union devoted its efforts to the day-to-day issues of pay, work week, working and safety conditions, and related problems.

Another attempt to include unskilled workers took place with the formation of the Canadian Congress of Labour (CCL) in 1940. This organization was the Canadian affiliate of the United States' Congress of Industrial Organizations (CIO). It resembled the Knights of Labour in that its aim was to organize all workers by plant and industry rather than by craft. However, the CCL, like the TLC, avoided the broad political emphasis that characterized the Knights of Labour, and the two main wings of the labour movement merged in 1956, forming the Canadian Labour Congress (CLC). A similar merger took place in the United States, creating the AFL–CIO.

It is interesting to compare the growth of unions in Canada and the United States. Strong membership growth occurred earlier in the United States, mainly because of legal differences. By 1935, American workers had acquired the legal right to strike, and in the same year, it became illegal for employers to fire pro-union employees. In Canada, such firings were not made illegal until 1939, and workers did not gain official

FURTHER DETAIL

WORKING CONDITIONS FIFTY YEARS AGO: ONE WORKER'S ACCOUNT

I started work for Stelco in 1940, and one of the jobs we had will give you an idea of conditions.

When the brick lining on the big open hearths would go down, all the labour gangs from all over the plant were called over to tear them down and to rebuild them. I was on the labour gang at the slag dump, and the foreman would come along about 4:00 in the afternoon and say: "You go home now and be back here at 6:00 and report over to open hearth." They didn't give you a chance to object at all. The inference was there—if you're not there at 6:00, don't bother to come back at all.

These furnaces had just been shut down, and they were still hot—I mean red hot, not white hot. The company didn't want to waste time. They didn't make any money when the furnaces were down.

You wore big wooden clogs on your feet, because your boots would start to burn if you didn't wear these clogs, and you wrapped a scarf around your ears and your ears would start to burn. You'd stand outside the door, and spot a brick. You'd spot the brick, because if you got in there and started to fish around, you started to burn. You couldn't stay in there any longer than 30 seconds or your clothes would start to smoulder. So you made up your mind—that's the brick right there! You had a big pair of tongs, and you made a lunge, and grabbed that brick, and ran right out. I've seen big, strong husky men — the heat would make them drop like flies. But there was a job that had to be done.

SOURCE: *Baptism of a Union: Stelco Strike of 1946*, W. Roberts (ed.), Department of Labour Studies, McMaster University. Reprinted with permission.

recognition of their right to organize until the war. As a result, union membership grew rapidly from 1935 to 1945 in the United States and from 1940 to 1950 in Canada.

The favourable public attitude toward unions in the United States soured somewhat after World War II, perhaps because of the rash of strikes that took place in 1946. One result of these strikes was the Taft-Hartley Act of 1947, which specified and outlawed certain "unfair labour practices" by unions. Specifically, the act severely limited the extent of the "closed shop" (under which only union members can be hired) and permitted state governments, at their discretion, to ban the "union shop"

Canadian Unions: Problems and Issues

The 1982 Charter of Rights is seen by many as limiting labour's rights. Most Supreme Court judgements defining how the Charter is to be interpreted have stressed individual rights. In a series of much-noted decisions in 1987, the court ruled that "the modern rights to bargain collectively and to strike are not fundamental rights and freedoms." Thus, the court has not interpreted "freedom of association" to include strike or bargaining and has ruled that governments have the right to curtail collective bargaining for public-sector workers by limiting salary increases, prohibiting strikes and lockouts, and imposing compulsory arbitration. The judgement is based on the proposition that restricting the right to strike is justified when "the effect of a strike would be especially injurious to the economic interests of a third party." The labour movement's reaction has been to try to arrange an amendment to the Charter specifying that its references to "everyone" include not only "individuals" and "corporations" but also labour's bargaining units.

A second discouraging set of developments for Canadian unions springs from trends in organized labour in other countries, as well as in the nature of jobs generally. The union movement was considerably weakened in the United States and Great Britain by the policies of Ronald Reagan and Margaret Thatcher, respectively. In addition, there has been a growing trend toward part-time work, which has not only kept average employment income from rising, but has also made it increasingly difficult for unions to organize workers.

Another impediment to Canadian unions is the general move toward freer trade and deregulation. Both require that the productivity of Canadian workers be increased through adjustments to production methods, such as increased use of robotics and computer-assisted design methods. But unions have tended to be suspicious of such changes. (This issue is discussed in greater detail in Chapter 32, at page 1032.)

Unions and Economic Nationalism

It is interesting to consider how labour's views on economic nationalism have changed over the years, as described in the following passages from an article by Professor Samuel Bowles of the University of Massachusetts.

A century ago there was a clear connection in the West between nationalism and political ideology. Conservatives were nationalists — businessmen warned their employees and fellow citizens against foreign agitators. Progressives and the labour movement, meanwhile, were internationalists.

Today it is business, not labour, that thinks in international terms. We find the labour movement, and the progressive political community in general, reeling before the challenges posed by the globalization of production.

Recognizing the gains to be made by redistributing income within a national economy, labour has increasingly embraced a nationalist position since the Second World War, while business, recognizing the profit opportunities in global capitalism, has tended to adopt internationalist positions.

The emergence of the welfare state defined national boundaries as the limits of redistribution. . . .

(continued)

(continued)

Both the economic effectiveness of the welfare state and the power of the labour movement required national boundaries, for in a world of cheap transport and cheap labour, the free movement of goods and labour jeopardizes the material gains of unions and social-program beneficiaries. A truly global system of economic competition would eventually force wage restraint and even concessions on the more well-to-do segments of the world's working class. . . .

As a result, multinational corporations are now portrayed as unpatriotic, and their global operations are the targets of uncommon criticism from labour. Asia-bashing has also seeped into labour's rhetoric.

From an egalitarian viewpoint, there are practical and moral problems with populist jingoism. It may promote tariffs and gain some short-run job protection, but it is divisive because it pits the interests of (often low-income) consumers of imported goods against those of workers. . . .

Tariff protection . . . is an unlikely foundation for a long-term populist coalition. As long as wages, working conditions and environmental protection in other parts of the world fall far short of North American standards, workers here will always be threatened with losing their jobs when their plants pack up and head overseas. Tariff protection can (and should) be used to promote smooth long-term economic adjustments, but it cannot protect the living standards of domestic workers in the long run.

Doing this requires two things: the maintenance of a high level of worldwide demand for developed countries' goods and services, and the spread of democratic and union rights and environmental protection throughout the world. Neither objective can be realized if workers in leading capitalist countries (and those who speak for them) adopt a "blame the Koreans" attitude.

SOURCE: Excerpted from Samuel Bowles, "Different Wavelengths," *The Globe and Mail*, December 8, 1988, page A7. Originally published in *Tikkun*, a journal of political and social criticism based in Oakland, California. Reprinted with permission.

(an arrangement that requires employees to join the union). These so-called right-to-work laws have since been adopted by many American states.

A rather different legal decision took place in Canada. In 1945, there was a long strike involving the workers of the Ford Motor Company of Canada over the issue of union security. The dispute was finally resolved by an arbitration decision within the Supreme Court. The resulting rules, which came to be known as the **Rand formula** (after the Supreme Court judge), made it illegal for workers to be forced to join a union, but at the same time made it compulsory for them to pay union dues, whether or not they were members. This decision had the effect of solidifying union rights. Various versions of the Rand formula have been adopted in collective agreements involving public-sector workers in many provinces, and its use is compulsory for many private-sector contracts.

The net result of the two countries' different laws and legal precedents is that only about 16 percent of American workers are union members, a much lower proportion than in Canada. Another difference between the two labour movements is that Canadian unions have maintained their historical involvement with general political reforms in a more direct way than have their American counterparts. The third and most immediate difference is that, today, public-sector unions are far more extensive in Canada than they are in the United States. One reason for this is that many more government employees, at all levels of government, are permitted to unionize in this country.

The largest membership growth in Canada since 1960 has been in the public sector. But this growth has just compensated for declining membership in other areas. Membership has fallen because there is now a lower percentage of workers in the heavy industries (where unions have been popular), a larger percentage of the work force is young and female, and a growing number of workers want part-time employment. These groups seem less attracted to unions. Finally, the deep recessions of the early 1980s and 1990s, as well as the widespread public frustration with visible public-sector unions such as the Canadian Union of Postal Workers, have made unions less popular.

UNIONS AS A LABOUR MONOPOLY

Unions require that we alter our economic analysis of the labour market in much the same way that monopolies required us to alter our analysis of the goods market. You will recall that in a monopolized product market, a firm selects the point on its demand curve that maximizes its profits. Much the same idea applies to unions, which are, after all, monopoly sellers of labour. They too face a demand curve—derived this time from the marginal productivity schedules of firms—and can choose the point on it that suits them best.

The problem for the economist trying to analyze union behaviour—and perhaps also for the union leader trying to select a course of action—is how to decide which point on the demand curve is "best." Unlike the case of the business firm, there is no obvious goal analogous to profit maximization that clearly delineates what the union should do. Instead, a number of alternative goals are plausible, partly because union members themselves differ in their objectives, particularly in the trade-off between higher wages and job security. If older workers are protected from being fired by seniority rules that require those who have held jobs longest to be the last to be dismissed, these older workers may give greater priority to high wages and pensions than do younger workers. Younger workers may be more concerned about job security, health and safety provisions, and working hours. The policy pursued by union leaders may depend on the relative power of the different groups of members in the union.

ALTERNATIVE UNION GOALS AND STRATEGIES

Differences in union goals can be illustrated with the aid of Figure 14-11, which depicts a demand curve for labour, labelled *DD*. The union leadership must decide which point on the curve is best. One possibility is to treat the size of the union as fixed and force employers to pay the highest wage they will pay and still employ all the union members. If, for example, the union has 4000 members, this would be point *A*, with a wage of $12 per hour. But this is a high-risk strategy for a union. Firms forced to pay such high wages will be at a competitive disadvantage compared with firms that have non-union labour, and may even be forced to shut down.

Alternatively, union leaders may be interested in increasing the size of their unions. In an extreme case, they might try to make employment as large as possible without pushing the wage below the competitive level. If the competitive wage would be $6 per hour in the absence of the union, this strategy would correspond to selecting point *C*, with employment for 8000 workers. In this case, the existence of the union would have no effect on wages or on employment.

An intermediate strategy that has often been suggested calls for the union to maximize the total income of all workers. This would dictate choosing point *B*, with a wage of $9 per hour and jobs for 6000 workers (since point *B* is where the demand elasticity is unity in this numerical

FIGURE 14-11

ALTERNATIVE GOALS FOR A UNION

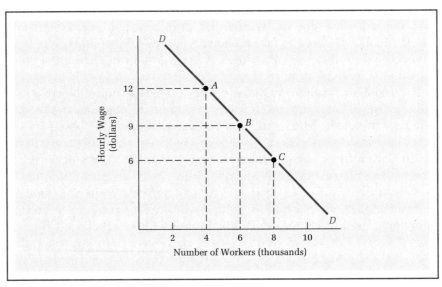

Line *DD* is the demand curve for labour in a market that becomes unionized. Point *C* is the equilibrium point before the union, when wages were $6 per hour. If the union wants to push wages higher, it normally will have to sacrifice some jobs. Points *A* and *B* show two of its many alternatives.

example). Other possible strategies can also be imagined, but these suffice to make the basic point clear.

Unions, as monopoly sellers of labour, have the power to push wages above the competitive levels. However, since the demand curve for labour is downward sloping, such increases in wages can normally be achieved only by reducing the number of jobs. Just as a monopoly firm must limit its output to push up its price, so the union must restrict employment to push wages up.

This can be seen clearly by comparing points B and A with point C (the competitive solution). If the union selects point B, it raises wages by $3 per hour, but at the cost of 2000 jobs. If it goes all the way to point A, wages are raised to twice the competitive level, but employment is cut in half.

What do unions actually try to do? There are probably as many different choices as there are unions. Some seem to pursue a maximum-employment goal much like point C, raising wages very little. Others seem to push for the highest possible wages, much like point A. Most probably select an intermediate route. This implies, of course, that the effects of unionization on wage rates and employment will differ markedly among industries.

How would a union that has decided to push wages above the competitive level accomplish this task? One approach is to restrict supply. By keeping out some of the workers who would like to enter the industry or occupation, the supply curve of labour is shifted inward. This sort of behaviour is often encountered in craft unions, which may require a long period of apprenticeship. Such unions sometimes offer only a small number of new memberships each year, largely to replace members who have retired or died. Membership in such a union is very valuable and is sometimes offered primarily to offspring of current members. Restricting supply is also practised within the medical profession (whose association operates like a union) by limiting enrollment in medical schools. Many other professional associations also perform the functions of unions for their members.

Instead of restricting supply, the union can simply set a high wage rate. In this case, it is the employers who will restrict entry into the job, because with wages so high, they will not want to employ many workers. This second strategy is more typically employed by industrial unions, like those representing automobile or mine workers. Either method can be used to achieve the desired point on the demand curve. Wages are raised only by reducing employment in either case.

In some exceptional cases, however, a union may be able to achieve wage gains without sacrificing employment. To do this, the union must be able to exercise effective control over the demand curve for labour. Union actions try to push the demand curve outward, simultaneously raising both wages and employment. This is usually difficult to do, but one way is by *featherbedding* — forcing management to employ more workers than are really needed.[9] Quite the opposite technique is to institute a campaign to raise worker productivity, which some unions seem to have been able to do. Alternatively, the union can try to raise the demand for the company's product either by flexing its political muscle (for example, by successfully lobbying for legislation to reduce foreign competition) or by appealing to the public to buy union products.

HAVE UNIONS REALLY RAISED WAGES?

The theory of unions as monopoly sellers of labour certainly suggests that unions have some ability to raise wages, but it also shows that they may be hesitant to use this ability for fear of reducing employment. To what extent do union members actually earn higher wages than non-members?

The consensus that has emerged from economic research on this question would probably surprise most people. A study by H. Gregg Lewis estimated that most union members earn wages about 15 percent higher than those earned by non-members (who are otherwise identical in skill level, geographical location, and so on).[10] While this figure is certainly not negligible, and while there are indications that it has been rising slightly, the differential can hardly be considered huge. This does not mean, however, that unions have raised wages by no more than 15 percent. Some observers believe that union activity has also raised the wages of non-unionized workers by forcing non-union employers to compete harder for their workers. If so, the differential between union and non-union workers must be less than the amount by which unions have raised wages overall. In addition, unions have improved the situations of their members, and perhaps of all workers, in other areas—for example, working conditions, health and safety measures, and the provision of pensions—that do not show up in pay cheques but do raise the cost of labour to the employer.

MONOPSONY AND BILATERAL MONOPOLY

While the analysis we have just presented has its applications, it oversimplifies matters in several important respects. For one thing, it envisions a market situation in which one powerful union is dealing with many powerless employers: The labour market is assumed to be monopolized on the selling side but competitive on the buying side. There are industries that more or less fit this model. The giant Teamsters union negotiates with a trucking industry that comprises thousands of firms,

---

9. The best-known example of featherbedding involved the railway unions, which for years forced management to keep "firemen" in the cabs of diesel engines, in which there were no burning fires. Similarly, the musicians' union requires the O'Keefe Centre in Toronto to hire a "house minimum" of twenty musicians each night, even if fewer are needed for a particular performance. Of course, it is not only labour that has tried to create an artificial demand for its services. Lawyers, doctors, and business firms, among others, have sought ways to induce consumers to buy more of their products and services. *EXERCISE:* Can you think of ways in which they have done this?

10. H.G. Lewis, *Union Relative Wage Effects: A Survey* (Chicago: University of Chicago Press, 1986).

most of them quite small and powerless. Similarly, most of the unions in the construction industry are much larger than the firms with which they bargain.

But there are many cases that simply do not fit the model. The large automakers do not stand idly by while the United Auto Workers union picks its favourite point on the demand curve. Nor does the steelworkers' union sit across the bargaining table from representatives of a perfectly competitive industry. In these and other industries, while the union certainly has a good deal of monopoly power over labour supply, the firms also have some **monopsony** power over the labour demand. Just as a monopoly union on the selling side of the labour market does not passively sell labour at the going wage, a monopsony firm on the buying side does not passively purchase labour at the going wage or at the wage suggested by the labour union. Analysts find it difficult to predict the wage and employment decisions that will emerge when both the buying and the selling sides of a market are monopolized — a situation called **bilateral monopoly**.

The difficulties here are similar to those we encountered in considering the behaviour of oligopolistic industries in Chapter 11. Just as one oligopolistic firm, in planning its strategy, is acutely aware that its rivals are likely to react to anything it does, a union dealing with a monopsony employer knows that any move it makes will elicit a countermove by the firm. This knowledge makes the first decision that much more complicated.

Still, it is possible to say something a bit more concrete about the outcome of the wage-determination process under bilateral monopoly. Where the demand for labour is highly competitive, we have seen that a union can generally achieve a higher wage rate only by paying the price — a reduction in employment. However, where the employer is a monopsonist, a union may be able to induce the firm both to raise wages and to increase employment. While the details of the analysis are better left to a more advanced course (or, perhaps, to classroom discussion), the underlying logic is simple enough to be explained here.

A monopsonist employer unrestrained by a union will use its market power to force wages down below the competitive level, just as a monopoly seller uses its market power to force prices higher. The monopsonist employer forces wages down by reducing its demand for labour below what would otherwise be the profit-maximizing amount, thereby cutting both wages and the number of workers employed. However, a union may be able to prevent this from happening. It can deliberately set a floor on wages, pledging its members not to work at all at any wage level below this floor. If the union's threat is credible to the employer, the firm will lose the incentive to cut its demand for labour, since that attempt will no longer force wages down. Consequently, the presence of a union may force the monopsony firm to pay higher wages and, simultaneously, to employ more workers than it would otherwise have employed.

Even though it is hard to think of industries that are pure monopsonists in their dealings with labour, these conclusions are nonetheless of

MONOPSONY refers to a market situation in which there is only one buyer.

BILATERAL MONOPOLY is a market situation in which there is a monopoly on the selling side and a monopsony on the buying side.

some importance in reality. The fact is that large oligopolistic firms often do engage in one-on-one wage bargaining with their employees' unions, and there is reason to believe that the resulting bargaining process resembles to a considerable degree the workings of the bilateral monopoly model that we have just described. (Even in the absence of a union [a monopoly seller], an increase in wages *can* lead to higher employment where a monopsonist employer is involved. This contrasts with the outcome in the competitive situation discussed earlier in this chapter, where a minimum-wage law was shown to cause lower employment. Thus, in a monopsony situation, a minimum-wage law need not involve a trade-off, since both wages and employment can be increased by such a policy.)

COLLECTIVE BARGAINING AND STRIKES

The process by which unions and management settle upon the terms of a labour contract is called **collective bargaining**. Unfortunately, nothing as straightforward as a supply–demand diagram exists in reality to tell us what wage level will emerge from a collective-bargaining session. Furthermore, actual collective-bargaining sessions range over many more issues than wages. For example, fringe benefits — such as pensions, health and life insurance, paid holidays, and the like—may be just as important as wages to both labour and management. Wage premiums for overtime work and seniority privileges are also commonly negotiated. Similarly, work conditions, such as the speed with which the assembly line should move, can be crucial issues. Many labour contracts specify in great detail the rights of labour and management to set work conditions —and also provide elaborate procedures for resolving grievances and disputes. The list could go on and on. The final contract that emerges from collective bargaining may well run to many pages of fine print.

With the issues so varied and complex and with the stakes so high, it is no wonder that both labour and management employ skilled professionals who specialize in preparing for and carrying out these negotiations, and each side enters a collective-bargaining session armed with reams of evidence supporting its positions.

The bargaining in these sessions is often heated, with outcomes riding as much on the personalities and skills of the negotiators as on cool-headed logic and economic facts. Negotiations may last well into the night, with each side seeming to try to wear the other out. Each side may threaten the other with grave consequences if it does not accept its terms. Unions, for their part, generally threaten to strike or to carry out a work slowdown. Firms counter with the threat that they would rather face a strike than give in or that they might even close the plant without a strike (an action that is called a "lockout").

MEDIATION AND ARBITRATION

Where the public interest is seriously affected or when the union and firm reach an impasse, government agencies may well send in a **mediator**, whose job is to try to speed up the negotiation process. This impartial observer sits down with each side separately to discuss its problems and tries to persuade each to yield a bit to the other. At some stage, when an agreement looks possible, the mediator may call the two sides back together for another bargaining session in his or her presence.

A mediator, however, has no power to force a settlement. Success hinges on his or her ability to smooth ruffled feathers and to find common ground for agreement. Sometimes, in cases where the union and the firm simply cannot agree and where neither wants a strike, differences are finally settled by **arbitration**—the appointment of an impartial individual empowered to settle the issues that negotiation could not resolve. In fact, in some vital sectors where a strike would be too injurious to the public interest, the labour contract or the law may stipulate that there must be *compulsory arbitration* if the two parties cannot agree. However, both labour and management are normally reluctant to accept this procedure.

STRIKES

Most collective-bargaining situations do not lead to strikes. But the right to strike remains fundamentally important for the bargaining process. Imagine, for example, a firm bargaining with a union that was prohibited from striking. It seems likely that the union's bargaining position would be quite weak. On the other hand, a firm that always capitulated rather than suffer a strike would be virtually at the mercy of the union. Thus, strikes (or, more precisely, the possibility of strikes) serve an important economic purpose.

For the families involved, work stoppages clearly represent major dislocations. Despite this and despite the headline-grabbing nature of major strikes, however, the total amount of work-time lost to strikes is small— far less, for example, than the time lost to coffee breaks! It is noteworthy, though, that Canada's record of time lost to strikes is not good compared with that of other countries. In recent years, for example, Canada has lost about half a day per worker per year because of strikes. The comparable figures for several other countries are as follows: Italy, four-fifths of a day per worker per year; Great Britain, two-fifths of a day; the United States and France, approximately one-tenth of a day; and Japan, one one-hundredth of a day.

Some analysts are concerned about Canada's labour relations as we move toward free trade with both the United States and Mexico. In the most recent year for which data are available, Canada had almost four times as many strikes and lockouts as Mexico and fourteen times as many as the United States. It is also disturbing that some Canadian labour leaders argue that the job losses suffered by their members are independent of the unions' wage claims. For example, in late 1992, a leader of the United Steelworkers of America blamed the layoffs of 630 Stelco workers in Hamilton on government policy. No reference was made to the fact that the union had run a 93-day strike two years earlier and had obtained a large wage increase. At that earlier time, the union executive claimed that they had "won" the strike and that they expected no permanent layoffs to follow from the higher wages.

Recent amendments to Ontario's Labour Relations Act that increase the power of unions have raised similar concerns among some analysts. If union leaders demonstrate disregard for two facts—that the demand curve for labour is negatively sloped and that capital migrates to profitable locations—then job creation efforts in Ontario may become more difficult.

COLLECTIVE BARGAINING IN THE PUBLIC SECTOR

We have argued that strikes serve an important function in private-sector bargaining as a way of dividing the fruits of economic activity between big labour and big business. But does the same rationale for strikes apply to the public sector, where strikes or work stoppages have become increasingly common among postal workers, garbage collectors, teachers, and others?

It is not clear that it does. In most private-sector strikes, labour and management are inflicting harm upon each other in a battle for the "survival of the fittest." Consumers normally suffer only mild inconveniences. When General Motors is on strike, many potential car buyers may be disappointed, but they can turn to Fords, Chryslers, or many imports. Similarly, when other products made by private firms disappear from the shelves because of strikes, the consumer can easily replace them with close substitutes. Thus, in many cases, we can think of consumers as being relatively unharmed spectators when large unions and large private firms slug it out.

But public-sector bargaining is different. Here, management does not represent the interests of capital against those of labour; rather, it represents the public. There is no pool of profits to be divided between the union and the shareholders. Instead, what management agrees to give the union comes out of the pockets of taxpayers.

Finally, it is quite clear that the public is not just a spectator in such strikes, but the primary victim. When police or fire-protection services are reduced, when mail delivery ceases, when public schools or airports shut down, consumers cannot find substitutes for these services. In a very real sense, then, strikes in the public sector are strikes against citizens, not strikes against management. They pit representatives of a particular group of workers against representatives of taxpayers as a whole.

For these reasons, the right of public employees to strike has traditionally been more limited than the corresponding right of private-sector workers. Nevertheless, employees under the federal government's jurisdiction were given the right to strike in the late 1960s. Partly as a result of this, the biggest growth in union membership has been in the public sector.

CORPORATISM AND INDUSTRIAL DEMOCRACY

Discussion of public-sector unions raises the more general issue of sectional interests. Trade unions are not the only institutions trying to acquire market power for the benefit of their restricted membership. Professional associations (such as those for doctors and lawyers) have the same purpose, as do firms that engage in takeovers and mergers to increase market share. All these institutions attempt to increase the general support for their actions by claiming that they act in the public interest. For example, firms are simply "trying to achieve the economies of large-scale operations" and the unions are "fighting a general battle for the working class."

The market mechanism limits the power of these institutions, since it facilitates the introduction of cheaper substitutes, such as goods from abroad or labour-saving production inputs. It is perfectly rational for self-seeking institutions to use the political process to limit the market's ability to undermine their market power. This is why both firms and unions call for increased protection through foreign tariffs and quotas, and why unions support minimum-wage legislation. If market power exists and the political process is used to maintain it, what is the prognosis for the price system?

One suggested solution is corporatism or tripartism. It was tried in England in the early 1970s by Prime Minister Edward Heath, when he asked employers and unions to "share fully with the government the benefits and obligations involved in running the national economy." The idea was to blunt the forces of special interest by making big business and big labour truly responsible for the public interest. For instance, it was hoped that this co-operative approach would reduce the excessive wage increases of particular labour groups (all of which had been justified by reference to the public interest). Margaret Thatcher's government discarded this approach, arguing that tripartism simply enabled private groups to strengthen their ability to use the political process for their own purposes.

Industrial democracy is another suggested institutional change that might solve these problems. It is based on the assumption that it is simply not feasible to dismantle the power of large firms and unions. Instead, workers should be allowed fuller participation in management decisions. The reasoning behind this suggestion is that only under a system of worker self-management will workers be forced to appreciate and accept the constraints of the market that employers normally face. There are several successful examples of this arrangement in Canada. Critics of industrial democracy worry that entrepreneurial drive would not be rewarded under such a system, and that it would consequently be diminished. The current state of Canadian labour relations suggests that these issues will continue to be actively debated.

SUMMARY

1. A person's income depends on the factors of production that he or she owns and on the prices that those factors command in the market. Short of redefining the ownership of factors, we can change the distribution of income by changing factor prices (an approach that can have undesirable side effects) or by transferring income from the rich to the poor by means of a very general tax system that does not differentiate among the alternative sources of income. We discuss factor pricing in this chapter, and general income redistribution in the next.

2. A profit-maximizing firm purchases the quantity of any input at which the price of the input equals its marginal revenue product.

3. The demand curve for labour, like the demand curve for any factor of production, is derived from the marginal revenue product curve. It slopes downward because of the "law" of diminishing marginal returns.

4. One reason that youth suffers from such high unemployment rates is that minimum-wage laws militate against the employment of low-productivity workers.

5. Increased demand for a good that needs land to produce it will drive up the prices of land either because inferior land will be brought into use or because land will be used more intensively.

6. Economic rent is any payment to the supplier of a factor of production that is greater than the minimum amount needed to induce the desired quantity of the factor to be supplied.

7. Factors of production that are unique in quality and difficult or impossible to reproduce will tend to be paid relatively high economic rents because of their scarcity. Factors of production that are easy to produce at a constant cost and that are provided by many suppliers will earn little or no economic rent.

8. Radical economists view marginal productivity theory as an instrument that promotes the interests of the capitalist class. They also criticize mainstream economists for having an unduly narrow focus; for accepting consumer tastes and human nature as "givens" rather than treating them as the results of the economic system; for stressing efficiency rather than equality as an economic goal; and for concentrating on increasing the quantity of output rather than the quality of life.

9. Interest rates are determined by the supply of and the demand for funds. The demand for funds is a derived demand, since these funds are used to finance business investment. Thus, the demand for funds depends on the marginal productivity of capital.

10. A dollar obtainable sooner is worth more than a dollar obtainable later because of the interest that dollar can earn in the interim.

11. Economic profits over and above the cost of capital are earned (a) by exercise of monopoly power, (b) as a payment for bearing risk, and (c) as the earnings of successful innovation.

12. The desirability of increased taxation of profits depends on its effects on the supply of entrepreneurial talent. If most profits are economic rents, higher profits taxes will have few detrimental effects. But if most profits are necessary to attract entrepreneurs into the market, higher profits taxes can threaten the capitalist system.

13. The supply of labour is determined by free choices made by individuals. Because of conflicting income and substitution effects, the quantity of labour supplied may rise or fall as a result of an increase in wages. Historical data show that hours of work per week have fallen as wages have risen, suggesting that income effects may be dominant in the long run.

14. In a free market, the wage rate and the level of employment are determined by the interaction of supply and demand. Workers in great demand or short supply will command high wages, and, conversely, low wages will be assigned to workers in abundant supply or with skills that are not in great demand.

15. Human-capital theory assumes that people make educational decisions in much the same way that businesses make investment decisions and tacitly assumes that people learn things in school that increase their productivity in jobs.

16. Other theories of the effects of education on earnings deny that schooling actually raises productivity. One view is that the educational system primarily sorts people according to their abilities. Another view holds that schools sort people according to their social class and teach them discipline and obedience.

17. According to the theory of dual labour markets, there are two distinct types of labour markets with very little mobility between them. The primary labour market contains the "good" jobs, where wages are high, prospects for advancement are good, and higher education pays off. The secondary labour market contains the "bad" jobs, with low wages, little opportunity for promotion, and little return on education.

18. About one-third of all Canadian workers belong to unions, which can be thought of as monopoly sellers of labour.

19. Analysis of union behaviour is complicated by the fact that a union can have many goals. For the most part, unions probably force wages to be higher and employment to be lower than they would be in a competitive labour market. However, there are exceptions.

20. Strikes (or at least the threat of strikes) play an important role in collective bargaining as a way of dividing the fruits of economic activity between big business and big labour. Strikes in the public sector, however, take on a different character because the adversaries are no longer "labour" versus "capital" but rather a particular group of labourers versus the general public.

CONCEPTS FOR REVIEW

Factors of production	Discounting	Dual labour markets
Marginal productivity principle	Entrepreneurs	Union
Derived demand	Risk-bearing	Rand formula
Minimum-wage law	Invention versus innovation	Monopsony
Marginal land	Income and substitution effects	Bilateral monopoly
Economic rent	Backward-bending supply	Collective bargaining
Investment	curve	Mediation
Capital	Investments in human capital	Arbitration
Interest	Human-capital theory	

QUESTIONS FOR DISCUSSION

1. A profit-maximizing firm expands its purchase of any input up to the point where diminishing returns have reduced the marginal revenue product so that it equals the input price. Why does it not pay the firm to "quit while it is ahead," buying so small a quantity of the input that diminishing returns do not set in?

2. Which of the following inputs do you think include a relatively large economic rent in their earnings?
   a. Nuts and bolts
   b. Petroleum
   c. A champion racehorse
   Use supply–demand analysis to explain your answer.

3. Three machines are employed in an isolated area. They each produce 1000 units of output per month, the first requiring $17 000 in raw materials, the second $21 000, and the third $23 000. What would you expect to be the monthly charge for the first and second machines if the services of the third machine could be hired at a price of $9000 a month? What part of the charges for the first two machines would be economic rent?

4. Economists conclude that a tax on the profits of firms will be shifted in part to consumers of the products of those firms, in the form of higher product prices. However, they believe that a tax on the rent of land usually cannot be shifted. What explains the difference?

5. Many economists argue that a tax on apartment houses is likely to reduce the supply of apartments but that a tax on all land, including the land on which apartment houses stand, will not reduce the supply of apartments. Can you explain the difference? How does your answer to this question relate to your answer to Question 4?

6. If you have a contract under which you will be paid $10 000 two years from now, why do you become richer if the rate of interest falls?

7. What is the difference between interest and profit? Who earns interest, in return for what contribution to production? Who earns economic profit, in return for what contribution to production?

8. Explain the difference between an invention and an innovation. Give an example of each.

9. "Marginal productivity does not determine how much a worker will earn — it determines only how many workers will be hired at a given wage. Therefore, marginal productivity analysis is a theory of demand for labour, not a theory of distribution." What, then, do you think determines wages? Does marginal productivity affect their level? If so, how?

10. In Canada today, the first $100 000 of income that an individual earns in capital gains is tax free. Some politicians argue that this tax shelter should be removed. Use supply–demand diagrams to determine the likely effects of such a tax change on the levels of savings, investment, and the rate of interest for both a closed and an open economy.

11. Universities are known to pay rather low wages for student labour. Can this be explained by the operation of supply and demand in the local labour market? Is the concept of monopsony of any use? How might things differ if students formed a union?

12. University professors are highly skilled (or at least highly educated!) labour. Yet their salaries are not very high. Is this a refutation of the marginal productivity theory?

13. The following table shows the number of pizzas that can be produced by a large pizza parlour employing various numbers of pizza chefs.

Number of Chefs	Number of Pizzas per Day
1	40
2	64
3	82
4	92
5	100
6	92

    a. Find the marginal physical product schedule of chefs.

    b. Assuming a price of $5 per pizza, find the marginal revenue product schedule.

    c. If chefs are paid $70 per day, how many chefs will this pizza parlour employ? How would your answer change if wages rose to $95 per day?

    d. Suppose the price of a pizza rises from $5 to $6. Show what happens to the derived demand curve for pizza chefs.

14. "Strikes are simply intolerable and should be outlawed." Comment.

15. "Public employees should have the same right to strike as private employees." Comment.

16. In which of the following industries is wage determination most plausibly explained by the model of perfect competition? the model of pure monopoly? the model of bilateral monopoly?

    a. Odd-job repairs in private homes.

    b. Manufacturing of low-priced clothing for women.

    c. Steel manufacturing.

17. In the bitter strike battle between Eastern Airlines and several of its unions, it was clear from the beginning that the airline was in serious financial trouble, with its survival and the survival of the jobs it provided apparently in question. Discuss what might nevertheless have led the unions to hold out so tenaciously.

18. Can you think of some types of workers whose marginal products were probably raised by computerization? Are there any whose marginal products were probably reduced? Can you characterize the difference between the two types of jobs in general terms?

THE TAX SYSTEM AND INCOME INEQUALITY

*The hardest thing in the world
to understand is income tax.*
ALBERT EINSTEIN

Chapter 12 examined several reasons why the government might want to interfere with the workings of the market mechanism. Some of these interferences involve levying taxes; for example, we noted that taxes may be useful in correcting misallocations of resources caused by externalities. Other interferences involve direct spending by government — the provision of public goods is a good example—and this spending, in turn, requires that taxes be levied to raise the necessary revenue. These, then, are two of the main reasons for taxes: to improve resource allocation and to raise revenue to pay for government expenditures. The third reason for levying taxes is to change the distribution of income. This objective can be accomplished in two ways: by imposing higher rates of taxation on the rich than on the poor, and by paying some of the tax revenue back (in the form of transfer payments) to citizens whose market income is deemed to be inadequate.

Our discussion in this chapter proceeds in four stages. First, we examine the general tax system in Canada. We consider the effects that our current taxes have on the allocation of resources and the distribution of income, and the principles that distinguish "good" from "bad" taxes. An understanding of these principles allows us to evaluate some of the federal government's recent tax reforms, such as the goods and services tax (GST).

The balance of the chapter is devoted to a broader exploration of the problem of income inequality. In the second major section, we consider the problem of poverty in Canada and explore the workings of our country's welfare system. Then, in the third section, we examine the issue of discrimination — a root cause of some of our problems of income inequality and one of the reasons that those problems cannot be solved fundamentally by means of transfer payments alone. Finally, in the last section of the chapter, we offer a full explanation of one of the twelve Ideas for Beyond the Final Exam: the fundamental trade-off between economic equality and economic efficiency. Taking for granted that equality and efficiency are both important social goals, we shall learn why policies that promote greater income equality (or less poverty or less discrimination) often threaten to interfere with economic efficiency. We shall explain why this is so and what can be done about it.

In a brief course, the two middle sections of the chapter (on welfare problems and discrimination, respectively, pages 496–514) may be omitted without loss of continuity. In other words, if necessary, the reader may move directly from the discussion of taxes in the first section to the examination of the trade-off between equality and efficiency in the last section.

TAXES IN CANADA

SOME FACTS AND DEFINITIONS

By international standards, Canadians are taxed rather heavily. Figure 15-1 compares the fraction of income paid in taxes in Canada with that paid by residents of some other industrialized nations. Canadians are not heavily taxed in comparison with the French (or citizens of some other

FIGURE 15-1

THE BURDEN OF TAXATION IN G7 COUNTRIES, 1991

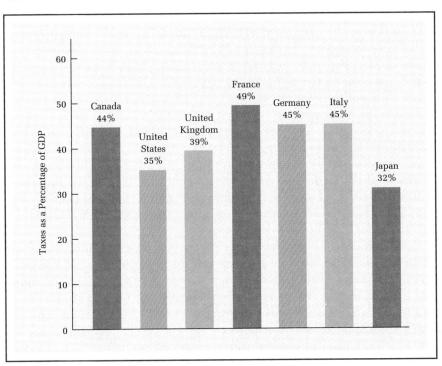

Canadians are not heavily taxed in comparison with the citizens of France, but we do pay more tax than the Americans and the Japanese.

SOURCE: Compiled from data in Canadian Tax Foundation, *The National Finances 1992* (Toronto: Canadian Tax Foundation, 1992), page 3:16, table 3.15.

non-G7 countries, like the Swedes or the Dutch), but we do pay more taxes than the British, the Americans, and the Japanese.

PROGRESSIVE, PROPORTIONAL, AND REGRESSIVE TAXES

Economists classify taxes as progressive, proportional, or regressive. Under a **progressive tax**, the fraction of income paid in taxes rises as a person's income increases. Under a **proportional tax**, this fraction is constant. And under a **regressive tax**, the fraction of income paid to the tax collector declines as income rises. Since the fraction of income paid in taxes is called the **average tax rate**, these definitions can be expressed as they are in the margin.

Often, however, the average tax rate is less interesting than the **marginal tax rate**, which is the fraction of each *additional* dollar that must be paid to the tax collector. The reason, as we will see, is that the marginal tax rate, not the average tax rate, most directly affects economic incentives.

DIRECT VERSUS INDIRECT TAXES

Another way to classify taxes is to divide them into two broad categories: **direct taxes** and **indirect taxes**. Direct taxes are levied directly on *people*. Primary examples are income taxes and inheritance taxes, although the notoriously regressive poll tax — which charges every person the same amount — is also a direct tax. In contrast, indirect taxes are levied on *goods and services*, such as gasoline, telephone use, home ownership, and so on. Sales taxes and property taxes are the most important indirect taxes in Canada. Many countries also rely heavily on the value-added tax, of which Canada's GST is one version. As a broad generalization, one can say that the Canadian and U.S. governments rely more heavily on direct taxation than do the governments of most other countries.

The federal government has relied heavily on direct taxes, while, in comparison, the provincial and municipal governments have depended more on indirect taxes and on transfers from the federal government. The three big direct taxes used by the federal government are the personal income tax, the corporate profits tax, and the payroll tax. Together, these taxes represented 60 percent of the overall tax revenue collected by all levels of government in 1991. The provincial governments have relied largely on sales taxes and related sources, such as natural-resource revenues and profits from liquor sales. The municipal governments depend on property taxes and grants from the provinces. A more complete breakdown of government revenue sources is given in Figure 15-2. Let us now look at the major taxes in some detail.

THE PERSONAL INCOME TAX

The tax on individual incomes began during World War I, and it is now the government's biggest revenue-raiser. It is well known that the per-

A **PROGRESSIVE TAX** is one in which the average tax rate paid by an individual rises as his or her income rises. A **PROPORTIONAL TAX** is one in which the average tax rate is the same at all income levels. A **REGRESSIVE TAX** is one in which the average tax rate falls as income rises.

The **AVERAGE TAX RATE** is the ratio of taxes to income.

The **MARGINAL TAX RATE** is the fraction of each additional dollar of income that is paid in taxes.

DIRECT TAXES are taxes levied directly on people. **INDIRECT TAXES** are taxes levied on specific economic activities.

FIGURE 15-2

THE COMPOSITION OF THE OVERALL TAX BILL, 1991

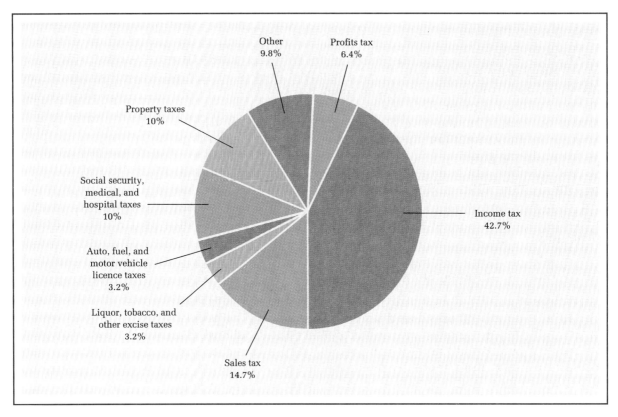

This diagram shows the share of each major tax in the overall tax bill for 1991.

SOURCE: Compiled from data in The Fraser Institute, *Tax Facts Eight*, 1992, page 5.

sonal income tax is progressive. Table 15-1 contains an abbreviated version of the tax table for 1992, showing only the rates for the amounts payable to the federal government. (Total income tax rates vary by province. For example, Ontario's income tax for each individual equals roughly 55 percent of his or her federal taxes. Nine provinces and the two territories allow the federal government to collect their income tax revenue for them. Quebec continues to levy and collect its own taxes and does not participate in the intergovernmental tax-collection agreements.) The progressivity is reflected in the way the average tax rate rises as income rises. In 1992, there were only three "tax brackets" in Canada: Incomes of $29 590 or less were taxed at the rate of 17 percent; incomes between $29 591 and $59 180, at 26 percent; and incomes of more than $59 180, at 29 percent.

Individuals can use various **tax shelters**, but lower-income earners are not able to take advantage of tax shelters as effectively as higher-income earners. Let us look at some of these tax shelters.

A TAX SHELTER is a special provision in the Income Tax Act that reduces or defers taxation if certain conditions are met.

TABLE 15-1

FEDERAL PERSONAL INCOME TAX RATES FOR THE 1992 TAX YEAR

Taxable Income (dollars)	Average Tax Rate (percent)	Marginal Tax Rate (percent)
25 000	17	17
45 000	20	26
75 000	23	29

SOURCE: Canadian Tax Foundation, *The National Finances 1992* (Toronto: Canadian Tax Foundation, 1992), page 7:3.

Capital gains and dividend income.   Canadian tax laws exempt from income tax the first $100 000 of **capital gains** earned during an individual's lifetime (although this exemption does not apply to capital gains derived from real estate investment beyond one's home). Above the exemption amount, capital gains are taxed at only two-thirds of the usual rate. Dividend income is also taxed at favourable rates. Most capital gains and dividends accrue to people in the upper income groups, so this tax shelter is the preserve of the rich. Why did the government create such a thing? The main reason is to encourage people to save and to invest in risky ventures.

A **CAPITAL GAIN** is the profit made from the sale of an asset at a higher price than was paid for it.

Tax benefits for home-owners.   Many individuals think that our income tax system should allow home-owners to deduct their payments of mortgage interest and property tax when calculating taxable income. After all, it is argued, such deductions are allowed in the United States and certain European countries, and it seems fair to treat home-owners in a way similar to shopkeepers. The fault in this reasoning is that unlike shopkeepers, home-owners already receive a tax shelter by not having to declare the income they earn by incurring these expenses. This is because the "income" from owning a home accrues not in the form of cash, but in the form of living without paying rent.

    An example will make things clear. Mutt and Jeff are neighbours. Each earns $30 000 a year, and each has just won a lottery and received $100 000 in cash. Mutt uses his winnings to buy a $100 000 house for cash. Thus, he has no mortgage or rent payments, but must pay $2000 per year in property tax. Jeff uses his winnings to buy a bond that yields 10 percent interest. Thus, his interest income is $10 000. Jeff rents the house next door to Mutt's, which is exactly the same and which rents for $12 000 per year. Most observers would agree that Mutt and Jeff *should* pay the same income tax. But, ignoring other deductions and exemptions, Mutt's taxable income is $30 000, while Jeff's is $40 000 (see Table 15-2).

    How could this disparity be rectified? One way would be to allow both home-owners and renters to deduct their expenses. This would make Mutt's taxable income fall by $2000 to $28 000, and it would allow Jeff's

TABLE 15-2
OWNING VERSUS RENTING A HOME

Item	Mutt (owner)		Jeff (renter)	
Income	$30 000		$30 000	
Interest income	—		10 000	
Property tax		2000		—
Rent				12 000
Taxable income	$30 000		$40 000	

taxable income to fall by $12 000 to $28 000. Another way would be to force home-owners to add their "imputed rent" to their income. In this example, Mutt would have to add the implicit rental income of $12 000 (that he is receiving from himself), but he would be allowed to deduct the expenses involved (the property tax of $2000). Thus, his taxable income would be $40 000, just like Jeff's. The fact that the implicit rental income of home-owners is not taxed represents a major tax shelter that favours the well-to-do. Home-owners get a further break since capital gains obtained from the sale of one's principle residence are exempt from taxation.

We could go on listing more tax shelters, but enough has been said to illustrate the point:

Our personal income tax has offered many opportunities to avoid payment of tax through tax shelters. Since most shelters are beneficial mainly to rich people, they have eroded the progressivity of the income tax quite seriously.

SALES AND EXCISE TAXES

Most provincial governments levy a broad-based sales tax on the purchase of goods and services. There are exceptions, such as food, children's clothing, services, and housing rents, so that slightly less than 50 percent of consumer expenditure is exempt. In 1992, sales tax rates ranged from zero in Alberta to 12 percent in Newfoundland. In addition, most provinces have special **excise taxes** on such things as tobacco products, liquor, gasoline, and luxury items. The federal government has, in the past, levied a general manufacturers' sales tax (MST), which in 1989 stood at a rate of 13.5 percent. It has also imposed excise taxes on a hodgepodge of miscellaneous goods and services, including cigarettes, oil and gasoline, and liquor, as well as on many imported products (in the form of tariffs and duties). In 1991, the federal government replaced the MST with a more general goods and services tax (GST), a variation on the **value-added tax** (VAT) that is levied in many countries around the world.

An **EXCISE TAX** is a tax levied on a particular commodity or service, as a fixed amount of money per unit of product sold or as a fixed percentage of the purchase price.

With a VAT, each firm is taxed only on the excess of its sales over the costs incurred in buying materials at earlier stages in the production process. Hence, there is a built-in incentive for compliance, since all participants have an interest in reporting to the government the full price of what they had to pay for partly fabricated products. In addition, a VAT is flexible, so exports can easily be exempted. Finally, the tax can be broadly based (that is, levied on a wide variety of goods and services, at primary, intermediate, and final production stages), and the more products and services it is levied on, the lower the tax rate can be to achieve the same revenue.

The main drawback of increased reliance on *any* form of sales tax is that sales taxes are regressive, meaning that they are unfair to low-income families. Since poor families cannot afford to save as much as richer families, they spend a larger proportion of their incomes on goods and services; hence, if the items they buy are taxed, they pay a larger proportion of their incomes in sales tax. Therefore, the federal government also introduced a personal income tax credit for low-income families to go hand-in-hand with the GST. According to government estimates, the two changes in the tax system have had the combined effect of lessening the overall tax burden on families earning up to about $30 000 and increasing the tax burden on families with higher incomes. But the progressivity of this tax package comes entirely from its tax-credit component; by itself, as we have already stated, a sales tax is regressive.

WHY DID THE GOVERNMENT REPLACE THE MST WITH THE GST?

As its name suggests, the MST was a tax levied on the sale of manufactured items. The problems caused by this tax stemmed largely from the fact that in a modern economy, the production process is divided into many stages. What is a final manufactured product for one company is, in fact, an input to production for another company; hence, in many cases, the MST amounted to a tax on business inputs. Consequently, the MST effectively raised the costs of production for Canadian manufacturers. In 1989, the Department of Finance estimated that 49 percent of MST revenues actually came from taxing business inputs.

Because other countries do not tax manufacturing inputs in this way, the MST effectively put Canadian firms at a cost disadvantage in relation to the foreign producers of our imports. (Indeed, the MST was often referred to as a "job killer.") Thus, despite the controversy surrounding the introduction of the GST, analysts agreed that the MST had to be changed. They were in favour of eliminating features of the tax system that limited the market's ability to create jobs, especially since no other industrialized country was imposing such an impediment on its own economy.

Short-run job creation was not the only thing at stake in this debate. In the longer term, labour income can be increased only if labour becomes more productive. For this to occur, firms must invest in new plant and equipment to give labour more productive capital to work with. In this regard, the usual argument in support of sales taxes as opposed to income taxes is that income taxes discourage saving and therefore restrict the funds available to finance firms' investments. Conversely, sales taxes, because they are paid only when income is spent (not when it is saved), encourage saving and result in more funds being made available to finance firms' investment expenditures. Compared with income taxes, then, sales taxes are supposed to raise the level of the country's future capital stock and increase potential gross domestic product (GDP) and per-capita incomes in the future. But because the MST taxed business inputs, which resulted in the taxation of about one-third of firms' investment expenditures, it failed to deliver this desirable outcome and instead restricted growth in potential GDP and labour earnings. The GST was designed to solve this problem.

Another undesirable feature of the MST was its unreliability as a source of revenue for the government. As of 1989, only about 70 000 firms actually paid some part of the tax, and 22 000 "special rulings" exempting firms from the tax or modifying its terms had been arranged with the Department of Finance. This administrative morass was a classic example of what can occur when a tax fails as a general scheme that all market participants must confront on an equal footing.

As a general value-added tax, the GST goes a long way toward solving these problems. Some goods and services, such as basic groceries, prescription drugs, medical devices, residential rents, legal-aid services, day-care services, and many health, dental, and educational services, are exempt from the tax. Where the tax does apply, it works as follows: If a household buys an item — say, a dishwasher — it pays the sales tax. If a business buys an item to be used as an input—say, a restaurant buys a dishwasher—it too pays the tax, but it can later claim a refund called an "input tax credit." This is how the GST avoids placing Canadian manufacturers at the competitive disadvantage that existed under the MST.

One problem with the GST is that it requires a great deal of paperwork. At the end of each accounting period, all firms must calculate the total GST that they have collected for the government in the course of making sales. They must also subtract the amount of the GST that they have paid on business inputs to other firms, for which they can claim a GST refund.

Hence, while it is true that 19 of the 24 most highly industrialized countries in the world had a VAT in place well before Canada introduced its GST, the GST is among the most cumbersome of such schemes to implement. This would not have been the case if the government's early attempts to design a co-ordinated federal and provincial sales tax program had succeeded. Under such a program, both federal and provincial sales taxes would have been collected with the aid of the same administrative machinery. In the face of provincial resistance to the plan, however, the federal government felt compelled to proceed on its own, in the hope that the provinces would agree to co-ordinate as time passed. So far, only Quebec has co-ordinated in this way.

ADVANTAGES AND DISADVANTAGES OF THE GST

To summarize, the main advantages of the GST are as follows:

1. It replaces an inefficient tax. By taxing business inputs, the MST led to job losses in the export sector and in the import-competing sector, and it restricted investment spending by firms. The GST, on the other hand, stimulates growth in potential output, and thus provides the main benefit expected of a sales tax.

2. On democratic grounds, a visible tax is better than a hidden one; and since it is paid at the retail level, the GST is highly visible.

The main disadvantages of the GST are as follows:

1. Like any sales tax, if it were not supplemented by a program such as the income tax credit for low-income earners, the GST would contribute to regressivity in the overall tax system. This is because the ratio of consumption to income is highest for low-income earners, so any type of sales tax scores well on efficiency grounds but poorly on equity grounds.

2. Many analysts have argued that the early 1990s — a period of economic slowdown — was not the time for implementing the GST, because, as we will explain in Chapter 22, increases in sales taxes are "stagflationary" in the short run.

3. Many individuals are opposed to the GST on the grounds that it could become an instrument facilitating a major "tax grab" by the government in the future.

The last two disadvantages are related. If we could assume that the government would *not* raise the GST rate in the future, we could safely conclude that the GST would not prove to be a strongly inflationary measure. In other words, since government revenues from the GST (minus expenditures on the accompanying tax-credit program) simply replace the revenues lost through the elimination of the MST, the GST should cause no increase in the overall payout by the private sector or in the overall cost of producing goods and services. But if the GST rate were to be raised in the future, the reform package would no longer be revenue-neutral, and inflationary consequences would have to be expected. Can we, then, predict whether or not the GST rate will be raised in the near future?

The experience of other countries can be cited in support of either possibility. For example, while New Zealand implemented a 10 percent VAT in 1986 and increased it to 12.5 percent by 1989, Spain and Greece implemented similar tax schemes at the same time and have not increased their rates since. A number of other countries, such as Germany and the United Kingdom, have had VAT schemes in place for many years and have raised their rates significantly over time. Brazil's VAT, on the other hand, has remained virtually constant for over 25 years. Thus, it is difficult to speculate on the implications of Canada's GST for the future.

OTHER TAXES

CORPORATE PROFITS TAX

The tax on corporate profits is considered a "direct" tax because corporations are seen as fictitious "persons" in the eyes of the law. The general federal tax rate is 28 percent of income, and the provincial rate varies from 10 to 17 percent. But the corporate tax rates are lower for manufacturing firms and small businesses. Corporate investments in certain depressed regions also qualify firms for a lower rate.

There are many tax shelters that permit large corporations to reduce their tax obligations. For example, some companies set up subsidiaries in other countries that have low corporate tax rates. Such companies then adjust the prices of their products or services among their various affiliates in such a way that most of their profits are officially recorded in the countries with the lowest tax rates. We shall discuss some of the difficulties that arise in taxing profits later in this chapter (pages 492–93).

PROPERTY TAXES

Municipalities raise revenue by taxing the value of properties, such as houses and office buildings. (Exemptions include educational institutions and church property. For some of these, the province makes grants to municipalities to make up for "lost" taxes.) The usual procedure assigns each taxable property an *assessed value* (originally intended to be an estimate of its market value), then imposes a tax rate, based on the community's total assessed value, that will yield enough revenue to cover expenditures on local services. Because properties are reassessed much less frequently than market values change and because market values are usually estimated by crude rules of thumb, certain inequities arise. For example, one person's house may be assessed at almost 100 percent of its true market value while another's may be assessed at little more than 50 percent.

The property tax is among the most controversial in the tax system. Some economists view it as a tax on one particular type of wealth—real estate. In this view, since families with higher incomes generally own much more real estate than do families with low incomes, the property tax is *progressive* relative to income; that is, the ratio of property tax to income rises as we move up the income scale. However, other economists view the property tax as an excise tax on rents; since expenditures on rent generally account for a larger fraction of the incomes of the poor than of the rich, this makes it seem *regressive* relative to income.

There is also political controversy over the property tax. Municipal property tax revenues (along with provincial grants) have been the traditional source of financing for public schools. As a result, wealthy communities with a lot of expensive real estate have been able to afford higher-quality schools than have poor communities. The reason can be made clear with a simple arithmetical example. Suppose that real estate holdings in a wealthy municipality average $300 000 per family, while in a poor municipality, they average only $100 000 per family. If both municipalities levy a 2 percent property tax to pay for their schools, the wealthy municipality will generate $6000 per family in tax receipts, while the poor one will generate only $2000.

PAYROLL TAXES AND SOCIAL BENEFITS

Canada has two important payroll taxes: contributions to the Canada (or Quebec) Pension Plan and contributions to the unemployment insurance program. The unemployment insurance account is supposed to run a surplus during years of reasonable economic growth, and a deficit during years of recession. However, the recession of the early 1980s was so severe and protracted that the government was compelled to supplement the unemployment insurance fund from general revenues—a practice that has continued ever since, despite significant increases in the contribution rate.

The other major payroll tax—employer and employee contributions to the Canada Pension Plan — is paid into another fund, which operates somewhat differently from the trust funds associated with most private pension plans. In the private plans, you pay in money while you are working, it accumulates at compound interest, and then you withdraw it bit by bit in your retirement years. The solvency of such a plan is not in doubt, since it does not involve a commitment to pay out more to the individual than he or she has put in, plus the accumulated interest.

With the Canada Pension Plan, however, people who are now retired receive funds from the contributions of those who are currently working. Thus, the solvency of the system depends on changes in the patterns of economic and population growth. The proportion of the Canadian population aged 65 or older rose from 6.5 percent in the 1940s to 9.5 percent in the 1980s, and is expected to rise to more than 11 percent in the 1990s. Unless economic growth occurs at a rapid rate, payroll taxes will have to be raised or pension levels will have to be cut if the Canada Pension Plan is to remain solvent. Although this is not an immediate problem, no economist expects sufficient economic growth in the longer term to counteract the underlying demographic trends.

The other federal government programs for retirement are the Old Age Security and the Guaranteed Income Supplement schemes. These are not financed by payroll tax contributions to trust funds but are paid for out of the federal government's current general revenues. There are, however, some provincially levied payroll taxes: workers' compensation in all provinces and health insurance premiums in Ontario, British Columbia, and Alberta.

FISCAL FEDERALISM

Grants from the federal government are a major source of revenue for provincial and municipal governments. In addition, grants from the provinces are vital to municipal governments. This system of transfers from one level of government to the next is referred to as **fiscal federalism** and has a long history in Canada.

FISCAL FEDERALISM refers to the system of transfer payments from one level of government to the next.

Under the Constitution, most government-funded social programs fall within the jurisdiction of the junior levels of government. Health care, education, and welfare programs are the most notable. As a result, the junior-level governments have faced an ongoing squeeze between the growth in their expenditure requirements and available revenues. The federal government has relieved this squeeze in several ways: by reducing federal government income tax rates (to "make room" for provincial tax-rate increases), by making transfer payments to the provincial governments, and by directly undertaking income-security programs (such as the Canada Pension Plan and the unemployment insurance program).

While the provinces have welcomed revenues from the federal government, they have often resented the loss of provincial discretion that is involved. Before 1977, there was a complicated set of transfer payments called **conditional grants**. Under these schemes, the federal government matched provincial government spending, according to various formulas, *if* the provinces spent their money in specified ways. The provinces often argued that the funds should have "no strings attached." The federal government discontinued conditional grants, because it objected to the power that this system gave the provinces in determining the size of the grants. The provinces received more **unconditional grants** and an increased share of the personal income tax in return. (Other aspects of federal–provincial co-ordination leave the federal government with some control over certain transfers.)

As the name implies, unconditional grants involve transfers from the federal government to the provinces, with no strings attached. The grants are paid out of general federal revenues, and many go only to provinces that would have to levy very high tax rates in order to raise per-capita revenues equal to the national average. Many different taxes are involved in these schemes, and the arrangements are revised every few years. In recent years, seven of the ten provinces (excepting British Columbia, Alberta, and Ontario) have received unconditional grants. The negotiations associated with revising these "equalization payments" are often the major source of dispute at federal–provincial conferences.

THE CONCEPT OF EQUITY IN TAXATION

Taxes are judged on the basis of two criteria: *equity* (Is the tax fair?) and *efficiency* (Does it interfere unduly with the workings of the market economy?). It is curious that economists have been concerned mostly with the latter, while public discussions about tax proposals almost always focus on the former. Let us, therefore, begin our discussion by investigating the concept of equitable taxation.

HORIZONTAL EQUITY

HORIZONTAL EQUITY is the notion that equally situated individuals should be taxed equally.

There are three distinct concepts of tax equity. The first is **horizontal equity**, which simply asserts that equally situated individuals should be taxed equally. When the principle is stated in this way, few quarrel with it. But it is often quite difficult to apply this principle in practice, and violations of horizontal equity can be found throughout Canadian tax laws.

Consider, for example, the personal income tax. Horizontal equity calls for two families with the same income to pay the same tax. But what if one family has eight children and the other has one child? Well, you answer, we must define "equally situated" to include equal family sizes, so only families with the same number of children can be compared on grounds of horizontal equity. But what if one family has unusually high medical expenses, while the other has none? Are they still equally situated? By now, the point should be clear: Determining when two families are equally situated is no simple task. In fact, the Canadian tax provisions involve many requirements that must be met before two families are construed to be "equal."

Another set of issues concerns the specific measures used to achieve horizontal equity in taxation. For example, if the goal is to ensure that families with many children are taxed fairly in comparison with smaller families, is it better to give relief to the former through a **tax exemption** —reducing taxable income by some amount—or through a **tax credit**— reducing the tax that is due by some amount? Some of the government's 1987 tax reforms focussed on just this issue, and as a result of the new legislation, credits replaced exemptions in our tax system.

The importance of this change is best explained with the aid of a numerical example. Consider two Ontario families, each with one employed parent, a second parent who does not work outside the home, and two young children. The families are alike in every way except that one has a gross income of $75 000 while the other has a gross income of $30 000. Under the pre-1988 system, the personal exemptions for a basic income earner, his or her spouse, and two children totalled roughly $10 000, so the taxable incomes for our two families would have been reduced to $65 000 and $20 000, respectively. The combined federal and provincial marginal tax rate would have been about 50 percent for the richer family and 20 percent for the poorer one. Thus, although the exemption of $10 000 would have reduced each family's tax base by the same amount, it would have saved the richer family $5000 in taxes and the poorer family only $2000.

Under the current credit system, the government may still give a total of $7000 in tax relief, but it distributes the funds differently. With credits, taxes are first calculated on the full amount of gross income—$75 000 and $30 000 in our example—but the amount of tax to be actually collected is reduced by the tax credit. If the credit were set at $3500 for a four-person family, both the high- and the low-income families would receive the same relief.

In brief, by removing the preferential treatment given to high-income earners under an exemption system, tax credits increase the progressivity of the tax system. In addition, tax credits set up an obvious and automatic mechanism for a system of *negative income tax*, a method of transferring funds to the poor that some people think would be easier and more equitable than are existing social-assistance schemes. Under a negative income tax scheme, almost every adult (not just those who owe tax) would fill out a tax form; tax credits and/or lack of income would result

A **TAX EXEMPTION** permits the reduction of an individual's or a firm's taxable income by some amount.

A **TAX CREDIT** directly reduces an individual's or a firm's tax obligation by a given amount that is independent of the tax rate. Some individual tax credits are *refundable*; if they reduce the tax owed to an amount less than zero, the government transfers that amount to the individual.

in some of them "owing" a negative amount, which would be paid to them by the government. The negative income tax proposal is discussed fully later in this chapter.

VERTICAL EQUITY

VERTICAL EQUITY is the notion that differently situated individuals should be taxed differently in a way that society deems to be fair.

The **ABILITY-TO-PAY PRINCIPLE** is the idea that people with greater ability to pay taxes should pay higher taxes.

The second concept of fair taxation seems to flow naturally from the first. If equals are to be treated equally, it appears that unequals should be treated unequally. This precept is known as **vertical equity**.

Just saying this, of course, does not get us very far. For the most part, vertical equity has been translated into the **ability-to-pay principle**, according to which those most able to pay should pay the highest taxes. But this still leaves a definitional problem similar to the problem of defining "equally situated": How do we measure ability to pay? The nature of each tax often provides a straightforward answer. In income taxation, we measure ability to pay by income; in property taxation, we measure it by property value; and so on.

A thornier problem arises when we try to translate the notion into concrete terms. Consider the three alternative income tax plans listed in Table 15-3. Under all three plans, families with higher incomes pay higher income taxes. Thus, all three plans could be said to operate on the ability-to-pay concept of vertical equity. Yet the three are quite different in their distributive consequences. Plan 1 is a progressive tax, something like the personal income tax in Canada: The average tax rate is higher for richer families. Plan 2 is a proportional tax: Every family pays 10 percent of its income. Plan 3 is quite regressive: Since tax payments rise more slowly than income, the tax rate for richer families is lower than that for poor families.

Which plan comes closest to the ideal notion of vertical equity? Many people find that Plan 3 offends their sense of "fairness," for it makes the distribution of income *after* taxes even more unequal than the distribution *before* taxes. But there is much less agreement over the relative merits of Plan 1 (progressive taxation) and Plan 2 (proportional taxation). Very often, in fact, the notion of vertical equity is taken to be synonymous with progressivity. Other things being equal, progressive taxes are seen as "good" taxes in some ethical sense because they make the distribution of income more equal. Conversely, regressive taxes are seen as "bad." On these grounds, advocates of greater equality of incomes support progressive income taxes and oppose sales taxes.

TABLE 15-3

THREE ALTERNATIVE INCOME TAX PLANS

Income	Tax Payments (dollars)			Average Tax Rates (percent)		
	Plan 1	Plan 2	Plan 3	Plan 1	Plan 2	Plan 3
10 000	300	1 000	1000	3	10	10
50 000	8 000	5 000	3000	16	10	6
250 000	70 000	25 000	7500	28	10	3

THE BENEFITS PRINCIPLE

Whereas the principles of horizontal and vertical equity, for all their ambiguities and practical problems, at least do not conflict with each other, the third principle of fair taxation often violates commonly accepted notions of vertical equity. According to the **benefits principle of taxation**, which is often applied when the proceeds from certain taxes are earmarked for specific public services, those who reap the benefits from government services should pay the taxes.

One clear example is admission fees to national parks. In 1992, the Ontario government announced its intention to charge tolls on all new limited-access highways. Most people seem to find the use of the benefits principle fair in such cases. But in other contexts — such as public schools, hospitals, and libraries—the body politic has been loath to apply the benefits principle because it clashes so dramatically with common notions of fairness. Thus, these services are normally financed out of general tax revenues, rather than by direct charges for their use. Even for health care, a strong case can be made on efficiency grounds for an increased use of the benefits principle. For a more detailed description of how the benefits principle can be applied in the medical field, without giving up on our principle of universal access, see the boxed insert on pages 979–80.

The **BENEFITS PRINCIPLE OF TAXATION** holds that people who derive the benefits from the service should pay the taxes that finance it.

THE CONCEPT OF EFFICIENCY IN TAXATION

The concept of economic efficiency is the central notion of Parts 2 through 4 of this book. The economy is said to be *efficient* if it has used every available opportunity to make someone better off without making someone else worse off. In this sense, taxes almost always introduce *inefficiencies*. That is, if the tax were removed, some people could be made better off without anyone being harmed.

However, a comparison of a world with taxes to a world without taxes is not particularly pertinent. The government does, after all, need to raise revenues to pay for the goods and services it provides. For this reason, when economists discuss the notion of "efficient" taxation, they are usually looking for the taxes that cause the *least* amount of inefficiency.

To explain the concept of efficient taxation, we need to introduce one new term. Economists define the **burden of a tax** as the amount of money taxpayers would have to be given to make them just as well off in the presence of the tax as they would be in its absence. An example will clarify this notion and also make clear why the burden of a tax normally exceeds the revenues it raises.

Suppose the government, in the interest of energy conservation, decides to levy a high tax on the biggest gas-guzzling cars, with progressively lower taxes on smaller cars (as some provinces do). For example, a simple tax schedule might be the following:

The **BURDEN OF A TAX** on individuals is the amount of money they would have to be given to make them just as well off with the tax as they would be without it.

Car Type	Tax
Cadillac	$1000
Taurus	500
Geo	0

Sandra has a taste for big cars and has always bought Cadillacs. (Sandra is clearly no pauper.) Once the new tax takes effect, she has three options. She can still buy a Cadillac Seville and pay $1000 in tax, she can switch to a Taurus and avoid half the tax, or she can switch to a Geo and avoid the entire tax.

If Sandra chooses the first option, we have a case in which the burden of the tax is exactly equal to the amount of tax the person pays. Why? Because if Sandra's rich aunt gives her $1000, Sandra winds up exactly as well off as she was before the tax was enacted.

Generally, when a tax induces no change in economic behaviour, the burden of the tax can be measured accurately by the revenue collected.

However, this is not what we normally expect to happen. Moreover, it is certainly not what the government intends by levying a tax on big cars. We normally expect taxes to induce some people to alter their behaviour in ways that reduce or avoid tax payments. Therefore, let us look into Sandra's other two options.

If she decides to purchase a Taurus, Sandra pays only $500 in tax. But this is an inadequate measure of the burden of the new tax because Sandra is greatly chagrined by the fact that she no longer drives a Cadillac. How much money would it take to make Sandra just as well off as she was before the tax? Only Sandra knows for sure. But we do know that it is more than the $500 tax that she pays. Why? Because, even if someone were to give Sandra the $500 needed to pay her tax bill, she would still be less happy, owing to the switch from a Cadillac to a Taurus, than she was before the tax was introduced. Whatever the (unknown) burden of the tax is, the amount by which it exceeds the $500 tax bill is called the **excess burden** of the tax.

The **EXCESS BURDEN** of a tax to an individual is the amount by which the burden of the tax exceeds the tax that is paid.

Sandra's final option makes the importance of understanding excess burden even clearer. If she switches to buying a Geo, Sandra will pay no tax. Are we therefore to conclude that she has suffered no burden? Clearly not, for she longs for the Cadillac that she no longer has. The general principle can be stated as follows:

Whenever a tax induces people to change their behaviour—that is, whenever it "distorts" their choices—the tax has an excess burden. This means that the revenue collected by the tax systematically understates the true burden of the tax.

The excess burdens that arise from tax-induced changes in economic behaviour are precisely the inefficiencies we referred to at the outset of this discussion. The basic precept of efficient taxation is to try to devise a tax system that *minimizes* these inefficiencies. (Another way of putting the same point is to say that the goal is to devise a tax system that minimizes the aggregate loss in consumer surplus. By recalling pages 107–11 in Chapter 4, you can see that as long as an industry has constant long-run average costs (so that the supply curve is horizontal), the excess burden of a sales tax is precisely measured as the loss in consumer surplus that results from the tax.)

In comparing two taxes that raise the same total revenue, the one that produces less excess burden is the more efficient.

Notice the proviso that the two taxes being compared must yield the same revenue. We are really interested in the *total* burden of each tax. Since

$$\text{Total burden} = \text{Tax collections} + \text{Excess burden},$$

only when tax collections are equal can we unambiguously state that the tax with *less* excess burden is more efficient. Since excess burdens arise when consumers and firms alter their behaviour on account of taxation, this precept of sound tax policy can be restated in the following way:

In devising a tax system to raise revenue, try to raise any given amount of revenue through taxes that induce the smallest changes in behaviour.

Of course, sometimes a tax is levied not primarily as a revenue-raiser but as a way of inducing individuals or firms to alter their behaviour. This case will be discussed in Chapter 17.

SHIFTING THE BURDEN OF TAXATION: TAX INCIDENCE

When economists speak of the **incidence of a tax**, they are referring to who actually bears the burden of the tax. In discussing the tax on gas-guzzling autos, we have adhered, so far, to what has been called the **flypaper theory of tax incidence**: that the burden of any tax sticks where the government puts it. In this case, the theory holds that the burden stays on Sandra. But often, things do not work out this way.

The **INCIDENCE OF A TAX** is an allocation of the burden of the tax to specific individuals or groups.

Consider, for example, what will happen if the government levies a $1000 tax on luxury cars like Cadillacs. Figure 15-3 shows this tax as a $1000 vertical shift of the supply curve. If the demand curve does not shift, the market equilibrium moves from point *A* to point *B*. The quantity of luxury cars declines as Sandras all over Canada react to the higher price by buying fewer luxury cars. Notice that the price rises from $30 000 to $30 500, an increase of $500. Thus, people who continue buying luxury cars bear a burden of only $500—just half the tax that they pay!

Does this mean that the tax imposes a negative excess burden? Certainly not. What it means is that consumers who refrain from buying the taxed commodity have managed to *shift* part of the burden of the tax

FIGURE 15-3

THE INCIDENCE OF AN EXCISE TAX

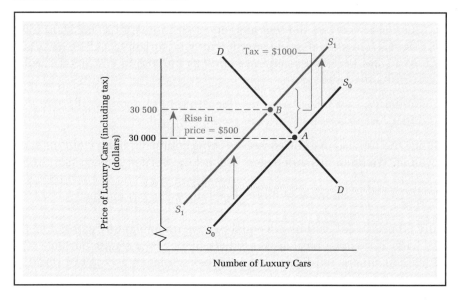

When the government imposes a $1000 tax on luxury cars, the supply curve relating quantity supplied to the price *inclusive of tax* shifts upward from S_0S_0 to S_1S_1. The equilibrium price in this example rises from $30 000 to $30 500, so the burden of the tax is shared equally between car sellers (who receive $500 less) and car buyers (who pay $500 more, including the tax). In general, how the burden is shared depends on the elasticities of demand and supply.

TAX SHIFTING occurs when the economic reactions to a tax cause prices and outputs in the economy to change, thereby shifting part of the burden of the tax onto others.

away from consumers generally, including those who continue to buy luxury cars. Who are the victims of this **tax shifting**? In our example, there are two main candidates. First are the car manufacturers or, more precisely, their shareholders. Shareholders bear the burden to the extent that the tax, by reducing car sales, cuts into their profits. The other principal candidates are auto workers. To the extent that their reduced production leads to layoffs or to lower wages, the auto workers bear part of the burden of the tax.

People who have never studied economics almost always believe in the flypaper theory of tax incidence, which holds that sales taxes are borne by consumers, property taxes by home-owners, taxes on corporations by shareholders, and so on. Perhaps the most important lesson to follow from our discussion of taxes is as follows:

The flypaper theory of tax incidence is often wrong.

Failure to grasp this basic point has led to all sorts of misguided tax legislation in which governments, thinking they were placing a tax burden on one group of people, inadvertently placed it squarely on another. Of course, there are cases where the flypaper theory of tax incidence comes very close to being correct. Let us consider some specific examples of tax incidence.

THE INCIDENCE OF EXCISE TAXES

Excise taxes have already been covered in our automobile example—Figure 15-3 could represent any commodity that is taxed. The basic finding is that part of the burden will fall on consumers of the taxed commodity (including those who stop buying it because of the tax) and part will be shifted to the firms and the workers who produce the commodity (see pages 134–38 for review).

The amount that is shifted depends on the slopes of the demand and supply curves. We can understand intuitively how this works. If consumers are so loyal to the taxed commodity that they will continue to buy almost the same quantity no matter what the price, it is clear that they will be stuck with most of the tax bill because they have left themselves vulnerable to it. Thus, we expect the following to be true:

The more inelastic the demand for the product, the larger the share of the tax that consumers will pay.

Similarly, if suppliers are determined to supply the same amount of the product no matter how low the price, most of the tax will be borne by suppliers:

The more inelastic the supply curve, the larger the share of the tax that suppliers will pay.

One extreme case arises if no one stops buying luxury cars when their price rises. The demand curve becomes vertical, like demand curve *DD* in Figure 15-4. In this case, there can be no tax shifting. The price of a luxury car (inclusive of tax) rises by the full amount of the tax—from $30 000 to $31 000—so consumers bear the entire burden.

The other extreme case arises when the supply curve is totally inelastic (see Figure 15-5). Since the number of luxury cars supplied is the same at any price, the supply curve will not shift when a tax is imposed. Consequently, car manufacturers must bear the full burden of any tax that is placed on their product. Figure 15-5 shows that the tax does not change the market price (including tax), which, of course, means that the price received by sellers must fall by the full amount of the tax.

Demand and supply schedules for most goods and services are not as extreme as those depicted in Figures 15-4 and 15-5, so the burden is shared by consumers and suppliers. Precisely how it is shared depends on the elasticities of the supply and demand curves.

THE INCIDENCE OF THE PAYROLL TAX

A payroll tax may be thought of as an excise tax on the employment of labour. As we mentioned earlier, the Canadian payroll tax comes in two parts: Some of it is levied on the employees (through payroll deductions) and the rest on employers. People who have never studied economics often fail to grasp this fundamental point:

FIGURE 15-4

AN EXTREME CASE OF TAX INCIDENCE

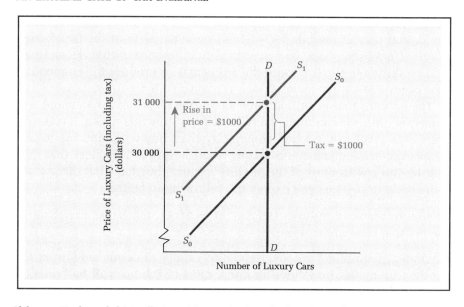

If the quantity demanded is totally insensitive to price (completely *inelastic*), the demand curve will be vertical. As the diagram shows, the price inclusive of tax rises, to $31 000 in this case, so buyers bear the entire burden of the tax. Since price exclusive of tax remains at $30 000, none of the burden falls on the sellers.

FIGURE 15-5

ANOTHER EXTREME CASE OF TAX INCIDENCE

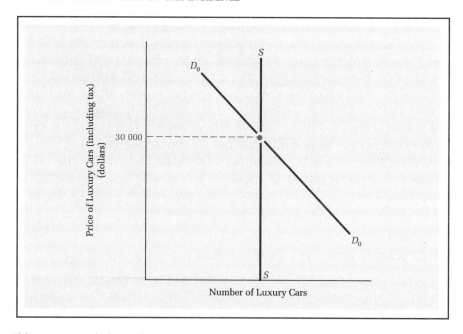

If the quantity supplied is totally insensitive to price, supply curve *SS* will be vertical and will not shift when a tax is imposed. The sellers will bear the entire burden, because the price that they receive net of tax (here, $30 000) is reduced by the full amount of the tax.

The incidence of a payroll tax is the same whether it is levied on employers or employees.

A simple numerical example can illustrate why this is so. Consider an employee earning $100 a day with a 14 percent payroll tax that is "shared" equally between the employer and the employee. How much does it cost the firm to hire this worker? It costs $100 in wages paid to the worker plus $7 in taxes paid to the government, for a total of $107 a day. How much does the worker receive? She gets $100 in wages paid by the employer less $7 deducted and sent to the government, or $93 a day. The difference between wages paid and wages received is $107 − $93 = $14.

Now suppose the government tries to "shift" the burden of the tax entirely onto firms by raising the employer's tax to $14 while lowering the employee's tax to zero. At first, the daily wage is fixed at $100, so firms' total labour costs (including tax) rise to $114 per day and workers' net incomes rise to $100 per day. The government seems to have achieved its goal.

But this is not an equilibrium situation. With the daily wage at $114 for firms and $100 for workers, the quantity of labour demanded by firms will be *less* and the quantity of labour supplied by the workers will be *more* than when the two wages were $107 and $93. There will therefore be a surplus of labour on the market (an excess of quantity supplied over quantity demanded), and this surplus will put downward pressure on wages.

How far will wages have to fall? It is easy to see that a wage of $93 will restore equilibrium. If the daily wage is $93, labour will cost firms $107 per day, just as it did before the tax change. Thus, firms will demand the same quantity as they did when the payroll tax was shared. Similarly, workers will receive the same $93 net wage as they did previously; quantity supplied will be the same as it was before the tax change. Thus, in the end, the market will completely frustrate the intent of the government.

The payroll tax is an excellent example of a case in which the government, misled by the flypaper theory of tax incidence, thinks it is "taxing firms" when it raises the employer's share and that it is "taxing workers" when it raises the employee's share. In truth, who is really paying depends on the incidence of the tax. But no difference results from a change in the employer's and the employee's shares.

Who, then, really bears the burden of the payroll tax? Like any excise tax, the incidence of the payroll tax depends on the elasticities of the supply and demand schedules. In the case of labour supply, a large body of empirical evidence points to the conclusion that the quantity of labour supplied is not very responsive to price for most population groups. The supply curve is almost vertical, like that shown in Figure 15-5. The result is that workers as a group are able to shift very little of the burden of the payroll tax.

But employers *can* shift it in most cases. Firms view their share of the payroll tax as an additional cost of using labour. Thus, when payroll taxes go up, firms try to substitute cheaper factors of production (capital) for labour wherever they can. This reduces the quantity of labour demanded, lowering the wage received by workers. And this is how market forces shift part of the tax burden from firms to workers.

To the extent that the supply curve of labour has some positive slope, the quantity of labour supplied will fall when the wage goes down, and in this way, workers can shift some of the burden back onto firms. But the firms, in turn, can shift that burden onto consumers by raising their prices. As we know from Part 2, prices in competitive markets generally rise when costs (such as labour costs) increase. It is doubtful, therefore, that firms bear any of the burden of the payroll tax. Here, the flypaper theory of tax incidence could not be further from the truth. Even though the tax is collected by the firm, it is really borne by workers and consumers.

THE INCIDENCE OF THE TAX ON CAPITAL

The corporate profits tax is difficult to analyze since it is partly a tax on pure economic profit and partly an excise tax on the employment of capital equipment. Also, as we note in Chapter 23 (page 789), the Canadian profits tax can have no effect on profits, or the earnings of capital, when it is levied on multinationals that receive a tax credit in their home country equal to the taxes paid in Canada. In the case of the multinationals, the burden of any unsheltered Canadian profits tax is squarely on the government (and therefore on the citizens) of the foreign country where the company is based. Our corporate tax simply lowers the tax revenue of the company's home country, dollar for dollar, as long as the company does not avoid paying the taxes to both governments. (Large corporations can avoid paying taxes by transferring portions of profits out of both Canada and the United States—which is usually the relevant home country—to affiliates in third countries where corporate tax rates are low.) Even for purely domestic firms that cannot escape taxes in this way, the flypaper theory of tax incidence is again far from the truth.

In the case of domestic firms, we can learn much about the incidence of the profits tax by treating it as a tax on the earnings of capital. The supply of capital to the Canadian economy is very elastic. If Canadian owners of capital cannot obtain an after-tax return in Canada equal to what is available elsewhere, they will invest elsewhere. Capital is far more mobile internationally than labour, and for a country as small as Canada, the minimum acceptable rate of return for capital is determined outside. Thus, we investigate the incidence of the tax on capital on the assumption that the supply is perfectly elastic, as shown in Figure 15-6.

Before the domestic tax is imposed, the supply of capital is perfectly elastic at a 10 percent rate of return (the return that we assume, for the purposes of this discussion, to be available in the rest of the world). Equilibrium in the capital market is initially at point A. If a 50 percent tax is imposed in Canada, capital owners require a 20 percent before-tax return to continue to employ their capital in Canada. Thus, the supply curve

FIGURE 15-6

THE INCIDENCE OF A TAX ON MOBILE CAPITAL

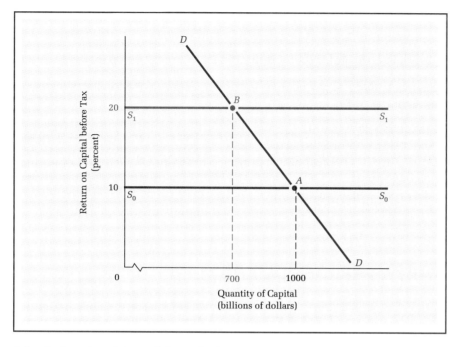

Before the domestic tax is imposed, the supply of capital is perfectly elastic at a 10 percent rate of return, the return assumed available in the rest of the world. If a 50 percent tax is imposed in Canada, capital owners require a 20 percent return before tax, so the supply curve shifts from S_0S_0 to S_1S_1, and the owners of capital bear none of the tax.

shifts upward from S_0S_0 to S_1S_1, and the equilibrium position after the tax is levied is given by point B. Since the before-tax rate of return rises by the full amount of the tax, the owners of capital completely escape the tax. The burden falls entirely on consumers and on the labour employed by the firms.

The conclusion is that it is difficult to impose a tax that sticks on the owners of capital.

WHEN TAXATION CAN IMPROVE EFFICIENCY

We have spent much of this chapter discussing the kinds of inefficiencies and excess burdens that arise from taxation. Before we finish this discussion, two things must be pointed out.

First, economic efficiency is not society's only goal. For example, the tax on gas-guzzling cars causes inefficiencies if it changes people's behaviour patterns. But this, presumably, was exactly what the government sought to accomplish. The government wanted to reduce the number of big cars on the road to conserve energy, and it was willing to tolerate some economic inefficiency to accomplish this end. We can, of course, argue whether this was a good idea—whether the conservation achieved was worth the efficiency loss. But the general point is as follows:

Some taxes that introduce economic inefficiencies are nonetheless good ideas, because they help achieve some other goal.

There is a second, and more fundamental, point to be made:

Some taxes that change economic behaviour may lead to efficiency *gains* rather than to efficiency losses.

As you might guess, this can happen only when there is an inefficiency in the system before the tax. In that case, an appropriate tax may help set things right. One important example of this phenomenon will occupy much of Chapter 17. There we will see that because firms and individuals who despoil clean air and clean water often do so without paying any price, these precious resources are used inefficiently. A corrective tax on pollution can remedy this problem.

EQUITY, EFFICIENCY, AND THE OPTIMAL TAX

In a perfect world, the ideal tax would reflect society's views on equity in taxation without inducing changes in economic behaviour and therefore without creating excess burden. Unfortunately, there is no such tax.

On the contrary, the taxes with the smallest excess burdens can be the most regressive. For instance, one option that has long been suggested is the head tax, which would, in principle, charge every person the same number of dollars. Although such a tax would be very regressive, it would also be quite efficient: Since there is no change in economic behaviour that would enable anyone to avoid the tax, there would be no reason for anyone to change his or her behaviour. In practice, because of the way head taxes are normally implemented, they do induce a change in behaviour. They are often called poll taxes because they are imposed on everyone listed to vote in elections. People can avoid the tax by giving up the opportunity to vote; if they do so, an excess burden exists after all.

In Great Britain, Margaret Thatcher's Conservative government imposed a poll tax in 1990 to pay for a reduction in property taxes. This tax substitution raises the tax burden on individuals who own low-valued property, unless they remove themselves from the voters' list. Given that a large percentage of the voters so affected had not traditionally supported Thatcher's party, it was doubtful that she regarded such a change in behaviour as a burden.

Fortunately, there is a tax that, while not ideal, scores very high on both the equity and the efficiency criteria: a comprehensive personal income tax with few shelters.

While it is true that income taxes can be avoided by earning less income, we have already observed that, in reality, the supply of labour is changed little by taxation. Investing in relatively safe assets (such as government bonds) rather than risky ones (such as common shares) is another possible reaction that would reduce tax bills, since less risky assets pay lower rates of return. But it is not clear that the income tax actually induces such behaviour because, while it taxes away some of the profits when investments turn out well, it also offers a tax deduction when investments turn sour.

The main argument against an income tax is that it reduces the return on saving. As noted earlier, many economists have worried that income taxes discourage saving and thus retard economic growth. This is the reason that many tax analysts in Canada favour the GST (which taxes only income that is spent, not income that is saved) and schemes such as extending the limits for tax-deductible contributions to registered retirement savings plans. However, other analysts doubt that the effect of the disincentive to save that accompanies income taxes is in fact large enough to cause concern. Consequently, they favour income taxes over sales taxes. Thus, although there are still unresolved questions, and research is continuing, many studies suggest as follows:

A comprehensive personal income tax with no unintended tax shelters induces few behavioural reactions that would reduce consumer well-being, and thus has a rather small excess burden.

On efficiency grounds, sales taxes score somewhat higher than does a general income tax. But on equity grounds, unless a sales tax is combined with a wealth tax (for example, an inheritance tax), it scores poorly. We know that personal income taxes can be made as progressive as society deems desirable, but if marginal tax rates on rich people get extremely high, some of the potential efficiency losses might become more serious than they now appear. On both efficiency and equity grounds, then, many economists—including both liberals and conservatives—view a comprehensive personal income tax as one of the best ways for a government to raise revenue.

THE REAL VERSUS THE IDEAL

That seems to be a cheerful conclusion, because the personal income tax is the biggest tax in the Canadian revenue system. Unfortunately, however, our actual tax system does not closely resemble an ideal, comprehensive income tax. For one thing, tax shelters make the income tax less progressive than it seems to be; for another, they make it far less efficient than it could be. The reason follows directly from our analysis of the incidence of taxation:

When different income-earning activities are taxed at different marginal rates, economic choices are distorted by tax considerations; this impairs economic efficiency.

Our present tax system encourages people to devote more time and energy to lightly taxed sources of income (such as capital gains) and less to heavily taxed activities (such as earning wages). Consequently, economic activity is distorted. The result is that the personal income tax, which could *in principle* raise a lot of revenue with little excess burden, in fact imposes considerable excess burdens on society. As a result, proposals for tax reform are continually being debated.

POVERTY AND THE WELFARE SYSTEM

POVERTY: THE FACTS

The **POVERTY LINE** is an amount of income below which a family is considered "poor."

The dividing line between the poor and the non-poor is called the **poverty line**. It is defined as the level of income at which a person or a family spends 59 percent of that income on the essentials of life (food, clothing, and shelter). (The average Canadian family spends 39 percent of income on these essentials.) For 1991, this definition meant that the poverty line for an individual was an income of $10 179 per year in rural areas and $14 951 per year in a large city. For a family of four, the corresponding low-income cutoffs were $20 192 and $29 661, respectively. Using these National Council of Welfare definitions, 16 percent of Canadian families were poor in 1991.

Substantial progress toward eliminating poverty was made during the 1970s; the percentage of persons in Canada living below the poverty line fell from 23 percent to 15 percent (see Figure 15-7). However, because of the severe recessions of the early 1980s and 1990s, the poverty rate in 1991 was higher than it was in 1980. Even before the recession of the early 1990s, one of every seven Canadians was living below the poverty line in 1989! This fact has worried many people. But some critics have argued that the official data may overstate the incidence of poverty, since the official definition is based only on cash income. A number of goods are received by the poor in kind: for example, public education, public housing, and health care.

This debate raises the fundamental question of how we define "the poor." Continuing economic growth will eventually pull almost everyone above any arbitrarily established poverty line. Does this event mark the end of poverty? Some would say yes. But others insist that the biblical statement is right: "The poor ye have always with you."

There are two ways to define poverty. The more optimistic definition uses an **absolute concept of poverty**: If you fall short of a certain minimum standard of living, you are poor; once you pass this standard, you are no longer poor. The second definition is based on a **relative concept of poverty**: The poor are those who fall too far behind the average income.

Each definition has its pros and cons. The basic problem with the absolute concept is that it is arbitrary. Who sets the line? Most of the people of Bangladesh would be delighted to live a bit below the Canadian poverty line and would consider themselves quite prosperous. Similarly, the standard of living that we now call "poor" would probably not have

FIGURE 15-7

PROGRESS IN THE REDUCTION OF POVERTY

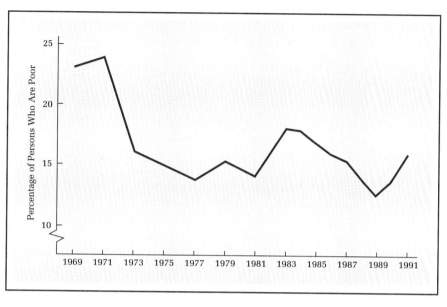

This figure charts the decline in the percentage of Canadians classified as "poor" by official definitions. While substantial progress was made before 1980, 16 percent of all Canadians remain below the poverty line.

SOURCE: Compiled from data in Economic Council of Canada, *The New Face of Poverty: Income Security Needs of Canadian Families* (Ottawa: Canada Communications Group, 1992).

been considered so in Canada in 1780 and certainly not in Europe during the Middle Ages. Different times and different places apparently call for different poverty lines.

The fact that the concept of poverty is culturally, not physiologically, determined suggests that it must be a relative concept. But recent debates in Canada suggest that many are uncomfortable with this proposition (see the boxed insert on the next page). Those who prefer the absolute concept estimate the poverty rate at only 2 percent.

How can we achieve some perspective on whether official estimates of the poverty line should be regarded as too low or too high? One way of providing an answer is to consider the Gallup poll taken in March 1986, which asked respondents what they considered the least amount of money a family of four needed to get along. The average answer was almost exactly equal to the official poverty line for 1986. Another standard of reference is provided by minimum-wage legislation. In most provinces, a full-time worker receiving the minimum wage earns an income below the poverty line. While this suggests that the poverty line may be a bit high, it must be remembered that most poor people earn incomes *significantly* below the poverty line.

Once we start moving away from an absolute concept of poverty toward a relative concept, the sharp distinction between the poor and the

PUBLIC CONTROVERSY

ABSOLUTE VERSUS RELATIVE DEFINITIONS OF POVERTY

The following excerpt from an editorial in The Globe and Mail *indicates the disagreement among Canadians concerning the extent of the poverty problem.*

An example of why relative measures of poverty fail to give an entirely honest picture: In 1951, the annual income of the average Canadian family, which at that time had almost exactly four members, was $3,535. Adjusting for inflation, that is equivalent to just over $20,000 in 1991 dollars. Compare that to today's poverty line. . . . According to current definitions of poverty, the average Canadian family of 1951 was very poor indeed. And compared to the average family of 1991—3.17 members with a combined average income of $53,131, per capita three times as wealthy as their counterparts of 40 years ago—they are clearly not as well off. But would Canadians who grew up middle-class in the 1950s agree with the current wisdom, which holds that the lower standard of living they enjoyed in their youth should be classified as poverty?. . .

According to statistics compiled by the National Council of Welfare, of those who were below the poverty line in 1988, 99 per cent had refrigerators, 50 per cent had washers and driers, nearly 20 per cent had dishwashers, 60 per cent had colour TV, 62 per cent had cable, 34 per cent had VCRs and 50 per cent had at least one automobile. Among families whose income was less than $5,000 (far, far below the low income cut off) fully 46 per cent were homeowners, 76 per cent mortgage free. "While it is possible to imagine some scenarios in which extreme poverty and mortgage-free home ownership might coin-

cide," wrote Christopher Sarlo in *Poverty in Canada*, "it is puzzling that one-third of Canada's most destitute families own their home outright." Prof. Sarlo also noted that, while 550,000 households headed by someone 65 years of age or older were considered poor, almost half of these (250,000) owned a home, 90 per cent mortgage free. . . .

Prof. Sarlo proposed a new definition, which would set the poverty line as the minimum income level required to adequately feed, clothe and shelter a Canadian family— and would give a more accurate picture of the number of poor in Canadian society. Whether Prof. Sarlo's poverty line is generous enough (setting it at $15,067 for a family of four in a mid-sized city, he's been accused of "drawing it one calorie above starvation") is clearly worth arguing. According to his definition, "less than two per cent of Canada's population lives in poverty." That too is debatable. But defining poverty as income insufficient to purchase healthy food, decent clothing and adequate shelter would surely be far superior to Statscan's confusing, misleading model.

Poverty is a problem in Canada. But advocates and lobby groups have exaggerated the situation, reckoning that hyperbole in a good cause is justified. Over the long-term, however, they are not doing anyone any favours. Relative definitions of poverty, substantially overstating the problem, will distort public policy and give Canadians a chronic case of compassion fatigue. Once that sets in, the pleas of those who are truly suffering will just sound like so much more crying wolf.

SOURCE: Editorial, *The Globe and Mail*, December 28, 1992, page A14. Reprinted with the permission of *The Globe and Mail*.

non-poor starts to evaporate. Instead, it is more constructive to think of a parade of people from the poorest soul to the richest millionaire. The "poverty problem," then, seems to be that the disparities in income are "too large" in some sense. The poor are so poor because the rich are so rich. If we follow this line of thought far enough, we are led away from the narrow problem of poverty toward the broader problem of inequality of income.

INEQUALITY: THE FACTS

Nothing in the market mechanism works to prevent large differences in incomes. On the contrary, it tends to breed inequality, for the basic source of the great efficiency of the market mechanism is its system of rewards and penalties. The market is generous to those who are successful in operating efficient enterprises that are responsive to consumer demands, and it is ruthless in penalizing those who are unable or unwilling to satisfy consumer demands efficiently. Its financial punishment of those who try and fail can be particularly severe. At times, it even brings down the great and powerful.

Most people have a good idea that the income distribution is quite spread out—that the gulf between the rich and the poor is a wide one. But few have any concept of where they stand in the distribution. In Table 15-4, you will find some statistics on the 1990 income distribution in Canada (the most recent data available when this book went to press). But before looking at these, try the following experiment. First, write down your family's before-tax income in 1990. (If you do not know, take

TABLE 15-4

DISTRIBUTION OF FAMILY INCOME IN CANADA, 1990, CANADIAN FAMILIES

Income Range (dollars)	Percentage of All Families in This Range	Percentage of Families in This and Lower Ranges
Under 10 000	2.6	2.6
10 000 to 19 999	10.8	13.4
20 000 to 29 999	13.4	26.8
30 000 to 39 999	14.3	41.1
40 000 to 49 999	14.4	55.5
50 000 to 59 999	12.8	68.3
60 000 to 74 999	13.6	81.9
75 000 and more	18.1	100.0

If your family's income falls close to one of the end points of the ranges indicated here, you can approximate the fraction of families with income *lower* than yours just by looking at the last column.

SOURCE: Compiled from data in Statistics Canada, *Income Distribution by Size in Canada*, 1990, catalogue no. 13-207, page 137. Used with the permission of the Minister of Industry, Science and Technology, 1993.

a guess.) Next, try to guess what percentage of Canadian families had incomes lower than this. Finally, if we divide Canada into three broad income classes—rich, middle class, and poor—to which group do you think your family belongs?

Once you have written down answers to these three questions, look at the income distribution data for 1990 in Table 15-4. If you are like most postsecondary students, these figures will contain a few surprises for you. First, if we adopt the tentative definitions that the lowest 20 percent are the "poor," the highest 20 percent are the "rich," and the middle 60 percent are the "middle class," many fewer of you belong to the celebrated middle class than thought so. In fact, the cutoff point that defined membership in the rich class in 1990 was about $72 000 before taxes, an income level exceeded by families of many students. (Your family may be shocked to learn that it is rich!)

Next, use Table 15-4 to estimate the fraction of Canadian families that have incomes lower than your family's. Most students who come from households of moderate prosperity have an instinctive feeling that they stand somewhere near the middle of the income distribution, so they estimate about half, or perhaps a little more. In fact, if your family earned a pretax income of $70 000 in 1990, more than 75 percent of Canadian families are poorer than yours!

This exercise has perhaps brought us down to earth. Let us now look past the average level of income and see how the pie is divided. Table 15-5 shows the shares of income accruing to each fifth of the population in 1990 and several earlier years. In a perfectly equal society, all the numbers in this table would be "20 percent" since each fifth of the population would receive one-fifth of the income. In fact, as the table shows, this is certainly not the case. In 1990, for example, the poorest fifth of all families had only 6.4 percent of the total income, while the richest fifth had 39.3 percent—six times as much.

DEPICTING INCOME DISTRIBUTIONS: THE LORENZ CURVE

Statisticians and economists use a convenient tool to portray data like those in Table 15-5 graphically. The device, called a **Lorenz curve**, is shown in Figure 15-8. To construct a Lorenz curve, we first draw a square with vertical and horizontal dimensions that both represent 100 percent. Then we record the percentage of families (or persons) on the horizontal axis and the percentage of income that these families (or persons) receive on the vertical axis, using all the data that we have. For example, point C in Figure 15-8 depicts the fact (known from Table 15-5) that the bottom 60 percent (the three lowest fifths) of Canadian families in 1990 received 36.7 percent of the total income. Similarly, points A, B, and D represent the other information contained in Table 15-5. We can list four important properties of a Lorenz curve:

TABLE 15-5

INCOME SHARES IN SELECTED YEARS

Income Group	1990	1985	1982	1979	1973	1965
Lowest fifth	6.4	6.3	6.3	6.1	6.1	6.2
Second fifth	12.4	12.3	12.6	13.0	12.9	13.1
Middle fifth	17.9	17.9	18.0	18.4	18.1	18.0
Fourth fifth	24.0	24.1	24.1	24.3	23.9	23.6
Highest fifth	39.3	39.4	38.9	38.3	38.9	39.0

SOURCE: Compiled from data in Statistics Canada, *Income Distribution by Size in Canada*, 1990, catalogue no. 13-207, page 45. Used with the permission of the Minister of Industry, Science and Technology, 1993.

1. It begins at the origin, because zero families naturally have zero income.

2. It always ends at the upper-right corner of the square, since 100 percent of the nation's families must necessarily receive all the nation's income.

3. If income were distributed equally, the Lorenz curve would be a straight line connecting these two points (the thin solid line in Fig-

FIGURE 15-8

A LORENZ CURVE FOR CANADA

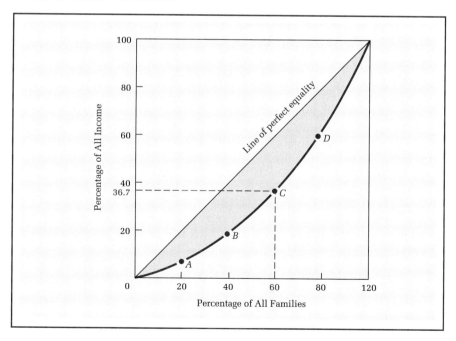

This Lorenz curve for Canada is based on the 1990 distribution of income given in Table 15-5. The percentage of families is measured along the horizontal axis, and the percentage of income that these families receive is measured along the vertical axis. Thus, for example, point *C* indicates that the bottom 60 percent of Canadian families received 36.7 percent of the total income in 1990.

"There is a perfect example of what is wrong with this country today."

"There is a perfect example of what is wrong with this country today."

Drawing by Mulligan. © 1978 The New Yorker Magazine, Inc.

ure 15-8). With everybody equal, the bottom 20 percent of the families would receive 20 percent of the income, the bottom 40 percent would receive 40 percent, and so on.

4. In a real economy, with significant income differences, the Lorenz curve will "sag" downward from this line of perfect equality. It is easy to see why this is so. If there is any inequality at all, the poorest 20 percent of families must get less than 20 percent of all the income. This corresponds to a point below the equality line, such as point *A*. Similarly, the bottom 40 percent of families must receive less than 40 percent of the income (point *B*), and so on.

In fact, the size of the area between the line of perfect equality and the Lorenz curve (the shaded area in Figure 15-8) is often used as a handy measure of inequality. The larger this area, the more unequal is the income distribution. For Canadian family incomes, this so-called area of inequality usually fills up about one-third of the total area underneath the equality line.

Standing by itself, the Lorenz curve tells us rather little. To interpret it, we must know what it looked like in earlier years or what it looks like in other countries. The historical data in Table 15-5 show that the Canadian Lorenz curve has not moved much at all in the last quarter-century. To some, this remarkable stability in the income distribution is deplorable. To others, it suggests some immutable law of the capitalist system. In fact, neither view is correct. The apparent stability in the income distribution is the result of a standoff between certain demographic forces that were pushing the Lorenz curve outward (such as more young people, more old people, and more families headed by women) and other forces that were pulling it inward (such as government antipoverty programs).

Comparing Canada with other countries is much harder, since no two countries use precisely the same definition of income distribution. In 1976, the Organization for Economic Co-operation and Development (OECD) made a heroic effort to standardize the income distribution data of its member countries so they could be compared.[1] In this analysis, Japan stood out as the industrialized country with the most equal income distribution, with Australia, West Germany, the Netherlands, and Sweden bunched closely for second place. Canada placed between this group and France and the United States, which seemed to have the most inequality. Before extrapolating from these findings, it should be pointed out that only twelve industrial countries were compared. Israel, which is often thought to have a most equal income distribution, is not in the OECD. Neither are any of the less developed countries, which are generally found to have much more inequality than the developed ones.

POLICIES TO COMBAT POVERTY

Let us take for granted that our nation has a commitment to reduce the amount of poverty. What are some policies that can promote this goal? Which of these does the least harm to economic incentives and is hence most efficient? The traditional approach to poverty fighting in Canada has used a variety of programs collectively known as *social assistance*. The best-known of these is the welfare system administered by the municipalities.

Our welfare system has been attacked as a classic example of an inefficient redistributive program. Why? One reason is that it provides little incentive for a welfare recipient to get a job and earn income. Only by acquiring skills on the job can welfare recipients ever break out of the unemployment–poverty circle. The following example was used by the Economic Council of Canada in its 1983 *Annual Review*: If a single mother with two dependent children works regularly as a sales clerk at half the average industrial wage, the family would still qualify for some welfare. However, for each dollar earned, welfare is reduced by 75 cents. Also, the woman would have to make contributions to unemployment insurance and to the Canada Pension Plan. Furthermore, her taxable income would have increased enough to cross the income tax threshold. When all these reductions in transfer payments and increases in taxes and contributions are added up, the effective tax rate on the women's earnings from the job would be 110 percent! The family's income position would actually be reduced by her working. Even today, working at the

1. Malcolm Sawyer, "Income Distribution in OECD Countries," *OECD Occasional Studies* (July 1976), pages 3–36.

minimum wage brings in less than does welfare in most provinces. Such disincentive effects make it essentially impossible for many individuals to escape the poverty trap. Some attempts have been made to ease this transition from welfare to paid employment, but very few individuals have been able to participate in the pilot projects.

Equally alarming is the fact that our existing federal legislation precludes any requirement that individuals engage in some work as part of their welfare program. This means that we cannot implement "workfare" programs such as those that have been in place in the United States for some years. In a workfare program, the government finds a job for the welfare recipient, and welfare payments continue only as long as the individual reports for work. Five-year studies have found that welfare rates dropped by one-third among individuals involved in these programs. Through being in a social setting with other working individuals and by developing contacts and skills, one-third of the welfare recipients found better jobs and dropped off the welfare rolls entirely.

In Canada, the federal government funds the provincial welfare schemes through the Canada Assistance Plan. The legislation that defines this plan states explicitly that provinces cannot require individuals to engage in a program of work as a prerequisite for receiving welfare assistance. Governments have, however, begun to experiment with work-incentive schemes. For example, in New Brunswick in 1993, individuals leaving welfare for low-paying jobs could receive an income supplement. Participants in this experiment receive a payment equal to 50 percent of the difference between their salary and the policy target level of income of $30 000. For example, a person accepting a $15 000 per-year-job receives $7500 from government, for a total income of $22 500. Without this scheme, the individual would have received $9864 on welfare. Thus, in arrangements of this sort, the individual receives a higher income (and some job experience), while governments save money.

The welfare system is not the only government program directed toward the relief of poverty. As we will explain in Chapter 18 (pages 634–37), the unemployment insurance system plays a role. Also, many of the poor are provided with a number of important goods and services either at no charge or at prices that are well below market levels. Subsidized day-care, free prescription drugs, and subsidized public housing are some notable examples. These programs significantly enhance the living standards of the poor. However, most of them offer benefits that decline as family income rises. As a result, these antipoverty programs accentuate the basic problem—that many poor families are *worse* off if their earnings rise. An effective tax rate of more than 100 percent creates a powerful incentive not to work.

THE NEGATIVE INCOME TAX

These problems and others like them have contributed to the "welfare mess" and have led to frequent calls to scrap the whole system and replace it with a simple structure designed to get income into the hands of the poor without providing such adverse incentives. The solution suggested most frequently, at least by economists, is the so-called **negative income tax (NIT)**. The Macdonald Commission, a federal royal commission of the mid-1980s charged with studying the country's economic affairs, endorsed this proposal, calling it the Universal Income Security Program. It was also endorsed in 1992 by the federal government, which called it the Guaranteed Annual Income Plan.

The name "negative income tax" derives from the scheme's similarity to the regular (positive) income tax. Let us illustrate how NIT would work. To describe a particular NIT plan, we require two numbers: a minimum income level below which no person or family is allowed to fall (the "guaranteed annual income") and a rate at which benefits are "taxed away" as income rises. Consider a plan with a $6000 guaranteed income (for an individual) and a 50 percent tax rate. A person with no earnings would then receive a $6000 payment (a "negative tax") from the government. A person earning $2000 would have the basic benefit reduced by 50 percent of his or her earnings. Since half of the earnings is $1000, the individual would receive $5000 from the government plus the $2000 earned income for a total income of $7000 (see Table 15-6).

Notice in Table 15-6 that with a 50 percent tax rate, the increase in total income as earnings rise is always half of the increase in earnings. There is always some incentive to work under an NIT system. Notice also that there is a "break-even" level of income at which benefits cease. In this case, the break-even level is $12 000. This is not just another number that policy-makers can arbitrarily select in the way they select the guarantee level and the tax rate. Rather, it is dictated by the choice of the guarantee level and the tax rate. In our example, $6000 is the maximum possible benefit and benefits are reduced by 50 cents for each $1 of earnings. Hence, benefits will be reduced to zero when 50 percent of earnings is equal to $6000. This occurs when earnings are $12 000 in our example. The general relation is as follows:

$$\text{Guarantee} = \text{Tax rate} \times \text{Break-even level}$$

The fact that the break-even level is completely determined by the guarantee level and the tax rate creates an annoying problem. If we are

TABLE 15-6

ILLUSTRATION OF A NEGATIVE-INCOME-TAX PLAN

Earnings (dollars)	Benefits Paid (dollars)	Total Income (dollars)
0	6000	6 000
2 000	5000	7 000
4 000	4000	8 000
6 000	3000	9 000
8 000	2000	10 000
10 000	1000	11 000
12 000	0	12 000

truly to make a dent in the poverty population through an NIT system, the guarantee will have to come fairly close to the poverty line. But then, if we are to keep the tax rate moderate, the break-even level will have to be far above the poverty line. This means that families that are not considered "poor" (although they are certainly not rich) will also receive benefits. For example, a low tax rate of 33.3 percent means that some benefits will be paid to families whose income is as high as three times the guarantee level.

But if we raise the tax rate to bring the guarantee and break-even levels closer together, the incentive to work—and with it, the principal rationale for the NIT in the first place—shrinks. Thus, the NIT is no magic cure-all. Difficult choices must still be made.

THE NEGATIVE INCOME TAX AND WORK INCENTIVES

For people now covered by welfare programs, the NIT would increase the incentive to work. However, we have just seen that it is virtually inevitable that a number of families who are now too well off to collect welfare would become eligible for NIT payments. For these people, the NIT would impose work disincentives, both because it would provide them with more income and because it would subject them to the relatively high NIT tax rate, reducing their after-tax wage rate.

These possible disincentive effects have worried both social reformers and legislators, so in the late 1960s, the government initiated a series of social experiments to estimate the effect of the NIT on the supply of labour. Families in several communities in Manitoba were offered NIT payments in return for allowing social scientists to monitor their behaviour. A matched set of "control" families, who were not given NIT payments, were also observed. The idea was to measure how the behaviour of the families receiving NIT payments differed from that of the families that did not receive them or received conventional welfare payments.

The experiments, like more extensive ones undertaken in the United States, lasted about a decade. While the Canadian data have never been fully analyzed (because of funding limitations), the related experiments in the United States have shown that the net effects of the NIT on labour supply were small—but certainly not zero. Members of families receiving NIT benefits did work slightly less than the others, but some obtained higher-paying jobs. The fears of those who predicted that NIT payments would induce widespread withdrawals from the labour force were unfounded. This, combined with the fact that some individuals were inspired to obtain higher-paying work, led many economists to conclude that the NIT should be adopted. The experiments show that, contrary to the worry of many government officials, the NIT *is* affordable. In addition, the only way to beat the poverty problem in the long run is to encourage people to acquire skills on the job that will improve their productivity.

OTHER TAX AND EXPENDITURE PROGRAMS

If we take the broader view that society's objective is not just to eliminate poverty but to reduce income disparities, the fact that many non-poor families would receive benefits from the NIT is perhaps not a serious drawback. After all, unless the plan were outlandishly generous, these families would still be well below the average income. Still, in general discussions, the NIT is largely thought of as an antipoverty program, not as a tool for income equalization.

By contrast, the personal income tax *is* thought to be a means of promoting equality. Indeed, it is probably given more credit for this than it actually deserves. The reason is that the income tax is widely known to be *progressive*. The fact that the tax is progressive means that incomes after tax are distributed more equally than incomes before tax, because the rich turn over a larger share of their incomes to the tax collector. This is illustrated by the two Lorenz curves in Figure 15-9. These curves, however, are not drawn accurately to scale. If they were, they would lie almost on top of each other because the degree of equalization that can be attributed to the tax system is very modest — one reason being the existence of tax shelters (which were discussed earlier in this chapter).

Most experts agree that the many other taxes in the Canadian system are decidedly regressive. Since low-income earners *spend* a larger portion of their incomes than do high-income earners, and since an especially high proportion of their incomes is spent on housing, both sales and property taxes can be quite regressive. On balance, the evidence suggests

FIGURE 15-9

THE EFFECT OF PROGRESSIVE INCOME TAXATION ON THE LORENZ CURVE

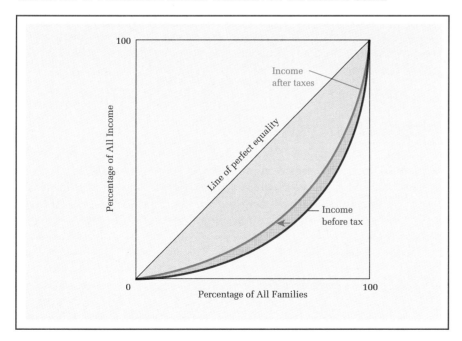

Since a progressive income tax takes proportionately more income from the rich than from the poor, it reduces income inequality. Graphically, this means that society's Lorenz curve shifts in the manner shown here. The magnitude of the shift, however, is exaggerated to make the graph more readable. In reality, the Canadian income tax has only a very small effect on the Lorenz curve.

that when the effects of these taxes are combined with those of the income tax, the tax system as a whole is only slightly progressive.

It is more difficult to measure the income distribution effects of government expenditure programs. Nevertheless, studies have been done to estimate which income classes benefit most from individual expenditure schemes, such as those that finance highways, postsecondary education, the protection of private property, and so on. These studies show that higher-income classes benefit to such an extent that government expenditures as a whole are regressive. In fact, they are so regressive that they outweigh the mildly progressive effect of total taxes, so that the overall income distribution effect of the entire set of government-sector initiatives is estimated to be slightly regressive.

As noted earlier in this chapter, one set of government transfer policies does not involve individuals directly. Instead, these schemes redistribute funds from the "have" provinces to the "have-not" provinces. The most important of these is the equalization program that involves grant payments from federal government revenues to all provincial governments except Ontario, British Columbia, and Alberta.

Finally, numerous regional programs offer incentives to companies that locate or expand in the so-called depressed regions. Unfortunately, there is a dearth of research on the effectiveness of these regional policies. Some economists have argued that transfers to the have-not regions have significantly reduced out-migration from these areas. This leaves the depressed regions with an excess supply of labour, with low wages, and with the slow growth that is usually associated with a state of dependency on the federal government. Other economists argue that the regional redistribution payments have stimulated much local economic activity, thereby lessening the general poverty problem. Further research is greatly needed in this area.

DISCRIMINATION

Some of the factors that lead to income differentials are widely accepted as "just." For example, few quarrel with the idea that it is fair for people who work longer hours to receive higher incomes. However, almost no one is willing to condone income inequalities that arise strictly because of discrimination.

DISCRIMINATION: THE FACTS

ECONOMIC DISCRIMINA-TION is defined as occurring when equivalent factors of production receive different payments for equal contributions to output.

The facts about discrimination are not easy to come by. We define **economic discrimination** as occurring when equivalent factors of production receive different payments for equal contributions to output. But this definition is hard to apply in practice because we cannot always tell when two factors of production are "equivalent."

Probably no one would call it "discrimination" if a woman with only a high-school diploma received a lower salary than a man with a university degree (though one might legitimately ask whether discrimination helps to explain the difference in their educational attainments). Even if they have the same education, the man many have ten more years of work experience than the woman. If they receive different wages for this reason, are we to call that "discrimination"?

Similar ambiguities plague discussions about racial discrimination. For example, if a Native person receives less pay than a white for the same job, it may be that the white has had more education and training, which make him more productive. Thus, it is not clear that the employer is discriminating. It may be that discrimination exists at the schooling level, and perhaps this is what caused the skill differential assumed in our example. But discrimination within the educational system is not the fault of an individual employer.

Ideally, we would compare men and women, or Natives and whites, whose *productivities* are equal. In this case, if women receive lower wages than men, or if Natives receive lower wages than whites, we would clearly call it discrimination. But discrimination normally takes much more subtle forms than the paying of unequal wages for equal work. For instance, employers can simply keep women or Natives relegated to inferior jobs, thus justifying the lower salaries they pay them.

One clearly incorrect way to measure discrimination is to compare the typical incomes of different groups. For example, in 1988, women's average earnings were about 71 percent of men's. Virtually everyone agrees that existing levels of discrimination are smaller than these differentials suggest, but far greater than zero. Precisely how much greater is a topic of continuing economic research. Several studies in the United States suggest that at least half of the observed wage differential between white women and white men is caused by discrimination in the labour market (although more might be due to discrimination in education, and so on). Other studies have reached somewhat different conclusions. While no one denies the existence of discrimination, its quantitative importance is a matter of ongoing controversy and research.

DISCRIMINATION: THE THEORY

Let us see what economic theory tells us about discrimination. In particular, consider the following two questions:

1. Must the existence of *prejudice*, which we define as arising when one group dislikes associating with another group, always lead to discrimination (unequal pay for work of equal value)?

2. Are there "natural" economic forces that tend either to erode or to exacerbate discrimination over time?

As we shall see now, the analysis we have provided in previous chapters sheds light on both these issues.

DISCRIMINATION BY EMPLOYERS

Most attention seems to focus on discrimination by employers, so let us start there. What happens if, for instance, some firms refuse to hire women for certain positions? Figure 15-10 will help us find the answer. Part (a) pertains to firms that discriminate; part (b) pertains to firms that do not. The supply and demand curves for labour in both parts are based on the analysis in Chapter 14. We suppose the two demand curves to be identical. However, the supply curve in part (b) must be farther to the right than the supply curve in part (a), because men *and* women can work in part (b), whereas only men can work in part (a). The result is that wages will be lower in part (b) than in part (a). Since all the women are forced into part (b), their wages are lower than the average wage of the men in parts (a) and (b), so we conclude that there is discrimination against women.

But now consider the situation from the point of view of the employers. Firms in part (a) of Figure 15-10 are paying more for labour; they are paying for the privilege of discriminating against women. The non-discriminatory firms in part (b) have a cost advantage. As we learned in earlier chapters, if there is effective competition, these non-discriminatory firms will tend to capture more and more of the market. The discriminators will gradually be driven out of business. If, on the other hand, many of the firms in part (a) have protected monopolies, they will be able to remain in business. But they will pay for the privilege of discriminat-

FIGURE 15-10

WAGE DISCRIMINATION

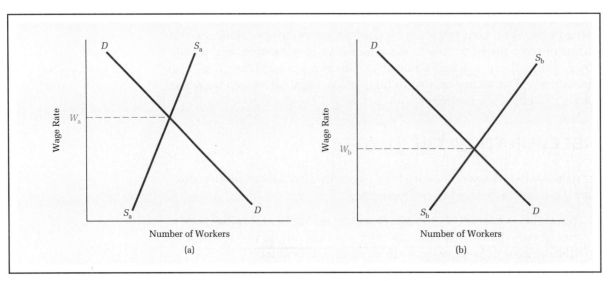

Part (a) depicts supply and demand curves for labour among discriminatory firms; part (b) shows the same for non-discriminatory firms. Since only men can work in part (a), while both sexes can work in part (b), the supply curve in part (b) is farther to the right than the supply curve in part (a). Consequently, the wage rate in part (b), W_b, winds up below the wage rate in part (a), W_a.

ing by earning lower monopoly profits than they otherwise could (because they pay higher wages than they would normally have to pay).

DISCRIMINATION BY FELLOW WORKERS

Competitive forces will tend to reduce discrimination over time if employers are the source of discrimination. Such optimistic conclusions cannot necessarily be reached, however, if it is the workers who are prejudiced. Consider what happens if, for example, men do not like to have women as their supervisors. If men do not give their full co-operation, female supervisors will be less effective than their male counterparts and, hence, will earn lower wages. Here, prejudice does lead to discrimination, even in the long run.

STATISTICAL DISCRIMINATION

A final type of discrimination, called **statistical discrimination**, may be the most stubborn of all and can exist even where there is no prejudice. Here is an important example. It is, of course, a fact that only women can have babies. It is also a fact that many, although certainly not all, working women who have babies quit their jobs (at least for a while) to care for their newborns. Employers know this. What they cannot know, however, is *which* women of child-bearing age are likely to drop out of the labour force for this reason.

STATISTICAL DISCRIMINA-TION is said to occur when the productivity of a particular worker is estimated to be low just because that worker belongs to a particular group (such as women).

Suppose three candidates apply for a job that requires a long-term commitment. Susan plans to quit after a few years to raise a family. Jane does not plan to have any children. Jack is the lone male candidate. If the employer knew all the facts, he would prefer either Jane or Jack to Susan but would be indifferent between Jane and Jack. Instead, he presumes that both Jane and Susan, being young women, are more likely to quit to raise a family than Jack is; therefore, he hires Jack, even though Jane is just as good a prospect. Jane is discriminated against. (Lest it be thought that this example justifies discrimination against women, it should be pointed out that women generally have less job turnover and absenteeism for non-pregnancy health reasons than men do. Furthermore, it can be argued that because society attaches utility to the continuation of the species, women produce external economies by having children and therefore are entitled to compensation by society in excess of their productivity within a firm.)

With regard to the two questions with which we began this section, then, we conclude that different types of discrimination lead to different answers. Prejudice often but not always leads to economic discrimination. Also, discrimination may occur in the absence of prejudice. Finally, the forces of competition tend to erode some, but not all, of the inequities caused by discrimination. And, as we have seen, the victims of discrimination are not the only losers; society as a whole loses whenever discriminatory practices impair economic efficiency. Hence, most observers feel that we should not rely on market forces alone to combat discrimination. The government has a clear role to play.

POLICIES TO COMBAT DISCRIMINATION

The policies that we considered earlier in this chapter for combatting poverty or reducing income inequality are all based on taxes and transfer payments—on moving dollars from one set of hands to another. This has not been the approach used to fight discrimination. Instead, governments have decided to make it illegal to discriminate.

Originally, it was thought that the problem could best be attacked by outlawing discrimination in rates of pay and in hiring standards—and by devoting resources to enforcement of these provisions. While progress toward the elimination of discrimination according to race and sex was made during the 1960s and 1970s and will undoubtedly continue under Canada's Charter of Rights and Freedoms, some people have felt the pace has been too slow. One reason is that discrimination in the labour market has proved to be more subtle than was first thought. Officials can rarely find proof that unequal pay is being given for work of equal value, because determining when work is "of equal value" has turned out to be a formidable task.

In the early 1970s in the United States, a new wrinkle was added. Firms and other organizations with a suspiciously small representation of minority groups or women in their work forces are now required not only to end discriminatory practices, but also to demonstrate that they are taking **affirmative action** to remedy this imbalance. That is, they have to prove that they are making efforts to locate members of minority groups and females and to hire them if they prove to be qualified.

AFFIRMATIVE ACTION refers to active efforts to locate and hire members of minority groups.

This approach to fighting discrimination is highly controversial. Critics claim that affirmative action really means hiring quotas and compulsory hiring of unqualified workers simply because they are female or members of a minority group. Proponents counter that, without affirmative action, discriminatory employers would simply claim they could not find qualified minority or female employees. The difficulty revolves around the impossibility of deciding, on purely objective criteria, who is "qualified" and who is not. What one person sees as government coercion to hire an unqualified applicant to fill a quota, another sees as a progressive policy forcing a discriminatory employer to mend his or her ways. Nothing in this book—or anywhere else—will teach you which view is correct in any particular instance.

PAY EQUITY involves classifying jobs by objective criteria and forcing employers to pay equal wages for the jobs judged to be of comparable worth.

A number of people have concluded that affirmative action will never put appreciable numbers of women into "men's jobs" and have sought to combat sex discrimination by setting wage rates according to some standard of **pay equity**. The argument, which has sparked acrimonious debate in recent years, runs as follows. Women are frequently discriminated against by being relegated to low-paying occupations while men get the better-paying jobs. To remedy the resulting wage disparities, the government should use job evaluations to decide which men's and women's jobs are comparable and then insist that employers pay equal wages for jobs judged to be of comparable worth.

Critics of pay equity scoff at the idea that the government can decide the relative values of different jobs on objective criteria. The forces of supply and demand described in Chapter 14, they argue, are the only sensible way to set relative wages. The wages that emerge from the marketplace reflect both the marginal revenue products in the various occupations and the availability of labour to each. Any other wages invite shortages in some occupations, and cause others to be besieged by a surplus of applicants.

The controversies over affirmative action and pay equity are excellent examples of the trade-off between equality and efficiency. Without a doubt, giving more high-paying jobs to members of minority groups and to women, or raising the wages of low-paid workers, would move society's Lorenz curve in the direction of greater equality. Supporters of pay equity and affirmative action seek this result. But if affirmative action disrupts industry and requires firms to replace "qualified" workers with "less-qualified" workers, the nation's productivity may fall. Further, if pay equity creates chronic surpluses in some occupations and shortages in others, economic efficiency may suffer. Opponents of these policies are greatly troubled by these potential losses. How far should such policies be pushed? A good question, but one without a good answer.

The experience of other countries provides some evidence on how pay equity works. Australia has had equal-pay legislation since 1969; since that time, women's pay has risen from 66 percent to more than 85 percent of men's (even though the legislation was phased in gradually over several years in the early 1970s). Major labour-market imbalances do not seem to have emerged. One thing that has helped the success of the Australian policy is that the country's wage-setting was already very centralized, so an institutional structure was already in place to permit the government to co-ordinate with firms and unions concerning job classifications. In contrast to Australia, the European Community (EC) has required member countries to have pay-equity legislation for both public and private sectors since 1975. But the European countries have few enforcement mechanisms, so the wage gap between men and women remains about equal to that observed in North America. Some changes are occurring, however. In Britain, for example, Prime Minister Margaret Thatcher toughened pay-equity laws in 1983 after the European Court ruled that the country was not complying with the EC requirements. In 1988, Ontario introduced the most thorough pay-equity laws in the world. The provincial legislation stipulates that government departments and agencies, along with the 700 private-sector companies in the province that employ more than 500 workers, must achieve pay equity by 1995. A discussion of the Canadian male–female wage gap is provided in the boxed insert on the next page.

"I am an equal opportunity employer. That's why I've decided to give all the other employers an equal opportunity at your services."

FURTHER DETAIL

SEX, STATISTICS, AND WAGES

It was reported that women's wages rose to 69.6 per cent of men's in 1991, from 67.6 per cent the year before. But what does that mean? For starters, it does *not* mean . . . that women are being paid nearly one-third less to do the same jobs. . . .

One would expect that, since society's attitudes towards women's work and education have changed relatively recently, the difference in average wages would be least among the young. And that is precisely what one finds: The hypothetical full-time working woman over age 55 earned 63.6 per cent of the income of her male counterpart in the same age bracket, while her granddaughter, aged 15 to 24, earned on average 86.4 per cent as much as a man in the same age group. . . .

[T]here is already almost no wage gap between single men and single women. In 1991, single women's average earnings were 91.1 per cent of those of their male counterparts. For some women, there was even less of a difference. Data compiled by Statistics Canada at The Globe and Mail's request show that the income of single women age 35 to 44 was 94.5 per cent of that earned by men of the same age. And looking only at the most educated members of that age group—single females with a university degree — women actually made six percent *more* money than single, 35 to 44 year-old, university-educated men. . . .

All of these numbers refer, of course, to full-time workers. But not all full-time workers work the same number of hours. On average, men work more than women: 40.4 hours vs. 35.2 hours a week. In other words, the average man works 12.9 per cent longer, explaining a large part of the wage gap.

But the biggest factor is marriage. The earnings of single women, single men and married women working full-time are roughly comparable. But the earnings of the average married man rise above those of everyone else. That is the only real "wage gap." Whether or not it is a problem is a subject worthy of discussion. Its existence suggests that, as one would expect, married men and women choose certain career and life paths, different from those chosen by singles. But why is it that many married women work only part-time, or adopt less time-consuming (and less well-paying) full-time careers? Are they forced to by their husbands? By circumstance? By entrenched social attitudes? . . .

In the debate that ought to take place around this issue, answering these questions would be a good place to start.

SOURCE: Editorial, *The Globe and Mail*, January 21, 1993, page A24. Reprinted with the permission of *The Globe and Mail*.

While it remains to be seen how the pros and cons of particular pay-equity laws work out, a more definite analysis can be given concerning other policies aimed at women's rights in the job market. For example, paternity leave should be as available as maternity leave. With only the institution of maternity leave, the demand for female labour is reduced because the relative cost of employing women is increased.

EQUALITY VERSUS EFFICIENCY

THE POLITICS AND ECONOMICS OF INEQUALITY

It is apparent that the trade-off between equality and efficiency is not widely understood. Social reformers often argue that society should adopt even the most outlandish programs to increase income equality or eradicate poverty, regardless of the potential side effects these policies might have. Defenders of the status quo, for their part, often seem so obsessed with these undesirable side effects—whether real or imagined —that they ignore the benefits of redistribution programs.

The continuing debate over supply-side economics is a good illustration. Many of the tax incentives supported by supply-siders, such as the elimination of taxes on the first $100 000 of capital gains, are clearly of greatest benefit to the wealthy. The poor, after all, do not own much corporate stock. On the other hand, measures such as this one are designed to increase the incentives to save and invest, and if they are successful, the whole nation will benefit from the resulting increase in productivity. The more zealous advocates of supply-side initiatives trumpet the hoped-for gains in productivity and show little appreciation of the harmful effects on income equality. Some of their opponents vocally decry the widening of income differentials and show little concern for increasing the nation's productivity. Each side claims to have a monopoly on virtue. Neither one has.

Economists try not to paint these issues in black and white. They prefer to phrase things in terms of trade-offs—to reap gains on one front, you must often make sacrifices on another. A policy is not necessarily ill-conceived simply because it has an undesirable effect on income equality, if it makes an important enough contribution to productivity. On the other hand, policies with very bad distributive consequences may deserve to be rejected, even if they would raise the gross domestic product.

Admitting that there is a trade-off between equality and efficiency— that while supply-side tax cuts may help solve the productivity problem, they may also increase income inequality—may not be the best way to win votes, but it does face the facts. In that way, the admission helps us make the inherently political decisions about what should be done.

THE OPTIMAL AMOUNT OF INEQUALITY

We have seen that substantial income inequality exists in Canada and have noted some reasons for it. Let us now ask a question that is loaded with value judgements, but to which economic analysis has something to contribute nonetheless: *How much inequality is the ideal amount?* We shall not, of course, be able to give a numerical answer to this question.

No one can do that. Our objective is rather to see the type of analysis that is relevant to answering the question. We begin in a simple setting in which the answer is easily obtained. Then we shall see how the real world differs from this simple model.

Consider a world in which there are two people, Smith and Jones, and suppose that we want to divide $100 between them in the way that yields the most total utility. Suppose further that Smith and Jones are alike in their ability to enjoy money; technically, we say that their marginal utility curves are identical. This identical marginal utility curve is depicted in Figure 15-11. We can prove the following result: The optimal distribution of income is to give $50 to Smith and $50 to Jones, which is point E in Figure 15-11.

To prove it, we show that if the income distribution is unequal, we can improve things by moving closer to equality. Suppose Smith has $75 (point S in the figure) and Jones has $25 (point J). Then, as we can see, because of the law of diminishing marginal utility, Smith's marginal utility (which is s) must be less than Jones's (which is j). If we take $1 away from Smith, Smith loses the low marginal utility, s, of a dollar to him. Then, when we give it to Jones, Jones gains the high marginal utility, j, that a dollar gives him. On balance, then, society's total utility must rise

FIGURE 15-11

THE OPTIMAL DISTRIBUTION OF INCOME

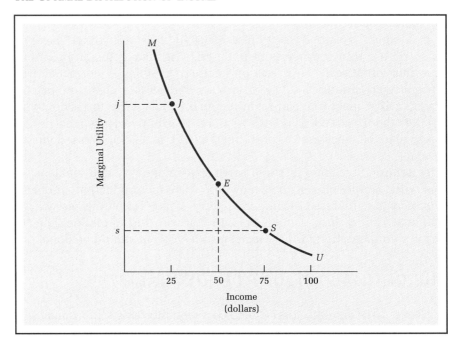

If Smith and Jones have the identical marginal utility curve (*MU*), the optimal way to distribute $100 between them is to give $50 to each (point *E*). If income is not distributed this way, their marginal utilities will be unequal, so that a redistribution of income can make society better off. This is illustrated by points *J* and *S*, representing an income distribution in which Jones gets $25 (and hence has marginal utility *j*), while Smith gets $75 (and hence has marginal utility *s*).

by $j - s$ because Jones's gain exceeds Smith's loss. Therefore, a distribution with Smith getting only $74 is better than one in which he gets $75. Since the same argument can be used to show that a $73–$27 distribution is better than $74–$26, and so on, we have established our result that a $50–$50 distribution—point E—is best.

Now, in this argument, there is nothing special about the fact that we assumed only two people or that exactly $100 was available. Any number of people and dollars would do as well. What *is* crucial is our assumption that the same amount of money would be available no matter how we chose to distribute it. Thus, we have proved the following general result:

To maximize total utility, the best way to distribute any fixed amount of money among people with identical marginal utility curves is to divide it equally.

THE TRADE-OFF BETWEEN EQUALITY AND EFFICIENCY

If we seek to apply this analysis to the real world, two major difficulties arise. First, people are different and have different marginal utility curves. Thus, *some* inequality can probably be justified. The second problem is much more formidable.

The total amount of income in our society is not independent of the ways in which we try to distribute it.

To see this vividly, ask yourself the following question: What would happen if we tried to achieve perfect equality by putting a 100 percent income tax on all workers and then dividing the tax receipts equally among the population? No one would have any incentive to work, to invest, to take risks, or to do anything else to earn money, because the rewards for all such activities would disappear. The gross domestic product would fall drastically. While the example is extreme, the same principle applies to more moderate policies to equalize incomes; indeed, it is the basic idea behind supply-side economics.

The Trade-Off between Equality and Efficiency

Policies that redistribute income reduce the rewards of high-income earners while raising the rewards of low-income earners. Hence, they reduce the incentive to earn high income. This gives rise to a trade-off that is one of the most fundamental in all of economics and one of our twelve Ideas for Beyond the Final Exam.

Measures taken to increase the amount of economic equality will often reduce economic efficiency—that is, lower the gross domestic product. In trying to divide the pie more equally, we may inadvertently reduce its size.

Because of this trade-off, the result that equal incomes are always optimal does not apply to the real world.

The optimal distribution of income will always involve *some* inequality.

But this does not mean that attempts to reduce inequality are always misguided. What we should learn from this analysis are two things:

1. There are better and worse ways to promote equality. In pursuing further income equality (or fighting poverty), we should seek policies that do the least possible harm to incentives.

2. Equality is bought at a price. Thus, like we would for any commodity, we must decide rationally how much to purchase. We will probably want to spend some of our potential income on equality, but not all of it.

Figure 15-12 illustrates both of these lessons. Curve *abcde* represents possible combinations of gross domestic product (GDP) and income equality that are obtainable under the present system of taxes and transfers. If, for example, point *c* is the current position of the economy, raising taxes on the rich to finance more transfers to the poor might move us downward to the right, toward point *d*. Equality increases but GDP falls

FIGURE 15-12
THE TRADE-OFF BETWEEN EQUALITY AND EFFICIENCY

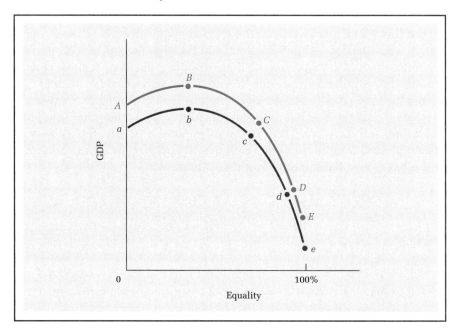

This diagram represents the fundamental trade-off between equality and efficiency. If the economy is initially at point *c*, movements toward greater equality (to the right) normally can be achieved only by reducing economic efficiency, and thus reducing the gross domestic product. The movements from points *C* and *c* toward points *D* and *d* represent two alternative policies for equalizing the income distribution. The policy that leads to *D* is preferred since it is more efficient.

as the rich react to higher marginal tax rates by producing less. Similarly, reducing both taxes and social-welfare programs might move us upward to the left, toward point *b*. Notice that, to the left of point *b*, GDP falls as inequality rises. This might be because very poorly paid workers are less productive as a result of inadequate investments in human capital, poor nutrition, or just a general sense of disaffection. Curve *ABCDE* represents possible combinations of GDP and equality under some new, more efficient, redistributive policy. It is more efficient in the sense that, for any desired level of equality, we can get more GDP with the policy represented by *ABCDE* than with the policy represented by *abcde*.

The first lesson is that we should stick to the higher of the two curves. Any point chosen on curve *abcde* can be improved upon by moving to the corresponding point on curve *ABCDE*. By picking the more efficient redistributive policy, we can have more equality *and* more GDP.

The second lesson is that neither point *B* nor point *E* would normally be society's optimal choice. At point *B*, we are seeking the highest possible GDP with utter disregard for whatever inequality might accompany it. At point *E*, we are forcing complete equality, even if work incentives vanish and a very low GDP is the result.

An astonishing degree of confusion results from the failure to understand these two lessons. Proponents of measures that further economic equality often feel obligated to deny that their programs will have any harmful effects on incentives. At times, these vehement denials are so obviously unrealistic that they undermine the very case that the egalitarians are trying to defend. Conservatives who oppose these policies also harm the strength of their case by making outlandish claims about the efficiency losses that are likely to arise from greater equality. Neither side, it seems, is willing or able to acknowledge the basic trade-off between equality and efficiency depicted in Figure 15-12. Hence, the debate generates more heat than light. Since these debates are sure to continue for the next ten or twenty years, and probably for the rest of your lives, we hope that some understanding of this trade-off stays with you well Beyond the Final Exam.

But just understanding the terms of the trade-off will not tell you the right answer. By looking at Figure 15-12, we know that the optimal amount of equality lies between points *B* and *E*, but we do not know what it actually is. Is it something like point *D*, with more equality and less GDP than we now have? Or is it a movement back toward point *B*? Everyone will have a different answer to this question, because it is basically a question of value judgement. Just how much is more equality worth to you?

We noted earlier in this chapter that many economists recommend a negative income tax (NIT) system. In terms of Figure 15-12, they believe that it would be more efficient to redistribute income through an NIT system than through the existing welfare system. The NIT is curve *ABCDE*, while the present system is curve *abcde*. If this view is correct, then by replacing the current welfare system with the NIT, we could have more equality *and* more efficiency at the same time. But this does not mean that equalization would become costless. Curve *ABCDE* still slopes downward—by increasing equality, we still diminish the GDP.

The late Arthur Okun, an influential American economist, used the following analogy to illustrate the issue. Imagine that money is liquid and that you have a bucket you can use to transport money from the rich to the poor. The problem is that the bucket is leaky. As you move the money, some drips away. Will you use the bucket if only 1 cent is lost for each 1 dollar you move? Probably everyone would say yes. But what if each dollar taken from the rich results in only 10 cents for the poor? Only the most extreme egalitarians will still say yes. Now try the hard questions. What if 20 to 40 cents is lost for each dollar that you move? If you can answer questions like these, you can decide how far down the hill from point *B* you think society should travel, for you will have expressed your value judgements in quantitative terms.

POSTSCRIPT ON THE DISTRIBUTION OF INCOME

Now that we have completed our analysis of the distribution of income, it may be useful to see how it all relates to our central theme: What does the market do well, and what does it do poorly?

We have learned that a market economy uses the marginal productivity principle to assign an income to each individual. In so doing, the market attaches high prices to scarce factors and low prices to abundant ones and thus guides firms to make efficient use of society's resources. This is one of the market's great strengths. However, by attaching high prices to some factors and low prices to others, the market mechanism often creates a distribution of income that is quite unequal; some people wind up fabulously rich while others wind up miserably poor. For this reason, the market has been widely criticized for centuries for doing a rather poor job of distributing income in accordance with commonly held notions of fairness and equity.

On balance, most observers feel that the criticism is justified: The market mechanism is extraordinarily good at promoting efficiency but rather bad at promoting equality. As we said at the outset, the market has both virtues and vices.

SUMMARY

1. Because of tax shelters, the personal income tax has not been as progressive as it might be. Nonetheless, it is a progressive tax. Many other taxes, by contrast, are regressive.

2. Sales taxes are more efficient than income taxes, since income taxes discourage saving. With lower saving, firms invest less in new plant and equipment, which results in lower

per-capita incomes in the future. The disadvantage of the sales tax, however, is that it is regressive.

3. The controversial goods and services tax (GST) was designed to replace the manufacturers' sales tax (MST)—a tax that raised the cost of business inputs and so put Canadian producers at a cost disadvantage in relation to foreign firms. The GST was supplemented by an income tax credit scheme, making the package less regressive than a sales tax is on its own. Nevertheless, the GST has remained very unpopular, because most Canadians regard it as a mechanism that could facilitate a big tax grab on the part of the government in the future.

4. There are three concepts of fair or "equitable" taxation that occasionally conflict. Horizontal equity simply calls for equals to be treated equally. Vertical equity, which calls for unequals to be treated unequally, has often been translated into the ability-to-pay principle—that people who are more able to pay taxes should be taxed more heavily. The benefits principle of tax equity ignores ability to pay and seeks to tax people according to the benefits they receive.

5. The burden of a tax is the amount of money an individual would have to be given to make the individual as well off with the tax as he or she was without it. This burden normally exceeds the taxes that are paid; the difference between the two is called the excess burden of the tax.

6. Excess burden arises when a tax induces some people or firms to change their behaviour. Excess burdens represent economic inefficiencies, so the basic principle of efficient taxation is to use taxes that have small excess burdens.

7. When people change their behaviour in response to a tax, they often shift the burden of the tax onto someone else. This is why the flypaper theory of tax incidence—the belief that the burden of any tax always stays where government puts it—is often incorrect.

8. The burden of a sales or excise tax is normally shared between suppliers and consumers. The manner in which it is shared depends on the elasticities of supply and demand.

9. A payroll tax is like an excise tax on labour services. Since the supply of labour is much less elastic than the demand for labour, workers bear most of the burden of the payroll tax. This includes both the employer's "share" and the employee's "share" of the tax.

10. The corporate profits tax can be treated like an excise tax on capital's services. Since the supply of capital is much more elastic than the demand for capital, buyers of the products produced by capital bear most of the burden of the tax.

11. Sometimes, "inefficient" taxes — that is, taxes that cause a good deal of excess burden — are nonetheless desirable because the changes in behaviour that they induce further some other social goal.

12. When there are inefficiencies in the system for reasons other than the tax system (for example, externalities), taxation can improve efficiency.

13. When both equity and efficiency are considered, many economists feel that a general personal income tax is one of the best ways to raise revenue. A sales tax may be superior on efficiency grounds (since it does not involve a disincentive for saving), but in the absence of a wealth tax (such as an inheritance tax), the sales tax is inferior on equity grounds.

14. Substantial progress toward eliminating poverty was made during the 1970s; the percentage of families living below the poverty line fell from 23 percent to 15 percent. However, because of the severe recession of the early 1980s, the poverty rate did not improve during that decade.

15. The difficulty in agreeing on a sharp dividing line between the poor and the non-poor

leads one to broaden the problem of poverty into the problem of inequality in incomes.

16. In Canada in 1990, the richest 20 percent of families received 39.3 percent of the income, while the poorest 20 percent of families received just above 6.4 percent. These numbers have changed little over the past twenty years and represent an average level of inequality when compared with statistics from other advanced industrial nations.

17. Individual incomes differ for many reasons, one of which is discrimination. Prejudice against members of a minority group or against women may lead to discrimination in rates of pay, or to segregation in the workplace, or to both. However, discrimination may also arise even when there is no prejudice (this is called statistical discrimination).

18. There is a trade-off between the goals of reducing inequality and enhancing economic efficiency: Policies that help on the equality front normally harm efficiency, and vice versa. This is one of the twelve Ideas for Beyond the Final Exam.

19. Because of this trade-off, there is an optimal degree of inequality for any society. Society finds this optimum in the same way that a consumer decides how much to buy of different commodities: The trade-off tells us how costly it is to "purchase" more equality,

and preferences then determine how much should be "bought." However, since people differ in their value judgements about the importance of equality, there will inevitably be disagreement over the ideal amount of equality.

20. There may, however, be some hope of reaching agreement over the policies to use in pursuit of whatever goal for equality is selected. This is because more-efficient redistributive policies let us buy any amount of equality at a lower price in terms of lost output. Economists claim on these grounds, for example, that a negative income tax is preferable to our current welfare system.

21. Even the negative income tax is no panacea, however. Its primary virtue lies in the way it preserves incentives to work. But if this is done by keeping the tax rate low, either the minimum guaranteed level of income will have to be very low or many non-poor families will become eligible to receive benefits.

22. The goal of income equality is also pursued through the tax system, especially through the progressive income tax. However, because of tax shelters, the equalization achieved by this tax is much less than is commonly believed. In addition, taxes other than income taxes are typically regressive, as are many government expenditure programs, so the government-sector initiatives overall are slightly regressive.

CONCEPTS FOR REVIEW

Progressive, proportional, and
  regressive taxes
Average and marginal tax rates
Direct and indirect taxes
Personal income tax
Tax shelters

Capital gain
Excise tax
Value-added tax
Corporate profits tax
Property tax
Payroll tax

Fiscal federalism
Conditional and
  unconditional grants
Horizontal and vertical equity
Tax exemptions and credits
Ability-to-pay principle

Benefits principle of taxation	Poverty line	Affirmative action
Burden of a tax	Absolute and relative concepts	Pay equity
Excess burden	of poverty	Optimal amount of inequality
Incidence of a tax	Lorenz curve	Trade-off between equality
Flypaper theory of tax	Negative income tax (NIT)	and efficiency
incidence	Economic discrimination	
Tax shifting	Statistical discrimination	

QUESTIONS FOR DISCUSSION

1. "If the federal government continues to raise taxes as it has been doing, it will ruin the country." Comment.

2. Using the following hypothetical income tax table, compute the marginal and average tax rates. Is the tax progressive, proportional, or regressive?

Income (dollars)	Tax (dollars)
10 000	0
20 000	2400
30 000	4800
40 000	7200

3. Which concept of tax equity, if any, seems to be served by each of the following?
   a. The progressive income tax
   b. The excise tax on liquor
   c. The property tax

4. Think of some tax that you personally pay. What steps have you taken or could you take to reduce your tax payments? Is there an excess burden on you? Why or why not?

5. Consider the supply and demand schedules for cigarettes given in the table opposite:
   a. What is the equilibrium price and equilibrium quantity?
   b. Now the government levies an excise tax of $1.25 per pack on cigarettes. What is the equilibrium price paid by consumers, price received by producers, and quantity now?
   c. Explain why it makes no difference whether the government levies the $1.25 tax on the consumer or the producer. (Relate your answer to the discussion of the payroll tax on pages 489–92.)
   d. Suppose the tax is levied on the producers. How much of the tax are they able to shift onto consumers? Explain how they manage to do this.
   e. Is there any excess burden from this tax? Why? Who bears this excess burden?
   f. By how much does cigarette consumption decline because of the tax? Why might the government be happy about this outcome, despite the excess burden?

Price per Pack (dollars)	Quantity Demanded (millions of packs per year)	Quantity Supplied (millions of packs per year)
3.00	360	160
3.25	330	180
3.50	300	200
3.75	270	220
4.00	240	240
4.25	210	260
4.50	180	280
4.75	150	300
5.00	120	320

6. The country of Taxmania produces only two commodities: rice and caviar. The poor spend all their income on rice, while the rich purchase both goods. Both demand for and supply of rice are quite inelastic. In the caviar market, both supply and demand are quite elastic. Which good would be heavily taxed if Taxmanians cared most about efficiency? What if they cared most about vertical equity?

7. Using the leaky-bucket analogy (page 520), explain why economists believe that replacing the present welfare system with a negative income tax would help reduce the "leak."

8. Suppose you were to design a system of negative income tax for Canada. Pick a guaranteed income level and a tax rate that seem reasonable to you. What break-even level of income is implied by these choices? For the plan you have just devised, construct a corresponding version of Table 15-6 (page 505).

9. What follows is a complete list of the distribution of income at Canada's Wonderland. From these data, construct a Lorenz curve for Canada's Wonderland.

Name	Income
Fred Flintstone	$100 000
Barney Rubble	172 000
Ticket taker	16 000
Yogi Bear	68 000
Boo-Boo	44 000

How different is this from the Lorenz curve for Canada (Figure 15-8, on page 501)?

10. Suppose you were assigned the task of defining the poor. Would you choose an absolute or a relative concept of poverty? Why? What would be your specific definition of poverty?

11. Discuss the concept of the "optimal amount of inequality." What are some of the practical problems in determining how much inequality really is optimal? Use the issue of capital gains taxation as an example to make your answer more specific.

REGULATION OF INDUSTRY AND COMPETITION POLICY

The free enterprise system is absolutely too important to be left to the voluntary action of the marketplace.

A U.S. CONGRESSMAN (1979)

B ecause the market system may not function ideally in monopolistic or oligopolistic industries, governments have frequently intervened in these areas. In Canada, such intervention has followed two basic patterns. The Competition Act seeks to prohibit the acquisition of monopoly power and to ban certain monopolistic practices. In addition, some firms have been subjected to **regulation**, which constrains their pricing policies and other decisions.

In the first part of this chapter, we discuss the reasons for, and the effectiveness of, regulation. We find that despite the good intentions of its designers, the regulatory mechanism, particularly in the form it took before the 1980s, was criticized on the grounds that while its cost to the consuming public was high, it did not protect their interests effectively. We explain the nature of the problems involved and the steps, many of them suggested by simple economic theory, that have been taken since the late 1970s to remedy those problems. We also discuss some recent moves toward deregulation (that is, reducing the number of regulations and the powers of the regulatory agencies) and privatization (that is, reversing earlier policy decisions to nationalize certain firms). Much of our discussion deals with regulatory restrictions of *pricing* by firms under regulatory control. Regulators control a variety of economic activities other than pricing, as we note, but price-setting rules and their consequences for economic welfare are most easily analyzed with the help of the tools studied in previous chapters of this book.

The second part of the chapter explores our Competition Act. This piece of legislation—the main instrument of the government's competition policy—attempts to control the growth of monopoly and to prevent firms from engaging in "undesirable" practices. Firms violating competition laws risk a lawsuit from the federal government, which can seek a ruling that both prevents the practice from recurring and punishes the offender by imposing fines or even prison terms. As in the first part of

REGULATION OF INDUSTRY is a process established by law that restricts or controls some specified decisions made by the affected firms. Regulation is usually carried out by a special government agency assigned the task of administering and interpreting the law. That agency also acts as a court in enforcing the regulatory laws.

the chapter, on regulation, we reach the conclusion that, thus far, government policy in this area has not been very successful.

MONOPOLY, REGULATION, AND NATIONALIZATION

In the western economies, certain industries have traditionally been run as monopolies. These include postal services, electricity generation, transportation, and gas supply. Since there are no competitive pressures to protect the interests of consumers from monopolistic exploitation in these cases, it is generally agreed that some substitute form of protection from excessive prices and restricted outputs is needed.

Most of Western Europe has adopted **nationalization** as its solution, which means that the state owns and operates certain monopolistic industries. In Canada, we seem to have been reluctant to go as far as the Europeans, but we have nonetheless had significant elements of nationalization. For example, most cities run their own public transportation systems, and numerous Crown corporations either exist today (for example, Via Rail) or have been recently privatized (for example, Air Canada).

The main instrument of control of public utility industries in Canada, however, is the regulatory agency. The federal and provincial governments have created a large number of agencies that regulate prices, standards of service, provisions for safety, and a variety of other aspects of the operations of telephone companies, radio and television stations, electric utilities, airlines, trucking companies, and firms in many other industries (such as car insurance, where, in some provinces, companies must comply with no-fault provisions). Many of these industries are not pure monopolies but include firms that are nevertheless suspected of possessing so much market power that their regulation is considered to be in the public interest.

A PUZZLE: INDUSTRY OPPOSITION TO DEREGULATION

An observer who knew nothing about regulated industries might expect that deregulation would be welcomed by the firms affected. After all, regulations curb their freedom of decision making in many ways.

Yet most companies—and their unions—fight bitterly against proposals for deregulation. Later, we will discuss some of the reasons for this opposition. But already we may surmise from this observation that regulation may, inadvertently or deliberately, have been serving the interests of some of the regulated firms, rather than making life harder for them.

THE DEGREE OF REGULATION IN CANADA

Regulation is extensive in Canada: The proportion of national product that is subject to direct regulation is 29 percent, and this figure does not record the share in gross domestic product of the industries that are "self-regulated." (Self-regulated industries are those that the elected bodies—in most cases, provincial legislatures—have given carte blanche to set their own rules of practice, and in many cases, their own charges. Industries that are self-regulated include law, medicine, and dentistry.)

In 1980, the Bureau of Competition Policy in the federal department of Consumer and Corporate Affairs established a Regulated Sector Branch. The staff of this branch appear before federal and provincial regulatory bodies to argue on behalf of greater competition. They have, for example, argued for greater recognition of the costs that agricultural marketing boards impose on the consumer.

Agricultural marketing boards are pervasive in Canada. The products they affect include chickens, turkeys, eggs, tobacco, and well over a hundred others. If it were not for the provincial marketing boards, which often set quotas for individual suppliers, these agricultural industries would be competitive. Hence, in these cases, the whole point of regulation is to *create* monopoly power, so that total market supply can be managed. The purpose of this policy is to create higher and more stable incomes for farmers. While consumers lose from this policy, and there are often calls to do away with agricultural marketing boards, these boards seem destined to survive until more-efficient and more-equitable methods of maintaining farm incomes are broadly understood to be available.

We limit our discussion of agricultural marketing boards to the boxed insert on pages 530–31, since, in this chapter, we wish to concentrate on government regulation that is at least intended to reduce monopoly practices.

WHY REGULATION?

As we learned in Chapter 10, one main reason for regulation of industry is the phenomenon of **natural monopoly**. In some industries, it is apparently far cheaper to have production carried out by one firm than by a number of different firms. This situation may occur for several reasons.

ECONOMIES OF SCALE AND SCOPE

One reason why this may occur is because of economies of large-scale production. An example of such **economies of scale** is a railroad track, which can carry 100 trains a day with total cost hardly higher than when it carries 1 train. Here is a case in which savings are made possible by expanding the volume of an activity—a case of economies of scale. As we saw in Chapter 7, scale economies lead to an average-cost (AC) curve that goes downhill as output increases (see Figure 16-1). This means that a firm with a large output can cover its costs at a price lower than that of a firm whose output is smaller. In Figure 16-1, point A represents the larger firm, whose AC is $5, while B is the smaller firm, with AC = $7.

ECONOMIES OF SCALE are savings that are acquired through increases in quantities produced.

FIGURE 16-1

ECONOMIES OF SCALE

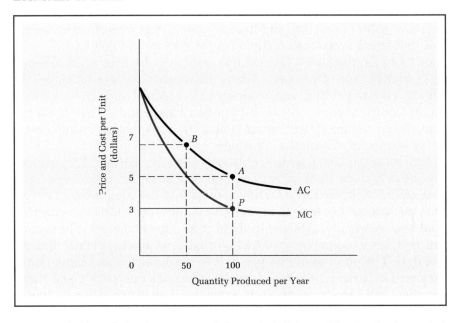

Economies of scale imply that the average-cost (AC) curve is declining, and therefore that the marginal-cost (MC) curve is below the AC curve. In such a case, the first firm to become large has the lowest costs and drives others out of business. If a regulator forces the remaining large firm to produce 100 units and charge a price equal to its marginal cost ($3 per unit), that firm will take in $300 in revenues. But, since its average cost at 100 units is $5 per unit, its total cost will be $500, and the firm will lose money.

ECONOMIES OF SCOPE are savings that are acquired through simultaneous production of many different products.

Another reason a single large firm may have a cost advantage over a group of small firms is that it is sometimes cheaper to produce a number of different commodities together than to turn them out separately, each by a different firm. The saving made possible by simultaneous production of many different products is called **economies of scope**, an example of which is the manufacture of both cars and trucks by the same producer. The techniques employed in producing both commodities are sufficiently similar to make specialized production by different firms impractical.

In industries where there are great economies of scale *and* scope, society will obviously incur a significant cost penalty if it insists on maintaining a large number of firms. Supply by a number of smaller competing firms will be far more costly and use up much larger quantities of resources than will supply by a monopoly. Moreover, in the presence of strong economies of scale and scope, society will not be able to preserve free competition, even if it wants to do so. The large, multiproduct firm will have so great a cost advantage over its rivals that the small firms will simply be unable to survive. We say in such a case that free competition is *not sustainable*.

Where monopoly production is cheapest and where free competition is not sustainable, the industry is a natural monopoly. Because monopoly is cheaper, society may not want to have competition; if free competition is not sustainable, society will not even have a choice in the matter.

But even if society reconciles itself to monopoly, it will generally not want to let the monopoly firm do whatever it wants to with its market power. Therefore, it will consider either regulation or nationalization of these firms.

UNIVERSAL SERVICE AND RATE AVERAGING

A second reason for regulation is the desire for "universal service"—that is, the availability of service at "reasonable prices" even to small communities where the small scale of operation makes costs extremely high. In such cases, regulators have sometimes encouraged a public utility to supply services to some consumers at a financial loss. But a loss on some sales is financially feasible only when the firm is permitted to make up for it by obtaining higher profits on its other sales.

This process of **rate averaging** of gains and losses, also referred to as **cross subsidization**, is possible only if the firm is protected from price competition and free entry of new competitors in its more profitable markets. If no such protection is provided by a regulatory agency, potential competitors will sniff out the profit opportunities in the markets where service is supplied at a price well above cost. Many new firms will enter the business and cause prices to be driven down in those markets. This practice is referred to as "cream skimming." The entrants choose to enter only into the profitable markets and skim away the cream of the profits for themselves, leaving the unprofitable markets to the supplier who had attempted to provide universal service. This phenomenon is one reason why regulatory rules, until recently, made it very difficult or impossible for new firms to enter when and where they saw fit.

> **RATE AVERAGING** or **CROSS SUBSIDIZATION** means selling one product at a loss, which is balanced by higher profits on another product.

Airlines and telecommunications are two industries in which these issues have arisen. In both cases, fears have been expressed that without regulation of entry and rates or the granting of special subsidies, less-populous communities would effectively be isolated, losing their airline services and obtaining telephone service only at cripplingly high rates. Many economists question the validity of this argument for regulation, which, they say, calls for a hidden subsidy of rural consumers by all other consumers. In the United States, airline-deregulation legislation provided for government subsidies to help small communities attract airline service. In fact, this market has been taken over to a considerable extent by specialized "commuter" airlines flying much smaller aircraft than do the major airlines, which have withdrawn from many such routes.

A similar issue affects our postal service, which charges the same price to deliver a letter anywhere within the country, regardless of the distance or the special difficulties and costs of a particular route. To maintain this pricing scheme, the law must protect Canada Post from direct competition in many of its activities; otherwise, its extreme form of uniform pricing would soon deprive it of its most profitable routes.

FURTHER DETAIL

AGRICULTURAL MARKETING BOARDS

The thrust of the government's overall regulatory program is to reverse or forestall monopoly behaviour—that is, to force prices and profit levels down. Similarly, the Competition Act itself, which we study later in this chapter, is intended to stop firms from colluding and operating like a monopolist. But concern for low incomes in agriculture has led to the opposite approach in the regulation of many agricultural industries. In this area, our laws permit firms to band together as a monopoly in what are known as marketing boards. If a majority of firms producing a particular farm product vote in favour of the formation of a marketing board, all such firms are required by law to sell through the board and adhere to the quotas on sales that it imposes.

To see why a marketing board establishes and enforces quotas, consider the accompanying diagram. Part (a) depicts the demand and supply curves of a competitive industry, while part (b) shows the situation of one of the numerous firms within that industry. Assume that the competitive industry is in full long-run equilibrium—at point A in both diagrams — before the marketing board is formed.

Now suppose the producers band together and the executive of the newly formed marketing board decides to dictate a higher price, indicated by the horizontal blue line in the diagram. This rise in price causes buyers of the industry's product to decrease their quantity demanded (to point B in part (a)), so that industry output and sales are cut in half. To make sure that this cutback in production occurs, the marketing board imposes a quota on the output of each individual firm in the industry. The quota for each firm is equal to the horizontal distance from the origin to the vertical blue line in part (b). Each firm then operates at point B, and earns above-normal profits (indicated by the shaded rectangle).

Without the quotas, such profits could not persist. For one thing, price exceeds marginal cost at the output level given by point B, so firms that are already in the industry would, under normal circumstances, expand output. With all firms acting in this manner, the market price would be driven back down. A second consideration is that new firms, in the hope of acquiring a share of the above-normal profits that result from the quotas, would be tempted to enter the industry. Such an influx of new firms would also have the effect of driving the market price back down. However, the quota system is designed to preclude this possibility: New entry will *not* occur, because only the pre-existing firms are assigned a quota.

In recent years, agricultural marketing boards have come under attack, most often for the following four reasons. First, as in other industries, consumers prefer to have access to more goods at lower prices—that is, they dislike monopolies. Second, the imposition of quotas can have certain consequences that do not meet with public support—for example, millions of "unwanted" eggs and large quantities of cheese are known to have been destroyed when quotas were exceeded. The third reason frequently cited in support of eliminating marketing boards is that their existence makes it very difficult for Canada to be taken seriously when we argue in trade negotiations with other countries that *they* are indulging in too much protection of their agricultural industries. For example, in interna-

(continued)

(continued)

tional negotiations pertaining to the wheat industry (an industry in which we have no marketing boards), Canada has been a leader in calling for all countries to reduce government subsidization of farmers. But our credibility is undermined — and any hope for improvements for our wheat farmers therefore severely threatened — when other countries can justifiably argue that Canadian authorities intervene extensively in other areas of agriculture in Canada through our system of marketing boards.

The fourth problem with marketing boards that makes them vulnerable to criticism is that, in the long run, they in fact fail to raise producer incomes. Let us consider why this is so. Quotas can be bought and sold. When a person wants to enter the industry, he or she must buy both a farm property and a quota (the right to sell the product). Competition forces the price of the quota up to equal the present value of the stream of extra profits that is generated by the quota—a value, for

each period, equal to the shaded profit area in the diagram. This higher purchase price raises the new owner's fixed costs, causing the farm's AC curve to move up to the level at which it will cross through point *B*. Hence, those who buy into the industry *after* the quotas have been assigned get no financial benefits from them; the only beneficiaries of the quota system are the individuals who owned their farms when the marketing board was originally established. Also, these original owners benefit from the system only in their role as landowners; as current producers, they gain nothing because their AC curves (which are based on opportunity costs) have been pushed up just as much as those of the new farm owners. Hence, the quota system provides a one-time windfall gain for the preexisting farm owners; as producers in any year thereafter, they do not benefit at all. Ultimately, then, the quota system is difficult to defend: It imposes real costs on society, yet fails to benefit current farmers in their role as producers.

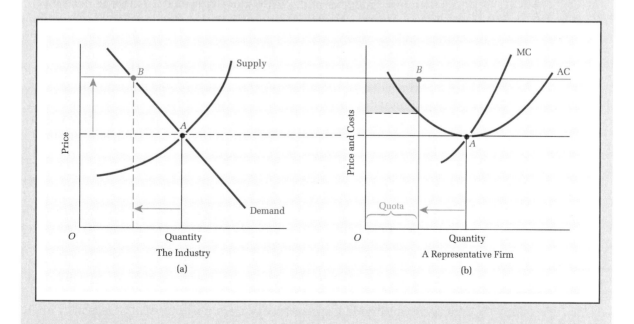

The Industry
(a)

A Representative Firm
(b)

We conclude that the goal of "universal service" leads to regulatory control of entry and exit, and not just to control of prices.

SELF-DESTRUCTIVE COMPETITION

A third reason for regulation is to help prevent **self-destructive competition**, which, for example, economies of scale make possible. In an industry such as rail transportation, equipment—including roadbeds, tracks, switching facilities, locomotives, and cars—is extremely expensive. Suppose that two railways, having been built and equipped, are competing for some limited business that happens to be insufficient to require using their total facilities to anything near capacity. That is, to meet this level of consumer demand, each railway may have to run only 40 percent as many trains over the track as can conveniently be scheduled over that route. The management of each railway will feel that, with its unused capacity, any business will be worthwhile, provided that it covers more than its short-run marginal costs—fuel, labour, and expenses other than plant and equipment. If the short-run marginal cost of shipping an additional tonne of, say, coal is $5, either railway will be happy to lure coal-shipping customers away from the other at a price of, say, $7 per tonne, even though that price may not cover the entire cost of track and equipment. Each tonne of business that pays $7 when marginal cost is $5 will put the railway $2 ahead of where it would have been without the business. The new business does not contribute much to the cost of the tracks or locomotives or other equipment, which must be paid for whether that business is acquired or not. Thus, even if the new business pays only for its own marginal cost and a little more, it seems financially desirable.

But the temptation to accept business on such terms will drive both firms' prices down toward their marginal cost, and, in the process, both railways are likely to go broke. If there are no customers paying for the track, the roadbed, and the equipment, the railway will simply be unable to continue. Thus, some believe that regulation of rates can be sensible, even in industries subject to competitive pressures, simply to protect the firms from themselves. Without this regulation, self-destructive competition could end up sinking those industries financially, and the public would thereby be deprived of vital services.

MANAGEMENT OF A PUBLIC RESOURCE

A fourth reason often given for public regulation is that some industries base their operations on a public resource of limited capacity, so that a public agency must intervene to ration out that resource "fairly." The most notable example of the need for this type of rationing is radio and television broadcasting. The frequency spectrum that is currently used for broadcasting is limited, so it must be divided up among the users. If it were not divided up, and entry were not limited, the airwaves might become crowded and interference of broadcasters with one another's transmissions would undermine the quality of reception and perhaps even make the airwaves totally useless.

Many economists have argued that government has no business allocating scarce resources like the radio and TV spectrum among commercial users who employ such public resources for a profit. These economists argue that government rationing of the airwaves is a giveaway of public resources to favoured individuals, who then grow rich at the public's expense—even though the Canadian Radio-television and Telecommunications Commission, in return, does retain some right to regulate the content of broadcasts. Rather, many propose that firms be required to bid against one another for licences to run radio and TV stations. In that way, the licences would go to those who could make the best use of them—an ability that would be determined by their bids. The profits would then go into the public treasury rather than into private pockets, and could be used to finance non-profit, public-interest activities such as public broadcasting.

PROTECTION AGAINST MISINFORMATION

A final reason for regulation is the danger that consumers will be misinformed or cheated; that consumers, employees, or the environment will be threatened by unscrupulous sellers; or that even conscientious sellers will be forced to keep up with the questionable practices of less-scrupulous rivals. Because some of these issues will be illustrated and examined in detail in Chapter 17 on environmental protection, the subject will not be discussed further in this chapter.

To summarize, there are five basic reasons for the activities of regulatory agencies:

1. The desire to prevent excess profits and other undesirable practices in an industry that is considered to be a natural monopoly.
2. The desire for universal service—that is, the desire to provide service at relatively low rates to customers whom it is particularly expensive to serve, and to do so without government subsidy.
3. The desire to prevent self-destructive price competition in multifirm industries with large capital costs and low marginal costs.
4. The desire to allocate fairly public resources or facilities of limited capacity.
5. The desire to protect customers, employees, and the environment from damage resulting from inappropriate behaviour by firms.

WHY REGULATORS SOMETIMES RAISE PRICES

It has been suggested that regulation sometimes results in prices higher than those that consumers would pay in its absence. One of the most widely publicized illustrations of this tendency was the difference in U.S. air fares between San Francisco and Los Angeles and between Washington, D.C., and New York City before the United States deregulated airlines. The former fare was never regulated by the Civil Aeronautics Board because the flight is contained entirely within the state of California, whereas the board did control the interstate flight between New York and Washington. The California flight is nearly twice as long as the East Coast flight, and neither route is sparsely travelled nor beset by any other noteworthy features that would make for substantial differences in cost. Yet at the time of deregulation, fares were a little higher than $40 for the long California trip and a little higher than $50 for the short Washington–New York trip.

Why would regulators ever push for a price floor rather than a price ceiling? (This relates to the puzzle mentioned near the beginning of this chapter.) The answer is that they typically do so when they want to introduce or preserve competitors in an industry. We saw earlier that strong economies of scale and scope make it impossible for a number of smaller firms to survive. The largest firm in the industry will have such cost advantages over its competitors that it will be able to drive them out of the market while still operating at prices that are profitable. Most observers applaud low prices and price cuts that reflect such cost advantages. However, a firm that wants the market for itself may conceivably engage in price-cutting even when such cuts are not justifiable in terms of cost.

The reason such price-cutting may not reduce the overall profits of a regulated firm is that regulation often imposes an upper limit on the amount of profit a firm is permitted to earn. To see the connection, consider a regulated firm that produces two commodities, A and B, and that is setting each price below its profit-maximizing level in order to limit profits to the allowable ceilings. The firm may be able, without loss of profit, to cut the price of A even below its marginal cost and make up for any resulting decrease in profit by a sufficient rise in the price of B. In other words, the firm has instituted a *cross subsidy* from the consumers of product B to the consumers of product A. Consumers of B are paying an excessive amount for their purchase in order to make up for the deficit in the sale of product A.

Why would any firm want to do this? Suppose A is threatened by competition while B has no competitors on the horizon. Then, a cross subsidy from B to A may be a way of preventing the entry of the potential competitors of A or even of driving some current competitors out of the field.

But regulation sometimes goes beyond the prevention of cross subsidy. Firms that feel they are hurt by competitive pressures will complain to regulatory commissions that the prices charged by their rivals are "unfairly" low. The commission, afraid that unrestrained pricing will reduce the number of firms in the industry, then attempts to "equalize" matters by imposing price floors that permit all the firms in the industry to operate profitably.

Many economists maintain that this approach to pricing is a perversion of the idea of competition. The virtue of competition is that, where it occurs, firms force one another to supply consumers with products of high quality at low prices. Any firm that cannot do this is driven out of business by market forces. If competition does not do this, it loses its purpose, because, to the economist, it is a means to an end, not an end in itself.

An arrangement under which firms are enabled to co-exist only by preventing them from competing with one another preserves the appearance of competition but destroys its substance.

SOME PRICING ISSUES

Consider the natural monopoly depicted in Figure 16-2. If this firm is left unregulated, it will choose to operate at output level *OA*, since this is the point at which MR = MC. This firm will charge a price equal to *OF* and earn an amount of profit equal to the shaded red area in the graph. Let us compare this unregulated outcome with the outcomes that would follow from several possible price-setting rules.

FIGURE 16-2

ALTERNATIVE REGULATIONS FOR A NATURAL MONOPOLY

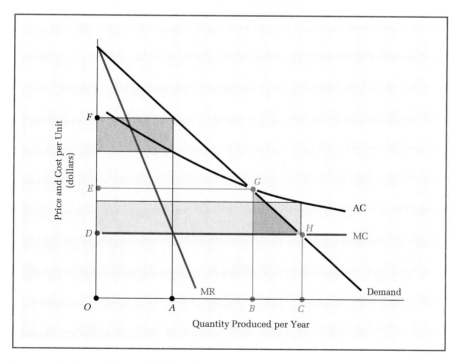

An unregulated natural monopoly obeys the MR = MC rule, setting price to equal distance *OF* and quantity produced to equal distance *OA*, and earning profits equal to the shaded red area. If regulated and subject to the rules of average-cost pricing, the firm is allowed to earn no more than normal (that is, zero) economic profits; it must therefore set its price equal to distance *OE* and produce a quantity equal to distance *OB*. Alternatively, if the firm is subject to the rules of marginal-cost pricing (facing a *P* = MC constraint), society's optimal-resource-allocation rule (MU = MC) is satisfied, but the firm must be subsidized by an amount equal to the area of the gold rectangle.

AVERAGE-COST PRICING

Suppose the regulator stipulates that price can be no higher than the level that just permits the firm to earn a normal rate of profit. In the economist's language, this regulation allows zero economic profits, meaning that the stipulated price is equal to average cost. This price is shown by the height of the horizontal blue line connecting points E and G in Figure 16-2. The monopoly firm is forced to operate at the price and quantity given by point G. Consumers appear to be better off with this outcome than with the one that occurs without regulation, since price is lower (distance OE is less than distance OF) and the quantity of the good available for consumption is greater (distance OB is greater than distance OA). Furthermore, society's sense of fairness is more likely to be satisfied, since monopoly profits are eliminated.

There are three problems with this average-cost pricing approach, however. The first is simply a problem of implementation. Consider that almost every company produces a number of different varieties and qualities of some product, and many firms produce thousands of different products, each with its own price. Even General Motors, a fairly specialized firm, produces many makes and sizes of cars and trucks in addition to refrigerators, washing machines, and various other things. In a multiproduct firm, we cannot even define AC = TC/Q, since to calculate Q (total output), we would have to add up all the apples and oranges (and all the other different items) that the firm produces. But we know that one cannot add up apples and oranges. Thus, since we cannot calculate AC for a multiproduct firm, it is hardly possible for the regulator to require P = AC for each of the firm's products, although regulators sometimes *think* they can do so.

Even if we ignore this implementation issue, there is a second problem: The maximum-profit constraint removes the incentive for firms to invest in cost-saving innovations. After all, if whenever a firm successfully lowers the position of its AC and MC curves, the regulator automatically lowers the allowed-price line (to continue to satisfy the P = AC rule), the firm gains nothing from investing in the cost-saving innovation. This means that our comparison of the regulated firm and the unregulated firm in Figure 16-2 is somewhat misleading, in that the unregulated firm could conceivably lower its cost curves enough that it could charge a lower price and produce a higher quantity than it could under regulation.

Here again, an actual implementation issue arises. In a number of regulated industries, a proposed change in rates is likely to require a minimum of several months to get through the regulatory machinery. This phenomenon, known as **regulatory lag**, is perhaps the main reason that profit regulation has not eliminated all rewards for efficiency and all penalties for inefficiency.

Suppose, for example, that the regulatory commission approves a set of prices calculated to yield exactly the "fair rate of return" to the company—say, 10 percent. If management then invests successfully in new processes that reduce its costs sharply, the rate of return under the old prices may rise to, say, 12 percent. If it takes two years for the regulators to review the prices they previously approved and adjust them to the new cost levels, the company will earn a 2 percent bonus reward for its efficiency during the two years of regulatory lag. Similarly, if management makes a series of bad decisions that reduce the company's return to 7 percent, the firm may well apply to the regulator for some adjustments in prices to permit it to recoup its losses. If the regulator takes eighteen months to act, the firm suffers a penalty for its inefficiency. It may be added that where mismanagement is clearly the cause of losses, regulators will be reluctant to permit the regulated firm to make up for such losses by rate adjustments. But in most cases, it is difficult to pinpoint responsibility for a firm's losses.

All in all, those who have studied regulated industries have come away deeply concerned about the effects of regulation upon economic efficiency. Although some regulated firms seem to operate very efficiently, others seem to behave in quite the opposite way.

Although regulatory lag does permit some penalty for inefficiency and some reward for superior performance by regulated firms, the arrangement works only in a rough-and-ready manner. It leaves unsolved one of the fundamental problems of regulation—the provision of incentives for efficiency.

The third problem with average-cost pricing is that, even if it did not involve a disincentive effect on investment in cost-saving innovations or any implementation difficulties with regard to multiproduct firms, its outcome would still be inefficient. The reason for this will become clear in the following discussion of an alternative regulation strategy—marginal-cost pricing.

MARGINAL-COST PRICING

As noted in Chapter 10, economic efficiency requires that MU equal MC, but at point *G* in Figure 16-2 (the outcome point under average-cost pricing), MU exceeds MC. This inefficiency can be eliminated only by expanding output to amount *OC*. It seems clear, then, that the regulator should set the maximum price at the level indicated by the height of the marginal-cost curve in Figure 16-2. We can also see that at this price, society would benefit from the increase in quantity produced that is represented by distance *BC*. The value of this extra output to consumers is equal to the area below the demand curve between points *B* and *C*. Further, since it costs society only the amount equal to the area below the marginal-cost curve between points *B* and *C* to produce the extra output, the benefits to society of this higher level of output exceed the costs by an amount equal to the blue triangular-shaped area in the graph. Thus, marginal-cost pricing is indeed preferable to average-cost pricing.

There is, however, a problem with marginal-cost pricing for a firm with a natural monopoly. Since the MC curve is forever below the AC curve, the firm would be forced to cease operation if it were confronted by this regulation. To operate at $P = $ MC would cause the firm to incur losses (equal to the area of the gold rectangle in Figure 16-2). Thus, if marginal-cost pricing is to be pursued in a natural monopoly situation, the private firm must be either subsidized or replaced by a Crown corporation that would continue to operate at a loss.

THE RAMSEY PRICING RULE

In recent years, economists have been attracted to a very imaginative third approach to the problem of pricing in regulated industries that produce a multiplicity of products. This approach derives its name from its discoverer, Frank Ramsey, a brilliant English mathematician who died in 1930, at the age of 26, after making several enduring contributions to both mathematics and economics.

The basic idea of Ramsey's pricing principle can be explained in a fairly straightforward manner. As we just explained, prices must be set *above* marginal costs if a firm with increasing returns to scale is to break even. But how much above? In effect, Ramsey argued as follows: The reason we do not like prices to be above marginal costs is that such high prices distort the choices made by consumers, leading them to buy "too little" of the goods whose prices are set way above MC. Yet, it is necessary to set prices somewhat above marginal costs to allow the firm to survive. Therefore, it makes sense to raise prices *most* above marginal cost where consumers will respond the *least* to such price increases—that is, where the elasticity of demand is the lowest—so that price rises will create the least distortion of demand. This line of argument led Ramsey to formulate the following rule:

Ramsey pricing rule: Where prices must exceed marginal cost in order to permit the regulated firm to break even, the ratios of P to MC should be largest for those products with the smallest elasticities of demand.

Many economists accept this pricing rule as the correct conclusion on theoretical grounds. It has even been proposed for postal and telephone pricing.

CONSTRAINED MARKET PRICING AND STAND-ALONE COST CEILINGS

In the regulation of railways in the United States, that country's Interstate Commerce Commission has recently adopted a new approach to regulation explicitly derived from the theory of contestability that we mentioned in Chapter 11 (see page 329). In its decisions, the commission has recognized the value of the Ramsey pricing rule as a general guideline for policy. But the commissioners felt it was not practical to calculate statistically and update constantly all the demand-elasticity numbers and marginal-cost figures that use of the Ramsey rule requires. Instead, they decided to adopt a four-part rule known as **constrained market pricing**. The intent was to compel the U.S. railways to set the prices they would have set if all of their activities were contestable—that is, to set prices as if entry into freight transportation were everywhere sufficiently easy that the railways would be subjected to a perpetual and constant threat of new competition. The four parts of the rule are as follows:

1. For types of freight and routes where competition happens to be substantial and effective, the railways should be deregulated; that is, market forces should be allowed to do the job of policing the railways' behaviour.

2. Where competition is inadequate, a floor and a ceiling should be set for each and every railway price, with the railway companies left free to select any price level they wish within those bounds.

3. The price floor should be the lowest level to which price could fall in the long run under perfectly competitive conditions. This provision, in effect, prohibits a railway from adopting any price below marginal cost. It is designed to provide adequate and defensible protection for any railway's rivals against any attempt at unfair competitive price-cutting.

4. The price ceiling should be the cost that a *hypothetical* (that is, imaginary) efficient entrant would have to bear to supply each specific service. In other words, for activities where entry is difficult or impossible, the idea is to prohibit the railways from charging more than they could get away with if entry were easy and cheap. The hypothetical cost figure for the efficient entrant is called the **stand-alone cost** of the service. It is the cost that would be required if an efficient entrant were to supply only the service or group of services in question. This provision is intended to protect the interests of railway customers, guaranteeing them prices no higher than those that might be charged if the markets were effectively competitive.

Most economists who have studied the issue seem to approve of this new approach to rate regulation, although there are still some disputes about the details of its operation. Given the historical similarity between the American and Canadian approaches to regulation, we may expect this approach to receive attention in Canada.

REACTIONS TO THE PROBLEMS OF REGULATION

DEREGULATION PLUS INCREASED COMPETITION

One of the most widespread approaches to solving the problems of regulation is to have regulators get out of the business, leaving much more (if not all) of the task of looking after consumer interests to the natural forces of competition. This approach is promising in areas of the economy in which competition can be expected to survive without government intervention—for example, in freight transportation, airlines, and pipelines. As a consequence, a number of economists representing a broad range of political views have been advocating at least some deregulation in these fields.

Throughout the 1980s, a significant amount of deregulation took place within the United States, and some occurred in Canada as well. It is interesting to note one aspect of this experience: In a number of cases, we observed both an increase in quantity of service and a decrease in price. Our analysis has shown that this combination of results can be explained by only two possibilities:

1. that the incentive to avoid cost-saving innovations under regulation is quantitatively important; and/or

2. that new firms successfully entered these deregulated industries. This development proves that the industries in question were not natural monopoly situations after all. In such instances, the regulatory board must have functioned as a *preserver* of monopoly power, which would explain why firms in these industries resisted deregulation. This provides one answer to the puzzle of industry opposition to deregulation, which we noted at the beginning of this chapter.

In a number of cases, then, deregulation has been deemed successful.

Of course, deregulation will not work in industries in which self-destructive competition is likely to occur in the absence of government regulation. The experience of the U.S. airlines after the industry was deregulated offers some evidence to support this assertion. While considerable competition continues to prevail, many of the new airlines established since the end of regulation have gone bankrupt or have been purchased by the older firms. On many routes, the number of competitors has decreased sharply. This has given rise to concerns about the ability of competition to continue to protect consumer interests, at least on some of the routes. In other industries, competition is considered sufficiently weak that many think some continued regulation is indispensable. Thus, the question remains: Which controls in those fields will not destroy incentives for efficiency?

PERFORMANCE CRITERIA FOR THE PERMITTED RATE OF RETURN

The argument for deregulation addresses itself to all of the problems discussed in the previous section, but there are other proposals that are concerned with only one or another of these problems. We turn now to proposals designed to prevent profit controls from discouraging efficiency.

Some observers have advocated that the legally permitted rate of return not be set at a fixed number—say, 10 percent—but that it be varied from firm to firm, depending on the firm's record of efficiency and performance. That is, if some measure of quality of performance can be agreed upon (a measure that should take account of cost efficiency as well as product and service quality), then the better the performance score of the regulated firm, the more it would be permitted to earn. A firm that performed well in a given year might be permitted 12 percent profits for that year, whereas a firm that did badly might be allowed only 8 percent, and a firm that performed abominably might be permitted only 4 percent.

However, financial incentives cannot easily be built into rate-of-return formulas that contain no good objective criteria of performance (for example, in the railway industry, the number of minutes that trains come in behind schedule). Moreover, it is difficult to balance incentives for different aspects of performance. For example, if the formula assigns too much weight to product quality and too little to low cost, the firm will be encouraged to incur costs that are unjustifiably high from the point of view of public welfare in order to turn out products of slightly higher quality.

INSTITUTIONALIZED REGULATORY LAG

A previous edition of this book described a third alternative, which, in the last several years, has been adopted in Great Britain for airport services and in the United States for telephone rates. The basic idea is for regulation to consciously take advantage of the incentive for efficiency provided by regulatory lag. Under such a program, the regulators assign ceilings (*price caps*) for the product prices of the firms they oversee.

However, the price caps (measured in inflation-adjusted *real* terms) are lowered each year at a rate based on the rate of cost reduction (productivity growth) previously achieved by the regulated firm. Thus, if in the future the regulated firm can manage to achieve cost savings (by innovation or other means) greater than those it obtained in the past, the firm's real costs will fall faster than its real prices and it will be permitted to keep the resulting profits as its reward for having implemented cost-reduction programs. Of course, the catch for the regulated firm is that if it proves able to reduce its costs by, say, 2 percent per year (in real terms), but has its regulatory price cap cut by 3 percent per year on the basis of its past record, it will lose profits. Consumers, however, will continue to benefit from the cuts in real prices. Thus, in order to earn economic profits, management is constantly forced to look for ever more economical ways of doing things.

This approach clearly gives up any attempt to limit the profit of the regulated firm. Nonetheless, it protects the consumer by controlling the firm's prices — indeed, it makes those prices lower and lower, in real terms.

THE PATENT SYSTEM

One form of incentive that government has long employed is the **patent** system, which rewards innovative firms by granting them a temporary monopoly. The patent restricts imitation and is designed to offer small-firm innovators the same advantages from their research activities as are enjoyed by innovators in industries that contain no competitors ready to

A **PATENT** is a temporary grant of monopoly rights over an innovation.

erode profits by imitation. The idea is that, with the incentive of patent protection, these smaller firms will dare to challenge the larger, more monopolistic firms. Thus, somewhat ironically, while government tries to limit existing monopolies, it also creates and guarantees monopoly power for other firms. A patent acts as a temporary barrier to entry, thereby providing society with the benefits of firms' increased expenditures on innovation while protecting society from the costs associated with long-term monopoly power. Of course, sometimes the protected firms themselves grow big with the help of the protection. Once-small firms like Polaroid and Xerox grew into industrial giants with the help of government protection through patent laws.

Questions have been raised about the effectiveness of patents in promoting expenditure on research and development, and the evidence certainly does not provide overwhelming support for the view that patents constitute a strong stimulus for innovation. Questions have also been raised about the desirability of granting an innovator an unrestricted monopoly for twenty years, as the patent program now does in Canada. Similar issues have been raised about copyright (and related) laws, which restrict reproduction of written and artistic works, trademarks, and registered industrial designs.

SOME EFFECTS OF DEREGULATION

Deregulation of industries is much more advanced in the United States than it is in Canada, although even there, it is too early to reach a final evaluation of its consequences. Nonetheless, several conclusions are becoming clear from the American experience of the past decade, and these should be borne in mind when considering the pros and cons of deregulation in Canada.

1. ***Effects on prices and local services.*** The first key effect of deregulation (which we have already noted above) is that prices have decreased significantly. Originally, it was feared that smaller and more isolated communities would be deprived of service because the small number of customers and the new, lower prices would make service unprofitable. It was said that airlines, railways, and telephone companies would withdraw from such communities once they were no longer forced to stay there by the regulators.

   These worries have largely proved groundless. True, the larger airlines have left the smaller communities, as predicted. But they have usually been replaced by smaller commuter airlines that have provided, on the average, more frequent service than did their regulated predecessors. Of course, a few communities have been left without service or with service of poorer quality, but other locations have benefited considerably.

2. ***Effects on profits.*** Just as deregulation went into effect in the United States, a severe recession hit the North American economy.

The profits of the older firms in the industry fell sharply and, in many cases, turned into losses. Whether deregulation or recession or both are responsible is much disputed. Some experienced observers argue that without deregulation, losses would have been even worse, but no one can be sure.

What was surprising was that deregulation turned out, even during the recession, to be profitable to many new entrants. A number of new airlines, trucking companies, and telephone companies either showed a profit almost at once or showed promise of becoming profitable very soon. Indeed, in airlines, trucking, and bus transportation, the new entrants, instead of suffering from a cost handicap, often had a substantial cost advantage over the older firms. The reason was that the older firms had agreed to costly union contracts under regulation.

3. ***Effects on the unions***.   Deregulation has badly hurt unions such as the Teamsters (of the trucking industry) and the Airline Pilots Association. In the new competitive climate, firms have been forced to make sharp cuts in their work forces and to resist wage increases and other costly changes in working conditions. Indeed, there has been strong pressure for retrenchment on all these fronts.

4. ***Concentration and mergers***.   Particularly in aviation and rail-freight transportation, deregulation in the United States was followed by a wave of mergers in which two firms agreed to join together or one firm agreed to be bought out by another.

That this has happened should not be surprising since, as we saw earlier in the chapter, industries with important economies of scale are the most likely targets for regulation. It was to be expected that, once freed from regulatory constraints, firms in such industries would try to take advantage of the opportunity to achieve cost reductions through rapid expansion or by means of mergers.

Evaluations of the merger movement have differed sharply. Some observers have concluded that mergers threaten to increase monopoly power and exploit the public. Others have argued that indirect competitive pressures (for example, barges and trucks are rivals of large railways) remain strong and that economies of scale resulting from the mergers will be passed on to the consuming public.

Critics of deregulation have placed a good deal of emphasis on such things as reduced passenger comfort in the airline industry, but economists argue that competition would not bring such results unless passengers as a group preferred lower fares to the greater standards of luxury that preceded them.

In addition, some observers have been concerned about the safety effects of deregulation, suggesting, for example, that the incidence of accidents may increase if airlines cut expenditures on safety to keep prices low. Despite the fact that the U.S. evidence displays no such trend for the years since deregulation was introduced, special vigilance may nonetheless be required to guard against neglect of safety as a cost-cutting measure. The expense of additional governmental inspection can be considered a required cost of deregulation.

Perhaps we can achieve some perspective on deregulation by considering a very specific example, such as municipal transportation. Most cities limit the number of taxi licences in order to keep taxi services orderly and keep driver incomes from falling because of overcompetition. But since most drivers can afford to own neither the car they drive nor the licence, they must rent both from the central dispatcher (the taxi company). In early 1993 in Toronto, the going price for a licence was about $50 000. This was much lower than the price in 1989 ($100 000). The difference between these amounts reflected the state of demand. In the boom year of 1989, we might have expected cab drivers to earn higher incomes. In fact, much of the potential increase in incomes was used up by drivers' having to pay higher rental fees. When demand for taxis fell during the recession of the early 1990s, the value of a licence (and therefore the amount of rental fees) fell. The existence of regulation (the fact that the quantity of licences is limited) means that the bulk of the high incomes that occur in boom years go to licence owners, not drivers.

London, England, has no such licence system for taxis, yet both residents and visitors are served by a stable and efficient service. Another English city, Manchester, has even deregulated the municipal bus service. There are seven separate bus companies competing for riders, and Manchester residents seem entirely satisfied with the results. Having studied numerous specific industries like these taxi and bus services, many economists have concluded that deregulation is often recommended.

A WORD ON NATIONALIZATION

As we indicated at the beginning of the chapter, in industries in which monopoly or near monopoly offers cost advantages to society over competition, there is an alternative to regulation. This alternative is *nationalization*—that is, government ownership and operation of the firms in such industries. A number of cities operate their own public transport facilities, collect their own garbage, and offer other services that elsewhere are provided by private enterprise.

It is an almost instinctive reaction among people in Canada to consider such public enterprises as being prone to extreme mismanagement and waste. Indeed, the near-legendary problems of Canada Post do seem to support this supposition. However, here too, one should be careful not to jump to conclusions. It is true that, for many years, visitors found the nationalized French telephone system a model of chaos and mismanagement. But at the same time, the Swedish telephone system, which is also nationalized, has consistently been smooth-working and efficient. Also, the French government-supplied electricity system has set world standards in its use of the most modern analytic techniques of economics and engineering and has adopted innovative pricing policies that promote efficiency.

Despite these accomplishments, nationalized industries continue to be hampered by weak incentives for efficiency. First, governments virtually never permit a nationalized firm to go bankrupt, and, as a result, the firm's management is deprived of one of the most powerful motivations for the minimization of costs. Second, no one has yet found a systematic incentive mechanism for efficiency that can do for nationalized industries what the profit motive does for private enterprise. Where the market is unsparing in its rewards for accomplishments and in its penalties for poor performance, one can be quite sure that a firm's inefficiency will not readily be tolerated. But nationalized industries have no such automatic mechanism to hand out rewards and penalties dependably and impartially. We have seen, however, that there are analogous problems under regulation: Where profits are controlled by the regulator, the rewards for efficiency are also far from automatic. Hence, the relative efficiency of a nationalized firm versus a regulated private firm is far from clear.

By now, several dozen studies have compared the efficiency of private unregulated, private regulated, and nationalized firms.[1] While a majority conclude that the costs of unregulated private firms are the lowest, they find considerably more variation in the relative performance of nationalized and private regulated firms. Results seem to vary by type of industry, by country, and by size of enterprise.

One industry that has been studied is residential garbage collection, a relatively homogeneous service that is carried out by both government and private firms and thus seems particularly well suited for comparing the costs of competition, private monopoly, and government monopoly. A study of the relative costs of private and public collection of garbage in about 300 municipalities in the United States found that collection costs were about the same whether the job was done by government or by a group of competing firms.[2] Competition was expensive because each firm served only scattered customers, and there was much duplication of routes. On the other hand, the costs of both government collection and competitive private collection were some 34 percent higher than the costs of service by a private monopoly collector working under contract to a municipal government. The government services typically had significantly larger crews, higher rates of employee absenteeism, smaller trucks, and less-frequent use of incentive systems than did the private collectors.

Another study, however, compared the costs of 33 private electric utilities and 23 public ones in the United States.[3] On the basis of a

1. For a good survey of these studies, see Yair Ahorani, *The Evolution and Management of State Owned Enterprises* (Cambridge, Mass.: Ballinger Publishing Company, 1986), pages 197–204.

2. E.S. Savas, "Evaluating the Organization of Service Delivery: Solid Waste Collection and Disposal: A Summary." (New York: Center for Government Studies, Graduate School of Business, Columbia University, April 1978).

3. See D.R. Pescatrice and J.M. Trapani III, "The Performance and Objectives of Public and Private Utilities Operating in the United States," *Journal of Public Economics* 13 (1980), pages 259–78.

sophisticated statistical analysis, the authors concluded that publicly owned electric utilities perform better than their privately owned regulated counterparts. The costs of the government-owned firms were 24 to 33 percent lower than those of the private firms, a difference similar to that found in other studies of the issue. Thus, at least for the electric utilities they studied, the authors judged that public ownership is a better choice than production by regulated private firms.

In sum, it is by no means clear that the regulatory approach always serves the public better than does nationalization. In both cases, much seems to depend on the rules employed by the pertinent government agency.

THE MOVEMENT TOWARD PRIVATIZATION

In a number of countries, a trend to move sharply away from nationalization has been apparent. Among free-market economies, Great Britain is the prime example. The Conservative government of Margaret Thatcher **privatized** about 40 percent of the industries that were nationalized between 1945 and 1979. The list includes telecommunications; oil and gas production; airports and airlines; trucking; rail hotels; seaports; shipbuilding; and the aerospace, automobile, and semiconductor industries. Under "Thatcherism," bus and coach routes were also deregulated; local governments began to contract services out to private contractors; privatization of pension plans, health care, and education increased; and more than a million public housing units were sold to tenants. Television broadcasting, formerly the exclusive province of the British Broadcasting Corporation, a government-owned entity, fell increasingly into private hands. The results of privatization are still the subject of heated debate.

However, it is in the formerly centrally planned economies of Eastern Europe that the movement away from nationalization has come to sound like a stampede. Plans, and actions already taken, to transform these economies into free-market systems imply extreme disillusionment with the performance of government-owned industry.

The Canadian government is similarly convinced that some of the country's nationalized firms should be privatized. Since the mid-1980s, it has sold off a number of companies, of which Air Canada, sold in 1989, is perhaps the most notable.

Cynics claim that the only reason for these sales is to provide funds to reduce the budget deficit. In fact, only limited funds can be provided in this way. When the government sells a company, it must subtract the asset's book value from the sale proceeds before it can apply the remaining funds to reducing the deficit. Instead, in promoting the principle of privatization, the government typically offers the following five justifications:

1. The economic environment has changed. In Canada's early years, state intervention was deemed necessary for opening the country to commerce (through the development of canals, railways, a national

PUBLIC CONTROVERSY

SELL REVENUE CANADA AND COLLECT TAXES AS THE ROMANS DID

The following newspaper article was written by Professor Trevor Hodge of Carleton University. Besides being amusing, it shows that the nationalization-versus-privatization debate has been waged for many years.

There is one simple and obvious way of reforming the tax system, a way that would be agreeable to business, welcome to taxpayers and pleasing to Conservatives, a way that Finance Minister Michael Wilson probably hasn't even considered. Privatize it. Sell off Revenue Canada, and entrust tax collection to the private sector.

Mr. Wilson may be forgiven for not having looked at this attractive option, but anyone with the benefit of a classical education can tell you that was how the ancient Romans did it. And given the fractious state of national unity, no lessons from a prosperous multicultural empire that lasted 1000 years are to be sneezed at. . . .

It worked like this. . . . The government set the tax rates and every year auctioned off to the highest bidder the right to collect them. The actual collection was done by private companies in competition (and sometimes in cahoots) with each other. Shares in them were traded publicly. You could buy into a tax company and . . . the more tax that was wrung out of the taxpayers, the better a dividend you got.

In theory, a profit margin of half a percent was built into the contract price. In reality, you bid as high as you dared to land the contract and then stung the taxpayers for every cent you could get, since everything over the contract price was gravy.

In the provinces, where you were not dealing with Roman citizens, this meant that claims for a refund were often settled by the tax inspector arriving on the doorstep accompanied . . . by half a dozen goons from the Roman army barracks down the road. In this healthy demonstration of the spirit of free enterprise, an amicable settlement would be reached right speedily.

As with all private ventures, there was, of course, a risk. To avoid the trap of overbidding, you had to have some idea of how much blood really could be squeezed from the stone. Most companies accordingly ran a kind of private intelligence service, with agents reporting on how the harvest was shaping up, and other potential plums for the picking. . . .

But man is fallible, and sometimes an incautiously high bid led to a situation distressingly reminiscent of Dome Petroleum, de Havilland Aircraft, Maislin trucking and other familiar names on the Canadian economic scene. In 59 BC, the Roman government found itself faced with an appeal from the tax-collecting companies operating in the province of Asia. They had committed themselves to what they now saw was a grossly optimistic contract and, if held to it, they were staring bankruptcy in the face. Speakers urged that . . . a contract was a contract, but students of political economy won't be surprised to learn the companies were bailed out by remission of one-third of the debt. . . .

What the ordinary taxpayer thought of it all is perhaps summed up in one word. The Latin term for the tax companies and their representatives was *publicani*. All it really means is "public servants," but it normally appears in the New Testament as "publicans" (and it's not necessary to read very far to find what kind of reputation they enjoyed among their friends and neighbours).

SOURCE: Excerpted from A. Trevor Hodge, "Sell Revenue Canada and Collect Taxes as the Romans Did," *The Globe and Mail*, June 18, 1987, page 7. Reprinted with the permission of *The Globe and Mail*.

broadcasting system, and so on); today, this involvement is no longer necessary.

2. The test of market competition can improve efficiency.

3. A number of Crown corporations need sizable amounts of funds to expand and meet competition. The government cannot afford to raise these funds, and the firms themselves, as Crown corporations, are prevented from acquiring equity funds elsewhere.

4. Management style in the private sector is more conducive to risk-taking.

5. It is unfair to use tax dollars raised in the private sector to fund Crown corporations that compete directly with private firms.

Some Canadians agree with these government beliefs. Others disagree—in principle or with respect to specific cases. Undoubtedly, these views will be fully debated over the coming years.

THE COMPETITION ACT

Competition cases in the courts are likely to be well publicized because the accused firms are often household names. For example, in the last several years, each of the following companies has been found guilty of either misleading advertising or some improper pricing practice: The Brick, Commodore Business Machines, Chrysler, K Mart, Krazy Kelly's, Sears, Toshiba, and Zellers. But the vast majority of competition cases investigated by the government do not even come to trial, let alone result in a conviction. A classic example of the delays and expenses involved in the pursuit of cases of unfair competition was the government's attempted prosecution of five major moving companies for price fixing. The combines investigation began in 1966, but a guilty plea without trial was not entered until December 14, 1983.

What are the specific purposes of our competition laws? Also, how well has the government's competition policy program succeeded in practice? These questions are the main concerns of the remainder of this chapter. Starting with a little history, we describe how competition policy has fared over the century since its inception. We outline the activities that are currently prohibited by law and how recent amendments to the Competition Act have changed the nature of our competition policy. Then we re-examine the role of monopoly in the economy and the pros and cons of the competition policy program from the viewpoint of economic analysis.

THE ORIGIN AND DEVELOPMENT OF COMPETITION POLICY

In 1888, a Select Committee of the House of Commons investigating alleged combinations (monopolies and mergers) in the manufacturing, trade, and insurance industries reported that combines existed in thirteen commodities or industries in Canada (including, for example, sugar, groceries, coal, and stoves). As a result, in 1889, Parliament passed into law An Act for the Prevention and Suppression of Combinations in Restraint of Trade. Thus, Canada's formal competition policy predated that of the United States—the Sherman Act—by one year.

The Canadian legislation became part of the Criminal Code and provided as follows:

> Every person who conspires, combines, agrees or arranges with any other person . . . unlawfully . . . to restrain or injure trade or commerce in relation to any . . . article or commodity; to unduly prevent . . . [its] manufacture or production . . . , to unreasonably enhance [its] price . . . or to unduly prevent or lessen competition in [its] production, manufacture, purchase, barter, sale, transportation or supply . . . is guilty of a misdemeanor and liable on conviction to a penalty not exceeding $4,000 and not less than $200, or to imprisonment for any term not exceeding 2 years. And if a corporation, it is liable on conviction to a penalty not exceeding $10,000 and not less than $1,000.

Note the words "unduly" and "unreasonably." They still exist in important sections of current legislation and have been the cause of great concern because, in criminal law, it is necessary to prove guilt beyond a reasonable doubt—a difficult task given the vagueness of these words.

In any case, the original legislation was not effective because no machinery was set up to secure evidence. Not until 1910, at the peak of a merger movement in Canada, was a formal process of investigation enacted. Under the terms of the legislation, six citizens could apply to a judge to appoint a board of investigation. This board, if approved, would submit a report and could recommend fines. However, the mere publication of a report was considered to be the main punishment.

Over the years, a number of amendments were made to the existing legislation, which by the 1970s had been renamed the **Combines Investigation Act**. However, the government remained dissatisfied with the legislation because the rules relied on criminal, rather than civil, law (the implications of which will be explained shortly). As a result, the government was losing *all* of its major cases. In 1971, in an attempt to rectify this and a number of other weaknesses, the government introduced a new bill that was intended to facilitate the prosecution of major forms of anticompetitive behaviour. The introduction of the bill sparked one of the largest lobbying efforts in Canadian history. The business community, in particular, opposed any strengthening of the law and in the end was at least partially successful. After more than three years, the government split the legislation into two parts (Stage 1 and Stage 2) and passed only the first (less controversial) stage into law in 1976. Stage 2 did not become law until 1986; hence, our current **Competition Act** is indeed a recent law, and is therefore only now in the process of being interpreted through judicial decisions.

CURRENT LEGISLATION

The Competition Act deals with events that change the structure of the economy, such as mergers or monopolization, and with conduct in business that is considered not to be to the benefit of the economy as a whole. Examples of such conduct include agreements to restrict competition and certain problematic pricing, distribution, and sales practices.

ABUSE OF DOMINANT POSITION

Only one conviction had been obtained, after trial, under the monopoly section of the old Combines Investigation Act. In 1952, the Eddy Match company was found guilty of monopolizing the market for wooden matches over a twenty-year period. It had maintained its monopoly by buying up rivals and carrying out industrial spying, among other things.

Nine other cases were brought to trial under the old act and, in five of them, the companies were acquitted. In one of the remaining four, the company pleaded guilty without trial. In the other three, the companies involved agreed to the terms of a *prohibition order* (an order forbidding the repetition or continuation of an offence) without admitting guilt.

Generally, prosecutions failed under the old act because, while the government could often show that monopolies existed, it was not able to prove that monopolies were operating to the detriment of the public. As a result, in the K.C. Irving case, the company was found innocent even though, from 1944 to 1971, it had acquired all five of the English-language daily newspapers in New Brunswick. Because of such problems, our new act contains no awkward "detriment-of-the-public" clause. Instead, section 50 of the Competition Act defines a monopoly as any abuse of a dominant position. Explicitly included as abuses are the following practices:

> Squeezing . . . the margin available . . . for the purpose of impeding or preventing . . . entry into, or expansion in, a market; . . . pre-emption of scarce facilities or resources required by a competitor for the operation of a business, . . . adoption of product specifications that are incompatible with products produced by any other person and are designed to prevent his entry into, or to eliminate him from, a market; . . . requiring or inducing a supplier to sell only or primarily to certain customers, or to refrain from selling to a competitor, with the object of preventing a competitor's entry into, or expansion in, a market; . . . selling articles at a price lower than the acquisition cost for the purpose of disciplining or eliminating a competitor.

Another problem with the old act was that its monopoly provisions were part of the Criminal Code, as opposed to the civil law. Criminal law requires that guilt be proved beyond a reasonable doubt, a requirement unsuited to economic issues. Whether competition has been unduly eliminated is always a matter of judgement, resting on a comparison of the advantages of possible economies of scale and superior competitive performance and the disadvantages of possible anticompetitive behaviour.

Furthermore, the empirical information on which such a comparison must be based is normally quite limited. In civil law, the Crown must establish only a balance of probability that competition has been significantly lessened.

One final problem that limited effectiveness of the old Combines Investigation Act was that its fines were very small compared with the benefits that could be had by breaking the law.

MERGERS

Mergers have long been regarded with suspicion by competition-policy authorities. Particularly when a merger is **horizontal**, it is often feared that because the number of competing firms in the industry is reduced (that is, concentration is increased), competition will decline.

The authorities do not wish to impede mergers that seem likely to increase efficiency by improving the co-ordination of production activities, permitting economies of scale, getting one of the firms out of financial difficulties, or facilitating operations in a variety of other ways. But the authorities do want to prevent mergers that threaten to reduce competition.

Although by no means unanimous on the subject, most economists agree that mergers sometimes reduce competition, particularly in a market that is not contestable, so that threats of entry do not prevent the merged firm from raising prices above competitive levels. This danger is particularly acute if the number of firms is sufficiently small to make collusion a real possibility.

On the other hand, where there is reason to believe that a merger will *not* reduce competition, many economists oppose impediments to it, arguing that mergers that are not undertaken to reduce competition have only one purpose—to achieve greater efficiency. For example, the larger firm that results from a merger may enjoy substantial economies of scale not available to smaller firms. The two merging companies may learn special skills from one another, or they may offset one another's risks. Mergers have sometimes proved disappointing and have brought little cost saving. But a recent U.S. study of roughly 22 000 large manufacturing establishments, of which 1100 had been purchased and merged ("taken over") between 1981 and 1986, found that the merged manufacturing plants subsequently had rates of productivity growth some 14 percent higher than the others in the same industry.[4]

In Canada, because of the relatively small size of the market, government policy has long been favourable to the existence of large firms, and a reflection of this general policy can be seen in the results of attempts to prosecute certain mergers under the terms of the old Combines Investigation Act. Before 1986, only six merger prosecutions were undertaken. One resulted in a guilty plea before trial, but the others resulted in acquittals.

A MERGER occurs when two previously independent firms are combined under a single owner or group of owners. A HORIZONTAL MERGER is a merger of two firms producing similar products, as when one toothpaste manufacturing firm purchases another. A VERTICAL MERGER involves the joining of two firms, one of which supplies an ingredient of the other's product, as when an automaker acquires a tire manufacturing firm. A CONGLOMERATE MERGER is the union of two unrelated firms, as when a defence industry firm joins a firm that produces compact discs.

---

4. Frank Lichtenberg and David Siegel, "The Effects of Leveraged Buyouts on Productivity and Related Aspects of Firm Behavior," NBER Working Paper no. 3022, 1989.

The reason for the lack of success in prosecutions and for the apparent unwillingness of the government to initiate new cases under the old act can be found in the courts' interpretation of the law. Just as in the case of monopoly, a finding of guilty under the old law required proof that, because of a merger, competition was or was likely to be lessened to the detriment of the public. The courts interpreted the latter phrase to mean the existence of a virtual monopoly. Thus, in the case of British Columbia Sugar, even though it was shown that the company, through merger, had gained a near monopoly over sugar sales in the four western provinces, the presiding judge decided that the eastern sugar companies presented a viable source of potential competition.

Shortly after the proclamation of the new act, there was a merger conviction: A funeral home company in Hamilton pleaded guilty to limiting competition by buying up funeral homes in the area until it controlled 70 percent of the Protestant market. The company was fined $200 000.

Under the new act, mergers come under the jurisdiction of the Competition Tribunal, which is composed of federal judges and laypeople appointed by the government. Decisions by the tribunal cannot be appealed to the Cabinet — only to the Federal Court of Appeal. As we have noted in earlier chapters, it is difficult to determine what output levels are required for firms to realize fully the economies of larger-scale operation. Thus, it is fortunate that the new act shifted mergers from a criminal to a civil offence. The wording of the act carefully notes that mergers have both costs and benefits, and these contradictory features make the civil law jurisdiction absolutely necessary. The tribunal must judge the relative size of the gains in efficiency and international competitiveness (which are particularly stressed in the opening clause of the act) versus the increase in industry concentration within the domestic market. Section 68 of the Competition Act states as follows:

> The Tribunal shall not make an order . . . if it finds that the merger or proposed merger . . . is likely to bring about gains in efficiency that will be greater than, and will offset, the effects of any prevention or lessening of competition that will result or is likely to result from the merger.

Under the new act, the Bureau of Competition Policy must be notified before a merger occurs if the parties have Canadian assets or sales of more than $400 million or if the deal itself involves assets or sales of more than $35 million. Between 1986 and 1992, the bureau has examined 944 mergers, and has challenged or asked for changes regarding 20 of these mergers.

Agreements to Restrict Competition

Section 32 of the Competition Act provides as follows:

> Everyone who conspires, combines, agrees or arranges with another person . . . to . . . restrain or injure competition unduly . . . is guilty of an indictable offence and is liable to imprisonment for five years or a fine of one million dollars or to both.

Under the old Combines Investigation Act, the government was successful in approximately 75 percent of the nearly 100 cases brought under section 32. At a certain point, however, two cases—those of Aetna and of Atlantic Sugar—produced judgements that made successful prosecution virtually impossible thereafter. The problem arose in the added requirement of *proof of double intent*. Before these cases, it was sufficient for the government to prove that the parties in the conspiracy intended to enter an agreement. It was not necessary to show that they intended to limit competition. After the precedent had been set by the Aetna and the Atlantic Sugar cases, both conditions were required for a conviction. The presiding judge in the Atlantic Sugar case held that, although the companies shared virtually the entire market (each having had a constant market share for a quarter of a century), they should be acquitted of conspiracy charges because "the reason for maintaining traditional market shares was to avoid a price war which would have resulted had the accused taken the only method of increasing them by price cutting through excessive discounts."[5] Notice that there was no mention of consumer interest.

Under the new Competition Act, agreements to limit competition are still classified as offences under the Criminal Code, but now only proof of single intent is required; for example, all the government has to prove is that price-fixing occurred, not that prices were being fixed for a particular reason.

Consumer advocates also welcomed the raising of the maximum fine, although the nature of this change can still be criticized on two counts. First, in principle, the fines should bear some relationship to the economic cost to consumers of the anticompetitive behaviour. Second, the maximum fines are often not imposed. Fines of around $200 000 are not uncommon now, but this is an amount that some firms may still regard as a reasonable cost of doing business. More recently, however, larger fines *have* been levied: In late 1990, Canada's three largest flour-milling companies were each fined $1 million for price-rigging. In September 1991, the government successfully prosecuted Union Carbide for fixing the price of compressed gas. The result was a record single-company fine of $1.75 million. These fines are consistent with the Bureau of Competition Policy's stated objective to "get the fines up to a level that is more than a permit or fee for companies to break the law."[6]

PRICING PRACTICES

The Competition Act deals with several pricing practices that are assumed to reduce competition.

---

5. See G. Kaiser, *World Law of Competition*, vol. 3A: Canada (New York: Matthew Bender, 1982), for an account of this and other relevant cases.

6. Howard Wetston, Director of the Bureau of Competition Policy, as quoted in Jock Ferguson and Drew Fagan, "Mills Fined for Rigging CIDA Bids," *The Globe and Mail*, December 8, 1990, pages A1, A9.

RESALE PRICE MAINTE-
NANCE involves forcing
retailers to keep the price of a
product at or above that specified by the wholesaler.

Resale price maintenance.

This pricing practice typically involves the manufacturer's forcing retailers to maintain the price of a product at, or at least not below, some specified amount. If a retailer refuses to carry out the manufacturer's wishes, the manufacturer normally cuts off the supply of the product. This practice has been illegal in Canada since 1952, despite many analysts' expressed concern that this part of the law may actually lessen competition. These analysts note that the discounters who undercut the manufacturer's stipulated price cut corners in customer service, offering little help in product selection, installation, or repair. Also, the discounters make it difficult for full-service retailers to survive. Potential customers go to a full-service department store for product information and then buy the item from a discounter. The final result, it is claimed, can be a decrease in competition, as the full-service retailer is forced out of the particular business. Given the ambiguity that surrounds the question of whether resale price maintenance is indeed a reprehensible practice, it is ironic that, in contrast to prosecutions under other sections of the old Combines Investigation Act, prosecutions against resale price maintenance were generally successful. Fines were usually assessed, and prohibition orders often issued.

PREDATORY PRICING refers
to price cuts that are undertaken only to keep other firms
from entering the industry.

Predatory pricing.

This term refers to price cuts by existing firms when such cuts are effected in an attempt to keep other firms from entering the industry. Unfortunately, a crucial element in this section of the act states that prices cannot be "unreasonably low." In addition, to obtain a conviction, it has to be proved that the predatory-pricing practice is part of a policy and that competition is or can be threatened or destroyed by that policy.

Three major cases falling under this section of the act have reached full trial. In one of these, the Hoffman–La Roche case, the company was found guilty because, for a six-month period, it had adopted a policy of giving away one of its products (Valium) to hospitals in order to build up a consumer preference. It was noted at trial that a zero price was certainly a large drop from regular prices. In a second case, Consumers Glass Company, a producer of cup lids, was charged with lowering prices unreasonably in order to drive out a competitor. However, the company successfully argued that, because of excess capacity in the industry, it was merely lowering its prices to make the maximum possible recovery of its fixed costs. That is, given the market situation, it was "loss minimizing" by charging a price greater than average variable cost but less than what was called average total cost.

PRICE DISCRIMINATION
involves charging different
prices, relative to costs, to
different buyers of the
same product.

Price discrimination.

The intent of this section of the act is to ensure that a seller does not sell products of like quality to competing buyers at different prices. Such a practice confers an undue advantage to the buyer paying the lower price. This section of the old act was not used to a great extent because of difficulties in dealing with matters such as whether the buyers are competitors (which involves defining relevant markets). In fact, only two cases were brought to trial under this section of the old act, with one conviction and one acquittal being recorded.

Many economists find the legal definition of price discrimination misleading. Suppose, for instance, that one person lives on a mountaintop far from the place where a good is produced, and another customer is located in an area that enjoys easy access to the good in question. Economists would say that it is not discriminatory to charge each a different price. On the contrary, economists hold that, in such cases, it is discriminatory to charge both customers the same price, because one price would not account for the substantial difference in the two delivery costs.

Even more important than this definitional argument, however, is the issue of the desirability or undesirability of discrimination. The word *discrimination* has been called a "persuasive term"—in this case, a word that automatically implies gross misconduct. But, in fact, price discrimination can sometimes be beneficial to all parties to a transaction.

Suppose, for example, that a commodity is available to the poor only if it is sold at a relatively low price, but one that still more than covers the good's marginal cost (the cost incurred in expanding into the lower-income market). In this case, the contribution from the lower-income market may permit *some* reduction in price to the rich, since the firm might not be able to cover its total cost if it were to charge the rich the *same* low price necessary for entry into the low-income market. The result is that everyone—the poor, the wealthy, and the selling firm—will benefit from this discriminatory pricing.

The pricing practices of doctors before the existence of universal medicare offer an example of the situation described above. At that time, doctors were known to charge higher fees to their wealthy patients than to their poor ones. The reduced fees presumably permitted more poor patients to visit them, and doctors may thus have been able to earn an even better income than they could by charging a uniformly high fee to everyone. Even the fee to the rich may have gone down in the process because of the doctors' increased earnings from their enlarged pool of poor patients. Discrimination led to lower fees for everyone and all parties were made better off. It is therefore difficult to understand why the government should prohibit such behaviour. Note also that it is this sort of ambiguity that makes it difficult to obtain a judgement "beyond reasonable doubt," as is required under criminal law—the domain within which these cases continue to be tried.

DISTRIBUTION PRACTICES

The following distribution practices are subject to review by the Competition Tribunal: tied selling, exclusive dealing, consignment selling, refusal to supply, and market restriction. Being "reviewable" means that these practices are not considered to be offences under the Competition Act. There is basically no appeal from a decision by the tribunal, and it may issue only remedial orders.

These practices deal generally with **vertical marketing** arrangements, which are considered harmful to competition in that they might allow the wholesaler or retailer to gain a local monopoly on the sale of a product or permit the supplier to abuse a monopoly position.

Two cases will illustrate the nature of these practices. In the case of Bombardier Ltée., the company's exclusive dealing practices in snowmobiles were brought under review. The company admitted that it had supplied dealers with its snowmobiles under the explicit condition that they would not handle any other brand of snowmobiles. Eight dealers had had their franchises terminated for breaching this contract. Although the Restrictive Trade Practices Commission, the forerunner of the Competition Tribunal, agreed that Bombardier controlled a substantial share of the snowmobile market (50 percent in Quebec, Ontario, and Atlantic Canada), it found that this fact had not produced a substantial lessening of competition. Accordingly, the case was dismissed.

In a case dealing with tied selling, the results were different. The Bureau of Broadcast Measurement is a major supplier of television rating services and the sole supplier of radio rating services in Canada. The company required that anyone desiring its radio ratings, over which it had a monopoly, would also have to purchase its television ratings. The commission held that this practice was unfair to an existing competitor and would impede entry into or expansion within the ratings market. It therefore issued a prohibition order in this matter.

MISLEADING ADVERTISING AND UNFAIR TRADE PRACTICES

Other sections of the Competition Act contain provisions dealing with misleading advertising and deceptive marketing practices. It is important that any violations in these areas be prosecuted in order to protect a fundamental principle on which our economic system is based: the assumption that the buyer is "knowledgeable."

These sections have spawned more prosecutions and convictions since 1976 than have any other sections of the Competition Act. Nevertheless, a lack of resources precludes investigation into all but a small percentage of the thousands of complaints about misleading or deceptive advertising that reach the bureau each year. One case that was followed closely by the media in late 1992 illustrates the problems involved. The bureau felt that it could not proceed with a case against the tobacco industry. The complaint had been that the industry's advertised claim that increased provincial taxes on cigarettes would not reduce smoking was factually incorrect. Despite the fact that industry officials had publicly stated on earlier occasions that rising taxes had been accelerating the decline in smoking, government officials knew that the specific advertisement could be interpreted as stating that taxes only cause people to smuggle more cigarettes from the United States (rather than reduce overall smoking).

PENALTIES AND EXEMPTIONS

When guilty verdicts are obtained, competition policy is enforced by one or more of the penalties provided for in various sections of the Competition Act:

1. Fines—the limit varies with the section of the act and is unlimited in some sections of the act.

2. Divestiture—convicted companies are forced to sell some of their assets.

3. Prohibition orders—the order prohibits the repetition or continuation of an offence.

4. Restitution—payment of sums are ordered to certain persons identified by the court.

5. Interim injunctions—the order prevents certain activities pending a trial.

6. Post-conviction reporting.

7. Declaring invalid patents or trademarks.

8. Imprisonment to a maximum of five years.

In a precedent-setting case in late 1992, the Bureau of Competition Policy granted its first immunity-from-prosecution arrangement. The case involved bid-rigging among companies that were offering to provide the insecticide that is used by several government departments. Under this new policy, a company that is involved in conspiracy and bid-rigging can receive immunity if three criteria are satisfied: It did not initiate the illegal activity, it assists in the subsequent investigation, and it provides full restitution to any victims.

In addition to fines, private damage actions can be based on a breach of the Competition Act. However, class actions, which are available in the United States, are not provided for in the Canadian act.

While this list of penalties sounds imposing, it must be remembered that the government has achieved very few prosecutions, except under the sections of the act pertaining to resale price maintenance and unfair trade practices. In addition, many activities are currently exempt from the act, including the following:

1. The formation of labour unions.

2. Any association between people who fish and fish processors.

3. The operation of shipping conferences (cartels of ship owners who collude on prices).

4. Competition-reducing agreements in the professions.

5. The conduct of firms that are effectively regulated.

6. Monopoly behaviour of firms holding a valid patent or trademark.

7. With some exceptions, agreements among exporters.

It was only with the passage of the new act in 1986 that banks and Crown corporations came under the jurisdiction of competition policy.

THE ADMINISTRATION OF COMPETITION POLICY

The federal minister charged with the responsibility of administering competition policy in Canada is the minister of consumer and corporate affairs. The day-to-day administration of this program is carried out by the director of investigation and research under the auspices of the Bureau of Competition Policy (one of the three bureaus in Consumer and Corporate Affairs Canada). The bureau had an authorized strength of 260 person-years at the start of this decade. The majority of these personnel are situated at headquarters in Hull, Quebec, while the remainder constitute the field staff of the Marketing Practices Branch.

An inquiry into any alleged violation of the Competition Act can be initiated in one of three ways: by the director, at the direction of the minister, or in response to a formal request by six Canadian residents. (For example, if you felt moved to initiate an inquiry into a case of misleading advertising or deceptive marketing practices, you and five friends could do so by writing to the following address: Marketing Practices Branch, Bureau of Competition Policy, Consumer and Corporate Affairs, 50 Victoria Street, 19th floor, Hull, Quebec, K1A 0C9 [phone: (819) 997-4282]. You could also contact one of the regional offices, located in major centres across Canada.) The vast majority of inquiries are initiated by the director, often in response to complaints by companies or individuals regarding alleged violations.

In general, bureau staff carry out a preliminary inquiry into a complaint, and if the preliminary evidence gives the director reason to believe that a violation has in fact been committed, he or she initiates a formal inquiry. Once an inquiry has become formal, evidence can be obtained by searching premises, formally requesting data, or holding hearings under the auspices of the Competition Tribunal.

If the formal investigation finds sufficient evidence of wrongdoing, the director can refer the case either to the Competition Tribunal, if the alleged offence is reviewable, or to the attorney general of Canada, to be considered for the laying of criminal charges (since some prohibitions under the act are still criminal issues).

The attorney general reviews the case (a time-consuming process ranging from several months to several years) and decides either to drop it or to lay formal charges. (Note that the attorney general, not the director of investigation and research, lays charges and formally prosecutes the cases.) Once charges are laid, cases travel along the normal route of criminal justice in Canada.

JUDICIAL INTERPRETATIONS OF THE COMPETITION ACT

Several years have now passed since the current Competition Act became law, and we are starting to see how the courts are interpreting its provisions. In our legal system, these precedent-setting decisions are very important in determining whether the current law will represent any real increase in effectiveness over the former legislation, the Combines Investigation Act.

For a while, things did not look good for the new act. In 1990, several court cases ruled that aspects of the new Competition Tribunal were unconstitutional. One issue was the Charter of Rights and Freedoms—because of the Charter, the tribunal did not have the ability to investigate a company's files. In one case, the Federal Court of Appeal ruled against the tribunal regarding the latter's attempt to file a contempt charge against Chrysler Canada Ltd. for ignoring an order it had issued. In explaining the court's decision, the chief justice stated as follows:

> I cannot find . . . a clear expression of an intention to confer on the tribunal the power to punish for contempt those who fail to comply with the tribunal's order. . . . Granted it might be desirable that the tribunal possess such a power, but it seems that Parliament thought otherwise.[7]

Clearly, without this authority, the tribunal would be useless.

Other cases (in Quebec and Nova Scotia in 1990) concerned price-fixing. The initial rulings found the heart of the new legislation—the conspiracy section concerning business collusion—unconstitutional.

The government did receive some good news in 1990. The NutraSweet case—the first to come to trial under the new Abuse of Dominant Position section of the Competition Act—was completed, and the government won a conviction against the firm. After NutraSweet's Canadian patent on aspartame (an artificial sweetener) had expired, the company was alleged to have engaged in a series of unfair trade practices to maintain its 95 percent share of the Canadian market.

The government received more good news in 1992. In that year, the Supreme Court of Canada overturned all of the unconstitutionality rulings that were reached in 1990. As a result, the Director of Investigations has referred to 1992 as a watershed year in the evolution of our competition law. The power of the new tribunal is now secure, and a more potent competition policy may finally be in store for Canada.

ISSUES IN CONCENTRATION OF INDUSTRY

Having reviewed our competition policy and its interpretation by the courts, we have reached the conclusion that, prior to 1992, it was not very successful. One very rough way to measure the success of anti-combines legislation, especially on the merger–monopoly front, is to look at what has happened to the share of Canadian business in the hands of the largest firms.

First, we can compare the degree of domination by large firms in the Canadian economy with that in other countries. A second method of evaluation involves observations of firms over a long period of time. Some observers, particularly Marxist economists, have predicted that capitalism will have a basic tendency toward **concentration of industry**. They argue that because small firms are increasingly driven out of business, especially during economic crises, large firms consequently acquire

---

7. As quoted in *The Globe and Mail*, July 11, 1990, page A1.

ever-larger shares of the market. One can therefore investigate whether such a tendency has been observed in Canada. If, in fact, concentration has not increased, someone who holds these views might be led to surmise that competition policy has had a hand in preventing the growth of monopoly. But first, we should consider what might have been expected to happen to concentration in Canada in the absence of any countermeasures by government. Is there good reason to expect an inexorable trend toward bigness, as the Marxists suggest?

There are two basic reasons why the larger firms in an industry may triumph over the small. First, larger firms may obtain monopoly power, which they can use to their advantage. They can force sellers of equipment, raw materials, and other inputs to give them better terms than are available to small competitors, and they can also force retailers to give preference to their products. These are, of course, the sorts of advantages to bigness that the anticombines laws are intended to eliminate.

The second reason an industry's output may tend to be divided among fewer and larger firms with the passage of time has to do with technology. In some industries, fairly small firms can produce as cheaply as, or more cheaply than, large ones, while in other industries, only rather large firms can achieve minimum costs. By and large, the difference in the number of firms from one industry to another has tended to correspond to the size of firm that is least costly. Automobile, steel, and airplane manufacturing are all industries in which tiny companies cannot hope to produce economically, and indeed, these are all industries made up of a relatively few large firms. In clothing production and many personal-service industries, matters go the other way.

Frequently, innovation seems to have increased the plant size that minimizes costs. Such examples as automated processes or assembly lines suggest that new techniques always call for gigantic equipment, but this is not always true. For example, the introduction of truck transportation took much of the freight-shipping market away from the giant railways and gave it to much smaller trucking firms. Technological change also seems to have favoured the establishment of small electronics firms. Similarly, the continuing development of cheaper and smaller computers is likely to provide a competitive advantage to smaller firms in many other industries.

If innovation provides increased cost advantages to larger firms, the growth of firms will be stimulated. But a fall in the number of firms in the industry need not inevitably result. If demand for the industry's output grows faster than does the optimal size of the firms, we may end up with a larger number of firms, each of them bigger than before but each having a smaller share of an expanded market.

For example, suppose in some industry a new process is invented that requires a far larger scale of operation than is currently typical. Specifically, suppose that the least-costly plant size becomes twice as large. If demand for the industry's product increases only a little, we can expect a decrease in the number of firms. But if demand for the industry's product happens to triple at the same time, the optimal number of firms will in fact increase to one and a half times the original number—each firm will be twice as big as before, so that together they will serve three times the volume. In such a case, each firm's share of industry output will in fact have declined.

In the twentieth century, technological developments do seem to call for larger firms, which are best adapted to take advantage of the resulting economies of scale. Perhaps this has somewhat outstripped the rate of growth in output—that is, the growth of gross domestic product. If so, we should expect some fall in the number of firms in a typical industry, as many Marxists expect. However, as was just noted, not all technological change has worked in this direction. For example, many firms in the electronics industry are relatively small, and some observers argue that new techniques will permit smaller firms to supply some telecommunications services without incurring high costs. We must turn to the evidence to judge whether or not Canadian industry has grown more concentrated.

EVIDENCE ON CONCENTRATION IN INDUSTRY

There have been many statistical studies of concentration in Canadian industry. One common way of measuring concentration is to calculate the share of the industry's output produced by the four largest firms in an industry, the so-called **concentration ratio**. Of course, there is no theoretical reason why the three or five or ten largest firms could not be used for the purpose, but conventionally, four firms are used as the standard. In Canada, the use of four firms is also dictated by the Statistics Act, which, for reasons of confidentiality, does not permit publication of more detailed information regarding individual companies.

Four-firm concentration ratios in Canada range from 99 (for tobacco products manufacturers and breweries), 93 (for motor vehicle manufacturers), 77 (for makers of major appliances), and 62 (for petroleum refining) to 33 (for bakeries), 21 (for logging), and 6 (for machine shops and women's clothing factories). But only comparisons over time and by geographic area can reveal the most significant implications of these figures. Here, the available evidence suggests that concentration in Canadian industry is somewhat higher than it is in the United States and the United Kingdom. The relatively small size of the Canadian market (which has been somewhat insulated from world markets by tariffs and quotas) and the virtual absence of an effective Canadian merger policy have been put forward as two major explanations for this fact. However, some of the differences are also likely to be the result of different methods of measurement.

A **CONCENTRATION RATIO** is the percentage of an industry's output produced by its four largest firms. It is intended to measure the degree to which the industry is dominated by large firms— that is, how closely it approximates a monopoly.

In Canada, there has been no trend whatsoever in the *average* four-firm concentration ratio over time: It has been stuck at 50 for decades.

CONCENTRATION AND MARKET POWER

Why should anyone care about concentration ratios? One should care about them if they are a good measure of market power. **Market power** is the ability of a firm to raise its price significantly above the competitive price level and to maintain this high price profitably for a considerable period. The question, then, is this: If an industry becomes more concentrated, will the firms necessarily increase their ability to institute a profitable rise in price above the competitive level?

Many economists have concluded that this does not necessarily happen. Specifically, the following three conclusions are now widely accepted:

1. If, after an increase in concentration, an industry still has a very low concentration ratio, its firms are very unlikely to have any market power either before or after the rise in concentration.

2. If circumstances in the industry are in other respects favourable for successful price collusion (tacit or explicit agreement on price), a rise in concentration will facilitate market power. It will do so by reducing the number of firms that need to be consulted in arriving at an agreement and by decreasing the number of firms that have to be watched to make sure they do not violate the collusive agreement.

3. Where entry into and exit from the industry are easy and costless—that is, where the market is highly *contestable*—then even when concentration increases, market power will not be enhanced. This is because an excessive price will attract new entrants, who will soon force the price down.

As long as barriers to foreign trade do not prevent foreign firms from entering Canadian markets, the openness of the economy should permit many of our markets to be contestable. Tariffs and quotas limit this process, however, and so they raise the likelihood that high concentration truly does represent significant market power. Thus, tariff cuts can be used as a substitute for the traditional legal and regulatory approaches to competition policy that we have considered in this chapter. Further, given that the latter approaches have met with limited success, as we have just learned, many economists *favour* the free trade approach. It relies on the internal discipline of competition rather than on the externally imposed discipline of the regulator or the legal system.

The inability of any one country's legal system to control companies that are involved in cross-border alliances with companies based in other countries makes this market-oriented approach to competition policy even more important. Nevertheless, many are uneasy about this trend away from relying on their own government for protection (see the boxed insert opposite).

MARKET POWER is the ability of a firm to raise its price significantly above the competitive price level and to maintain this high price profitably for a considerable period.

WHEN COUNTRIES OPEN THEIR BORDERS, LEADERS AND CITIZENS ARE SOON PARTED

The first trend identified at the World Economic Forum in Switzerland earlier this year [1993] was "the complete breakdown of the credibility of political leadership almost everywhere in the world." . . .

What explains it? Why were Brian Mulroney, John Major, François Mitterrand, Helmut Kohl and George Bush so unpopular? What do these leaders have in common?

They lead governments. What is the primary role of governments? To serve and protect the public interest. It follows that populations in the leading industrial democracies do not feel their leaders are serving and protecting the public interest very well. Call a referendum on almost anything (Maastricht, the Charlottetown accord) and the public will vote in protest.

What are they protesting against? Here we enter the realm of speculation, but a common factor in all these countries is their leaders' commitment to closer economic integration. Free trade. Monetary union. Open borders. Our political leaders are among the leading proponents of globalization.

The role of the state in a globalizing economy deserves more reflection than it has received. Over the past decade, the role has been quite simple: Get out of the way. Politicians, starting with Margaret Thatcher and Ronald Reagan, launched a campaign against public ownership and regulation that soon extended into vastly larger free-trade and common-market areas. The long-term economic wisdom in these policies is quite clear, but the deference of the state to unpredictable external forces marks a significant change from its role in modern history.

Citizens traditionally regard the state as a defence against external threats. But for a decade now, most citizens of industrial democracies have seen their leaders dismantle the walls of economic, political and even cultural protection that constitute one of the state's fundamental purposes. Leaders say that lowering walls is in the long-term economic and social interest of the citizens, but citizens feel increasingly insecure and hostile to politicians who seem intent on relinquishing national power (Charlottetown again).

It is more than the economic dislocations of globalization that touch a popular nerve. Values are at stake. There is a sense that the healthy proportion between urban and rural, small and big, familiar and unfamiliar, old and new is eroding. Government leaders tend to come across as agents of this erosion, often lecturing their populations about the need to give up even more control over their communities' fate in the name of long-term economic growth.

Thus, historian Paul Kennedy (*Rise and Fall of the Great Powers*) noted [in Switzerland] that the daily newspaper tends to express two contradictory messages about globalization. The international pages are filled with stories of passionate conflict among cultures, religions and even civilizations, while the business pages are filled with stories of promising new global alliances and exchange. One cannot help but notice that the "bad" news exists in the arena of human values, while the "good" news exists in the arena of economic ones. In this context, economics and business enjoy the moral upper

(continued)

(continued)
hand in modern life, while culture and values fuel the immorality of hate and destruction.

All this raises the question of the role of the state in a globalized economy. Is it simply to withdraw and allow market forces, including population movements, to wash over old sovereignties in the faith that economic growth and social betterment will eventually follow?

At the broadest level, this seems to be the view of current political leaders. The first sign of change in this consensus may be the election of Bill Clinton in the United States — not a protectionist, but speaking the language of protection geared to the realities of a different age.

SOURCE: William Thorsell, "When Countries Open Their Borders, Leaders and Citizens Are Soon Parted," *The Globe and Mail*, February 13, 1993, page D6. Reprinted with the permission of *The Globe and Mail*.

SUMMARY

1. Regulation has three primary purposes: to put brakes on the decisions of industries with monopoly power; to contribute to public health and safety; and to manage market supply so that producer incomes (for example, those of farmers) can be raised and stabilized.

2. Agriculture, railways, trucking, telecommunications, and gas and electricity supply are among the industries that are directly regulated in Canada.

3. In recent years, there has been a major push toward reduction of regulation, except in agriculture and self-regulated areas such as law and medicine.

4. Many agricultural products are sold through marketing boards — that is, monopoly sales outlets that set quotas for all individual producers. While other government regulatory agencies are intended to limit and reduce monopoly power, marketing boards are designed to create and maintain monopoly power.

5. Among the major reasons given for regulation are (a) economies of scale and scope, which make industries into natural monopolies; (b) the danger of self-destructive competition in industries with low (short-run) marginal costs; (c) the desire to provide service to isolated areas where supply is expensive and unprofitable; (d) the desire for fair allocation of scarce resources (such as radio and television airwaves); and (e) the protection of consumers, employees, and the environment.

6. The standard rule for reaching the optimal allocation of society's resources — that is, that quantity produced in each industry should be set at the level given by MU = MC — cannot be applied in the case of a natural monopolist. Since AC exceeds MC, the marginal-cost pricing rule would cause such a firm to operate at a loss.

7. Price regulations that limit firms to a normal rate of profit remove the incentive for them to invest in cost-reducing innovations. Deregulation is one approach to this problem, and institutionalized regulatory lag is another.

8. Deregulation in the United States has clearly reduced costs and prices. However, it has also reduced "frills" in service to customers

and has been followed by a substantial number of mergers.

9. Nationalized (government-run) industries are frequently suspected of being wasteful and inefficient, but the evidence is not uniform and there are cases in which nationalized firms seem more efficient than similar regulated firms.

10. Competition policy refers to programs designed to control the growth of monopoly and to prevent big business from engaging in "undesirable" practices.

11. The Combines Investigation Act was replaced by the Competition Act in 1986. The most important revisions to the competition policy laws were
   a. Changing many of the laws to civil rather than criminal provisions (although conspiracy, bid-rigging, price discrimination, predatory pricing, resale price maintenance, and misleading advertising remain criminal offences).
   b. Changing the legal interpretation of monopoly mergers so that "complete elimination" of competition is not a requirement for prosecution.

c. Raising the fines involved for breaking the competition laws.

12. By 1990, the new Competition Act had run into several constitutional challenges. But by 1992, the government had won their appeal to the Supreme Court in all these cases, so, perhaps for the first time in Canada's history, we now have a powerful and flexible instrument for conducting competition policy.

13. The evidence indicates that there has been no significant increase in the concentration of individual Canadian industries into larger firms during the twentieth century. Direct evidence regarding whether competition policy has been effective in preventing monopoly is inconclusive, but it is generally agreed that Canada has not had an effective merger policy.

14. High concentration ratios for domestic industries do not necessarily mean that the larger firms in those industries wield excessive market power, since markets can still be contestable through the elimination of foreign trade barriers.

CONCEPTS FOR REVIEW

Regulation of industry	Marginal-cost pricing	Vertical merger
Nationalization	Ramsey pricing rule	Conglomerate merger
Natural monopoly	Constrained market pricing	Resale price maintenance
Economies of scale	Stand-alone cost	Predatory pricing
Economies of scope	Patent	Price discrimination
Cross subsidy	Privatization	Vertical marketing
Self-destructive competition	Combines Investigation Act	Concentration of industry
Average-cost pricing	Competition Act	Concentration ratio
Regulatory lag	Horizontal merger	Market power

QUESTIONS FOR DISCUSSION

1. Why is a hydro-electric company in a city usually considered to be a natural monopoly? What would happen if two competing hydro-electric companies were established? How about telephone companies?

2. In some regulated industries, prices are prevented from falling by the regulatory agency and, as a result, many firms open up business in that industry. In your opinion, is this competitive or anticompetitive? Is it a good idea or a bad one?

3. List some industries with regulated rates whose services you have bought. What do you think of the quality of their service?

4. In which, if any, of the regulated industries mentioned in your previous answer is there competitive rivalry? Why is regulation appropriate in these cases? (Or *is* it inappropriate in your opinion, and if so, why?)

5. Do you think it is appropriate for local users of telephone service to be cross subsidized by other telephone users?

6. Can you think of a way in which a new rural telephone subscriber contributes a beneficial externality? If so, does it make sense to provide a subsidy to rural subscribers? Who should pay the subsidy?

7. How might one go about distinguishing "predatory" from "non-predatory" pricing?

8. To provide incentives for increased efficiency, several regulatory agencies in the United States have eliminated ceilings on the profits of regulated firms but instead put caps on their prices. Suppose a regulated firm manages to cut its prices in half but, in the process, doubles its profits. Should rational consumers consider this to be a good or a bad development? Why?

9. Suppose Sam lives downtown while Fran's home is far away, so that it requires much more gas to deliver newspapers to Fran than to Sam. Yet the newspaper charges them exactly the same amount. Would the courts consider this to be price discrimination? Would an economist? Would you? Why?

10. A shopkeeper sells her store and signs a contract that restrains her from opening another store in competition with the new owner. The courts have decided that this contract is a reasonable restraint of trade. Can you think of any other types of restraint of trade that seem reasonable? Any that seem unreasonable?

11. Why do you think some industries are highly concentrated?

12. Do you think it is in the public interest to launch a combines suit that costs a billion dollars? What leads you to your conclusions?

13. In Japan and a number of European countries, the competition laws are much less severe than those in North America. Do you think this helps or harms North American industry in its efforts to compete with foreign producers? Why?

14. Do you think government authorities should interfere more than they do now in corporate takeover activities? What are some of the pros and cons of either alternative?

ENVIRONMENTAL PROTECTION AND RESOURCE CONSERVATION

We learned in Chapter 12 that externalities (the incidental benefits or damages imposed upon people not directly involved in an economic activity) can cause the market mechanism to malfunction. The first part of this chapter discusses a particularly important application of the analysis of externalities — the problem of environmental deterioration. The second half addresses the closely related subject of natural-resource depletion and the interwoven questions of energy use and environmental decay.

Environmental protection is one of the critical issues of our era, and one in which there is naturally a great deal of public interest. As concerned citizens, you will be called upon to participate, in one way or another, in the global effort to curb the growing problems in this area, and your understanding of the economic principle of externalities and of the related issue of property rights will enable you to come to a better-informed position on the subject. We have chosen to end the microeconomics part of our textbook with this chapter precisely because it so clearly embodies our belief that you will be able to apply the ideas you have learned here "beyond the final exam."

Everything's a trade-off. If you want a high standard of living, you have to settle for a low quality of life.

OVERHEARD CONVERSATION
REPORTED AT A MEETING
OF THE AMERICAN
PHILOSOPHICAL SOCIETY

THE ECONOMICS OF ENVIRONMENTAL PROTECTION

Environmental problems are by no means new. What *is* new and different is the amount of attention that society is now prepared to give them. Perhaps much of this increased interest can be attributed to rising incomes, which have freed people from the more urgent concerns about food, clothing, and shelter, allowing them the luxury of concentrating on the next level of needs—the *quality* of their lives.

Economic thought on the environment preceded the outburst of public concern about the subject by nearly half a century. In 1911, a noted British economist, A.C. Pigou, wrote a remarkable book called *The Economics of Welfare*, which offered an explanation of the market economy's poor environmental performance that is still generally accepted by economists today. Moreover, the same book outlined an approach to environmental policy that is still favoured by most economists and that is beginning to win over lawmakers as well. Pigou suggested that a system of charges on emissions would be an effective and efficient means of controlling pollution. In this way, the price mechanism can remedy one of its own shortcomings.

The most common method for controlling water and air pollution in Canada is for the provincial governments to issue specific discharge limits for each individual firm. Often, each firm in an area or an industry is required to reduce its pollution by the same percentage amount. The analysis in this chapter will enable us to see why this assignment of equal percentage reductions is both inefficient and inequitable.

THE ENVIRONMENT IN PERSPECTIVE: IS EVERYTHING GETTING STEADILY WORSE?

Much of the discussion of environmental problems in the popular press leaves the reader with the impression that matters have been growing steadily worse and that pollution is largely a product of the profit system and modern industrialization. As we will see, there are environmental problems today that are both enormous and pressing, but in fact pollution is nothing new. Medieval cities were pestholes—the streets and rivers were littered with garbage and the air stank of rotting wastes. At the beginning of the eighteenth century, a German traveller reported that to get a view of London from the tower of St. Paul's, one had to get there very early in the morning "before the air was full of coal smoke." Early in the twentieth century the automobile was hailed as a source of major improvement in the cleanliness of city streets, where residents had been fighting a losing battle against the proliferation of horse dung.

Since 1960, there has been progress in solving some pollution problems, much of it the result of concerted efforts to protect the environment. The quality of the air in most Canadian cities has improved. In Toronto, for example, the concentration of suspended particulates, or soot, in the air has fallen dramatically since the Grey Cup "Smog Bowl" of 1962. On that weekend, the air pollution index rose to 155. To put this figure in perspective, it should be noted that the current health-advisory level for the index is 32. At a level of 58, people with chronic respiratory diseases may be affected. At 100, even healthy people may be affected by prolonged conditions, and those with cardiac and respiratory diseases could suffer severe effects. Depending on weather conditions, readings in excess of 50 can trigger a first alert and cause industrial operations to be curtailed. At 100, the air pollution threat is considered serious and the province can order a stoppage of all operations not essential to public health and safety.

Such regulations are improving the situation. Recently in Toronto, for example, the index has exceeded 32 on just several days each year. Similar improvements have occurred elsewhere in Canada and in other industrialized countries. Even the famous, or rather infamous, "fogs" of London are almost a thing of the past. There have been two high readings of particular note in the British capital: in 1959 (when the index rose to 275 and there was a 10 percent increase over the normal number of deaths) and in 1962 (when the index rose to 575 and there was a 20 percent increase in mortality). But more recently, London's cleaner air has resulted in an astounding 50 percent increase in the number of hours of winter sunshine. In short, pollution problems are not a uniquely modern phenomenon, nor is every part of the environment deteriorating relentlessly.

Environmental problems have not occurred exclusively in capitalist economies. For example, in the People's Republic of China, coal soot from factory smokestacks in Beijing envelops the city in a thick black haze. Similarly, smoke from brown-coal furnaces pollutes the air almost everywhere in Eastern Europe (these countries adopted capitalist approaches only very recently). The Polish government has declared Bogomice and four other towns "unfit for human habitation" because of heavy-metal particles suspended in the air and deposited in the soil by emissions from nearby copper-smelting plants, and it has been estimated that a third of Poland's citizens live in areas of "ecological disaster." In December 1987, the Soviet newspaper *Pravda* stated that the industrial city of Ufa, with a population of nearly one million, had also become unfit for human beings. The citizens of Leipzig, a major industrial city in what was formerly East Germany, have a life expectancy a full six years shorter than the national average. The Iset and Volga rivers in the former Soviet Union are so filled with chemicals that they have actually caught fire!

In the preceding discussion, we have tried to put matters into perspective, but we do not mean to suggest that all is well with the environment in market-oriented economies or that there is nothing more to do. While there have been some improvements, serious problems remain. Our world is now subject to a number of new pollutants, most of which are far more dangerous than those we have reduced, even though they may be less visible and less malodorous.

A variety of highly toxic substances—PCBs (polychlorinated biphenyls), chlorinated hydrocarbons, dioxins, heavy metals, and radioactive materials—are dumped carelessly, left to cause cancer and threaten life and health in other ways. Some of these substances linger in the environment so long that they are likely to constitute a threat for many thousands of years. The accumulation of these and other by-products of modern technology may well cause damage that is all but irreversible.

Ironically, although successful clean-up of conventional water pollutants has returned fishlife to some previously "dead" waterways, those fish are sometimes inedible because they are so contaminated with toxic substances. This is true of the Great Lakes, where vast quantities of toxic pesticides and other chemicals remain trapped in bottom sediments. But even these problems pale in comparison with the environmental issues discussed in the boxed insert on pages 575–77. There, we consider acid rain, the problem of carbon dioxide buildup in the earth's atmosphere (and the resulting increase in global temperatures that some scientists predict), the expanding hole in the ozone layer of the atmosphere, and toxic wastes.

While environmental problems are neither new nor confined only to capitalist, industrialized economies, these facts are not legitimate grounds for complacency. The potential damage that we are inflicting on ourselves and on our surroundings is very real and very substantial.

THE LAW OF CONSERVATION OF MATTER AND ENERGY

The physical law of conservation of matter and energy tells us there is no way that objects can be made to disappear — at most, they can be changed into something else. Oil, for instance, can be transformed into heat (and smoke) or into plastic — but it will never vanish. After a raw material has been used, either it must be used again (recycled) or it becomes a waste product that must somehow be disposed of.

If any input used in the production process is not recycled, it must ultimately become a waste product. It may end up on the garbage heap of some municipal dump. It may literally go up in smoke, contributing its bit to the pollution of the atmosphere. Or it may even be transformed into heat, warming up adjacent waterways and killing aquatic life in the process. The laws of physics tell us there is nothing we can do to make used inputs disappear altogether from the earth.

In fact, only a small proportion of the economy's inputs are made up of recycled materials, and although recycling rates for such commonly used materials as aluminum, paper, and glass appear to be rising in many industrial countries, only one country—the Netherlands—recovers more than half of these products, which are relatively easy to recycle. Canada's current recycling rates are among the worst in the industrialized world; we recycle only 3 percent of such goods, on average. Things are improving, however. During the 1980s, more than 250 Canadian municipalities (about 200 of them in Ontario) launched voluntary recycling programs. A more aggressive approach is being adopted in the United States. There, at least 30 states have adopted laws requiring the recycling of wastes. Recycling laws and municipal garbage fees are hitting people where it hurts: in the pocketbook. In one town, residents must pay by the bag to have their garbage taken away, instead of paying a flat annual fee for whatever amount of trash they produce. The switch to the pay-by-the-bag system has reduced trash volume by 25 percent, as people are induced to recycle, compost, and perhaps refrain from purchasing "over-packaged" products. These examples are typical of what is starting to happen in many communities.

Nevertheless, as we discussed in Chapter 3, the recent public enthusiasm for recycling can create a glut of recycled items, with the result that the existing system does not have the capacity to process all of them, and some portion is simply dumped as usual (see page 76). Hence, average recycling rates of 40 percent are considered very successful. Although this does represent an important step in the right direction, we must realize that, with output growing over time and with input use consequently increasing, waste disposal and pollution are virtually certain to be growing problems.

Many people think of industry as the primary villain in environmental damage. But although private firms have done their share in harming the environment, private individuals and government have also been prime contributors. The emissions of private passenger cars play an important role in the air pollution problems of most major cities; wastes from residential washing machines contribute to their water pollution problems. Governments are guilty as well. Major hydro-electric power projects usually alter entire ecosystems fundamentally, and the wastes of municipal sewage-treatment plants are a major source of water pollution. Worse still, many municipalities continue to dump untreated sewage into lakes and rivers. Consider conditions in Quebec: In 1990, only one-sixth of that province's towns and cities were equipped with sewage-treatment plants, and less than half of Montreal's sewage was being treated. (To keep matters in perspective, we should note that this problem is not exclusive to Canada: 70 percent of the cities on the Mediterranean pump unprocessed sewage into the sea. If the governments of the developed world have such poor records, what can we reasonably expect of the less developed countries?) Even more threatening than inadequate sewage treatment, however, are government-run nuclear power plants that produce radioactive materials, which are among the most dangerous of all wastes. And the problem of their disposal is far from solved.

ENVIRONMENTAL DAMAGE AS AN EXTERNALITY

We have already indicated that our very existence means that some environmental damage is inevitable. Products of the earth must be used up, and wastes must be generated in the process of creating the means of subsistence.

There is no question of reducing environmental damage to zero. As long as the human race survives, complete elimination of such damage is impossible. Indeed, it is not even desirable to get as close as possible to zero damage. Some pollutants in small quantities are quickly dispersed and rendered harmless by natural processes, and it is not worth the opportunity cost to eliminate others that cause only slight damage. Use of a large quantity of resources for this purpose could so limit their supply that there would not be materials available for the construction of hospitals, schools, and other things more important to society than the elimination of some pollutants.

The real issue, then, is not whether pollution should exist at all, but whether environmental damage in an unregulated market economy tends to be more serious and widespread than the public interest can tolerate. This issue immediately raises three key questions. First, why do economists believe that environmental damage is unacceptably severe in terms of the public interest? (And how do they measure "the public interest"?) Second, why does the market mechanism, which is so good at providing about the right number of toasters and trucks, generate too much pollution? (What goes wrong with the system?) Third, what can we do about it?

Economists do not claim any special ability to judge what is good for the public interest. They normally prefer to accept the wishes of the members of the public as adequate indicators. When the economy reflects these wishes as closely as it can, given the resources and technology available, economists conclude that it is working effectively. When it operates in a way that frustrates the desires of the people, they conclude that the economy is functioning improperly. Why, then, do economists believe that the market mechanism generates "too much" pollution?

To answer this, we must deal with the fundamental analysis of A.C. Pigou, to which we referred at the beginning of this chapter. In Chapter 12, we discussed some of the failures of the market mechanism and singled out externalities as a primary cause. An **externality**, it will be recalled, is an incidental consequence of some economic activity that is either beneficial or detrimental to someone who neither controls the activity nor is intentionally served by it. The emission of pollutants constitutes one of the most clear-cut examples of a detrimental externality. The smoke from a chemical plant affects people other than the management of the plant or its customers. Because the incidental damage done by the smoke does not enter the financial accounts of the firm whose plant produces the emissions, the owners of the firm have no financial incentive to restrain those emissions, particularly since emission control costs money. Instead, they will find it profitable to produce their chemical product and to emit their smoke as though it caused no external damage to the community.

One can argue that this is a failure of the pricing system. Through the smoke externality, the business firm is able to use up some of the community's clean air without paying for the privilege. Just as the firm would undoubtedly use oil and electricity wastefully if they were obtainable at no charge, the firm uses the community's air wastefully, despoiling it with smoke far beyond the level that the public interest can justify. Rather than being at the (low) socially desirable level, the quantity of smoke is at whatever (usually high) level is necessary to save as much money as possible for the firm that emits it, because the external damage caused by the smoke costs the firm nothing.

The achievement of any solution to this externality problem is particularly difficult when the smoke crosses political boundaries. This represents a very large problem for Canada, as the boxed insert on pages 575–77 indicates.

Externalities

Externalities play a crucial role in affecting the quality of life. They show why the market mechanism, which is so efficient in supplying consumers' goods, has a much poorer record in terms of its effects on the environment. The problem of pollution illustrates the importance of externalities for public policy and indicates why their analysis is one of our twelve Ideas for Beyond the Final Exam.

SUPPLY–DEMAND ANALYSIS OF ENVIRONMENTAL PROBLEMS

Basic supply–demand analysis can be used to explain both how externalities lead to environmental problems and how these problems can be cured. As an illustration, let us look at the problem of solid wastes—and the damage that the massive generation of garbage is doing to our environment.

In Figure 17-1, we see a demand curve, *DE*, for garbage removal. As usual, this curve has a negative slope, meaning that if the price of garbage removal is set sufficiently high, people will become more sparing in the amount of garbage removal they order. They may more often bring papers, bottles, and cans to recycling centres and public dumps; they may repair broken items rather than throw them out; and so on. In short, a higher price for garbage removal can be expected to reduce the quantity demanded of garbage-removal services.

The graph also shows the supply curve, *SS*, that we can expect to prevail in an ideal market for garbage removal. Garbage disposal is expensive to society—it requires people and trucks to haul it away; garbage dumps occupy valuable land; and the use of fire or other means to get rid of the garbage creates pollution that, as we have seen, has a high real cost to the community. As we saw in our analysis of competitive industries (Chapter 8), the position of the market's supply curve depends on the marginal cost of garbage removal. If suppliers have to pay the full costs of garbage removal, the supply curve will be comparably high (as drawn in the graph) and have a positive slope, meaning that the marginal cost of garbage disposal rises as the quantity rises. We see that, for the community depicted in the graph, the price of garbage removal will be *P*

FIGURE 17-1

FREE DUMPING OF POLLUTANTS AS AN INDUCEMENT TO ENVIRONMENTAL DAMAGE

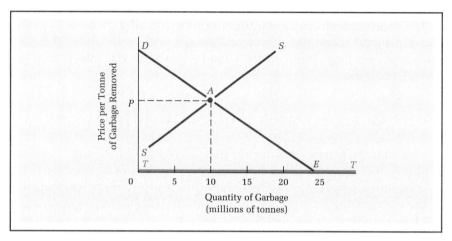

Whether wastes are solid, liquid, or gaseous, they impose costs upon the community. If the emitter is not charged for the damage, the resulting wastes are effectively being removed at zero charge to the polluter (blue removal supply curve *TT*). The polluter is thus induced to pollute a great deal (25 million tonnes in the figure). If the charges to the polluter reflected the true cost to the community (supply curve *SS* of waste removal), it would pay to emit a much smaller amount (10 million tonnes in the figure).

dollars per tonne, and at that price, 10 million tonnes will be generated (point *A*).

But what if the community's government decides to remove garbage "free"? Of course, that means the government is really charging the consumer for the service in the form of taxes, but not in a way that makes each consumer pay for the quantity of garbage that he or she produces. The result is that the supply curve is no longer *SS*. Rather, it becomes the blue line, *TT*, which lies along the horizontal axis, because any household can increase the garbage it throws away and still face a zero cost. Now the intersection of the supply and demand curves is no longer point *A*. Rather, it is point *E*, at which the price is zero and the quantity of garbage generated is 25 million tonnes — an amount substantially greater than would be produced if those who made the garbage had to pay the cost of getting rid of it.

Similar problems occur if the community offers the oxygen of its waterways and the purity of its atmosphere without charge to all who choose to use them. The amount that will be wasted and otherwise used up is likely to be enormously greater than it would be if users had to pay for the cost of their actions to society. That, in the view of economists, is one major reason for the severity of our environmental problems. Three conclusions follow:

1. The magnitude of our pollution problem is attributable in large part to the fact that the market lets individuals, firms, and government agencies deplete such resources as oxygen in the water and pure air without financial charge.

FURTHER DETAIL

THE THREATENED ENVIRONMENT

In recent years, we have come to realize that several threats to the environment are fundamental. One is acid rain, which is created by the millions of tonnes of sulphur dioxide and nitrogen oxides spewed out of North American smokestacks and automobile exhaust pipes (globally, more than 4.5 billion tonnes of carbon are injected into the earth's atmosphere each year). The oxides mix with water vapour in the air to form weak sulphuric and nitric acid, which later falls as acid rain. The result is increased acidity in lakes, which has curtailed the ability of many fish to reproduce, and in the soil, which has slowed the growth of trees and increased their vulnerability to disease. The taller the smokestacks and the stronger the prevailing winds, the farther away from the source of the pollution the damage is likely to occur. Fifty percent of the acid rain that falls in Canada comes from American sources, and about 10 percent of the acid rain that falls in the eastern United States comes from Canada. From a purely national point of view, it does not pay Americans to spend a lot to limit acid rain, when Canadians get much of the benefit.

Clearly, one reason that pollution issues are so difficult to solve is that they are rife with problems of externality, which stem from the fact that clear property rights do not exist. Who owns the air or the rivers: the general public or the owners of the firms that dis-charge the waste? It is very difficult to come to an agreement that establishes such property rights, especially when more than one country is involved.

When problems are fairly localized, agreements are more feasible. For example, the governments of Ontario, New York state, Canada, and the United States have agreed to cut pollution in the Niagara River by 50 percent by 1996. But when more jurisdictions are involved—as is the case in Europe — agreements are more difficult to reach. For example, Germany and Austria regularly complain of acid rain and river contamination from the Czech Republic and Slovakia, yet nothing has been done to eliminate the problem.

With every news report, the externality dimension of environmental problems seems to become clearer. For instance, Lapp villagers in northern Sweden and Norway were forbidden to eat local reindeer meat after their herds became contaminated by fallout from the nuclear accident at Chernobyl in far-off Ukraine. Similarly, Canadian wildlife scientists have found high levels of PCBs and other contaminants in polar-bear livers.

The lack of established property rights is an age-old factor in the destruction of common resources. When European settlers moved across the plains of North America, their cow herds, being privately owned, were

(continued)

(continued)

not killed off. The buffalo were publicly owned, however, so it was in no particular hunter's interest to preserve the herds. It is therefore not surprising that the buffalo no longer roam.

It may be that people are becoming increasingly aware of the need to establish property rights for the environment. No-smoking areas are spreading at a rapid rate, as people understand more about the effects of second-hand smoke.

But some pollution problems involve such dramatic externalities that the whole world is affected. One example is the greenhouse effect. The steadily rising and essentially irreversible concentration of carbon dioxide in the earth's atmosphere causes it to trap increasing amounts of the heat radiated by the planet. The general warming trend is expected to have disastrous effects, including mass starvation in some less developed countries, flooding of entire coastal areas, and severe droughts on the Canadian prairies, perhaps within the next 50 years.

Another worldwide threat is in the upper atmosphere — the thinning of the layer of ozone, a bluish gas that shields the earth from the sun's ultraviolet rays. Synthetic chemicals called chlorofluorocarbons (CFCs) are depleting the ozone layer. The chance of getting skin cancer is now estimated to be much higher than it was 50 years ago. The Montreal Protocol, an international treaty ratified by Canada and 46 other nations (effective 1989), calls for a 50 percent reduction in the production and use of CFCs by 1998, and for a total halt in their production two years later.

Hazardous wastes (such as those from nuclear plants, industrial manufacturing, laboratories, and medical institutions) represent yet another critical environmental problem: Improperly disposed, they can threaten all forms of organic life. Unfortunately, little has been done so far to solve this problem. Indeed, there are many instances in which industrialized countries have literally just shipped the problem off to the poorest of the less developed countries — countries unequipped with the necessary storage and treatment facilities, and certainly too poor to deal with the serious environmental problems that will follow. For example, in 1988, the government of Guinea-Bissau signed a contract with two British firms to receive 15 million tonnes of pharmaceutical wastes over a five-year period. While this arrangement was very inexpensive from the firms' point of view, the payments to Guinea-Bissau totalled more than four times that country's national product. Solving the problem is difficult when parts of the world are so poor that they are forced to regard such transactions as "good deals."

The users of the world's resources simply must be compelled to take the external costs of their actions into consideration when making their decisions. The people who are hacking down the world's rain forests at the rate of 1200 hectares an hour are literally cutting away the lungs of the earth, since rain forests contribute a large percentage of the oxygen in the earth's atmosphere. But these individuals are not evil; in many cases, they are forced to overuse the environment for their own or their country's immediate survival. For example, some developing countries' needs for foreign exchange to pay for imports compel them to cut timber faster than it can be regenerated. They simply cannot afford to worry about the future.

Obviously, many of these problems cannot be solved without political decisions to redistribute income to the less developed countries, and to define property rights. But the right kinds of political and institutional changes will be forthcoming only if they are rooted in an understanding of the externality dimension of environmental issues.

Countries in the developed world must therefore learn to co-operate in order to

(continued)

(continued)

devise a sufficiently comprehensive program of income redistribution to the less developed countries. Without help from the developed world, these poorer countries cannot possibly make the sacrifices that the human race must make *collectively* to reverse the deterioration of the environment. Calculations by the Organization for Economic Co-operation and Development (OECD) show that if its 24 rich members managed to keep their carbon dioxide emissions at their 1990 levels for an entire decade, this would reduce the global total only by about 11 percent from what it would otherwise be by the year 2050. The reason is that any such reduction is projected to be swamped by the increase in emissions from developing countries. It is estimated that China's emissions alone will equal those of the entire OECD by 2050.

It is clear that the degree of global income redistribution required is vast, and that we must consequently ensure that the pollution-abatement strategies we adopt involve the least possible costs in terms of job and income losses. That is why we argue so forcefully later in this chapter for the most efficient pollution-abatement schemes available.

2. One way of dealing with pollution problems is to charge those who emit pollution (or despoil the environment in other ways) a price commensurate with the costs they impose on society.

3. This is another instance in which higher prices—on environmentally damaging activities—can be beneficial to the community.

BASIC APPROACHES TO ENVIRONMENTAL POLICY

In broad terms, three general methods have been proposed for the control of activities that damage the environment:

1. *Voluntary programs*, such as non-mandatory investment in pollution control equipment by firms that decide to act in a manner that meets their social responsibilities, or voluntary separation of solid wastes by consumers for recycling.

2. *Direct controls*, which either impose legal ceilings on the amount any polluter is permitted to emit or specify how particular activities must be carried on—for example, they may prohibit backyard incinerators or the use of high-sulphur coal, or require smokestack "scrubbers" to capture the emissions of electricity-generating installations.

3. *Taxes on emissions*, or the use of other monetary incentives or penalties to make it financially unattractive for emitters of pollutants to continue to pollute as usual.

Each of these methods has its place. If used appropriately, together they can constitute an effective and efficient environmental program. Let us consider each of them in turn.

VOLUNTARISM

Voluntary control of pollution has usually proved to be weak and unreliable. Voluntary programs for the collection and separation of garbage into different and easily recyclable materials have rarely managed to reroute more than a small fraction of a community's wastes from the garbage dump to the recycling plants. Some business people with strong consciences have manifested good intentions and made sincere attempts to improve the practices of their companies. Yet competition has usually prevented them from spending more than token amounts for this purpose. No business, whatever its virtues, can long afford to have the prices of its products undercut by rival suppliers. As a result, voluntary business programs have often been more helpful to the companies' public relations activities than the environment. Firms with a real interest in environmental protection have called for legislation that *requires* all firms, including competitors, to undertake the same measures, thereby subjecting all firms in the industry to similar handicaps.

Yet voluntary measures do have their place. They are appropriate where alternative measures are not readily available. Where surveillance and, consequently, enforcement are impractical, as in the prevention of littering by campers in isolated areas, there is no choice but an appeal to people's consciences. In brief but serious emergencies, in which there is no time to plan and enact a systematic program, there may also be no good substitute for voluntary compliance. Several major cities have, for example, experienced periods of temporary but dangerous concentrations of pollutants when the authorities were forced to appeal to the public to avoid activities that would aggravate the problem. One can easily cite cases in which the public response to appeals requiring co-operation for short periods was enthusiastic and gratifying. Let's summarize:

Voluntary programs are not dependable ways to protect the environment. However, in brief, unexpected emergencies or where effective surveillance is impossible, the policy-maker may have no other choice. Sometimes, in these cases, voluntary programs work.

Incidentally, government spending policies can create incentives for voluntary action in the private sector (or at least minimize private-sector resistance to non-voluntary changes). For example, in 1993, the Ontario government announced its intention to purchase all of its paper from pulp and paper mills that do not use chlorine for bleaching. This policy effectively undercuts industry arguments that a shift toward unbleached paper is unaffordable (on profitability and job-creation grounds).

DIRECT CONTROLS

Direct controls have been the chief instrument of environmental policy in Canada. Under the Constitution, legislative authority for the environment is shared between the provincial and federal governments. The job of enforcing federal standards often falls to the provinces. Probably the best-known of these controls are automobile emissions standards. The federal government establishes emissions standards for new vehicles being sold in Canada, but the provincial governments are responsible for the control of pollution after the vehicles have been sold.

Control measures in provincial legislation, such as Ontario's Environmental Protection Act, include control orders, stop orders, and program approvals. These restrictions focus on the *results* of pollution. Such was the case on October 13, 1970, when the Ontario government ordered 48 firms and institutions in Toronto and Hamilton to reduce operations because the air pollution index exceeded 50.

Since then, major operations such as Ontario Hydro, Inco, Falconbridge and Algoma Steel have co-operated with a 1986 Ontario statute that required them to reduce sulphur dioxide pollution by 67 percent in stages between 1986 and 1994. This step was significant because these four companies produced 80 percent of the acid gas pollution in the province. Reliance on direct controls continues. For example, in 1993, the Ontario government announced that all pulp and paper mills in the province must cut chlorine discharges by 40 percent in 1995 and by 68 percent in 1999, and that firms must submit plans for the complete elimination of chlorine by 2002.

TAXES ON EMISSIONS

Most economists agree that a nearly exclusive reliance on direct controls is a mistake and that, in most cases, financial penalties on polluters can do the same job more dependably, more effectively, and more economically. The most common suggestion is that firms be permitted to pollute all they want but be forced to pay a tax for the privilege, to make them *want* to pollute less. A tax on emissions requires the polluter to install a meter that records emissions in the same way that a hydro meter records the use of electricity. At the end of the month, the government automatically sends the polluter a bill charging a stipulated amount for each litre of waste (the amount must also vary with the quality of the wastes—a higher tax rate being imposed on wastes that are more dangerous or unpleasant). Thus, the more damage a polluting firm does, the more it must pay. Such taxes are deliberately designed to encourage the use of a glaring loophole—polluters can reduce the tax they pay by decreasing the amount they emit. In terms of Figure 17-1, if the tax is used to increase the payment for waste emissions from zero (blue supply line *TT*) and instead forces the polluter to pay their true cost to society, emissions will automatically be reduced from 25 million to 10 million tonnes.

Firms do respond to such taxes. The most widely publicized example comes from the Ruhr River basin in Germany, where emissions taxes have been used for almost four decades. Although the Ruhr is one of the world's most concentrated industrial centres, those of its rivers that are protected by taxes are sufficiently clean to be usable for fishing and other recreational purposes. Firms have found it profitable to avoid the taxes by extracting pollutants from their liquid discharges and recycling.

It is encouraging that political leaders on both sides of the border in North America have embraced the idea of using taxes as a lever to achieve environmental goals. It is hoped that they will study the success of such schemes as Singapore's charging of a toll on vehicles entering the downtown area with fewer than four passengers. The day the policy went into effect in Singapore, there was a 50 percent drop in the number of cars entering the city. To put this matter in perspective, note that in the absence of such a scheme, Toronto's ground-level ozone readings in 1988 exceeded federal maximum guidelines on more than 100 occasions.

EMISSIONS TAXES VERSUS DIRECT CONTROLS

It is important to see why taxes on emissions may prove more effective and reliable than direct controls. Direct controls rely essentially on the enforcement mechanism of the criminal justice system. Rules are set up that the polluter must obey. If a polluting firm violates those rules, it must be caught. Then, the regulatory agency must decide whether it has enough evidence to prosecute. Next, it must win its case before the courts. Finally, the courts must impose a penalty that is more than a token gesture. If any one of these steps does not occur, the polluter gets away with damaging activities.

ENFORCEMENT ISSUES

The enforcement of direct controls requires vigilance and enthusiasm by the regulatory agency, which must assign the resources and persons needed to carry out the task of enforcement. Yet experience indicates that regulatory vigour is far from universal and often evaporates as time passes and public concern recedes. In many cases, the resources devoted to enforcement are pitifully small. Also, there are often lags in the court process, and legislation has typically prescribed ridiculously light penalties for violators.

The following facts illustrate some of these problems. The province of Quebec has some of the toughest environmental laws in Canada, with fines ranging up to $1 million per day, but little effort seems to go into enforcing the laws. For example, in 1987, fewer than half of the companies required by law to submit an environmental report complied. In Ontario, surveys by the Ministry of the Environment showed that half of the province's industries and one-third of the municipal sewage plants violated water pollution guidelines in 1988. However, some progress is being made: In 1989, Ontario became the first province to jail a corporate executive for a pollution-related offence (the firm repeatedly ignored a court order to curtail emissions). Since corporate executives are directly responsible for actual decision making, the threat of imprisonment is one aspect of the legal approach that might indeed represent a more effective disincentive than do the prevailing, relatively small, fines and penalties.

But even when the legal machinery is set in motion, the laws often seem rigged in favour of polluters. For example, early in 1990, an arsonist set fire to 15 million used tires at the five-hectare Tyre King dump in Hagersville, Ontario. The fire—the largest of its kind in North American history—burned for seventeen days, and forced the evacuation of the area. A major component of tires is a petroleum-based substance that is highly flammable and almost impossible to extinguish once it catches fire. The flames release toxic gases and a dioxin-laced oil that contaminates the water system. In 1987, Tyre King had been issued a control order to stack the tires in hundreds of piles separated by fire lanes, and to fence the site. The company appealed the order, and when the fire broke out three years later, a hearing date had yet to be set. By allowing the activity in question to continue until an appeal is heard, current laws give polluters an incentive to appeal rather than to obey the law.

In contrast to direct control, pollution taxes are automatic and certain. No one need be caught, prosecuted, convicted, and punished. The tax bills are just sent out automatically by the untiring tax collector. The only sure way for polluters to avoid or reduce pollution charges is to cut down their emissions.

EFFICIENCY IN CLEAN-UP

A second difference between direct controls and taxes is worth noting. Suppose there is a ruling under a program of direct controls that Filth, Ltd., must cut its emissions by 50 percent. That firm has absolutely no motivation to go one drop further. Why should it cut its emissions by 55 or even 52 percent when the law offers it neither reward nor encouragement for going beyond the stipulated quota? Under a system of emission taxes, however, the more the firm cuts back on its pollution, the more it saves in tax payments.

A third important difference between direct controls and taxes on emissions is the greater efficiency of the latter in the use of resources. The tax approach can probably do the job far more cheaply, saving labour, fuel, and raw materials, which can instead be used to build, say, schools, hospitals, and housing for low-income groups. Statistical estimates for several pollution-control programs suggest that the cost of doing the job through direct controls can easily be twice as high as under the tax alternative.

Why should there be such a difference? The answer is that under direct controls, the job of cutting back emissions is apportioned among the various polluters on the basis of some principle (usually intended to approximate some standard of fairness) selected by the regulators. This approach rarely assigns the task in accordance with the firm's ability to carry it out cheaply and efficiently. Suppose it costs Firm A only 2¢ a litre to reduce emissions while Firm B must spend 10¢ a litre to do the same job. If both firms spew out 2000 litres of pollution a day, a 50 percent reduction in pollution can be achieved by ordering both firms to limit emissions to 1000 litres a day. This may or may not be fair, but it is certainly not efficient. The social cost will be 1000 times 2¢, or $20, to Firm A and 1000 times 10¢, or $100, to Firm B—a total of $120.

If, instead, a tax of 5¢ per litre is imposed, all the work will be done by Firm A—which can do it more cheaply. Firm A will cut its emissions out altogether, paying the 2¢ a litre this requires, to avoid the 5¢-per-litre tax. Firm B will probably go on polluting as before, because it is cheaper to pay the tax than the 10¢ a litre it costs to control its pollution. In this way, under the tax, total daily emissions will still be cut by 2000 litres a day. But the entire job will be done by the polluter who can do it more cheaply, and the total daily cost of the program will therefore be $40 (2¢ × 2000 litres) instead of the $120 it would cost under direct controls.

The secret of the efficiency induced by a tax on pollution is straightforward. Only polluters who can reduce emissions cheaply and efficiently can afford to take advantage of the built-in loophole—the opportunity to save on taxes by reducing emissions. The tax approach simply assigns the job to those who can do it most effectively.

EQUITY ISSUES

Under direct controls, the authorities usually aim at an *equitable* assignment of emissions quotas. For example, they may require all polluters to reduce their discharges by the same percentage. However, the attempt to put this rule into practice almost always results in complaints, political pressures, renegotiation of quotas, and a consequent set of assignments that seem to have been designed with the aid of a roulette wheel rather than a deliberate decision-making process.

Why are equal-percentage reductions in emissions not generally equitable? We have already seen one reason: Costs of reduction are not the same for all industries or all plants in an industry. For example, the cost for a typical beet sugar plant to reduce its emissions (as measured in terms of the oxygen these wastes use up) is only about one-sixth as large as an equivalent reduction for a petroleum refinery. A modern paper plant can usually decrease its discharges at much less cost than can an antiquated plant in the same industry. Is it really fair to require all these firms to cut back their emissions by the same amounts when, through no fault of their own, the resulting financial burden and loss of jobs is so different?

There are even clearer examples of the potential inequity in equal-percentage reductions. Consider two companies, one run by a conscientious environmentalist who has voluntarily installed substantial amounts of equipment to cleanse and reduce emissions, and the other by an irresponsible management that has continued to allow as much garbage to pour into the public waterways as maximum profitability requires. Is it really fair for both of these firms to be told to cut back equally?

Once such problems and others like them are recognized, and an attempt is made to reassign emissions quotas accordingly, it will become clear that each emitter is a special case requiring special treatment. The regulator is almost forced to proceed case by case, and the resulting quotas end up following complex patterns that are at best difficult to defend in terms of equity or efficiency.

The pollution tax avoids these problems by leaving to the individual firm the choice of whether to pollute and pay the tax or to clean up.

ADVANTAGES AND DISADVANTAGES

Given all these advantages of the tax approach, why would anyone want to use direct controls? There are three general and important situations in which direct controls have a clear advantage:

1. Where an emission is so dangerous that a decision is made to prohibit it altogether. Here, there is obviously nothing to be gained by installing complicated procedures for the collection of taxes that will never be paid because there will be no emissions.

2. Where a sudden change in circumstances—for example, a dangerous air quality crisis—calls for prompt and substantial changes in conduct, such as temporary reductions in the use of cars or incinerators. It is difficult and clumsy to change tax rules, and direct controls will usually do a better job here.

3. Where effective and dependable metering devices have not been invented or are prohibitively costly to install and operate. In such cases, there is no way to operate an effective tax program; if the amount of wastes that the polluting firm has emitted cannot be determined, its tax bill cannot be calculated. In that case, the only effective option may be to require it to use "clean" fuel or to install emissions-purification equipment.

In reality, there is often no device analogous to a gas or water meter that can be used to measure pollution emissions cheaply and effectively. For example, to evaluate emissions in waterways, the standard procedure is to take samples, bring them to a laboratory, and subject them to a series of complicated tests (which often take weeks to carry out) to determine the chemical contents of the emissions. For a polluter whose emissions are very large, this may be worth doing. But for the emitter who spews out only a few litres of pollutants a day, the cost of such a complex process is likely to exceed the benefits. Whatever their other inefficiencies, direct controls are likely to do the job of controlling such sources of pollution more cheaply. On the other side of the argument, however, is the possibility that the widespread adoption of emissions charges and the resulting rise in demand for metering devices could lead to research and development that produces cheaper and more effective meters.

OTHER FINANCIAL DEVICES TO PROTECT THE ENVIRONMENT

The basic idea underlying the emissions-tax approach to environmental protection is that it provides financial incentives for polluters to reduce the damage they do to the environment. But emissions taxes are not the only form of financial inducement that has been proposed. At least two others deserve consideration: *subsidies for reduced emissions* and the requirement of *emissions permits* for polluters, with each permit authorizing the emission of a specified quantity of pollutant. Such permits would be offered for sale in limited quantities fixed by the authorities, at prices set by demand and supply.

Subsidies

Subsidies are already in use. Their advocates say that financial inducements can be just as effective when they take the form of a reward for good behaviour as when they take the form of a penalty (taxes) for harmful behaviour. One can induce a donkey to move forward by dangling a carrot in front of its nose just as surely (and with much less unpleasantness) as by applying a stick to its rump. Environmental subsidies usually take one of two forms:

1. partial payment of the cost of installation of some sort of pollution-control equipment, or
2. the offer of a fixed reward for every reduction in emissions from a base level, usually some amount that the polluter emitted in the past.

A subsidy to help defray the cost of control equipment can be effective when the purchaser of the equipment was considering doing it anyway but did not because of the high cost. This may be the case for a municipality that wants to treat its wastes more thoroughly but has not found a way to afford the cost. It may also be the case in private industry, where collection of the wastes can yield products that are valuable and reusable but the equipment required for the process is too costly. But where the polluter gains nothing from such control, a partial subsidy for the purchase of control equipment is not likely to be very effective. It simply reduces the cost of something the polluter does not want to do in any event.

The second type of subsidy—a reward based on quantity of reduced emissions—does indeed have the same sort of incentive effects for *individual* polluters as does a tax. In both cases, the more polluters emit, the worse off they are financially, either because they receive a smaller subsidy payment or because their tax bill is higher. But as far as the industry is concerned, there is a world of difference between the effect of a tax and the effect of a subsidy. A tax discourages the output of commodities whose production causes pollution, whereas a subsidy encourages such output to expand. If you need to review the proof of this point, refer back to Chapter 8, pages 248–49.

Emissions Permits

A third type of financial inducement strongly advocated by some economists is the sale of **marketable emissions permits**. Under this arrangement, the environmental agency decides what quantity of emissions per

FURTHER DETAIL

PUTTING IVORY-TOWER THEORY TO THE TEST

One remedy for pollution long advocated by economists as an alternative to direct controls is the issuance of a limited number of pollution permits to be sold on a free market. Almost twenty years ago, the U.S. Environmental Protection Agency (EPA) began to experiment with a program of emissions trading. Our reprint of a newspaper advertisement is an example of this program. Any firm that purchased the "pollution offset credit" could construct a new factory or other source of pollution in areas where pollution standards were not met, as long as its emissions were more than offset by reductions in pollution elsewhere. Experts have concluded that the emissions-trading program has "clearly afforded many firms flexibility in meeting emission limits, and this flexibility has resulted in significant aggregate cost savings—in the billions of dollars."*

Classified advertisement in *The Wall Street Journal*, June 5, 1986, page 32.

---

*Robert W. Hahn, "Economic Prescriptions for Environmental Problems: How the Patient Followed the Doctor's Orders," *Journal of Economic Perspectives*, vol. 3, no. 2 (Spring 1989), page 101.

One way to test the efficiency of marketable emissions permits is by running experiments (see the boxed insert on experimental economics in Chapter 3, pages 77–78). Extensive simulations have been studied at universities in Arizona and Colorado in the United States as well as Hamilton's McMaster University. The results of these experiments suggest that the more complicated the institutional framework for the trading of emissions permits, the less effective that approach will be. Nevertheless, even the least effective schemes have helped managers of experimental firms to achieve 50 percent of the efficiency gains that are possible compared to a direct-control approach that forces equal-percentage cutbacks for all participants.

Journalists in Canada have started calling for Canadian policy-makers to follow the American experience with marketable emissions permits, as the following editorial makes clear.

What Price Pollution?
Tired of the same old stocks, bonds and securitized credit-card receivables? Investors will soon have a new market to play: pollution futures.

Almost unnoticed in the events of the past week was the launch of a revolution in envi-
(continued)

(continued)

ronmental regulation, with the first annual auction of sulfur dioxide emissions permits by the Chicago Board of Trade. The U.S. Environmental Protection Agency offered 150,000 permits for sale, each entitling the bearer to spew one ton of the compound into the air per year. Another 125,000 units were put up by power utilities around the U.S., out of the allotments they were given earlier by the EPA under the 1990 Clean Air Act.

While some private trading of emissions permits has already taken place, the EPA auction is intended to make a more liquid market, with better information on prices. By next month, the CBOT hopes to have established a secondary market writing futures contracts on the permits, allowing utilities planning investments to lock in prices in advance.

Putting a price on the right to pollute will strike some as the darkest emanation yet of capitalism's calculating soul. Yet many environmentalists applaud the plan. For by harnessing the logic of the market to environmental ends, it offers the most cost-effective path to the Clean Air Act's goal of cutting total sulfur-dioxide emissions in half by the year 2000.

Put a price on anything, and people are induced to minimize their consumption of it. This is the principle behind other attempts to use price signals for green ends, such as the White House's new energy tax. Industry and consumers are free to search out the most cost-effective ways to conserve, rather than accepting the prescriptions of the regulators. Instead of grudgingly complying with the standards, moreover, they have every incentive to exceed them.

Unlike other schemes, however, the emissions permits plan allows the market to set the levy, recognizing that the same reduction in emissions costs different amounts to different plants. Firms may compare the marginal cost of reducing their emissions with the price of buying more credits. So long as it is less, they will go on reducing, and sell the credits thus "earned" to others at a profit. Plants that find it more costly to reduce can pay to shift the burden of compliance onto plants that can make greater reductions at lower cost.

Indeed, not only the industry can get into the game. One of the participants in the Chicago auction was a Cleveland-based environmental group, which put in a bid for 1100 permits. This may be the start of something big. By buying up emissions permits, those who place a high value on clean air can drive up the price of polluting it, and so make cleaning up more profitable for more plants. At long last, environmentalists can put their money where their mouth is.

SOURCE: Editorial, *The Globe and Mail*, April 7, 1993, page A18. Reprinted with the permission of *The Globe and Mail*.

unit of time (say, per month) is tolerable and then issues a batch of permits authorizing just that amount of total pollution. The permits are offered for sale to the highest bidders. Their price is therefore determined by demand and supply. It will be high if the number of permits offered for sale is small and there is a large number of industrial firms that must use the permits. Similarly, the price of a permit will be low if many permits are issued but the number of polluters demanding them is small.

In many ways, the emissions permit works the way a tax does — it simply makes it too expensive for polluters to continue emitting as much as they would have without it. In addition, the permit offers two clear advantages over the tax approach. First, it reduces uncertainty about the quantity that will be emitted. Under a tax, we cannot be sure about this in advance, since it depends on the extent to which polluters respond to the tax rate that is selected. In the case of permits, the ceiling on emissions is decided in advance by the environmental authorities, who enforce the ceiling simply by issuing permits authorizing a specific total quantity of emissions.

Second, any given tax on emissions will be eroded and made ineffective by inflation. For example, a tax of X dollars will become insignificant as inflation erodes the value of the dollar, even though it may have been effective when it was first enacted and the price level was much lower. With an emissions-permit system, however, as long as there is no change in the quantity of emissions authorized by licence, inflation will obviously have no effect on the amount of pollution. It will simply raise the price of a licence along with the prices of other commodities.

A shortcoming of the pollution-licence idea is its apparent political unattractiveness: Many people react indignantly to the notion of "licences to pollute." Yet the U.S. Environmental Protection Agency has introduced measures that are close approximations to a market in emissions permits (see the preceding boxed insert). These measures have been embraced by several international conferences on pollution problems in recent years.

TWO CHEERS FOR THE MARKET

We have seen that protecting the environment is one task that cannot be left to the free market; because of the important externalities involved, the market will systematically allocate too few resources to the job. This problem is particularly difficult to solve politically when the pollution extends beyond national borders. However, if pollution is localized, the market failure does not imply that the price mechanism must be discarded. On the contrary, we have seen that a legislated market solution —based on pollution charges—may well be the best way to protect the environment. At least in this case, the power of the market mechanism can be harnessed to correct its own failings.

THE ECONOMICS OF ENERGY AND NATURAL RESOURCES

We turn now, in the second half of this chapter, to the case of natural resources, where the market mechanism also plays a crucial role. The "energy crisis" of the 1970s, during which the price of oil leapt dramatically upward, had profound effects throughout the world—one of which was a marked change in our tendency to think that unlimited stocks of natural resources are simply ours for the taking. Indeed, in the mid-1970s, there was near-panic about the prospect of running out of a number of commodities. In fact, humanity has a long history of panicking about imminent exhaustion of natural resources. In the thirteenth century, a large part of Europe's forests was cut down, primarily for use in metal-working (much of it for armour). Wood prices rose, and there was a good deal of talk about the depletion of fuel stocks.

In this part of the chapter, we will try to sort out such matters. On the one hand, natural resources have always been scarce, and one can argue with good reason that they have been used wastefully. On the other hand, we are *not* about to run out of most vital resources, and there is reason to be optimistic about the availability of substitutes.

A PUZZLE: THOSE RESILIENT RESOURCE SUPPLIES

It is a plain fact that the earth is endowed with only finite quantities of such vital resources as oil, copper, lead, coal, and many others. This fact has fascinated pessimists through the years. In 1972, extreme pessimism assumed its most scientific guise in a publication by the Club of Rome called *The Limits to Growth*. Using computers to project future world conditions, the authors concluded "with some confidence" that if there is "no major change in the present system . . . industrial growth will certainly stop within the next century, at the latest." At the core of the problem, they said, would be our running out of resources.[1]

Table 17-1 shows the sort of data that are frequently used to support such doomsday forecasts. The bottom line of the table shows for four minerals the number of years of consumption (assuming unchanged rates of use) that could be met by known reserves of these resources as of 1980. Reading this table without knowing what lies behind it can indeed be alarming. It seems to say that we will run out of all of these vital minerals by the year 2051.

But now compare the two rows of the table. Surely something mysterious is going on! We see that, in 1960, only about a 24-year supply of zinc apparently remained. Yet 20 years later, despite all the zinc that had

---

1. Donella H. Meadows et al., *The Limits to Growth* (New York: Universe Books, 1972), pages 125–26.

TABLE 17-1

EXPECTED LIFE (IN YEARS) OF SOME WORLD MINERAL RESERVES, 1960 AND 1980 ESTIMATES

	Zinc	Nickel	Lead	Copper
1960	24	43	19	37
1980	42	71	47	59

Notice that we had more years' supply of each of these depletable resources in 1980 than in 1960, despite twenty years of consumption!

SOURCE: Bureau of Mines, U.S. Department of the Interior, *The Domestic Supply of Critical Minerals*, 1983, page 21.

been used in the meantime, the reserves of zinc were estimated to last another 42 years! Each of the other resources also had *larger* reserves in 1980 than in 1960, even though rates of consumption had risen in the interim. This does seem a funny way to keep score.

In part, we can ascribe this puzzle to the misleading nature of figures on "known reserves," although these are the sorts of statistics on resource depletion that are commonly cited by pessimists. But economic principles also help a great deal in clearing up the mystery.

THE FREE MARKET AND PRICING OF DEPLETABLE RESOURCES

If figures on known reserves behave as peculiarly as those we have just seen, one begins to doubt their ability to indicate whether we are really coming uncomfortably close to running out of certain resources. Is there some other indicator of growing scarcity that seems more reliable? Most economists agree that there is—that the price of the resource serves this function well.

As a resource becomes scarcer, we expect its price to rise for several reasons. One is that, for most resources, the process of depletion is not simply a matter of gradually using up the supply of a homogeneous product, every unit of which is equally available. Rather, the most accessible and highest-quality deposits of the resource are generally used up first; then industry turns to less accessible locations and/or deposits of lower purity or quality, and then finally to deposits that are still harder or more costly to extract or of still poorer quality. Oil is a clear example of this. First, Canadians relied primarily on the most easily found domestic oil wells. Then they turned to imports from South America and elsewhere, with their higher transport costs. At that point, it was not yet profitable to embark on the dangerous and extremely costly process of bringing up oil from the ocean floor off Newfoundland. We know that Canada still possesses huge stocks of petroleum embedded in the Alberta tar sands and in the Arctic, but until recently, they have been too difficult and therefore too costly to reach.

Increasing scarcity of a resource such as oil is not usually a matter of imminent and total disappearance. Rather, it takes the form of exhaustion of the most accessible and cheapest sources so that new supplies become more costly.

A second reason for rising resource prices is hidden in the operation of the supply–demand mechanism. To see how it works, let us consider the simpler (if less realistic) case in which extraction of a resource does not grow increasingly difficult as its reserves dwindle. That is, we envision the earth's supplies of a mythical mineral, Zipthon, whose reserves are of uniform quality and can be extracted and delivered to market with negligible extraction and transportation costs. How quickly will the reserves of Zipthon be used up, and what will happen to the price of the mineral with the passage of time?

If the market for Zipthon is perfectly competitive, we can provide a remarkably concrete answer about the behaviour of prices. The answer, which was discovered by American economist Harold Hotelling, tells us that as long as the supply of Zipthon lasts, its price must rise at a rate equal to the rate of interest. That is, if in 1990 the price of Zipthon is $100 per tonne and the rate of interest is 10 percent, its price in 1991 must be $110.

Under perfect competition, the price of a depletable resource whose costs of transportation and extraction are negligible must rise at the rate of interest. If the rate of interest is 10 percent, the price of the resource must rise 10 percent every year.

Why is this so? The answer is simple. People who have money tied up in inventories of Zipthon must earn exactly as much per dollar of investment as they would by putting their money into, say, a government bond. Suppose that $100 invested in bonds would next year rise in value to $112, while $100 in Zipthon would grow only to $110, and suppose the two investments were equally risky. What would happen? People who owned Zipthon would obviously find it profitable to sell the Zipthon and put their money into bonds instead.

But as more Zipthon was dumped on the market, it would become increasingly abundant for the present and increasingly scarce in the future. Thus, its expected future price would rise while its actual current price would fall. This and other associated changes in Zipthon prices and bond prices would continue until there was no further advantage in the one investment against the other—that is, until both offered the same rate of return per dollar of investment.

The same process, working in reverse, would apply if Zipthon prices were rising faster than the rate of interest. Investors would switch from bonds to Zipthon, and with more Zipthon held for investment rather than released for current consumption, current prices of Zipthon would rise. At the same time, the abundance of future stocks would be increased and thus expected future prices would fall.

Following this fundamental principle about the pricing of a scarce resource with fixed extraction costs, let us see what will happen to the price of $100 worth of Zipthon over the course of, say, four years. We have the following pattern of Zipthon prices:

Initial Date	One Year Later	Two Years Later	Three Years Later	Four Years Later
$100	$110	$121	$133.10	$146.41

These prices follow from the fact that $110 is 10 percent higher than $100, $121 is 10 percent higher than $110, and so on. Note that, because of the compounding effect, the dollar amount of the price increase is greater each year. Zipthon rises in value by $10.00 in the first year, $11.00 in the second year, $12.10 in the third, $13.31 in the fourth, and so on indefinitely. Thus, we conclude as follows:

The basic law of pricing of a depletable resource tells us that, as its stocks are used up, its price in a perfectly competitive market will rise every year by greater and greater dollar amounts.

Notice that we have been able to make these predictions about the price of Zipthon without any knowledge about the supply of Zipthon or consumer demand for it. This is remarkable. But if we want to go on to determine what will happen to the consumption of Zipthon—the rate at which its inventory will be used up—we need to know something about supply and demand.

In Figure 17-2(a), there is a demand curve for Zipthon, *DD*, which shows the amount that people want to use up per year at various price levels. On the vertical axis, we show how the price must rise from year to year in the pattern we have just calculated—from $100 per tonne in the initial year to $110 in the next year, and so on. Because of the negative slope of the demand curve, it follows that, each year, consumption of Zipthon will fall. That is, if there is no shift in the demand curve, consumption will fall from 100 000 tonnes initially, to 95 000 tonnes in the next year, and so on.

FIGURE 17-2

CONSUMPTION OVER TIME OF A DEPLETABLE RESOURCE

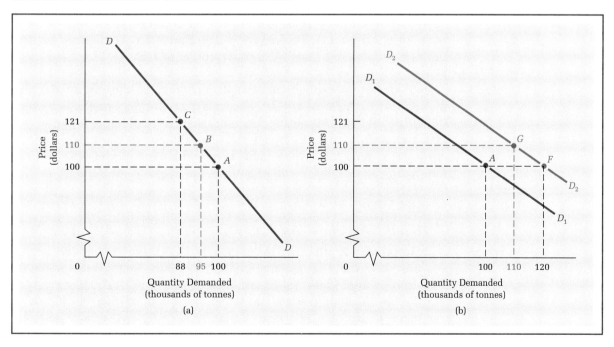

The price of the resource must rise, year after year (from $100 to $110 to $121, and so on). If the demand curve does not shift (part (a)), quantity demanded will be reduced every year. Even if the demand curve does shift outward (as in part (b)), the increasing price will keep any rise in quantity demanded lower than it would otherwise have been.

But in reality, such demand curves rarely do stay still. As the economy grows and population and per-capita incomes increase, demand curves can be expected to shift outward. Further, there is every reason to believe that this has been true of the demand for most scarce resources. Shifts in the demand curve naturally tend to increase consumption, thereby offsetting at least part of the reduction in quantity demanded that results from rising prices. Nevertheless, it remains true that rising prices do help to cut back consumption growth relative to what it would have been if price had remained constant. In Figure 17-2(b), we depict an outward shift in demand from curve D_1D_1 in the initial period to curve D_2D_2 a year later. If price had remained constant at the initial value, $100 per tonne, quantity consumed per year would have risen from 100 000 tonnes to 120 000 tonnes. But since, in accord with the basic principle, price must rise to $110, quantity demanded increases only to 110 000 tonnes — which is smaller than 120 000 tonnes. Thus, whether or not the demand curve shifts, we reach this conclusion:

The ever-rising prices that accompany increasing scarcity of a depletable resource discourage consumption (encourage conservation). Even if quantity demanded is growing, it will grow less rapidly than if prices were not rising.

How do the facts match up with this theoretical analysis? Their correspondence is very poor indeed. For example, the real prices of zinc and lead (that is, after the effects of general inflation or deflation have been eliminated) have remained roughly constant during this century, while other resource prices, such as the price of crude oil, have experienced large shifts (both up and down) every few years. Thus, in reality, resource prices have not risen steadily, as our simple theory might have led us to expect.

How does one explain the actual behaviour of the prices of finite resources, which surely are being used up, even if only gradually? What this price behaviour indicates is that reality is much more complicated than our simple analytic model and that sometimes the complications grow so extreme that prices behave very differently from what simple theory predicts. Of these complications, we mention only three:

1. *Unexpected discoveries of reserves whose existence was previously not suspected.* If we were to stumble on a huge and easily accessible reserve of Zipthon, which came as a complete surprise to the market, the price of Zipthon would obviously fall. This is illustrated in Figure 17-3, where we see that people originally believed the available supply curve to be that represented by curve S_1S_1. The discovery of the new Zipthon reserves leads them to recognize that the supply is much larger than they had thought (curve S_2S_2). Like any outward shift in a supply curve, this can be expected to cause a fall in price.

2. *The invention of new methods of mining or refining that may significantly reduce extraction costs.* This, too, can lead to a rightward

FIGURE 17-3

PRICE EFFECTS OF A DISCOVERY OF ADDITIONAL RESERVES

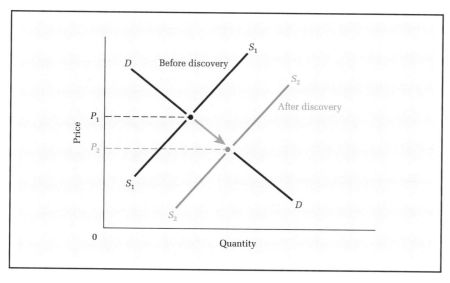

A discovery causes a rightward shift in the supply curve of the resource. Because the cost to suppliers of any given quantity of the resource is reduced by the discovery, it will pay them to supply a larger quantity at any given price. This must lead to a price fall (from P_1 to P_2).

shift in the supply curve as it becomes profitable for suppliers to deliver a larger quantity at any given price. The situation can also be represented by Figure 17-3, only it is now a reduction in cost, not a discovery of new reserves, that shifts the supply curve to the right.

3. *A government subsidy.* From the point of view of the supplier, a government subsidy is exactly the same as a reduction in mining or processing costs — either technological improvement or a handout from the government will decrease the cost per tonne of supplying the resource. Thus, the supply curve will shift to the right (from S_1S_1 to S_2S_2 in Figure 17-3) and the price will fall.

Yet, despite these influences, which postpone the price rises in depletable resources predicted by the theory, both logic and evidence indicate that in the long run, as a resource really becomes scarce and costly to obtain, its price must ultimately rise.

THE FREE MARKET AND RESOURCE DEPLETION

Popular views of the process of depletion of a vital resource envision a scenario in which consumption grows year after year and stocks of the item dwindle as a result until, one day, quantity supplied can no longer keep up with quantity demanded. From then on, the nation faces a history of steady shortfalls, with rationing or chaos being the inevitable result. Economists pay little attention to such scenarios. Although the following seems implausible to anyone who has not studied economics, it is nevertheless true:

In a free market, quantity demanded can never exceed quantity supplied, even if a finite resource is undergoing rapid depletion. The reason is simple: In any free market, quantity demanded must always equal quantity supplied, for price will automatically adjust to eliminate any difference between them.

In fact, there have been cases of real shortages in the past. For example, twice during the 1970s, the quantities of gasoline supplied were, in many parts of the United States, lower than the quantities demanded, and chaos did indeed result. There were long lines of cars at those gas stations that remained open, and huge amounts of petroleum and time were wasted in the process as the cars inched forward (sometimes for hours) toward the gas pumps. During World War II, meat, sugar, and other commodities were in short supply, and there was a period in the 1970s when supplies of paper, copper, and other commodities were inadequate to meet demand. But in every such case, there were regulations or laws that prohibited full adjustment of prices. In a sense, then, it was these price regulations, and not any disappearance of resources, that were responsible for the shortages.

In theory, any shortage—any excess of quantity demanded over quantity supplied—must be artificial; that is, it must be ascribed to a decision to prevent the price mechanism from doing its job.

To say that the cause is artificial does not, of course, settle the basic issue—whether freedom of price adjustments is desirable when resource depletion is under way, or whether interference with the pricing process is justified. We will see that there are, in fact, valid grounds on which to question the desirability of completely unrestricted freedom of pricing in such circumstances.

Many economists, however, believe that this is another of those cases in which the cure—deregulation of prices—is better than the disease—shortages and the resulting dislocations in the economy. They hold that the general public is misguided in its clamour against the rising prices that must ultimately accompany depletion of a resource, and that people are mistaken in regarding these price rises as the problem when in fact they are part of the cure.

It is, of course, easy to understand why no consumer loves a price rise. It is also easy to understand why many consumers ascribe any such price rise to a plot—to a conspiracy by greedy suppliers who somehow deliberately arrange shortages in order to force prices upward. Sometimes, this view is correct. For example, the members of the Organization of Petroleum Exporting Countries (OPEC) have openly and frankly undertaken to influence the flow of oil in order to increase the price they receive for it. But it is important to recognize from the principles of supply and demand that when a resource grows scarce, its price will tend to rise automatically, even without any conspiracies or plots.

Let us first see how economists can possibly say that rising prices for scarce resources are good for the economy. Then we will consider some valid reservations about the desirability of an unfettered-market solution as we discuss the controversy over Canadian energy policy.

ON THE VIRTUES OF RISING PRICES

Rising prices help control the process of resource depletion in three basic ways:

1. They discourage consumption and waste and provide an inducement for conservation.

2. They stimulate more efficient use of the resource by industry, providing incentives for the employment of processes that are more sparing in their use of the resource or that use substitute resources.

3. They encourage innovation—the discovery of other, more abundant resources that can do the job and of new techniques that permit these other resources to be used economically.

Let us examine each of these more carefully.

It used to be said that consumer demand for oil was highly *inelastic* —that prices would never make a significant dent in consumption of petroleum. Recent events seem to have proved otherwise. With rising fuel prices, people have begun to insulate their homes, to keep home temperatures lower, to take fewer shopping trips, and to buy smaller automobiles. Moreover, in the long run, we can expect even more demand adjustment—that is, the long-run demand curve for oil is probably more elastic than the short-run curve. As the nation's fleet of cars wears out, they will gradually be replaced by vehicles that economize on fuel. New homes will be built more snugly to save on heat, and they will be located closer to the workplace to save on fuel in transportation.

Evidence indicating how much difference price can make is provided by the pattern of fuel consumption in Europe. There, fuel taxes have long habituated the public to high gasoline prices, and fuel consumption per capita is much less than it is in North America.

The second way in which a price increase helps to conserve a scarce resource is through its effect on industrial usage. Like a final consumer, a business firm can economize on its use of a resource. It can use more fuel-efficient means of transportation and more insulation. It can locate its new plants in ways that reduce the need for transportation. And it can substitute labour and other inputs for scarce resources. The use of a pick and shovel involves the employment of more labour to save the fuel that might have been used by a bulldozer. Farmers who gather manure save the fuel necessary to produce chemical fertilizers. U.S. oil-consumption data provide clear evidence of the overall responsiveness of the demand for oil to its price. Between 1960 and 1973, U.S. demand increased by more than 75 percent, but after the OPEC price increases, from 1973 to 1985, demand declined by 10 percent.

Finally, rising prices help to slow the disappearance of a resource by stimulating the production of substitutes and even by inducing more production of the resource itself. The last statement is paradoxical — if a resource is finite, how can more be produced? Certainly, it can be extracted and sold faster, but that only hastens the process of depletion. How can we get more of a finite resource? Of course, we cannot. But rising prices make it feasible to use repositories of the resource that otherwise would have been considered not worth the effort. It has recently become economically feasible, for example, to extract oil from Canada's tar sands—formations that were formerly too expensive to exploit. Similarly, piping natural gas from the Arctic has long been talked about, but only higher prices will make it feasible.

Higher prices of a vanishing resource also stimulate research and development, leading to the emergence of substitute products. It is high oil prices that will transform solar energy, wind energy, and biomass energy from romantic notions, which cynics can deride as impractical, into effective sources of fuel that may someday make substantial contributions to the economy's energy flows. At the oil prices in effect during the 1960s, these sources simply could not compete.

A final word on the price mechanism and resource conservation is in order. One often hears about the rape of our natural resources by greedy owners who rush to exchange them for profits without any thought for the needs of the future. But the price mechanism has built-in incentives to prevent this from happening. We have seen how a resource's price can be expected to rise automatically as its stocks dwindle. Obviously, when the price rise is sufficiently rapid, it becomes more profitable to leave more of the resource underground for future extraction than to sell it at today's lower prices. One may legitimately object to this for many reasons, but surely not on the grounds that oil supplies are being squandered by excessive and irresponsible rates of extraction.

Freedom of pricing of a dwindling resource induces conservation by consumers and by industry; it encourages the introduction of substitute products; and it induces moderation in rates of extraction by the owners of the resources.

GROWING RESERVES OF EXHAUSTIBLE RESOURCES: OUR PUZZLE REVISITED

We began the second part of this chapter with a brief discussion of the more pessimistic views about future resource supplies, including an estimate made in 1960 that, by 1985, we would have run out of zinc and lead and would have only eighteen years of nickel reserves and twelve years of copper reserves left. Yet in Table 17-1 (page 588), we saw that between 1960 and 1980, the reserves of all of these finite resources actually increased.

This paradox, as we have seen, has a straightforward economic explanation: Rising reserves are a tribute to the success of exploration activity that took place in the meantime. Minerals are not discovered by accident. They are discovered by difficult and costly work requiring the services of geologists and engineers and the use of extremely expensive machinery. Exploration requires an enormous expenditure, which industry cannot justify when reserves are high and mineral prices are low.

Consequently, over the course of the twentieth century, proven reserves have not changed very much. Every time some mineral's known reserves fell, particularly if its price therefore tended to rise, exploration increased until the decline was offset.

CONTROVERSIES OVER CANADIAN RESOURCE POLICY

DEPLETABLE RESOURCES

Let us now consider how some of these arguments apply to the Canadian experience. Our 1974–84 controversy over oil prices stemmed from four basic facts. First, many Canadian consumers of oil felt that the high world price was artificial: It had been caused by a monopolistic cartel in foreign lands. Since Canada has the resources to be self-sufficient in oil, many felt that we should not be "held to ransom" by such monopoly practices. After all, the only reason we import oil in the East and export it in the West is that we lack sufficient pipeline facilities. It was argued that if we could solve this problem, our self-sufficiency in oil would permit a lower, "made in Canada" price.

The second major influence in the oil price debate was the fear of unemployment expressed by many workers in manufacturing firms in Central Canada and in the energy industries of the West. The concern in Central Canada was that large increases in energy prices would force firms to lay off some of their workers. We will see in Chapter 18 that this reasoning is correct: Rising costs of energy cause an inward shift of the aggregate supply curve, leading simultaneously to a rise in the overall price level and to a fall in real gross domestic product. But the decrease in output for the country as a whole would be much smaller than that which would occur in Central Canada. Meanwhile, energy workers in the West feared that low prices for energy in Canada would eliminate the profit incentive for their employers, so that exploration and other activities would diminish, with a consequent loss of jobs in the West. We learned earlier in this chapter that this reasoning is also correct. Thus, fear of unemployment and lower incomes boiled down to a distribution problem: Whose incomes should the governments protect — those of workers in Central Canada or those of workers in the West?

The third major issue in the oil price discussions was the fight between the federal and provincial (mainly Alberta) governments concerning tax revenue. Both levels of government wanted the tax revenue that could stem from higher oil prices. Natural resources are owned by the provinces, which can impose various taxes (known as royalties) on producers operating on provincial lands. But the federal government has jurisdiction over international and interprovincial trade, so it can levy export and import taxes and subsidies as oil crosses provincial and international borders. The two levels of government were forced to negotiate, because there is a limit to the total amount of tax that can be imposed. If taxes are very high, consumer prices must also skyrocket to provide some operating revenue to the producer. Thus, the total tax is bounded by concern for both consumers and producers.

The fourth important factor in the oil price issue was the high degree of foreign ownership in the energy industry. Approximately 70 percent of the shares of oil companies operating in Canada were foreign-owned. The federal government thought a low oil price was a good idea because it would limit the profits of these companies and so preclude a large transfer of income from Canadians to foreigners.

How did the energy policy of the Liberal federal government accommodate these four concerns? The Canadian price of oil was allowed to increase, but only very gradually, so that by 1981, it was at only half the level of world oil prices. This pricing policy followed from two considerations: (1) the federal government's sympathy with the view that Canadian resource endowments give us the right and ability to ignore world prices, and (2) its view that potential unemployment in manufacturing operations in Ontario was more important, on political grounds, than potential unemployment in the energy industries in the West. The government's attempt to overcome the problem of the lack of a pipeline to Atlantic Canada involved imposing export taxes on oil and gas from the West to pay for an import subsidy for foreign oil purchased in the East.

With regard to the distribution of energy tax revenues between Ottawa and the provinces, the federal government simply saw the world price developments as an opportunity to tap a lucrative new tax source. It imposed the Petroleum and Natural Gas Revenue Tax at such a level that producer returns became negative.[2] This forced provincial governments (principally Alberta's) to reduce their taxes, simply to try to stimulate economic activity within their own regions.

Two components of the federal National Energy Program were directed at the issue of foreign profits. One was direct purchases of oil operations from foreigners (this included such measures as the creation of Petro-Canada), and the other involved levying a tax on producing firms that was designed to avoid limiting the return on *new* exploration and development. The idea in this case was to tax oil discovered before 1981 much more heavily than that found later. The "old" oil is produced at much lower cost than that from recent operations. Thus, economic rents exist on these older operations, since the going market price is sufficient to

---

2. See Brian L. Scarfe, "The National Energy Program after Three Years: An Economic Perspective," *Western Economic Review*, 1984.

make viable the more recent, more expensive extractions. From a micro-economic point of view, the attempt to tax only rents made sense, as long as the tax was not set too high (review Chapter 14, pages 421–27, if necessary).

How did the federal government's decisions turn out? Were they consistent with sound economic analysis? Again, let us consider each part of the problem in turn. Of course, our energy supplies make it *possible* for Canadians to pay a price below world levels. Nevertheless, the option of selling at the world price was available, so it represented the true opportunity cost of Canadians' using domestic energy. (Consuming energy resources domestically means that we cannot sell those resources to foreigners at the world price. The world price therefore represents the buying power that we forego.) A lower price simply prevented the "correct" signals of relative scarcities from reaching individual Canadian decision-makers. Only if the high world price could have been viewed as very temporary (say, because of an expectation that OPEC would collapse as a result of internal struggles over production quotas for member countries) would it have made sense to insulate our economy from a needless series of adjustments.

The federal government's views concerning unemployment in central Canada versus unemployment in the West appear to have been somewhat short-sighted. Job prospects are not enhanced in Canadian manufacturing if artificially low energy prices encourage the perpetuation of production techniques that are inefficient by international standards. Finally, unemployment in central Canada was increased when the depressed energy industry in the West sent fewer orders back East for industrial equipment and when job-seekers ceased their migration to the West.

Some "Canadianization" of the energy industry did follow from the National Energy Program, but any contribution this might have made to establishing "security of supply" was certainly nullified in the short run by the cutbacks in exploration and development that stemmed from low producer prices and high taxes. Unfortunately, the nationalization program and the retroactive taxing of the oil industry's most profitable operations (involving "old" oil) came at a most inopportune time—just as deregulation was occurring in the United States. Combined with the negative returns, this was enough to cause a significant shift in economic activity to the United States.

In summary, with the passage of time, any validity of the "made in Canada" oil price diminished. By late 1984, Canadian prices were roughly in line with world prices, but the lag in getting there had been too long. Among the problems that resulted from this lag were a cutback in oil development, a delay in moving toward less energy-intensive production methods, and a setback in federal–provincial co-operation. When the Conservatives came to federal power in 1984, they reversed many of the Liberal policies. By 1986, all of the major components of the National Energy Program had been dismantled.

RENEWABLE RESOURCES

In the 1990s, it seems that more attention is being paid to several other Canadian resources — fisheries, fresh water, and forests. In principle, these are all renewable resources, but there is serious concern that, in practice, depletion is foreseeable in these areas as well. For example, our fishery stocks are certainly being run down and, again, a fundamental externality problem is involved. To protect the size of the stocks in the future, we need government regulations today limiting the size of current catches. But property rights cannot be easily defined, since the fish swim on both sides of the boundary that separates Canadian and international waters. In 1990, for example, the countries of the European Community decided to take three times more fish from the international waters off Newfoundland than the amount recommended by the North Atlantic Fisheries Organization, a seventeen-member international agency to which the European Community belongs. There is no mechanism allowing Canada to appeal this sort of transgression. Hence, to ensure our resources of fish are protected for the future, our government has little option but to impose stiffer quotas on domestic fishing. For some communities in Atlantic Canada, the effect of these developments is devastating.

Similar problems plague our supply of fresh water. The St. Lawrence River—the source of drinking water for about half of Quebec's 6.7 million people—is so polluted that beluga whales are dying at a rapid rate. Similarly, in British Columbia, Greenpeace calls the Fraser River "the biggest sewer line" in the province.

With regard to forests, public concern had become so great by 1990 that proposals for a significant slowdown in the rate of future development of our forestry resources were under serious consideration. One example of the problems involved comes from Alberta. In an attempt to prevent the province's economy from becoming too dependent on a single resource — oil — the Alberta government sold forest-cutting rights on a grand scale: Between 1987 and 1990, rights for an area almost the size of Great Britain were sold off. In addition to the threat of deforestation, other environmental concerns ensued. In 1990, the federal government intervened in the provincial government's activities to investigate the environmental impact of a large pulp-mill complex that was planned on the Athabasca River about 100 kilometres northeast of Edmonton. Pulp mills introduce hundreds of chemical compounds known collectively as organochlorines—a major source of dioxins—into the water system.

The dispute over this kind of resource development represents the classic trade-off: short-run job creation versus potentially long-term environmental damage (in this case, to drinking water and Native fisheries). Central Canada could ease the terms of this trade-off for Alberta — and the similar trade-off facing Atlantic Canada that we discussed earlier — by facilitating the diversification of those regional economies. If the more environmentally friendly economic activities that are currently more prevalent in central Canada were encouraged throughout the country, the

burden of protecting our resource stocks would be more evenly distributed, and would consequently be made more manageable.

SERIOUS PROBLEMS REMAIN

We close this chapter with some thoughts about the future. First, we
might note that there are some grounds for optimism about the availability of energy. Past history and research already under way suggest that
new techniques will become feasible as higher prices encourage the
development of alternative energy sources. Already, solar heating has
become economically viable in certain cases (especially for private homes
in sunny climates), and its use can be expected to spread. Also, scientists
are studying the use of geothermal energy, and nuclear fusion promises
a virtually unlimited supply of energy if we can learn to harness it. In
all these ways, then, higher prices will lead to a lower quantity demanded
and a greater quantity supplied of energy, thus helping to avert an
"energy crisis."

Yet we certainly do not want to paint too rosy a picture. Adjustment
to higher relative prices can be painful, as owners of gas-guzzling cars
and fuel-inefficient homes have already found out. In peering into the
crystal ball, we can see that goods and services that rely either directly
or indirectly on fossil fuels are likely to be relatively more expensive.
This can hardly be considered good news. But the point to emphasize is
that we *can* see an end to this process. And this end is not a cataclysmic
one in which we run out of energy and industrial activity ceases. Instead,
it is one in which new technology based on non-depletable energy
resources, such as the sun and the atom, takes over the business of pow-
ering vehicles, heating homes, and turning the wheels of industry. Energy
will probably be more expensive than it is today, but it will be available.

The truly cataclysmic possibilities that follow from natural-resource
use are not generally problems of availability; rather, they are the effects
on the environment of using these resources. For example, earlier in this
chapter, we mentioned that burning fossil fuels is raising the concentration of carbon dioxide in the earth's atmosphere, thereby increasing
global temperatures (the greenhouse effect). As we noted, many observers
now predict that, within 50 years, gradually increasing temperatures may
well have disastrous effects on crops, will begin to melt the polar icecaps
(causing massive flooding along coastlines), and will have other calami-
tous consequences. The reason we cannot expect the market mechanism
to prevent these problems automatically is because of the *externalities*
involved.

There are two dimensions to the externality issue. One is the cross-
country spillover problem that we have already discussed. The other is
a cross-generations spillover. Conventional cost–benefit study involves
discounting all future effects back to the present. This convention implicitly gives the present generation preferential treatment concerning the use
of environmental resources (compared to future generations). Also, since

investments in environmental improvement usually involve large initial costs but benefits that can be measured only imprecisely and that can be expected to materialize only after several years, often these investments appear to be "not worth the costs." But these "biases" in conventional cost–benefit study *can* be avoided, as long as we use a very low discount rate in the calculations.

ALTERNATIVES FOR THE FUTURE

We hope that the analysis contained in this chapter will help you come to a reasoned view on these very serious issues. The global nature of externality effects and the magnitude of the income redistribution to the less developed countries that must occur if those countries are to take part in the limiting of pollution are cause for great concern. But there is no point in *not* doing whatever it is possible to do *now*, and in this regard, the most fundamental decision confronting us is whether the very nature of our economic system is at fault.

Many observers, including scientist, author, and broadcaster David Suzuki, argue that our environmental problems call for an entire reorientation of human nature and economic life. According to this widespread view, we must

1. purge our system of its dependence on human greed as a motivating factor;
2. reject economic growth as a goal for society; and
3. reject mainstream economics as a useful discipline in the area of environmental protection.

For example, Suzuki writes as follows:

> Economists consider the environment to be essentially limitless, endless, self-renewing, and free. . . .
>
> Economic growth has become an end in itself, a mindless goal that is sought by every country in the world and the very measure of progress. Yet any thoughtful person knows that it is a deadly notion that cannot be sustained in a finite world.[3]

Not surprisingly, many economists think that this criticism of their discipline goes too far. It is true that only fairly recently have people—including economists — appreciated how far-reaching and essentially irreversible some of our environmental and resource-conservation problems are. But we must also appreciate that some economic growth is required to enable the less developed countries to play their very necessary part in the solution to these problems.

3. David Suzuki, "Reflections: You Can't Put a Price on Earth," *The Hamilton Spectator*, September 9, 1989.

ECONOMICS AND THE ENVIRONMENT: A RECONCILIATION?

Most people see an unbridgeable chasm between the desire of ecologists and environmentalists to have clean air and water and to control toxic wastes, on the one hand, and the pursuits of economists and business people concerned with economic development and prosperity, on the other hand. These two views are seen as impossible to reconcile, and the attitude of most people is that one of them has to give way to the other. I suggest that it is possible to reconcile the two—a reconciliation that upholds the goals of environmentalists but not necessarily their means. . . .

The first principle [that guides this analysis] is that of private property and the incentives engendered thereby. . . .

[Take] . . . the case of Soviet agriculture. In the pre-*perestroika* days . . . on the 98 percent of the land that was communally owned, only 75 percent of the crops were produced. On the 2 percent of the land that was privately owned in the form of small gardens around the workers' houses, fully 25 percent of the crops were grown. This illustrates the difference in incentives that operates when something is privately owned versus when it is publicly owned. . . .

The second principle is the tragedy of the commons. One way to illustrate this is to suppose that we are all shepherds, grazing our sheep on a common meadow. Some public-spirited citizen decides that the grass is being grazed too closely by the sheep. He takes his sheep elsewhere, at some expense, in order to preserve the meadow. But what typically happens is that other people then allow their sheep to graze on the meadow that has just been vacated by this public-spirited citizen, and the grass is not saved. As you can see, there is very little incentive to act in a public-spirited way in a common meadow. If you owned the entire meadow and saw that it was becoming overgrazed, you would stop the sheep from grazing there and let that grass build up while they grazed elsewhere. That you will not do so under the institution of public property is the tragedy of the commons.

Perhaps a more direct illustration of this principle is to imagine four or five children age 10 or 12, each sipping a soda pop. They each have their own can and are drinking at their own rates. That is scenario one. In scenario two, we take the soda pop cans away from them, pour all the soda into a common cup, and give each child a straw. Then we watch them go at it. What differences are we likely to see? These little kids are going to be sucking up the pop at a much greater rate. Those of you who have children will realize that the rate of drinking will be very different. In scenario two, if you don't drink it very

(continued)

(continued)

quickly, you can't have it later; someone else will grab it in the meanwhile. . . .

Let us now consider species extinction. Thanks to the modern miracle of television we have all seen the results of actions of poachers in Africa, the herds of elephants left to die with

their tusks cut off with a chain saw. Pregnant cows are killed, the meat and leather go to waste, and the tusks don't get their true market value but only their black market value. Entire herds of elephants have been killed in this fashion.

Here we have a problem of the tragedy of the commons and a lack of the incentives that only private ownership can supply. The poachers are aided and abetted in their activities by the villagers because these elephants are not privately owned. Villagers cannot profit from the elephants. Instead, the central governments of these African republics expropriate the value. The poachers in the African jungle see these animals as predators. The elephants destroy the crops of the villagers. So there are costs to the villagers of the elephants but no gains for them. The incentive is to encourage poachers to slaughter elephants. . . .

Several African countries have . . . allowed privatization of the animals. Hunting rights are sold to the native peoples, who can then rent them out to people who want to join safaris. These countries have given an incentive to their people to preserve the elephants because now they have a value to them. Under such conditions, elephant herds are actually increasing. . . .

Some people say that the reason the elephant is being hunted to extinction is because of its highly valued ivory tusk or, in the case of the rhinoceros, because of its horn. This is true under a regime of non-ownership. But when these animals are privately owned, the ivory tusk is the reason for their preservation. When people have an incentive and can profit from the existence of the elephant, they will protect it and make sure that pregnant females are not killed. Are the cow, goat, and chicken harmed to the point of extinction because of their value to us? On the contrary, they are preserved because of this value. . . .

Let's now look briefly at recycling and hazardous wastes. Here, again, the market is blamed. People point to plastic foam cups and plastic bags and other items that are not biodegradable [or] environmentally friendly and suggest it is an evil chase after the "unholy buck" that explains their presence. I would like to offer a different assessment of this problem. . . .

The . . . government has engaged in nationalizing or municipalizing or socializing the solid waste management industry. It costs you no more to put plastic into your curbside garbage can than it does to put in paper. . . .

Suppose private enterprise was in total control of the disposal of solid wastes. Then the person with whom you contract to pick up your garbage at the curbside would say to you: "If I accept your plastic—and I am willing to do that—when I bring it to the dump, the dump owner will charge me for the plastic because it will ruin his land, so I will have to charge you more for it, householder." Under this scenario, the next time you are faced with the choice of a plastic or paper bag, the true costs of your choice will impinge upon you, and you will act environmentally rationally

(continued)

(continued)

or at least you will tend in that direction. Right now there is no financial incentive to do so. . . .

The next issue I'd like to address is the greenhouse effect and the ozone layer. . . .

One proposed solution to the greenhouse effect is to maintain large acreages devoted to forests because trees take in carbon dioxide and give off oxygen. This raises the question of why our forests are disappearing. I think the culprit is government ownership of forest preserves, not greed and profits, as people like David Suzuki maintain. . . .

If a forestry company owns a hundred square miles of forest and cuts it all down without replanting, the present discounted value of that land plummets. If a company does that once too often, it risks courting bankruptcy. In sharp contrast, suppose the government owns the land and gives the company a contract to do with that land as it wishes for six months. In this situation it is in the best interests of the company to clear cut, and the economic incentives to reforest are greatly attenuated. . . .

There are many serious environmental groups with impeccable credentials that have seen that the best way to preserve woodlands is to buy them and administer them. The Audubon Society has a vast holding in Alabama and oil was discovered on it. Instead of saying that oil is evil and we're not going to have anything to do with it, they made a deal with an oil company to exploit this resource, in a very clean way, so they could buy more property for wildlife preserves. People open to the evidence will eventually be convinced that there is a case to be made for employing the tools and analysis of economics in the marketplace to preserve these holdings.

SOURCE: Walter E. Block, "Environment Problems, Free Market Solutions," *Fraser Forum*, The Fraser Institute (February 1990), pages 4–17. Reprinted with the permission of The Fraser Institute.

Thus, we have chosen to end the microeconomics part of this book with the preceding boxed insert, which presents excerpts from one of the published responses to critics such as Suzuki. The article is by economist Walter Block of the Fraser Institute in Vancouver, an economic research and educational institution dedicated to directing public attention to the positive contribution that competitive markets can make to economic well-being. Some readers will find Block's enthusiasm for unfettered private markets to be somewhat exaggerated. The important thing is that, by now, you will have developed an understanding of the issues and arguments involved, and of the ways in which mainstream economics can contribute to sorting them out.

Our problems in the areas of pollution and resource conservation are indeed serious, but as a method of scientific inquiry, the discipline of economics does *not* perpetuate these problems. On the contrary, by focussing as they do on incentive mechanisms, economists can make, and have made, very constructive suggestions about the ways in which some of our laws and our tax system might usefully be changed. Indeed, as we try to demonstrate throughout this book, experience has shown that the public interest is best served when we accept human nature as we know it and when we design our laws and institutions in such a way that private interests and the public interest are made to coincide.

SUMMARY

1. Pollution is as old as human history, and both planned and market economies suffer from substantial environmental problems.

2. The production of commodities *must* cause waste-disposal problems unless everything is recycled. Even recycling processes cause pollution (and use up energy).

3. Industrial activity causes environmental damage, but so does the activity of private individuals (as when they drive cars that emit pollutants). Government agencies also damage the environment (as when municipal sewage is dumped untreated or a hydroelectric project floods large areas).

4. Pollution is an externality—when a factory emits smoke, it may damage the health of people who neither work for the factory nor buy its products. Hence, pollution control cannot be left to the free market. This is one of our twelve Ideas for Beyond the Final Exam.

5. Pollution can be controlled by voluntary programs, direct controls, taxes on emissions, or other monetary incentives for the reduction of emissions. Most economists believe that the tax approach (or the related but more flexible emissions-permit system) is the most efficient and effective way to control detrimental externalities.

6. The quantity demanded of a scarce resource can exceed the quantity supplied only if something prevents the market mechanism from operating freely.

7. As a resource grows scarce on a free market, its price will rise, inducing increased conservation by consumers, increased exploration for new reserves, and increased substitution of other items that can serve the same purpose.

8. In fact, in the twentieth century, the relative prices of many resources have remained roughly constant, largely because of the discovery of new reserves and because of cost-saving innovations.

9. The price mechanism and rationing are the only known alternatives to chaos in the allocation of scarce resources.

10. In the 1970s, OPEC succeeded in raising the relative price of petroleum, but the rise in price led to a substantial decline in world demand as well as to an increase in production in countries outside OPEC.

11. Canada's energy policy during the late 1970s and early 1980s kept domestic energy prices below world levels, while producers were heavily taxed. Energy consumers obtained a short-term benefit, but longer-run costs included a cutback in exploration and development and reduced investment in energy-efficient production techniques in Canadian manufacturing.

12. Some commentators argue that concern for the environment and acceptance of mainstream economic analysis are somehow incompatible. According to this view, environmental problems cannot be solved until the existing focus on private profit is eliminated and individuals are persuaded to care more about the "public good." Mainstream economics rejects this view, arguing that success in solving these problems is facilitated by *harnessing* the profit motive rather than wishing it were not with us. The goal of mainstream economic policy is to arrange our laws in such a way that the public interest and private interests complement, rather than compete with, each other.

CONCEPTS FOR REVIEW

Externality
Direct controls

Pollution charges (taxes on
  emissions)
Marketable emissions permits

Paradox of growing reserves
  of finite resources

QUESTIONS FOR DISCUSSION

1. What sorts of pollution problems would you expect in a small African village? In a city in India? In communist China? In Toronto?

2. Suppose you are assigned the task of drafting a law to impose a tax on the emission of smoke. What provisions would you put into the law?
   a. How would you decide the size of the tax?
   b. What would you do about smoke emitted by a municipal electricity plant?
   c. Would you use the same tax rate in densely and sparsely settled areas?
   What information would you need to collect before determining what you would do about each of the preceding provisions?

3. Production of commodity X creates 10 kilograms of emissions for every unit of X produced. The demand and supply curves for X are described by the following table:

Price (dollars)	Quantity Demanded	Quantity Supplied
10	80	100
9	85	95
8	90	90
7	95	85
6	100	80
5	105	75

   What are the equilibrium price and quantity, and how much pollution will be emitted?

4. If the price of X to consumers is $9 and the government imposes a tax of $2 per unit, show that because suppliers get only $7, they will produce only 85 units of output, not the 95 units of output they would produce if they received the full $9 per unit.

5. Show that, with this tax, the equilibrium price is $9 and the equilibrium quantity demanded is 85. How much pollution will not be emitted?

6. Compare your answers to Questions 3 and 5 and show how large a reduction in pollution emissions occurs because of the $2 tax on the polluting output.

7. Discuss some valid and some invalid objections to letting rising prices eliminate shortages of supplies of scarce resources.

8. Describe what must be done by a government agency that is given the job of rationing a scarce resource.

9. Some observers believe that a program of rationing may work fairly satisfactorily for a few months or for one or two years, particularly during an emergency period when patriotic spirit is strong. However, they believe that over longer periods and when there is no upsurge of patriotism, it is likely to prove far less satisfactory. Do you agree or disagree? Why?

GLOSSARY

A 45° line A ray through the origin with a slope of +1. It marks off points where the variables measured on each axis have equal values, assuming that both variables are measured in the same units. (27)

Ability-to-pay principle of taxation The idea that people with greater ability to pay taxes should pay higher taxes. (484)

Absolute advantage One country is said to have an absolute advantage over another in the production of a particular good if it can produce that good using smaller quantities of resources than can the other country. (365)

Abstraction Ignoring many details in order to focus on the most important factors in a problem. (13)

Affirmative action Active efforts to locate and hire members of minority groups. (512)

Aggregate demand The total amount that all consumers, business firms, government agencies, and foreigners are willing to spend on final goods and services. (670)

Aggregate demand curve Graphic presentation of the quantity of national product that is demanded at each possible value of the price level. (615)

Aggregate supply The total amount that all business firms are willing to produce. (734)

Aggregate supply curve Graphic presentation, for each possible price level, of goods and services that all the nation's businesses are willing to produce at given factor prices. (615, 734)

Aggregation Combining many individual markets into one overall market. Economic aggregates are the focus of macroeconomics. (613)

Allocation of resources The decision regarding how to divide the economy's scarce input resources among the different outputs produced in the economy and among the differ-

ent firms or other organizations that produce those outputs. (39)

Appreciation (of a nation's currency) Is said to occur when exchange rates change so that a unit of its own currency can buy more units of foreign currency. (855)

Asset An item of value that an individual or a firm owns.

Automatic stabilizer Any arrangement that automatically supports aggregate demand when it would otherwise sag and holds down aggregate demand when it would otherwise surge ahead; thus, it reduces the sensitivity of the economy to shifts in demand. (901)

Autonomous increase in consumption An increase in consumer spending without any increase in incomes. It appears on a graph as a shift of the entire consumption function. (724)

Average-cost (AC) curve Shows, for each output, the cost per unit, that is, total cost divided by output. (168)

Average physical product (APP) Total physical product (TPP) divided by the quantity of input used. Thus, $APP = TPP/Q_i$, where Q_i is the quantity of input. (161)

Average propensity to consume (APC) The ratio of overall consumption to disposable income. (682)

Average propensity to save (APS) The ratio of overall savings to disposable income. (682)

Average revenue (AR) Total revenue (TR) divided by quantity. (204)

Balance of payments *See* Deficit, balance-of-payments; Surplus, balance-of-payments.

Balance sheet An accounting statement listing the values of all the assets on the left-hand side and the values of all the liabilities and net worth on the right-hand side. (832)

Bank of Canada Canada's central bank. (847)

Bank rate The rate of interest charged by the Bank of Canada when

reserves are loaned to the chartered banks (advances from the central bank). It is used as a signal of the direction of monetary policy. (853)

Barter A system of exchange in which people directly trade one good for another, without using money as an intermediate step. (821)

Benefits principle of taxation The idea that people who derive the benefits from a service should pay the taxes that finance it. (485)

Bilateral monopoly A market situation in which there is a monopoly on the selling side and a monopsony on the buying side. (461)

Bond A corporation's promise to pay the holder a fixed sum of money at the specified *maturity* date, and some other fixed amount of money (the *coupon* or *interest payment*) every year up to the date of maturity. (801)

Brain drain Occurs when the educated natives of a less developed country emigrate to wealthier nations. (1054)

Budget deficit The amount by which the government's expenditures exceed its receipts during a specified period of time, usually one year. (958)

Budget line A graphic representation of all the possible combinations of two commodities that a household can purchase, given the prices of the commodities and some fixed amount of money at its disposal. (116)

Burden of a tax The amount of money individuals would have to be given to make them just as well off with the tax as they would be without it. (485)

Capital The inventory (stock) of plant, equipment, and other productive resources held by a business firm, an individual, or some other organization. (435)

Capital gain An increase in the market value of a piece of property, such as a common share of stock or a parcel of land, that occurs during the period between when it is bought and when it is sold; also, the profit made on the sale of such an asset. (477, 786)

Capital good An item that is used to produce other goods and services in the future, rather than being consumed today. (45)

Capital loss A decrease in the market value of a piece of property that occurs between the time it is bought and the time it is sold; also, the loss incurred on the sale of such an asset. (786)

Capitalism Method of economic organization in which private individuals own the means of production, either directly or indirectly through corporations. (273)

Cartel A group of sellers of a product who have joined together to control its production, sale, and price in the hope of obtaining the advantages of monopoly. (320)

Central bank A bank for banks. Canada's central bank is the Bank of Canada. (847)

Commodity money An object in use as a medium of exchange that also has a substantial value in alternative (non-monetary) uses. (822)

Common stock A piece of paper that gives the holder a share in the ownership of a corporation. (801)

Comparative advantage One country is said to have a comparative advantage over another in the production of a particular good relative to other goods it can produce if it produces that good least inefficiently in comparison with the other country. (365)

Competition policy Government policy that attempts to control the growth of monopoly and to prevent firms from engaging in "undesirable" practices through the use of legislation and various programs. (548)

Complements Two goods are called complements if an increase in the price of one reduces the quantity demanded of the other, all other things remaining constant. (147)

Concentration of industry The share of the industry's total output (in money terms) supplied by some given number (usually four) of its largest firms. (559)

Concentration ratio The percentage of an industry's output produced by its four largest firms. It is intended to measure the degree to which the industry is dominated by large firms—that is, how closely it approximates a monopoly. (561)

Consumer expenditure (consumption) The total amount spent by consumers on newly produced goods and services (excluding purchases of new homes, which are considered investment goods). Symbolized by the letter C. (670)

Consumer Price Index The most popular index number for the price level. Its weights are based on the spending patterns of a typical urban household. (664)

Consumer sovereignty Consumer preferences determine what goods shall be produced, and in what amounts. (261)

Consumer surplus The amount by which an individual's total willingness to pay for an item exceeds what he or she has to pay to buy it. (107)

Consumption function The relationship between total consumer expenditure and total disposable income in the economy, holding all other determinants of consumer spending constant. (680)

Consumption good An item that is available for immediate use by households and that satisfies wants of members of households without contributing directly to future production by the economy. (45)

Corporation A firm that has the legal status of a fictional person. It is owned by shareholders and run by elected officers and a board of directors, whose chairperson often influences the affairs of the firm. (799)

Correlation Two variables are said to be correlated if they tend to go up or down together. But correlation need not imply causation. (17)

Cost disease of personal services Tendency of the cost of services such as auto repair and legal counsel to rise faster than the economy's overall inflation rate because it is difficult to increase productivity (output per person hours) in these services. (355)

Countervailing duty A tariff levied on imports to offset the effects of what are perceived as unrealistically low prices set by producers in the exporting country. (390)

Cross elasticity of demand The cross elasticity of demand for product X to a change in the price of another product, Y, is the ratio of the percentage change in quantity demanded of product X to the percentage change in the price of product Y that brings about the change in quantity demanded. (147)

Cross subsidization (rate averaging) Selling one product at a loss, which is balanced by higher profits on another product. (531)

Crowding out Occurs when deficit spending by the government forces private investment spending or exports to contract. (974)

Cyclically adjusted budget The hypothetical budget we *would* have if the economy were operating with an average level of unemployment. (966)

Deficit, balance-of-payments The amount by which the quantity supplied of foreign exchange (per year) falls short of the quantity demanded. Balance-of-payments deficits arise whenever the value of foreign exchange is pegged at an artificially low level—that is, when the value of the *domestic* currency is pegged at an artificially high level. (858)

Deflating (by a price index) Dividing some nominal magnitude by a price index in order to express that magnitude in dollars of constant purchasing power. (665)

Deflation A sustained decrease in the general price level. (622)

Demand curve A graphical depiction of a *demand schedule*. It shows how the quantity demanded of some product during a specified period of time will change as the price of that product changes, holding all other determinants of quantity demanded constant. (61)

Demand, "Law" of States that a lower price generally increases the amount of a commodity that people in a market are willing to buy. So, for most goods, demand curves have a negative slope. (133)

Demand schedule A table showing how the quantity demanded of some product during a specified period of time changes as the price of that product changes, holding all other determinants of quantity demanded constant. (60)

Depletability An attribute of private goods, as opposed to public goods. A commodity is depletable if it is used up when someone consumes it. (343)

Deposit creation Process by which the banking system turns a dollar of reserves into several dollars of deposits. (833)

Deposit insurance A system that guarantees that depositors will not lose money even if their bank goes bankrupt. (830)

Deposit-switching The Bank of Canada's switching of Government of Canada bank balances between the central bank and the private chartered banks. (852)

Depreciation allowances Tax deductions that businesses may claim when they spend money on investment goods. (695, 785)

Depreciation (of capital goods) The value of the portion of the nation's capital equipment that is used up within the year. It indicates how much output is needed just to keep the economy's capital stock intact. (656)

Depreciation (of a nation's currency) Is said to occur when exchange rates change so that a unit of its own currency can buy fewer units of foreign currency. (855)

Diminishing marginal utility, "Law" of Asserts that additional units of a commodity are worth less and less to a consumer in money terms. As the individual's consumption increases, the marginal utility of each additional unit declines. (103)

Direct taxes Taxes levied directly on people. (473)

Discounting Process of determining the present worth of a quantity of money receivable or payable at some future date. (405, 437)

Discouraged worker An unemployed person who gives up looking for work and is therefore no longer counted as part of the labour force. (630)

Discrimination, economic Occurs when equivalent factors of production receive different payments for equal contributions to output. (508)

Discrimination, statistical Occurs when the productivity of a particular worker is estimated to be low just because that worker belongs to a particular group (such as women). (511)

Disguised unemployment Occurs when tasks are carried out by a larger number of persons than the number that can complete them most efficiently. (1052)

Disposable income The sum of the incomes of all the individuals in the economy after all taxes have been deducted. (659, 671)

Diversification An increase in the number and variety of stocks, bonds, and other such items in an individual's portfolio of investments. (805)

Division of labour Breaking up a task into a number of smaller, more **specialized** tasks so that each worker can become more adept at his or her particular job. Division of labour creates efficiency and increases productivity. (48)

Dual labour market theory A theory asserting that workers generally work in one of two types of jobs—those that offer opportunities for acquisition of skills and promotions, and "dead end jobs," which offer little scope for improvement. (451)

Dumping Selling goods in a foreign market at lower prices than those charged in the home market. (395)

Economic growth Occurs when an economy is able to produce more goods and services for each consumer. (45)

Economic model A representation of a theory or part of a theory, often for the purpose of illuminating some aspect of the economy. Economic models are often expressed in equations, by graphs, or in words. (17)

Economic profit The total revenue a firm or an industry derives from the sale of its products minus the total cost of its inputs, including the opportunity cost of any inputs supplied by the proprietors. (203, 228)

Economic rent What is said to be earned whenever a factor of production receives a reward that exceeds the minimum amount necessary to keep the factor in its present employment. (425)

Economies of scale (also referred to as *increasing returns to scale*) Savings acquired through increases in quantities produced; in other words, when all input quantities are doubled, the quantity of output is more than doubled. (183, 529)

Economies of scope Savings acquired through simultaneous production of many different products. (528)

Efficiency The absence of waste, achieved primarily by gains in productivity resulting from specialization, division of labour, and a system of exchange. (47)

Efficient allocation of resources One that takes advantage of every opportunity to make some individuals better off, in their own estimation, while not worsening the lot of anyone else. (255)

Elasticity of demand, (price) The ratio of the *percentage* change in quantity demanded to the *percentage* change in price that brings about the change in quantity demanded. (138)

Entrepreneurship The act of starting new firms, introducing new products and technological innovations, and, in general, taking the risks that are necessary in seeking out business opportunities. (442)

Equation of exchange Statement that the money value of GDP transactions must be equal to the product of the average stock of money times velocity—that is, $M \times V = P \times Y$. (884)

Equilibrium A situation in which there are no inherent forces that produce change. Changes away from an equilibrium position occur only as a result of outside events that disturb the status quo. (65, 698)

Equilibrium level of GDP (on the demand side) Level of GDP that makes aggregate demand equal to production. (699)

Equilibrium price Price at which quantity demanded and quantity supplied are equal. This common quantity is called the *equilibrium quantity*. (65)

Excess burden of a tax The amount by which the burden of a tax exceeds the tax that is paid. (486)

Excess capacity theorem Asserts that monopolistic competitive firms will tend to produce outputs lower than those that minimize average costs; that is, that they will tend to produce less than their capacity. (316)

Excess reserves Reserves held in excess of what are needed to satisfy customer-service needs. (833)

Exchange A mechanism by which workers can trade the various products resulting from specialization and the division of labour. (49)

Exchange controls Laws restricting the exchange of one nation's currency for another's. (944)

Exchange rate The price at which one currency can be bought, stated in terms of another currency. (86, 738, 854)

Exchange rates, fixed Rates set by government decisions and maintained by central bank actions. (857)

Exchange rates, floating or flexible Rates determined in free markets by the law of supply and demand. (855)

Excise tax A tax levied on a particular commodity or service as a fixed amount of money per unit of product sold or as a fixed percentage of the purchase price. (134, 478)

Excludability An attribute of private goods, as opposed to public goods. A commodity is excludable if someone who does not pay for it can be kept from enjoying it. (343)

Expansion path The locus of a firm's cost-minimizing input combinations for all relevant output levels. (196)

Exponential growth Growth at a constant percentage rate. (1035)

Export-led growth The strategy of emphasizing the production of goods for export. (279)

Export subsidy A payment by the government to exporters to permit them to reduce the selling price of their goods so they can compete more efficiently in foreign markets. (375)

Externality, beneficial or **detrimental** Result of an activity that causes incidental benefits or damages to others, and no corresponding compensation is provided to or paid by those who generate the externality. (337)

Fiat money Money decreed as such by the government. It is of little value as a commodity, but it maintains its value as a medium of exchange because people have faith that the issuer will stand behind the pieces of printed paper and limit their production. (823)

Final goods and services Those that are purchased by their ultimate users. (617)

Fiscal federalism The system of transfer payments from one level of government to the next. (481)

Fiscal policy The government's plan for spending and taxation. It is designed to steer aggregate demand in some desired direction. (763)

Fixed costs Unavoidable overhead costs that do not vary when the firm's output level changes. (169)

Fractional reserve banking A system under which bankers keep in their vaults as reserves only a fraction of the funds they hold on deposit. (829)

Game theory Analyzes the behaviour of competing firms mathematically, treating it as analogous to the strategies of rival players in a competitive game. (324)

Gold-exchange system (Bretton Woods system) International monetary system that prevailed from 1944 to 1971. Under this system, the United States fixed the value of the dollar in terms of gold, and other countries fixed the values of their currencies in terms of the U.S. dollar. (942)

Gold standard System in which exchange rates are set in terms of gold and pegged by buying or selling gold as necessary. (940)

Government purchases All the goods and services purchased by all levels of government. Transfer payments to individuals (such as welfare benefits) and payments from one level of government to another are not included. Symbolized by the letter *C*. (670)

Gross domestic product (GDP) The sum of the money values of all final goods and services produced in the economy during a specified period of time, usually one year. (616)

Gross domestic product deflator Price index obtained by dividing nominal GDP by real GDP. (665)

Gross domestic product (GDP) per capita The economy's total output divided by the number of people among whom it will be distributed —that is, the economy's population. (1023)

Gross domestic product, nominal The economy's total output valued at current prices. (617)

Gross domestic product, potential The real GDP that the economy would produce if its labour and other resources were fully employed. (639)

Gross domestic product, real The economy's total output valued at the prices that prevailed in some agreed-upon year (currently 1986). (617)

Gross national product The total income created by the employment of all factors of production owned by a nation's people. In contrast, *gross domestic product* is the amount of employment-creating production activity that takes place *within* the nation. (618)

Growth, disembodied Increases in an economy's output that can occur without being accompanied by (embodied in) additional capital stock. (1040)

Growth, embodied Increases in an economy's output that are made possible by increased or improved plant, equipment, or other forms of capital. (1040)

Horizontal equity The notion that equally situated individuals should be taxed equally. (482)

Human capital theory A theory interpreting education as an investment in a human being's earning power, just as an improvement in a factory is an investment in the factory's earning capacity. (450)

Incidence of a tax An allocation of the burden of the tax to specific individuals or groups. (487)

Income effect A portion of the change in quantity of a good demanded when its price changes. A rise in price cuts the consumer's purchasing power (real income), which leads to a change in the quantity demanded of that commodity. That change is the income effect. (112)

Income–expenditure diagram (45° line diagram) A plotting of total real expenditure (on the vertical axis) against real income (on the horziontal axis). The 45° line marks off points where income and expenditure are equal. (704)

Incomes policy A generic term used to describe a wide variety of measures aimed at curbing inflation *without* reducing aggregate demand. (1010)

Incomes policy, tax-based (TIP) Use of the tax system to provide incentives favouring non-inflationary behaviour. (1013)

Increasing costs, principle of As the production of a good expands, the opportunity cost of producing another unit of this good generally increases. (42)

Increasing returns to scale *See* Economies of scale

Index number A number indicating the percentage change in some variable (such as the price level) between the base period and some other period. Typically, the value of the index number in the base period is arbitrarily set to 100. (663)

Indexing Provisions in a law or a contract whereby monetary payments are automatically adjusted whenever a specified price index changes; sometimes called *escalator clauses.* (1014)

Indifference curve Line connecting all combinations of the commodities that are equally desirable to the consumer. (119)

Indirect taxes Taxes levied on specific economic activities. (473)

Induced increase in consumption An increase in consumer spending that stems from an increase in consumer incomes. It appears on a graph as a movement along a fixed consumption function. (724)

Induced investment That part of investment spending that rises when GDP rises, and falls when GDP falls. (702)

Inferior good A commodity whose quantity demanded falls when the

purchaser's real income rises, all other things remaining equal. (111)

Inflation A sustained increase in the general price level. (615)

Inflation accounting Adjusting standard accounting procedures for the fact that inflation lowers the purchasing power of money. (963)

Inflation, creeping Inflation that proceeds for a long time at a moderate and fairly steady pace. (649)

Inflation, expected rate of Forecasted rate of price change. Also, the difference between the nominal interest rate and the real interest rate. (646)

Inflation, galloping Inflation that proceeds at an exceptionally high rate, perhaps for only a relatively brief period. (649)

Inflationary gap The amount by which equilibrium real GDP exceeds the full-employment level of GDP. (709)

Innovation The act of putting a new idea into practical use. (443)

Input Any item that the firm uses in its production process. Inputs, also called the means of production, are the natural resources, labour, and produced plant and equipment used to make outputs. (38, 161)

Interest The payment for the use of funds employed in the production of capital; it is measured as a percentage per year of the value of the funds tied up in the capital. (436)

Intermediate good A good purchased for resale or for use in producing another good. (618)

International Monetary Fund (IMF) International organization set up originally to police and manage the gold-exchange system. (942)

Invention The act of generating a new idea. (443)

Investment The flow of resources into the production of new capital. (435)

Investment good *See* Capital good

Investment, gross private domestic Sum of business investment expenditures on plant and equipment, residential construction expenditures, and inventory change. (655)

Investment schedule Table or curve showing how investment spending depends on GDP. (700–701)

Investment spending The sum of the expenditures of business firms on

new plant, equipment, and inventories, plus the expenditures of households on new homes. Financial "investments" are not included, nor are resales of existing physical assets. Symbolized by the letter *I.* (670)

Isoquant (sometimes called a *production indifference curve*) A curve in a graph showing quantities of *inputs* on its axes. Each isoquant indicates *all* combinations of input quantities capable of producing a *given* quantity of output. (193)

Labour force The number of people employed or seeking employment. (629)

Labour productivity Productivity, of labour.

Laissez faire A program of minimal interference with the workings of the market system. (260)

Less developed countries (LDCs) Countries whose share of output composed of agricultural products, mining, and the like is relatively high; that engage in relatively little industrial high-technology activity; and whose per-capita incomes are generally comparatively low. (1044)

Liability An item of value that an individual or a firm owes. Many liabilities are known as "debts." (831)

Liability, limited The legal obligation of a firm's owners to pay back company debts only with the money they have already invested in the firm. (799)

Liability, unlimited The legal obligation of a firm's owners to pay back company debts with whatever resources they own. (797)

Liquidity, of an asset The ease with which the asset can be converted into cash. (828)

Long run A period of time long enough for all of the firm's sunk commitments to come to an end. (174)

Lorenz curve Graph depicting the distribution of income. (500)

M1 The narrowly defined money supply, which is the sum of all coins and paper money in circulation, plus pure chequing deposits at chartered banks. (827)

M2 The broadly defined money supply, which is the sum of currency in public hands, plus chequing and all savings deposits at chartered banks. (827)

Macroeconomics The study of the behaviour of entire economies. (612)

Marginal-cost (MC) curve Shows, for each output, the increase in the firm's total cost required if it increases its output by an additional unit. Geometrically, MC is the slope of the TC curve. In symbols, $MC = \Delta TC/\Delta Q$. (168)

Marginal land Land that is just on the borderline of being used. (423)

Marginal physical product (MPP) The increase in total output that results from a one-unit increase in an input, holding the amounts of all other inputs constant. Geometrically, it is the slope of the TPP curve. In symbols, $MPP = \Delta TPP/\Delta Q_i$. (163, 414)

Marginal private cost (MPC) *See* Marginal social cost.

Marginal profit The addition to total profit resulting from one more unit of output. (208)

Marginal propensity to consume (MPC) The ratio of the change in consumption to the change in disposable income that produces the change in consumption. On a graph, it appears as the slope of the consumption function: $MPC = \Delta C/\Delta DI$. (680)

Marginal propensity to save (MPS) Graphically, the slope of the saving function, which indicates how much more consumers will save if disposable income rises by one unit. (682)

Marginal rate of substitution In relation to two commodities, the maximum amount of one commodity that the consumer is willing to give up in exchange for one more unit of the other commodity. Geometrically, it is represented by the *slope of an indifference curve.* (121)

Marginal returns, "Law" of diminishing Asserts that if the quantities of all other inputs are held constant, the employment of additional quantities of any one input by a firm or an industry will eventually yield smaller and smaller (marginal) increases in output. (164)

Marginal revenue (MR) The *addition* to total revenue resulting from the addition of one more unit to total output. Geometrically, marginal revenue is the *slope* of the total-revenue curve. The formula is $MR = \Delta TR/\Delta Q$. (205)

Marginal revenue product (MRP) The additional revenue earned as a result of increased sales when an additional unit of an input is used. $MRP = MPP \times$ price of product. (166, 414)

Marginal social cost (MSC) The sum of the *marginal private cost (MPC)* (the share of an activity's marginal cost paid for by those who generate the activity) and the *incidental cost* (the share borne by others). (338)

Market The set of all sale and purchase transactions that affect the price of some commodity. (228)

Market-demand curve Shows how the total quantity demanded of some product during a specified period of time changes as the price of that product changes, other things being constant. (132)

Market power The ability of a firm to raise its price significantly above the competitive price level and to maintain this high price profitably for a considerable period. (562)

Market system A form of organization of the economy in which decisions on resource allocation are made independently by individual producers and consumers acting in their own best interest without central direction. (51)

Maximin criterion Selecting the strategy that yields the maximum payoff, on the assumption that your competitor will do as much damage to you as it can. (327)

Merger The combining of two previously independent firms under a single owner or group of owners. (551)

Merger, conglomerate The union of two unrelated firms. (551)

Merger, horizontal A merger of two firms producing similar products. (551)

Merger, vertical The joining of two firms, one of which supplies an ingredient of the other's product. (551)

Microeconomics The study of the behaviour of individual decision-making units, such as farmers or consumers. (612)

Minimum-wage law Requires all employees (with some specified exceptions) to be paid at least some fixed given dollar amount per hour. (418)

Monetarism Mode of analysis that uses the equation of exchange to organize macroeconomic predictions. (889)

Monetary policy Actions that the Bank of Canada takes in order to change the equilibrium of the money market—that is, to alter either the money supply or the exchange rate. (865)

Monetizing the deficit The effect of the central bank's purchasing the bonds that the government issues. (972)

Money The standard object used in exchanging goods and services. In short, money is the *medium of exchange*. (822)

Money fixed asset An asset with a face value fixed in terms of dollars, such as money itself, government bonds, and corporate bonds. (685)

Monopolistic competition Competition among firms, each of which has products that are somewhat different from those of its rivals. (312)

Monopoly, natural An industry in which the advantages of large-scale production make it possible for a single firm to produce the entire output of the market at lower average cost than could a number of firms each producing a smaller quantity. (292)

Monopoly, pure An industry in which there is only one supplier of a product for which there are no close substitutes, and in which it is very hard or impossible for another firm to co-exist. (290)

Monopsony A market situation in which there is only one buyer. (461)

Moral hazard The tendency of insurance to discourage policyholders from protecting themselves from risk. (349)

National debt The federal government's total indebtedness at any given moment in time; results from the accumulation of previous deficits. (958)

National income The sum of the incomes of all individuals in the economy earned in the forms of wages, interest, rents, and profits. It excludes transfer payments and is calculated before any income taxes have been deducted. (659, 671)

National income accounting Book-keeping and measurement system for national economic data. (654)

National product The total production of a nation's economy. (613)

Nationalization Government owner-ship and operation of business firms. (526)

Near moneys Liquid assets that are close substitutes for money. (828)

Negative income tax (NIT) Transfer program under which families with incomes below a certain threshold (the "breakeven level") would receive cash benefits from the government; these benefits would decline as income rose. (505)

Net exports The excess of foreign expenditures on our products over our purchases of foreign goods (Canadian exports minus Canadian imports). Symoblized by $X - IM$. (670)

Net worth The value of all assets minus the value of all liabilities. (832)

Normative question One that involves a value judgement. (20)

Oligopoly A market dominated by a few sellers, at least several of which are large enough relative to the total market to be able to influence the market price. (318)

Open-market operations The Bank of Canada's purchase or sale of government securities through transactions in the open bond market. (850)

Opportunity cost The foregone value of the next best alternative that is not chosen. (37)

Origin The lower left-hand corner of a graph where the two axes meet. In two-variable diagrams, both variables equal zero at the origin. (22)

Output The goods and services that consumers want to acquire and that firms produce; also, the quantity of the good or service that a firm produces. (38, 161)

Paradox of thrift The fact that an effort by a nation to save more may simply reduce national income and fail to raise total savings. (727)

Partnership A firm whose ownership is shared by a fixed number of proprietors. (798)

Patent A temporary grant of monopoly rights over an innovation. (541)

Pay equity Classifying jobs by objective criteria and forcing employers to pay equal wages for the jobs judged to be of comparable worth. (512)

Perfectly contestable market One in which entry and exit are costless and unimpeded. (329)

Personal income A measure of income derived by subtracting corporate profits, retained earnings, and payroll taxes from national income, then adding in transfer payments. Personal income measures the income that actually accrues to individuals. (659)

Phillips curve A graph depicting the rate of unemployment on the horizontal axis and either the rate of inflation or the rate of change of money wages on the vertical axis; it is normally downward sloping, indicating that higher inflation rates are associated with lower unemployment rates. (990)

Phillips curve, vertical (long-run) Shows the menu of inflation/unemployment choices available to society in the long run; it is a vertical straight line at the natural rate of unemployment. (997)

Ploughback *See* Retained earnings

Positive question One that can be assessed by evaluating its consistency with logic and factual evidence. (20)

Poverty line The amount of income below which a family is considered "poor." (496)

Predatory pricing Price cuts that are undertaken only to keep other firms from entering the industry. (554)

Price ceiling Legal maximum price that may be charged for a commodity. (79)

Price discrimination Charging different prices, relative to costs, to different buyers of the same product. (554)

Price floor Legal minimum price that

may be charged for a commodity. (84)

Price leadership One firm sets the price for the industry and the others follow. (321)

Price war Each competing firm is determined to sell at a price that is lower than the prices of its rivals, usually regardless of whether that price covers the pertinent cost. (322)

Private good A commodity or service whose benefits are depleted by an additional user and for which other people are excluded from its benefits. (343)

Production function Indicates the *maximum* amount of product that can be obtained from any specified combination of inputs, given the current state of knowledge. (179)

Production possibilities frontier A graphical representation of the different combinations of various goods that a producer can turn out, given the available resources and existing technology. (40)

Productivity The amount of output produced by a unit of input. (738)

Productivity, of labour The amount of output produced per hour (or week or year) of labour input. It can be measured as total national output (GDP) in a given year divided by the total number of hours of work performed for pay in the country during that year; that is, labour productivity is defined as *GDP per labour hour*. (1023)

Profit-sharing A system of compensating labour in which workers receive both a fixed base wage and a share of the firm's profits. (1013)

Progressive tax One in which the average tax rate paid by an individual rises as his or her income rises. (473)

Property tax A tax on the assessed value of real property. (480)

Proportional tax One in which the average tax rate is the same at all income levels. (473)

Public good A commodity or service whose benefits are *not depleted* by an additional user and for which it is generally difficult or *impossible to exclude* people from its benefits, even if they are unwilling to pay for them. (343)

Purchasing power The purchasing

power of a given sum of money is the volume of goods and services it will buy. (640)

Purchasing-power parity theory (of exchange rates) Theory that the exchange rate between any two national currencies adjusts to reflect differences in the price levels of the two nations. (934)

Quantity theory of money A simple theory of aggregate demand based on the idea that velocity is constant, so that nominal GDP is proportional to the money stock. (884)

Quota A specification of the maximum amount of a good permitted into a country from abroad per unit of time. (375)

Random walk The time path of a variable, such as the price of a stock, when its magnitude in one period equals its value in the preceding period plus a completely random number. (814)

Rate averaging *See* Cross subsidization.

Rate of interest, nominal The percentage by which the money the borrower pays back exceeds the money that he or she borrowed, making no adjustment for any fall in the purchasing power of money that results from inflation. (646)

Rate of interest, real The percentage increase in purchasing power that the borrower pays to the lender for the privilege of borrowing. It indicates the increased ability to purchase goods and services that the lender earns. (646)

Rational decision A decision that best serves the objective of the decision-maker, whatever that objective may be. The term *rational* connotes neither approval nor disapproval of the objective itself. (37)

Rational expectations Forecasts that, while not necessarily correct, are the best that can be made given the available data. Rational expectations cannot err *systematically*. If expectations are rational, forecasting errors are pure random numbers. (1005)

Ray through the origin (or ray) A straight line emanating from the origin, or zero point on a graph. (26)

Real wage rate The wage rate adjusted for inflation. It indicates the volume of goods and services that the money wage will buy. (640)

Recession A period of time during which the total output of the economy declines. (616)

Recessionary gap The amount by which the equilibrium level of real GDP falls short of potential GDP. (708)

Regressive tax One in which the average tax rate falls as income rises. (473)

Regulation of industry A process established by law that restricts or controls some specified decisions made by the affected firms. (525)

Relative price The price of an item in terms of some other item, rather than in terms of dollars. (642)

Rent-seeking Unproductive activity in the pursuit of economic profit, that is, profit in excess of competitive earnings. (301, 350)

Required reserves The minimum amount of reserves (in cash or the equivalent), mandated by law, that banks in some countries must maintain. Historically, in Canada, required reserves were proportional to the volume of deposits, but Canada no longer has restrictions of this sort. (831)

Resale price maintenance Forcing retailers to keep the price of a product at or above that specified by the wholesaler. (554)

Research and development (R & D) Systematic efforts undertaken to invent new or improved products or productive techniques and to make them ready to market or for use in production processes. (1027)

Resources The instruments, provided by nature or by people, that are used to obtain the goods and services humans want. The three types of resources are often referred to as "land" (natural resources), "labour," and "capital" (resources made by people, such as factories and machines). (36)

Retained earnings (ploughback) The portion of a corporation's profits that management decides to keep and invest back into the firm's operations rather than pay out directly to the shareholders in the form of dividends. (801)

Run on a bank An event that occurs when many depositors withdraw cash from their accounts simultaneously. (820)

Sales-maximizing firm One whose objective is to sell as much of its output as possible (measured in terms of the revenue it brings in) rather than to maximize the company's profit. (322)

Scatter diagram A graph showing the relationship between two variables. Each year is represented by a point in the diagram. The co-ordinates of each year's point show the values of the two variables in that year. (676)

Self-correcting mechanism The economy's way of curing inflationary or recessionary gaps automatically via inflation or deflation. (750)

Service industry One that does not turn out any physical products (for example, telecommunications, medical care, teaching, police protection, and the legal profession). (1028)

Short run A period of time briefer than the long run, so that some, but not all, of the firm's sunk commitments will have ended. (174)

Shortage An excess of quantity demanded over quantity supplied. When there is a shortage, buyers cannot purchase the quantities they desire. (65)

Slope of a budget line Amount of one commodity the market requires an individual to give up in order to obtain one additional unit of another commodity without any change in the amount of money spent. (121)

Slope of a curved line At any particular point, the slope of the straight line that is tangent to the curved line at that point. (24)

Slope of a straight line The ratio of the vertical change to the corresponding horizontal change as we move to the right along the line. The ratio of the "rise" over the "run." (24)

Slope of an indifference curve *See* Marginal rate of substitution

Socialism Method of economic organization in which the state owns the means of production. (273)

Sole proprietorship A business firm owned by a single person. (797)

Specialization The practice of devoting a country's energies and resources to only a small proportion of the world's productive activities. (363)

Speculation Investment in risky assets in the hope of obtaining a profit from the expected changes in the prices of these assets. (810)

Stabilization policy The name given to government programs designed to prevent or shorten recessions and to counteract inflation (that is, to *stabilize* prices). (627)

Stagflation Inflation that occurs while the economy is growing slowly ("stagnating") or having a recession. (626, 745)

Store of value An item used to store wealth from one point in time to another. (822)

Substitutes Two goods are called substitutes if an increase in the price of one raises the quantity demanded of the other, all other things remaining constant. (147)

Substitution effect The change in quantity demanded of a good resulting from a change in its relative price, exclusive of whatever change in quantity demanded may be attributable to the associated change in real income. (112)

Sunk cost A cost to which a firm is precommitted for some limited period, either because the firm has signed a contract to make the payments or because it has already paid for some durable item and cannot get its money back except by using that item to produce output for some period of time. (174)

Supply curve A graphical depiction of a *supply schedule*. It shows how the quantity supplied of some product during a specified period of time will change as the price of that product changes, holding all other determinants of quantity supplied constant. (62)

Supply–demand diagram Diagram showing both a supply curve and a demand curve. (64)

Supply schedule A table showing how the quantity supplied of some product during a specified period of time changes as the price of that product changes, holding all other determinants of quantity supplied constant. (62)

Surplus An excess of quantity supplied over quantity demanded. When there is a surplus, sellers cannot sell the quantities they desire to supply. (65)

Surplus, balance-of-payments The amount by which the quantity supplied of foreign exchange (per year) exceeds the quantity demanded. Balance-of-payments surpluses arise whenever the value of foreign exchange is pegged at an artificially high level—that is, when the value of the *domestic* currency is pegged at an artificially low level. (858)

Tariff A tax on imports. (375, 778)

Tax credit Reduction of an individual's or a firm's tax obligation by a given amount that is independent of the tax rate. Some individual tax credits are *refundable;* if they reduce the tax owed to an amount less than zero, the government transfers that amount to the individual. (483)

Tax exemption Permits the reduction of an individual's or a firm's taxable income (tax base) by some amount. (483)

Tax rate, average The ratio of taxes to income. (473)

Tax rate, marginal The fraction of each *additional* dollar of income that is paid in taxes. (473)

Tax shelter A special provision in the Income Tax Act that reduces or defers taxation if certain conditions are met. (474)

Tax shifting Occurs when the economic reactions to a tax cause prices and outputs in the economy to change, thereby shifting part of the burden of the tax onto others. (488)

The multiplier The ratio of the change in equilibrium GDP (Y) divided by the original change in spending that causes the change in GDP. (718)

Theory A deliberate simplification of factual relationships; its purpose is to explain how those relationships work. (16)

Time-series graph A type of two-variable diagram that depicts the change in a variable over time. The horizontal axis always represents time. (28)

Total-cost (TC) curve Shows, for each possible quantity of output, the total amount that the firm must spend for its inputs to produce that amount of output plus any opportunity cost incurred in the process. (168)

Total expenditure schedule Shows how total spending varies with the level of national income (GDP). (701)

Total physical product (TPP) curve Shows what happens to the quantity of the firm's output as one changes the quantity of one of the firm's inputs while holding the quantities of all other inputs unchanged. (161)

Trade adjustment assistance Special unemployment benefits, loans, retraining programs, or other aid provided to workers and firms that are harmed by foreign competition. (385)

Transfer payments Sums of money that certain individuals receive as grants from the government, rather than as payments for services rendered to employers. (483, 655, 673)

Transfer payments, regional A variety of programs for redistributing funds from the federal government to the provinces, especially the poorer ones. (481–82)

Unemployment, cyclical The portion of unemployment that is attributable to a decline in the economy's total production. Cyclical unemployment rises during recessions and falls as prosperity is restored. (632)

Unemployment, frictional Unemployment that occurs as a result of the normal workings of the labour market. It includes people who are temporarily between jobs because they are moving or changing occupations, or for similar reasons. (632)

Unemployment insurance Government program under which some, but not all, unemployed workers receive transfer payments. (634)

Unemployment, natural rate of Also referred to as the "full-employment" unemployment rate. The specific rate of unemployment toward which the economy's self-correcting mechanism tends to push the unemployment rate. (996)

Unemployment rate The number of

unemployed people, expressed as a percentage of the labour force. (629)

Unemployment, structural Unemployment of workers who have lost their jobs because they have been displaced by automation, because their skills are no longer in demand, or for similar reasons. (632)

Unit of account The standard unit for quoting prices. (822)

Utility, marginal The marginal utility of a commodity to a consumer (measured in money terms) is the maximum amount of money that he or she is willing to pay for *one more unit* of it. (101)

Utility, total The total utility of a quantity of goods to a consumer

(measured in money terms) is the maximum amount of money income that he or she is willing to give in exchange for it. (101)

Value added The value added by a company is its revenue from selling a product minus the amounts paid for goods and services purchased from other firms. (657)

Value judgement A proposition that cannot be proven true or false; it simply is or is not consistent with a particular moral code. (19)

Variable An object, such as price, whose magnitude is measured by a number, and for which one wishes to study what happens when the size of that number changes (varies). (22)

Variable cost Any cost that is not a fixed cost. (169)

Velocity The number of times per year that an "average dollar" is spent on goods and services. It is the ratio of nominal GDP to the number of dollars in the money stock —that is, Velocity = Nominal GDP/Money stock. (884)

Vertical equity The notion that differently situated individuals should be taxed differently in a way that society deems to be fair. (484)

Wage–price controls Legal restrictions on the ability of industry and labour to raise wages and prices. (1011–12)

Ability-to-pay principle, 484
Absolute advantage, 365, 370, 398
Absolute concept of poverty, 496–99
Abstraction, in economics, 12–16
Acid rain, 575
Adjustment assistance, 398, 399, *see also* Unemployment insurance
Adjustment costs, 393, 1057
Advertising, 312, 318–19
  misleading, 556
  and monopoly, 302
  and oligopoly, 318–19
Aetna (company), 553
Affirmative action, 416, 513
AFL–CIO, 453
Africa
  gross domestic product of, 1054–55
  population growth in, 1048, 1051
Aggregate demand, 635, 670–74, *see also* Demand; Demand management
  and economic growth, 1037–39
  and fiscal policy, 912–14, 919
  and foreign interest rates, 868, 870–71, 920, 925
  and inflation, 745–47, 984–85, 1006
  and monetary policy, 881–83, 914–20
  and stabilization policy, 627–29, 695, 697
  and taxes, 785–88, 790
Aggregate demand curves, 615, 706–708, 883
  and multiplier, 728–30
Aggregate supply, *see also* Supply
  and exchange rates, 738, 920–22
  and foreign interest rates, 923, 925–26
  and inflation, 985
  and input prices, 738
  and money wage rates, 736
  and sales taxes, 738
  and taxes, 784–90
Aggregate supply curves, 615, 734–39, 895–98
Aggregation, and macroeonomics, 612–14
Agricultural marketing boards, 310, 527, 530–31
Agricultural subsidies, 390
Air Canada, 526, 546
Airlines

  deregulation of, 529, 533–34, 540, 543–44
  fares, 71
Airports, 259
Allocation of resources, *see* Resource allocation
American Federation of Labor (AFL), 453, *see also* AFL–CIO
Analytical cost curves, *see under* Cost curves
Anti-Inflation Board (Canada), 1011
Anti-inflation policy, 627, 997–1001, 1008
Antipoverty programs, 503–508
Arbitration, 462–63
Assets, 831
Athabasca River, 600
Atlantic Sugar (company), 553
Australia
  income distribution in, 503
  equal pay legislation in, 513
Average costs (AC), 168–70, 172–74, 182–83
  long run, 175–76, 183–86
  and natural monopolies, 292–93
  short run, 175–76
Average data, relationship to marginal and total, 221–24
Average fixed costs (AFC), 171–72
Average physical product (APP), 161–63
Average propensity to consume (APC), 682
Average propensity to save (APS), 682
Average revenue (AR), 204–205
Average tax rate, 473
Average variable costs (AVC), 237

Baby boom, 91
Balance of payments, 857–59
  deficit in, 858–59
  and exchange rates, 939
  surplus in, 858–59
Balance sheets, of banks, 832
Bank Act (Canada), 842
Banking
  central, 847–71: and independence of, 848, 850
  fractional reserve, 829
  history of, 828–29
Bank of Canada, 633, 847–49
  and budget deficits, 971–73

  and exchange rates, 854, 869–70
  governors of, 848–49
  independence of, 848–49
  and inflation, 751
  and monetary policy, 916, 918
  and money supply, 849–62
Bank of Canada Act, 847, 849
Bank rate, 853–54
Bank regulation, 830–31
Banks
  assets of, 831–32
  chartered, 819–21
  competition among, 819–21
  liabilities of, 831–32
  and money supply, 825–28
  profits vs. safety of, 830
  runs on, 820–21
Barter, 821–22
Bastiat, Frédéric, 396
Beneficial externalities, 337, 338, 340–41, 342
Benefits principle of taxation, 485
Bilateral monopoly, 461
"Black" markets, 79, 80
Block, Walter, 605
The Body Shop, 52
Bombardier Ltée, 556
Bond prices, 805–808
  and interest rates, 803
Bonds, 800, 801–802, 803–805
  government, 849–52, 974
Bouey, Gerald, 849, 869
Boulding, Kenneth, 1041
Brain drain, 1054
Brazil
  value-added tax in, 479
Break-even analysis, 235
Bretton Woods system, 941–45
Britain, *see* United Kingdom
British Columbia Sugar (company), 552
Broadcasting, radio and television, 532–33
Broadfoot, Barry, 625
Budget, 763–64
  balanced, 757–58
  cuts to, 35–36
  cyclically adjusted, 965–67
  and fiscal policy, 958, 965–67
Budget deficits, 633, 790, 923, 957–80
  bogus arguments about, 968–70
  closing of, 976–78, 979–80

consequences of, 10
and inflation, 970–73
and interest rates, 973–75
interest rates on, 963–65
measurement of, 962–65
monetization of, 971–73
and recessions, 965–66
and trade deficits, 950–53
Budget lines, 115–18, 120–24
definition of, 116
isoquants and, 194–96
Bundesbank, 850, 870, 949
Burden of a tax, 485–87, 494
Bureau of Broadcast Measurement, 556
Bureau of Competition Policy (Canada), 552, 553, 558
Business confidence, 694
Business cycles, 621, 749, 958
Businesses, see Corporations

Caisses populaires, 827
Canada
balance of payments in, 939–40, 947–48
banks in, 819–20: regulation of, 830–31, 842–43
budget deficits in, 957–80
competition policy in, 548–59
economic growth in, 48–49
economic history of, 611, 621–27, 746, 750–52, 916–17, 998
energy policy in, 597–98
excise taxes in, 137–38
family income in, 499–503
federal/provincial relations in, 597–98
firms in, 796–800: foreign ownership of, 812
and foreign loans, 440–41
inflation in, 649–50, 641, 998
and international trade, 375–76
money in, 824–25
national debt in, 957–80
and nationalization, 546–48
oil pricing in, 257
pollution control in, 568
poverty in, 496
productivity in, 164, 1023, 1024, 1026–28, 1029
regional economic issues in, 924
regulation in, 526–27
services in, 1028
stock exchanges in, 808
tariffs in, 375–76
tax system in, 471, 472–96, 688
trade policy in, 361, 388–90
trade with Japan, 362–63, 380
trade with U.S., 390–95, see also Canada–U.S. Free Trade

Agreement
trade with Western Europe, 362–63
unemployment in, 629, 633–37, 998
unions in, 452–57
wage–price controls in, 1013
Canada Assistance Plan, 504
Canada Deposit Insurance Corporation (CDIC), 831, 842–43
Canada Employment Centres, 1009–1010
Canada Pension Plan (CPP), 481
Canada Post, 291, 531, 544
Canada–U.S. Free Trade Agreement (FTA), 362, 380, 385, 390–95, 926
Canadian Airlines, 749
Canadian Auto Workers union (CAW), 1032
Canadian Congress of Labour (CCL), 453
Canadian Dairy Commission, 85
Canadian Labour Congress (CLC), 453
Canadian Radio–Television and Tele-communications Commission (CRTC), 533
Capital, 435–36
and aggregate-supply curve, 739
incidence of taxes on, 492–93
in less developed countries, 1048–50
opportunity cost of, 245–46
Capital cost allowances, 785
Capital equipment, 1037–38, 1039–40
Capital gains, 475
taxes on, 786
Capital goods, 45, 436–37, 654
Capitalism, 52, 434, 1041–42
Cartels, 320–21
CATS (Computer Assisted Trading System), 809
Central planning, 264–65, 273, 352–53
Chamberlin, Edward, 312
Charter of Rights and Freedoms (Canada), 455, 559
"Cheap foreign labour" argument, 361, 362–63, 374, 397–98
Cheques, as money, 825–27
Chernobyl (Ukraine), 575
Chicago Board of Trade, 586
China
economy of, 277–78
pollution in, 569, 577
population control in, 1051
Choice
consumer, 99–129
rational, 4–5
and scarcity, 35–56
Circular flow diagrams, 671–74, 695, 697–99, 764
"Closed shop," 454
Club of Rome, 588

Collective bargaining, 452–60, 462–64
Coalitions, 327
Collusion, 562
and oligopoly, 319, 321–22
in pricing, 562
Combines Investigation Act (Canada), 549, 558
Commodities, see also Goods; Products
distribution of, 285–87
Commodity money, 822–23
Commodity prices, 1055
Common stocks, 801, see also Stocks
Comparative advantage, 8–9, 49, 51, 365–67, 369–72, 374, 398, 1033
Competition
agreement to restrict, 552–53
international, 1056–57
perfect, see Perfect competition
price, 531
self-destructive, 532, 540
Competition Act (Canada), 525, 548–59
Competition policy, 548–49, 557–58
exemptions from, 557
penalties and, 557
Competition Tribunal, 552, 556, 558
Complements, 147–48
Computer Assisted Trading System (CATS), 809
Computer industry, 75–76
Concentration of industry, 543, 559–64
Concentration ratio, 561–62
Conditional grants, 482
Conglomerate mergers, 551
Congress of Industrial Organizations (CIO), 453, see also AFL–CIO
Constant returns to scale, 185
Constrained market pricing, 539
Consumer behaviour, 688–89
Consumer choice, 99–129
Consumer expenditure, 143–45, 670
Consumer incomes
and demand, 69–70
Consumer preferences, 431–32
and demand, 70
and distribution of goods, 262
and indifference curve analysis, 118–22
and price mechanism, 262
Consumer price index (CPI), 664
Consumer sovereignty, 261
Consumer spending, see Consumption
Consumer surplus, 100, 107–11
Consumption, 671, 674–89, 697–98
autonomous increase in, 724
and economic growth, 1039–41
and income taxes, 675–76, 686–87, 688–89, 766–68

induced increase in, 724
  multiplier effect of, 724–26
Consumption function, 680–83, 730
  movements along, 683
  shifts of, 683
Consumption possibilities frontiers,
    371–72
Consumption goods, 45
Contour maps, 27–28
Co-ordination of economic activity,
    48, 51, 258, 260–63, 712
Corporate income taxes, 786, 788–89
Corporate profits taxes, 444, 473, 480,
    492, 799
Corporate takeovers, 811–12
Corporations, 796–97, 799–800, see
    also Partnerships; Sole
    proprietorships
  financing of, 800–801, 803–804,
    809–10
  foreign ownership of, 812
  multinational, 1049
Corporatism, 465
Correlation, 17
Cost advantages, and monopoly,
    291–92
Cost curves, 167–76, 182–83, 195–96
  analytical, 187–89
  average, 168–69, 172–74, 175–76
  long run, 175–76
  marginal, 168–70
  and monopoly, 302–303
  short run, 175–76
  total, 168, 172–74
  Cost minimization, 189–90, 195–96
Cost of living, 640
Costs, see also Opportunity costs
  historical, 187–89
  increasing, 42
  minimization of, 189–90, 195–96
  money, 37–38
  true economic, 4–5
Countervailing duties, 390, 394
Coyne Affair, 916, 918
Coyne, James, 848, 914
Credit cards, 828
Credit unions, 827
Cross elasticity of demand, 147, 149,
    151
Cross subsidization, 529, 534
Crow, John, 849, 869–70, 924–25,
    1000
Crowding-out effect, 974–75, 979,
    1027
Currency, 87, 826, 859, see also
    Exchange rates; Foreign exchange
  appreciation of, 855, 938
  depreciation of, 855, 938, 977
  devaluation of, 860, 942–43
  revaluation of, 860, 942–43

Current account, 939–40
Cycles, business, see Business cycles
Cyclically adjusted budget, 966–67
Cyclical unemployment, 632–33

Debt
  foreign-owned, 969
  in less developed countries, 949–50,
    970, 1049
  national, 957–80
  public and private, compared, 959
Defence, national, 386–87
Deficit spending, see Budget deficits
Deflating by price index, 665
Deflation, 622, 624, 747–50
Deflator, GDP, 665
Deindustrialization thesis, 1028
Demand, see also Aggregate demand;
    Supply and demand
  and advertising, 302, 318–19
  cross elasticity of, 147–48
  elasticity of, 138–48
  income elasticity of, 147
  for labour, 447–48, 457–59
  and land rent, 420–24
  law of, 133–34
  market, 131–58
  for money, 862–63
  price elasticity of, 138–53
  and prices, 137–38, 139, 146–48,
    150–53
  for related goods, 70–71
Demand curves, 22, 23, 61, 103
  of competitive firms, 231–32
  of complements, 147–48
  derived, 415–16, 438
  elasticity of, 138–53
  effect of excise tax on, 136–37
  horizontal, 231–32
  individual, 99–129, 132–33
  and inputs, 414–16
  and international trade, 372
  and investment, 694–95
  for labour, 457–59
  for loans, 437–38
  and marginal utility, 105–106
  of monopolies, 294, 302
  and monopolistic competition,
    314–16
  movements along, 68, 152
  and price changes, 124–26
  shifts of, 67–72, 151–52
  and time, 152–53, 156–58
  and utility, 103–106
Demand management, 628–29,
    674–76, 695, 749, 997,
    1006–1007, 1008–1009
Demand relationships, statistical anal-
    ysis of, 156–58
Demand schedules, 60–61

Demand-side equilibrium, 699–710
  and full employment, 708–10
Denmark, and the European Monetary
    System, 949
Depletability of commodities/private
    goods, 343
Deposit creation, 832–33
Deposit destruction, 838
Deposit insurance, 830–31, 842–43
Deposit-switching, 852–53
Depreciation, 656–57, 977, see also
    under Currency
  allowances, 695, 785
Deregulation, 525, 526, 539–40, see
    also Regulation
  of airlines, 529, 533–34, 540
  effects of, 542–44
  safety and, 543–44
Derived demand curves, 415–16, 438
Detrimental externalities, 337–38,
    338–39, 341, 342
Diamond–water paradox, 99, 106–107
Diefenbaker, John, 848
Diminishing marginal returns, 166
  and economies of scale, 186–87
Direct taxes, 473
"Dirty" floating, 947
Discounting, 405–406, 437
Discouraged workers, 630–31
Discrimination, 508–14
  economic, 420
  by employers, 510–11
  by fellow workers, 511
  policies to combat, 512–14
  price, 554–55
  statistical, 511–12
Disposable income, 659–60, 671,
    676–80, 767–68
Distribution
  economic, see Economic
    distribution
  of goods, 48, 285–87
  of income, see Income distribution
  of products, 262–63
Diversification, of investments, 805
Dividend income, and taxes, 475
Division of labour, 48–49
Double coincidence of wants, 821
Drug trade, 89–92
  deregulation of, 89
Dumping, 395–97, see also Wastes/
    waste disposal
Duopoly, 324, 326–27
Dutch auctions, 109

Earnings, retained, 801
East Germany, pollution in, 569
Econometric models, 903–904
Economic Council of Canada, 503,
    633, 977, 978

Economic distribution, 420, 508–14
Economic growth, 45–46, 1037–44
  interpretation of trends in, 28–32
  social costs of, 1042
  and stabilization policy, 628–29
  zero, 1042–44
Economic models, 17–18, 903–904
Economic nationalism, 455–56
Economic planning, *see* Central
  planning
Economic power, 432, *see also* Market
  power
Economic profit, 203, 442, *see also*
  Zero economic profit
Economic rent, 425–28
Economic theory, 16–17
Economics
  abstraction in, 12–16
  big issues vs. marginal changes, 431
  as a discipline, 12, 19
  and experimental methods, 77–78
Economies of scale, 159–61, 173,
  183–86, 527–28, 561
  decreasing returns to scale, 185
  and diminishing returns, 186–87
  and historical costs, 187–89
  increasing returns to scale, 185
  and monopoly, 292
Economies of scope, 528
Economists, agreement and disagreement among, 19
Eddy Match company, 550
Education
  and budget deficits, 980
  discrimination in, 509
  earnings and, 450–52
  as an investment, 449–52
  in less developed countries,
    1051–52
  and productivity, 1056–57
Efficiency, 46–47, 255–56, 400–401,
  see also Inefficiency
  and distribution of goods, 285–86
  and environmental issues, 581–82
  and equality, 272, 399, 400, 432,
    494–96, 513, 515–20
  and free markets, 254–72
  and government purchases, 1057
  and international trade, 366–67, 380
  and nationalization, 545–46
  and natural resources, 595
  and output selection, 266–69
  and perfect competition, 246–48,
    266–69
  and production planning, 286–87
  and profit regulation, 536–37,
    540–41
  and resource allocation, 254–56,
    264–67, 285–87, 334–37
  and taxation, 482, 485–87, 493–96

Egypt, population of, 1050–51
Elasticity of demand, 138–51
  cross, 147, 149, 151
  and consumer income, 147
  and demand curves, 138–43
  and the farm-income problem,
    150–51
  and legal cases, 148–49
  and price, 145–46, 148
Elasticity of supply, and price change,
  147
Emissions
  permits for, 584–86
  taxes on, 568, 577, 579–87
Employment, *see also* Unemployment
  equilibrium, 750
  full, 633–34, 695, 697, 708–11,
    741–45, 783
  and labour unions, 458–60
  programs, 1009–10
  and sales taxes, 477–78
Employment policy, 398, *see also*
  Adjustment assistance;
  Unemployment
Energy industry, foreign ownership in,
  598
Energy prices, *see under* Oil; Prices;
  Pricing; Resources
Engels, Friedrich, 230
Entrepreneurship, 442–44, 1053
Entry of firms into industry, 241–44
  barriers to, 291–92, 298, 304
  deterrence to, 325–26
  freedom of, 246, 313, 329–30
  and industry concentration, 562
  and regulation, 531, 540
Environmental policy, 577–80
Environmental protection, 567–87,
  601–605, 1041, 1043, *see also* Pollution; Wastes/waste disposal
  agreements on, 575
  and free trade, 388, 389
  and self-interest, 51, 52
Environmental Protection Agency
  (EPA), 585–86, 587
Equality, *see* Income distribution;
  Equity; Income inequality
Equalization payments, 482
Equilibrium, 65
  of competitive firm, 232–33,
    241–44, 246–48
  demand-side, 699–710
  employment, 708–11, 713, 741–45,
    750
  GDP, 697–713
  industry, 239–46
  in international trade, 776–78
  in labour market, 447–48
  long-run, 241–46, 315–16
  in money markets, 864–68

profit-maximizing, 294, 296
  sales-maximization, 323
  short-run, 232–33, 239–41, 314
  supply–demand, 372–74, 739–41,
    985–86
Equilibrium income, 697–99
  and exports, 776–78
  and government purchases, 763–66
  and imports, 776–78
  and tax policy, 768–70
Equilibrium price, 65–66, 69–71,
  372–74
Equilibrium quantity, 66, 69–71
Equity
  and environmental issues, 582–83
  horizontal, 482–83
  pay, *see* Pay equity
  in taxation, 482–85, 494–96
  vertical, 484
Escalator clause, 1014
*An Essay on the Principles of Popula-
  tion* (Malthus), 1034
European Community (EC), 391, 394
  and central bank, 849
  and fisheries, 600
  pay equity in, 513
  and single currency, 948
  trade restrictions in, 389–90
European Free Trade Association, 391
European Monetary System (EMS),
  948–49
Europe, Eastern
  and nationalization, 546
  pollution in, 569
Europe, Western, Canada's trade with,
  362–63
Excess burden of a tax, 486–87, 494
Excess reserves, 833
Exchange, *see also* Barter; Currency;
  Foreign exchange; International
  trade; Voluntary exchange
  equation of, 884–85
  medium of, 821–22
Exchange controls, 944
Exchange-rate policy, 866–71, 916–17,
  920, 922–23, 923–27
Exchange rates, 86, 854–60, 933–39,
  see also Currency
  and aggregate supply, 738, 920–22
  and Bank of Canada, 854, 869–70
  and economic activity, 937
  fixed (pegged), 86–87, 857–60, 868,
    912–13, 914–17, 919
  fixed vs. floating, 945–48
  flexible (floating), 855–57, 913–14,
    917–19, 920, 923, 947
  in free markets, 855–57, 938
  and inflation, 934–37
  and interest rates, 938
  in long run, 934–37

in medium run, 937
  purchasing-power parity theory of,
    934
  in short run, 938
  and speculation, 945–46
Excise taxes, 134–38, 303, 476
  incidence of, 489
Excludability of commodities/private
    goods, 343
Expansion path, 196
Exponential growth of population,
    1035–37
Export-led growth, 279
Exports, 670–71, 672
  and equilibrium income, 776–78
  net, 670
  subsidies and, 375
Externalities, 7–8, 337–42, 571–73,
    575–77, see also Environmental
    protection; Pollution

Factor payments, 656
Factors of production, 411, see also
    Capital; Entrepreneurship; Inputs;
    Labour; Land; Natural resources
  pricing of, 411–65
Farm incomes, 85, 150–51, 527
Farm prices, 85–86
Featherbedding, 459–60
Fiat money, 823, 825
Final goods and services, 617–18,
    654–55, 658–59
Firms, see Corporations; Partnerships;
    Sole Proprietorships; see under
    Perfect competition
Fiscal federalism, 481–82
Fiscal policy, 763–90, 890–95, see
    also Demand management; Stabi-
    lization policy; Tax policy
  and budget, 965–67
  contractionary, 780–81, 923
  and exchange rates, 912–14, 922
  expansionary, 779–80, 891–92, 913,
    924, 972–73, 976–77
  and inflation, 997–99
  and international trade, 398
  and monetary policy, 892–95, 977
  and tax policy, 781–82
Fisheries, 600
Fixed costs, 169–72, 211–14
Fly-paper theory of tax incidence,
    487, 488
Ford Motor Company, 1032
Forecasting, see also Inflationary
    expectations; Rational
    expectations
  economic, 783, 902
  of stock prices, 796, 814–15
Foreign-aid programs, 395, 1053–55
Foreign exchange, 849–50, 854–60,

  864–71, 923, 925, see also
    Exchange rates
  and balance of payments, 939
Forests, 600, 605
Forget Commission, 636
45° line diagrams, 704
Fractional reserve banking, 829
France
  electricity system in, 544–45
  and European Monetary System,
    949
  income distribution in, 503
  productivity in, 1023
  telephone system in, 544
Fraser Institute, 605
Fraser River, 600
Free markets, 254–72
  and exchange rates, 855–57
"Free rider" problem, 343–44
Free trade, 377–78, 384–86, 387–88,
    390–95, 400, see also Interna-
    tional trade; Protectionism;
    Quotas; Tariffs
  ethics of, 395
  and less developed countries, 395
  and poverty, 395
  and regional agreements, 391
Frictional unemployment, 632
Friedman, Milton, 842, 900

Galbraith, John Kenneth, 782
Galloping inflation, 649–50
Game theory, 324–30
Garbage collection, see Wastes/waste
    disposal
GATT (the General Agreement on Tar-
    iffs and Trade), 388, 388–89
GDP deflator, 665
The General Theory of Employment,
    Interest, and Money (Keynes), 624
George, Henry, 425
Germany
  and European Monetary System,
    949
  Great Depression and, 624
  inflation in, 650
  productivity in, 1023, 1024, 1029
  sales taxes in, 479
  services in, 1028
  wages in, 1031
Globalization, economic, 563–64, 1056
Gold, and money, 823, 828–29
Gold-exchange system, see Bretton
    Woods system
Gold standard, 941
Goods, see Capital goods; Consump-
    tion goods; Final goods and serv-
    ices; Private goods; Public goods
Goods and Services Tax (GST), 473,
    476, 477–79, 688

Government
  bonds, 849–52, 974
  expenditure and income distribu-
    tion, 508
  failure, 349, 351
  intervention, 349, 351
  radical vs. mainstream view of,
    434–35
  size of, 904
Government policy, 623
  and businesses in less developed
    countries, 1053
  changes in, 904–905
  econometric models and, 903–904
  economic theory and, 16–17
Government purchases, 655, 670, 671
  and budget deficits, 973–75, 977,
    979
  and efficiency, 1057
  and equilibrium income, 763–66
  and fiscal policy, 781–82, 784
Government spending, see Govern-
    ment purchases
Graphs, 22–23
  horizontal axis, of, 22
  interpretation of, 28–32
  origin on, 22, 26–27, 29–30
  steepness of, 30–32
  units of measurement, 30–2: per-
    centage increase, 32
  vertical axis on, 22
  Y-intercept on, 26
Great Britain, see United Kingdom
Great Depression, 623–25, 635, 750,
    941
Great Lakes, pollution of, 570
Greece, sales tax in, 479
Greenhouse effect, 576, 605
Greenpeace, 600
Gross domestic product (GDP), 433,
    611, 654–59, 673
  and accidents/disasters, 620
  and disposable income, 767
  equilibrium, 697–713
  and housework, 618, 619
  and income equality, 518–19
  and leisure, 620
  and national debt, 959, 961–62
  nominal, 617, 862, 890, 961
  per capita, 1023
  real, 617, 622, 734, 889, 890,
    985–86
  and stabilization policy, 612–29
  and unemployment, 638–40
Gross national product (GNP), 618,
    659–60, 673
Gross private domestic investment,
    655
Growth
  disembodied, 1040–41

embodied, 1040–41
  population, 1033–37, 1047–48,
    1050–51
Guaranteed Annual Income Plan, 505
Guaranteed Income Supplement, 481
Guinea–Bissau, waste disposal and,
  576
Gurley, John, 431

Head taxes, *see* Poll taxes
Health care, 356–57, 394, 979–80
Heath, Edward, 465
Hodge, A. Trevor, 547
Home-owners, and tax benefits, 475
Horizontal equity, 482–83
Horizontal mergers, 551
Housework, and GDP, 618, 619
Housing prices, 72
Human capital
  investments in, 449–52
  theory, 450
Hungary, inflation in, 650
Hurtig, Mel, 812

Imports, 670–71, 672
  and equilibrium income, 776–78
  prices of, 395, 397–98
Incidence of a tax, 487–93
Income, 876–77
  average, 400
  and budget lines, 115–18
  changes in, 111–12, 124
  determination, 702–706
  disposable, *see* Disposable income
  equilibrium, 697–99, 763–66
  future, 686–87
  and labour unions, 458–59
  vs. money, 876–77
  national, *see* National income
  per-capita, 1033–34, 1044, 1046–47
  personal, 659, 683–84
  and prices, 112–13
Income distribution, 7, 411–65, 614
  and efficiency, 400, 401
  and inequality, 499–508, 516–20
  and inflation, 644–45, 1016–17
  to less developed countries, 576–77
  and prices, 271–72
  and tax cuts, 788
Income effect, 112–15, 445, 447
Income–expenditure analysis, 704,
  706
Income inequality, 7, 788, 978
  and efficiency, 272, 399, 515–20
  and income redistribution, 499–508
  and product distribution, 262–63
  and tax cuts, 788
Incomes policy, 1010–13
Income taxes, personal, 473–76, 786
  comprehensive, 494–96

and consumer spending, 675–76,
    686–87, 688–89, 766–68
  and equality, 507
  and horizontal equity, 483
  indexing of, 648–49
  negative, 483–84, 504–506, 519–20
  and return on saving, 495
Increasing returns to scale, 185
Indexing, for inflation, 648–49, 663,
    1014–15
Index numbers, 663
India
  national product and population,
    1033–34
  population of, 1050, 1051
Indifference curve analysis, 100,
    118–24
Indirect taxes, 473
"Indispensable necessity" syndrome,
    35–36
Individual-demand curves, 99–129,
    132–33
Indonesia, population of, 1050–51
Induced investment, 702
Industrial democracy, 465
Industrial strategy, 1038
Industry and Labour Adjustment Pro-
    gram, 1010
Industry, competitive
  supply curves of, 238–39, 242–45
Inefficiency, 47, 255, 269, 272, *see*
    also Efficiency
  and externalities, 338–41
  and international trade, 384
  and monopoly, 300–301
  and taxes, 493–94
  and welfare system, 503
Infant-industry argument, 387
Inferior goods, 111–12, 113, 124
Inflation, *see also* Anti-inflation
    policy
  and budget deficits, 970–73
  and consumption, 685–86
  creeping, 615, 649–50
  and demand, 745–47
  demand-side, 984–85, 987–88, 991
  and exchange rates, 934–37
  and fiscal policy, 997–99
  galloping, 615, 649–50
  and income distribution, 644–45
  indexing for, 648–49
  and inflationary gap, 742–45
  and interest rates, 9–10
  and loans, 644, 649
  and monetary policy, 648, 881–82,
    997–99
  and multiplier, 754–57
  and purchasing power, 640–41, 642,
    645
  rate of, 685–86, 1006–1007: actual,

1006; expected, 645–46,
    1006–1007
  and savings, 676
  supply-side, 984–85, 992–94
  and tax system, 646–49
  and unemployment, 9, 611, 613,
    614, 627, 708–10, 712, 971,
    983–1017
  and Vietnam war, 626
  and wealth distribution, 644–45
  and World War II, 626
Inflationary expectations, 1002–1005,
    1011
Inflationary gaps, 709, 741–45, 995–97
Information
  asymmetric, 350–51
  imperfect, 19–20, 348, *see also*
    Value judgements
  symmetric, 350–51
Infrastructure
  physical, 352–53
  social, 1039
Inheritance taxes, 473
Innovation, 443–44, 1023, 1037–38,
    1040, 1056, *see also* Technology
  and monopoly, 303
  and productivity, 1023, 1025–26
  and regulation, 536, 540
  and size of firm, 560–61
Input–output analysis, 264–65
Input prices, 413
  and aggregate supply curve, 738
  changes in, 179, 196–97
  and supply curves, 75
Inputs, 38, 39–41
  allocation/assignment of, 261–62,
    287, *see also* Production
    planning
  combinations, choice of, 176–90,
    194–95
  decisions regarding, 159–98
  optimal quantity of, 165–66, 177–79
  single, 186
  single-variable, 161–67
  substitution, 179, 180, 197
Insurance, 349, 637, *see also* Unem-
    ployment insurance
Interest, 435–44
Interest-rate differentials, 870–71, 938
Interest rates, 435–41, *see also* Bank
    rate; Usury laws
  and bond prices, 803
  and budget deficits, 963–65, 973–75
  ceilings on, 439–40
  and consumption, 684
  control of, 58
  foreign, 440–41, 866–68, 870–71,
    923, 925–26
  illusion of high, 9–10, 648
  and inflation accounting, 963–65

and investment, 695
and monetization, 972–73
nominal, 646, 647–48, 676, 963, 1014
real, 646, 647–48, 676, 963, 1014
and resource allocation, 345–46
and total expenditure, 877
and velocity of circulation, 888
Intermediate goods, 618, 657, 658–59
International Monetary Fund (IMF), 859, 942
International monetary system, 933–53
International trade, 51, 363–64, 777–79, *see also* Exports; Free Trade; Imports
and equilibrium income, 776–78
equilibrium price in, 372–74
and industry concentration, 562
and less developed countries, 395, 503, 1054
and medical assistance programs, 394
mutual gains from, 364
restrictions on, 361, 374, 376–88, 389–90, 926–27, 935, 937
and social programs, 394
supply–demand equilibrium and, 372–74
trade deficits, 950–53
Interstate Commerce Commission (U.S.), 538
Invention, 443
Inventories, 654
Investment, 435–36, 655, 671, 701–702, 730, *see also* Bonds; Stocks
gross private domestic, 655
in human capital, 449–52
induced, 702
in less developed countries, 1048–50
and multiplier, 717–19
and productivity, 1027, 1038
and resource allocation, 346–47
and saving, 710–12
and tax policy, 695
variability of, 694–95
Investment goods, *see* Capital goods
Investment spending, 670, 674
"Invisible hand," 50, 57, 258, 268–69, 285–87
Ireland, and European Monetary System, 949
Irreversible decisions, 347
Isoquants, 193–97
Israel, income distribution in, 503
Italy, and European Monetary System, 949
Ivory trade, 89

Japan
economy of, 48–49, 278–81
productivity in, 1023, 1024, 1025, 1037
profit-sharing in, 1013–14
services in, 1028
trade: with Canada, 362–63, 380; with United States, 952–53
Job creation, *see* Employment policy
Job losses, *see* Employment policy; Unemployment
Johnson, Harry, 1013
Johnson, Lyndon B., 675

K.C. Irving case, 550
Kennedy, John F., 675
Kennedy, Paul, 563
Keynesian model, 877–83
fiscal policy in, 877–82
vs. monetarism, 889–99
monetary policy in, 877–82
Keynes, John Maynard, 624, 626, 694, 696–97, 749–50, 816
Knights of Labour, 453

Labour
and aggregate supply, 739
and budget deficits, 979
costs of, 460
dehumanization of, 433–34
demand for, 447–48
division of, 48–49
foreign, 362–63, 374, 397–98
and minimum-wage legislation, 418–20, 421
motivations of, 431–32
productivity of, 10–11, 1023–24
in service sector, 354–55
skilled, 418–19, 1056
supply of, 445–47, 459
unskilled, 418–20, 1056
Labour force, 629, 631, 633
Labour markets, 445–65
discrimination in, 509, 510–11
dual, 451–52
primary, 451–52
secondary, 452
Labour Relations Act (Ontario), 464
Labour-supply paradox, 446–47
Labour unions, 452–65
and deregulation, 543
public-sector, 464
Lags
in productivity, 1030–31, 1032
in stabilization policy, 893–95, 899–901, 902
Laissez faire, 253–72
vs. economic planning, 253–54
Land rents, 420–25, 425–26
and land use, 424–25

Latin America, population of, 1051
Law of comparative advantage, 8–9, 49, 51, 361–62, 366
Law of conservation of matter and energy, 570–71
Law of demand, 133–34
Law of diminishing marginal returns, 164–65, 173, 186, 1034
Law of diminishing marginal utility, 102–104, 105–106, 107
Law of supply and demand, 5–6, 58, 66, 257, 260
Leisure, and GDP, 620
Lemieux, Mario, 425–27
Leontief, Wassily, 264
Less developed countries (LDCs), 1044–55
aid to, 1053–55
and debt problem, 949–50, 970, 1049
education in, 1051–52
and environmental issues, 576–77
foreign investment in, 1048–50
and GDP, 619–20
impediments to development in, 1048–53
income redistribution to, 576–77
and international trade, 395, 503
living standards in, 1044–46
per-capita income in, 1033–34, 1044, 1046–47
and population, 1035, 1047–48, 1050–51
productivity in, 1026
training in, 1050, 1051–52, 1054
unemployment in, 1052–53
women in, 1045
Liability, 831
limited, 799
unlimited, 797, 798
Licence fees, 303–304
Limited liability, 799
Lindbeck, Assar, 81
Liquidity, 828
Living standards, *see* Standards of living
Loans, 427–41, *see also* Debt; Interest rates
foreign, 440–41
Loblaws, 52
Longfield, Mountifort, 256
Long run, 174–76
Lorenz curve, 500–503
Losses, short-run, 234–35
Lucas, Robert E., 903–904

M1, 827–28
M2, 827–28
Macdonald Commission, 505, 636–37
Macdonald, Sir John A., 388

Macroeconomics, compared with microeconomics, 612–13

Mainstream economics vs. radical economics, 429–35

Malthus, Thomas R., 368, 1034, 1035–36

"Managed" float, 947

Management, motivations of, 431–32

Manufacturers' sales tax (MST), 476, 477–79

Manufacturing sector, and productivity growth, 1029

Mao Tse-tung, 277–78

Marcet, Jane, 368

Marginal analysis, 6, 99–101, 106–109, 207–18, 221–24
vs. big economic issues, 631

Marginal costs (MC), 6, 168–70, 210–15, see also under Cost curves

Marginal data, relationship to average and total, 221–24

Marginal land, 423

Marginal physical product (MPP), 163–65, 412

Marginal private cost (MPC), 338–39

Marginal productivity theory, 412–35

Marginal profit, 208–10

Marginal propensity to consume (MPC), 680–83, 720, 723–24

Marginal propensity to save (MPS), 682–83

Marginal rate of substitution, 121–22, 124

Marginal revenue (MR), 205, 210–11, 232–33
and monopoly, 294–95

Marginal revenue product (MRP), 166, 412, 414, 430, 436–37

Marginal social cost (MSC), 338–39

Marginal tax rate, 473

Marginal utility, 101–109

Market activity, and GDP, 619–20

Market controls, 399–400, see also Minimum-wage legislation; Quotas; Tariffs

Market demand, 131–58

Market-demand curves, 132–34, 302

Market mechanism, 7, 333–59, 499
pollution and, 572
and price controls, 78–86
shortcomings of, 333–59

Market power, 562–64

Markets
"black", 79, 80
movement in unison, 613

Market structures, 228–29, see also Monopolistic competition; Oligopoly; Perfect competition; Pure monopoly

Market system, 51–54
and environmental issues, 51

Marxist economics, 416, 559–61

Marx, Karl, 1041–42

Maximin criterion, 327

Mediation, 462–63

Medical care, see Health care

Mergers
and competition policy, 551
conglomerate, 551
and deregulation, 543
horizontal, 551
vertical, 551

Mexico, foreign debt of, 949

Microeconomics, compared with macroeconomics, 612–13

Mill, James, 368

Minimum-differentiation principle, 328

Minimum-wage legislation, 6, 86, 400, 418–21, 497

Misinformation, and regulation, 533

Monetarism, 888–906
vs. Keynesian model, 889–99

Monetary policy, 841, 865–66, 890–91, see also Demand management; Stabilization policy
and central banking, 847–71
contractionary, 865–66, 916–17
and exchange rates, 914–19, 922
expansionary, 865–66, 881–82, 918, 977
and fiscal policy, 892–95, 977
and inflation, 648, 881–82, 997–99
and international trade, 398
in Keynesian model, 877–82

Monetization, 971–73

Money, 49, 821–28, 876
circulation, velocity of, 883–88
commodity, 822–23
demand for, 862–63
fiat, 823
gold and silver as, 823, 828–29
income vs., 876–77
as medium of exchange, 821–22
quantity theory of, 883–85
as store of value, 822
as unit of account, 822

Money costs, 37–38

Money creation, 832–38, 840–41

Money fixed assets, 485

Money market, equilibrium in, 864–68, 870–71

Money supply, 825–28, 881–83
Bank of Canada and, 850–62
banks and, 825–28
multiple contractions of, 838–40
and open-market operations, 850–52

Money values and GDP, 616–18

Money wages, 736–37

Monopolistic competition, 228–29, 311, 312–17
excess-capacity theorem of, 316–17
compared with perfect competition, 311–14, 316

Monopoly, 526, see also Natural monopoly; Pure monopoly
barriers to entry and, 291
bilateral, 461
and competition policy, 525, 550, 560
cost advantages and, 291–98
and discrimination, 510–11
and inefficiency, 300–301
compared with perfect competition, 298–301
and profits, 442, 444
unions as, 457–60

Monopoly policy, 303–305, 361
and pollution, 289–90, 305–307

Monopsony, 460–62

Montreal Stock Exchange, 808

Moral hazard, 349

Morgenstern, Oskar, 324

Multinational corporations, and less developed countries, 1049

Multiplier analysis, 717–18

Multipliers
and aggregate demand curve, 728–30
and inflation, 754–57
and international trade, 777–78
and tax policy, 770–71

NAFTA (North American Free Trade Agreement), 362, 391, 395

National-accounts vs. public-accounts methods of measurement, 963

National Citizens' Coalition, 636

National Council of Welfare, 496

National debt, 957–80
burden of the, 968–70, 975–76

National Energy Program, 598, 599

National income, 659, 671, 672, 700

Nationalization, 526, 544–46

National product, 613, 659, 671, 672, 673

Natural monopolies, 292–93, 303, 527, 538
regulated, 292–93

Natural resources, 587–605

Near moneys, 828

Negative income tax (NIT), 483–84, 504–506, 519–20

Netherlands, the
central bank in, 850
income distribution in, 503
recycling in, 570

Net worth, 832

Neumann, John von, 324

"The New Economics," 626
New Zealand
  economy of, 980
  sales taxes in, 479
Niagara River, 575
Nominal GDP, 617, 862, 889, 890, 961
Nominal rate of interest, 646, 647–48, 676, 963, 1014, 1016–17
Normal goods, 112
Normative questions, 20
North Atlantic Fisheries Organization, 600
North–South controversy, 1055
NutraSweet case, 559

Ocean Ranger disaster, 620
OECD (Organization for Economic Co-operation and Development), 85, 503, 577, 619
Oil prices, 257, 589, 597–99, 752–54
  and Iranian revolution, 627, 752
  and Israel–Arab war 1973, 626
  and OPEC 1973 agreement, 752
  and productivity, 1027
Okun, Arthur, 520
Old Age Security Program, 481
Oligopoly, 228–29, 311, 318–22
  and interdependence, 320–24
OPEC (Organization of Petroleum Exporting Countries), 257, 320–21, 594, 599, 626, 627, 752
Open-market operations, 849–52
Opportunity costs, 4–5, 37–42, 335
  of capital, 245–46
  and comparative advantage, 369–71
  and economic growth, 45, 46
  of holding money, 862
  and money costs, 37–38
Optimal purchase rule, 100, 104–106
Output(s), 38, 39–41, 161–63, 182–83
  government, 654
  increase in, 7
  and monopolistic competition, 314–17
  and monopoly, 296–98, 298–99
  per-capita, 1023, 1029–30
  profit-maximizing, 211–14, 232–35, 296–98
  selection, 260–61, 265–67
  and total profit, 206
Output–price decisions, 199–224, 314–16
Ozone layer, 576, 605

Pacific Rim countries, and trade, 1054
Paradox of thrift, 726–27
Partnerships, 798–99
Patents, 291, 541–42
Pay cheques, and velocity of circulation, 885–87

Pay equity, 512–14
Payments mechanism, and velocity of circulation, 887
Payoff matrix, 324, 326–27
Payroll taxes, 481, 787
  incidence of, 489–92
Per-capita income, 1033–34, 1044, 1046–47
Perfect competition, 227–51, 266–69
  compared with monopolistic competition, 311–14, 316
  compared with monopoly, 298–301
  and oligopoly, 318
  and supply curves of competitive firm, 237–39
  and supply curves of competitive industry, 238–39, 242–45
Perfectly contestable markets, 329–30
Permits, for emissions, 584–85
Personal income taxes, see Income taxes, personal
Petro-Canada, 598
Petroleum and Gas Revenue Tax, 598
Phillips, A.W., 18
Phillips curve, 18, 990–97
  and demand-side inflation, 990–92
  and inflationary expectations, 1002–1005
  and rational expectations, 1006–1007
  and supply-side inflation, 992–94
  vertical (long-run), 996–97
Phillips machine, 18
Pigou, A.C., 568, 572
Ploughback, 801
Poland, 276
  pollution in, 569
Politicians, role of, in economic policy, 905
Poll taxes, 473, 494
Pollution, 337–41, 568–70, see also Wastes/waste disposal
  charges for, 227–28, 289–90, 305–307, 342, 568, 574, 577
  direct controls on, 577, 578–79, 580–83
  and GDP, 621
  across international borders, 575–76
  and monopoly, 289–90, 305–307
  permits for, 579, 585
  subsidy to cut, 248–49
  voluntarism and, 577, 578
Population
  aging, 978
  and demand, 70
  growth of, 1033–37: exponential, 1035–37; zero, 1035
  and less developed countries, 1035
  and wages, 1034
Porter, Michael, 1056

Portfolio investment, 805–808
Portugal, and European Monetary System, 949
Positive questions, 20
Potential GDP, 638–39, 708
Poverty, 401, 496–508, see also Anti-poverty programs
  absolute concept of, 496–99
  relative concept of, 496–99
Poverty line, 496, 497, 506
Power, economic, 432, see also Market power
Predatory pricing, 534
Prejudice, 509, 511
Price ceilings, 5, 78–82, 269–71, 534, 539, 541
Price changes, 111–15, 124–26
  and budget line, 117–18
  and consumer expenditure, 143–45
  and elasticity of demand, 138–41, 143–45
  and income effect, 112–15
  and substitution, 112–15
Price controls, 5–6, 57–58, 59, 78–86, 87–88, 90, 531–32
  and auxiliary restrictions, 88
  and inflation, 1010–13
  unenforceable, 87–88
  during World War II, 626
Price discrimination, 554–55
Price elasticity of supply, 147
Price floors, 5–6, 84–86, 534, 539
Price indexes, 665, see also Consumer price index
  deflating by, 665
Price leadership, 321–22
Price level, 644, 685, 1017
  in Canada, 621–23
  and economic growth, 985–86
  in income–expenditure analysis, 706
  and recessionary gap, 748–50
  and supply, 734–36
Price making, 294
Price mechanism, 6
Prices
  of bonds, 805–808
  and cartels, 320–21
  and consumer preference, 262
  and consumption, 685
  and demand, 133–37, 139, 146–48, 150–53
  and deregulation, 542
  and economic co-ordination, 258, 260
  and efficiency, 256–57, 259
  of imports, 395, 397–98
  and income distribution, 271–72
  and inflation, 640, 642–44
  and input assignment, 262

and international trade, 362, 377–83
and marginal utility, 105
and monopolistic competition, 313–16
and monopoly, 294–95, 297–98, 298–99, 304–307
and oligopoly, 318–19
profit-maximizing, 211–15
and public goods, 343–44
and quantity demanded, 145–46
relative, 642–44
and resource allocation, 260–71, 336–37
and resource depletion, 593–602
of stocks, 805–808, 814–16
effect of weather on, 72
Price system, 52, 57–58, 83–84, 253–88, 572–73
Price taking, 230, 232
Price wars, 322
Pricing, 535–39
average-cost, 536–37
collusion in, 319, 321–22, 562
and consumer surplus, 108–11
and competition reduction, 553–55
decisions on, 199–208
of depletable resources, 587–92
and factors of production, 411–65
marginal-cost, 537–38
and oligopolies, 318–19, 326–27
peak/off peak, 271–72
predatory, 554
Ramsey rule of, 538
and regulation, 533–34
restrictions on, 525
Principle–agent problems, 356
Principle of increasing costs, 42
Principle of marginal productivity, 412–16
"Prisoners' dilemma," 327, 328
Private goods, 343
Privatization, 546–48
Product differentiation, 313, 318–19
Production costs, 159–98, 303
Production factors
pricing of, 412–65
Production, flexible methods of, 1032
Production function, 179–82, 184–87, 193
Production planning, 261–62
and central planning, 264–65
and input–output analysis, 263–65
Production possibilities frontiers, 40–47, 48, 335–36, 369–72
Productivity, 738, 1021–33
and aggregate supply, 738
communications and, 1025–26
convergence in, 1025–26
and education, 1051–52, 1057
growth of, 10–11, 356

investment and, 1027
of labour, 10–11, 355, 1023–24
and labour unions, 460
lagging, 1030–31, 1032
in less developed countries, 1026
marginal, 412–16
and services, 1031
slowdowns in, 1026–28, 1056–57
technology and, 1025–26, 1037
and unemployment, 1029–30
and wages, 749
Products, see also Complements;
Goods; Substitutes
continuous shift in, 1031, 1033
distribution of, 262–63
Profit maximization, 202–203, 206–15
and monopoly, 294, 295, 296–98, 304–305
compared with sales maximization, 322–24
Profits, 441–44, 673
of banks, 830
and deregulation, 542–43
and entry of firms into industry, 241–44, 543
and interest rates, 442–43
and monopolistic competition, 313–14
and monopoly, 294, 298, 443, 444
regulation of, 535–38, 540–91
short-run, 234
taxation of, 444
Profit-sharing, 1013–14
Progressive taxes, 473, 474, 476, 480–81, 484, 507–508
Property rights, 337–38, 575–76, 603–605
Property taxes, 480–81, 494
Proportional tax, 473
Proprietorships, sole, 797–98
Protectionism, 384–86
infant-industry argument, 387
and monopoly, 398
Public-accounts vs. national-accounts methods of measurement, 963
Public goods, 343–44
Public interest
and efficiency, 256–57
and environmental damage, 572–73
and monopolistic competition, 329
and oligopoly, 329
and pricing, 256–57
radical vs. mainstream view of, 434–35
Public resources, regulation of, 532–33
Public sector
collective bargaining in, 464
size of, 904
Public utilities, 526

Purchasing power, 640–41, 642, 645
Purchasing-power parity theory, 934–37
Pure monopoly, 228–29

Quantity demanded, 67–71
and demand, 60
and income change, 111–15
and price change, 111–15, 124–26
Quantity supplied, 72–73
and price, 62
and supply, 62–63
Quantity versus quality, 433–34
Quotas, 374–83
vs. tariffs, 379–81

Radical economics vs. mainstream economics, 429–35
Radicalism, 53
Railways, pricing of, 538–39
Rain forests, 576
Ramsey, Frank, 538
Ramsey pricing rule, 538–39
Rand formula, 456
Random walks, 814–16
Rasminsky, Louis, 848–49
Rate averaging, 529, 534
Rate of return, 540–41
Rational choice, 4–5
Rational decisions, 37
Rational expectations, 1005–1008
Rationing, 1012
Reagan, Ronald, 563, 675
Real GDP, 617, 622, 734, 889, 890, 985–86
Real rate of interest, 646, 647–48, 676, 963, 1014, 1016–17
Real wage rate, 640, 1002–1005
Recessionary gap, 708, 741–42, 747–50, 971, 994–95
Recessions, 611, 615–16, 710, 983
and budget, 965–66
and inflation, 623, 627, 997–99
and national debt, 623, 627, 959, 965–66
and stabilization, 628, 635, 637
Recycling, 76, 78, 570–71, 578, 604, 1041
Redistribution of income, see Income distribution
Regional redistribution payments, 508
Regressive taxes, 473, 477, 480–81, 484, 507–508
Regulated Sector Branch (Canada), 527
Regulation of industry, 525–48, see also Deregulation
of municipal transportation, 544
and productivity, 1027
of railways, 538–39

Regulatory lag, 536, 541
Reich, Robert, 1056
Relative concept of poverty, 496–99
Relative prices, 642–44
Rent controls, 5–6, 79–81, 428
Rent, land, 421–25
Rent-seeking, 301, 348, 429
Required reserves, 842
Resale price maintenance, 554
Research and development (R & D),
    1027, 1037, 1040, 1054
Reserves
    excess, 833
    required, 831, 842
Resource allocation, 39, 45, 88–89,
    614
    efficient, 254–56, 264–71, 285–87,
        334–37
    inefficient, 300–301
    and laissez faire economy, 260–63,
        272
    and monopolistic competition,
        316–17
    and monopoly, 300–301
    and oligopoly, 319
    and regulation, 532–33
    and time, 344–47
Resource utilization, 48
Resources, 36
    conservation of, 595, 596
    depletable, 588–93, 597–99
    depletion of, 593–97, 1040–41
    exhaustible, 596–99
    industry royalties, 597–98
    and monopoly, 291
    public, 532–33
    renewable, 600–601
    scarcity of, 35, 36–37
Restrictive Trade Practices Commis-
    sion, 556
Retained earnings, 801
Returns to scale, 186–87, see also
    Economies of scale
Revenue Canada, 545
Ricardo, David, 366, 368, 376
Right-to-work laws, 454, 456–57
Risk-taking, see also Entrepreneur-
    ship; Speculation
    and income, 443
Robinson, Joan, 312
Roosevelt, Franklin Delano, 624
Royal Commission on Employment
    (Newfoundland), 636
Ruhr river basin, taxes on emissions
    in, 579
Rules-versus-discretion debate,
    899–901, 902, 904–906
Runs on banks, 820–21

Sales maximization, 322–24

Sales taxes, 476–77, 676, 687–88, 787,
    see also Goods and Services Tax;
    Manufacturers' sales tax; Value-
    added tax
    and aggregate supply, 738
    and employment, 477–78
    and income taxes, 478, 495
Sarlo, Christopher, 498
Satisficing, 202
Savings, 671, 676, 682–83, 726–27
    and income tax, 495
    and investment, 710–12
    taxes on income from, 786
Scarcity, 107
    and choice, 35–56
    and economic co-ordination, 258,
        260
    of natural resources, 587–89, 595
Scatter diagrams, 676–80
Schumpeter, Joseph, 303
Self-correcting mechanism, 750–52,
    757, 901–902, 994–97, 1001
Self-interest, 50, 51
Self-regulated industries, 527
Services, 81–82, see also Final goods
    and services
    cost of, 11, 354–57
    and deregulation, 542
    deterioration of, 354
    outside market, 81–82
    and productivity, 1028–29
    universality of, 110, 531–32
    user charges for, 110–11
    wait for, 81–82
Shares, see Stocks
Sherman Act (U.S.), 549
Shortages, 65, 260
    and corruption, 87
    and favouritism, 87
    and price controls, 79, 80, 81–82
    of resources, 594
    and speculation, 813–14
Short run, 174–76
Shut-down analysis, 235–37, 238
Singapore
    population control in, 1051
    toll on vehicles downtown, 580
Slopes, 23–26
    of curved lines, 24–26: tangent to
        the curve, 25
    infinite, 24
    negative, 24
    positive, 24
    of straight lines, 24
    zero, 24
Smith, Adam, 48–49, 50–51, 57–58,
    99, 230, 253, 364, 376, 1033
Social assistance, see Social programs;
    Welfare system
Social marginal costs, see Marginal

social cost
Socialism, 273
Social programs, 394, 400, 482, 483,
    629, 979–80, see also Education;
    Health care; Welfare system
Softwood lumber dispute, 380
Sole proprietorships, 797–98
Solow, Robert, 433
Soviet Union
    economy of, 273–77, 1039–40
    pollution in, 569
Spain
    in European Community, 389–90
    and European Monetary System,
        949
    sales taxes in, 479
Specialization, 48–49, 51, 363–64,
    365–67, 369, 384
Stabilization of commodity prices,
    1055
Stabilization policy, 612, 627–29, 695,
    697, 757, 782, 1017
    for a closed economy, 875–906
    and fiscal policy, 892–95
    and gross domestic product, 612–29
    and Keynesians, 895–99
    lags in, 873–95, 899–901, 902
    and monetarists, 895–99
    and monetary policy, 892–95
    for a small open economy, 911–27
Stabilizers, automatic, 901
Stagflation, 626, 734, 752–54, 745–47
Stagnation, 1041–42, 1045
Stalin, Joseph, 273
Stand-alone costs, 539
Standards of living, 1022–24, 1031,
    1034–35, 1044–46
State, the, see Government
Statistical discrimination, 511–12
Statistics Canada, 616, 630–31
Stelco, layoffs at, 463
St. Lawrence River, 600
Stock exchanges, 808–10
Stock markets, 795–96, 805–808, 816
Stocks, 795, 800, 801–802, 803–805
    prices of, 805–808, 814–16
Store of value, 822
Strikes, 453, 454, 456, 462, 463–64
Structural unemployment, 632
Subsidies
    agricultural, 390
    and environmental issues, 584
    export, 377
    on goods and services, 504
    and less developed countries, 1054
    per-unit, 301–302
    "unfair," 393–94
Substitutes, 147
    and elasticity of demand, 146,
        147–48

and monopoly, 304, 305
Substitution effect, 112–15, 445, 447
Sunk costs, 171, 174, *see also* Fixed costs
Supply
    and monopoly, 293–94
    price elasticity of, 147
Supply and demand, 57–95, 611, 613
    and baby boom, 91
    equilibrium of, 63–67, 372–74, 739–41
    laws of, 5–6, 66, 90–92
    in macroeconomics, 614–16
Supply curves, 62
    of competitive firms, 238–39
    of competitive industry, 238–39, 242–45
    effect of excise tax on, 135–36
    of labour, 446
    for loans, 439
    long-run, 242–45
    movements along, 72
    shifts of, 72–76, 78
    short-run, 238–39
Supply–demand analysis, 57
    and environmental problems, 573–74
    and factor prices, 412–65
    and resources pricing, 589–92
Supply–demand diagrams, 64–65
Supply schedules, 62
Supply-side economics, 515, 517
Supply-side equilibrium, 733–45
Supply-side inflation, 984–85, 992–94
Surpluses, 65, 84, 85, *see also* Consumer surplus
    disposal of, 84
Suzuki, David, 602, 605
Sweden
    and European Monetary System, 948
    income distribution in, 503
    inflation in, 649
    and interest rates, 938
    national product and population, 1033–34
    telephone system in, 544

Taft–Hartley Act (U.S.), 454, 456
Takeovers, corporate, 811–12
Tariffs, 361–62, 374–83, 392, 398, 400, 778, 926–27, 1054
    vs. quotas, 379–81
Taxation
    ability-to-pay principle, 484
    and aggregate supply, 784–90
    average tax rate, 474
    benefits principle of, 485
    and economic behaviour, 494–96
    efficiency and, 482, 485–87

and equilibrium income, 768–70
equity in, 482–85
and fiscal policy, 781–82
and inflation, 646–49
and investment, 695
marginal tax rate, 473
multipliers for, 770–71
and profit-maximizing price, 214–15
Tax-based incomes policy (TIP), 1013
Tax credits, 477, 483, 787
Tax cuts, 785–90
Taxes
    burdens of, 485–87, 494
    on capital, 492–93
    on capital gains, 786
    and consumption, 686–89
    on corporate income, 788–89
    on corporate profits, 444, 473, 480, 492, 799
    direct, 473
    dividend income, 475
    excess burdens of, 485–87
    excise, 134–38, 303, 476, 489
    on goods and services, 473, 476
    on income, personal, *see* Income tax, personal
    incidences of, 487–93
    indirect, 473
    inheritance, 473
    negative income, 483–84
    payroll, 473, 481, 489–92, 787
    on personal income, *see* Income tax, personal
    poll, 473, 494
    and productivity, 1038–39
    progressive, 473
    property, 473, 480, 494
    proportional, 473
    regressive, 473, 477, 480–81, 484
    sales, 473, 787
    on savings income, 786
    value-added, 473, 476–77
    on wealth, 495
Tax exemptions, 483
Tax policy, 668–71, 781–82
Tax shelters, 376, 399, 474–76, 480, 494–95
Tax shifting, 488, 491–92
Technology, *see also* Innovations
    and aggregate supply, 738
    and concentration of industry, 560
    and monopoly, 292
    and productivity, 1925–26, 1037
    and size of firm, 560–61
    and supply curves, 74–75
Telecommunications industry, 187–89, 531
Ten Lost Years (Broadfoot), 625
Thatcher, Margaret, 465, 494, 513, 546, 563

Thorsell, William, 564
Thrift, *see* Paradox of thrift; Savings
Thurow, Lester, 1056
Time
    and demand curves, 150, 152–53
    and resource allocation, 344–47
Time period, choice of, 29
Time–series graphs, 28–32
Tobacco industry, and advertising, 556
Tobin, James, 431
Total cost (TC), 167–69, 172–74
Total data, relationship to average and marginal, 221–24
Total expenditures, 697, 718, *see also* Consumption; Investment
    and interest rates, 877
Total expenditure schedule, 700–702
Total fixed costs (TFC), 171–72
Total physical product (TPP), 161–63
Total-product curve, 167
Total profit, 203–208
    maximization of, 208–10
Total revenue (TR), 203–206
Total utility, 101–102, 104, 106–107
Total variable costs (TVC), 237
Towers, Graham, 848
Toxic wastes, *see* Wastes/waste disposal
Trade, *see* Exchange; Free trade; International trade
Trade adjustment assistance, 385
Trade policy, 387–90
Trades and Labor Congress of Canada (TLC), 453
Trade unions, *see* Labour unions
Training, 398
    in less developed countries, 1050, 1051–52, 1054
Transactions, limitation of volume of, 88
Transfer payments, 481–82, 508, 655, 673, 771–72, 980
    indexing of, 1014, 1016–17
Transportation, *see also* Airlines; Railways
    municipal, 544
    pricing of, 271–72
Treasury bills, 854
Trotsky, Leon, 253
Tyre King, 581

Unconditional grants, 482
"Underground economy," 620
Unemployment, 350, 611, 784, *see also* Employment
    and budget deficits, 966–67, 977
    cyclical, 632–33
    economic costs of, 637–40
    and economic policy, 399
    and energy prices, 597, 599

and equilibrium, 750
and free trade, 384–85
frictional, 632
"hidden," 631, 1052
and inflation, 9, 611, 613, 614, 615,
    627–28, 712, 971, 983–1017
and international trade, 393, 398,
    400
in less developed countries,
    1052–53
measurement of, 630–32
and minimum-wage legislation,
    417–20, 634–35
and minority groups, 420
natural, 996
and productivity growth, 1029–30
rate of, 629, 633–34
and recessionary gaps, 747–50
and stabilization policy, 629
structural, 632
and youth, 417–18, 640
Unemployment insurance, 626, 629,
    633, 634–37
Unfair trade practices, 377, 394, 556
Union Carbide, 553
Unions, see Labour unions
"Union shop," 454
Unit costs, see Average costs
United Kingdom
    and European Monetary System,
        949
    and inflation, 627
    pay equity in, 513
    privatization in, 546
    productivity in, 1024, 1025, 1029,
        1030–31
    unemployment in, 1030
    value-added tax in, 479
    wages and prices in, 749, 1012,
        1031
United Nations Development Report,
    1047
United States

bank failures in, 830
economic policy in the 1980s, 950,
    951, 952
and foreign exchange, 942, 943
Great Depression and, 624
and income distribution, 503
and income tax changes, 675,
    686–87
and inflation, 627
and labour unions, 453–57
and loan markets, 440–41
oil prices and, 752
productivity in, 1023, 1024, 1025,
    1029, 1037
services in, 1028
stagflation in, 752
trade: with Canada, 390–95; with
    Japan, 952–53
wage and price controls in, 1013
and wage and price levels, 749
United Steel Workers of America, 463
Unit of account, 822
Universal Income Security Program,
    505
Universality, 110, 529, 980
User charges, 109–10
Usury laws, 435–37, 439–40
Utilities, electric, 545–46
Utility, 100, 101–109, see also Mar-
    ginal utility; Total utility

Value-added tax (VAT), 476–77, 478,
    479
Value judgements, 19
Values added, 657–59
Variable costs, 169–72, 235
Variables, 22
    in graphs, 22–23
Velocity of circulation, 883–88
Vertical equity, 484
Vertical mergers, 551
Voluntarism, and pollution control,
    578

Voluntary exchange, mutual gains
    from, 5, 49, 109, 364

Wage rate, 350–51, 447–49, 748–50
    and ability, 448–49, 449–52
    changes in, 445–47
    controls on, 1010–13
    and education, 450–52
    and inflationary expectations,
        1002–1005
    and labour unions, 458–60
    and money, 736–37
    and productivity, 1031
    real, see Real wage rate
Wages
    determination of, 447–60, 461–62
    and inflation, 640–42, 1001
    and labour supply, 458–60
    and population growth, 1034
Warehousing, 184
Wastes/waste disposal, 109–10, 545,
    569–71, 573–74, 576
Water, 600
Wealth, 683–84
    and economic growth, 1041–44
    taxes on, 495
West Germany, income distribution in,
    503
The Wealth of Nations (Smith), 50
Welfare system, 503–506
Work conditions, 462, 1032
Work ethic, and productivity, 1037
"Workfare," 504
Work incentives, 503–504, 519
World Bank, 1054
World Bank Development Report,
    1037
World War II, 626, 941–42, 959, 960,
    975

Zero economic growth, 1042–44
Zero economic profit, 245–46
Zero population growth, 1035

CREDITS

Page 18 The London School of Economics Photo Unit; page 50 Stock Montage, Inc.; page 52 Loblaw Companies Limited. The copyright in the photograph and the packaging of the photographed products is the property of Loblaw Companies Limited, 1993, © All Rights Reserved. The trademarks "President's Choice," "G.R.E.E.N.," and all other trademarks appearing in the photograph are the property of Loblaw Companies Limited; page 59 Stock Montage, Inc.; page 76 J. Lauzon/Publiphoto; page 77 David Brownell/The Image Bank Canada; page 90 Health and Welfare Canada; page 148 AP/Wide World Photos; page 180 Jeff Hunter/The Image Bank Canada; page 259 The Image Bank Canada; page 350 Janeart/ The Image Bank Canada; page 368 Stock Montage, Inc.; page 425 Canapress Photo Service; page 454 Wood engraving by Rosemary Kilbourn, from William Kilbourn, *The Elements Combined: A History of the Steel Company of Canada* (Toronto: Clarke, Irwin & Company, 1960). Used with the permission of the author; page 571 Cralle/The Image Bank Canada; page 575 Hans-Jurgen Burkard/Bilderberg/SABA; page 581 *The Globe and Mail*, Toronto; page 585 Kay Chernush/The Image Bank Canada; page 603 Basin/Publiphoto; page 604 Canapress Photo Service; page 625 Dept. of National Defence/National Archives of Canada/PA-035132; page 636 Canapress Photo Service; page 642 From *The Wall Street Journal* —reprinted with the permission of Cartoon Features Syndicate; page 650 Stock Montage, Inc.; page 696 Stock Montage, Inc.; page 712 Gregory Heisler/The Image Bank Canada; page 788 Reprinted with permission— The Toronto Star Syndicate; page 815 KAL, Cartoonists & Writers Syndicate; page 824 Currency Museum, Bank of Canada, photographs by James Zagon; page 826 The University Museum, University of Pennsylvania; page 842 Alvis Upitis/The Image Bank Canada; page 850 Bernard Roussel/The Image Bank Canada; page 869 Currency Museum, Bank of Canada, photograph by William McElligott; page 903 Toronto Argonauts Football Club, photograph by John Sokolowski; page 936 McDonald's Restaurants of Canada Limited; page 952 Canapress Photo Service; page 977 Canapress Photo Service; page 1016 Photograph courtesy of the Canadian Council of Catholic Bishops; page 1032 Canapress Photo Service.

Readers wishing further information on data provided through the co-operation of Statistics Canada may obtain copies of related publications by mail from Publications Sales, Statistics Canada, Ottawa, Ontario K1A 0T6, by phone at 1-613-951-7277 or toll-free 1-800-267-6677. You may also fax your order to 1-613-951-1584.

READER REPLY CARD

We are interested in your reaction to *Economics: Principles and Policy*, Fourth Canadian Edition, by William J. Baumol, Alan S. Blinder, and William M. Scarth. You can help us to improve this book in future editions by completing this questionnaire.

1. Which version of the text did you use?
   ☐ full text   ☐ microeconomics split edition   ☐ macroeconomics split edition

2. What was your reason for using this book?
   ☐ university course   ☐ college course   ☐ continuing education course
   ☐ professional development   ☐ personal interest   ☐ other _____ _____

3. If you are a student, please identify your school and the course in which you used this book.

4. Which chapters or parts of this book did you use? Which did you omit?

5. What did you like best about this book?

6. What did you like least?

7. Please identify any topics you think should be added to future editions.

8. Please add any comments or suggestions.

9. May we contact you for further information?

   Name: _____

   Address: _____

   _____

   Phone: _____

(fold here and tape shut)

0116870399-M8Z4X6-BR01

Scott Duncan
Publisher, College Division
HARCOURT BRACE & COMPANY, CANADA
55 HORNER AVENUE
TORONTO, ONTARIO
M8Z 9Z9